Modern Japan

GARLAND REFERENCE LIBRARY OF THE HUMANITIES (VOL. 2031)

Modern Japan

An Encyclopedia of History, Culture, and Nationalism

Editor
James L. Huffman

GARLAND PUBLISHING, INC.
A MEMBER OF THE TAYLOR & FRANCIS GROUP
New York & London
1998

Library of Congress Cataloging-in-Publication Data

Modern Japan: An encyclopedia of history, culture, and nationalism / editor,
   James L. Huffman
            p.   cm. — (Garland reference library of the humanities ; vol.
2031)
      Includes bibliographical references and index.
      ISBN 0–8153–2525–8 (alk. paper)
      1. Japan—Encyclopedias. 2. Japan—History—1868–   3. Nationalism—
Japan.   I. Huffman, James L., 1941–   .   II. Series.
DS805.M63   1997
952—dc21   97–21910
                                                                              CIP

Cover art: Photograph of buildings in Shinjuki, Tokyo, Japan by Brett Froomer,
          The Image Bank, NY.
Cover design: Robert Vankeirsbilck.

Printed on acid-free, 250-year-life paper
Manufactured in the United States of America

NOV 19 1998

Contents

Introduction

Informed that an encyclopedia was being prepared on Japanese nationalism, a scholar-friend of mine inquired, in the well-honed, reflexive manner of a good teacher: "How do you define nationalism?" Then, barely pausing for a reply, he continued: "That's really interesting; it's such an important topic. Let's have a talk." His response was typical. Scholars might argue interminably about definitions, yet they and other opinion leaders have agreed for decades that nationalism lies at the core of Japan's modern development. Elusive or not, nationalism is one of those topics that anyone seeking to explain the Pacific archipelago's last century and a half simply dare not ignore.

Almost as soon as U.S. Commodore Matthew Perry arrived in Edo Bay in the 1850s, a variety of antiforeign nationalism, or xenophobia, reared its head. Even the commoner-inspired broadsides *(kawaraban)* that enlivened the streets of the Tokugawa capital berated the foreign devils. Three-quarters of a century later, after Japan had experienced massive doses of modernization, the journalist Kanesada Hanazono noted, with neither approbation nor reproach, that "the two salient features of the Japanese press are that it has been struggling for the extension of the people's rights and has always been nationalistic."[1]

As the twentieth century neared its end, after decades of remarkable economic growth, the Japanese were once again producing thousands of articles and hundreds of books on nationalistic topics—everything from analyses of what makes Japanese culture unique *(Nihonjinron)*, to neo-nationalist appeals by men such as Ishihara Shintarō and Ikutarō Shimizu, who wish Japan to take a more aggressive stance against varied international pressures. If an inchoate sense of Japan's specialness has vaguely undergirded much of Japanese policy since Shōtoku Taishi sent his unwelcome greetings from the "land of the rising sun" to the "land of the setting sun" (China) in the seventh century A.D., something akin to our modern definitions of nationalism has motivated most of Japan's decision makers precisely, and often urgently, at least since the mid-nineteenth century.

This chronology helps account for the fact that a fairly rich, if highly uneven, literature in English exists on Japanese nationalism. The classic study, indeed the only overall treatment, is Delmer Brown's *Nationalism in Japan* (Russell and Russell, 1955), which traces nationalism from the earliest times to the immediate post–World War II years. Among studies of specific topics and periods, the largest volume of work has been done on the ultranationalism of the tumultuous prewar decades of the 1920s and 1930s. This literature includes Maruyama Masao's *Thought and Behaviour in Modern Japanese Politics* (Oxford University Press, 1969), Richard Storry's *The Double Patriots: A Study of Japanese Nationalism* (Greenwood Press, 1973), Hugh Byas's more journalistic *Government by Assassination* (Allen and Unwin, 1943), and Ivan Morris's *Nationalism and the Right Wing in Japan* (Oxford University Press, 1960), which focuses on the connections between postwar nationalism and the prewar era.

A second spate of literature on nationalist movements has appeared in more recent years. These discuss the many national self-analyses that preoccupied many Japanese from the mid-1970s to the beginning of the 1990s. On a popular level, works such as Ezra Vogel's *Japan As Number One* (Harvard University Press, 1979) and Ishihara's *The Japan That Can Say No* (Simon and Schuster, 1991) have captured huge readerships by evoking a Japan sufficiently strong to lead the world. On a more analytical level, Peter Dale's *The Myth of Japanese Uniqueness* (Croom, 1986) and Yoshino Kosaku's *Cultural Nationalism in Contemporary Japan* (Routledge, 1992) have sought the roots and meaning of Japan's national self-obsession.

Fewer scholarly works exist on early modern nationalism, although several superb studies have examined other, specific, national developments with a direct bearing on nationalism. The most notable such book is Carol Gluck's *Japan's Modern Myths: Ideology in the Late Meiji Period* (Princeton University Press, 1985), a seminal work that traces the rise of Japan's *tennōsei* (emperor system) ideology in the late nineteenth and early twentieth centuries. Kenneth B. Pyle's *The New Generation in Meiji Japan* (Stanford University Press, 1969), a study of the identity search of Japanese who came into their own in the 1880s, raises important issues related to nationalism in the nineteenth century, as do Donald Rodin's *Schooldays in Imperial Japan* (University of California Press, 1980), which examines the creation of elite culture in Japan's first government-sponsored school for promising young men; Bob Tadashi Wakabayashi's *Antiforeignism and Western Learning in Early-Modern Japan* (Harvard University Press, 1986), a study of the "New Thesis" of Aizawa Seishisai; Stefan Tanaka's important work, *Japan's Orient* (University of California Press, 1993), which looks at historical discussions of the nature of Japan and China in the Meiji era (1868–1912); and H.D. Harootunian's analysis of the ideas of the late-Tokugawa national-learning (*kokugaku*) scholars in *Things Seen and Unseen* (University of Chicago Press, 1988).

Although these studies of nationalism vary widely in their analyses of what the subject means and whence it evolved, the peculiar turns of Japan's modern history have dictated that almost all of them share one common, somewhat peculiar, characteristic. Regardless of the period or specific theme upon which they are focusing, writers on nationalism almost always use World War II as a point of reference. The neo-nationalists of the 1980s and their analysts hark back to a war era that either haunts or inspires evolving post-Shōwa (1926–89) expressions of national pride. Discussions of *tennōsei* rarely move far from the question of how such attitudes helped trigger the ultranationalism that led Japan into a major war against the world. Pyle's new generation reacts to Westernization in ways that portend a later, more extremist recipe for cultural chauvinism. This focus may be inevitable, given the cataclysmic effects of Japan's empire-mongering. It also has a regrettable side; we probably will not be able to develop a full and balanced understanding of the role that nationalism played until what the Japanese call the Great Pacific War (1937–45) ceases to loom so large in our consciousness.

Another problem that characterizes studies of nationalism is the difficulty of defining the term. During the search for contributors for this encyclopedia, no question arose more frequently than how nationalism was to be defined. The concept is inherently complex, even elusive. The effort to define it is hampered by the significant differences in the varieties of nationalism from era to era and from place to place. Clarity also is rendered difficult by the many varieties of nationalism that appear within identical eras and locales. The issue revolves around cultural definitions of the national self, the political activities of the state, and the intellectual debates of academic elites. Nationalism may be located in military, intellectual, economic, or literary guises. Sometimes it springs from fear, often from pride, frequently from a need for political cohesion, and at times from rank ignorance.

All—or nearly all—scholars do agree that the concept of nationalism includes a body of people, called the nation, who, in the words of Yoshino, see themselves as "a distinct community with distinctive characteristics."[2] To define nationalism simply as a commonly shared love of, and identification with, the nation sounds vague and simplistic, but although more will be said later in this essay about specific guises that nationalism took in different eras, the broad definition probably is the only sensible one in a work such as this one, in which the editor included writings from nearly every academic discipline, touching on developments across the entire modern period.

One need not employ such wide brushstrokes, however, in discussing certain issues that appear repeatedly in most examinations of Japanese nationalism—and in the more than 425 entries that make up the body of this encyclopedia. A careful reading of the materials that follow should reinforce a number of standard conceptions regarding modern Japanese development, including the idea that particularly close ties exist between nationalism and the emperor system in Japan, as well as the idea that one feature of being Japanese is to query repeatedly what it *means* to be Japanese. But that careful reading also should challenge some of our assumptions and raise several new questions, particularly as they relate to the sources and uses of nationalism.

One of the first impressions is the variety and richness of the styles of nationalism that have flourished on Japanese soil since the mid-1850s. Pyle wrote an influential essay in the 1970s illustrating this fact. He examined six different ways in which analysts tend to appraise nationalism: the "idea," or intellectual, approach; the functional approach; structural analyses; "interest theories," which perceive nationalism growing from the needs of certain groups; "strain theories," which trace nationalism to clashes or conflicts in society; and the cultural approach.[3] Pyle focused on analytical methods rather than on nationalism itself, but his examples make it abundantly clear—as do the entries in this encyclopedia—that the varieties of nationalism are nearly limitless.

Mutsu Munemitsu, Japanese foreign minister in the 1890s, is described in the entries following as a pragmatic nationalist, scarcely interested in emotional attachments to the country but eager to utilize popular loyalties in making Japan powerful. Nakano Seigō, a right-wing activist of the 1930s, represents popular nationalism, an emotive and extremist brand that most officials eschewed even during the war years. Kita Ikki, a similarly extremist exponent of nationalism in the same period, illustrates the hold that nationalism had on many socialists and other left-wingers. Natsume Sōseki espoused a type of cultural nationalism that rejected chauvinism and all political forms of nationalism. Others have championed GNP nationalism, pressure nationalism (a response to international criticism of Japanese economic policies in the 1980s), agrarian nationalism, imperialistic nationalism, *tennōsei* nationalism, neo-nationalism, and a score of others. Charles Yates's entry on the old samurai Saigō Takamori shows a man who deeply loved the emperor yet was not a nationalist in any meaningful sense, because he had no "specific idea of Japan as a distinct and coherent political entity, or of the Japanese as a people united by a shared sense of nationhood." The point is that no single conception of the term can encompass all of its many uses and facets. The broad definition posited above—of nationalism as mere love of country—may well fit them all, but beyond that it is impossible to go, because the different needs of different eras, places, and peoples have dictated vastly divergent meanings of the term.

Even more striking, and less often discussed, is the fact that differences in the guises worn by nationalism have corresponded directly with the differences in Japan's modern eras themselves. Many scholars commit the error of identifying a Meiji nationalism as either a sibling or a parent of the various forms operating in the 1990s, while in truth it was probably no more than a distant cousin. Maruyama wrote of a "cycle of nationalism: birth, maturity and decline," which he saw as completed with Japan's defeat in World War II.[4] He obviously was thinking of political nationalism, the variety that helped leaders unify the state, then propelled that state into the quest for territory and into war. For Maruyama, the nationalism of the 1870s was no different fundamentally from that of the 1930s. Viewed from another perspective, it seems clear that nationalistic movements and impulses not only underwent different stages but also encompassed vastly different content in successive decades and eras.

One scheme of nationalism might postulate four varieties: (1) incipient, fear-driven nationalism, from 1850 to 1868, when a changing elite was forced to deal with new and immensely threatening international incursions into the sacred homeland; (2) nation-building nationalism, from 1868 to 1900, when the Meiji oligarchs directed frenetic efforts to shape Japan's people into a coherent, strong state worthy of recognition as an equal by the Western powers; (3) empire-building nationalism, from 1900 to 1945, when Japan sought to expand its territories and to defeat the world in war; and (4) market-building nationalism, since 1945 (or at least 1952), as Japan has flung its energies into economic dominance. Although each of these eras had similarities, such as a somewhat parallel commitment to the Japanese nation-state, at heart the differences probably have been greater than the similarities.

In the first period, potentially national symbols such as mutual allegiance to the emperor (*tennō*) may have made the anti-Tokugawa movement possible, but the rebels' driving forces had more to do with family or regional allegiances and fears of foreigners than with any coherent idea of a Japanese nation. In the early Meiji years, nationalism was essentially a domestic phenomenon, wrapped in intense arguments over the nature of sovereignty, the structure of Japan's *kokutai* (national polity), the relationship between the governors and the governed—and, above all, how to define "Japan" as one among many nation-states of the world.

By the twentieth century, the questions and foci had changed dramatically. On the one hand, nationalists now talked increasingly about Japan's rightful place in the world order, not just where it fit but what lands it ought to acquire. By the 1930s, the focus was not only on uniqueness and the nature of Japan's polity but also on superiority: divine origins and superior values. After the war and a period of deep national angst, the nationalism that reemerged from the 1950s onward was of yet a different order. Discussions of superiority were resurrected, but the focus now was not on the emperor or on the divine origins of the Japanese nation but on the values of the Japanese *people*, values such as hard work, a willingness to sacrifice individual interests to the broader group, and a capacity for making wise economic decisions. The goal, at least until the 1990s, was almost exclusively economic.

There is no denying the links between these different forms; nor should one overlook how what may have been tangential ideas in one period survived to become central in another. But too often, experts have erred in not identifying carefully enough the distinctive characteristics of each period. It is in this vein that Yoshino is helpful. He points out that the cultural nationalism inherent in most *Nihonjinron* of the 1980s had little to do with the more political, more aggressive empire-building nationalism of the 1930s (his "primary nationalism"). The cultural nationalists at the time of the death of the Shōwa Emperor (more popularly known in the West as Hirohito) in 1989 may or may not have desired greater independence for Japan in foreign-policy considerations, but they generally had only limited interest in strengthening the emperor's role at the core of the Japanese state. And Yoshino sees little chance for a linking of the old and new forms.[5]

A third point that emerges repeatedly in the entries that follow has to do with causes. At times, external forces and domestic traditions may have produced a responsive populace ready to participate in seemingly spontaneous nationalist movements. The underlying reality consistently was that the forces of nationalism were created and directed (though often with unintended consequences) by the governing elite. This probably will surprise no one who is interested primarily in the ultranationalism of the 1930s. Accounts of the War Ministry issuing pamphlets about war as the father of creation and the Education Ministry filling textbooks with patriotic paeans have become standard in studies of that era. Less well known, but just as apparent in the entries following, are the strenuous efforts that the earlier Meiji government exerted in the creation of nationalism.

Eric Hobsbawn has written that, although modern countries "generally claim to be . . . rooted in the remotest antiquity," and although they proclaim themselves to be "human communities so 'natural' as to require no definition other than self-assertion," the opposite often is true: These states *invent* traditions to lend themselves legitimacy.[6] Although his illustrations are drawn exclusively from the West, Hobsbawn might as well have been describing nineteenth-century Japan.

Terrified by foreign threats, convinced that the masses were "unlearned, powerless fools,"[7] and worried that the people and the government were "separated from each other by ten million miles, from above the heavens to underneath the earth,"[8] the early Meiji officials endeavored to bind the *heimin* (masses) emotionally to the new state by creating traditions, symbols, and institutions that would foster nationalism. Best known are the military-draft and compulsory-education systems, both designed to enlighten the masses and bind them to their country. Less well known, at least to general readers, are the carefully calculated attempts to create symbols of the nation—ceremonies, events, and holidays that appealed to the hearts and senses more than to the intellect. In 1870, these officials adopted a national flag; in 1873, they made a public holiday out of *Kigensetsu* (Empire Day), commemorating the descent from the heavens of the first emperor, Jimmu, to assume the Japanese throne); in 1890, they issued the Imperial Rescript on Education, which made loyalty to family, emperor, and state the people's central value; in 1893, schools ordered children to sing "Kimi ga yo," the national song, on all holidays. And so it went; by 1906, in the words of one pleased statesman, "the Japanese now are all a loyal and patriotic people."[9]

Nor was it the government alone that built nationalism among the masses. Intellectuals of later periods would argue about the acceptable forms, indeed the very efficacy, of nationalism, but these years found the elites in all fields, official and nonofficial alike, cooperating to bring their "lower fellows" into the national circle. Village headmen west of Tokyo would devise constitutional schemes to spread national consciousness among the commoners of their own regions; in the world of journalism, Tokutomi Sohō would publish for the express purpose of "nurturing feelings of mutual affection among the people,"[10] and art historian Okakura Kakuzō would rewrite the history of Japanese art "to stir an interest in and understanding of Japan's national past."[11] By establishment consensus, Japan was fragmented and backward, and the Confucian-educated elites of the late nineteenth century saw the building of nationalism as a first priority in correcting that flaw.

Whether the cultural and economic forms of postwar nationalism have been quite so carefully and consciously nurtured is less clear. It is apparent, however, in entries as diverse as those by Harumi Befu, Bradford L. Simcock, Mikiso Hane, and J. Victor Koschmann that many elite institutions have striven mightily to counteract what they perceive as undue individualism in contemporary society and to encourage a return to "Japanese" values. In fact, many respected intellectuals found business and political manipulation even in the supposedly spontaneous outpouring of national sympathy at the time of the Shōwa Emperor's death.[12] We are probably too close to this period to determine whether new forms of nationalism are indeed being created from above, or whether *Nihonjinron* and the more political, traditional forms of nationalism are spontaneous, popular expressions. The experience of the earlier eras suggests that scholars need to pay careful attention to the motives and activities of the elites when analyzing the sentiments of the masses.

A fourth issue raised in these entries is the often-noted, but nonetheless remarkable, connection in all eras between the emperor system and Japanese nationalism. Already in the 1850s and 1860s, at the dusk of the feudalistic Edo era, it was the unique, unbroken line of the imperial family that restorationist forces invoked most effectively in their efforts to protect the country and throw out what they considered the Tokugawa usurpers. After 1868, the new government took Shinto, which had been essentially a shamanist spiritual institution, and politicized it; the officials made Meiji a modern *emperor*, then dispatched him on more than 100 tours of the countryside to review troops, award titles, and show the people that they had a ruler. In other words, to stimulate nationalism, they turned the Tokugawa-era high priest into a Meiji-era state sovereign.[13]

By the 1930s, the *tennō* had become not only priest and ruler but teacher and father as well. As a result, absolute loyalty to him had become the ultimate test of genuine nationalism. Inadequate loyalty to the emperor sent holiness pastors and Communists alike to jail. It should not be surprising then, that scholars often regard the Shōwa Emperor's renunciation of divinity on January 1, 1946, as the prime symbol of a new national spirit at the end of World War II or that they consider the massive attention paid to his 1989 death, along with the heavy dose of Shinto rituals included in his funeral, as a key symbol of resurgent nationalism in the late twentieth century.

Observers might disagree on what attachment to the imperial symbol means. Some might see it as a harmless, or even positive, national glue; others might fear that it portends a return to militarism or to an acceptance of authoritarianism. But there is unanimity—among the contributors in this encyclopedia as well as among scholars at large—about the complex, but unalterably close, relationship between the imperial system and all forms of Japanese nationalism. The historian Takeda Kiyoko, writing about the 1930s, asserted that the Shōwa Emperor "was, in effect, used as a tool for clarification of the fundamental nature of the Japanese state."[14] The same could be said about the use of each emperor in every modern era.

In Japan, as in so many countries in the twentieth-century, nationalism has proved to be the most enduring of all value systems. It has taken the place of older allegiances to family and lord, giving to the idea of Nihon (Japan)—the spiritual force reserved in other places only for gods or God. The forms, meanings, and purposes of nationalism have varied markedly from era to era and from group to group. Its wellsprings have been anything but natural; indeed, nationalism might be compared to a traditional Japanese garden, intentionally devised and carefully nurtured to make it *appear* as if it were natural. But none of these facts negates the most important reality of all, that what Maruyama calls the "spiritual motive force"[15] of nationalism has dominated Japan's political and social evolution for more than a century and a half. For that reason alone, the entries in this encyclopedia deserve careful examination. Taken individually, they present important, often curious, images. As a whole, they demonstrate a massive and complex phenomenon that must be studied in greater detail if the reality that is modern Japan is to be grasped.

James L. Huffman

Notes

1. Kanesada Hanazono, *Journalism in Japan and Its Early Pioneers* (Osaka: Osaka Mainichi, 1926), 2.
2. Yoshino Kosaku, *Cultural Nationalism in Contemporary Japan* (London: Routledge, 1992), 6.
3. Kenneth B. Pyle, "Some Recent Approaches to Japanese Nationalism," *Journal of Asian Studies*, Vol. 31 (November 1971), 5–16.
4. Maruyama Masao, *Thought and Behaviour in Modern Japanese Politics* (London: Oxford University Press, 1969), 7–8.
5. Yoshino, 219–22.
6. Eric Hobsbawn, *The Invention of Tradition* (Cambridge: Cambridge University Press, 1984), 14.
7. Editorial in *Yūbin Hōchi Shimbun*, April 4, 1875.
8. Tokutomi Sohō, *Shorai no Nihon* (The Future Japan), in *Tokutomi Sohō shū* (Collected Works of Tokutomi Sohō), Vol. 34 of *Meiji bungaku zenshū* (Complete Works of Meiji Literature) (Tokyo: Echima Shobō, 1974), 106.
9. Ōkuma Shigenobu, quoted in Carol Gluck, *Japan's Modern Myths: Ideology in the Late Meiji Period* (Princeton, NJ: Princeton University Press, 1985), 35.
10. Journal *Kokumin no Tomo*, January 3, 1890, quoted in Okano Takeo, *Meiji genron shi* (History of the Meiji Press) (Tokyo: Hō Shuppan, 1974), 112.
11. Stefan Tanaka, "Imaging History: Inscribing Belief in the Nation," *Journal of Asian Studies*, Vol. 53, No. 1 (February 1994), 40.
12. Watanabe Osamu, "The Sociology of *Jishuku* and *Kichō*: The Death of the *Shōwa Tennō* as a Reflection of the Structure of Contemporary Japanese Society," *Japan Forum*, Vol. 1, No. 2 (October 1989), 275–89.
13. For a discussion of the conflicting "political" and "natural" roles of the emperor, see Igarashi Akio, "Kindaishi no seitōka ni hatasu 'junsuisei' no ayausa," *Asahi Jānaru*, Vol. 31, No. 4 (January 25, 1989), 94–99.
14. Takeda Kiyoko, "Emperor Hirohito and the Turbulent Shōwa Era," *Japan Foundation Newsletter* (June 1989), 3.
15. Maruyama Masao, *Studies in the Intellectual History of Tokugawa Japan* (Tokyo: University of Tokyo Press, 1974), 324.

Subject List

Anti-Nationalist Activities
Ampo Movement
Atomic Bombs
Bikini Atomic Tests
Holiness Band Oppression
Ienaga Saburō
Kanno Suga (Sugako)
Kawai Eijirō
Kawakami Hajime
Kiryū Yūyū
Kōtoku Shūsui
Miki Kiyoshi
Nakano Seigō
Ōe Kenzaburō
Ōsugi Sakae
Ōyama Ikuo
Pacifism
Popular Front Incident
Professors' Group Affair
Saitō Takao
Toranomon Incident
Uchimura Kanzō
Yanaihara Tadao
Yosano Akiko
Yoshimoto Takaaki

Censorship (see Government Control)

Communications
Adachi Kenzō
Akiyama Teisuke
Associated Press of Japan
Censorship
Commoners' Newspaper
Dōmei News Agency
Friend of the Nation
Fukuchi Gen'ichirō
Fukuzawa Yukichi
Itō Miyoji

Iwanaga Yūkichi
Japan Telegraphic News Agency
Kiryū Yūyū
Kokumin Shimbun
Kokusai News Agency
Kuroiwa Shūroku
Maruyama Masao
Miyake Setsurei
Nakano Seigō
Nihon Hōsō Kyōkai (NHK)
Saionji Kinmochi
Sakai Toshihiko
Tokutomi Sohō
Yamaji Aizan
Yokohama Incident

Communism (see Socialism)

Concepts
Agrarian Nationalism
Bushidō
Debate on Japanese Capitalism
Dutch Studies
Family State
Fascism
Folklore Studies
Internationalization
The Japanese
Japanese Monroe Doctrine
Kamikaze
Labor Farmer Faction
Mito Learning
National Essence
Nativism, National Learning
New Nationalism
New Order in East Asia
Nihonjinron
Organ Theory
Overcoming the Modern

Pacifism
Rich Country, Strong Army
Shōwa Research Association
Shōwa Restoration
Society for Political Education
Spencer, Herbert
Spirit of Japan

Cultural Nationalism
Academy for the Love of One's
  Community
Agrarian Nationalism
Cardinal Principles of the National Polity
Emperor System
Family State
Folklore Studies
Great New Food Festival
Harvest Festival
Hinomaru
Inoue Nisshō
Ishihara Shintarō
The Japanese
Japanese Language
Japanese Romantic School
Kawabata Yasunari
League of the Divine Wind
Mishima Yukio
Mito Learning
Miyake Setsurei
Moral Education
Nakano Seigō
National Essence
Nativism, National Learning
Nihonjinron
Nishimura Shigeki
Nitobe Inazō
Okakura Kakuzō
Rice
Sake
Shiga Shigetaka
Shinto
Society of the People's Friends
State Foundation Society
Sugiura Shigetake
Sumo
Tanigawa Gan
True Japan Society
Watsuji Tetsurō
Yanagita Kunio

Culture and Society
Citizens' Movements
Civilization and Enlightenment
Conciliation Movement
Deer Cry Pavilion

Emperor's Birthday
Empire Day
Expo '70
Folklore Studies
Foreign Employees
Great New Food Festival
Harvest Festival
Information Society
Internationalization
Japanese Language
Korean Minority in Japan
Levellers Society
Nihon Hōsō Kyōkai (NHK)
1980s
Okakura Kakuzō
Olympic Games, 1964
Rice
Sake
"The Sovereign's Reign"
Student Movements
Trade and Economic Development
Value Creation Society
War Songs

Decrees, Documents, Treaties
Article Nine
Charter Oath
Constitution (1947)
Imperial Rescript on Education
Imperial Rescript to Soldiers and Sailors
Japan-U.S. Security Treaties
Meiji Constitution
Peace Preservation Law (1925)
Peace Regulations (1887)
Root-Takahira Agreement
San Francisco Peace Treaty
Shimonoseki Treaty
Taft-Katsura Agreement
Tanaka Memorandum
Versailles Peace Treaty
Yamagata-Lobanov Convention

Diplomacy (see International Relations)

Economics
Federation of Economic Organizations
Financial Clique
Foreign Aid (ODA)
Foreign Labor (Unskilled)
Greater East Asia Coprosperity Sphere
Ikeda Hayato
Inoue Junnosuke
Ministry of International Trade and Industry
  (MITI)
New Nationalism

1980s
Nixon Shocks
Oil Crisis
Reverse Course
Rice Riots
Rich Country, Strong Army
Shibusawa Eiichi
South Manchurian Railway
Takahashi Korekiyo
Trade and Economic Development

Education
Cardinal Principles of the National Polity
First Higher School
Fukuzawa Yukichi
Fundamental Law of Education
Gakuren Incident
Hiraga Purge
Ienaga Saburō
Imperial Rescript on Education
Inoue Kowashi
Ministry of Education
Minobe Tatsukichi
Moral Education
Mori Arinori
Motoda Eifu
Nishimura Shigeki
Nitobe Inazō
Shimoda Utako
Sugiura Shigetake
Takigawa Affair
Textbook Controversy
Textbooks
Yamawaki Fusako
Yanaihara Tadao
Yoshioka Yayoi

Emperor System
Agrarian Nationalism
Emperor System
Emperor's Birthday
Empire Day
Greater Japan Federated Youth Association
Harvest Festival
Heisei
Hozumi Yatsuka
Imperial Household Ministry
Imperial Military Reservist Association
Imperial Rescript on Education
Imperial Rescript to Soldiers and Sailors
Kido Kōichi
Meiji Emperor
Motoda Eifu
National Essence
National Socialism Movement

Nativism, National Learning
Nogi Maresuke
Organ Theory
Privy Council
Saigō Takamori
Shinto
Sovereign's Reign, the
State Shinto
Textbooks
Toranomon Incident

Eras
Meiji Era
Occupation (Allied)
Shōwa Era
Taishō Era

Ethnic Issues and Groups (see Social Issues)

Government Control
Cabinet Information Bureau
Cardinal Principles of the National Polity
Censorship
"Change of Direction"
Cooperation and Harmony Society
Dōmei News Agency
Emperor System
Gakuren Incident
Hiraga Purge
Holiness Band Oppression
Home Ministry
Imperial Rule Assistance Association
Kiryū Yūyū
March 15 Incident
Military Police
Ministry of Education
Moral Education
National Mobilization Law
New Order Movement
Peace Preservation Law (1925)
Peace Regulations (1887)
Popular Front Incident
Professors' Group Affair
Public Peace Police Law
Purges During the Allied Occupation (1945–
    52)
Red Flag Incident
Special Higher Police
Terauchi Masatake
Textbooks
United Church of Christ in Japan
Yamagata Aritomo
Yokohama Incident

Imperialism

Colonialism (1895–1945)
Concordia Society
Conquer Korea Argument
Crisis of 1873
East Asia Common Culture Society
East Asian League
Ishiwara Kanji
Japanese Monroe Doctrine
Komura Jutarō
Korea
Lytton Commission
Manchukuo
Manchurian Incident
Mutual Friendship Society
New Order in East Asia
Seven Professors Incident
Shanghai Incident
Shimonoseki Treaty
Siberian Intervention
Sino-Japanese War (1894–95)
South Manchurian Railway
Taiwan
Tanaka Memorandum
Tōyama Mitsuru
Triple Intervention
Twenty-One Demands
World War I
World War II

Incidents

Asanuma Inejirō
February 26 Incident
Inukai Tsuyoshi
League of Blood Incident
Kyoto University Incidents
March 15 Incident
March Incident
Marco Polo Bridge Incident
Maria Luz Incident
May Day Incident
May 15 Incident
Meiji Restoration
Mishima Yukio
Nagasaki Flag Incident
Narita Airport Dispute
Normanton Incident
October Incident
Ōi Kentarō
Political Crisis of 1881
Popular Front Incident
Professors' Group Affair
Red Flag Incident
Rice Riots

Seven Professors Incident
Shanghai Incident
Shimanaka Incident
Shimpeitai Incident
Siemens Incident
Sōmagahara Incident
Sorge Incident
Takigawa Affair
Textbook Controversy
Toranomon Incident
Triple Intervention
Twenty-One Demands
Yokohama Incident

International Relations

Anglo-Japanese Alliance
Anticomintern Pact
Coalition Movement
Conquer Korea Argument
Deer Cry Pavillion
East Asia Common Culture Society
Foreign Aid
Foreign Employees
Fresh Wind Society
Hirota Kōki
Iwakura Tomomi
Japan-U.S. Security Treaties
Japanese Monroe Doctrine
Korea
League of Nations
London Naval Treaty
Lytton Commission
MacArthur, Douglas
Manchukuo
Maria Luz Incident
Matsumoto Shigeharu
Matsuoka Yōsuke
Mori Arinori
Mutsu Munemitsu
Mutual Friendship Society
Nagai Ryūtarō
Nagasaki Flag Incident
Nakasone Yasuhiro
National Seclusion
New Nationalism
1980s
Nitobe Inazō
Nixon Shocks
Normanton Incident
Occupation (Allied)
Oil Crisis
Perry, Matthew Calbraith
Portsmouth Treaty
Potsdam Declaration

Root-Takahira Agreement
Ryūkyū, Disposition of
Sakuma Shōzan
San Francisco Peace Treaty
Shidehara Kijūrō
Shigemitsu Mamoru
Soejima Taneomi
Sōmagahara Incident
Taft-Katsura Agreement
Taiwan
Tanaka Giichi
Tanaka Memorandum
Tatekawa Yoshitsugu
Territorial Disputes
Textbook Controversy
Three Nonnuclear Principles
Tōgō Shigenori
Treaty Revision
Tripartite Pact
Triple Intervention
Versailles Peace Treaty
Washington Conference
Yalta Agreement
Yamagata-Lobanov Convention
Yoshida Shigeru

Journalism (see Communications)

Labor
Akamatsu Katsumaro
Cooperation and Harmony Society
Factory Girls
Kagawa Toyohiko
Kawai Eijirō
Labor Movement (postwar)
Labor Movement (prewar)
Ōyama Ikuo
Public Peace Police Law
Suzuki Bunji

Literature
Hayashi Fusao
Ishihara Shintarō
Japanese Romantic School
Kawabata Yausnari
Mishima Yukio
Natsume Sōseki
Naturalism
Ōe Kenzaburō
Takeuchi Yoshimi
Tanigawa Gan
Tanizaki Jun'ichirō
Yosano Akiko
Yoshimoto Takaaki

Military
Aizawa Saburō
Anami Korechika
Araki Sadao
Article Nine
Boshin War
Bushidō
Control Faction
Imperial Military Reservist Association
Imperial Rescript to Soldiers and Sailors
Imperial Way Faction
Ishiwara Kanji
Kamikaze
Katō Hiroharu
Koiso Kuniaki
Manchukuo
Manchurian Incident
Marco Polo Bridge Incident
Mazaki (Masaki) Jinzaburō
Miura Gorō
Mutō Akira
Nagata Tetsuzan
National Defense State
New Nationalism
Nishida Mitsugi (Zei, Mitsugu)
Nogi Maresuke
Obata Toshirō
Okada Keisuke
Portsmouth Treaty
Power of Supreme Command
Russo-Japanese War
Saga Rebellion
Saigō Takamori
Saitō Makoto
Satsuma Rebellion
Shanghai Incident
Shimonoseki Treaty
Shrine of the Peaceful Country
Siberian Expedition
Sino-Japanese War
Sōmagahara Incident
Suzuki Kantarō
Taiwan
Takashima Shūhan
Tanaka Giichi
Tatekawa Yoshitsugu
Tōgō Heihachirō
Tōjō Hideki
Tokyo War Crimes Trials
Triple Intervention
Ugaki Kazushige
Washington Conference
World War I
World War II

Yamagata Aritomo
Yamamoto Gonnohyōe (Gonbei)
Yamamoto Isoroku
Yonai Mitsumasa
Young Officers' Movement

Organizations and Political Parties
Academy for the Love of One's Community
All-Japan Student Federation
Amur River Society
Cherry Blossom Society
Conciliation Movement
Concordia Society
Cooperation and Harmony Society
Endure Society
Federation of Economic Organizations
Great Japan National Essence Association
Greater East Asia Society
Greater Japan Federated Youth Association
Greater Japan National Defense Women's
  Association
Greater Japan Women's Association
Greater Japan Youth Party
Home Ministry
Imperial Military Reservist Association
Imperial Way Faction
Institute of the Golden Pheasant
Jimmu Society
League for the Study of Government
Meiji Six Society
National Foundations Society
Nonchurch Christian Movement
Patriotic Women's Society
Public Party of Patriots
Shōwa Research Association
Society for Political Education
Society of Patriots
Society of the People's Friends
State Foundation Society
Ultranationalist Groups
United Church of Christ in Japan
Women's Movements

Philosophy and the World of Ideas
Abe Isoo
Fukuzawa Yukichi
Gondō Seikyō
Hirano Yoshitarō
Hiratsuka Raichō
Hozumi Yatsuka
Ienaga Saburō
Inoue Kowashi
Ishihara Shintarō
Itō Noe
Kanno Suga (Sugako)

Katō Hiroyuki
Kawai Eijirō
Kawakami Hajime
Kinoshita Naoe
Kita Ikki
Kōtoku Shūsui
Maruyama Masao
Miki Kiyoshi
Minobe Tatsukichi
Miyake Setsurei
Nishida Kitarō
Nishimura Shigeki
Okakura Kakuzō (pen name Tenshin)
Shiga Shigetaka
Shimizu Ikutarō
Spencer, Herbert
Sugiura Shigetake
Takabatake Motoyuki
Takamure Itsue
Takeuchi Yoshimi
Tanigawa Gan
Uesugi Shinkichi
Watsuji Tetsurō
Yanagita Kunio
Yanaihara Tadao
Yoshino Sakuzō

Politics and Government
Adachi Kenzō
Bureau of Rites
Constitution
Constitutional Democratic Party
Etō Shimpei
Freedom and People's Rights Movement
Friends of Constitutional Government Party
Hiranuma Kiichirō
Hirota Kōki
Ikeda Hayato
Imperial Rule Assistance Association
Inoue Junnosuke
Inoue Kaoru
Inoue Kowashi
Inukai Tsuyoshi
Ishibashi Tanzan
Ishihara Shintarō
Itagaki Taisuke
Itō Hirobumi
Itō Miyoji
Katō Hiroyuki
Katō Takaaki
Katsura Tarō
Kido Kōichi
Kido Takayoshi
Kishi Nobusuke
Kiyoura Keigo

Koiso Kuniaki
Komura Jutarō
Konoe Fumimaro
Matsuoka Yōsuke
Meiji Constitution
Meiji Restoration
Miura Gorō
Nagai Ryūtarō
Nakano Seigō
Nakasone Yasuhiro
1980s
Occupation (Allied)
Ōi Kentarō
Okada Keisuke
Ōkubo Toshimichi
Ōkuma Shigenobu
Ono Azusa
Ōyama Ikuo
Ozaki Yukio
Political Crisis of 1881
Public Party of Patriots
Reverse Course
Saigō Takamori
Saigō Tsugumichi
Saionji Kinmochi
Saitō Makoto
Saitō Takao
Satō Eisaku
Senior Statesmen
Shidehara Kijūrō
Shigemitsu Mamoru
Social Masses Party
Society of Patriots
Soejima Taneomi
Suzuki Kantarō
Takahashi Korekiyo
Tanaka Giichi
Terauchi Masatake
Tōjō Hideki
Ugaki Kazushige
Yamagata Aritomo
Yamamoto Gonnohyōe (Gonbei)
Yonai Mitsumasa
Yoshida Shigeru

Popular Movements and Uprisings
"Ain't It Great"
All-Japan Student Federation
Citizens' Movements
Coalition Movement
Freedom and People's Rights Movement
Hibiya Riots
League for Establishing a National Assembly
League of the Divine Wind
May Day Incident

Narita Airport Dispute
Portsmouth Treaty
Revere the Emperor and Expel the Barbarians
Rice Riots
Saga Rebellion
Satsuma Rebellion
Student Movements
Tachibana Kōzaburō
Women's Movements

Religion
Aum Supreme Truth Religion
Conference of Three Religions
Deguchi Nao
Holiness Band Oppression
Kagawa Toyohiko
Meiji Shrine
Nichiren Sect
Nonchurch Christian Movement
Shinto
Shrine of the Peaceful Country
State Shinto
Uchimura Kanzō
United Church of Christ in Japan
Value Creation Society

Scandals
Akiyama Teisuke
Kodama Yoshio
Lockheed Scandal
Political Crisis of 1881
Siemens Incident
Toshiba Scandal

Social Issues
Ainu
Anti-Semitism
Conciliation Movement
Factory Girls
Foreign Labor
Korean Minority in Japan
Levellers Society
Mutual Friendship Society
Ryūkyū, Disposition of
Three Nonnuclear Principles

Socialism
Akamatsu Katsumaro
Akao Bin
Ampo Movement
Asanuma Inejirō
Debate on Japanese Capitalism
Gakuren Incident
Hirano Yoshitarō
Itō Noe

Chronology

1853 Tokugawa Iesada became shogun; U.S. Commodore Matthew Perry arrived in Japan.

1854 Kanagawa Treaty signed with the United States, opening Japan; Yoshida Shōin attempted to stow away to America.

1858 Commercial treaty signed with the United States, then other countries.

1860 Chief minister Ii Naosuke assassinated by antiforeign extremists; Japan's first mission sent to the West.

1862 Unsuccessful attempt made to join the court and the Tokugawa *bakufu*; British merchant Charles Richardson killed by Satsuma samurai.

1863 Battles fought between Western powers and Satsuma and Chōshū domains.

1864 Chōshū domain rebelled unsuccessfully against *bakufu*.

1866 Secret Satsuma-Chōshū alliance forged against *bakufu*; Tokugawa attack on Chōshū failed.

1867 Mass *eejanaika* movements began; Tokugawa Keiki resigned as shogun.

1868 Meiji Restoration; Charter Oath issued.

1869 Government forces won Boshin War over pro-Tokugawa troops; imperial capital moved from Kyoto to Tokyo.

1871 Iwakura Mission began to study Western nations; prefectures replaced feudal domains; Japan's first daily newspaper, *Yomiuri*, started; feudal domains abolished.

1872 Compulsory education decreed; *Maria Luz* Incident occurred.

1873 Universal military draft established; Iwakura Mission ended; Saigō Takamori left government over handling of relations with Korea.

1874 Taiwan expedition led to Japanese control of Ryūkyū Islands.

1875 Society of Patriots formed, disbanded.

1877	Saigō Takamori and followers rose up in unsuccessful Satsuma Rebellion.
1878	Home Minister Ōkubo Toshimichi assassinated.
1879	Okinawa Prefecture established.
1881	Political Crisis of 1881 yielded promise of constitution; Jiyūtō (Liberal Party) formed; Black Sea Society (Gen'yōsha) founded.
1882	Rikken Kaishintō (Constitutional Reform Party) and Teiseitō (Constitutional Imperial Party) formed; Imperial Rescript to Soldiers and Sailors issued.
1883	Rokumeikan built.
1884	Farmers rebelled in Chichibu; Jiyūtō disbanded.
1886	Normanton Incident sparked treaty-revision movement.
1887	Peace Regulations moved government opponents from Tokyo region; Tokutomi Sohō launched *Kokumin no Tomo*.
1889	Meiji Constitution promulgated; newspaper *Nihon* launched; Education Minister Mori Arinori assassinated.
1890	Imperial Rescript on Education promulgated; first Diet (legislature) convened.
1894	First Sino-Japanese War began.
1895	Shimonoseki Treaty gave Japan Taiwan and Liaodong Peninsula; Triple Intervention returned Liaodong to China.
1900	Japan participated in ending China's Boxer Rebellion.
1901	Patriotic Women's Society formed; Dentsū News Agency launched; Amur River Society founded.
1902	Anglo-Japanese Alliance signed.
1903	Japan's first socialist paper, *Heimin Shimbun*, founded.
1904	Russo-Japanese War began.
1905	Portsmouth Treaty gave Japan Russian holdings in Manchuria; Hibiya Riots protested treaty's weakness.
1908	Gentlemen's agreement ended Japanese laborers' immigration to United States; Red Flag Incident occurred.
1909	Itō Hirobumi assassinated in Manchuria.
1910	Korea annexed.
1911	Socialist/anarchist group executed for alleged plot against emperor; tariff autonomy obtained with Western nations.

1912	Meiji Emperor died; first labor union, Yūaikai, began; Taishō era began.
1913	Taishō crisis resulted in fall of Katsura Tarō cabinet.
1914	Siemens Incident erupted over bribery of naval officials; World War I began.
1915	Twenty-One Demands made on China.
1918	Riots occurred across Japan over high rice prices; Hara Takashi became first true political-party prime minister.
1920	Japan joined League of Nations.
1921	Hara Takashi assassinated; Washington Conference limited naval construction, replaced Anglo-Japanese Alliance.
1923	Great Kantō Earthquake devastated Tokyo.
1925	NHK (Nihon Hōso Kyōkai) began broadcasting; Peace Preservation Law issued; universal male suffrage enacted.
1926	Taishō Emperor died; Shōwa era began.
1928	March 15 Incident occurred.
1930	London Naval Treaty continued naval restrictions; Prime Minister Hamaguchi Osachi shot for agreeing to them.
1931	March Incident and Manchurian Incident occurred.
1932	League of Blood Incident took place; Prime Minister Inukai Tsuyoshi assassinated in May 15 Incident; Manchukuo established as Japanese puppet state in Manchuria.
1933	Japan left League of Nations; Takigawa Affair occurred.
1936	Young Officers staged February 26 Incident; Japan and Germany signed Anticomintern Pact; Dōmei News Agency formed.
1937	Second Sino-Japanese War began with Marco Polo Bridge Incident; government cracked down on leading leftists.
1938	Prime Minister Konoe Fumimaro announced new order in East Asia.
1939	Japanese and Soviet forces battled in Nomonhan region of southern Manchuria.
1940	Tripartite Pact signed by Japan, Germany, and Italy.
1941	Nonaggression Pact signed with Russia; Japan invaded Indochina; Tōjō Hideki became prime minister; Pearl Harbor bombing initiated Great Pacific War.
1942	Battle of Midway turned war's tide against Japan; Greater Japan Women's Association formed to support war effort.
1944	United States began bombing Japanese mainland.

1945	Okinawa invaded by Allies; atomic bombs dropped on Hiroshima, Nagasaki; Japan surrendered; Allied Occupation began.
1946	Land reform began; war crimes trials opened; new constitution approved.
1947	1947 Constitution took effect; postwar Diet opened; general strikes banned by Occupation forces; socialists briefly took power.
1948	War crimes trials ended, seven executed.
1949	American Joseph Dodge took charge of economy; MITI (Ministry of International Trade and Industry) created to encourage trade.
1950	Sōhyō (General Council of Trade Unions) labor union formed; widespread purge of communists undertaken; Korean War began.
1951	San Francisco Peace Treaty signed; Japan-U.S. Security Treaty signed.
1952	Occupation ended; May Day Incident took place.
1953	NHK began TV broadcasting. Korean War ended.
1954	Self-Defense Forces formed out of old Police Reserve Force; Bikini atomic tests conducted.
1955	Liberal Democratic Party organized.
1956	Japan joined United Nations.
1957	Sōmagahara Incident occurred over U.S. troop activities in Japan.
1958	Nagasaki Flag Incident took place.
1959	Intense debate waged over Japan-U.S. Security Treaty.
1960	Revised Treaty of Mutual Cooperation and Security led to resignation of Prime Minister Kishi Nobusuke; socialist leader Asanuma Inejirō assassinated.
1961	Prime Minister Ikeda Hayato announced income-doubling goal.
1964	Bullet train began operation; Summer Olympic Games held in Tokyo.
1968	Kawabata Yasunari won Nobel Prize in literature; student demonstration began at many universities.
1969	Citizens movements spread over environmental issues.
1970	Japan launched first satellite; Expo '70, Japan's first world fair, held in Osaka; novelist Mishima Yukio committed suicide.
1971	Yen allowed to float against other currencies; Japan experienced "Nixon shocks" over unilateral U.S. policies affecting Japan.
1972	Okinawa returned to Japan by United States; Winter Olympic Games held in Sapporo;

diplomatic relations with China normalized.

1973   Oil-price crisis triggered sharp inflation.

1974   Tanaka Kakuei forced from office by financial scandals.

1976   Lockheed scandal broke over bribery for military procurements.

1978   Tokyo International Airport at Narita opened.

1981   "GNP nationalism" became popular.

1982   Nakasone Yasuhiro became prime minister, calling for greater involvement in world leadership; controversy erupted over revision of school textbooks.

1987   Toshiba scandal occurred.

1988   Hiring of foreign laborers became controversial issue.

1989   Shōwa emperor (Hirohito) died; Heisei era began.

1993   Liberal Democratic Party lost power for first time since 1950s.

1994   Murayama Tomiichi became Japan's second socialist prime minister; Nobel Prize in Literature won by Ōe Kenzaburō.

1995   Hanshin earthquake killed more than 5,000 in western Japan; Aum Shinrikyō mounted poison gas attacks on Tokyo subway system.

1996   United States moved some bases from Okinawa, following widespread demonstrations.

Contributors

David Abosch
State University of New York
Buffalo, New York

Stephen J. Anderson
International University of Japan
Tokyo, Japan

Jackson H. Bailey
Earlham College
Richmond, Indiana

Andrew E. Barshay
University of California
Berkeley, California

Lawrence W. Beer
Lafayette College
Easton, Pennsylvania

Harumi Befu
Stanford University
Stanford, California

John H. Boyle
California State University
Chico, California

Sidney DeVere Brown
University of Oklahoma
Norman, Oklahoma

Thomas W. Burkman
State University of New York
Buffalo, New York

Ardath Burks
Rutgers University
New Brunswick, New Jersey

George C.C. Chang
University of Pennsylvania
Philadelphia, Pennsylvania

Parks M. Coble
University of Nebraska
Lincoln, Nebraska

Ellen T. Conant
Art historian
New York, New York

Hilary Conroy
University of Pennsylvania
Philadelphia, Pennsylvania

Sandra T.W. Davis
American International Underwriters
New York, New York

Joseph DeChicchis
Hiroshima University
Hiroshima, Japan

John W. Dower
Massachusetts Institute of Technology
Cambridge, Massachusetts

H. Byron Earhart
Western Michigan University
Kalamazoo, Michigan

Lane R. Earns
University of Wisconsin
Oshkosh, Wisconsin

David G. Egler
Western Illinois University
Macomb, Illinois

Robert D. Fiala
Concordia College
Seward, Nebraska

William Miles Fletcher III
University of North Carolina
Chapel Hill, North Carolina

Carolyn Bowen Francis
Okinawa Christian Center
Naha, Okinawa, Japan

Wilbur M. Fridell
University of California
Santa Barbara, California

Theodore Friend
Eisenhower Exchange Fellowships
New York, New York

Takashi Fujitani
University of California
Santa Cruz, California

Shigeko Fukai
Auburn University
Auburn, Alabama

Andrew G. Gordon
Harvard University
Cambridge, Massachusetts

Roger F. Hackett
University of Michigan
Ann Arbor, Michigan

Ellen H. Hammond
Chiba Keiai Junior College
Chiba, Japan

Mikiso Hane
Knox College
Galesburg, Illinois

Helen Hardacre
Harvard University
Cambridge, Massachusetts

Ann M. Harrington
Loyola University
Chicago, Illinois

Sally A. Hastings
Purdue University
West Lafayette, Indiana

Bill Heinrich
Columbia University
New York, New York

David Hewitt
Wittenberg University
Springfield, Ohio

Crayne Horton
Hiram College
Hiram, Ohio

Germaine A. Hoston
University of California
San Diego, California

John F. Howes
Obirin University
Tokyo, Japan

James L. Huffman
Wittenberg University
Springfield, Ohio

G. Cameron Hurst III
University of Pennsylvania
Philadelphia, Pennsylvania

Ken K. Ito
University of Michigan
Ann Arbor, Michigan

Kinko Ito
University of Arkansas
Little Rock, Arkansas

Yoshio Iwamoto
Indiana University
Bloomington, Indiana

Luo Jiu-jung
Institute of Modern History
Academia Sinica

Noriko Kamachi
University of Michigan
Dearborn, Michigan

Gregory J. Kasza
Indiana University
Bloomington, Indiana

W. Dean Kinzley
University of South Carolina
Columbia, South Carolina

J. Victor Koschmann
Cornell University
Ithaca, New York

Jacob Kovalio
Carleton University
Ottawa, Ontario, Canada

Ellis S. Krauss
University of California
San Diego, California

In-ha Lee
Tsuda College
Tokyo, Japan

Michael Lewis
Michigan State University
East Lansing, Michigan

Terry MacDougall
Stanford Japan Center
Kyoto, Japan

Byron K. Marshall
University of Minnesota
Minneapolis, Minnesota

James I. Matray
New Mexico State University
Las Cruces, New Mexico

Wayne M. McWilliams
Towson State University
Baltimore, Maryland

Frank O. Miller
College of Wooster
Wooster, Ohio

Barbara Molony
Santa Clara University
Santa Clara, California

Joe B. Moore
University of Victoria
Victoria, British Columbia, Canada

James R. Morita
Ohio State University
Columbus, Ohio

Kate Wildman Nakai
Sophia University
Tokyo, Japan

Ian Neary
Essex University
Colchester, United Kingdom

George M. Oshiro
Obirin University
Tokyo, Japan

Wayne Patterson
St. Norbert College
De Pere, Wisconsin

Louis G. Perez
Illinois State University
Normal, Illinois

Tracy Pollard
Wittenberg University
Springfield, Ohio

Cyril H. Powles
Trinity College
University of Toronto
Toronto, Ontario, Canada

Roger W. Purdy
John Carroll University
University Heights, Ohio

J. Mark Ramseyer
University of Chicago Law School
Chicago, Illinois

Laurel Rasplica Rodd
Arizona State University
Tempe, Arizona

Donald Roden
Rutgers University
New Brunswick, New Jersey

Jay Rubin
Harvard University
Cambridge, Massachusetts

Richard Rubinger
Indiana University
Bloomington, Indiana

J. Wayne Sabey
Western American Language Institute
Salt Lake City, Utah

Yoshiko Yokochi Samuel
Wesleyan University
Middletown, Connecticut

Wesley Sasaki-Uemura
University of Utah
Provo, Utah

Michael A. Schneider
Knox College
Galesburg, Illinois

Bradford L. Simcock
Miami University
Oxford, Ohio

Richard J. Smethurst
University of Pittsburgh
Pittsburgh, Pennsylvania

Stephen R. Smith
Wittenberg University
Springfield, Ohio

Robert M. Spaulding
Oklahoma State University
Stillwater, Oklahoma

M. William Steele
International Christian University
Tokyo, Japan

Patricia G. Steinhoff
University of Hawaii
Honolulu, Hawaii

Ronald Suleski
Pergamon Press
Tokyo, Japan

Eugene Swanger
Wittenberg University
Springfield, Ohio

Peter Swanger
Cleary-Gottleib Inc.
Tokyo, Japan

Koji Taira
University of Illinois
Champaign, Illinois

E. Patricia Tsurumi
University of Victoria
Victoria, British Columbia, Canada

Michael Umegaki
Keio University
Tokyo, Japan

Sinh Vinh
University of Alberta
Edmonton, Alberta, Canada

Bob Tadashi Wakabayashi
York University
North York, Ontario, Canada

Anne Walthall
University of California
Irvine, California

Michael Waxman
Marquette University Law School
Milwaukee, Wisconsin

Martin E. Weinstein
University of Illinois
Champaign, Illinois

John A. White
University of Hawaii
Honolulu, Hawaii

George M. Wilson
Indiana University
Bloomington, Illinois

Harry Wray
Nanzan University
Nagoya, Japan

Tien-wei Wu
History Department
Southern Illinois University

Masato Yamazaki
Aquinas College
Grand Rapids, Michigan

Guy Yasko
Cornell University
Ithaca, New York

Richard Yasko
University of Wisconsin
Whitewater, Wisconsin

Charles Yates
Earlham College
Richmond, Indiana

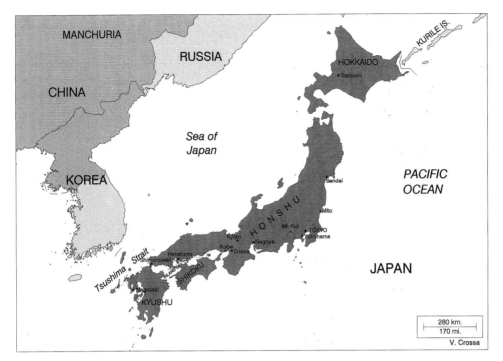

Map 1. *Japan in the world of East Asia.*

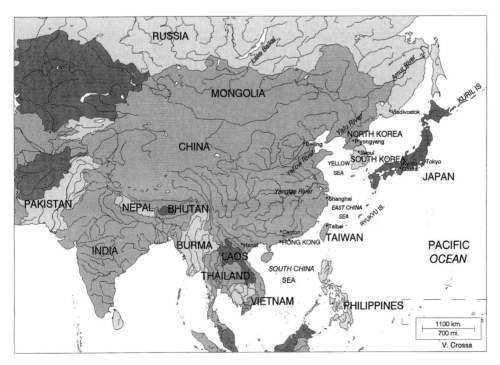

Map 2. *Contemporary Asia.*

Modern Japan

A

Abe Isoo (1865–1949)

Early socialist leader who opposed militarist nationalism. Born in Fukuoka and educated at Dōshisha University, he taught from 1903 to 1926 at Waseda University. He helped found many socialist organizations, including Japan's first officially recognized socialist party, the Shakai Minshūtō (Socialist People's Party), in 1901; a successor Shakai Minshūtō in 1926; and the Shakai Taishūtō (Social Masses Party) in 1932. He also participated in early labor organizations and served in the Diet (legislature) from 1928 until 1940. Abe consistently insisted on a moderate approach to socialism, even when his peers turned radical. A Christian, he opposed the Russo-Japanese War (1904–05) and remained a lifelong pacifist, emphasizing Japan's peaceful traditions and resigning from the Diet in protest as war approached in 1940.

James L. Huffman

Bibliography

Powels, C.H. "Abe Isoo: The Utility Man." *Pacifism in Japan: The Christian and Socialist Tradition.* Ed. N. Bamba and J. Howes. Kyoto: Minerva Press, 1978.

Abolition of Domains, Establishment of Prefectures (*Haihan Chiken*)

In August 1871, the Meiji government abolished the 270 feudal domains (*han*) and instituted in their places prefectures (*fu* and *ken*). A series of mergers in the subsequent months reduced the number of the newly established prefectures to a little more than 40, and set up the basic alignment of the prefectural system that remains today. These mergers left in their wake few marks of the *han* that had survived the fall of the Tokugawa shogunate in 1868. The mergers instituted the framework for the centralized modern state, whose massive modernization efforts would continue for generations to come.

The move to abolish the feudal domains, however, did not follow naturally from the fall of the shogunate during the Meiji Restoration in 1868. In the first few years of its existence, the Meiji government, in fact, could not challenge the continuation of the feudal domains, some of which—mainly, Satsuma, Chōshū, Tosa, and Saga—provided the bulk of its governmental and military strength. Prior to the summer of 1871, the Restoration leaders could make only modest attempts to make the authority and legitimacy of the imperial government uncontested from within. The most significant attempt was the *hanseki hōkan* (Petition to Return the Domains to the Emperor). In the spring of 1869, the leaders from Satsuma, Chōshū, and Tosa initiated a move to return their fiefs to the emperor, which was subsequently emulated by the rest of the domains. The key effect of the *hanseki hōkan*, however, was to make the daimyo the imperial governors of their own domains. There was little indication of the coming of the *haihan chiken* at this point.

The decision to terminate the domains, then, did not emerge from any continuous or focused effort by the Restoration leaders to centralize political control in the hands of the imperial government. Instead, several complex factors were at work. Among them was the foreign powers' pressure upon the Restoration leaders to make the imperial government responsible for the administrative and financial affairs of Japan in general. Another was the increasing awareness that the continuation of the feudal domains perpetuated the rivalry among the Restoration leaders within the imperial government, on the basis of their own domain affiliations. Still another factor was the financial collapse of the feudal-domain governments, which removed the possibility of any effective resistance by the feudal domains against the decision to terminate them.

The *haihan chiken* had many short-term and long-term effects. Former daimyo joined the ranks of the nobility; the imperial government began a systematic interference in local affairs by way of, among others, the centrally appointed governors; interlocal mobility among the populace increased; and a number of reform policies aimed at modernizing the society and the economy were now possible with little or no preferential considerations toward specific localities. The most significant consequence may be found in the fact that the populace in general and the former samurai in particular, who were to make up the pool of political leaders, were freed from the provincial loyalism that the continuation of the feudal domains would have preserved. As one Restoration leader put it, the *hainhan chiken* was a "second Restoration."

Michael Umegaki

Bibliography
Umegaki, Michio. *After the Restoration: The Beginning of Japan's Modern State*. New York: New York University Press, 1988.

Academy for the Love of One's Community (*Aikyō Juku*)

A school dedicated to promoting ultranationalism. The nationalistic activist Tachibana Kōzaburō founded this small school in the city of Mito in 1930, with financial assistance from Ibaraki Prefecture, to teach farming techniques, Japanese history, and national ethics to young people. The school propounded the typical ideas of *nōhonshugi* (agrarian nationalism), including communal-village rule, eradication of peasant debts, and the Shōwa Restoration. The teachers and students were nonrevolutionary at first, but they soon began to advocate violent activism on behalf of their cause. The 23 Aikyō Juku students provided much of the manpower for attacks on Tokyo power stations during the 1932 May 15 Incident. Tachibana was imprisoned for his role in the episode, which led to the decline of the school and its disbanding in March 1933.

James L. Huffman

Bibliography
Storry, Richard. *The Double Patriots: A Study of Japanese Nationalism*. Westport, CT: Greenwood Press, 1973.

Adachi Kenzō (1864–1948)

Nationalistic leader of the Rikken Minseitō (Constitutional Democratic Party). Born in Kumamoto Prefecture, he spent his early years as a patriotic journalist, promoting revision of the unequal treaties with Western countries, reporting on the Sino-Japanese War (1894–95), founding newspapers in Korea, and playing a role in the assassination of Korea's Queen Min. In 1902, he was elected to the Diet (legislature), where he became known as the "king of elections" for his effectiveness in building the parliamentary strength of the Kenseikai (Constitutional Association) and, later, the Rikken Minseitō. Between 1925 and 1931, he served several times as home minister and minister of communications, maintaining close ties to war industries. In 1931, he helped bring down his own party's cabinet in the aftermath of the September 18 Manchurian Incident by insisting, unsuccessfully, that the major parties form a joint government to meet the international crisis. Ever an ally of nationalist elements, he left the Minseitō and formed the ultranationalist Kokumin Dōmei (National People's Alliance), a small party that advocated the creation of a war economy and a Japan-Manchuria economic bloc. Adachi retired from politics in 1940.

James L. Huffman

Bibliography
Berger, Gordon. *Parties Out of Power in Japan, 1931–1941*. Princeton, NJ: Princeton University Press, 1977.

Agrarian Nationalism (*Nōhonshugi*)

Utopian, nationalistic philosophy. Throughout the modern period, utopian thinkers rose from time to time to herald the special, superior qualities of traditional rural life and values in Japan, generally as a contrast or antidote to the onslaught of industrialization, urbanization, and modernization. Many of the modern proponents of *nōhonshugi* evoked the late-Tokugawa-era teachings of Ninomiya Sontoku, who emphasized rural self-sufficiency, hard work, frugality, and social harmony. Although some of these ideas advocated formal governmental programs to stimulate rural productivity and undergird modern industry, the majority adhered to the more sentimental, popular form of agrarianism that pitted village against city, Japan against the West, and farming against industry.

Nōhonshugi was a particularly influential doctrine among many of the right-wing nationalists of the 1920s and 1930s. Young soldiers who had lived on Japan's farms, nearly all of which were devastated by depression during those decades, frequently were drawn by the ideas of men such as Tachibana Kōzaburō and Gondō Seikyō. Tachibana, a native of Ibaraki Prefecture, warned against the evils of materialistic capitalism. He called for the love and cooperation of the ideal village, putting his ideas into practice by creating his own producers' cooperative. His Aikyō Juku (Academy for the Love of One's Community) not only taught farming methods and bred patriotism but also provided participants for the bloody May 15 (1932) Incident in which Prime Minister Inukai Tsuyoshi was assassinated. Gondō, who was of a more theoretical bent, wrote widely, urging the removal of all levels of government intervening between the emperor and the village. Nearly all of the *nōhonshugi* advocates believed in the supremacy of the emperor and the spiritual superiority not only of the village over the city but of Japan over all other countries. As a way of thought, *nōhonshugi* largely withered after World War II.

James L. Huffman

Bibliography
Havens, Thomas. *Farm and Nation in Modern Japan: Agrarian Nationalism, 1870–1940*. Princeton, NJ: Princeton University Press, 1974.

Ain't It Great (*Eejanaika*)

Waves of frenzied dancing from the seventh month of 1867 to the fourth month of 1868 following a sudden decline in what had been extraordinarily high food prices, which caught up hundreds of thousands of commoners across domainal boundaries, beginning in the post stations along the Tokyo-to-Kyoto Tokaidō highway near Nagoya and spreading from there west through the villages in Omi to Kyoto and Ise, the northern shore of Shikoku, and as far as Hiroshima; they also spread east to Yokohama and Edo. In each place, the discovery of lucky charms (*ofuda*) from Ise and other shrines and various Buddhist temples led people to believe that a new world (*yonaoshi*) saturated with the divine spirit in which they would be liberated from the old status order was in the offing. Houses on which the charms fell offered the dancers food and drink in thanksgiving for this blessing.

At Numazu, a wood-block print turned up among the falling objects bearing the motto "exterminate the aliens," (*ijin taiji*), the commoners' equivalent to the nativist call to "revere the emperor and expel the barbarians" (*sonnō jōi*). The participants acted out the expulsion of foreigners from Japan's sacred soil by throwing stones at the unfortunates who happened to get in their way and forecast the downfall of the *bakufu* by parading a coffin through the streets bearing the posthumous name for Tokugawa Ieyasu (1542–1616). In this joyous carnival-like atmosphere, men dressed as women and women as men, they ate and drank their fill, and they engaged in licentious, rowdy behavior, sometimes threatening to smash up the homes of the wealthy who hesitated to bless them with the appropriate food and drink. Meiji Restoration leader Iwakura Tomomi (1825–83) believed that this popular craze lasted long enough to be useful to the forces trying to bring about an imperial restoration.

Anne Walthall

Bibliography
Wilson, George. "*Ee ja nai ka* on the Eve of the Meiji Restoration in Japan." *Semiotica* Vol. 70, No. 3–4 (1988), 301–19.
———. "Pursuing the Millennium in the Meiji Restoration." *Conflict in Modern Japanese History: The Neglected Tradition*. Ed. Tetsuo Najita and J. Victor Koschmann. Chicago: University of Chicago Press, 1982.

Ainu

The Ainu are the indigenous people of Hokkaido, Japan's second-largest island. Former Ainu habitation of southern Kamchatka, the Kuril Islands, Sakhalin Island, and Japanese Honshu also has been documented. Archaeological evidence links the Ainu to the Neolithic Jōmon, who inhabited all of the major Japanese islands in prehistoric times. Linguistic affinities with Altaic or Turkic-Mongolic groups and cultural affinities with Pacific island popula-

Traditional Ainu ceremony in Hokkaido. Courtesy Consulate General of Japan, N.Y.

tions have also been noted. Evidence of early recorded history suggests the gradual incorporation of the Honshu Ainu into the general Japanese population, and evidence of great similarity between Ainu physical features and samurai characteristics has prompted speculation that such assimilation may have followed lines of social stratification.

In the post-Columbian era of European exploration and conquest, the Ainu were still a linguistically and racially distinct people, apart from, and independent of, the Japanese, who called the Ainu nation Ezo. The eastward expansion of Russia and the northward extension of Japan precipitated a 400-year encroachment on, and acculturation of, the Ezo population following the Tokugawa assumption of power in 1600. Especially harsh was the treatment of the Ainu following the 1868 consolidation of Meiji rule. Subsequent appropriation of Hokkaido lands, bans on traditional ways of hunting and fishing, forced introduction of agriculture, and other legislation of that era have continued to haunt and embitter the Ainu. Japanese treaties with Czarist and Soviet regimes

partitioned the Ainu homeland without Ainu consent or consultation; advocates of Ainu rights consider illegitimate such Russo-Japanese appropriation and exchanges of Ainu territory, the most recent of which precipitated the expatriation of Sakhalin Ainu at the close of World War II. Japanese assimilation policies have been effective for the most part: The Ainu speak Japanese (only a handful of aging native Ainu speakers remain), and most Ainu can no longer be reliably distinguished on the basis of physiology from other Japanese (although many Ainu retain prototypical features).

By the mid-1990s, the Ainu, as a Japanese social group defined by a common ethnolinguistic history, numbered more than 50,000. Since the end of World War II, Ainu intellectuals and political leaders have instilled pride in their people and worked to redress historical wrongs and continued discrimination by government agencies. Ainu groups have increasingly sought relief via the Japanese judiciary, especially in disputes over land use and ecology. The major Ainu-rights organization, the Utari Kyōkai, which has represented the Ainu at the United

Nations and other international forums, tirelessly petitions the Japanese government to recognize the need for Ainu representation in the national and prefectural governments and the basic right of the Ainu to be educated in their own language. Ainu pride focuses on Ainu linguistic heritage, which features the elaborate *yukar* and other less stable oral forms. A movement to revive the language began gaining momentum in the late 1980s. One Ainu author and religious leader, Kayano Shigeru, produced videotape lessons and presented a weekly radio course for learning Ainu from 1989 to 1993, and other Ainu broadcasts continued after that. A member of the Diet (legislature) since 1994, Kayano has pushed for regular Ainu-language television broadcasts; Ainu speech contests and other cultural events have been nationally televised. Although proscribed by the Ministry of Education for the elementary and secondary curriculums, Ainu language studies may be pursued at several major universities in Japan.

Joseph DeChicchis

Bibliography
DeChicchis, Joseph. "The Present State of the Ainu Language." *Journal of Multilingual and Multicultural Development.* Vol. 16 (1995), 103–24.
Takakura, Shin'ichirō. *The Ainu of Northern Japan: A Study in Conquest and Acculturation.* Trans. John A. Harrison. Philadelphia: Transactions of the American Philosophical Society, 1960.
Watanabe, Hitoshi. *The Ainu: A Study of Ecology and the System of Social Solidarity between Man and Nature in Relation to Group Structure.* Tokyo: Faculty of Science, University of Tokyo, 1972.

Aizawa Saburō (1889–1936)

Military officer and assassin. An ultranationalist lieutenant colonel stationed at Fukuyama on the Inland Sea, Aizawa was distressed by government moves in 1935 to strengthen the role of the army's Tōseiha (Control Faction) within the military. He protested publicly when one of his heroes, Mazaki Jinzaburō, was removed as inspector general of military training, then decided to take action against the man he considered responsible for the removal, after learning that he himself was being reassigned to Taiwan. On August 12, Aizawa entered the office of Nagata Tetsuzan, chief of the Military Affairs Bureau, and stabbed him to death. His trial became a platform for the patriotic views of the Kōdōha (Imperial Way Faction) and aroused wide public sympathy. However, the infamous February 26, 1936, mutiny a few months later precipitated a new public impatience with extremism, and Aizawa was found guilty and executed on July 7, 1936.

James L. Huffman

Bibliography
Butow, Robert. *Tōjō and the Coming of War.* Stanford, CA: Stanford University Press, 1961.

Akamatsu Katsumarō (1894–1955)

Proletarian-nationalist political leader. A native of Yamaguchi Prefecture and a graduate of the University of Tokyo, Akamatsu made a shift to nationalism that was typical of many socialist leaders in the 1930s. Following a brief career in journalism, he spent his early years leading the Japan Communist Party, the Japan Federation of Labor and the Shakai Minshūtō (Socialist People's Party). After the Manchurian Incident in 1931, however, he left the Shakai Minshūtō to help form the Nihon Kokka Shakaitō (Japan National Socialist Party), which advocated state socialism. Moving even further toward traditional patriotism, in 1933 he created the Kokumin Kyōkai (Nationalist Association), which focused on the emperor's "divinity" and encouraged direct action by nationalists. He was elected to the Diet (legislature) and became head of the Nihon Kakushintō (Japan Reform Party) in 1937, then served in a planning section of the Imperial Rule Assistance Association during World War II. Postwar Allied Occupation authorities barred him from politics.

James L. Huffman

Bibliography
Storry, Richard. *The Double Patriots: A Study of Japanese Nationalism.* Westport, CT: Greenwood Press, 1973.

Akao Bin (1898–1990)

Right-wing politician, activist, and founder of the Greater Japan Patriots Party (Dainihon Aikokutō). He began his political career as a Communist and was jailed in the 1920s as a result of participation in one of his repeated clashes with the Japanese police. In his incarceration, he read the writings of fascist Italian leader Benito Mussolini and changed his political orientation to become an extreme right-wing activist. In 1942, he was elected to a seat in the lower house of the Japanese Diet (legislature) but was expelled for publicly criticizing Prime Minister Tōjō Hideki. In 1952, he founded the Greater Japan Patriots Party; as its president, he became noted as one of Japan's most colorful and eccentric politicians. In 1960, one of his followers, Yamaguchi Otoya, assassinated Asanuma Inejirō, chairman of the Japan Socialist Party. Throughout the postwar period, Akao was a perennial losing candidate for a seat in the Diet, noted for touring Tokyo in a minibus delivering passionate harangues against communism and socialism and in favor of emphasizing duty over rights and reestablishing the emperor as Japan's supreme political authority.

J. Wayne Sabey

Bibliography
Okada, Keisuke. "Bin Akao, Quixotic Politician, Dies at 91." *Japan Times* (February 19–25, 1990), 8.

Akiyama Teisuke (1868–1950)
Journalist and politician. Reared in Kurashiki, Okayama Prefecture, and graduated from Tokyo University, he worked briefly in the government audit bureau, then launched the *Niroku Shimpō*, one of Japan's most popular newspapers, in the early 1900s. He was a pioneer of controversial, sensational reportorial styles, with campaigns attacking the Mitsui financial clique's business practices, fighting prostitution and advocating labor solidarity. Elected to the Diet (legislature) in 1902, he attacked the Katsura government's spending policies and negotiating style during the Russo-Japanese War (1904–05). Angered officials circulated rumors that he was a Russian spy and attacked him in the Diet. The rumors were damning, given the overcharged patriotic mood of the period: Akiyama was forced to resign from the Diet in 1904 and his newspaper was temporarily suspended the same year. Later, it resumed publication under the name *Tokyo Niroku Shimpō*, but Akiyama never regained his earlier prominence.

James L. Huffman

Bibliography
Huffman, James L. *Creating a Public: People and Press in Meiji Japan.* Honolulu: University of Hawaii Press, 1997.

All-Japan Student Federation (*Zengakuren*)
Student federation—abbreviation for Zen Nihon Gakusei Jichigai Sōrengō (All-Japan Federation of Student Self-Governing Associations). Created in September 1948, this organization is the national coordinating body of the local *jichikai* (self-governing associations) of the separate faculties of individual universities in Japan. From its inception, it has been dominated by the left wing, and although all students belong to their own campus *jichikai*, by virtue of having dues collected as part of university tuition, most shun Zengakuren or its local units. Zengakuren's strength has fluctuated considerably over the years, depending on the national mood and the issues of the day. The organization also has been subject to numerous schisms. At the beginning, the Japan Communist Party (JCP) controlled it; then, in 1958, the anti-JCP Communist League took over. In the 1960s, numerous splits occurred, with one part of Zengakuren controlled by pro-JCP students and another divided among New Left elements. Indeed, by the 1980s, Zengakuren had bred at least 32 factions, many of which had produced their own multiple splits.

During the 1950s and 1960s, Zengakuren and its affiliated groups dominated many of Japan's most explosive political and social struggles. They had opposed the government's early efforts to reinstitute moral education in the public schools. In the late 1950s, they were among the most radical opponents of the revised Japan–U.S. Security Treaty, against which they demonstrated by the thousands in cities across Japan. And in the 1960s, they played the central role in demonstrations against the Vietnam War.

Zengakuren activities also sparked the student protest movements that brought higher education almost to a standstill after the mid-1960s. Demonstrating against tuition rises, the continuance of the Security Treaty system, "feudal" university governance structures, declining educational quality, and a host of other issues, thousands of Zengakuren-led students carried out strikes, boycotts, sitdowns, and armed clashes with riot police. They temporarily closed scores of campuses and nearly paralyzed the university system. Not until riot police launched a massive attack on students occupying Yasuda Auditorium at Tokyo University in January 1969 did the movement begin to dissipate. By then, 152 universities had been struck and 10,000 students arrested.

Zengakuren has continued to agitate for leftist causes, but, having been plagued by sometimes violent disputes within and by rising national affluence without, it has lost much of its former influence and support.

James L. Huffman

Bibliography

Dowsey, Stuart, ed. *Zengakuren: Japan's Revolutionary Students*. Berkeley, CA: Ishi Press, 1970.

Steinhoff, Patricia. "Student Conflict." *Conflict in Japan*. Ed. Ellis Krauss et al. Honolulu: University of Hawaii Press, 1984.

Ampo Movement

A movement in opposition to the treaty signed in 1951 together with the San Francisco Peace Treaty, which gave the United States the right to station military forces in Japan indefinitely. (The term "Ampo" is an abbreviation for Nichibei Anzen Hoshō Jōyaku, or Japan-U.S. Security Treaty.)

Although presented as a necessary counterbalance to Japan's renunciation of military forces in Article 9 of the postwar constitution, the treaty did not oblige the United States to defend Japan. Negotiations during 1958–59 revised the treaty to add a U.S. obligation to defend Japan and a Japanese obligation to defend U.S. bases from attack. The treaty justified the bases for the maintenance of peace and security in the Far East, not solely for the security of Japan. Its duration was set at 10 years, after which either side could abrogate with one year's notice.

The People's Council to Prevent the Security Treaty Revision, with 134 member organizations led by the socialist and Communist parties and Sōhyo (General Council of Trade Unions), coordinated massive public protests against the treaty in 1959 and 1960. After U.S. ratification of the treaty in January 1960, the Ampo movement intensified. On May 19, 1960 the Kishi Nobusuke cabinet and the Liberal Democratic Party (LDP), which supported the treaty, summoned police into the Diet (legislature) to end the opposition parties' obstruction of a vote. The next day, with opposition parties boycotting the session, the lower house approved the treaty. Insisting that the passage was invalid, the People's Council organized demonstrations of 200,000–300,000 people around the Diet building every day for one month. On June 15, the mainstream faction of Zengakuren (All-Japan Student Federation) forced its way into the Diet and clashed with police, resulting in the death of one woman student.

The treaty was automatically ratified by constitutional provision on June 19 without a vote by the upper house. The Ampo movement was unable to block the treaty, but the massive public protests led to the cancellation of U.S. President Dwight D. Eisenhower's planned visit to Japan for the ratification ceremony and to the downfall of the Kishi cabinet.

As the treaty's 10-year limit neared late in the 1960s, strong Japanese resistance developed to the U.S. use of Japanese bases as a rear staging area for operations in Vietnam. The U.S. launching of B-52 bomber strikes on Vietnam from its bases in Okinawa, nuclear-weapons storage there, and the U.S. insistence that Okinawan bases continue under the security treaty also complicated negotiations for the return of Okinawa to Japanese control. A further source of friction was the U.S. refusal to acknowledge whether its naval vessels making port calls in Japan under the treaty carried nuclear weapons, in defiance of Japan's strong antinuclear position.

From 1967 to 1970, massive public protests against these interrelated issues surpassed the 1960 Ampo movement in scale and violence, but the protests were no longer coordinated by a single council, and they had even less effect than previously. The Japan-U.S. Security Treaty was automatically extended on June 23, 1970, and when administrative control over Okinawa returned to Japan in May 1972, the treaty provisions covered U.S. bases there.

The automatic extension of the treaty has effectively prevented the mobilization of an antitreaty campaign since 1970. The Ampo movement is no longer active, but termination of the treaty remains an issue for the Japanese left. An English-language journal, *Ampo*, continues to be published quarterly by veterans of the 1970 movement.

The Ampo movement's connection to nationalism is complex. The treaty has been a persistent source of friction and anti-American sentiment, but, in postwar Japan, anti-Ameri-

A

can sentiment does not necessarily equate with traditional nationalism. The treaty is a product of Japan's defeat in World War II, so one might expect opposition to have come from those seeking a revival of wartime nationalism. Yet the relatively conservative LDP, which ruled Japan for nearly all of the last half of the 1900s, carried the mantle of traditional nationalism, and consistently supported the treaty, while the parties of the Left, fearing a revival of militaristic nationalism, consistently opposed the treaty. There is unquestionably a nationalistic theme in the desire to free Japan of U.S. military and political dominance, but it is a distinctively postwar Japanese nationalism, the rhetoric of which is not derived from earlier cultural expressions of nationalism.

Patricia G. Steinhoff

Bibliography

Havens, Thomas. *Fire Across the Sea: The Vietnam War and Japan, 1965–1975.* Princeton, NJ: Princeton University Press, 1987.

Packard, George. *Protest in Tokyo: The Security Treaty Crisis of 1960,* Princeton, NJ: Princeton University Press, 1966.

Amur River Society (*Kokuryūkai*)

Ultranationalist society dedicated to Japanese expansion onto the Asian continent (*dai-Ajia shugi*) from its founding in 1901 to the end of World War II. Its ideological leader was Tōyama Mitsuru; its political head, Uchida Ryōhei. The literal translation of its name as Black Dragon Society conjured up Western comparisons with Chinese secret societies. However, it openly sought its objectives through political pressure and intimidation. During the group's early years, Uchida was particularly concerned with halting Russian expansion into East Asia, and he identified the Amur River, which forms the northern boundary of Manchuria, as a defense line for Japan that should mark the maximum advance of the Russian empire. The Kokuryūkai was virulently anti-Russian, engaged in an ambitious program to gather intelligence on Russian activities in Asia, published a large volume of anti-Russian propaganda in Japan, and often resorted to intimidation and violence to seek support for its objectives.

Following Japan's victory in the Russo-Japanese War (1904–05), Kokuryūkai pressed for Japanese annexation of Russian territory as far west as Lake Baikal and led antigovernment demonstrations when the war-ending Portsmouth Treaty (1905) achieved far less than that. Its members then campaigned for Japanese annexation of Korea and supported Asian revolutionaries such as China's Sun Yatsen and Emilio Aguinaldo of the Philippines in the hope that they would accept Japanese leadership in East Asia. Kokuryūkai members also engaged in a broad program of domestic propaganda designed to lionize the leaders and members of the right-wing movement, attack leftist leaders, and thought, and stress national reconstruction based on an emperor-centered ideology. Through the leadership of Uchida and close ties to high government, military, and business officials, the Kokuryūkai became one of the most influential and important of prewar Japan's ultranationalist societies. It was disbanded by the Allied Occupation in 1945.

J. Wayne Sabey

Bibliography

Sabey, J. Wayne. "The Gen-yōsha, the Kokuryūkai and Japanese Expansionism." Unpublished doctoral dissertation, University of Michigan, 1972.

Anami Korechika (1887–1945)

General; army minister at the end of World War II. An Ōita native, he supported the "kamikaze spirit" in military education, the takeover of Manchuria, and Ishiwara Kanji's East Asian League (Tōa Renmei), though he opposed the rebels in the failed but pivotal February 26, 1936, coup attempt.

As vice army minister in 1940, Anami cooperated in toppling the Yonai Mitsumasa cabinet in an effort to accelerate movement toward an Axis alliance. As army minister in the 1945 cabinet of Prime Minister Suzuki Kantarō, he ordered the arrest of the highly placed diplomat (and later prime minister) Yoshida Shigeru to prevent him from persuading the emperor to accept peace. He also opposed peace overtures through Sweden and the Soviet Union until early August 1945.

At August imperial conferences on the Potsdam Declaration, which outlined World War II surrender terms for Japan, Anami had to reconcile his own divided loyalties as army leader, first opposing surrender then favoring it. Ultimately, he allowed the Suzuki cabinet to continue (by not resigning as army minister), seconded the document of surrender, then committed suicide. His suicide foiled a coup attempt by a group of young officers opposed to the surrender.

Jacob Kovalio

Bibliography
Shillony, Ben-Ami. *Politics and Culture in Wartime Japan.* Oxford: Oxford University Press, 1981.

Anglo-Japanese Alliance (*Nichibei Dōmei*)

Japan's first equal alliance with any major Western country, signed in 1902. Several circumstances combined at the turn of the twentieth century to make an alliance mutually beneficial to Great Britain and Japan, the two archipelago countries on the extremes of the Eurasian landmass. Both had developed major navies; both had important interests in China; and, above all, both were anxious about Russian advances in the region. Of special concern was Russia's refusal to withdraw troops from Manchuria in the aftermath of the 1900 Boxer Rebellion.

As a result, negotiations led to the signing on January 30, 1902, of the first modern alliance between a strong Asian and a major European country. The alliance recognized both states' special interests in China and Japan's interests in Korea. It also pledged both partners to joint action if Russia joined any other party in actions against either Japan or Great Britain. The five-year pact was extended twice and continued in force until 1923.

Initially hailed in both countries for stabilizing their roles in Asia while reducing the sums that the British in particular had to spend on an Asian navy, the treaty was causing considerable uneasiness in Great Britain by the 1910s, as Japan appeared to use it to justify expansiveness in China and the Pacific region. Of particular concern was Japan's invocation of the treaty in taking over German holdings in China and in the Pacific islands during World War I. The fact that the Russian threat had diminished after the Russo-Japanese War (1904–05) also made the alliance seem less necessary to the British.

As a result, the pact was replaced by the Four Power Treaty of Great Britain, France, the United States, and Japan that grew out of the 1921 Washington Conference. The new treaty was vague and relatively unspecific, pledging each of the four participants to respect the others' rights in northeast Asia. The termination of the Anglo-Japanese Alliance left many Japanese dissatisfied, but the alliance had served its purpose in helping Japan become a major force in Asia's multipolar world.

James L. Huffman

Bibliography
Nish, Ian. *The Anglo-Japanese Alliance: Diplomacy of Two Island Empires.* London: Athlone Press, 1985.

Ansei Purge (1858–59)

A crucial turning point that led to the Meiji Restoration of 1868 in Japan. The Ansei Purge involved the punishment by the Tokugawa *bakufu* of nearly 100 activists from outside feudal domains, from the imperial court at Kyoto, and from the *bakufu* itself. Though not bloody by twentieth-century standards, the purge claimed a dozen lives and altered the complexion of Japanese politics. As a result, trust in the *bakufu* diminished, and its legitimacy came into question.

Two interrelated issues generated this crisis: commercial relations with the outside world and succession to the ailing Tokugawa shogun. These twin problems crystallized in 1857 when U.S. Consul Townsend Harris tried to cajole Japan into a trade agreement. Chief *bakufu* leader Hotta Masayoshi went to Kyoto to gain the emperor's approval of the agreement but was turned down. At the same time, the court backed a plan to have Hitotsubashi Yoshinobu, son of former Mito daimyo Tokugawa Nariaki, become the next shogun. Treaty backers thought that this succession scheme would secure court support for the treaty. When the new *bakufu* strongman Ii Naosuke signed the Harris treaty in 1858 without court approval, criticism of the *bakufu* mounted. During the purge, such luminaries of the late-Tokugawa reform movement as Hashimoto Sanai and Yoshida Shōin were executed. In retaliation for his bold confrontational policy, Ii was assassinated in 1860 by samurai who opposed his arbitrary rule.

George M. Wilson

Bibliography
Wilson, George M. "The Bakumatsu Intellectual in Action: Hashimoto Sanai in the Political Crisis of 1858." *Personality in Japanese History.* Ed. A.M. Craig and D.H. Shively. Berkeley: University of California Press, 1970.

Anticomintern Pact (1936)

Agreement drawing Japan and the Axis powers together before World War II. Signed between Japan and Germany on November 25, 1936, and joined by Italy a year later, the pact was intended to counter aggressive activities of the Soviet Union. Among other provisions, it called for the signatories to share information and to collaborate to prevent Soviet aggression abroad. A secret protocol also pledged each of the three partners to refuse cooperation with the Soviets if the U.S.S.R. threatened or attacked any of them. Among the most vocal advocates of the pact was Oshima Hiroshi, the ultranationalist Japanese military attaché to Germany.

James L. Huffman

Bibliography

Feis, Herbert. *The Road to Pearl Harbor.* Princeton, NJ: Princeton University Press, 1950.

Anti-Japanese Boycott

In the first half of the twentieth century, popular nationalism became a potent force in Chinese politics, particularly in urban areas. Students, professionals, and businessmen fought to "save China" at a time of weakness and foreign invasion. One important component of this nationalist force was the anti-Japanese boycott, which figured prominently in such events as the May Fourth Movement and the May Thirtieth Movement. The boycotts were particularly significant because they attracted the support not only of radical groups, such as the students, but usually had the backing of more conservative elements, such as chambers of commerce and business guilds. Chinese capitalists often faced stiff competition from foreign businesses, and boycotts were a way of opening the door for Chinese manufacturing and commerce.

Although the anti-American boycott of 1905 is generally considered the first such significant action in China, Japan was the most frequent target of boycotts. The *Tatsu Maru* Incident of February 1908, in which the Qing government apologized for alleged slights to the Japanese flag, occasioned the first serious boycott aimed at Japan. A more successful boycott occurred in 1915 in response to Tokyo's Twenty-One Demands, which reduced Japanese exports to China for several months.

The May Fourth Movement of 1919, in response to Japanese actions in Shandong province, led to a renewal of the boycott. Student groups throughout China organized the boycott, the effects of which were felt until 1921. As was often the case with boycotts, however, the goal of the organizers was not simply to damage Japanese economic interests but also to pressure the Chinese government to resist Japanese encroachments. The Beiyang government in Beijing became as much the students' target as the Japanese. The cycle of boycotts continued throughout the 1920s. Although Great Britain became the primary target in the anti-foreign boycott at the time of the May Thirtieth Movement of 1925, the original target had been Japan, which was responsible for the killing of Chinese workers striking at a Japanese mill in Shanghai. Anti-Japanese actions resumed in 1928–29 following the Jinan Incident.

The intense boycott movements of the 1920s played into the hands of the Guomindang government in Canton. Allied with the new Chinese Communist Party, the Guomindang (GMD) tapped into the large pool of activists which grew out of the May Fourth–May Thirtieth tradition. After Chiang Kaishek's break with the Communists in April 1927, however, the GMD found the boycott movement a mixed blessing. As head of a new, and relatively weak, government in Nanjing, Chiang sought to avoid antagonizing his powerful neighbor by settling the Jinan Incident (1928) on terms favorable to Japan. The boycott activity, moreover, was a mass movement of the type which Chiang came increasingly to distrust.

The contradictions between Chiang's goals and those of boycott organizers became clear in the 1930s. The summer of 1931 saw the beginnings of what would become the most intense and successful of all the anti-Japanese boycotts. Beginning with the Wanbaoshan Incident of July 1931, the movement peaked with the Manchurian Incident in September and the fighting between China and Japan at Shanghai in early 1932. After the fighting at Shanghai ended and the League of Nations was unable to force a Japanese withdrawal from the northeast, Chiang decided upon a policy of appeasing Japan and pursuing the civil war against the Communists. Under such conditions, the GMD government found itself in the mid-1930s in the awkward position of trying to terminate the anti-Japanese boycott movement. Japanese sales in China had fallen by as much as 75 percent in the year following the Manchurian Incident, and Tokyo made suspension of the boycott a condition for coexistence with Chiang.

Beginning in May 1932, therefore, the Nanjing government actively suppressed anti-Japanese boycott activity. Throughout the remaining years of the Nanjing Decade, when calls for boycotting Japanese products followed in the wake of new Japanese pressures, such as the war at the Great Wall in 1933 and the Amo Statement of 1934, Chiang was placed in the awkward position of opposing the boycott, while simultaneously depicting himself as the leader of Chinese nationalism. Groups sympathetic to the CCP used this issue to embarrass Chiang.

The anti-Japanese boycott movement failed to stop Japanese imperialism in China. Although Japan's exports to China often decreased for months at a time because of the boycotts, Japanese business eventually recovered. More importantly, Japanese extremists used the anti-boycott movement to justify a more aggressive policy toward China. Only through armed conquest of China, they argued, could Chinese resistance to "economic cooperation" with Japan be ended. In retrospect, the most important legacy of the boycott movement was not its effectiveness in halting Japanese imperialism but its politicization of China's urban populace. Boycotts allowed ordinary people to participate in "saving the nation," and contributed to the growth of nationalism in China. In the 1920s this sentiment fueled the Guomindang's "National Revolution"; in the 1930s, it aided the Communists.

Parks M. Coble

Bibliography

Coble, Parks M. *Facing Japan: Chinese Politics and Japanese Imperialism, 1931–1937*. Cambridge: Harvard University Press, 1991.

Jordan, Donald. *Chinese Boycotts versus Japanese Bombs: The Failure of China's "Revolutionary Diplomacy," 1931–1932*. Ann Arbor: University of Michigan Press, 1991.

Remer, C.F. *A Study of Chinese Boycotts with Special Reference to Their Economic Effectiveness*. Taipei: Cheng-wen Publishing Co., 1966.

Anti-Semitism

Imported from Europe, anti-Semitism never has been official government policy. Though propagated at times by influential anti-Semitic publications, it has not flourished among the citizenry, due to Japan's nonmonotheism and the absence of a large Jewish minority.

Japanese-Jewish contacts began in the Meiji era (1868–1912), and the first negative ideas about Jews followed an 1877 translation of Shakespeare's *The Merchant of Venice*. Anti-Semitic ideology also was imported by soldiers returning from the Siberian intervention (1918–22), where they had had contacts with "White" czarist forces. In the 1920s, right-wing circles referred to Jews in terms of "Jewish peril" (*yudayaka*), "redding" (*sekika*, suggesting Jewish responsibility for the Bolshevik Revolution and Communism), and a "conspiracy to rule the world" (*sekai shihai inbō*) by dominating the League of Nations, world finances, and the media. The liberal scholar Yoshino Sakuzō criticized anti-Semitism in the 1920s, as did the nationalist Mitsukawa Kametarō, whereas other writers, such as Koibe Zen'ichirō, promoted the idea of a "common Jewish-Japanese ancestry" (*dōsoron*). Within the military, such experts in Jewish affairs as Colonel Yasue Norihiro, who visited Palestine and met Zionist leaders, and navy Captain Inuzuka Koreshige were anti-Semitic but ready to cooperate with Jews for Japan's benefit.

In Japanese Manchuria and China, anti-Semitism was in the 1920s and 1930s fomented by White Russian fascists. Publicizing their views through the newspaper *Our Way*, they carried out ransom kidnappings and killed many wealthy Jews, encouraged by the slow initial reaction of the Kwantung army. In Japan itself during these years, anti-Semitism was influenced by Nazi Germany, due to the 1936 Anticomintern Pact, which drew Japan and the Axis powers together. Adolf Hitler's *Mein Kampf* was translated, and anti-Semitism became part of a general anti-Western and anti-Communist campaign. Freemasons, the Rotary organization, American actor Charlie Chaplin, jazz, and pornography all were attacked in books and the press as vehicles of "Jewish conspiracy."

The Kokusai Seikei Gakkai (International Political and Economic Association) and its organ *Yudaya Kenkyū* (Jewish Research) became central anti-Semitic tools. Lieutenant-General Shiōden Nobutaka was the most important anti-Semitic activist in the prewar era; other leading anti-Semites included politician Kishi Nobusuke, ultrarightist Sasakawa Ryōichi, journalist Tokutomi Sohō, and diplomat Shiratori Toshio.

The government itself did not adopt anti-Semitic policies; it allowed Jews to settle in the empire and refused Nazi demands for deportation or extradition of Jewish refugees.

After the Pacific War, Japanese interest in the Jews focused on the Holocaust, Israel, the kibbutz, Anne Frank, and the trial of Nazi war criminal Adolf Eichmann. In 1970, the bestseller *The Japanese and the Jews,* by an anonymous author using the pseudonym Isaiah Ben-Dasan, used the historic Jewish plight as a counterpoint to emphasize Japan's own felicitous circumstances.

In the mid-1980s, anxiety over trade frictions with the United States and rapid revaluation of the yen caused a "Jewish boom" in the publishing world. A number of books praising Jewish economic, scientific, and religious contributions appeared, but many more best-sellers were anti-Semitic; they rehashed versions of prewar publications emphasizing the "Protocols," "Jewish domination of the United States through Freemasonry," and contemporary "Jewish conspiracies." They accused the Jews of attempting to dominate the world through Israel, of destroying Japan's exports through reevaluating the yen and supporting the South Korean economy, and of preventing German reunification. Prominent anti-Semitic writers in this decade included Shinto priest Yamakage Motohisa, journalist Akama Gō, and especially former teacher Uno Masami, whose Institute for Research of Middle East Problems and Ribachi (Liberty) Research Institute produced nine books (the Know the Jews series has sold millions of copies), the anti-Semitic monthly *Enoch,* and the English-language *The New American View*, prepared in collaboration with American racist groups. While the popularity of these books stems partly from genuine anti-Semitism, much of it can be attributed to a simple fascination with an unknown culture.

Jacob Kovalio

Bibliography
Shillony, Ben-Ami. *Politics and Culture in Wartime Japan.* Oxford: Oxford University Press, 1981.
Uno, Masami. *Yudaya ga wakaru to nihon ga miete kuru* (If You Understand the Jews, You Will Understand Japan). Tokyo: Tokuma, 1986.

Araki Sadao (1877–1966)

Ultranationalist general and politician. A native of Tokyo, he served as army minister (1931–34), member of the Supreme War Council (1934–36), and education minister (1938–39). He also was vice president of the right-wing Kokuhonsha (National Foundations Society).

An admirer of "peasant values" and a critic of capitalism, Communism, and fascism, Araki stressed spiritual training (*seishin kyōiku*) in military and civilian education. He also supported numerous slogans that emphasized the imperial institution as a way of guaranteeing Japan's spiritual superiority: imperial way (*kōdō*), imperial fatherland (*kōkōku*), and imperial military (*kōgun*). He was close to Generals Mazaki Jinzaburō, Hayashi Senjurō, and Obata Toshirō and is known as a leader of the army's Kōdōha (Imperial Way Faction).

As army minister, Araki promoted the development of Manchuria as Japan's lifeline, called for the establishment of Manchukuo under army jurisdiction, urged rejection of the 1932 Lytton Report, which condemned Japan's expansion into Manchuria, and advocated Japan's withdrawal from the League of Nations in 1933. He also supported the building of a Japan-Manchukuo-China bloc, preparations against potential Soviet aggression in 1935–36, and establishment of a Five Ministers' Conference for quick decision making. As education minister, he promoted the nationalistic *Kokutai no Hongi* (Cardinal Principles of National Polity) and the purge of "unpatriotic" university professors.

Though ineffective as a politician, Araki became popular due to his nationalistic bombast. Initially a hero of the *seinen shōkō* (young officers) plotting a Shōwa Restoration in the mid-1930s, he became an object of scorn when they realized that he saw the slogan only as a rallying cry but opposed extremist violence. He was sentenced by the Tokyo War Crimes tribunal to life imprisonment in 1947 as a Class A war criminal, then was released in 1955.

Jacob Kovalio

Bibliography
Kovalio, Jacob. "Personnel Policies of Army Minister Araki Sadao." *Tradition and Modern Japan.* Ed. P.G. O'Neill. Vancouver: Norbury, 1981.

Article 9

Added to the 1947 Japanese Constitution under pressure from the American-dominated Occupation government, Article 9 purports to limit Japan's ability to maintain a military force. The article declares that "the Japanese people forever renounce war as a sovereign right of the nation and the threat of force as means of settling international disputes." It then provides that "land, sea, and air forces, as well as other war potential, will never be maintained."

The article could hardly be much clearer. Yet, Japanese nationalists have not thought the ban clear enough to prevent rearmament. To them, the article has been a sore reminder of the war Japan lost, and they have searched hard for ways around the apparent ban on military force. Generally, the courts have upheld their efforts, explaining that Article 9 excepts self-defense, ruling that Japan may both maintain forces for "self-defense" and contract with the United States for additional military protection.

Japan fields a formidable war machine. By the end of the 1980s, it spent 3.9 trillion yen on its euphemistically labeled "Self-Defense Force." At the then-current exchange rate, this made Japan's military budget the third largest in the world. Japan had 250,000 personnel, more than 1,000 tanks, several hundred combat aircraft, and one of the largest navies in the world. But such numbers miss the quality, for Japan boasted much of the latest in hi-tech weaponry, from F15 fighters and early-warning spy planes to an elaborate array of missiles and antisubmarine equipment.

Despite this powerful military force, Article 9 still has some residual effect. In order to maintain the fiction of self-defense, Japan has not bought the equipment it would need to expand its power overseas. The Japanese military lacks aircraft carriers and long-range strategic bombers, for example, and the crucial support craft necessary to resupply its warships in battle. And despite the strength of the nationalists, pacifists continue to have some effect. As of the late 1990s, Japan had no nuclear weapons; its ammunition stockpiles remained small; and its reserves numbered only 50,000.

To assuage fears that the Japanese military was growing too large, the Miki Takeo cabinet announced in 1976 that it would cap military spending at 1 percent of the Japanese GNP (gross national product). This "lid" was always something of a fiction. It was never legal or constitutional and always required some dubious accounting. Yet, for many years it provided a political compromise between the nationalists, who hoped to consolidate Japan's role as an international military power, and the leftists, who feared the domestic consequences of a large military force. Nonetheless, it was an unstable compromise. Economic growth slowed during the 1980s, while military spending continued to grow at more than 5–6 percent per year. By 1987, the military budget had passed the 1 percent mark, and the compromise seemed to have unraveled.

J. Mark Ramseyer

Bibliography

Henderson, D.F. *The Constitution of Japan: Its First Twenty Years*. Seattle: University of Washington Press, 1968.

Ward, Robert, and Sakamoto Yoshikazu, eds. *Democratizing Japan: The Allied Occupation*. Honolulu: University of Hawaii Press, 1987.

Asanuma Inejirō (1898–1960)

A charismatic activist in the socialist movement. His life and death exemplified the tensions between Japan's nationalism and socialism. After failing the examination for officer school several times, he graduated from Waseda University in political economy in 1923, having become involved in the student movement there. He joined the Communist Party in 1922 but left it in 1924, focusing his energies on tenant organizing and then proletarian politics. By the late 1920s, he had made party organizing his primary focus. He was elected to the Tokyo City Council in 1933 and to the lower house of the Diet (legislature) in 1936 and 1937 representing the Social Masses Party (SMP). After World War II, he helped found the Japan Socialist Party (JSP) and was returned to the Diet seven times from 1946 to 1958, becoming secretary general of the party in 1948 and party president in March 1960.

Before World War II, he marched in step with his mentor Aso Hisashi as he swung from an anti-imperialist stance in the 1920s to support for Japan's role in promoting an "independent" Manchuria by 1932, to fervent embrace of the so-called Holy War in China by 1938. Asanuma was a leader in the effort of some in the SMP to bring about a merger with the right-wing Tōhōkai (Far East Society), and he joined his party in censuring Saitō Takao for his anti-war speech in the Diet in 1940. As a leader of the postwar socialists, however, Asanuma spearheaded JSP opposition to rearmament and visited China as the head of JSP delegations in 1957 and 1959. During the latter trip to China, he issued a tough critique of American imperialism in Asia, which helped win him the post of party president. As president, he led the struggle against the renewal of the Japan-U.S. Security Treaty (*ampo*) in the spring of 1960. In an incident that shocked the Japanese nation later that year, he was stabbed to death by a rightist during an election speech.

A masterful organizer, Asanuma lived in modest public housing all of his adult life, in an old working-class ward of Tokyo, and was extremely popular among wage workers and shopkeepers. One consistent thread in his political thinking was the idea of independence for Asia.

Andrew G. Gordon

Bibliography

Gordon, Andrew. *Labor and Imperial Democracy in Prewar Japan*. Berkeley: University of California Press, 1991.

Associated Press of Japan
(*Nihon Shimbun Rengōsha*)

In 1926, Iwanaga Yūkichi, general manager of the Kokusai Tsūshinsha (International News Agency), reorganized the agency into the Nihon Shimbun Rengōsha, a nonprofit newspaper cooperative popularly known as Rengōsha. Iwanaga hoped that Rengō, modeled after the American Associated Press, could better meet Japan's domestic and foreign news needs and break the Reuter New Agency's grip on news dissemination.

For more than 15 years, Japanese businessmen, government leaders, and journalists had protested Reuter's restriction of the flow of news in and out of Japan. AP General Manager Kent Cooper shared similar complaints about Reuter's domination of the flow of international news, and he and Iwanaga sought to free themselves from Reuter's restrictions. The Japanese agency was especially vulnerable because violation of the Rengō-Reuter agreement could result in cancellation of Reuter's economic news, Rengō's only profitable service. In 1933, Iwanaga and Cooper allied their agencies, thus finally breaking Reuter's control of news be-

tween Rengō and the AP. The two agencies now could exchange news directly with each other, without having to go through Reuter. This act shattered the domination of the global news network cartel established by Reuter, the French agency Havas, and the German agency Wolff, in the 1870s.

On the home front, Rengō found itself in stiff competition with Nippon Denpō Tsūshinsha, the other major Japanese news agency, popularly known as Dentsū. Dentsū had a strong power base among the provincial press. Rengō's main clients were the major Osaka and Tokyo dailies; it had only a few provincial papers. Because of its goal of influencing the international news network, Rengō enjoyed financial and moral support from the Foreign Ministry; assistance for Dentsū came from the military. Rengō had a close association with the AP, and Dentsū with the United Press (UP). The rivalry between the Japanese news agencies ended in 1936, when they merged as the Dōmei Tsūshinsha (Dōmei News Agency).

Roger W. Purdy

Bibliography

Cooper, Kent. *Barriers Down*. New York: Farrar and Rinehart, 1942.

Atomic Bombs

At 8:15 in the morning on August 6, 1945, the American bomber *Enola Gay* dropped an atomic bomb over Hiroshima. Constructed of Uranium-235, the bomb detonated about 1,900 feet above the city with a destructive force equivalent to about 12.5 kilotons of TNT. Best estimates place the number of people physically present in Hiroshima on August 6 at 340,000–350,000. Of those, it is thought that between 90,000 and 120,000 died instantly or within the first two months after the bombing. Then, at 11:02 on August 9, the American bomber *Bock's Car* released a second atomic weapon, over Nagasaki. This bomb used Plutonium-239. It exploded about 1,650 feet above the city with the force of about 20 kilotons. Probably 260,000–270,000 people were in Nagasaki at the time of the blast, and it is estimated that 60,000–70,000 died within two months. Thousands of others in both cities suffered from severe radiation sickness, burns, and other injuries, and many victims who survived the first two months succumbed later.

On September 19, 1945, little more than a week after they arrived in Japan, U.S. General Douglas MacArthur's Occupation forces laid down a stringent Press Code. The code prohibited any publication, including those dealing with the atomic bombings, that was judged to be contrary to the interests of the Allied forces or that might incite resentment. While the full impact of the censorship is difficult to measure, the policy clearly impeded the broad dissemination of information about the bombs' effects and inhibited attempts to integrate the atomic-bomb experience into nation-centered narrative accounts of the war. A few literary works were published in 1947 and 1948, but censorship was not entirely relaxed until the final stages of the occupation in the early 1950s.

It was not the bombings themselves that first directed broad public attention to nuclear warfare as a significant *national* concern but an incident in the hydrogen-bomb race of the 1950s. On March 1, 1954, the United States tested a hydrogen bomb on a small Pacific Island in the Bikini group. Radioactive fallout from the test rained down for several hours on a Japanese tuna boat, the *Lucky Dragon V*, whose crew apparently had been fishing about 90 miles from the explosion. The crew of 23 suffered acute burns and radiation sickness, and, on September 23, the radio operator died. Opposition parties, fishermen's associations, and Japanese consumers protested immediately. Many municipal assemblies passed resolutions against the military use of nuclear energy, and both houses of the Japanese Diet (legislature) called for international regulation of weapons tests. But the most important long-range result of the controversy was a nationwide signature campaign for nuclear disarmament that began among housewives in the suburban Suginami Ward of Tokyo. Within one year, the signatures reportedly numbered 32 million, a figure equal to more than half the registered voters in Japan at the time. The campaign was followed by the first annual World Conference against Atomic and Hydrogen Bombs, convened in Hiroshima on August 6, 1955.

By the mid-1950s, the experience of victimization through nuclear warfare was fast becoming a central element in the national self-consciousness of postwar Japanese. Indeed, for the next 20 years, the antinuclear movement played a major role in what might be called left-wing nationalism, often with a strong anti-American tone. Japan's antinuclear national identity was also manifested to some extent in government policy. Prime Minister Hatoyama Ichirō gave initial impetus to the principle that nuclear weapons should not be brought into Japan when he refused to accept American Honest John missiles in the mid-1950s. Then, in 1967, Prime Minister Satō Eisaku first enunciated the "three nonnuclear principles"— against manufacturing, possessing, or permitting the introduction of nuclear weapons—and these principles have remained a stable aspect of government policy ever since.

Attitudes toward the atomic bombings have changed markedly since the early postwar period. When officials of the U.S. Strategic Bombing Survey interviewed 5,000 Japanese just a few months after the end of the war, they found that only about 20 percent professed resentment against the United States for the bombings. Instead, the respondents often blamed Japan's own wartime leaders. However, since the early 1970s, members of postwar generations who have been influenced by the "atomic diplomacy" thesis of revisionist historians are cynical about U.S. policy since Vietnam and, affected by rising nationalism, have tended to assign more blame to the United States. The young are also more receptive to the view that racism played a role in wartime American decision making.

Nationalism associated with the bombings has most often been channeled into pride in Japan's Peace Constitution and the three nonnuclear principles. In 1980, however, sociologist Shimizu Ikutarō offered the opposite argument, asserting that, since Japanese were the first victims of nuclear weapons, there should be no objection if they also were among the first to manufacture and possess such weapons. Shimizu's contention was still considered extremist in the early 1990s. Nevertheless, an increasingly large number of Japanese think that Japan will inevitably go nuclear some day.

J. Victor Koschmann

Bibliography

Asada, Sadao. "Japanese Perceptions of the A-Bomb Decision, 1945–1980." *The American Military and the Far East*. Ed. Joe C. Dixon. Washington, DC: U.S. Government Printing Office, 1980, 198–217.

Committee for the Compilation of Materials on Damage Caused by the Atomic Bombs in Hiroshima and Nagasaki, ed. *The Impact of the A-Bomb: Hiroshima and Nagasaki, 1945–85*. Trans. Eisei

Ishikawa and David L. Swain. Tokyo: Iwanami Shoten, 1985.

The Meaning of Survival: Hiroshima's 36-Year Commitment to Peace. Hiroshima: Chugoku Shimbun and the Hiroshima International Cultural Foundation, Inc., 1983.

Aum Supreme Truth Religion (*Aum Shinrikyō*)

Religious sect. Led by Asahara Shōkō, who was born as Matsumoto Chizuo in 1955 in Kyushu, the sect blends aspects of Buddhism, Hinduism, Judaism, Christianity, and Asahara's own pet ideas. It began to grow in the mid-1980s, following an extended stay by Asahara in India, and was officially recognized as a religious organization in 1989. Like numerous others of the decade's "new new religions," it attracted significant numbers of highly educated, affluent young professionals who appeared to be searching for deeper values to counter the rushing materialism and political confusion of the time.

What set Aum Shinrikyō apart was its aggressive, often paranoid, militant style. Many of its members lived in communes, spartan style, at the Aum headquarters in the village of Kamikuishiki near Mt. Fuji. After faring disastrously in an effort to get sect members elected to the Diet (legislature) in 1990, Aum Shinrikyō was tied in public accounts to acts of violence, including the disappearance of an attorney who was investigating the sect. Asahara began to use the image of Armageddon and the end of humankind in his speeches. He also set up manufacturing plants to produce weapons and proselytized heavily in the former Soviet Union.

The Aum Shinrikyō ranks were devastated after March 1995, when the sect was charged with carrying out poison-gas attacks at Tokyo subway stations. The attacks resulted in 12 deaths and 5,000 hospitalizations and struck decisively at the Japanese sense of safety and invulnerability. Nearly all of the sect's leaders were arrested, and Asahara went on trial for the killings in 1996. Aum Shinrikyō's status as a religious organization also was taken away by the government in that year.

James L. Huffman

Bibliography
Kurimoto, Shin'ichirō, and Serizawa Shunsuke. "The Pathology of a Peculiar Sect." *Japan Echo* (Autumn 1995), 54–62.

B

Bakufu

The term *bakufu* has traditionally been used to represent the military government of Japan, which originated with the Kamakura period (1185–1333). At that time, *bakufu* referred to the household government of the shogun, who was the supreme military commander in the field. In this sense, the *bakufu* performed the functions of a private household administration managing the affairs of the shogun and his *gokenin* (direct retainers). The *bakufu* ran the military administration of Japan from the late twelfth century through the mid-nineteenth century. Originally, it was established as a purely military institution centered on the relationship between the shogun and his vassals. Over the course of time, the military responsibilities of the *bakufu* were gradually augmented by its increasingly widespread jurisdiction over land-tenure and civil matters. Despite its increasing national authority and role in integrating the country, however, the *bakufu* inhibited the growth of nationalism in several significant ways by perpetuating the regionalism of the country's earlier eras.

From its inception, the *bakufu* existed in a dynamic balance between its own authority over Japan's military class and the spiritual authority of the imperial court in Kyoto. During the Kamakura period, it developed as a challenger to the national authority of the emperor and the nobility. Through the appointment of *jitō* (estate stewards) and *shugo* (military governors), the *bakufu* gradually extended its military authority over land tenure and judicial matters, at the expense of the more public authority and the economic interests of the imperial civil government. Despite the emperor's role as the source of legitimation from which the

bakufu's authority originated, the court increasingly found itself on the defensive in seeking to protect its ancient prerogatives.

Throughout the Muromachi period (1133–1573), in which the Ashikaga family dominated shogunal politics, the *bakufu* and the military class it represented continued to extend their control over land tenure and the public functions of the imperial court. By the late fifteenth century, the balance between court and *bakufu* had shifted decidedly in favor of the warrior class, while the imperial institution was left with little more than a ceremonial role. However, this is not to say that the private household administration of the Ashikaga shoguns had been successful in establishing itself as the undisputed national government of Japan. On the contrary, during the Muromachi period, while the imperial court was being shunted aside as a significant contender for national authority, a new dynamic balance developed between the central authority of the *bakufu* and the increasingly independent authority of local or regional military leaders such as the *shugo daimyō*. As long as this separation between central and local authority continued, Japan could not develop into a unified country with a dominant set of national priorities and interests.

The balance that characterized the Muromachi *bakufu* was eventually disrupted in the mid-sixteenth century by an intense period of centralization under the unifiers Oda Nobunaga (1534–1582) and Toyotōmi Hideyoshi (1536–1598). It may be argued that, with Hideyoshi's leadership, Japan displayed many of the conditions necessary for the rise of nationalism. However, Hideyoshi's full ambitions remain unclear and his objectives were not realized. After his death, Tokugawa Ieyasu

(1542–1616) and his successors established the *bakuhan* system that institutionalized a new balance between the central authority of the *bakufu* and the local authority of the daimyo.

During the Tokugawa period (1600–1868), the *bakufu* made significant efforts to restore the imperial institution to its traditional role as the sacred legitimizer of public authority in Japan. These efforts were never intended to suggest that the imperial house represented an alternative to the *bakufu* around which a government with truly national authority might be established. On the contrary, the *bakufu* was simply acting to enhance its own authority in the balance of power inherent in the *bakuhan* system. Furthermore, while this balance of *bakufu* and daimyo authority was maintained, the rise of nationalism in Japan continued to be inhibited in significant ways by a separation of interests between Edo, the *bakufu* capital, and the domains. It would not be until the early nineteenth century that certain members of Japan's warrior class would come to recognize a shared national interest, stemming from the threat of Western imperialism. Under these conditions, and given the imperial institution's identification with legitimate authority, it was natural that the emperor should be seized upon as the focus for national loyalty and unity and that it was the *imperial* institution that consequently gave rise to the full development of Japanese nationalism in the late nineteenth century.

Crayne Horton

Bibliography

Hall, John W. *Government and Local Power in Japan*. Princeton, NJ: Princeton University Press, 1966.

Hall, John W., and Jeffrey P. Mass, eds. *Medieval Japan: Essays in Institutional History*. Stanford, CA: Stanford University Press, 1975.

Mass, Jeffrey P., and William B. Hauser, eds. *The Bakufu in Japanese History*. Stanford, CA: Stanford University Press, 1985.

Bikini Atomic Tests (1946 and 1954)

Bikini atoll in the Marshall Islands saw nuclear tests in 1946 and 1954. In March 1954, the United States detonated a hydrogen bomb. At 15 megatons, the new bomb had double the predicted power, and, as a result, the Japanese crew of the tuna fishing boat *Lucky Dragon V* (*Fukuryū Maru*), although well outside the authorized danger zone, was dusted with radioactive ash. All 23 men manifested radioactive illness, and one died in late September. National attention raised a host of touchy issues, including the morality of the Hiroshima and Nagasaki bombings, pollution from nuclear testing, and interruption of fishing. Indignation gave shape to one of the most enduring bases of postwar Japanese nationalism: antinuclear pacifism. Housewives began a petition campaign, protesting tests and circulating petitions demanding abolition of all nuclear bombs, which eventually garnered 30 million signatures, the largest grassroots protest in Japanese history embracing a broad cross section of Japanese society.

By 1960, the movement came to oppose the Japan-U.S. Security Treaty as well, but, as the pacifist movement became enmeshed in elective politics, it lost some of its idealistic focus. It continues as a general peace lobby pressuring the government in areas of military policy and atomic energy; it also lends Japanese national identity an idealistic, almost utopian, vision of neutrality among the military superpowers.

David G. Egler

Bibliography

Bradley, David. *No Place to Hide, 1946/1984*. Hanover, NH: University Press of New England, 1983.

Imai, Ryukichi. *The Outlook for Japan's Nuclear Future*. Santa Monica, CA: California Seminar on Arms Control and Foreign Policy, 1975.

Black Sea Society (*Gen'yōsha*)

Japan's pioneering ultranationalist group. During the years following the Meiji Restoration (1868), Tōyama Mitsuru, Hiraoka Kōtarō, and others who advocated the expansion of the Japanese empire onto the Asian continent (*dai-Ajia shugi*) supported armed insurrections against the government to press their case. Tōyama, in fact, was imprisoned in 1876 for his role in these uprisings. He was released from prison the following year after the failure of the great Satsuma Rebellion (1877), which led him to conclude that attempts to overthrow the government were futile. Thus, in 1881, he joined with Hiraoka in forming the Gen'yōsha, hoping that it would become instrumental, through political education, lobbying, and intimidation, in influencing Japan's leaders to more strongly support *dai-Ajia shugi*.

Even the name members chose for their society indicated their concern with expansionism since it was derived from the Genkai Sea off northwestern Kyushu, an important ocean link between Japan and the continent. They produced an enormous amount of domestic propaganda, participated in acts of violence and intimidation, such as the attempted assassination of Foreign Minister Ōkuma Shigenobu, and, while engaging in extensive intelligence gathering on the Asian continent, also agitated for military action there. Moreover, they strongly opposed liberalism in Japan and spawned such other affiliated right-wing societies as the Kokuryūkai (Amur River Society) and the Dainihon Seisantō (Greater Japan Production Party).

Tōyama, who avoided violent acts following his imprisonment, eventually became the senior statesman of the right wing in Japan, and Gen'yōsha members Hirota Kōki and Nakano Seigō became prominent and highly influential politicians. In fact, the primary impact of the Gen'yōsha came through the personal influence of Hirota, Nakano, Tōyama, and Uchida Ryōhei, whom it chose to become the leader of the Kokuryūkai. Following World War II, the Allied Occupation (1945–52) disbanded the Gen'yōsha.

J. Wayne Sabey

Bibliography

Sabey, J. Wayne. "The Gen'yōsha, the Kokuryūkai and Japanese Expansionism." Unpublished doctoral dissertation, University of Michigan, 1972.

Boshin War (1868–69)

The name, derived from the reading for the cyclic characters for the year 1868, given to the civil war that resulted in the defeat of the Tokugawa shogunate and its allies and the restoration of imperial rule. It was a series of military engagements lasting 17 months, from the battle of Toba-Fushimi south of Kyoto in January 1868 to the final surrender of pro-Tokugawa forces on the island of Hokkaido in June 1869. This desultory civil war moved through four distinct phases, each coinciding with the shift of hostilities eastward, from the Kyoto-Osaka area, to the Kantō region, to the northeast provinces of the main island, and, finally, to Hokkaido.

In the battle of Toba-Fushimi, 4,500 numerically inferior but better disciplined and led troops of Satsuma, Chōshū, and Tosa domains, under an imperial prince flying the "brocade banner," defeated 15,500 daimyo units loyal to the shogun and French-trained Tokugawa units. The victory set the course for a military settlement rather than a political compromise, gave the imperial forces confidence in their superiority, and brought into line any southwestern daimyo who were sitting on the fence, thereby consolidating the new imperial government in western Japan.

Although the peaceful surrender of Edo on May 3, 1868, was approved by Keiki, the last shogun, who then went into seclusion in Mito domain, a split occurred among Tokugawa followers. Those left in Edo who bitterly resented the negotiated surrender organized themselves as a fighting unit and rallied around the abbot of the temple (who was an imperial prince) at the Tokugawa mausoleum in Edo. With defeat in the battle of Ueno on July 4, 1868, and the destruction of the temple, all organized resistance in Edo ended. Before all hostilities in the Kantō region ceased, however, imperial forces made up of contingents from Satsuma, Chōshū, Tosa, and other domains of western Japan were dispatched to defeat troops in northern Honshu, which had formed a league, under the lord of Aizu domain, to resist the newly declared imperial regime. During the summer and autumn of 1868, this confederation of domains, reinforced by former Tokugawa retainers and stragglers from earlier engagements, stubbornly defended many of the northern castle towns, producing a temporary stalemate in the civil war that checked the process of unification. Superiority in numbers, weapons, and strategy finally enabled the contingents flying the imperial banner to capture Wakamatsu castle of the Aizu daimyo on November 6, 1868. Resistance in the north quickly collapsed as one daimyo after another surrendered to the new government. Most of them were placed under arrest, and their territories split and drastically reduced in size.

The final episode in the Boshin war took place on the northern island of Hokkaido (then known as Ezo). It presents an intriguing story of resolute resistance that prolonged the civil war more than half a year beyond the cessation of hostilities in Japan. Enomoto Takeaki, a loyal Tokugawa retainer and the leading naval commander under the shogunate, withdrew the bulk of the Tokugawa fleet northward, captured Hokkaido as a territory for Tokugawa supporters, and established a separate government in defiance of the new regime. For the first half of 1869, a base was established, with Hakodate as headquarters, for keeping the spirit of resistance alive. A republic was formed, with Enomoto as the elected president, a petition was sent to the Meiji (imperial) government to permit a separate regime, and foreign powers were appealed to for recognition. The requests were denied, and, in due course, the exiled government was defeated in a series of land and sea engagements. On June 26, 1869, when Enomoto surrendered at Hakodate, the Boshin civil war came to an end; it had lasted 17 months, with total casualties estimated at 8,200 killed and more than 5,000 wounded. In this sense, the Meiji Restoration was hardly a bloodless coup carried out without opposition; it was a severe, though unsuccessful, conflict waged against the new government by adherents of the old order.

Roger F. Hackett

Bibliography

Sheldon, Charles. "The Politics of the Civil War of 1868." *Modern Japan: Aspects of History, Literature and Society*. Ed. W.G. Beasley. Berkeley: University of California Press, 1975.

Bureau of Rites (*Jingikan*)

The highest organ of state in the Meiji government, from 1868 until 1871. The Jingikan was the power base for the *kokugakusha* (nativist scholars), and was the most ideologically pure of the new government's organs, some of which leaned toward pragmatism. The early Meiji government modeled its Jingikan after the supreme organ of state during the reign of the legendary first emperor, Jinmu, which also was known as the Jingikan. The mission of the Jingikan was to unify Shinto rites so that they might form the national ritual that nativists thought necessary for proper government. Due to the Restoration government's ebbing interest in nativism, as well as resistance from the houses that had administered rites up to the establishment of the Jingikan, the Jingikan failed to achieve its goal of establishing a national code of rites. The government stripped it of its supreme power in 1871 and, in the following year, abolished it altogether. Shinto priests and nativist thinkers campaigned to bring the Jingikan back, but it was not until the establishment of the Jingiin (Board of Rites) in 1940 that their project was fully realized.

Guy Yasko

Bibliography

Hardacre, Helen. *Shinto and the State, 1868–1988*. Princeton, NJ: Princeton University Press, 1989.
Koschmann, J.V. *The Mito Ideology*. Berkeley: University of California Press, 1987.

Bushidō

A Japanese term meaning the "way of the warrior," which has in the narrowest sense little connection with Japanese nationalism. It refers to the ideals of the warrior class (*bushi*, more often called samurai in the West) of medieval and early-modern Japan. It is a relatively recent term, not popularized until the twentieth century. But by a curious twist of fate, it became intermingled with the rise of nationalism in the late nineteenth and early twentieth centuries and then became linked with the militarism of the 1930s and 1940s.

From the late-twelfth until the mid-nineteenth century, Japan was normally ruled by the warrior class through three successive *bakufu* (military governments). Samurai of different eras lived under varied conditions and thus exhibited differing values and behaviors. For much of the period, warfare was endemic, and warriors were expected not only to be skilled in the military arts but also to exhibit courage on the battlefield, personal honor, and, perhaps above all, loyalty to their lord, even to the point of sacrificing themselves in battle or through ritual suicide.

Various formulations of the ethical behavior expected of the samurai survive, although the term *bushidō* seems not to have been used in the Kamakura and Muromachi eras (1185–1573). Instead, the ideals were described in terms such as "practices of those who carry bows and arrows" in order to distinguish them from the ways of the courtier. Idealized warrior behavior was glorified in war tales (*gunki monogatari*); other formulations survive in feudal codes issued by successive *bakufu* and in house laws and precepts written by lords intent on controlling their vassals or guiding heirs in the maintenance of the fief. Texts often present an idealized form of medieval ethical imperatives for warriors. The many codes, formulated with different emphases, underscore the lack of a universal standard of behavior held in common by the warriors of medieval Japan.

Vague though such ideals may have been, chief among the virtues extolled by various sources was the samurai's loyalty to his lord. Late-twentieth-century academic opinion maintains that the unconditional loyalty often portrayed in war tales and prescribed by codes was by no means universally observed in medieval Japan but varied widely depending upon the specific relationship between samurai and lord.

By the late sixteenth century, the word *bushidō* began to appear in texts, with a focus upon loyalty, bravery, and honor as a warrior's desirable qualities. But in an age of turmoil, when powerful barons (daimyo) vied to win control of the entire country, skilled warriors were at a premium, and the lords competed to surround themselves with such retainers. Some warriors would offer uncompromising loyalty to daimyo of notable character, but many others changed masters in order to improve individual or family positions. The fact that many contemporary documents stress the virtue of loyalty suggests that it did not often obtain in the real world.

In the subsequent Edo period (1600–1868), when the Tokugawa family established a peace that lasted two and a half centuries, the warrior class lost much of its fighting readiness and was converted into a service bureaucracy. Martial skills now developed into martial arts, although the samurai never lost their function as paramilitary personnel. Scholars turned to defining the role of the samurai in an era when they rarely risked their lives in support of their lords. Most writings on the role and ethics of the samurai class emerged from a Confucian point of view, neo-Confucianism having been adopted by the Tokugawa *bakufu* as essentially a civil religion.

Among the virtues expected of Tokugawa samurai, certainly loyalty was crucial. But the nature of loyalty had changed. With the freezing of the social order, daimyo became hereditary heads of fiefs owing fealty to the shogun, and each samurai inherited the lord of his respective father. Samurai were born into a rigidly stratified society. No matter how lacking in charisma or military skill, the lord was a samurai's hereditary lord, and exhortations to loyal service were all the more necessary.

Common Edo-period terms for samurai ethics were *budō* and *shidō*, also translated as "way of the warrior." These were highly Confucianized views of the expected behavior of the samurai, expounded by such thinkers as Yamaga Sokō, Kaibara Ekken, and Nakae Tōju, in which the samurai was urged to hone his martial skills while practicing the civil virtues of the scholar official. The joint ways of civil and military virtues (*bunbu ryōdō*) were frequently likened to the two wheels of a cart or the two wings of a bird. This Confucianized form of warrior ethics was the dominant stream of Tokugawa thought.

Bushidō was a little-used term during the period. It appeared in a few works, such as Yamamoto Tsunetomo's *Hagakure* (1716), famous for the ringing opening quote: "The way of the samurai lies in death." But this *bushidō* was a narrow stream of thought that sought to recapture an idealized, sacrificial form of loyal service to a lord, a way of life that was all but impossible under the changed social conditions in which the samurai actually functioned.

Given this background, why is there a tendency in Japan and abroad to assume that the Tokugawa warrior class had a clearly articulated set of ethical rules called *bushidō*, which was bequeathed to the modern era and even influenced the Japanese behavior in World War II?

The popularization of the term *bushidō*, and the concept of a "way" of the warrior, owe much to the Christian scholar and educator Nitobe Inazō (1862–1933), who wrote *Bushidō: The Soul of Japan* in 1900. Nitobe produced this volume in response to questions posed by Westerners about how moral education was inculcated in the Japanese populace when there was no religious instruction in the Meiji school system. A perplexed Nitobe explained that *bushidō* breathed a "sense of right and wrong into my nostrils." He cited the existence of a consistent body of ethical teachings, called *bushidō*—which he always capitalized to emphasize its importance—shared by the samurai class in Tokugawa times. Although he noted on several occasions that *bushidō* was an unformulated teaching, he nonetheless listed seven virtues of *bushidō*, which have been quoted by authors ever since: justice, courage, benevolence, politeness, veracity, honor, and loyalty.

According to Nitobe, these virtues had not disappeared with the end of the samurai class after the Meiji Restoration of 1868. In fact, they had been inherited and adopted by the Japanese populace as a whole. Nitobe argued that *bushidō* had become Japan's "animating spirit" even before it was formulated into a code—that it was the moral force motivating Japan's behavior.

Nitobe's book proved to be influential worldwide. It was translated into many Western languages and even recommended by U.S. President Theodore Roosevelt as the key to understanding Japan. It was written and subsequently popularized during a period of rising nationalism, which accompanied Japan's meteoric rise to international importance with victories over two giant neighbors, first China and then Russia.

Bushidō was part of the rediscovery of the past by Japanese scholars and popular writers, who had for some time rejected tradition in favor of Western ideas and institutions. A sudden flood of literature on *bushidō* inundated bookstores early in the twentieth century. The nationalist philosopher Inoue Testujirō compiled a collection of works on *bushidō* (*Bushidō sōsho*) in order to develop Japan's national defense by inculcating a *bushidō* spirit. Japanese of all persuasions came to see *bushidō* as embodying traditional Japanese values. Other scholars took Nitobe one step further: Nakariya Kaiten wrote of *bushidō* as the religion of Japan, while Takagi Takeshi compared it to European chivalry. Nitobe's fellow Christian, the famous journalist Uchimura Kanzō, went so far as to call *bushidō* Japan's "finest product" and to suggest grafting Christianity onto *bushidō*.

As Japan increasingly headed down the path of ultranationalism and expansion in the 1930s, young military officers read Nitobe or studied *Hagakure* to inculcate bravery and to imbue themselves with a sense of loyalty to the emperor as the embodiment of the nation. As anthropologist Ruth Benedict observed in her influential *Chrysanthemum and the Sword* (1946), *bushidō* is a "publicist's inspiration" turned into a "slogan of the nationalists and militarists." For many Japanese, it came to represent a sense of traditional martial culture, loyalty to the nation, and the spiritual toughness necessary for this small Asian power to triumph in an increasingly hostile international arena. Connecting historical *bushidō* with Japanese militarism involved a selective borrowing from the past, a reinterpretation for modern needs, and then a twisting of it for the needs of the state. Thus did *bushidō* become linked to Japanese nationalism.

The word still has an ugly connotation for those who remember the World War II era. It conjures up images of kamikaze pilots, harakiri, and fanatical sacrifice for Japan's cause. The initial goal of the U.S. Occupation of Japan (1945–52) was to demilitarize the country. So strong was the suspicion of Japan's martial spirit that Occupation authorities even prohibited the martial arts of *kendō* and judo, which were suspected to be conducive to developing a militaristic spirit.

Save for the glorification of the *Hagakure* text in the postwar period by such avowed nationalists as Mishima Yukio, *bushidō* has been largely discredited. But considerable apprehension at home and abroad persists that expanding Japanese military contributions in response to pressure from the international community may reawaken a militaristic spirit. Such is the legacy of *bushidō* in its connection with World War II.

G. Cameron Hurst III

Bibliography

Collcutt, Martin. "*Bushidō*," Encyclopedia of Japan. Vol. 1. Tokyo: Kodansha International, 1983, 221–23.

Hurst, G. Cameron, III. "Death, Honor, and Loyalty: The *Bushidō* Ideal," *Philosophy East and West*. Vol. 40, No. 4 (October 1990), esp. 516–19.

Nitobe, Inazo. *Bushidō: The Soul of Japan*. Rutland, VT: Charles E. Tuttle, 1969.

C

Cabinet Information Bureau (1936–45)

In the 1930s, military officers and state bureaucrats advocating imperialist expansion usurped much of the policy-making authority of the Japanese legislature. They organized new interministerial agencies in the cabinet to mobilize the country for war. The Cabinet Information Bureau *(Naikaku Jōhōkyokū)* (CIB) was the agency that controlled the mass media.

Founded as a modest committee in 1936, the CIB had become a major department of 510 officials by 1940. Its power extended over radio, film, the press, music, the theater, and the state news agency, paralleling the jurisdiction of Nazi Germany's Ministry of Propaganda, which provided a model for the CIB's establishment.

The CIB's goals transcended the mere censorship of government critics. Its aim was to transform all public expression into enthusiastic support for official policy. To this end, the CIB consolidated all news film companies into a state monopoly and helped coerce the dissolution of 25,000–30,000 newspapers and magazines. It had the power to blacklist journalists and other media people from practicing their professions and became the final arbiter of programs broadcast over radio and films shown in movie theaters.

Radio policy illustrates well the strong nationalistic bent of the CIB's "revolutionist" *(kakushin)* officials. Religious broadcasts in the late 1930s gradually excluded Christian subject matter and degenerated into patriotic pep rallies. The news was systematically distorted to conform with government propaganda, and the CIB even ordered the newscaster's tone of voice to be a "war cry."

Musical broadcasts deleted most songs sung in foreign languages as well as performances on foreign instruments such as the banjo, the ukulele, and the steel guitar. In their place, officials promoted such traditional Japanese instruments as the *shakuhachi*, the *koto*, and the *shamisen*. Military marches became standard fare in radio entertainment. One CIB document stated: "Apart from its political nature, culture does not exist."

The CIB's management of the mass media was a major cause of the strong public support for Japan's disastrous nationalistic crusade in Asia. The CIB was disbanded at the conclusion of World War II.

Gregory J. Kasza

Bibliography

Kaza, Gregory J. *The State and the Mass Media in Japan, 1918–1945.* Berkeley: University of California Press, 1988.

Cardinal Principles of the National Polity (*Kokutai no Hongi*)

A perfect expression of wartime Japanese nationalism, this document was published by the Bureau of Thought Control of the Ministry of Education *(Mombushō)* on March 30, 1937, a time when conflict with China was intensifying and friction with Great Britain and the United States had increased. Because it contained extreme nationalistic, militaristic, and anti-Western sentiments, the Occupation forces banned it specifically in the December 15, 1945, decree abolishing governmental sponsorship, support, perpetuation, control, and dissemination of State Shinto.

The *Kokutai no Hongi* went through three major draftings. Hisamatsu Sen'ichi, a Tokyo Imperial University scholar of the Japanese classics, was commissioned by the Bureau of Thought Control to write the first draft. Subsequently, a 14-member committee, including Hisamatsu, philosopher Wastsuji Tetsurō, nationalistic historian Kuroita Katsumi, and two members of the Research Section of the National Spiritual Culture Research Institute (NSCRI), Yoshida Kumaji and Yamada Yoshio, were designated to revise Hisamatsu's draft. Technically, the last draft was written by a second board of 10 specialists, including members of the NSCRI, the Mombushō, school inspectors, and supervisors of libraries. In fact, the chief of the Bureau of Thought Control, Itō Enkichi, a member of the committee, rewrote large sections even after the manuscript was in galley proofs. Five persons from the original drafting committee were purged during the Occupation, and at least three others might have been purged, but they had died. None, however, was purged specifically because of helping write *Kokutai no Hongi*.

The importance of *Kokutai no Hongi* as an instrument for propaganda can be seen by the Mombushō's dispatch in 1937 of 300,000 copies to public and private teachers from the elementary school to the university level as well as to prefectural governors, school principals, and university presidents. Eventually, 1.9 million official copies were sold, but the book was also circulated by private publishers. *Kokutai no Hongi* was used as a textbook or supplementary textbook at middle and higher schools and at technical schools. In fact, probably few persons ever read it in its entirety because the style and content were ponderous, abstruse, filled with honorifics, and, in Robert King Hall's words, "puzzling and contradictory."

The introduction proclaimed that it was written "to cultivate and awaken national sentiment and consciousness" and to clarify the *kokutai* (national polity). For that reason, it took the reader through the mythical origins of Japan's creation and strongly emphasized the imperial throne "coeval with Heaven and Earth" and Japanese virtues, such as loyalty and filial piety. The authors consistently attacked individualism and justified Japan's "mission" and military actions. They asserted that the bankruptcy of individualism caused the growth of Nazism, fascism, and Communism as well as mistaken Japanese conceptions of the nature of the state and the relationship of the individual to it. Similarly, *Kokutai no Hongi* proclaimed: "It is in the subduing of those who refuse to conform to the august influence of the emperor's virtue that the mission of our Imperial Military Forces lies . . . [and the military] hold a position of responsibility in which their duty is to make our national prestige greatly felt within and without our country to preserve the peace of the Orient in the face of the world powers."

The line between a nation claiming uniqueness and claiming superiority is narrow and can be dangerous. The *Kokutai no Hongi* repeated ad nauseam the uniqueness of Japanese institutions, virtues, and history. It crossed that line and descended into nationalistic propaganda. Nonetheless, it is a valuable historic document in which many Japanese ways of thinking may be found.

Harry Wray

Bibliography

Hall, Robert King. *Education for a New Japan.* New Haven, CT: Yale University Press, 1949.

———, ed. *Kokutai no Hongi* (Cardinal Principles of the National Entity of Japan). Trans. John Owen Gauntlett. Belmont, MA: Crofton, 1974.

Censorship (*Ken'etsu*)

Since the end of World War II, Japan's citizens have enjoyed unprecedented freedom of expression under the 1947 Constitution of Japan:

> Article 21. Freedom of assembly and association as well as speech, press and all other forms of expression are guaranteed. 2. No censorship shall be maintained, nor shall the secrecy of any means of communication be violated.

Censorship refers to governmental prior restraint or punishment of public expression in the mass media, art, or speech. Three sources of restriction may be distinguished, the last of which is most important in the constitutional politics of Japan's nationalism:

1. Restrictive administrative acts pursuant to law and constitution. In Japan's democratic polity, minimum official restraint in respect for others' rights (for example, a ban on pornography vending machines near schools) is not improper "censorship," but many question seizure by the Customs Office of imported

erotica as censorship. In a partly or comprehensively authoritarian legal system, freedom of expression is subordinated with varying regularity to other state priorities, such as control of dissent, public order, or national security. Nearly all contemporary governments claim that their censorship systems are morally and legally justified.

2. Restrictions on expression imposed by society, with or without official sanction. From a democratic perspective, social cultures tend to censor both good and bad ideas that are incompatible with currently dominant views. A democratic government's role may be to counteract social intolerance for minorities or unfamiliar art or ideas or to buttress the political consensus by banning expression that would endanger democracy. Majorities in democratic societies sometimes favor social censorship, whether or not it is legal.

3. Restrictions by integrated government and sociopolitical action on expression inimical to, or insufficiently supportive of, a particular collectivity's sense of national identity. The very discussion of important related topics may be taboo, as in the case of the "Emperor factor" in modern Japan. Official constraints and societal censorship in Japan's law and politics seem most noteworthy when clothed in nationalistic garb. Elites still contend over Japan's self-definition within a mental framework established long ago.

Confronted in the 1860s with an unprecedented challenge to national independence and identity by Western military and technological power, and by radically alien Western notions of law, society, and the state (both democratic and autocratic in substance), Japan's oligarchs drew brilliantly on select aspects of traditional emperor Shinto (as opposed to local shrine-based Shinto), and neo-Confucianism in transforming a powerless emperor into the foundation institution for a modern Japanese state, thus assuring national independence in the face of unequal treaties and international power. The 1889 Constitution of the Empire of Japan located full sovereignty in the emperor (*tennō*) without putting effective checks on the government power of those who acted in his name. Over subsequent decades, modern means of

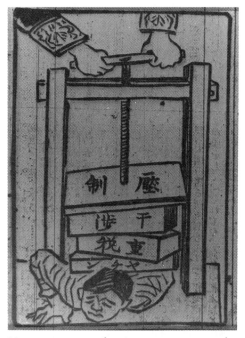

Newspaper cartoon decrying government control of citizenry, Niroku Shimpō, *March 21, 1902. Courtesy Meiji Shimbun Zasshi Bunkō.*

mass indoctrination and state control gradually changed the typical Japanese response to the emperor from an almost casual disinterest to an officially mandated reverence and absolute loyalty. The touchstone for the good and appropriately nationalistic Japanese became adherence to the will of a benevolent, paternal, quasi-divine emperor presiding over an organically related national family (*kokka* [the state]) in the divine land of Japan; that is, obedience to the government.

A subject's freedom of expression or religion under law did not include freedom from unquestioning conformity with State Shinto. The practical test for correct thought and action was compatibility with the dictates of the increasingly sophisticated and restrictive system of legal, administrative, social, and academic censorship. The aim went beyond coercive control to gaining willing self-sacrifice for the emperor-state in both domestic and foreign affairs. In the wartime period of the "dark valley" (1930–45), no force in the power structure provided a meaningful restraint on extreme emperor-centered nationalism (*kokutai*). Japan's prewar censorship system was one of the most refined ever developed by a large modern country.

More important than defeat itself, 1945 brought the collapse of the nationalistic thought structure behind censorship, the demystification of government and the emperor, and a weakening of that modern sense of national identity carefully nurtured since the nineteenth century. Besides numbness in devastation, the pain of first and total defeat, and the inherent pleasures of peace and freedom, the essential catalytic element in the revolutionary transition from an oppressive regime to a free democracy was the benevolently activist Allied Occupation dominated by the United States (1945–52). Attempts at censorship by holdovers in Japan's government in the fall of 1945 were immediately squelched by Occupation officials, and the machinery of control was disassembled.

The revolution of freedom has continued under the 1947 Constitution of Japan, coauthored by Americans and Japanese, popular from its first publication, and now the most respected and trusted of Japan's national institutions. Paradoxically, the Occupation leadership, which conferred freedom on all but extreme nationalists, itself censored comment on the Occupation in 1945 and, with the advent of the Cold War and the Korean War (1950–53), later restricted some leftist groups. Nevertheless, in the immediate postwar years most censorship ended, and freedom of expression, along with other human rights, a unique form of state pacifism (see ARTICLE 9 entry), and a powerless emperor became (and remains) the constitutional foundation for Japan's sense of national identity. No other sacred writ or state doctrine rivals the Peace Constitution in legitimacy among Japan's citizens.

However, from the 1950s until the 1980s, leaders of the ruling Liberal Democratic Party (LDP) generally advocated revision of the constitution along nationalistic lines, with some favoring less freedom. They always lacked broad popular support on this issue and the necessary parliamentary votes for constitutional amendment. A small but persistent and vocal minority in the LDP and in a large number of small extremist patriot groups has continued to advocate a rekindling of nationalist fires as Japan has regained great power status, a restoration of the emperor to his prewar modern status (of puppet king), state funding of Shinto shrines to the war dead, an end to constitutional pacifism, increased military power, less stress on freedom of expression, and censorship of written and oral discourse about the emperor and Japanese history.

To simplify, a complex war continued in the 1990s in party politics, in the government ministries, in the courts, and in public discourse between incompatible definitions of Japan's national identity: nationalistic visions stressing Japan's ethnic separateness and nostalgia for an assumed community coherence and national glory under the prewar emperor system; and a more matter-of-fact understanding grounded in internationalism, prosperity, and respect for human rights. Many symbols continued to reflect this deep division: perennial opposition to legal establishment of the wartime national anthem and flag; Shinto shrine visits by cabinet members; court decisions that give preferred status to Shinto in apparent violation of the requirements for state-religion separation; ceremonies surrounding the 1989 funeral of Emperor Hirohito and the accession of Emperor Akihito, which tampered with tradition to *remystify* the institution; a long series of court cases challenging apparent censorship of Japanese history textbooks by the Education Ministry; and rightists' harassment of scholars, journalists, and politicians for critical comment about the emperor.

Examples of the latter two restraints illustrate the linkages between censorship and nationalism against the background described above. To rightist groups, irreverent discourse on the emperor is taboo. In 1987, An *Asahi Shimbun* newspaperman was shot to death by such extremists. Although Emperor Akihito has clearly defended free discourse about his father the late Emperor Hirohito, Mayor Hitoshi Motoshima of Nagasaki was shot and seriously wounded by rightists in January 1990, for commenting that Hirohito bore some responsibility for the war. Rather than government or law, the main threat to free speech, censorship by intimidation, is practiced by small extreme nationalist groups or by individuals in the private sector. Their violent views and actions are more a symptom of political pathology than a portent of future mainstream Japanese politics.

Much more important are the *Ienaga Textbook Review Cases*, which began wending their way through the courts in 1965. Professor Ienaga Saburō, like other authors, was required repeatedly to make changes in the revisions of his popular high-school history textbook. The Education Ministry textbook examiners took issue with his representation of the ancient history of the imperial family and of Japan's modern wartime history, but Ienaga and others charging censorship accused the ministry of obfuscating history and attempting to cover up Japan's World War II atrocities in Asia. Both the ministry and Ienaga won points in court, but the ministry's right to require revisions was finally affirmed by the Supreme Court early in the 1990s.

No consensus had emerged by the latter 1990s, however, on whether the system of textbook-manuscript review constitutes inherently objectionable censorship. The Education Ministry, textbook authors, and precollegiate educators have not been consistently forthright in choosing well-established historical truth over nationalistic presentation of Japan's modern history and the emperor institution. Since 1982, Japan's Asian neighbors have repeatedly protested the ministry's treatment of wartime events, such as the Nanjing Massacre (1937) and the long occupation of Korea (1910–45). Japan's prime minister and foreign minister have acted to mitigate these concerns, but a restrictive bureaucratic nationalism lodged among officials in the Education Ministry may remain the single most important source of censorship in one of the world's most libertarian constitutional states.

Lawrence W. Beer

Bibliography

Beer, Lawrence W. *Freedom of Expression in Japan*. Tokyo: Kodansha International, 1984, chaps. 2, 7.

Hata, Ikuhiko. "When Ideologues Rewrite History." *Japan Echo*. Vol. 13, No. 4 (1986), 73.

Mitchell, Richard H. *Censorship in Imperial Japan*. Princeton, NJ: Princeton University Press, 1983.

Charter Oath

An "Oath in Five Articles" (*Gokajō no seimon*) pledged by the young Emperor Meiji to give direction to the new government on April 6, 1868, in Kyoto. The oath, later misinterpreted as promising parliamentary democracy, was misnamed the Charter Oath in English as if comparable to the Magna Carta. Such fantasies were facilitated by the ambiguity of the oath, which reads: "(1) An assembly shall be widely convoked, and all measures shall be decided by open discussion. (2) High and low shall be of one mind, and the national economy and finances shall be greatly strengthened. (3) Civil and military officials together, and the common people as well, shall all achieve their aspirations, and thus the people's minds shall not be made weary. (4) Evil practices of the past shall be abandoned, and actions shall be based on international usage. (5) Knowledge shall be sought all over the world, and the foundations of imperial rule shall be strengthened."

The drafters of the oath, Yuri Kimimasa (1829–1909) of Echizen, Fukuoka Takachika (1835–1919) of Tosa, and Kido Takayoshi (1833–77) of Chōshū, hoped that it would help unify a coalition government fighting a civil war with borrowed money and a borrowed army. The intent of Article 1 was not to promise an elected parliament but to have decisions made by leaders from all anti-Tokugawa domains, not merely those from Satsuma and Chōshū, who had provided the imperial army. Articles 2 and 3 were appeals for outside money and support. Article 4 warned against antiforeign violence that was jeopardizing foreign support. Article 5 endorsed undefined Westernization but only to strengthen imperial rule.

Although too vague to have much effect on government actions, the oath was an important step in building a nationalism transcending feudal loyalties to region and class.

Robert M. Spaulding

Bibliography

Spaulding, Robert M. "The Intent of the Charter Oath." *Studies in Japanese History and Politics*. Ed. Richard K. Beardsley. Ann Arbor: University of Michigan Press, 1967.

Cherry Blossom Society (*Sakurakai*)

Ultranationalist organization. On September 30, 1930, 25 young army officers created the Sakurakai, under the leadership of Lieutenant Colonel Hashimoto Kingorō of the army general staff, to agitate for the reorganization of the Japanese state along military lines. The society, formed to abolish civilian party governments and expand Japanese influence in Asia, limited membership to soldiers of the rank of lieutenant colonel and below. Drawing members from the general staff, the War Ministry, military police headquarters and various army schools, it never numbered more than 100.

With most members committed to violence if necessary, the Sakurakai worked with other ultranationalists in 1931 to plan the March and October Incidents, both aborted attempts to overthrow the government and replace it with a military-led cabinet. Several of its leaders were convicted after the October Incident, and the society dissolved.

James L. Huffman

Bibliography
Storry, Richard. *The Double Patriots: A Study of Japanese Nationalism.* Westport CT: Greenwood Press, 1973.

Citizens' Movements (*Shimin Undō*)

Japan's unprecedentedly rapid economic and industrial growth in the 1960s was expected to enrich consumers' living standard. In the late 1960s and early 1970s, however, many Japanese experienced relative deprivation and increased social problems: high commodity prices, poisonous industrial wastes, inflation, lack of public welfare, urban crowding, housing problems, controversy over "the right to sunshine," and environmental pollution.

As a result, many formerly submissive Japanese citizens joined movements designed to improve the quality of daily life. These *shimin undō* (citizens' movements) became politically mobilized and organized and championed such causes as peace, opposition to nuclear weapons and the Vietnam War, pollution controls, and consumer protections.

By the late 1960s, Japan faced particularly serious environmental problems because of its limited size, industrial concentration, intensive urbanization, and rapid industrialization. For the residents of certain regions, pollution became a life-and-death issue. Many Japanese suffered from such industrial-poisoning afflictions as Minamata disease (mercury poisoning, which injured nervous systems and caused spasms), *itai itai* disease (cadmium pollution, which made bones brittle), and asthma.

One response was the rise late in the 1960s of *jūmin undō* (residents' movements) organized by local fishermen, farmers, and peasants to deal with such local issues as industrial poisoning and overcrowding. The first pollution lawsuit by *jūmin undō* lawyers, filed in 1967, was followed by numerous legal and political actions throughout Japan. By the 1970s, the term *jūmin undō* had come to be used nationally, often interchangeably with *shimin undō*.

These movements attracted participants from the ordinary citizenry rather than from Japan's more usual sources of protest, such as radical labor unions, intellectuals, leftist parties, and student movements. As a result, they tended to be issue-oriented, nonideological, voluntary community organizations rather than political groups. They also were highly effective—so much so that by 1973 Japan's six largest cities had progressive mayors supported by the citizens' movements.

At first, many of the citizen protesters were sharply criticized by a populace long accustomed to order and passive acceptance of what life gave. Some were ostracized; some, bullied by victims who often blamed themselves for their diseases and difficulties. They also faced the intransigence of an unresponsive government headed by officials, both local and national, who feared that action would retard economic growth. Pollution, many argued, was part of the price of industrial nationalism and rapid progress.

Increasingly, however, citizens' movements gained respectability and influence. By the early 1970s, they were creating new forms of organization, developing creative protest strategies, and making themselves heard loudly in the legal and the political spheres. At their peak, in 1973, an estimated 3,000 such movements operated. Among the groups' more important accomplishments were the passage of the 1968 Basic Law for Environmental Pollution, which set new environmental pollution standards, and the approval of 14 antipollution laws by the 1970 "Pollution Diet" (legislature). Among these, one law, the first of its kind in the world, designated an act of pollution that damaged human health as a crime. The Environmental Agency was established in 1971, and a law recognizing victims of pollution went into effect in 1973. Another achievement was the Environmental Agency's adoption of some of the world's strictest automobile-emission standards. The citizens' movements declined significantly by the mid-1970s, although local activism has continued from time to time on specific issues.

Kinko Ito

Bibliography
McKean, Margaret A. *Environmental Protest and Citizen Politics in Japan.* Berkeley: University of California Press, 1981.

Artist's conception of "civilized" Ginza street in Tokyo, 1870s. Courtesy Mainichi Shimbunsha Shi Henshūshitsu.

Pempel, T.J. *Policy and Politics in Japan: Creative Conservatism*. Philadelphia, PA: Temple University Press, 1982.

Civilization and Enlightenment (*Bunmei Kaika*)

Widely used phrase in the Meiji era (1868–1912) signifying the government's efforts to educate Japan's general populace about Western civilization. In fact, the movement was limited to the upper classes of the great cities and flourished from the early 1870s to the late 1880s, when it was overwhelmed by a revival of cultural nationalism. Its counterpart in the political sphere was the *fukoku kyōhei* (rich country, strong army) policy.

Civilization and enlightenment by government decree resulted in elimination of the *chonmage* (topknots) of the samurai in favor of short Western-style haircuts in 1871; making Western clothing compulsory for government officials in 1872; and the adoption of the solar calendar on January 1, 1873. Members of the elite began to grow beards, carry gold watches, and drop English phrases into their Japanese conversation. Such persons were deemed to be *hai kara* (high collar) after the foreign shirts they wore. Baseball was introduced in 1873 for young men needing a game to replace the mar-tial arts, which had fallen out of fashion with the abolition of the samurai class, and the American pastime was soon on its way to becoming the national sport of Japan.

Another aspect of *bunmei kaika* was the introduction of Western technology; a children's song of the time enumerated its 10 most desirable objects: gas lights, steam locomotives, horse-drawn carriages, cameras, the telegraph, lightning rods, newspapers, schools, the postal service, and steamboats.

Western liberal ideology was also introduced at this time by Fukuzawa Yukichi and the members of the Meirokusha (Meiji Six Society). In his *Encouragement of Learning* (1876), Fukuzawa stressed that all were equal at birth and that their differences resulted from their education. The public bought 3.5 million copies of Fukuzawa's books on Western thought and civilization espousing scientific, rational learning and the independence of the individual. Translations of Western classics on self-help, utilitarianism, and natural rights abounded in the period, including Meirokusha member Nakamura Masanao's 1872 version of John Stuart Mill's *On Liberty*.

"Civilization and enlightenment" flourished during the age as students went abroad or studied English at home; missionaries such as Guido Verbeck lectured on the American

Constitution to 1,000 young samurai in the Kyushu city of Saga; and foreign technical experts such as the agronomist William Smith Clark inspired his Sapporo Agricultural College students with the admonition, "Boys, be ambitious!"

A reaction set in during the 1880s against excesses, highlighted by the destruction of traditional art treasures; the advocacy of the exclusive use of the Roman alphabet and of intermarriage with Caucasians to strengthen the Japanese stock; and, most notably, the promotion by government leaders of social dancing to Western music at the Rokumeikan hall in Tokyo, where weekly soirées were held for Western diplomats. The cultural reaction that followed all but submerged *bunmei kaika*.

Sidney DeVere Brown

Bibliography
Blacker, Carmen. *The Japanese Enlightenment*. Cambridge: Cambridge University Press, 1964.
Hirakawa, Sukehiro. "Japan's Turn to the West." Trans. Bob Tadashi Wakabayashi. *Cambridge History of Japan*. Vol. 5, *The Nineteenth Century*. Ed. Marius B. Jansen. Cambridge: Cambridge University Press, 1989, 432–98.

Coalition Movement
(*Daidō Danketsu Undō*) (1886–90)

Antigovernment political association. Faced with the promised promulgation of the Meiji Constitution, Gotō Shōjirō, Hoshi Tōru, and 70 other former political party members (mostly from the old Jiyūtō [Liberal Party]) met on October 24, 1886, to create a movement capable of fighting government policies in the coming national legislature. They attempted, in particular, to gain popular support by inciting nationalistic opposition to the unequal treaties that had been forced on Japan by Western countries. The peak of the movement came in late 1887 and 1888, with fervent speeches across the country by Gotō and others. The government attempted to suppress the movement, particularly with the harsh *hoan jōrei* (Peace Regulations) in December 1887. The primary undoing of the movement, however, was factionalism and the opportunism of leaders such as Gotō, who entered the Kuroda Kiyotaka cabinet as minister of communications in 1889.

The movement helped lay the groundwork for eventual party politics.

James L. Huffman

Bibliography
Mason, R.H. *Japan's First General Election, 1890*. Cambridge: Cambridge University Press, 1969.

Colonialism (1895–1945)

Into the mid-1990s still the only non-Western colonial power, Japan became a ruler of other peoples and lands when it was itself still in a semicolonial state under the unequal treaty system. With the memory of that humiliating subservience dimming only slightly over the years, Japan administered five colonies: Taiwan, acquired in 1895; Guandong (Kwantung) Leased Territory and Karafuto (the southern half of Sakhalin), in 1905; Korea, in 1910; and Nan'yō (Pacific Islands), in 1914.

All five were acquired by force and, with the exception of Karafuto, a colony of Japanese settlers, were ruled mainly by military administrators (usually army men, but navy men in Nan'yō) or their protégés. Serious attempts to introduce genuine civilian administrations—especially in Taiwan during the 1920s—did not survive the growing militarization of Japan itself during the 1930s. With the exception of Nan'yō, all of Japan's colonies were countries or parts of countries that nearly touched Japan's borders. After the Meiji Restoration of 1868, Japan's new leaders described Korea as "a dagger pointing at the heart of Japan" and declared control of that country to be necessary protection against further erosion of Japan's autonomy. In the north, Karafuto was intended to be another buffer. Although Guandong was part of the outer ring of defense of the home islands, along with Taiwan it also represented the offensive side of Japanese colonialism: military dominance of weaker countries and their populations.

Since convincing the West that Japan deserved to be treated as an equal was a major motive for joining the imperialists' club in the first place, it is not surprising that Japanese colonialism began with an examination of European colonial institutions: The Bureau of Taiwan Affairs, hastily organized in 1895 to draw up plans for the first territory, immediately undertook a detailed study of French, British, Dutch, Spanish, and other Western colonial records. Administrators such as Gotō Shimpei, who laid the foundations of Japan's rule of Taiwan between 1898 and 1905, were diligent students of comparative colonialism. Like later colonial officers, he enthusiastically endorsed the elitist mentality of Europeans overseas and the treatment of subject peoples as lesser beings that was a part of this mentality. The imposing buildings erected to serve as central headquarters of the governments-general of Taiwan, Guandong, Korea, and later of the administration of Nan'yō were intended to instill awe of Japan and the Japanese in the minds of non-Japanese subjects. Like European colonials elsewhere, the bureaucrats who worked in these buildings and other Japanese residents carefully cultivated their superior status and enjoyed their many privileges.

Western models were important, but they were not to be uncritically imitated or merely modified by refinements that promised more orderly, sanitary, and economically productive satellites than those governed by British, French, or Dutch mentors. One major reason for paying so much attention to Western colonialism was to learn what was to be avoided, and the Japanese found much to be avoided. For instance, while fashioning plans to resist rapidly growing demands for self-rule in Korea during the early 1920s, Japan's chief of police forces in Korea, Maruyama Tsurukichi, held up British rule in India as the great negative example for colonial rulers facing the nationalism of indigenous populations.

Positive or negative, Western colonialism was by no means the only source of models. The nation building begun after the Meiji Restoration of 1868 also provided important guidelines. State initiative, the major engine of political, economic, and social development in Japan during the Meiji era (1868–1912), was the primary force in colonial development. As in Meiji Japan, not only did government provide Japanese capitalists with infrastructure such as police protection, railroads, stable currency, credit and banking facilities, uniform weights and measures, favorable laws, and so forth, but colonial administrations also invested directly in the economies under their control. Much of the colonial government's outlays went into trying to make the colonies financially independent and to improve agriculture that would guarantee exports of rice, sugar, and other foodstuffs to Japan. But industry was not neglected: Japan is the only colonial power to have located heavy industries, such as steel, chemicals, and hydro-electric power, in its colonies. These were developed by public and private capital late in the colonial period, but by 1945 they probably accounted for about one-quarter of Japan's industrial base.

National education, a key contributor to Japanese development after 1868, was a major concern of colonial governments. In Karafuto, education meant extending the public-school facilities of the main islands to the Japanese settlers in the new frontier. In Guandong, administrators also concentrated their efforts upon schools for Japanese children, although they encouraged the local people to send their children to these as well. Elsewhere, however, Japanese colonial education meant much more than providing the children of Japanese residents with some of the amenities of the ruling country: Japanese education for indigenous populations, especially elementary schooling, was a tool of modernization and nationalization. In Taiwan, Japanese educators began with overtures to the children of the local Chinese literati and ended up with a system of Japanese-language elementary schools attended by about 65 percent of Taiwanese children, including more than half of the female elementary school-age population. The story was similar in Korea, where more than half of all Korean school-age children were attending elementary school by 1940. (Despite strong campaigns to get them into Japanese schools, Koreans favored private schools operated by their fellow Koreans, but all private institutions were required to teach the Japanese language and arithmetic curricula of the Japanese schools.) The standards in Nan'yō's public schools for Micronesian children may have been lower, but they, too, offered modified versions of subjects taught in the primary schools of the Japanese archipelago. In 1937, more than 20 percent of the native islanders were in Nan'yō government schools, with only a slightly higher percentage of male pupils than female pupils attending. This schooling was designed to impart the new skills and attitudes needed to succeed in the modern society that colonial rulers were determined to create. It was also to be the vehicle by which subject peoples were to be transformed into loyal Japanese.

Policymakers and enactors envisioned assimilation, mainly through education, as a long-range process. In 1898, Gotō Shimpei had cautioned against rapid assimilation of Taiwan's

Chinese population: "You cannot change a flounder into a sea bream overnight." This approach was rarely questioned until 1919, when the home government changed official policy for Taiwan, Korea, and Nan'yō to one of accelerated assimilation. From 1919, Tokyo repeatedly instructed the governments-general of Taiwan and Korea to pursue rapid Japanization largely through education, popularization of Japanese customs, and gradual application of the laws of the ruling country. Nan'yō experienced the same policy change, but, in the South Seas, expectations of Japanization were lower because the Micronesians were considered to be less advanced than the Koreans and Taiwanese of Chinese ancestry who shared a common East Asian heritage with the Japanese.

Whether gradual or accelerated, assimilation, in theory, meant that affinities of race and culture between Japan and its non-Japanese subjects (excepting Micronesians) could bring subjects and rulers together in one identity that was entirely Japanese. Equal under one emperor, Japanese and non-Japanese "imperial peoples" (kōmin) would be imbued with the same nationalism. In practice, assimilation always meant assimilation at the bottom of colonial political, economic, and social hierarchies while old patterns of discrimination—in schooling, employment, and other areas—remained strong. The kōminka (imperialization of subject peoples) movement played a central role in accelerated Japanization during the 1930s, but the union of Asian peoples it advocated was in reality a unity under Japanese leadership. By the mid-1930s, kōminka was just another Japanese tool in the use of colonies as launching pads for economic, political, and military expansion in East and Southeast Asia.

In spite of Japanese schooling and other enticements, the subjects of assimilation remained lukewarm toward Japanese nationalism. As early as 1914, public opposition to Japanese rule surfaced in Taiwan; by 1920, a Taiwanese nationalist movement, many of whose leaders were Japanese educated, was challenging Japan's right to rule the island. Since the radical wing of this movement sought full independence for Taiwan, it faced persistent attacks from the colonial police. Radicals worked within organizations formed to raise Taiwanese consciousness and in peasant unions until mass arrests in 1931 and 1932 immobilized most of the colony's leftists. The mainstream fought for home rule through petitions to the national Diet

(legislature) in Tokyo and campaigns aimed at winning public opinion in the ruling country and publicizing their cause in Taiwan. By the mid-1930s, the government-general had put a halt to these activities, too, perhaps partly because they exposed the hollowness of the kōminka claims.

In Korea, opposition to Japan's annexation of the country was fierce, although the Japanese military ruthlessly suppressed all manifestation of it. After World War I, the doctrine of self-determination of peoples proclaimed by President Woodrow Wilson of the United States caught the attention of Korean intellectuals.

On March 1, 1919, Japanese overreaction to a peaceful demonstration and proclamation that Korea hoped to gain independence touched off the famous March First Movement. No armed uprising had been planned, but the Japanese police fired on the peaceful demonstrators and signaled to the army and navy for help. The result was countrywide defiance: More than a million Koreans joined in demonstrations or supported the movement in other ways. Suppression was brutal and bloody, with thousands of Koreans killed, arrested, and prosecuted. The government-general was able to halt organized anti-Japanese resistance and to entice some Koreans to collaborate with the regime, but the March First Movement inspired many people to passively resist. Kōminka policies did little to arrest a growing Korean consciousness.

Japanese colonialism was itself like Japanese nationalism in that it was fostered by a need to respond to Western aggression and by a growing urge to dominate other—mostly Asian—peoples. Even as the cession of Taiwan from China in 1895 was seen as an opportunity to begin Japan's climb toward nationhood, so the League of Nations' designation of the colony of Nan'yō as a Japanese mandate at the end of World War I was interpreted as irrefutable evidence of Japan's arrival as a world power. Yet, in its attempts to win colonized peoples to the cause of Japanese nationalism, Japanese colonialism failed miserably. For the people it ruled, it provided an anti-Japanese focus for their own nationalism.

E. Patricia Tsurumi

Bibliography

Kublin, Hyman. "The Evolution of Japanese Colonialism." *Comparative Studies in Society and History.* Vol. 2 (1959), 67–84.

Myers, Ramon H., and Mark R. Peattie, eds. *The Japanese Colonial Empire, 1895–1945*. Princeton, NJ: Princeton University Press, 1984.

Commoners' Newspaper (*Heimin Shimbun*) (1903–05)

Pacifist, socialist newspaper. A weekly mouthpiece of the socialist Heiminsha (Society of Commoners), this paper served as the leading antiwar vehicle during the Russo-Japanese War (1904–05). It was published 64 times between November 15, 1903, and January 29, 1905, proclaiming its commitment to "liberty, equality, and fraternity" along with "commonerism, socialism, and pacifism," and boasting a circulation of 3,000–4,000. The chief writers were Kōtoku Shūsui and Sakai Toshihiko.

Heimin was constantly in trouble with the authorities. After he wrote a March 27, 1904, editorial decrying the high taxes caused by the war, Sakai was given two months in jail, and officials tried to ban the paper, only to be blocked by the courts. Articles in the November 6, 1904, issue attacking patriotism and calling for primary-school teachers to propagate socialism also drew official ire, and, when the paper published the *Communist Manifesto* the following week, officials gave Kōtoku five months in prison and shut the paper down, this time with court acquiescence. The last issue, published in red, came on January 18, 1905. *Heimin* was succeeded by another socialist organ, *Chokugen* (Straight Talk), and, in 1907, by a daily *Heimin Shimbun,* but both of these also fell afoul of the authorities and lasted but a few months.

James L. Huffman

Bibliography

Notehelfer, Fred. *Kōtoku Shūsui: Portrait of a Japanese Radical*. Cambridge: Cambridge University Press, 1971.

Conciliation Movement (*Yūwa*)

From the late nineteenth century, groups of young Burakumin, Japan's outcast class, emerged determined to fight to protect their rights. The response of first local, then central, government was to channel and control these groups by creating Yūwa (conciliation) groups.

In some areas, local governments tried to control Buraku organizations by placing them under the leadership of trusted members of the community—perhaps teachers or police officers. Following the nationwide rice riots of 1918, in which the Burakumin were thought to have played a major role, central government made its first direct cash contribution to projects that aimed at the material improvement of the Buraku environment. Four years later, worried by the moves being made to organize what became the pro-Burakumin Suiheisha (Levellers Society), the government tried to launch its own movement, the Dainihon Byōdōkai (Greater Japan Equality Association). It was unsuccessful, but it was followed by a reorganization of the Home Ministry section that kept an eye on the Buraku communities, provided some funds to assist with improvements, and backed a number of central and local Yūwa groups.

By the mid-1920s, a number of Yūwa organizations had produced considerable duplication of effort. In 1927, the government consolidated all of them into the Chūō Yūwa Jigyō Kyōkai (Central Conciliation Project Association). Chairman of the new body was Hiranuma Kiichirō (1867–1952), former law minister, vice chairman of the Privy Council, and leader of the right-wing Kokuhonsha (National Foundations Society). His deputy was Arima Yoriyasu (1884–1957), who had served in the lower (elected) house of the Diet (legislature) before succeeding to a hereditary title in 1927 and taking his seat in the House of Peers. These two leaders represented the nationalist and the liberal elements, respectively, within the movement. Liberal ideas remained strong until the 1930s, but thereafter the nationalist ideology dominated.

By the mid-1930s, the Yūwa movement was an integral part of local government; most prefectures had their own Yūwa office. In 1935, a Ten-Year Plan repackaged the existing schemes into a single, coherent program. The scanty new funds may have been used more efficiently by a new Yūwa administration hierarchy, which strengthened central control over this sector of the community. This new structure accommodated the national wartime mobilization introduced after 1938. Henceforth, the Yūwa movement lost any independence, and, in 1940, the Imperial Rule Assistance Association absorbed it.

Ian Neary

Bibliography

Yoshino, I. Roger, and Sueo Murakoshi. *The Invisible Visible Minority: Japan's Burakumin*. Osaka: Buraku Liberation Research Institute, 1977.

Concordia Society (*Kyōwakai*)

A nationalistic organization for mass political mobilization in Manchuria after its occupation by the Japanese Guandong army in the Manchurian Incident of September 1931. Founded by Japanese civilian residents of Manchuria, the association endeavored to enlist support of other resident ethnic groups—Chinese, Koreans, Manchus, Russians, Mongols, and Turkic tribes—for a permanent Japanese presence in Manchukuo (as the nominally autonomous entity was called). Their appeal was to pan-Asian doctrines of *minzoku kyōwa* (racial harmony).

The genesis of Kyōwakai lay in the Manchuria Youth League, which, in the late 1920s, lobbied strongly for an independent state in Manchuria that was free of nationalist China and of warlords. In theory, Japanese economic leadership within Manchuria would create progress and prosperity for all and draw support for a cooperative interethnic nationalism. In practice, Kyōwakai became a totalitarian arm of the military-dominated Manchukuo government, which launched many social, economic, and political programs from 1932 to 1945. Membership reached 3.5 million by the end of World War II.

David G. Egler

Bibliography

Peattie, Mark. *Ishiwara Kanji and Japan's Confrontation with the West*. Princeton, NJ: Princeton University Press, 1975.

Conference of Three Religions (*Sankyo Kaido*)

A conference of Buddhist, Christian, and Shinto leaders with government representatives, called on February 25, 1912, by the home minister, Hara Kei, and his vice minister, Tokonami Takejirō. Following the Russo-Japanese War (1904–05), Japan experienced economic instability and social unrest, which the government attempted to counter by strong action against radical and subversive groups. Certain leaders perceived a need to strengthen the spiritual—that is, ideological—foundations of the emperor-state. Tokonami had been impressed while visiting the United States by the social influence of Christianity there, and the idea of religion as an instrument of political control had a long history in Japan. The inclusion in this conference of Christianity, which had hitherto been treated as a subversive influence, marked a new recognition of its standing. Seven Protestant leaders accepted, seeing the invitation as a chance to become less marginalized and to integrate more fully into Japanese society.

The conference, of little significance in itself, is remembered as a symbolic watershed in Christian history. It represented a new recognition of Christianity as one of the three "official" religions of the country. It marked the beginning of a process of co-opting the churches into the nationalistic structure of the emperor system (*tennōsei*). It signaled the growth of nationalistic sentiment (*nipponteki kirisutokyō*) within Christianity itself. And it marginalized those individuals and groups who strove to maintain emphases such as personal freedom, pacifism, and social action within the Christian tradition.

Cyril H. Powles

Bibliography

Kishimoto, Hideo, and John F. Howes, eds. and trans. *Japanese Religion in the Meiji Era*. Tokyo: Obunsha, 1956.

Conquer Korea Argument (*Seikan Ron*)

Government debate in 1873 over Japanese policy toward Korea. The argument, which occurred in 1873 when the precedent-setting, fact-finding Iwakura Mission returned to Japan from its world tour, was primarily between Saigō Takamori, the Satsuma samurai leader who had been commander of the Imperial (Meiji) Restoration army that ousted the Tokugawa shogunate in 1868, and Prince Iwakura Tomomi, head of the mission abroad and the imperial Restoration leader at whose residence in Kyoto much of the scheming to overthrow the Tokugawa had taken place. Saigō, left behind by the Iwakura Mission in command of the new imperial government recently established in Tokyo, had decided, and obtained the Meiji Emperor's approval, to conquer Korea and/or die there to avenge the Korean king's refusal to offer respect to the Meiji Emperor. Saigō also wanted to give the emperor's increasingly restive samurai army a mission to accomplish.

Iwakura, however, had seen the world and knew Japan's weakness in comparison with Western countries, and he challenged Saigō and the emperor's decision. Unfortunately for Saigō, his fellow Satsuma clansman

Ōkubo Toshimichi, who had been abroad with Iwakura, sided with Iwakura and drew up a list of Seven Reasons for Opposing the Korean Expedition, which stressed the great need for reform and rebuilding in Japan before any foreign adventures could be undertaken.

The defeated Saigō quit the government and retired to his own Satsuma domain, where disaffected samurai persuaded him to lead them in the abortive 1877 Satsuma Rebellion against the Tokyo government. Saigō died by suicide, but his memory lived on, and he became a kind of patron saint of future Japanese ultranationalist-expansionist organizations, such as the Gen'yōsha (Black Sea) and Kokuryūkai (Amur River) societies.

Hilary Conroy

Bibliography

Conroy, Hilary. *The Japanese Seizure of Korea, 1868–1910*. Philadelphia: University of Pennsylvania Press, 1960.
Mayo, Marlene. "The Korean Crisis of 1873 and Early Meiji Foreign Policy." *Journal of Asian Studies*. Vol. 31, No. 4 (1972), 793–820.

Constitution (*Shōwa Kenpō*) (1947)

The 1947 Constitution of Japan established a constitutional monarchy during the Allied Occupation following World War II. Ensuring a separation of powers among the Diet (legislature), the bureaucracy, and the courts, the constitution reflects the legal system and values of the occupiers much more than those of the occupied. Contrasted with the Meiji Constitution, adopted voluntarily in 1889, the imposed Shōwa Constitution has left far less opportunity to exploit the legal and governmental structure to further nationalistic tendencies. Many of the attempts to reform the Shōwa Kenpō have involved efforts to revive the legal framework that supported prewar nationalistic interests. An analysis of the elements of the Shōwa Kenpō that have received the most persistent initiatives at reform demonstrates the barrier that this document has been to the successful revival of Japanese nationalism.

The drafters of the 1947 Shōwa Kenpō wrought three major changes in the Meiji Constitution. First, Articles 1 and 8 of the postwar constitution removed the legal recognition of the emperor's divinity. This involved two significant elements: the separation of religion and state (Article 2); and the right of direct judicial review of acts carried out in the government's (formerly emperor's) name (Article 75). These two articles removed the opportunity to hide behind the emperor's invulnerable status as "god," thereby exposing nationalistic fervor to open legal examination. Although the Diet never enacted a system requiring judicial review of all processes launched by the bureaucracy, the Shōwa Kenpō gave the Diet the power to effectuate and maintain a balance among the elements of government. The lack of such power by the courts and the Diet under the Meiji Kenpō had created an unchecked breeding ground for government-engendered nationalism.

Second, Articles 10–40 established fundamental human rights, including equal personal rights; freedom of speech, religion, and association; and the opportunity for expressing legitimate dissent. Indeed, following the enactment of the Shōwa Constitution, significant voices of dissent, including open protests by socialist and Communist groups, labor organizations, and academics, became rampant—and it was the American Army of Occupation, not the Shōwa Constitution, that permitted the Japanese government to rein in the protests.

The conservative and rightist elements of Japanese society, fearing rebellion, willingly used the emergency powers provided by SCAP to limit these anti-nationalistic dissenters. Although Japanese values and laws have permitted a number of conservative judicial interpretations, the bureaucracy has prudently remained within the limits of administrative discretion permitted by the Diet in order to avoid embarrassing entanglements. This generally has been true even with such touchy issues as minority and women's rights, as well as with the political rightists' blaring loudspeaker demands for repeal of the "American-imposed constitution," which have been a constant on city streets ever since the 1950s.

Third, Article 9 of the Shōwa Kenpō renounces war and the maintenance of war potential and thereby attempts to restrict Japan's ability to develop an imperialistically minded military force. In addition to limiting military expenditures, the effect of this clause has been to deflect society's values from nationalistic wars of conquest and control. Even the name of Japan's military body (the Self-Defense Force) implies the goal of limiting the revival of nationalistic fervor.

Although no constitution can effectively prevent the rise of nationalism, the Shōwa Kenpō has so immersed Japanese society in its pacifist values that certain nationalistic behaviors, such as carrying out ceremonies honoring the war dead at the Shinto Yasukuni Shrine in Tokyo, have been challenged as being socially and legally inappropriate. Considering how improper and difficult it is to challenge the hierarchy in Japan, the growing willingness of people to demand examination of administrative action, express dissent, and resist a return to an uncontrolled military presence may be seen as resulting from the moderating, neutral spirit of the Shōwa Kenpō and its continuing strength.

Michael Waxman

Bibliography

Inoue, Kyoko. *MacArthur's Japanese Constitution*. Chicago: University of Chicago Press, 1991.

Constitutional Democratic Party (*Rikken Minseitō*)

Political party. Formed on June 1, 1927, by a merger of the Kenseikai (Constitutional Association) and the Seiyū Hontō (True Friends of Government), it was the more liberal of Japan's two main parties in the years leading to World War II. Its president, Hamaguchi Osachi, became prime minister in July 1929, after the Tanaka Giichi cabinet fell due to the assassination by extremist army officers of warlord Zhang Zuolin in Manchuria. The party, whose platform called for democratic politics, peace based on international justice, equal educational opportunity, and social cooperation, followed urban, business-oriented policies under Hamaguchi. His cabinet ended the gold embargo and pushed through the Diet (legislature) the unpopular London Naval Treaty, which maintained British and American superiority on the seas. After Hamaguchi was shot by a nationalistic extremist in November 1930, Wakatsuki Reijirō became prime minister, but his cabinet fell following the September 1931 Manchurian Incident, which triggered Japanese expansion in Asia, and the party lost its Diet majority in the 1932 elections. The Minseitō recovered later in the decade, winning the largest number of Diet seats in the 1936 and 1937 elections.

While the party remained more moderate in its international policies than the rival Rikken Seiyūkai (Friends of Constitutional Government Party), a significant number of its members gradually gave in to military control of the government. The Minseitō held out longer against the rising antiparliamentary tide than others, but it disbanded on August 15, 1940, and became part of the Imperial Rule Assistance Association (Taisei Yokusankai). The party's major postwar descendant was the Minshūtō (Democratic Party), which formed the Ashida Hitoshi cabinet in March 1948. The Minshūtō went into decline after scandal toppled Ashida in October of that year, and in 1950 it dissolved.

James L. Huffman

Bibliography

Scalapino, Robert A. *Democracy and the Party Movement in Prewar Japan*. Berkeley: University of California Press, 1967.

Control Faction (*Tōseiha*)

Army faction. The term was used to identify the army opponents of the extreme Kōdōha (Imperial Way Faction), which fanned ultranationalist flames throughout Japan in the 1930s. Led by officers such as Nagata Tetsuzan, Tōjō Hideki (later prime minister), and Mutō Akira, the faction advocated centralized control in order to mobilize Japan for war.

The Tōseiha emerged primarily in reaction against the policies of Army Minister Araki Sadao. Its members generally came from the Army Ministry or the general staff, held ranks between major and lieutenant-general, and favored the building of a national defense state through constitutional means—in contrast to the Kōdōha willingness to use terrorism. Tōseiha supporters also tended to favor expanded activity in China, curtailment of Western influences in East Asia, and accommodation with the Soviet Union. Many Tōseiha supporters came from central and northeastern Japan.

The nature of the Tōseiha was complex. There never was a formal organization; indeed, its name began as a derisive label applied by Kōdōha zealots to their rivals. Moreover, many of those identified with theControl Faction actually agreed with some Kōdōha positions, including expansion in Manchuria and the need to prepare for a total war. Many of the rifts related as much to personalities and factionalism as to ideology. Nagata generally supported

Araki's policies, prior to a schism in the mid-1930s over Araki's aggressive anti-Soviet policies, and an army pamphlet issued under Nagata's inspiration in 1934 was filled with Kōdōha nuances. Yet a Kōdōha member assassinated Nagata in 1935 because of his role in dismissing an Imperial Way leader, Mazaki Jinzaburō, from the Military Affairs Bureau. Similarly, Ishiwara Kanji, an important Tōseiha strategist, considered the Soviet Union a major threat and articulated many Kōdōha positions in his earlier years. The *Kōdō-Tōsei* struggle ended following the February 26, 1936, uprising, when the government purged most Imperial Way leaders for their attempts to overthrow the regime.

Jacob Kovalio

Bibliography

Crowley, James. "Japanese Army Factionalism in the Early 1930s." *Journal of Asian Studies*. Vol. 21, No. 3 (May 1962), 309–26.

Cooperation and Harmony Society (*Kyōchōkai*)

An organization officially established in December 1919 intended to foster industrial harmony. Home Minister Tokonami Takejirō and business leader Shibusawa Eiichi were the chief sponsors of the Kyōchōkai's creation. During the 1920s and into the 1930s, the society pushed for legal reforms in such areas as the Factory Law, health insurance, and severance pay. It also established settlement houses and employment bureaus and frequently provided a forum for strike mediation. But the Kyōchōkai devoted its greatest effort to inculcating the ideal of harmonism (*kyōchōshugi*), which it regarded as the foundation of the organic moral community that was its social ideal. In various schools, public lectures, popular magazines, and even in movies it produced, the Kyōchōkai led a rising chorus of voices supportive of what the organization's leaders defined as traditional national values.

The Kyōchōkai leadership, while committed to social reform, was convinced that meaningful reform had to rest on traditionalist ideals of harmony and cooperation. These values were not to be merely instrumental; they were presented as normative values central to the very nature of Japaneseness. They were not merely traditions but part of the fabric of national identity itself. Thus, the activities of the Kyōchōkai were linked to the larger Japanese obsession with national ethics training (*shūshin*) in prewar Japan, which aimed at the inculcation of the sanctified values of the emerging authoritarian states. The Kyōchōkai and the ideal of industrial harmony that it fostered were constituent elements of prewar ultranationalism.

W. Dean Kinzley

Bibliography

Garon, Sheldon. *The State and Labor in Modern Japan*. Berkeley: University of California Press, 1987.

Kinzley, W. Dean. *Industrial Harmony in Modern Japan: The Invention of a Tradition*. London and New York: Routledge, 1991.

Crisis of 1873

The leadership of early Meiji Japan was split asunder by the debate of October 14–23, 1873, in the Council of State over the proposed invasion of Korea. When the peace party won, half of the privy councilors resigned, as did important officers in the imperial guard, thus consolidating the leadership faction and setting the stage for later civil rebellions.

Korea had refused to recognize the new Meiji government and had given harsh treatment to Japanese envoys who were sent to Seoul periodically after 1868. On August 17, 1873, Saigō Takamori, leader of the war party, obtained the emperor's permission to head a mission to seek an apology. He recognized that in Seoul he might well be assassinated by xenophobes, providing a *casus belli*, which he desired mainly as a device to divert the attention of the large, disaffected class of former samurai, whose status had been undermined by Meiji government policies. War would provide employment for former samurai and restore official discipline.

The emperor's one restriction on Saigō, who dominated a caretaker government, was that he must await the return of the remaining leaders of the Iwakura Mission to America and Europe (1871–73) before going to Korea. Those leaders, however, having observed the gap between Japan and the advanced countries, now gave priority to internal development, and adamantly opposed actions that might cause a foreign war. Prince Iwakura Tomomi himself argued that Russia in the north was a greater threat than Korea, but he boldly maneuvered to avoid war with either. Ōkubo Toshimichi, fresh from studying industry and banking in the West, contended in an eloquent state paper that Japan must pursue a policy of mercantilism to build up its own industry and its merchant marine and must pay its foreign debt on schedule to avoid intervention. The ailing junior councilor Kido Takayoshi made a dramatic reversal of position while abroad and now realized that war with Korea would not strengthen the Japanese government and military system as he once thought, but might stir popular risings if accompanied by tax increases. Kido's priorities in 1873 were a system of public education and implementation of the first stages of constitutional government.

When it appeared that the war party would carry the day, Iwakura, Ōkubo, and Kido offered their resignations; dismayed Prime Minister Sanjō Sanetomi suffered a collapse, which German physician Theodore Hoffmann diagnosed as a nervous breakdown. Minister of the Right Iwakura became interim prime minister, asserted his opposition to what he called the "wild ideas" of Saigō, and recommended to the emperor that the Korea mission be canceled. The united peace party prevailed over the disparate elements of the war party and drove Saigō, who had staked his political life on the issue, out of government, along with fellow officials Itagaki Taisuke, Gotō Shōjirō, Soejima Taneomi, and Etō Shimpei.

Saigō and Ōkubo, who headed the rival camps in the 1873 debate, had been boyhood friends in Satsuma and fellow revolutionaries before the political crisis of 1873 separated them forever. Saigō returned to Kagoshima castletown, where he championed the cause of the *shizoku* (former samurai), headed an unsuccessful rebellion in 1877, and died a warrior's death by suicide. Ōkubo became home minister, dominating the modernizing cabinet for four-and-a-half years before he was assassinated by disgruntled *shizoku* in 1878 as he proceeded to the palace in his English carriage.

The imperial loyalty and expansionism espoused by Saigō remained a powerful undercurrent in Japanese politics and, for a time in the twentieth century, submerged the moderate policy, but Ōkubo's industrial policy became the mainstream force in modern Japan. Once he was anathema to his native Kagosha for crushing Saigō's rebellion; now he is honored there for the success of his economic policies with a dramatic bronze statue in foreign dress near his birthplace in the old samurai quarter.

Sidney DeVere Brown

Bibliography

Conroy, Hilary. *The Japanese Seizure of Korea, 1868–1910*. Philadelphia: University of Pennsylvania Press, 1960.
Mayo, Marlene. "The Korean Crisis of 1873 and Early Meiji Foreign Policy." *Journal of Asian Studies*. Vol. 31, No. 4 (1972), 793–820.

D

Debate on Japanese Capitalism
(*Nihon Shihonshugi Ronsō*)

Launched late in 1927 by Japanese Marxists, the debate centered on the nature and rate of capitalist development in Japan. It was silenced by the intensified repression of the Special Higher (Thought) Police (*tokkō*) in the mid-1930s, but it reemerged after World War II and has continued into the 1990s in somewhat attenuated form.

The controversy was intimately linked to Japanese nationalism both in its genesis and in its content. First, it was launched in response to two major developments, one internal and the other external. Ostensibly, it was the external stimulus that prevailed: the publication of the Communist International's 1927 Theses on the revolution in Japan, calling for a two-step—first bourgeois-democratic, then proletarian-socialist—revolution in Japan. The Comintern view that Japan remained socioeconomically backward in comparison with Russia on the eve of the 1917 October Revolution was repudiated by Yamakawa Hitoshi, Arahata Kanson, and other Japanese Communist Party members as based on an inadequate appreciation of Japan's spectacular capitalist economic growth since the Meiji Restoration in 1868. They promptly seceded from the party, launching their own opposition journal, *Rōnō* (Labor-Farmer), and the group came to be known as the Rōnōha. These Marxists immediately set out to produce an alternative interpretation of the development of Japanese capitalism, one that would sustain their contention that Japan was already ripe for a socialist revolution.

Meanwhile, internally, by the mid-1920s, Japanese scholars had assimilated fundamental principles of Marxist economics, and the first efforts were made, by Sano Manabu and others, to apply the method and analytical concepts of Marxism to Japan's own attempts to establish a thriving capitalist economy since the Meiji era (1868–1912). Takahashi Kamekichi was among these pioneers. But his application of Marxism to Japan led him to articulate a thesis that Japanese expansionism on the Asian mainland did not fit V.I. Lenin's theory of imperialism because it was not motivated by a capitalist economy that was as mature as that of the imperialist countries of Western Europe. Takahashi's thesis challenged Japan's indigenous Marxists to devise alternative Marxist interpretations of Japanese development that would be critical, rather than supportive, of Japanese expansionism.

Reflecting these stimuli, the controversy directly addressed issues related to the legitimacy of Japanese nationalism. Before World War II, the participants in the debate were alone in questioning the legitimate origins and nature of the Japanese state, as they debated the economic bases of the imperial system. After the war, the resurrected controversy attacked the question of the origins of Japan's wartime "fascism." Throughout, scholars of the Rōnōha and the opposing, "feudal" Kōzaha attacked the issue of the particularity versus the universality of Japan's historical experience, extending their discussions to the treatments of the weaknesses of Japanese democracy in the late twentieth century. In this respect, they addressed the issue of Japanese uniqueness that has been at the heart of Japanese nationalism.

Germaine A. Hoston

Bibliography

Hoston, Germaine A. *Marxism and the Crisis of Development in Prewar Japan*. Princeton, NJ: Princeton University Press, 1986.

Deer Cry Pavilion (*Rokumeikan*)

Conceived by Foreign Minister Inoue Kaoru and designed by the British architect Josiah Conder, this two-story Italianate brick building was erected across the street from Tokyo's Hibiya Park in 1883 to bring prominent Japanese and Westerners together for social events. Inoue, who was heavily involved in the effort to revise the unequal treaties that Western powers had imposed on Japan after the opening of the country in 1853, envisioned Rokumeikan events as useful in demonstrating how civilized Japan had become and thus influencing foreign diplomats to respond more favorably in negotiations. Complete with ballroom, reading room, music room, guest suites, and an alabaster bathtub, the building was the site of gala dances, bazaars, and garden parties during the Rokumeikan era (1883–87), the heyday of Western faddishness. In the late 1880s, the national mood turned against the excessive Western orientation, and patriots made treaty revision their most potent antigovernment issue. As a result, the Rokumeikan lost its luster. It became the Peers' Hall in 1890 and was torn down in 1941.

James L. Huffman

Bibliography

Barr, Pat. *The Deer Cry Pavilion*. London: Macmillan, 1968.

Deguchi Nao (1837–1918)

Religious leader. Born in Fukuchiyama (Kyoto Prefecture), she was widowed at the age of 51. Poverty and difficulties with her children drove her to seek religious experiences, and, in 1892, she began to see visions and to serve as a mouthpiece for the god Ushitora no Konjin. She put the divine messages into writing and developed a following that eventually took the name Ōmoto-kyō (Teaching of the Great Origin). Deguchi's message was messianic, proclaiming that the evil, decaying world soon would be renewed and that an era of peace would be ushered in with the appearance of a savior. Ōmoto-kyō was critical of the Shinto-based emperor system and, under the leadership of her son-in-law, Deguchi Onisaburō, became the subject of severe government oppression in the 1920s and 1930s.

James L. Huffman

Bibliography

Thomsen, Harry. *The New Religions of Japan*. Rutland, VT: Charles E. Tuttle, 1963.

Deguchi Onisaburō (1871–1948)

Religious leader. A native of Kyoto Prefecture who was named Ueda Kisaburō, he pursued a teaching career. Late in the 1890s, he had several mystical experiences and became a Shinto preacher prior to meeting the religionist Deguchi Nao in 1898. He was attracted to her messianic teachings and joined her group, eventually marrying her daughter Sumi and taking on the Deguchi name. Under his organizational skills, the religious group came to be known as Ōmoto-kyō (Teaching of the Great Origin) and took on a much more popular nature, with an emphasis on mystical healing and shamanistic ceremonies. By the 1920s, it claimed 2 million adherents.

Ōmoto-kyō began to attract government suspicion early in the 1900s as a result of its criticism of the emperor system (*tennōsei*) and of the government's use of poor peasants in the Russo-Japanese War (1904–05). Official opposition increased when Onisaburō began to put on "imperial" airs, riding a white horse and using motorcycle escorts for his travels. He was imprisoned twice (1921, 1935–42) for lèse majesté, and Ōmoto-kyō was brutally repressed, with its headquarters buildings dynamited by authorities in 1935. Onisaburō also attempted to link Ōmoto-kyō to other world religions, took up the use of Esperanto in 1923, and published his spiritual ideas in 81 volumes. He attempted to revive the religion after World War II, but his death in 1948 kept Ōmoto-kyō from ever approaching its prewar strength.

James L. Huffman

Bibliography

Thomsen, Harry. *The New Religions of Japan*. Rutland, VT: Charles E. Tuttle, 1963.

Dōmei News Agency (*Dōmei Tsūshinsha*)

Japan's wartime news agency, established in 1936. It resulted from the efforts, dating to the 1910s, of many Japanese journalists and business and government leaders to create a national representative news agency (*kokka daihyō tsūshinsha*) in Japan that could successfully counter Reuter's and other international news agencies' control of the global news network.

Japan's need for a national news agency was intensified following the Manchurian Incident in 1931. Iwanaga Yūkichi, president of the Nihon Shimbun Rengōsha news agency, proposed the merging of the Rengō and Nippon Denpō Tsūshinsha (Dentsū) news agencies. Despite governmental support, merger attempts were stymied by the reluctance of Dentsū's founder, Mitsunaga Hoshiro, to give up his agency and Dentsū's clients and by the provincial press's fear of the potential loss of its long-standing advertising agreements with Dentsū, making it vulnerable to the major metropolitan dailies. Rengō reorganized as the Dōmei News Agency in January 1936. As a compromise, Dentsū's dual operations were split. Its news operations merged with Dōmei in July and its advertising brokerage continued by itself.

During the war, Dōmei, as "the ears and voice of the nation," was the chief purveyor of international news for Japan, broadcasting news in Asian and European languages. It dispatched reporters to all major Allied and neutral countries, established an extensive radio network throughout East Asia, and supervised the news agencies in Manchuria and northern and southern China. It was also given full responsibility by the military for developing the news media in Singapore and Malaysia. In Japan, Dōmei also constructed a radio network with the metropolitan and provincial papers, supplying national and foreign news. Following Japan's defeat in 1945, Dōmei soon ran afoul of the Occupation government's press regulations. Seeing its imminent demise, Furuno Inosuke, Dōmei's second president, dissolved Dōmei, which was then reorganized as the Kyōdō and Jiji news agencies.

Roger W. Purdy

Bibliography

Purdy, Roger W. "The Ears and Voice of the Nation: The Dōmei News Agency and Japan News Network, 1936–1945." Unpublished doctoral dissertation, University of California, Santa Barbara, 1987.

Dutch Studies (*Rangaku*)

The early modern study of Western learning and technology through the medium of the Dutch language. Developing from the mid-eighteenth century, such studies were a primary vehicle for late Tokugawa acquisition of knowledge about the West. From the 1640s on, the Dutch were the only Europeans to maintain regular contact with Japan. To manage communications with them, the Tokugawa shogunate maintained a body of translators specializing in the study of the Dutch language. Through their knowledge of Dutch, some of them also acquired a degree of familiarity with Western branches of learning, such as medicine, pharmacology, astronomy, and geography. This knowledge gradually extended to a wider circle, and, from the mid-1700s, a number of scholars began to study Dutch to learn more about Western sciences. By the 1830s, schools established by Rangaku scholars were attracting an increasing number of students.

As the Western powers encroached steadily on Japanese isolation in the late eighteenth and early nineteenth centuries, the shogunate saw the need for better information about the West and, beginning in 1811, sponsored the study of Rangaku through the establishment of a succession of official translation bureaus. But, while recognizing the value of Western science and technology and of knowledge about the West, the Tokugawa government remained highly suspicious of direct contact with Westerners; in 1828 and 1839, it cracked down on Rangaku scholars for exceeding the established framework of dealings with the West. Once the Western powers forced open the country through gunboat diplomacy in the 1850s, however, Rangaku scholars provided an important pool of talent for more wide-ranging and intensive study of the West.

Kate Wildman Nakai

Bibliography

Keene, Donald. *The Japanese Discovery of Europe.* Stanford, CA: Stanford University Press, 1969.

Wakabayashi, Bob Tadashi. *Anti-Foreignism and Western Learning in Early-Modern Japan: The New Theses of 1825.* Cambridge: Harvard University Press, 1986.

E

East Asia Common Culture Society (*Tōa Dōbunkai*)

The Tōa Dōbunkai was founded in November 1898 by prominent Japanese, including Konoe Atsumaro, chairman of the House of Peers, as a medium for helping China toward progress and modernization and protecting it from the ravages of Western imperialism. The society's ideals were articulated by Ōkuma Shigenobu, leader of the Reform Party (Kaishintō), that same year. During World War II, it served to promote Japanese interests in Asian expansionism.

In the beginning, Chinese political refugees Kang Youwei and Liang Qichao were in the formative inner circle, but the society adopted a "no politics" rule and relegated them to associate membership status. Over the next three decades, prominent Japanese such as Count Makino Nobuaki, General Abe Nobuyuki, and later Prime Minister Konoe Fumimaro served as officers, while a research institute headquarters operated in Shanghai, and related training schools for students were established in Nanjing, Tianjin, Hankow, Shanghai, and Tokyo. By 1945, when it was closed down with Japan's defeat in the Pacific War, the society had produced more than 100 publications and the schools had graduated more than 4,000 students, many of them Chinese, as China-Japan cultural relations experts. Most Americans of Japan's Occupation days (1945–52) considered the Tōa Dōbunkai a sophisticated Japanese propaganda tool, but it is clear that some of the Japanese involved were sincere advocates of Japan-China friendship and progress.

Hilary Conroy
George C.C. Chang

Bibliography
Coox, Alvin D., and Hilary Conroy, eds. *China and Japan: A Search for Balance Since World War I*. Santa Barbara, CA: ABC-Clio, 1978.
Iriye, Akira, ed. *The Chinese and the Japanese*. Princeton, NJ: Princeton University Press, 1980.

East Asian League (*Tōa Renmei*)

Nationalist organization. The league was formed in 1939 by Kimura Takeo and other followers of the ultranationalist General Ishiwara Kanji, ostensibly to support Prime Minister Konoe Fumimaro's expansionist policy of forming a New Order in East Asia. In reality, its aim was to propound Ishiwara's belief that the countries of East Asia (particularly Manchukuo, China, and Japan) must coordinate their resources in humankind's "final war" to drive out Western imperialism. It called for political autonomy for each country, under Japanese leadership. The league created branches in at least 20 prefectures and had 100,000 members at its peak. Nationalistic Japanese officers in China also promoted the Tōa Renmei, and several branches were formed there with Wang Jingwei as chair. The Japanese cabinet regarded the group as extremist and a threat to established policy, and, after Tōjō Hideki became prime minister in 1941, the government actively opposed it. The Tōa Renmei was disbanded in 1942, though it later was reorganized to deal with domestic issues. It was banned again after World War II, only to reemerge in 1952, after the Allied Occupation, as an advocate of rearmament.

James L. Huffman

Bibliography

Peattie, Mark. *Ishiwara Kanji and Japan's Confrontation with the West*. Princeton, NJ: Princeton University Press, 1975.

Eight Cords, One Roof (*Hakkō Ichiu*)

Nationalist slogan used widely during World War II to justify aggression abroad. The phrase first appeared in an eighth-century *Nihon Shoki* (Chronicle of Japan) reference to the legendary first emperor, Jimmu, when he was building his capital. He reportedly used it vaguely, possibly as a call to complete the construction of the palace, perhaps to indicate his desire to complete the conquest of the Japanese islands. During the 1930s, it was dusted off by nationalists to signify the idea of "one roof, eight corners," or a world of eight directions, all under Japanese control. That use became widespread after the second Konoe Fumimaro cabinet invoked Jimmu's phrase in its "Fundamental National Policy," announced on August 1, 1940. The document proclaimed Japan's goal as the "establishment of world peace in accordance with the great spirit of *hakkō ichiu* on which the country was founded." The phrase continues to be used occasionally as a reference to universal peace or shared humanity.

James L. Huffman

Bibliography

Holton, Donald. *National Faith of Japan: A Study of Modern Shinto*. New York: Paragon, 1965.

Emperor System (*Tennōsei*)

In response to the particular pressures generated by its international and domestic environments, Japanese nationalism began to develop certain distinct features as a national unifying force in the late nineteenth century. One such feature was *tennōsei*, which encompassed the complex of Japan's prewar political institutions along with their accompanying ideological foundations.

The development of modern nationalism in Japan was largely a response to the impact of Western powers in the late Tokugawa and early Meiji era. At that time, Japan's political and intellectual elites came to share a growing sense of national consciousness as they were compelled to consider Japan's position within an international community fraught with new dangers and opportunities. It was not difficult for the Meiji leaders to perceive that Japan's very survival as a sovereign state and their own political dominance depended on their ability to generate and mobilize nationalistic sentiment throughout society. Eventually, this task would be accomplished through the creation of formal political institutions, which could be used as the focus of national loyalty.

During the first two decades of the Meiji period (1868–1912), Japan's leaders undertook the responsibility of fashioning the institutions of a modern state. It was in this era that the formal structures of *tennōsei* were first articulated. While designing the necessary political and social institutions, the Meiji oligarchs logically turned to Japan's Imperial House as the foundation of the new Japanese state. It had been in the emperor's name that the Meiji Restoration forces had justified their resistance to the Tokugawa *bakufu* (military government), and this identification with the Imperial House was repeated in the Meiji Emperor's Charter Oath of 1868. Consequently, it was the precedent of Japan's traditional political culture that led the Meiji oligarchs to once again rely on the emperor as the unifying focal point around which a modern constitutional government would be built.

The Meiji Constitution of 1889 was the formal capstone of the emperor system and the new Japanese state. At its center resided the emperor, whose legal, inviolable sovereignty was established by the constitution, which was offered as a gift to his subjects and which only he could amend. Within the constitution were provisions for the establishment of a bicameral legislature (the Diet) and a separate cabinet appointed by, and directly responsible to, the emperor. A Privy Council had been created in April 1888 to deliberate on the draft constitution and later to advise the emperor on important policy issues. The Privy Council was largely comprised of members of the peerage and upper bureaucracy who, through their formal and informal powers, exercised significant influence over the decision making of the emperor system. In addition to its participation in the Privy Council, Japan's peerage was provided with further access to formal authority and specific constitutional powers through its membership in the upper house of the Diet.

To enhance imperial sovereign authority and their own coercive power as the de facto representatives of the emperor, the Meiji oligarchs stipulated within the constitution that the emperor had direct responsibility of the army and navy. The Imperial Rescript to Soldiers and Sailors of 1882 and the constitution placed the military beyond the legal control of either the cabinet or the Diet. In this manner, the oligarchs sought to assure the military's allegiance to the emperor and the nation, without the interference of partisan politics and civilian control in the Diet.

According to the constitution, the Japanese Diet was granted only limited powers of veto over the annual national budget. However, despite the restricted range of its legal authority, the Diet managed to make good effect of its veto powers in circumstances in which the costs of state building, industrial development, and war required the Diet's cooperation in securing ever larger annual budget allocations. As a result of their control over the size of the national budget, the parties in the Diet managed throughout the Meiji and the Taishō (1912–26) periods to increase the scope of their influence within the emperor system.

Despite the limited nature of the powers granted to Japan's parliamentary parties, the Meiji oligarchs were deeply concerned by the specter of partisan politics within the new Diet. To balance this potentially disruptive force in society, the oligarchs determined to create a professional national bureaucracy as the core of the executive branch. Toward this end, the civil service regulations of 1887 instituted a system of higher civil-service examinations. It was the oligarchs' intention to produce a depoliticized body of upper-level bureaucrats who, like the military, were considered to be directly responsible to the emperor, rather than to the general public or their representatives in the Diet. In 1889, the new constitution further strengthened the authority and autonomy of the bureaucracy, which would subsequently develop into one of the key centers of segmented institutional power within the emperor system.

Prior to 1890, the Meiji leaders were employed designing and positioning the political institutions that made up the formal state structure of the emperor system. Nevertheless, they did not neglect what was considered the equally important task of articulating and disseminating the ideological principles of Japanese nationalism that would serve as the foundation of this system.

The stimulus for growth of modern nationalism in Japan was twofold. Initially, the impact of Western powers led Japanese elites in the 1870s to think in terms of Japan as a nation–state interacting with other members of the international community. Less spontaneously, during the late 1880s, the Meiji leaders, in anticipation of major changes in society and significant societal unrest following the inauguration of the Meiji Constitution, determined to forestall unnecessary conflict through a conscious manipulation of nationalistic symbols. In both cases, Japanese elites envisioned Japan's foreign and domestic environments as hierarchies of superiors and inferiors. Given Japan's traditional Confucian political culture, this response was natural.

At the domestic level, the natural sociopolitical hierarchy embodied by Japan's traditional culture was institutionalized by the Meiji Constitution. Within his person, the emperor combined the spiritual authority of a Shinto deity and the transcendent moral authority of a Confucian sage, with the national sovereignty of a Western-style constitutional monarch. In this manner, the Meiji oligarchs had succeeded in uniting supreme moral and political authority within the imperial institution, which could then be used as the focus of national loyalty and the temporal manifestation of Japan's *kokutai* (national polity). To reinforce this relationship, the 1890 Imperial Rescript on Education affirmed the emperor's role as father figure presiding over a *kazoku kokka* (family state). In a reciprocal fashion, it reinforced each citizen's patriotic responsibility and moral obligation of filial piety and self-sacrifice to the emperor.

The final layer of ideological cement applied by the Meiji oligarchs to reinforce Japan's *kokutai* and mobilize nationalistic sentiment behind the emperor system was the establishment of State Shinto. The Home Ministry assumed the responsibility of organizing a national network of local shrines as the physical focal points of emperor worship.

In the Meiji period, Japan's leaders sought to create a stable domestic order presided over by the emperor and those nonparliamentary institutions directly responsible to him. In practice, the Meiji oligarchs did not anticipate the emperor playing an active role in the political arena, which they and the *genrō* (elder statesmen) did their best to dominate. Political activity never escaped the stigma of being unpatriotic and selfish, particularly for those members of the Diet in opposition to the government. However, despite the efforts of the oligarchs to manipulate the imperial symbols and limit the arena of politics, by the early Taishō period nationalist ideology was being generated at the lower levels of society as well as from the top.

By the early Taishō period, the institutional structures and ideological foundations of the emperor system were well in place. The nationalist ideology of *tennōsei* and the value system that supported it were a natural reflection of the political culture, immanent in all levels of Japanese society. The traditional norms of filial piety and an adherence to hierarchical authority structures were fundamental characteristics of Japan's peasant-based society in the prewar period. Therefore, *tennōsei* ideology must be seen as a product of reciprocal communication among all levels of society. The Meiji government did make a concerted effort to foster emperor worship throughout Japan to legitimize its own authority, promote social stability, and generate a spirit of self-sacrifice among the citizenry, which was necessary for national development.

However, this is only part of the story. Within the villages of Japan's largely rural society, *tennōsei* ideology was being generated and sustained by the Japanese people themselves and their local elites through a process of societal discourse in which village officials, Shinto priests, schoolteachers, and other local elites not only served to transmit the official orthodoxy to local communities, but also acted as a conduit of rural values and nationalist sentiment that they communicated back up to the government.

Finally, we must consider the underlying objectives of the Meiji oligarchs that the emperor system and Japanese nationalism were intended to help achieve. Modern Japanese nationalism was partly a spontaneous reaction to the impact of foreign powers on Japan and partly a deliberate policy goal of the Meiji oligarchs. The institutions and ideology of the system were designed to help ensure the success of Japan's modernization process and Japan's eventual ability to compete in the international arena. Just as the Meiji oligarchs were inclined to view Japan's domestic environment in hierarchical terms, they likewise envisioned the international system in terms of a natural hierarchy of superior and inferior powers. They were determined that Japan should achieve an international position befitting its imperial institution, rather than suffer the Chinese fate of dismemberment at the hands of morally inferior Western nation–states.

In response to the potential dangers and opportunities inherent in the international environment of the late nineteenth century, the Meiji oligarchs mobilized the imperial symbols to encourage a spirit of nationalism and self-sacrifice necessary to achieve great power status. By the early Taishō period, the requisite institutional and ideological structures of *tennōsei* had successfully demonstrated their ability to mobilize society in pursuit of perceived national interests. In the 1930s, the basic ideological structures of *tennōsei* would be rearticulated with a greater sense of urgency by those who had come to perceive Japan's national objectives in terms of broader imperialistic objectives. In this period, *tennōsei* ideology would be hardened into an uncompromising ideological orthodoxy based on the concept of *kokutai* that has been identified with wartime ultranationalism.

With Japan's defeat in 1945, the formal political institutions of *tennōsei* were dismantled in favor of a new constitutional order that located sovereignty in the people themselves. Likewise, the ideological foundations of *tennōsei* were eliminated when, on January 1, 1945, the Shōwa Emperor publicly renounced his divinity.

Crayne Horton

Bibliography

Gluck, Carol. *Japan's Modern Myths: Ideology in the Late Meiji Period.* Princeton, NJ: Princeton University Press, 1985.

Maruyama, Masao. *Thought and Behavior in Modern Japanese Politics.* London: Oxford University Press, 1963.

Emperor's Birthday (*Tenchōsetsu*)

An ancient expression for the emperor's birthday. Derived from a passage in the *Lao-tzu*, the term was used in China to designate the monarch's birthday. Its use in Japan is recorded for the Emperor Kōnin in 775. The expression was revived for the Meiji Emperor, and the day (November 3) was included in the list of national holidays promulgated by the new government in 1873. Early celebrations of the festival cast the emperor in the role of a modern military leader. He reviewed the troops in the morning and then gave a luncheon for his high officials and the diplomatic corps. In the evening, the foreign minister gave a ball for Japanese and foreign persons of high rank. By the turn of the twentieth century, the day was celebrated in schools by a ritual reading of the highly patriotic, moralistic Imperial Rescript on Education (1890) before the imperial portrait.

The Taishō Emperor's birthday was August 31, but it was celebrated on October 31. Beginning in 1927, the festival was held on Emperor Hirohito's birthday, April 29. After the war, the emperor's birthday (*tennō tanjōbi*), no longer enhanced with flowery Chinese language, was retained as a national holiday. Hirohito's birthday became most notable as one of three holidays within one week (the other two were Constitution Day on May 3 and Children's Day on May 5) that constituted Golden Week, a major break in the working year. Since 1990, current Emperor Akihito's birthday has also been celebrated, on December 23.

The original Chinese expression was linked to a parallel phrase, resulting in the term *chikyūsetsu* for the empress's birthday. Although it never became a national holiday, *chikyūsetsu* provided a focus for activities related to women. In the Meiji era (1868–1912), it fell on May 28; in the Taishō era (1912–26), on June 25; and during the Shōwa era (1926–89), on March 6. Christian women first initiated celebration of the day in 1891, and women's magazines and female educators unsuccessfully advocated its designation as a national holiday. In the 1930s, the Aikoku Fujinkai (Patriotic Women's Society) promoted celebrations that included worship at shrines and mass rallies.

Sally A. Hastings

Bibliography
Jōya, Mock. *Things Japanese*. Tokyo: Japan Times, 1985.

Empire Day (*Kigensetsu*)

A national holiday (February 11) established by the Meiji government in 1873 to commemorate the foundation of the Japanese empire, traditionally held to have occurred in 660 B.C. with the accession of the emperor Jimmu. The holiday was one of a series designed to link the ritual life of the emperor to that of the people and give him high visibility as priest of the nation. The emperor promulgated the Meiji Constitution on this date in 1889, and, by the turn of the century, the day was celebrated in schools with a reading of the hortatory call to national loyalty, the Imperial Rescript on Education (1890), before the emperor's portrait. During the Taishō era (1912–26), public ceremonies celebrated the establishment of the constitution as well as the imperial institution. In 1948, when the Diet (legislature) approved a new schedule of national holidays in keeping with the spirit of the new, more democratic constitution, *Kigensetsu* was abolished. A 1966 revision of the law permitted restoration of the February 11 holiday under the new designation National Foundation Day (*Kenkoku Kinenbi*).

Sally A. Hastings

Bibliography
Crump, Thomas. *The Death of an Emperor*. Oxford: Oxford University Press, 1991.

Endure Society (*Yūzonsha*)

Political society, active from 1919 to 1923 in Japan's radical nationalist movement. Founded by Ōkawa Shūmei and Mitsukawa Kametarō, its members included Kita Ikki as well as adventurers such as Shimizu Yukinosuke and Iwata Fumio. Inheriting the continental tradition of the Gen'yōsha (Black Sea Society) and the Kokuryūkai (Amur River Society), the Yūzonsha made a clean break with earlier groups. Departing from their emphasis on Japanese expansion in Asia, it turned inward to promote radical reorganization at home. The name *yūzon* comes from a Chinese poem and refers to "enduring" elements (what "still exists") in a cultural tradition under attack.

At the close of World War I, Japan underwent rapid socioeconomic change, a turn to party government, and, in 1918, widespread rice riots. Into this charged atmosphere came Ōkawa and Kita with overlapping but dissimilar agendas. Ōkawa was a pan-Asianist who had studied ancient Indian philosophy at the University of Tokyo. Kita was a soldier of fortune who had participated in the Chinese revolutionary movement. Whereas Ōkawa allied himself with high political and military officials, Kita looked to junior officers as beacons of domestic reorganization. The Yūzonsha succeeded the Rōsōkai (Old and Young Society [1918–19]) and yielded to the Kōchisha (Activist Society [1924–32]), when Kita and Ōkawa disagreed over whether Japan should compromise with Russia.

George M. Wilson

Bibliography
Wilson, George. "Kita Ikki, Ōkawa Shūmei, and the Yūzonsha." *Papers on Japan*. [Harvard University], Vol. 2 (1963), 139–81.

E

Etō Shimpei (1833–74)

Meiji-era political leader, most noted for his support of *seikan ron*, the call for military action to chastise Korea in 1873, and for the role he played in the Saga Rebellion in 1874. A samurai from Saga domain, Etō joined the Meiji government in 1870 and was elevated to the post of minister of justice in 1872. In that capacity he led Japan's first attempt to modernize its penal codes using Western models. This work was cut short, as was his career, in October 1873, when he resigned from the government, after the plan for launching a war against Korea was rescinded. Upon learning that *shizoku* (former samurai) back in Saga were stirred up over this policy reversal and were conspiring to organize their own army to make an assault on Korea, Etō violated a government order requiring him to remain in Tokyo and went to join his Saga comrades, many of whom looked up to him as their leader. Although he claimed that his purpose was to quiet the tempers and prevent a revolt, Etō soon found himself leading the insurrection, the Saga Rebellion, which broke out in February 1874. The hastily assembled rebel force was quickly defeated by a force dispatched by the Meiji government. Etō, however, fled to Kagoshima, where he failed in an attempt to enlist the popular ex-official Saigō Takamori's support for his lost cause, and then to Kōchi, where he was finally captured. Etō, only recently the country's minister of justice, was quickly tried, sentenced, and beheaded. He nonetheless remained a patriotic hero in his native Saga—much like Saigō Takamori, hero of the unsuccessful 1877 Satsuma Rebellion, in Kagoshima.

Wayne M. McWilliams

Bibliography

McWilliams, Wayne C. "Etō Shimpei and the Saga Rebellion," *Proceedings of the First International Symposium on Asian Studies,* Vol. 2, 1979. Hong Kong: Asian Research Service, 1979, 465–77.

Expo '70

Japan's first world's fair, held in Osaka. Like the 1964 Olympics, this international exhibition, the first of its kind ever held in Asia, was an immense source of national pride. Japan had participated in similar fairs ever since the 1867 Paris exhibition and had been scheduled to host its own in 1940, when world tensions forced a cancellation. Now, two-and-a-half decades after World War II, the Japanese threw themselves into producing one of the most successful expositions ever. The theme of the event was the

Opening ceremony, Expo '70. Asahi Shimbun Photo.

"progress and harmony of mankind." Exhibits focused on technology and the future, with a stone brought back by astronauts from the moon drawing particular interest. Much attention also was paid to the moving sidewalk and the monorail, as well as to the use of computers in handling visitors—all heralded as signs of a bright technological future.

Some Japanese groups, including Christian seminarians, protested Expo '70, attacking the government's close ties to the United States, which was then fighting in Vietnam. But for most Japanese, the event was a source of pride. Exhibits were offered by 77 countries and a host of Japanese firms and organizations, at a cost of more than $330 million. Fair visitors numbered more than 50 million.

James L. Huffman

Bibliography
Allwood, John. *The Great Exhibitions*. London: Studio Vista, 1977.

E

F

Factory Girls (*Kōjo*)

As Japanese industrialization was launched during the Meiji period (1868–1912) to serve the nationalist goals of the country's rulers it is not surprising that the rulers tried to pass on these goals to the new country's first industrial workers, the majority of whom were female. Hundreds of thousands of female factory operatives, called *kōjo* (factory girls) whether employed in a large plant or a small workshop, were subjected to intense nationalistic indoctrination for decades beyond the Meiji era.

Such indoctrination began in the early 1870s when the government called upon families to send young women to the model silk mill at Tomioka and to other public filatures to learn the machine-reeling skills needed to generate profits that could finance nation building. By the turn of the twentieth century, when textile and other industries that employed *kōjo* had become privately owned, private enterprise had largely taken over the task. Factory women were ordered to "work with all your might for the country's sake, allowing Japan to become the greatest country in the world." As a text for *kōjo* indoctrination published in 1910 put it: "Many soldiers died in the Sino-Japanese War and much money was spent in order that Japan would become a first-class country. So let's work hard, make good thread, sell it abroad, and take those high foreign noses down a peg." Companies taught their hands songs that carried patriotic messages: "Factory girls, / We are soldiers of peace. / The service of women is a credit to the Empire and to yourselves. / There are trials and hardships, yes, / But what do they matter?" In the 1920s, a music professor in Tokyo not only composed such songs but

also made the rounds of city factories to teach them to *kōjo* there.

Despite their heavy exposure to such patriotic messages, it is unclear how "nationalistic" the *kōjo* of the pre–World War II era actually were. Memoirs of those daughters of former samurai and prosperous commoner families who during the early 1870s answered the government's call declare that such recruits were honored to go to reel for the nation. From the 1880s on, however, daughters of the poor, increasingly recruited from the poorest rural areas, replaced these proud pioneers in Japan's expanding industries. Often illiterate and usually ill-schooled, the hundreds of thousands of later *kōjo* have left few documentary records. In the one extant source of their thoughts and feelings that exists in some abundance—collections of hundreds of the anonymous work songs they composed and sang as they struggled to maintain the rhythms of their demanding tasks—there are no patriotic themes.

E. Patricia Tsurumi

Bibliography

Tsurumi, E. Patricia. *Factory Girls: Women in the Thread Mills of Meiji Japan.* Princeton, NJ: Princeton University Press.

Family State (*Kazoku Kokka*)

Term used to describe the Japanese polity as envisioned by nationalist thinkers such as Hozumi Yatsuka and Inoue Tetsujirō. Family-state ideology held that the Japanese polity was a series of concentric circles, with the imperial family at the core. Under this scheme, the emperor was patriarch to the whole of the Japanese people. The idea of the family state rested on modern ideas of the family, as well as the modern nation–state. Family-state ideology sprang up as the Meiji state was codifying a modern Japanese family system in the Household Register Law of 1871 and the Civil Code of 1898, both of which strengthened a legally sanctioned head of the family. Drawing an analogy between the head of the family and the emperor, advocates of the family state demanded that Japanese people accord the emperor the same respect due the family head in the new bourgeois version of Confucianism. This ideology supported many of the ultranationalist writers and activists of the 1920s and 1930s.

Guy Yasko

Bibliography

Gluck, Carol. *Japan's Modern Myths*. Princeton, NJ: Princeton University Press, 1985.

Irokawa, Daikichi. *The Culture of the Meiji Period*. Princeton, NJ: Princeton University Press, 1985.

Fascism

Most scholars use the term "fascism" in reference to two phenomena: (1) a particular brand of ultranationalistic political movement that arose mainly in Europe between the two world wars, and (2) the political regimes established by this type of movement in Fascist Italy and Nazi Germany. The debate over whether this term is applicable to Japan has always revolved around the issue of how closely Japan's civilian rightist groups and political regime of the 1930s resembled those of European fascism. This debate is as alive in the late twentieth century as it was in the interwar period.

According to historian Stanley Payne, fascism as a political movement appeared in more than 20 European countries and manifested these traits: opposition to liberalism, Communism, and conservatism; a military style; the aim of mass mobilization; the idealization of the nation or race, violence, masculinity, and youth; a charismatic, personal mode of command; the goals of a new nationalist autocratic state, a regulated economic structure, and empire. Fascism is not synonymous with extreme nationalism per se but is a specific form of it.

There were violent, nationalistic elements on the Japanese right in the early 1930s, but few Japanese groups matched the profile of fascism. This is not surprising, since Italian Benito Mussolini's Fascist Party had little impact as a model in Japan, and the critical period of growth for Japan's rightist groups occurred just after the Manchurian Incident of 1931, before Adolf Hitler came to power in Germany.

Unlike fascists, most Japanese rightists did not engage in violence, strive to form mass organizations, or advocate a new economic structure along national corporatist or national socialist lines. Only a minority of rightist groups, those labeled "national socialist" by the police, were exceptions. Moreover, all Japanese rightists eulogized the emperor as the supreme political leader, whereas fascists typically distanced themselves from the monarchical right. In short, the majority of Japan's rightists, even those such as the mutineers of February 1936 who assassinated state leaders, were more conservative in their ideology and positive program than European fascists.

In the late 1930s, several political movements emerged in conscious emulation of the Nazi Party; the most noteworthy was Nakano Seigō's East Asia Society (Tōhōkai). These organizations, however, did not practice violence, and they made little political headway.

Fascism in the form of a political regime in Italy and Germany had a much greater impact in Japan. Japan's military-bureaucratic leaders borrowed many new policies and institutions from Germany. For example, the control associations (*tōseikai*) imposed upon Japanese industry were patterned after Germany's *Wirtschaftsgruppen,* or economic groups, and the Greater Japan Industrial Patriotic Service Society (Dainihon Sangyō Hōkokukai) for workers was modeled after the German Labor Front. In neither instance was the Japanese structure a mirror image of its German counterpart, but the German inspiration for these innovations is well documented.

This institutional borrowing by state leaders was rooted in many shared conceptions of the nation. The new economic institutions were designed to replace market competition and trade unions with an economy reflecting the unitary interest of the nation. It was Germany's example that convinced many Japanese statesmen that this new "national defense state," which would integrate the entire nation into a great fighting machine, was superior to liberal democracy.

Still, there remained profound differences between the Japanese and Nazi regimes. Nazi Germany was ruled by a fascist political movement that seized power. Its members, who numbered 6.5 million by 1941, penetrated to the grass roots of society. Japan was ruled by career military officers and bureaucrats who took power by outmaneuvering rivals in the political elite. While in Japan the cabinet was the top authority, in Germany it was a single individual, Hitler, who did not even permit his cabinet to meet after 1938. Regarding fascism as a political movement, then, only a minority of Japan's rightist groups manifested most of the defining traits of fascism.

Regarding fascism as a political regime, however, many Japanese statesmen sympathized with the Nazis' conception of the nation as an armed camp and borrowed institutions accordingly. Their refusal to emulate many basic features of the Nazi system may advise against labeling Japan's entire political economy "fascist," but Japanese public policy after 1933 cannot be adequately understood without reference to fascist models.

Gregory J. Kasza

Bibliography

Kasza, Gregory J. "Fascism from Below? A Comparative Perspective on the Japanese Right, 1931–1936." *Journal of Contemporary History.* Vol. 19, No. 4 (October 1984), 607–29.

Maruyama, Masao. *Thought and Behaviour in Modern Japanese Politics.* Expanded and Ed. Ivan Morris. London: Oxford University Press, 1969.

February 26 Incident (*Niniroku Jiken*)

Unsuccessful military coup d'état, launched February 26, 1936, by 1,400 right-wing troops. Intending to install a more actively pro-military government, the rebels assassinated three leading officials and captured central Tokyo before the coup was crushed on February 29.

The uprising was led by a number of junior army officers and grew out of the Young Officers' Movement, which had formed late in the 1920s as a response to leftist activities and general unrest then on the rise. Following the Manchurian Incident when young Japanese officers precipitated an advance into China in 1931, many of them talked nostalgically of the samurai tradition that led to the Meiji Restoration and became active supporters of terrorism as a means of creating a stronger, more emperor-centered Japan. They were supported, tacitly, by several senior military officials, particularly those in the ultranationalist Kōdōha (Imperial Way Faction).

When their supporters in the government began to lose out to more moderate forces in 1935, the young officers became restive. And when they learned that the army's First Division, to which most of them belonged, was to be transferred to Manchuria, they decided on a coup.

They succeeded in killing Saitō Makoto, the lord keeper of the privy seal; Takahashi Korekiyo, the finance minister; and Watanabe Jōtarō, inspector-general of military education, as well as Prime Minister Okada Keisuke's brother (whom they mistook to be the prime minister himself). They also captured the Diet building, the War Ministry, metropolitan police headquarters, and the prime minister's residence.

The response of the military authorities was ambivalent at first, with several officials urging a moderate response to avoid civil war. The young Shōwa Emperor, however, made it clear that he regarded the young officers as traitors who should be crushed. As a result, the army surrounded the rebels on February 29 and demanded that they surrender or be shot. The majority complied, and the incident came to a quick end.

In contrast to earlier perpetrators of violence, the young officers were dealt with forcefully. They were given secret court-martials, with 19 sentenced to death and 70 given prison terms. Probably the best known among those executed was Kita Ikki, longtime advocate of national socialism. Senior officers known to have sympathized with the young officers were forced out of their posts, and the First Division was, indeed, transferred to Manchuria.

The incident greatly undercut the influence of the Kōdō faction in the army. At the same time, it increased the role of the mainstream military leadership in the government, as civilian officials depended more and more on the army to maintain stability. The episode also captured the public mind, taking its place in the gallery of "noble failures" that have long evoked pathos and admiration in Japan.

James L. Huffman

Bibliography

Shillony, Ben-Ami. *Revolt in Japan: The Young Officers and the February 26, 1936, Incident.* Princeton, NJ: Princeton University Press, 1973.

F

Federation of Economic Organizations (*Keidanren*: Abbreviation for *Keizai Dantai Rengōkai*)

A private and nonprofit economic organization established in August 1946 through the merger of several prewar economic and industrial groups, Keidanren is one of Japan's most powerful business organizations. Headed by internationally acknowledged leaders of the business community, it was composed in the mid-1990s of 122 industrial, commercial, and financial associations and 939 corporate members, encompassing virtually all the major businesses in Japan.

Although Keidanren is private and independent, its views and recommendations are well taken by the government (particularly MITI, the Ministry of International Trade and Industry). Keidanren is generally recognized as the "main temple" of the business community and its chairman as the business world's "prime minister." Among the five chairmen of Keidanren in a typical year, 1991, three were former bureaucrats and four were graduates of Tokyo University. All of them worked closely with the government. Many senior leaders of Keidanren have not only excellent academic training but also a broad vision for the future.

In addition to Keidanren, there are three other nationwide organizations of the *zaikai* (economic community), which serve different purposes but maintain close contact and cooperative relations with Keidanren on matters of common and mutual interest: Nisshō (Japan Chamber of Commerce and Industry, for the various regional economic problems of small- and medium-scale businesses), Nikkeiren (Japan Federation of Employers' Associations, for problems of labor-management relations), and Keizai Dōyōkai (Japan Association of Corporate Executives, for individual business executives' concerns about various economic and social problems). Among these four organizations, Keidanren is the most powerful and prestigious.

Keidanren makes an effort to influence the government (primarily MITI) to adopt policies that reflect the consensus within the business community. To effectively accomplish this objective, Keidanren has more than thirty committees, which cover the entire span of economic issues and maintain close contact with bureaucrats in relevant government ministries. Keidanren committee staffs particularly stay in constant contact with MITI by exchanging documents and arranging meetings, and Keidanren occasionally makes proposals to the government concerning economic matters of general interest to the business community.

Keidanren also facilitates political contributions from the business community to the Liberal Democratic Party (LDP) through the National Association, which was established to channel funds to the LDP. This financial contribution is said to tend to influence the government to consider the interests of the business community as a whole rather than to favor those of a particular segment.

The influence of Keidanren and the other economic organizations began to decline somewhat early in the 1990s, for several reasons: (1) The government policy-making process has become more complex and bureaucratized; (2) the growth of the economy has made Japanese industry far less dependent on economic organizations and government assistance; (3) the increasingly pluralistic nature of the business community has undermined the organizations' ability to create a consensus; and (4) the loss of several key personalities due to age and death has affected business-government interactions.

To meet the need of the pluralistic business community, Keidanren has expanded its activities as liaison between Japanese and foreign businesses, helping ensure the success of large-scale Japanese investment programs abroad. Also, to meet the need of the internationalization of the economy, Keidanren has established committees on relations with Southeast Asian and Latin American countries and on cooperation with African states. Keidanren has also provided new staff sections and committees to deal with the newer economic issues such as pollution control, consumer protection, and energy resources. Keidanren's new directions, which reflect changes in the society, have emphasized much broader issues for the long-range future of the Japanese economy. Keidanren is likely to continue to perform an important role for the business community, though its earlier consensus-mobilizing role is largely gone.

Masato Yamazaki

Bibliography

Lincoln, J. Edward. *Japan Facing Economic Maturity*. Washington, DC: Brookings Institution, 1988.

Vogel, F. Ezra. *Modern Japanese Organization and Decision-Making*. Tokyo: Charles E. Tuttle, 1980.

Financial Clique (*Zaibatsu*)

The precursor of the *zaibatsu* form of business organization, which dominated Japan's pre–World War II financial and business worlds, were the family enterprises paralleling Japan's traditional extended family, consisting of the stem (*honke*), its branches (*bunke*), and its affiliates (*bekke*) related by blood, marriage, adoption or putative kinship. Formalized under the Company Law of 1893, these enterprise groups became diversified joint-stock companies wholly or partly owned and controlled by a family-owned holding company. The strong dynastic flavor of this form of organization justifies the use of *batsu* (clique), which implies a tie more binding than a network of contractual business relationships.

Modern organizational concepts such as the holding company, the joint-stock company, controlling stock shares, and interlocking stock holdings helped promote the expansion of the *zaibatsu* in the twentieth century, relieving it from the sociobiological constraints on growth inherent in mere kinship organizations. Four preeminent *zaibatsu* emerged in prewar Japan: Mitsui, Mitsubishi, Sumitomo, and Yasuda.

Regardless of the business branches that engendered a *zaibatsu* (Mitsui: retail; Mitsubishi: shipping; Sumitomo: copper mining; Yasuda: banking), the *zaibatsu* tended to diversify into a wide range of activities in mining, industry, trade (domestic and foreign), transportation, shipping, finance, and insurance. The use of diversification as a primary thrust of expansion, in contrast to the typical Western drive for a monopoly in a given market, was another peculiar characteristic of *zaibatsu*; this made it impossible to measure any given clique's concentration of economic power by simply looking at its share of a particular market. A *zaibatsu* firm had to compete with kindred *zaibatsu* enterprises, as well as with the large, more specialized firms and numerous smaller businesses. Some of the specialized (less diversified) groups almost equaled *zaibatsu* in size and reputation. Furukawa, for example, excelled in copper mining and electrical power; Kawasaki, in shipbuilding, locomotives, and steel; and Shibusawa, in banking and engineering.

A few extraordinary entrepreneurs built mighty combines relatively quickly in the late nineteenth and early twentieth centuries, because businessmen then generally shunned the risks of modern business, and large-scale entrepreneurship was scarce. Likewise, during the 1930s, when imperialism and colonial development demanded investment in military industries, the established *zaibatsu* hesitated, but newcomers seized the opportunity and built new *zaibatsu*, including Ayukawa of Nissan, Noguchi of Japan Nitrogen (Chisso), and Mori of Shōwa Electric (Shōden).

After World War II, the Allied Occupation authorities dissolved *zaibatsu* and many giant firms in an effort to democratize Japan. Numerous independent companies emerged. However, their prewar connections reunited them, and they formed new groups through cross-holdings of stocks and mutual preferences in transactions. *Zaibatsu* names reappeared this time as group designations, such as Mitsui Group and Mitsubishi Group. As of 1996, six great enterprise groups dominated Japanese business: the Big Four (Mitsui, Mitsubishi, Sumitomo, and Yasuda), and two bank-centered groups, Daiichi-Kangin and Sanwa. Each member firm of a group is a giant enterprise in its own right and heads a pyramidlike *keiretsu* (system) consisting of many tiers of subcontractors, affiliates, suppliers, and distributors. The late-20th-century enterprise groups and *keiretsu* may even have surpassed the prewar *zaibatsu* in terms of cliquishness and solidarity.

Koji Taira

Bibliography

Hadley, Eleanor. *Antitrust in Japan*. Princeton, NJ: Princeton University Press, 1970.

Hirschmeier, Johannes, and Tsunehiko Yui. *The Development of Japanese Business*. Cambridge: Harvard University Press, 1975.

First Higher School (*Ichikō*)

Prewar Japan's premier secondary school for university-bound men. Founded in 1886 as one of five original preparatory institutions, each identified with a number, the First Higher School drew special acclaim for its close ties with Tokyo Imperial University, its prestigious faculty, and its illustrious graduates, whose ranks included seven prime ministers and such literary giants as Akutagawa Ryūnosuke, Tanizaki Jun'ichirō, and Kawabata Yasunari. Until its dissolution in 1949, the First Higher School provided a curricular and extracurricular model for the other elite preparatory schools, whose numbers increased fivefold by the late 1920s.

The early headmasters of First Higher conceived of their school as a flagship in the campaign for national strength and honor. As one administrator, Kuhara Kyūgen, put it in 1889: "Our school must never be satisfied with the mere pursuit of higher learning; we must always recognize our responsibility to cultivate national spirit through moral training" (Roden, 61–62). Accordingly, students and faculty rallied around a school flag that explicitly identified "the protection of the nation" with the responsibility of the institution. Throughout the late Meiji and pre-World War II years, in an array of flag-bearing ceremonies, military exercises, and even baseball games with American teams in Yokohama, the First Higher students demonstrated their commitment to the nation. Still, most alumni prefer to recall their "mother school" less as an incubator for nationalist ferment, and more as what Hayashi Kentarō called "an isolated castle of freedom" within a society that, after 1930, fell under the sway of totalitarianism. While not everyone agrees with Hayashi's charitable assessment of his own fellow graduates, most First Higher students did believe that their futures lay in a tolerant environment of institutional stability and international peace rather than mass mobilization and total war.

Donald Roden

Bibliography

Roden, Donald. *Schooldays in Imperial Japan*. Berkeley: University of California Press, 1980.

Folklore Studies (*Minzokugaku*)

The scientific study of Japanese legends, tales, customs and manners, recreation and games, folk religions, rituals, festivals, and folk medicine. Focusing on everyday life and the formation of the Japanese people, *minzokugaku* researchers obtain data by observing local customs and habits and by studying oral narrative traditions. According to leading folklorists, ancient legends and traditional narratives make it clear that the Japanese have remained a culturally unified, single people across the centuries, despite regional, climatic, and dialectal differences. Even the incursion of foreign ideas and modern industry in the twentieth century has not eradicated the society's distinctively Japanese essence.

Japanese *minzokugaku*, which drew inspiration from pioneering British folklore studies, developed around 1930 under the guidance of Yanagita Kunio (1875–1962) and Origuchi Shinobu (1887–1953). Yanagita's scholarship had antimodern overtones, coinciding with Japan's drive for modernization and growing confrontation with the Western powers. After World War II, ethnology and cultural anthropology greatly stimulated the discipline; yet it continued to grow into a distinctively Japanese branch of studies. As of the late 1990s, Japan was the only Asian country with an established science of folklore studies.

Yanagita, who called his *minzokugaku shin kokugaku* (new national learning), wished to revive the study of ancient and medieval Japanese history as a positivistic discipline based on Japanese traditions pursued by Japanese scholars, in order to inculcate a Japanese identity and encourage self-knowledge. Yanagita feared that rapid modernization and Westernization would negate Japan's history and cultural heritage.

As a governmental agriculture official, the young Yanagita had come into frequent contact with farmers and peasants in various villages. These experiences encouraged his fieldwork approach, which utilized the research method and framework of British folklore studies through the collection and recording of local tales and customs. Yanagita's first book, *Tonō monogatari* (Tales of Tono, 1910), a collection of folktales based on ethnographic data gathered in northwestern Japan, became the basis for *minzokugaku*. Yanagita helped establish *Kyōdō Kenkyū*, a *minzokugaku* journal, in 1914.

Japan's unconditional surrender in World War II in 1945 devastated most people and brought back earlier feelings of inferiority and anomie. The Japanese experienced seven years (1945–52) of Allied Occupation, causing Yanagita and other *minzokugaku* scholars to reflect deeply upon the significance of Japanese indigenous culture. More than ever before, they were determined to prove that Japan had its own unique and respectable culture.

As a result, Yanagita's postwar *minzokugaku* was focused to a significant degree on Shinto, the indigenous religion of Japan, and on *kokugaku*. Recognizing that many of the theories and doctrines of Shinto were on the verge of dissolution due to the religion's association with prewar extremism, Yanagita focused on Shinto as a folk religion—as a popular institution that served, along with the Japanese language, as an important source of continuity with the nation's past. Yanagita's research into Shinto resulted in the formulation of a cultural theory that emphasized the uniqueness of Japan's folk culture and encouraged the study of rice cultivation. Its proponents regarded rice as the symbol of national solidarity and of the sovereign power of the emperor.

Minzokugaku should be regarded both as a social science and as a field of study with sociopolitical implications. The interest of *minzokugaku* scholars in village studies and indigenous culture has helped fuel certain types of postwar conservatism, even as it has served as a counterweight to the heavy modernist emphasis of mainstream scholars on central institutions. Many late-twentieth-century folklorists fear that the field is in danger of being subsumed by the more traditional disciplines, such as anthropology and ethnology.

Kinko Ito

Bibliography

Dorson, Richard M., ed. *Studies in Japanese Folklore*. New York: Arno Press, 1980.

Gluck, Carol. "The People in History: Recent Trends in Japanese Historiography," *Journal of Asian Studies*. Vol. 38, No. 1 (November 1978), 25–50.

Foreign Aid (ODA) (*Keizai Enjo*)

Japan first surpassed the United States to become the largest donor of official development assistance (ODA) in the world in 1989. The funds provided ($8.965 billion) amounted to .32 percent of GNP, a ratio ranking Japan 12th among major Organization for Economic Cooperation and Development (OECD) donors. The following year, Japan's contribution increased to $9.24 billion, but the United States recovered the top ranking. By the mid-1990s, Japan's annual ODA had surpassed $11 billion, tops among all nations. Japan was a major recipient of foreign aid after World War II, with the United States providing the bulk of resources to stabilize the economy during the Occupation period (1945–52) and multilateral lending, such as World Bank loans, contributing to economic recovery into the 1960s.

Japan's ODA and other assistance to less-developed countries since the late 1950s has been pursued with an eye to the economic, political, and strategic benefits gained or perceived. The postwar foreign-aid program is often considered an outgrowth of the war reparations programs begun by Japan to assist Southeast Asian countries, such as the Philippines, Indonesia, and Malaysia, in the 1950s. Japanese ODA has been concentrated in Asia, particularly Southeast Asia, where it has become part of the web of economic linkages formed since the war. This was most pronounced during the 1960s, when ODA was linked to the export-promotion drive of Japanese industry. ODA funds tied to procurement contracts for domestic firms helped spur the export of plant and equipment for infrastructure projects throughout Asia. ODA assisted in the drive to open markets, secure supplies of natural resources, and provide a suitable climate for private investment. The self-interested nature of this type of assistance irritated many Southeast Asians and sparked anti-Japanese rioting in several Southeast Asian countries in the mid-1970s.

The export-promotion strategy shifted in the 1970s to an emphasis on assuring stable supplies of natural resources, particularly energy, as shown especially in the aggressive ODA program for the Mideast that emerged after the 1973 oil crisis. During the 1980s, the ODA effort diversified, with the need to recycle Japan's huge foreign-exchange surpluses becoming an important motivation. Japan's foreign aid has, however, continued to be dogged by complaints of economic nationalism and lack of quality. Japan has at times used ODA in pursuit of political aims—to respond to or preempt international criticism, to reward or punish policies adopted by recipient countries, or to support the security interests of the United States in an effort at "burden sharing."

More important, perhaps, is the way foreign aid has been used as a tool to forge a postwar political presence and identity. Involvement in donor activities has helped Japan rehabilitate itself in the eyes of the international community after World War II. Ever increasing levels of foreign aid have attested to Japan's emergence as a major economic power on a par with other members of the OECD. The program receives a high level of public support domestically, bolsters Japan's prestige externally, and provides an identity consistent with the image of Japan as a peacefully inclined, responsible member of the world community.

Ellen H. Hammond

F

Bibliography
Rix, Alan. *Japan's Economic Aid*. London: Croon Helm, 1980.
Yasutomo, Dennis T. *The Manner of Giving: Strategic Aid and Japanese Foreign Policy*. Lexington, MA: Lexington Books, 1986.

Foreign Employees (*Yatoi Gaikokujin*)

Often rendered with a slightly sarcastic honorific, *oyatoi gaikokujin*. The term came to be applied specifically to foreigners (*kanyatoi*) employed by the government in the nineteenth century. In the last years of the Tokugawa regime (1600–1868), 200 technical advisers (Dutch, French, British, American, and others) worked for the shogunate. François Coignet (in Japan 1868–77) was probably the first *yatoi* employed by the new Meiji (1868–1912) government. Scholars have identified about 2,000 individual, professional *yatoi* in Meiji public service. More impressive were the estimated 9,500 person-years of service offered to the Meiji modernizers. Although William Elliot Griffis (in Japan 1871–74) often referred to himself as the first *yatoi* in the Meiji era, more accurately he became far better known as America's first "old Japan hand" and the pioneer chronicler of the alien advisers.

Hired foreigners were, in most cases, useful teachers, and many became valuable advisers; the most influential were missionary and political advisor Guido Verberck (1830–98), constitutional scholar Herman Roesler (1834–94), and foreign-affairs consultant Henry Willard Denison (1864–1914). In one sense, however, all *yatoi* were imperialists, even if the term is softened by calling them cultural imperialists. Especially in the early period, they came to Japan sponsored by their respective countries and, for a time, became parties to pressure being applied to Japan to follow a Western path toward modernization.

To the Meiji government, the *yatoi* were a necessary evil, regarded as only a little less undesirable than foreign loans. They were eventually replaced by trained Japanese (in many cases, *ryūgakusei*, Japanese educated abroad). By the end of the nineteenth century, only a few alien advisers remained, as Japan reasserted its own national identity in modernization.

The *yatoi* were nonetheless significant actors in a drama involving a striking, possibly the earliest, historical example of the use of foreign technical assistance. Moreover, they were pioneers in explaining the Japanese lifestyle to their Western compatriots. Their memoirs and letters became primary sources, alongside Japanese material, to document the important transition from feudal Japan to the Meiji nation-state. *Yatoi* experiences also became the stuff of legend, even among Japanese. "With some temperaments and characters," as Griffis put it, the Japanese had "their hands full" (Burks, 195–96).

Ardath Burks

Bibliography
Beauchamp, Edward R., and Akira Iriye, eds. *Foreign Employees in Nineteenth-Century Japan*. Boulder, CO: Westview, 1990.
Burks, Ardath W., ed. *The Modernizers: Overseas Students, Foreign Employees and Meiji Japan*. Boulder, CO: Westview, 1985.

Foreign Labor (Unskilled)

Japan experienced a dramatic increase in the number of unskilled foreign workers seeking jobs there after the mid-1980s. Nearly all of these workers entered the country illegally, since Japanese immigration law forbade the entry of unskilled laborers. Most came on short-term student or tourist visas, then remained after their visas had expired, while a few posed as refugees or "boat people." Experts estimated the number of illegal foreign workers in Japan early in the 1990s at nearly 300,000, most of them from China, the Philippines, Thailand, Iran, Malaysia, South Korea, and Bangladesh, with a significant number of arrivals also from Latin America.

The primary cause of this influx lay in the contrasting economies of Japan and many Asian countries. While numerous countries were experiencing increasing unemployment, Japan was undergoing a serious labor shortage, particularly in low-paid jobs in construction, service, and factory work. The Industrial Bank of Japan estimated in 1989 that, by the early twenty-first century, at least 2 million jobs would be unfilled. For thousands of foreigners, the opportunities were too enticing to ignore. One result was that the government became more aggressive in deporting illegal aliens, sending home 22,626 persons in 1989, for example—more than a 50 percent increase over the previous year. The government also passed a new immigration-control law late in 1989, strengthening the ban on the entry of unskilled labor and imposing penalties on employers of illegal entrants.

The issue sparked a lively national debate, much of it centering on the nature of Japanese society and the meaning of "Japaneseness." While some scholars and officials called for a loosening of restrictions on foreign labor, many others insisted that the prohibition be maintained. In addition to arguing that an influx of foreigners might cause labor exploitation, undermine Japanese workers' wages and lead to more ghettos and crime, some writers raised the issue of ethnic homogeneity, arguing that large-scale immigration could lead to a sizable ethnic minority and to an increased "mixed race" population. The early 1990s saw a lessening of the tension, as the economy slowed down and fewer jobs were made available to outside workers. The volatility of the issue continued throughout the decade, however, in episodes such as the national government's 1996 refusal to allow its regional offices to hire foreigners in key posts and the continuing, regular deportation of illegal immigrants.

James L. Huffman

Bibliography

Shimada, Haruo. *Japan's "Guest Workers": Issues and Public Policies*. Tokyo: University of Tokyo Press, 1994.

Freedom and People's Rights Movement (*Jiyū Minken Undō*)

The name given to the political movement to establish a constitution and parliamentary government in early Meiji Japan (1874–90). It had its origins in the 1874 petition to the Meiji Emperor by former government leaders, including Itagaki Taisuke, Etō Shimpei, Gotō Shōjirō, and Soejima Taneomi, calling for the immediate establishment of a representative national assembly, and it continued sporadically in two stages (1874–81 and 1881–90) until the promulgation of the Meiji Constitution in 1889 and the first Diet (legislature) of 1890.

Despite its ideological rhetoric of "freedom and people's rights," the leadership was much more interested in wresting political power for itself from the *Sat-Chō hambatsu* (Satsuma and Chōshū-dominated oligarchy) and in preserving the political and economic power of its own social class, the *shizoku* (former samurai), than it was in empowering commoners. The movement, however, can be said to have been a major catalyst in the formulation and articulation of modern Japanese nationalism in that it engendered a political dialogue forcing the ruling oligarchy to reconsider, redefine, and refine its vision of Japan's place in the world.

After the return of the Iwakura Mission, in which leading officials had studied Western institutions in Europe and America between 1871 and 1873, the Meiji leadership split on the issue of a proposed punitive expedition to Korea (*Seikan ron,* 1874). The "outs," who had left the government, selected the issue of a national assembly as a method to force the "ins" to share power. Those in power were initially caught off guard because the "outs" had couched their petition in loyalist-nationalist language. Therefore, they could not be dismissed as disloyal to the emperor, because they had merely called for the realization of the goals expressed in the emperor's own Charter Oath of 1868, which called for national matters to be "decided by public discussion" and for "all classes, high and low," to "unite in vigorously carrying out the administration of affairs of state."

The oligarchy then was forced to rearticulate the principles of an emperor-centered, yet constitutionally limited, monarchy and to redefine Japanese nationalism in a more rational and coherent manner than had been previously attempted. For the next decade, the political debate was carried out in the press. The argument centered primarily on the tension between *kokken* (national rights) and *minken* (popular rights). More conservative intellectuals such as Inoue Kowashi and Kaneko Kentarō were assisted by two German political scientists, Hermann Roesler and Albert Mosse, who insisted that loyalty to the sovereign superseded individual rights.

The *minken* leaders were assisted by their own more liberal thinkers, such as Kōno Hironaka, Fukuzawa Yukichi, and Ueki Emori, who argued that one could be loyal to the emperor and the nation without surrendering individual political rights. The fact is that the *minken* "outs" and the *kokken* "ins" were quite close in their basic political assumptions. They both wanted a strong, prosperous, and independent Japan. Both groups would later demonstrate that their visions of an economically and militarily expansionist Japan in Asia were strikingly similar. Both hated the feudal and familial autocracy of the previous three centuries that had stifled individual political expression; yet, they both feared the excesses of the "rabble" masses, preferring a strong political leadership of educated elite. What they differed on, of course, was who should rule in the name of the emperor.

In the first stage of the movement (1874–81), the leaders of the "outs" formed a number of political associations, such as the Aikokusha (Society of Patriots), to agitate and petition for political liberalization. The government response was to make some minor concessions, to issue vague promises, and to attempt a suppression of the movement through bribery, intimidation, and a series of repressive laws.

The watershed came in 1881, when the oligarch Ōkuma Shigenobu clashed with the rest of the government in his advocacy of a British-style parliamentary democracy. When Ōkuma was ousted from the government that fall, the *minken* movement moved into the second phase, that of preparation for the constitutional government that had been promised by the emperor. During this stage, two main political parties—Jiyūtō (Liberal Party) led by Itagaki and Ōkuma's Rikken Kaishintō (Constitutional Reform Party)—competed for popular support.

If the actual goal of the movement was to force the oligarchy to broaden its base of leadership, then it can be considered a limited success. If, however, its goal was to win "freedom and people's rights," the movement must be judged a failure, and that failure must be attributed to at least six factors. First, the leadership of the movement was more interested in personal political power than in the extension of popular rights and freedoms. Second, the leadership tacitly supported the antigovernment rebellion of *shizoku* led by Saigō Takamori, who had no intention of empowering commoners, in the unsuccessful Satsuma Rebellion of 1877. Without doubt, this severely undercut the movement's claims of nationalist legitimacy because the oligarchy could, and did, point to this disloyalty as proof that the "outs" were not worthy of power. Third, the fact that the leaders occasionally accepted positions in the government as individuals rather than present a united opposition indicates that personal goals were paramount to ideological ones. Fourth, those "defections" of individuals to join the government seriously demoralized the more liberal intellectuals and thereby robbed the movement of considerable energy. Fifth, those leaders who joined the *hambatsu* often acquiesced in, and occasionally employed repressive laws to stifle, political dissent. Sixth, the leadership of the movement feared the specter of mass political power as much as the oligarchy did. The most powerful political party, Jiyūtō, disbanded in 1884, in part because it could no longer control the masses it had stirred up in two popular uprisings, the Chichibu and Kabasan Incidents of that year.

Had the parties been true to their stated ideological goals of promoting freedom and people's rights, the oligarchy might have been forced to share power with these nascent parties. Instead, the government was able to arrogate for itself the right to speak for the emperor as to what type of constitutional monarchy would best serve national goals.

Louis G. Perez

Bibliography

Akita, George. *The Foundations of Constitutional Government in Japan, 1868–1900.* Cambridge: Harvard University Press, 1967.

Bowen, Roger. *Rebellion and Democracy in Meiji Japan.* Berkeley: University of California Press, 1980.

Fresh Wind Society (*Seirankai*)

Nationalistic organization formed in July 1973 by 24 relatively young (average age 48) Liberal Democratic Party (LDP) politicians. At an initiation ceremony, where each member sliced his little finger with a razor blade and signed the membership roster in blood, the new organization pledged itself to promote relations with the non-Communist world, national morality, stronger national defense, educational reform, income redistribution, domestic law and order, constitutional revision, and the eradication of facile, bureaucratic compromise in policy-making. During the first year or so of its existence, the group blocked a visit to the People's Republic of Korea by an official LDP delegation, vigorously supported two defense appropriations bills and a health insurance bill in the Diet (legislature), campaigned for conservative local candidates, and twice aggressively confronted Prime Minister Tanaka Kakuei concerning his policy of reestablishing relations with the People's Republic of China (PRC).

Seirankai members have been vehemently nationalistic in many of their policies and statements, especially in promoting education oriented toward Japanese values and national morality, a stronger national defense establishment, and an independent foreign policy. The Seirankai emphasizes foreign policy. Indeed, U.S. President Richard Nixon's unannounced visit to the PRC in July 1971, which led to the normalization of U.S.-China relations, played an important role in the formation of the group. Although the LDP conservatives had traditionally provided the main bulwark of support for a pro-American foreign policy, many, including Seirankai members, began to distrust the United States when Nixon carried out the visit against the background of detente and the American withdrawal from Vietnam. This unexpected American policy shift caused a sea change in the LDP in favor of improving Japan's relations with the PRC and caused party "hawks," who staunchly supported the Republic of China (ROC) in Taiwan, to become increasingly isolated. This change also contributed to the 1972 fall of the Satō Eisaku government, bringing Tanaka Kakuei to the premiership partly on the strength of political sentiment in favor of diplomatic relations with Peking. As a consequence, Seirankai's nationalism has been directed not only against Japan's Communist neighbors but implicitly against the United States, which some Seirankai members have characterized as a decadent, corrupt, and licentious society from which Japan should declare its independence.

The Seirankai founder and early leader Ishihara Shintarō made news in 1989 as a result of a series of exchanges with Morita Akio, chairman of Sony Corporation, which were circulated in the United States in unauthorized English translations. In the exchanges, Ishihara emphasized Japan's superiority in production technology, charged Americans with racial prejudice, and asserted the need for Japan to learn to say "no" to the United States.

J. Victor Koschmann

Bibliography
Koschmann, J. Victor, "Hawks on the Defensive: The Seirankai." *The Japan Interpreter.* Vol. 8, No. 4 (Winter 1974), 467–77.

Friend of the Nation (Kokumin no Tomo)

Opinion journal. Founded on February 15, 1887, by then 24-year-old journalist Tokutomi Sohō, and his Min'yūsha (Society of the People's Friends), it has been called Japan's first *sōgō zasshi* (composite magazine). Its name was taken from American journalistic pioneer Edwin Godkin's *Nation.* Like other journals, it concentrated on politics, but its essays were exceptionally wide ranging, covering art, science, literature, social issues, and economics. Expounding Tokutomi's youthful antigovernment ideas, which he labeled *heiminshugi* (democracy; literally, commonerism), it was known for lively writing, low subscription rates, and heavy advertising; it quickly became Japan's largest magazine, attaining a circulation of 25,000 at its peak. As Tokutomi moved in an increasingly nationalistic—and progovernment—direction after the Sino-Japanese War (1894–95), *Kokumin no tomo* experienced a sharp decline in circulation. It discontinued publication in August 1898.

James L. Huffman

Bibliography
Pierson, John. *Tokutomi Sohō, 1863–1957.* Princeton, NJ: Princeton University Press, 1980.

Friends of Constitutional Government Party (Rikken Seiyūkai)

The most prominent political party of the prewar era. The party was formed by Itō Hirobumi in 1900 in an effort to combine bureaucratic forces and conservative politicians, largely from the old Kenseitō (Constitutional Party), into a party that would provide a bulwark of support for government policies. From then until its demise in 1940, it remained generally conservative, with a strong base in rural constituencies.

After Itō resigned in 1903, the presidency was taken by Saionji Kinmochi, who formed cabinets in 1906 and 1911. The most effective president in the early years was Hara Takashi, who managed most party affairs for Saionji, then became president in 1914. Under Hara, the party helped topple the Katsura Tarō government in the Taishō Political Crisis in 1913 and took full control of the cabinet (with all but three of the posts) when Hara became prime minister in 1918, ushering in the era of party cabinets. Despite continued advocacy of parliamentary control, the Seiyūkai pursued policies under Hara that were conservative: The government opposed universal male suffrage, cracked down on organized labor, and engaged heavily in pork barrel politics. The party declined somewhat after Hara's assassination late in 1921 and suffered a split in 1924. It recouped its losses under Tanaka Giichi, whose cabinet (1927–29) strengthened the repressive 1925 Peace Preservation Law and initiated new expansionist policies in China.

The last Seiyūkai cabinet was formed by Inukai Tsuyoshi late in 1931, following the shooting of Hamaguchi Osachi. By this time, the party was strongly antileftist and had opposed the arms limitations of the 1930 London Naval Treaty, which maintained British and American supremacy over Japanese shipping. When Inukai was assassinated on May 15, 1932, by even more conservative nationalists, the era of party-led governments terminated. The Seiyūkai became increasingly divided and disbanded in July 1940, with most of its members joining the Imperial Rule Assistance Association (Taisei Yokusankai) that autumn.

James L. Huffman

Bibliography

Berger, Gordon. *Parties out of Power in Japan, 1931–1941*. Princeton, NJ: Princeton University Press, 1977.

Duus, Peter. *Party Rivalry and Political Change in Taishō Japan*. Cambridge: Harvard University Press, 1968.

Najita, Tetsuo. *Hara Kei and the Politics of Compromise*. Cambridge: Harvard University Press, 1967.

Fukuchi Gen'ichirō. Courtesy Mainichi Shimbunsha Shi Henshūshitsu.

Fukuchi Gen'ichirō (1841–1906)

Journalist, playwright, and politician. Born in Nagasaki, he was a translator for the Tokugawa government early in the 1860s, then was jailed in 1868 for publishing the antigovernment newspaper *Kōko Shimbun* in the wake of the Meiji Restoration that same year. After shifting to the government side, he assumed the editorship of *Tokyo Nichi Nichi Shimbun* in 1874 following a brief tenure in the Finance Ministry. At that paper, he became the country's leading journalist, espousing a "gradualist" position that involved steady movement toward constitutional, parliamentary government. He also founded and led the first progovernment political party, Rikken Teiseitō (Constitutional Imperial Party), in 1881–83. After resigning from *Nichi Nichi* in 1888, he wrote novels, history books, and kabuki plays, helped build the Kabukiza theater, and was elected to the Diet (legislature) in 1904. Fukuchi was a trenchant editorialist—one of the first to employ the idea of *kokutai* (national polity) as a defense for making imperial sovereignty the cornerstone of the Meiji Constitution. He also helped in 1882 to draft the highly patriotic Imperial Rescript to Soldiers and Sailors (Gunjin chokuyu), which guided military behavior until World War II.

James L. Huffman

Bibliography

Huffman, James. *Politics of the Meiji Press: The Life of Fukuchi Gen'ichirō*. Honolulu: University Press of Hawaii, 1980.

Fukuzawa Yukichi (1835–1901)

Journalist, educator, and leading modernizer of the Meiji era (1868–1912). Born to a lower-ranking samurai family in Fukuoka Prefecture in Kyushu, he rejected traditional learning as a youth and gravitated to the new ideas of the West. After studying Western gunnery in Nagasaki and Dutch at the Ogata Kōan school in Osaka, he moved to Edo in 1858 to begin a Dutch-language school for his fief, then accompanied the first Japanese mission to the United States in 1860 and the first to Europe in 1862. On the basis of these trips and another journey to America in 1867, he wrote the widely acclaimed three-volume *Seiyō Jijō* (Conditions in the West) at the end of the decade, explaining Western customs in a style understandable to average citizens.

Fukuzawa Yukichi. Courtesy Asahi Shimbun.

lar rights) movement. He was an active advocate of national expansion in the 1890s, supporting the Sino-Japanese War (1894–95) effort and calling for Japan to adopt an aggressive continental policy that would make it a leader of Asian modernization.

James L. Huffman

Bibliography

Blacker, Carmen. *The Japanese Enlightenment: A Study of the Writings of Fukuzawa Yukichi.* Cambridge: Cambridge University Press, 1969.

Kiyooka, Eiichi, trans. *The Autobiography of Yukichi Fukuzawa.* New York: Columbia University Press, 1966.

Fundamental Law of Education (*Kyōiku Kihon Hō*)

Established on March 31, 1947, just one month before the promulgation of the postwar constitution, this is the fundamental law on which Japan's contemporary education system is based, the foundation for all educational laws and directives issued since then. Its contents, strongly influenced by the American-directed Occupation (1945–52), were drawn up in 1946 by the Education Reform Council and adopted by the Diet (legislature). Intended to replace the nationalistic Imperial Rescript on Education, which had guided the country's schools since 1890, it focused on democracy, individual dignity, and world peace as the basic goals of education.

The Fundamental Law contained a total of 11 articles in addition to a preamble. It demanded that education be used not to train loyal subjects, but to inspire the quest for truth and to create an independent spirit. The individual articles applied this theme to various components of the educational structure. Article 3 called for equal opportunity for all and forbade discrimination. Article 4 made education compulsory for all children. Article 8 said students should be given enough political knowledge to become good citizens, but it enjoined teachers from partisanship in the classroom. Article 9 required separation of church and state. And Article 10 (administration) ordered schools to be "directly responsible to the whole people." The Kyōiku Kihon Hō inspired considerable controversy as various groups interpreted it in their own ways in an effort to influence educational changes during the post-

During the 1870s, Fukuzawa became Japan's leading nonofficial proponent of Westernization, advocating the spread of practical knowledge (*jitsugaku*), an independent spirit, and scientific learning. His writings, which included *Gakumon no Susume* (An Encouragement of Learning) and *Bunmei no Gairyaku* (An Outline of a Theory of Civilization), called for citizen rights, the creation of a popular assembly, and an improvement in the conditions of women. Though making a point of avoiding public office, he maintained close ties to the political establishment, accepting membership in the first Tokyo city assembly in 1878 and agreeing two years later to edit a government gazette (*Kampō*) before that project fell through.

His greatest influence probably came through his school, renamed Keiō Gijuku in 1868, where he trained a generation of public servants, and at *Jiji Shimpō*, the newspaper he founded in 1882. At *Jiji*, he called for a new brand of nonpartisan journalism, though the paper discussed political issues forcefully and remained close to the views of the progressive politician Ōkuma Shigenobu. Fukuzawa grew more conservative in his later years, possibly because the times themselves had changed so rapidly, opposing what he viewed as the extremism of the *jiyū minken* (popu-

Occupation era. Its democratic, antinationalist thrust, however, has continued to exert a significant influence on Japan's schools.

James L. Huffman

Bibliography
Duke, Benjamin. *Japan's Militant Teachers.* Honolulu, HI: University Press of America, 1973.

G

Gakuren Incident (*Gakuren Jiken*)

Early on the morning of December 1, 1925, police rounded up 37 students at Kyoto University and other schools in that area. It was the first official attempt to eradicate left-wing student movements under the Peace Preservation Law (1925), which made the advocacy of socialist or unpatriotic laws illegal. The Kyoto police, who had been monitoring the pro-Communist Gakusei Shakai Kagaku Rengōkai (Student Social Science Federation, abbreviated as Gakuren), arrested the students and searched their dormitory rooms for incriminating evidence. The authorities expected their search to turn up evidence that would lead to prosecution under the new Peace Preservation Law, but the materials they found provided scant damaging evidence, and the raids sparked a wave of protest from students, faculty, and the general press. All the students were released within a week.

Police surveillance continued, though, and a second roundup began on January 15, 1926. This time, 38 were arrested, press coverage was banned, and within a year all had been given sentences of eight to twelve months for violating the Peace Preservation Law.

James L. Huffman

Bibliography

Dewitt Smith, Henry, II. *Japan's First Student Radicals*. Cambridge: Harvard University Press, 1972.

**Gentlemen's Agreement
(*Nichibei Shinshi Kyōyaku*)**

Informal diplomatic agreement limiting Japanese laborers' immigration to the United States, 1907–08. Antagonism toward Japanese immigrants had existed in California since the late 1800s, occasionally leading to violence. When the San Francisco school board decided to segregate the 93 Japanese school children there in October 1906, the Japanese government and public protested, claiming that the action violated the 1894 treaty that guaranteed Japanese residents of the United States the same liberties as Americans. Stung by the high feelings, U.S. President Theodore Roosevelt vigorously sought a compromise. After publicly criticizing the act of segregation, he brought the school board to Washington and persuaded it to rescind its decision. He also secured congressional passage of a bill that allowed the president to prohibit certain classes of laborers from coming to the United States.

Japan and the United States then exchanged six notes, jointly known as the Gentlemen's Agreement; in it, Japan agreed not to give passports to workers intending to go to the continental United States, and the Americans agreed not to prevent the immigration of laborers who already were in the United States or of resident Japanese workers' immediate family members. The short-term effect was to calm the tensions, both in Japan and on the U.S. West Coast. The improvement in feelings was temporary, however. When Japanese workers began bringing picture brides in significant numbers, Californians accused them of skirting the agreements. And when Congress banned all Japanese immigration to the United States in 1924, the Japanese felt that they had been duped—and singled out for discrimination. The general impact of the entire episode was to exacerbate the Japanese sense of unfair treatment at the hands of a supposed ally.

James L. Huffman

Bibliography

Esthus, Raymond. *Theodore Roosevelt and Japan*. Seattle: University of Washington Press, 1966.

Gondō Seikyō (pen name Nariaki) (1868–1937)

Agrarian nationalist thinker and writer. Born in Fukuoka, the young Gondō spent time in Korea as an intelligence agent and became an advocate of Japanese expansion in Asia. Back in Japan, he edited *Tōa Geppō* (East Asian Monthly News) for the rightist Kokuryūkai (Amur River Society) and became a leading exponent of agrarian nationalism (*nōhonshugi*), calling for a decentralized, village-based society operating directly under the emperor without prefectural or national governmental structures to intervene. In 1920, Gondō formed the Jichi Gakkai (Self-Rule School) to propound his views. He also wrote several books, including *Jichi minpan* (People's Guide to Self-Rule). Though he remained nonviolent personally, his ideas had great impact on right-wing activists such as Kita Ikki, Tachibana Kōzaburō, and Ōkawa Shūmei. For this reason, he was detained in connection with two rightist incidents in the early 1930s but then released.

James L. Huffman

Bibliography

Storry, Richard. *The Double Patriots: A Study of Japanese Nationalism*. Westport, CT: Greenwood Press, 1973.

Gotō Shimpei (1857–1929)

Leading bureaucrat. A medical doctor who began government service as an innovative health administrator, Gotō Shimpei encountered General Kodama Gentarō in 1895 while organizing army quarantine work. From 1898 to 1906, under Kodama, Gotō laid the foundations of Japan's colonial development of Taiwan. After the Russo-Japanese War (1904–05), as the first president of the South Manchurian Railway Company, he made the company a major vehicle for Japan's continental expansion.

As foreign minister in late 1918, Gotō advocated improving Japanese-Russian relations to strengthen Japanese control of China. He attempted to use the 1918 intervention in Russia by Western capitalist powers and Japan to gain Japanese influence in Russia. When this attempt failed, he urged speedy normalization of diplomatic and commercial connections with the Soviet Union. As mayor of Tokyo in 1923, Gotō offered his services as a private mediator between Japan and the Soviet Union. This initiative eventually contributed to the formal Russo-Japanese negotiations that produced the Basic Convention of 1925, which restored normal relations between the two countries.

E. Patricia Tsurumi

Bibliography

Hayase, Yukiko. "The Career of Gotō Shimpei: Japan's Statesman of Research, 1857–1929." Unpublished doctoral dissertation, Florida State University, 1974.
Tsurumi, E. Patricia. *Japanese Colonial Education in Taiwan, 1894–1945*. Cambridge: Harvard University Press, 1977.

Grand Shrines of Ise (*Ise Jingū*)

The Grand Shrines of Ise, considered the heart of Shinto and closely connected to the imperial house, are divided into two major complexes. The older inner shrine (*naiku*) was established in the early fourth century. It serves as the abode of Amaterasu-o-mi-Kami, the principal deity of the imperial family. Of lesser importance, the outer shrine (*geku*), established by the Emperor Yuryaku (456–79), houses the deity Toyuke Okami, responsible for a plentiful food supply for the nation.

From 1871 to 1945, the Grand Shrines of Ise were central to State Shinto, a term used to designate the use of Shinto by the state to promote a strong sense of national unity and purpose. With the intention of making palpable the sense that all Japanese were connected to Ise, amulets (*ofuda* and *omamori*) from Ise were distributed annually throughout Japan. The amulets were to be placed on the household altar (*kamidana*) that every household was expected to have. Although a government order in 1878 proclaimed the principle that people could refuse the amulets, most families accepted them and performed obeisance before them daily.

To symbolically integrate local areas into the national cult of Ise, beginning in the early Meiji era, outposts (*daijingu* or *kotai jingū*) of the Grand Shrines were established in every prefecture and were intended to be worshiped by the prefectural governors.

In accord with the ancient religious practice of periodically renewing the ontic power and purity of the shrines, the *naiku* and the *geku*

Grand Shrines of Ise. Courtesy Consulate General of Japan, N.Y.

are rebuilt in toto every 20 years. The present buildings, dedicated in 1993, cost more than $30 million, which was raised from individuals, groups, and corporations.

Eugene Swanger

Bibliography

Hardacre, Helen. *Shinto and the State: 1868–1988.* Princeton, NJ: Princeton University Press, 1989.

Picken, Stuart. *Shinto: Japan's Spiritual Roots.* Tokyo: Kodansha, 1980.

Great Japan National Essence Association (*Dainihon Kokusuikai*)

Prominent prewar ultranationalist group. In response to the growing power of Japan's political parties during the early years of the twentieth century, Nishimura Isaburō created the Dainihon Kokusuikai in 1919. Supported by Home Minister Tokonami Takejirō and other prominent politicians, it was strongly opposed to socialism and Communism and even objected to the more moderate views of many of Japan's party leaders. It also sought to make reverence for the emperor the focus of politics in Japan. Ultimately, it had more than 500,000 members. Although Suzuki Kisaburō, a man who had numerous connections with the party leaders of Japan, became its head in 1926, many of its members came from the laboring class and forsook mainstream politics, participating from time to time in violent clashes with individuals and groups they opposed. The most famous of these incidents occurred in 1924 in Nara when they attacked a group that was seeking to abolish national discrimination against outcasts. The Dainihon Kokusuikai was disbanded during the Allied Occupation (1945–52) after the end of World War II.

J. Wayne Sabey

Bibliography
Morris, Ivan. *Nationalism and the Right Wing in Japan.* London: Oxford University Press, 1960.

Great New Food Festival (*Daijōsai*)

The final and most elaborate of three Shinto ceremonies performed by a new emperor when assuming the throne. The first two are the *senso* (thread throne ceremony) and the *sokuirei* (ascend throne ceremony). The last *daijōsai* was performed by Emperor Akihito in November 1990.

In this rite, the new emperor, serving as the only intermediary between the Japanese people and the spirits who protect the nation, offers the rite of that year's harvest to Amaterasu-o-mi-Kami, the Sun Goddess and ancestor of the imperial family, to the other gods of heaven, and to those of the Japanese islands.

The rice fields where the largest portion of the rice used in this ceremony will be grown are chosen by divining their location from the cracks in the shoulder blade of a stag. Through this process, two fields are chosen, one somewhere in eastern Japan and one located in western Japan. Replicas of these fields are also laid out on the grounds of the imperial palace. After these fields are harvested in autumn, the farmers bring their grain to the palace.

The ceremony is held in three temporary shrines built expressly for this rite, the Yuki-den, representing the east; the Suki-den, representing the west; and the Kairyū-den, where the emperor rests.

The ceremony begins in the evening with the ritual bathing of the emperor in a wooden tub inside the Kairyū-den. The emperor then proceeds to the Yuki-den, where he offers to the gods bowls of boiled rice from the two chosen fields mixed with grains from the fields of each prefecture and a variety of other samples of cuisine from throughout Japan. The emperor himself partakes simply of boiled rice, millet, and dark *sake*. At midnight, he returns to the Kairyū-den, where he remains until 2:00 A.M., when he proceeds to the Suki-den to repeat the offering ritual. After finishing the second communion, the emperor withdraws, and all three structures are immolated.

The yearly equivalent of the *daijōsai*, the *niinamesai*, is held each November at the imperial palace, where the emperor invites Amaterasu and the other gods to a meal prepared, again, with the collected fruits of the nation's harvest. In the 1928 ceremony for the Shōwa Emperor, these products included not only the rice from the fields of each prefecture in Japan but also beans from Hokkaido, fish from Sakhalin, lily roots from Osaka, and bananas from Taiwan. Inclusion of offerings to the traditional gods of Japan from all Japanese lands serves to reaffirm in the minds of the Japanese their identity as members of the same nation, descendants of the same people.

Peter Swanger

Bibliography
Liscutin, Nicola. "Daijōsai: The Great Festival of Tasting the New Fruits." *Transactions of the Asiatic Society of Japan.* Ser. 4. Vol. 5 (1990), 25–52.
Packard, Jerrold M. *Sons of Heaven: A Portrait of the Japanese Monarchy.* New York: Charles Scribner's Sons, 1978.

Greater East Asia Coprosperity Sphere (*Dai-Tōa Kyōeiken*)

The Greater East Asia Coprosperity Sphere was the official name given Japan's drive to organize occupied territories during the Pacific War (1937–45) into a politically, economically, and culturally autarkic bloc. The concept of a cooperative supranational unit grew out of Japan's inability to defeat or accommodate Chinese nationalism. Simultaneously a critique of Western colonial empires and of revolutionary national independence movements, the coprosperity sphere sought an alternative through vague notions of moral advancement and spiritual unity subsuming the nations of East and Southeast Asia. In the confident days after Japan's December 7, 1941, attack on U.S. operations at Pearl Harbor, this meant mutual economic development within a strict racial hierarchy defined and headed by Japan. A new political and cultural order based on strident antipathy toward nationalism in Asia ultimately proved as difficult to implement as the thorough military and economic mobilization of the sphere.

As the war turned against Japan, attempts to clarify the structure of the new order caused

Tokyo to grant independence to Burma and the Philippines (summer 1943) and to make further concessions to Asian nationalism at the Greater East Asia Conference (November 1943), where Japan pledged its respect for the autonomy and cultural distinctiveness of member nationalities. Japan's formal colonial possessions (Korea, Taiwan, and Sakhalin), however, never achieved a separate identity within the coprosperity sphere, and acculturation and economic integration throughout the Japanese empire only intensified during the war.

Michael A. Schneider

Bibliography

Iriye, Akira. *Power and Culture: The Japanese-American War, 1941-1945.* Cambridge: Harvard University Press, 1981.

Lebra, Joyce C., ed. *Japan's Greater East Asia Co-Prosperity Sphere in World War II: Selected Readings and Documents.* Kuala Lumpur: Oxford University Press, 1975.

Greater East Asia Society (*Dai-Ajia Kyōkai*)

Ultranationalist society founded in March 1933 on the ideal of a Japanese-led league of Asian nations, the Dai-Ajia Kyōkai boasted many prominent members from all sectors of the Japanese elite, including Prince Konoe Fumimaro and General Matsui Iwane. The society shared ideas and members with the Tōa Renmei (East Asian League). Some of the pan-Asianist ideas of the Dai-Ajia Kyōkai were later incorporated into the Dai-Tōa Kyōeiken (Greater East Asia Coprosperity Sphere). The structure of nationalist thought in the Dai-Ajia Kyōkai illustrates the double structure of Japanese nationalism: Japanese nationalists were committed to rescuing Asia from Western colonialism, but their ideology placed Japan in the very imperialist position that Western powers had enjoyed in Asia.

Guy Yasko

Bibliography

Storry, Richard. *The Double Patriots: A Study of Japanese Nationalism.* Westport, CT: Greenwood Press, 1973.

Greater Japan Federated Youth Association (*Dainihon Rengō Seinendan*)

The Greater Japan Federated Youth Association was established in 1926 in an effort to bring preexisting local youth groups together into a centrally controlled organization to spread patriotic values. Youth organizations existed in villages and urban neighborhoods in the Tokugawa (1600–1868) and Meiji (1868–1912) eras, largely to perform local functions such as policing, road and irrigation-system repairs, and festival preparations. The need for home-front support during the Sino-Japanese (1894–95) and Russo-Japanese (1904–05) wars, the growing fear of civil unrest, and the spread among military leaders of the concept of spiritual mobilization for total war led Army, Home, and Education Ministry officials to establish a central youth-association headquarters in 1915 and the federated youth association in 1926. At the same time in the mid-1920s, the rise of progressive youth-association branches in some regions and the resistance among some civil bureaucrats, parliamentarians, and members of the press to army efforts to militarize the youth association led the army to establish its own youth-training centers that emphasized military drill, physical education, and even more intensive patriotic education. In the mid-1930s, the youth association and training centers enrolled 2.7 million members and 1 million members, respectively (although there was some overlap in membership). All such organizations were discontinued at the end of World War II.

Richard J. Smethurst

Bibliography

Smethurst, Richard J. *A Social Basis for Prewar Japanese Militarism.* Berkeley: University of California Press, 1974.

Greater Japan National Defense Women's Association (*Dainihon Kokubō Fujinkai*)

The National Defense Women's Association was founded in Osaka in 1932 to see off soldiers for the barracks or the front, to greet sick and wounded soldiers or the ashes of the war dead on their return home, to assemble and send "comfort bags" with daily necessities to the front, and to console the families of the war dead. The army's central authorities quickly recognized the value of the organization, brought it under central army control, and expanded it by establishing branches all over Japan as instruments to mobilize the home front during the war. At the local level, the army integrated the affairs of the women's group with those of the Imperial Military Reservists' Association. The image of the member, wearing over her white apron a white sash emblazoned with the words Greater Japan National Defense Women's Association, was a familiar one during the wartime years, and in early 1942 the defense women's organization had 15,699 branches and 9.25 million members. It was merged with the upper-class Patriotic Women's Society (Aikoku Fujinkai) and the Education Ministry's Confederated Women's Association in February 1942 to form the massive Greater Japan Women's Association (Dainihon Fujinkai).

Richard J. Smethurst

Bibliography
Smethurst, Richard J. *A Social Basis for Prewar Japanese Militarism.* Berkeley: University of California Press, 1974.

Greater Japan Women's Association (*Dainihon Fujinkai*)

Nationwide women's organization formed in February 1942 at government initiative from the merger of the Aikoku Fujinkai (Patriotic Women's Society), the Dainihon Kokubō Fujinkai (Greater Japan National Defense Women's Association), and the Dainihon Rengō Fujinkai (Federated Women's Association of Greater Japan). The tardiness of this incorporation into the war era's all-encompassing Imperial Rule Assistance Association (Taisei Yokusankai) was the result of friction among the three component organizations, which were sponsored by the Home, the Army, and the Education ministries, respectively. The regulations of the women's association stressed service to the emperor and society and familial ethics. In practice, this meant participation in neighborhood groups (*tonarigumi*), labor service outside the home, child care, and veneration of ancestors within. In fact, this organization, to which all women belonged, was one to which no woman belonged in reality. Deprived by the secrecy of troop movements of their duty to see soldiers off, women retreated from the streets into their traditional neighborhood organizations and homes to deal there with the shortage of goods. Nevertheless, the very existence of the organization bore witness to the government's eagerness to incorporate women into the war effort.

Sally A. Hastings

Bibliography
Havens, Thomas. *Valley of Darkness.* New York: Norton, 1978.

Greater Japan Youth Party (*Dainihon Seinentō*)

Right-wing organization, 1936–38. When Colonel Hashimoto Kingorō was removed from active military service for engagement in subversive activities following the abortive February 26, 1936, Incident, he formed his own Dainihon Seinentō, a small fascist organization that published a thrice-monthly magazine, *Taiyō Dainihon.* The party actively agitated for increased involvement of military officers in politics and for typical ultranationalist causes. Hashimoto disbanded the party in 1938, creating the equally rightist Dainihon Sekiseikai (Greater Japan Loyalty Society) in its place.

James L. Huffman

Bibliography
Storry, Richard. *The Double Patriots: A Study of Japanese Nationalism.* Westport, CT: Greenwood Press, 1973.

H

Hagi Rebellion

Hagi castletown in western Japan was the site of one of the lesser *shizoku* (former samurai) revolts against the new government of Meiji (1868–1912) Japan to protest abolition of their hereditary privileges. About 500 *shizoku* rose up in late October 1876, and were crushed by central-government forces by November 7; their leader, Maebara Issei, was pilloried and beheaded with six of his chief conspirators on December 3.

The rebellion lasted a mere 11 days. Its significance lay in its locale, Chōshū, one of two leading domains in the 1868 Meiji Restoration, and in the centralization resulting from its swift suppression. Modernizing Chōshū powerholders, led by Kido Takayoshi in Tokyo, overwhelmed discontented traditionalist *shizoku* left behind in Hagi. Kido entrapped Maebara with police spies, enticed a key conspirator to defect, and scattered the ragtag rebel army with modern military forces under Chōshū leadership, but he showed compassion for survivors. Chōshū forces never again challenged the central government.

Sidney DeVere Brown

Bibliography

Brown, Sidney DeVere. "Shizoku Dissidence: The Hagi Rebellion, 1876." *The Diary of Kido Takayoshi.* Vol. 3, *1874–1877.* Tokyo: University of Tokyo Press, 1986.

Hamaguchi Osachi (1870–1931)

Politician. Born to a poor official's family in Kōchi Prefecture on Shikoku, he graduated from Tokyo University in 1895 and spent some 20 years as a bureaucrat, working primarily in financial affairs. He joined the political party Rikken Dōshikai (Constitutional Society of Friends), and was elected to the Diet (legislature) in 1915. For the next decade and a half, he held numerous political and administrative positions, including home minister and finance minister, and in 1929 he was selected prime minister in the Minseitō (Constitutional Democratic Party) government. Known as "the lion" for his serious demeanor and principled behav-

Prime Minister Hamaguchi Osachi. Asahi Shimbun Photo.

ior, he consistently advocated fiscal retrenchment and international cooperation. He touched off a wave of protest by pushing through the 1930 London Naval Treaty, which kept Japan's naval tonnage at 60 percent of that of the U.S. and British navies. Though the emperor approved the treaty, Hamaguchi was shot by a zealous member of the Aikokusha (Society of Patriots) in November 1930. He continued as prime minister until April 1931, but he never recovered from the shooting and died that August.

James L. Huffman

Bibliography
Morton, William. *Tanaka Giichi, and Japan's China Policy.* New York: St. Martin's Press, 1980.

Hara Takashi (also Kei or Satoshi) (1856–1921)

The child of a samurai family in Iwate Prefecture, he spent his early adult years in a variety of fields: working at three different newspapers, including *Yubin Hōchi Shimbun* and *Osaka Mainichi Shimbun* (as editor in chief); serving as a diplomat in China, Korea, and France; and holding posts in the Agriculture and Commerce and Foreign ministries. His major life work commenced in 1900, when he assisted Itō Hirobumi in the creation of the Rikken Seiyūkai (Friends of Constitutional Government Party), one of Japan's early political parties. He gave the rest of his life to building the base of that party, gaining recognition as a key architect of party government. Three times (1906–08, 1911–12, and 1913–14), he served as home minister, using the patronage and appointment powers of that post to build Seiyūkai interests throughout Japan. Then, in 1918, following rice riots and the fall of the Terauchi Masatake cabinet, Hara was named prime minister, the first head of a majority party in the lower house of the Diet to attain that post. Widely known as the "commoner prime minister" because of his modest lifestyle and his refusal to accept a peerage, he opposed universal male suffrage but doubled the size of the electorate by lowering tax requirements. To the end, his main goal was the expansion of political party power. Hara was assassinated on November 4, 1921, by a deranged right-wing youth at the Tokyo train station.

James L. Huffman

Bibliography
Najita,Tetsuo. *Hara Kei in the Politics of Compromise.* Cambridge: Harvard University Press, 1967.

Hara Takashi. Asahi Shimbun Photo.

Harvest Festival (*Niinamesai*)

A festival dating to prehistoric times, its origins are probably to be found in the rhythms of rice agriculture, since a number of seasonal rites are linked to rice, especially transplanting in the spring and harvesting in the fall. Other popular harvest festivals also existed, but the *niinamesai* was especially linked to the emperor, who offered up rice for sacrifice as the season's first fruits and partook of this rice in a ritual act of sharing it with *kami* (divinities). In Japanese culture, rice has represented fertility and abundance. As the head of the country, the emperor was symbolically linked to rice, in effect assuming the responsibility for good crops and for thanking the *kami* after the harvest.

In ancient and medieval times, the festival may have assumed multiple significance as a rite of the new year and a cosmic renewal, as well as a celebration of the harvest. Since early in the Meiji period (1868–1912), the *niinamesai* has served as one of 13 official holidays. Unlike in the past, in modern times the emperor's celebration became public, and the populace was encouraged to worship the *kami* at this time. In this fashion, the Meiji government used the *niinamesai* to help merge Shinto ritual and local piety throughout the country and, simultaneously, to strengthen popular support for the emperor. This was one of the many ways in which the Meiji government helped develop a closer tie between ordinary citizens and the emperor as a means of promoting national unity. The *daijōsai* (Great New Food Festival), one of three Shinto ceremonies for a new emperor, is an elaboration of the *niinamesai*. The *daijōsai* is performed by the newly crowned emperor, who at the beginning of his reign offers up first fruits to the *kami*.

H. Byron Earhart

Bibliography

Ellwood, Robert S. *The Feast of Kingship: Accession Ceremonies in Ancient Japan.* Tokyo: Sophia University Press, 1973.
Hardacre, Helen. *Shinto and the State, 1868–1988.* Princeton, NJ: Princeton University Press, 1989.

Hashimoto Kingorō (1890–1957)

Army colonel and propagandist. Born in Okayama, he became one of the country's early agitators for more aggressive military policies. In 1927, he helped organize the Kinkikai (Society of the Imperial Flag), made up of army officers determined to overthrow the civilian government. In 1930, he and 25 others created the Sakurakai (Cherry Blossom Society), which aimed to replace party governments with military regimes. He also gave active assistance to the abortive March and October Incidents in 1931 and passive support to the February 26 Incident in 1936. Forced to retire from the military in August 1936, he formed the right-wing Dainihon Seinentō (Greater Japan Youth Party); when he was retired again for extremist activities after being recalled to fight in China in 1937, he gave himself to propaganda for ultranationalist issues. He was elected to the Diet (legislature) in 1944 from his Dainihon Sekiseikai (Greater Japan Loyalty Society), and in 1948 he was sentenced to life in prison as a Class A war criminal.

James L. Huffman

Bibliography

Storry, Richard. *The Double Patriots: A Study of Japanese Nationalism.* Westport, CT: Greenwood Press, 1973.

Hashimoto Sanai (1834–59)

Physician turned politician and exemplar of the type of enlightened young samurai who made the Meiji Restoration. Hailing from Fukui, a major Tokugawa collateral domain, Hashimoto studied from 1848 to 1852 at Ogata Kōan's school of Western-style medicine in Osaka. In 1857, he took part in a movement to win the shogunal succession for Hitotsubashi Yoshinobu, son of Mito domain's former daimyo, Tokugawa Nariaki. The movement sought the imperial court's support for Japan's first-ever commercial treaty, which U.S. Consul Townsend Harris was foisting on Japan. Hashimoto went to Kyoto to help get court approval, but the movement failed in 1858 when new shogunal regent Ii Naosuke signed the Harris treaty unilaterally in Edo.

Hashimoto strongly favored opening the country. In the broad view he took of the Mito idea of *sonnō jōi* (revere the emperor and expel the barbarians), Japan could best fend off Western imperialism by learning the secrets of the West and becoming an economic and technological power. He expressed this view much as his teacher Sakuma Shōzan did: Keep Japan's own ethics and values but adopt machines and techniques from the West.

During the Ansei Purge (1858–59) in which Ii banished more than 100 of his opponents from public life, Hashimoto was tried by a *bakufu* (military government) tribunal and executed. Regent Ii's harsh punishments and arbitrary rule only hastened the *bakufu*'s demise in the Meiji Restoration (1868) and made a martyr of Hashimoto Sanai.

George M. Wilson

Bibliography

Wilson, George M. "The Bakumatsu Intellectual in Action: Hashimoto Sanai in the Political Crisis of 1858." *Personality in Japanese History.* Ed. A.M. Craig and D.H. Shively. Berkeley: University of California Press, 1970, 234–63.

Hatoyama Haruko (1861–1938)

Educator and club woman. Born into a samurai family of Matsumoto Han, she studied the Chinese classics in a Matsumoto academy and English at the Takehashi Girls' School in Tokyo before entering the Tokyo Women's Normal School, from which she graduated in 1881. She joined the faculty there, only to resign the same year to marry Hatoyama Kazuo (1856–1911), who had studied law at Columbia and Yale Universities in the United States. She rejoined the Normal School faculty in 1884 and two years later cooperated with a dissident faculty group that founded the Kyōritsu Girls' Trade School, the first such school for girls in Japan. She was principal there from 1922 until her death. A founding member of the Aikoku Fujinkai (Patriotic Women's Society), she was also active in organizations to encourage women to study English, support relief work, maintain the home front in wartime, and advance women's education. Her son, Hatoyama Ichirō (1883–1959), was prime minister of Japan, 1954–56.

Sally A. Hastings

Bibliography

Sievers, Sharon L. *Flowers in Salt: The Beginnings of Feminist Consciousness in Modern Japan*. Stanford, CA: Stanford University Press, 1983.

Hatoyama Ichirō (1883–1959)

Prime minister (1954–56). A Tokyo native and son of the leading politician and educator Hatoyama Kazuo and pioneer women's leader Hatoyama Haruko, he spent his entire career in politics, serving 15 times in the Diet (legislature) after his first election in 1915. During the 1930s, Hatoyama was a strong nationalist, gaining a reputation for having liberal professors from Kyoto University dismissed during his tenure as education minister (1931–34).

He helped found the new Liberal Party immediately after the war and would have become prime minister in 1946 had he not been purged by Allied Occupation officials. His political rights were restored in 1951, and in 1954 he succeeded Yoshida Shigeru as prime minister. In office, he shifted Japan away from several Yoshida policies, moving toward a recentralization of police and education structures and unsuccessfully advocating revision of the 1947 Constitution to enable Japan to rebuild its military. He also restored diplomatic relations with the Soviet Union, led Japan's 1956 entry into the United Nations and brought the Japan Democratic Party and the Japan Liberal Party together in 1955 in the Liberal Democratic Party, which held power continuously for nearly four decades thereafter. He resigned from office in December 1956.

James L. Huffman

Bibliography

Nolte, Sharon. *Liberalism in Modern Japan*. Berkeley: University of California Press, 1987.

Hayashi Fusao (1903–75)

Writer who published *Kin'nō no seishin* (Loyalty to the Emperor, 1941) and *Dai-Tōa sensō kōteiron* (Affirmation of the Greater East Asia War, 1963–65). A native of Ōita Prefecture, Hayashi was active as a young writer in the Communist movement. He participated in strikes, wrote political essays, edited the Communist Party's journal, organized leftist writers' groups, and directed the Japan Proletarian Art League. The police imprisoned him three times between 1926 and 1934. Reemerging as a *tenkōsha* (convert), Hayashi now began ardently to support the government's war efforts and argued for *kin'nō* (loyalist) literature. *Seinen* (The Youth, 1932), a popular novel, treated Japan's rise as a modern country, expressing the author's admiration for the physical and spiritual beauty of Japan. After World War II, the Occupation forces purged him as an ultranationalist. Unlike other former leftists, he never reverted, and he continued to write nationalist fiction and essays, including his 1963–65 *Affirmation of the Greater Asian War*.

James R. Morita

Bibliography

Keene, Donald. *Dawn to the West: Japanese Literature in the Modern Era—Fiction*. New York: Henry Holt, 1984.

Heisei

Reign name of Akihito, who ascended to the Japanese throne on January 7, 1989. The name, taken from China's ancient Confucian classics, implies the maintenance of peace throughout the world and is the first chosen under a reign-name law adopted in 1979.

Heisei Emperor (Akihito). Asahi Shimbun Photo.

Supreme Truth Religion (Aum Shinrikyō) sect, which killed 12 and sent 5,000 to the hospital. Uncertainty over Japan's military relationship with the United States also raised questions during the middle of the 1990s, though most observers saw both the alliance and Japan's economic foundations as essentially solid.

James L. Huffman

Born in 1933, Akihito graduated from the Gakushūin High School in 1956 and captured the imagination of the country by marrying Shōda Michiko, the daughter of a wealthy commoner, three years later. He already was Japan's most widely traveled emperor when he took the throne, having visited nearly 40 countries on 22 state visits. Even before graduation from high school, he had represented his father at the coronation of Queen Elizabeth II of Great Britain. He is a marine biologist, a tennis player, a skilled amateur cellist, and the father of two sons and one daughter.

The early years of the Heisei reign were marked by considerable national difficulty, as the bubble of the 1980s burst, plunging Japan into an extended recession. The political world, too, experienced instability, with the Liberal Democratic Party temporarily losing its hold on power early in the 1990s and a succession of scandals bringing down government after government. The year 1995 was particularly difficult, with the Hanshin earthquake in western Honshu, which killed more than 5,000 people, and poison-gas attacks on Tokyo's subway system by the Aum

Hibiya Riots (*Hibiya Yakiuchi Jiken*)

Antigovernment riots, September 5–7, 1905. Heavy government censorship during the Russo-Japanese War (1904–05) led the populace to believe that Japan had won a more complete victory than it actually had. As a result, when the contents of the war-ending Treaty of Portsmouth became public, there was widespread discontent, particularly over the lack of an indemnity. Prime Minister Katsura Tarō succeeded in getting the Rikken Seiyūkai (Friends of Constitutional Government Party), the major opposition party, to accept the treaty, but the general public, encouraged by leading newspapers and some minor politicians, responded with an outcry of opposition. *Yorozu Chōhō*, Tokyo's largest newspaper, called for the country's flags to be flown at half-mast. And *Osaka Asahi Shimbun* declared, "We refuse to allow our inflamed flesh and blood to be turned into scorched earth."

On September 5, the day the treaty was signed, a rally was held at Hibiya Park by the hastily organized Kōwa Mondai Dōshi Rengōkai (Joint Council of Fellow Activists on the Peace Question) despite a government ban, with 30,000 gathering to hear speakers demand a rejection of the treaty and continuation of the war. Following a peaceful rally, 2,000 flag-carrying demonstrators headed toward the imperial palace, where they were confronted by police. A clash ensued, and violent episodes soon spread throughout the city, with 4,000 rioters assaulting Tokutomi Sohō's pro-government newspaper, *Kokumin Shimbun*, nearly 10,000 marching toward the official residence of the home minister, and thousands setting fires and storming buildings, often almost at random, across Tokyo. Riots and antitreaty demonstrations also occurred in other cities throughout Japan.

The government declared martial law on September 6, proscribing the publication of anything that might incite disturbances and restricting citizens' movement. Rains on September 7 also helped calm emotions. In all, 70 percent of

Tokyo's police boxes were burned, 350 buildings destroyed, 13 Christian churches demolished or burned—and more than 1,000 persons injured and 17 killed. As a foreshadowing of the 1930s, the riots gave chilling evidence of the difficulty of controlling patriotic passions once they had been stirred up by official policies and actions.

James L. Huffman

Newspaper accounts of 1918 riots at Hibiya and elsewhere. Courtesy Meiji Shimbun Zasshi Bunkō.

Bibliography

Okamoto, Shumpei. *The Japanese Oligarchy and the Russo-Japanese War*. New York: Columbia University Press, 1970.

Higashikuni Naruhiko (1887–1990)

Higashikuni was an uncle to Hirohito by marriage to Toshiko, the youngest daughter of the Meiji Emperor. As an army officer, Imperial Prince Higashikuni eventually rose to the rank of field marshal. He played a role, peripheral rather than leading, in many of the ultranationalist plots and intrigues of the 1920s and 1930s. These included the May 15 Incident (1932), when Prime Minister Inukai Tsuyoshi was assassinated and the February 26 Incident (1936), when 1,400 troops nearly brought down the government. On August 15, 1945, Higashikuni agreed to head a new government whose main task would be to turn control of Japan over to the Occupation forces under U.S. General Douglas MacArthur. After his resignation as caretaker prime minister in October 1945, he founded his own private religion (Higashikunikyō), but he did not play an important role in political affairs.

John H. Boyle

Bibliography

Shillony, Ben-Ami. *Revolt in Japan: The Young Officers and the February 26, 1936, Incident*. Princeton, NJ: Princeton University Press, 1973.

Hinomaru

National flag (*kokki*), consisting of a red disc on a white field, sometimes called the Rising Sun flag. The use of flags or banners by imperial and military families reportedly dates to the third century A.D., with the imperial family often using banners with the moon or the sun on them. The thirteenth-century Buddhist priest Nichiren is said to have given a *hinomaru* flag to the shogun when the Mongols invaded Japan in the late 1200s. Later military leaders, including Emperor Godaigo, Uesugi Kenshin, Date Masamune, Takeda Shingen, and Toyotomi Hideyoshi (during his Korean invasions in the 1590s) also used it, as did the early Tokugawa *bakufu* (1600–1868) on its ships. The first "national" use of the flag came in 1854, when the government ordered all Japanese ships to fly it to distinguish them from the newly arrived, flag-bearing Western ships. The Meiji government (1868–1912) made the *hinomaru* Japan's official flag in 1870. The Japanese military flag, which added 16 red rays to the disc, was widely used during World War II, then discontinued after Japan's defeat. The flying of the flag was forbidden for a time by the postwar Allied Occupation government, then resumed in 1949. As a patriotic symbol, the flag never has exerted the emotional impact in Japan that the Stars and Stripes does in the United States.

James L. Huffman

Bibliography

Aston, W.G. "The 'hi no maru,' or National Flag of Japan." *Transactions of the Asiatic Society of Japan*. Vol. 22, No. 1 (1894), 27–34.

Hiraga Purge (*Hiraga Shukugaku*)

Popular label for the events of early 1939 when the majority of the economics faculty at Tokyo University was removed by University President Hiraga Yuzuru (1873–1943). Hiraga, who had joined the faculty in 1931 after a career as a naval architect and then served as dean of engineering before his election to the presidency in 1938, sought to mobilize his campus behind the China War. He was particularly eager to end the factional strife among the economics faculty, and his first target was Professor Kawai Eijirō (1891–1944), under attack from the Right for defending his Marxist colleagues arrested in the Professors' Group Affair the previous year. The Home Ministry had banned four of Kawai's books, and the Justice Ministry placed him under investigation. Although a faculty committee of inquiry largely exonerated Kawai, President Hiraga nevertheless suspended him and then accepted the resignations of three economics professors who protested the action. Law Professor Rōyama Masamichi (1895–1980) was the only faculty member outside the Department of Economics to resign in protest.

This affair is often cited as signifying a government shift from targeting primarily Marxists to suppressing liberals, but two facts are noteworthy. First, Hiraga also suspended Professor Hijikata Seibi (1890–1975), the most outspoken nationalist within the department, and then accepted the resignations of nine other faculty and graduate assistants who were identified with the Right. Secondly, the purge was carried out in-house before Kawai was ever formally indicted—an unprecedented action at Tokyo University—and the faculty outside the Economics Department condoned the sacrifice of individuals to preserve some measure of institutional autonomy.

Byron K. Marshall

Bibliography
Marshall, Byron K. *Academic Autonomy and the Japanese Imperial University*. New York: Peter Lang, 1991.

Hirano Yoshitarō (1897–1980)
Communist scholar. The son of a wealthy entrepreneur and a graduate of (1921), then professor at, the University of Tokyo's Faculty of Law, Hirano studied abroad in the years 1927–1930 in Germany, the United States, and France, working most intensively with scholars of the Frankfurt School. He became a major figure in the "feudal" (*kōza*) school, which defended the Comintern orthodoxy of two-stage revolution during the debate in the late 1920s and 1930s on Japanese capitalism (*Nihon shihonshugi ronsō*). In the group's seven-volume *Nihon shihonshugi hattatsu shi kōza* (Symposium on the History of the Development of Japanese Capitalism), Hirano stressed the uniqueness of Japan's experience. During World War II, along with virtually all of his peers in the Communist movement, Hirano converted to the national cause and then turned his attention to the history of the Asiatic mode of production to the service of the war. Citing the scholarship of Marxist sociologist Karl Wittfogel and others, Hirano stressed the relative backwardness of China and Mongolia in a manner that supported Japanese expansionism. After the war, he promoted better Japanese-Chinese relations and critiqued the role of the state in capitalist society.

Germaine A. Hoston

Bibliography
Hoston, Germaine A. *Marxism and the Course of Development in Prewar Japan*. Princeton, NJ: Princeton University Press, 1986.

Hiranuma Kiichirō (1867–1952)
Nationalistic bureaucrat. Hiranuma controlled the Justice Ministry in the 1920s and 1930s, serving as justice minister, home minister, minister without portfolio (twice), and president of the Privy Council (1936–39). He was a prime minister from January to September 1939, and in 1924 he founded the Kokuhonsha (National Foundations Society) and several other nationalist organizations.

Born into an Okayama samurai family, Hiranuma graduated from the Tokyo Imperial University Law School in 1888. Alarmed at growing Western influence and lamenting the erosion of traditional Confucian ethics, he urged a return to Japan's unique cultural heritage embodied in the *kokutai* (national polity). Arguing that the moral familial nature of Japanese society made Japan different from all other nations, he called for Japan to purge itself of corrupting foreign ideas and reaffirm the moral relationship between the emperor and the people.

Hiranuma used this kind of nationalist rhetoric to attack political parties and party governments. Because of his antidemocratic position, he was widely regarded as a fascist during the 1930s. He denied these accusations, saying that fascism was a foreign totalitarian system unsuited for Japan. Convicted as a war criminal in 1948 by the International Military Tribunal for the Far East, he was sentenced to life imprisonment. He died at Keiō University Hospital in Tokyo, August 22, 1952.

Richard Yasko

Bibliography
Yasko, Richard. "Hiranuma Kiichirō and Conservative Politics in Pre-war Japan." Unpublished doctoral dissertation, University of Chicago, 1973.

Hiratsuka Raichō (1886–1971)
Feminist leader. Born in Tokyo, she was educated at Nihon Joshi Daigaku (Japan Women's University). Despite her youthful notoriety for an attempted suicide with male novelist Morita Shōhei, she emerged quickly as one of Japan's leading feminists. In 1911, she issued a famous feminist manifesto— "In the beginning, woman was the Sun"—in the journal *Seitō* (Bluestocking), which she had founded that year with other literary feminists.

"Motherhood protection" (*bosei hogo*) was Hiratsuka's major feminist cause. She debated the issue with poet Yosano Akiko and socialist feminist Yamakawa Kikue in articles in important journals between 1915 and 1919.

Hiratsuka, who had two children with painter Okumura Hiroshi, argued that the state owed support to mothers because their maternality benefited all of society. In 1919, she joined Ichikawa Fusae and Oku Mumeo in founding the Shin Fujin Kyōkai (New Women's Association) (NWA), which worked to abolish restrictions on women's participation in politics and to permit women to dissolve marriages or engagements with syphilitic men. The NWA disbanded in 1922 due to personal and philosophical differences among the founders.

Hiratsuka disagreed with Ichikawa's single-minded focus on suffrage and on equality with men, emphasizing instead women's special needs as mothers. For that reason, she played only a minor role in the suffrage activities of the 1920s. In the 1930s, however, she rejoined Ichikawa in the renewed "motherhood protection" movement. She actively supported the Bosei Hogo Renmei (Motherhood Protection League) founded in 1934 to prevent mother-child suicides by desperately poor mothers, especially widows and wives of Japanese soldiers in China. The league succeeded in having the Law for the Protection of Mothers and Children passed in 1937; even conservative Diet (legislature) members supported it because it did not undermine husbands' superiority in the family.

After World War II, Hiratsuka reemerged as a leader in the peace and women's movements. Mothers continued to be important for her; at the 1955 International Congress of Mothers, she called on "Mothers of the world [to] join hands" for peace. In 1962, she helped found the Communist-led Shin Nihon Fujin no Kai (New Japan Women's Association). She was president of the Nihon Fujin Dantai Rengōkai (Federation of Japanese Women's Organizations) in the late 1960s and served as vice president of the Kokusai Minshū Fujin Rengōkai (International Women's Democratic League).

Barbara Molony

Bibliography

Sievers, Sharon. *Flowers in Salt: The Beginnings of Feminist Consciousness in Modern Japan*. Stanford, CA: Stanford University Press, 1983.

Hirohito

See SHŌWA ERA (1926–89)

Hirota Kōki (1878–1948)

Politician, diplomat, foreign minister, and prime minister. A native of Fukuoka Prefecture, he was a friend of Tōyama Mitsuru and a member of the Gen'yōsha (Black Sea Society). He entered the Japanese diplomatic corps and was posted to brief terms in China, Great Britain, and the United States during 1929 and 1930, after which he became ambassador to the Soviet Union. These experiences led to his appointment as minister of foreign affairs in the cabinets of Admiral Saitō Makoto (1933–34) and Okada Keisuke (1934–36). Anti-Communist views and policies were a hallmark of his tenure in these positions, and he sought to bring China into an alliance with Japan against the advance of Communism. Following his appointment as prime minister in 1936, he greatly strengthened the military by large increases in its budgets, fostering the development of military industries and appointing only active officers as army and navy ministers in his cabinet. As prime minister, he is noted for signing the 1936 Anticomintern Pact with Germany and Italy. He later became foreign minister in the cabinet of Konoe Fumimaro (1937–39) and, in this post, tacitly approved the beginning of full-scale war in China following the Marco Polo Bridge Incident in 1937. Late in World War II, he sought Soviet intervention in an attempt to avoid unconditional Japanese surrender but failed. He was executed as a Class A war criminal by the International Military Tribunal for the Far East on December 23, 1948.

J. Wayne Sabey

Bibliography

Shiroyama, Saburō. *War Criminal*. New York: Kodansha International, 1977.

Holiness Band Oppression
(*Hōrinesu Bando Dan'atsu*)

The World War II Japanese government systematically oppressed and persecuted Holiness churches, which were forced, with all other Protestant churches, into a united Protestant church, the Nippon Kirisuto Kyōdan (United Church of Christ in Japan, Kyōdan hereafter) in June 1941, under the 1939 Religious Organizations Law. The former Holiness churches became Blocs 6 and 9 of the Kyōdan, which organized the former 34 denominations into 11 divisions along denominational lines.

Although the Kyōdan was officially registered and approved as a religious organization by the Ministry of Education in November 1941, from June 1942 authorities arrested 134 Holiness pastors for violating the Peace Preservation Law of 1925. This law, implemented in 1925 to suppress socialism and the Korean independence movement, was revised in 1941 to suppress Communists, intellectuals, and religious groups. Of those pastors arrested, 75 were indicted and sentenced under Article 7 of the law, which authorized "imprisonment of members, officials, and other leaders of associations organized for the purpose of disseminating statements that reject the national structure (*kokutai*) or desecrate the sanctity of Shintō shrines and of the Imperial Household." Seven pastors died while serving prison sentences.

The Ministry of Education revoked its approval of the Kyōdan, and the Ministry of Home Affairs ordered the dissolution of the 273 Holiness churches on April 7, 1943, using Article 8 of the same law, which forbade religious societies. Fearing that oppression would spread to all Protestant churches, Kyōdan leaders accepted the directive and removed Holiness churches and pastors from Kyōdan membership.

The oppression of Holiness churches warned all Christian churches that the government program to unify the country under the emperor system (*tennōsei*) would not tolerate dissent or opposition. Holiness churches and pastors became the target of persecution as a small minority within the Christian community. Interrogation of Holiness pastors usually focused on a basic tenet of faith, the second coming of Christ, which appeared to challenge the emperor's position as god and absolute leader of the nation. Questions frequently asked included: (1) The Bible says that all human beings are sinners. What about the emperor? (2) Sinners are saved by Christ. Does this include the emperor? (3) Christianity believes in only one God. Is the emperor not a living god, then? (4) The emperor sleeps and gets hungry. Is he, too, a human being? (5) When Christ comes again, will the emperor be judged? Will he become a follower of Christ?

Carolyn Bowen Francis

Bibliography

Murakami, Shigeyoshi, and Kashiwai Hajime. "The Footprints of the Holiness Band." *Japan Christian Quarterly* (Summer 1984), 147–52.

Home Ministry (*Naimushō*)

The abolition of the Naimushō (Home Ministry) in 1947 marked the end of an organization that had significantly contributed to the proliferation of nationalism in prewar Japan. The Home Ministry was just one government institution among several implicated by the Occupation authorities after World War II in their efforts to purge Japan of the force of ultranationalism. The military establishment, Education Ministry, and other government ministries were similarly targeted for either elimination or major reform, due to their perceived role in fostering a xenophobic form of nationalism among the Japanese people. In addition, various nongovernmental groups also were identified as having contributed to the rise of Japanese nationalism: the prewar financial clique (*zaibatsu*), members of the intellectual community, local village elites, and elements of the agricultural community. However, notwithstanding the importance of these many contributing agents, bureaucratic agencies played a unique role in the development of Japanese nationalism.

Hierarchical authority long has been taken seriously in Japan, with officials enjoying great respect and deference. This was particularly true of those who served in the prewar bureaucracy, designed by a group of Meiji oligarchs intent on creating a cohesive national system strong enough to enable Japan to gain respect and independence internationally. In anticipation of the new Diet (legislature) to be established by the Meiji Constitution of 1889, men such as Yamagata Aritomo (1838–1922) sought to create a neutral body of professional administrators, loyal to the emperor and above the partisan activities of political parties. The authority of these bureaucrats was buttressed by their designation as *tennō no kanri* (officials of the emperor), representing the imperial will and responsible to the emperor alone.

The relationship between the emperor and the national bureaucracy was one of reciprocal benefit. While bureaucrats acquired legitimate authority from their association with the imperial institution, they, in turn, helped transform the emperor into a figure of national reverence, the symbol of Japan's imperial ambitions and the focal point for the rise of Japanese nationalism. The Home Ministry played a major role in erecting the ideological framework of this symbiotic system—the *tennōsei* (emperor system), which represented the core of prewar Japanese nationalist ideology.

The Home Ministry made its most effective contribution to Japanese nationalism through its efforts to reorganize rural Japan and integrate village society into a national administrative hierarchy. Once integrated into this hierarchy, rural Japan could be much more effectively mobilized to achieve national goals, and the Home Ministry could use its new channels of access to disseminate *tennōsei* ideology at the grass-roots level.

The integration process began with the Town and Village Codes of 1888, which were designed to shift the loyalties of rural society from the traditional hamlet community to a newly established administrative hierarchy of towns and villages. In this fashion, the Home Ministry took the first crucial steps in creating channels of influence and control, to better mobilize the resources of rural society for the larger national effort at self-strengthening and international competition.

In the early twentieth century, Japan's rapid economic development and deepening involvement in the international arena created a new set of concerns and an increased sense of urgency within bureaucratic circles, leading to even greater Home Ministry efforts to strengthen *tennōsei* ideology. Among intellectuals and government officials there appeared a growing awareness that Japan was experiencing the first symptoms of *shakai mondai* (social problems), and, consequently, many prescriptions were recommended to treat this "disease." Within the Home Ministry, the primary target of a number of these preventive measures was rural society.

The causes identified for *shakai mondai* were broad. Industrialization was regarded as disrupting the natural order of society, leading to a widening generational rift, mounting class conflict, rural-versus-urban strife, and a host of other problems, including the erosion of Japan's traditional values system. To make matters worse, many officials feared that socialist ideology, which had gained support among intellectuals, was beginning to infect the working class. The belief that Japan faced a major domestic crisis was reinforced following the Russo-Japanese War (1904–05), when the Hibiya riots of September 1905 brought widespread violence to the streets of Tokyo, in opposition to the peace treaty (Portsmouth Treaty) that Japanese officials had negotiated with the Russians.

The Russo-Japanese War represented a turning point at which the Home Ministry began a more concerted effort to mobilize the hearts and minds of the Japanese people behind the symbols of *tennōsei* ideology. The ministry assumed a leading role in the preparation and dissemination of the *boshin shōsho* (Imperial Rescript on Diligence and Frugality) of 1908. This imperial rescript represented the bureaucracy's single best effort to establish the foundations of *tennōsei* ideology, linking the emperor and his subjects into a natural moral order, stretching in uninterrupted continuity from the mythical past into Japan's glorious future. The *boshin shōsho* was an instrument of mobilization, which not only established the ideological parameters of Japanese nationalism but also served to exhort Japanese citizens to ever greater sacrifices for emperor and nation.

The rescript was more than mere rhetoric: It was the cornerstone of the Home Ministry's efforts to achieve practical organizational benefits through the mobilization of Japan's spiritual and physical resources. At the local level, various patriotic self-help and agricultural-improvement programs were quickly created and integrated into a national hierarchy under central-government direction. The Local Improvements Movement, formally inaugurated by the Home Ministry in 1909, established a broad array of village associations designed to realize nationalist ideals and implement the practical objectives of the *boshin shōsho*. Many of these associations were organized from the ground up by government officials who sought such practical objectives as the encouragement of savings, local self-reliance, and educational reforms. Other organizations, such as the *hōtoku* (rural self-help societies), also were used by the Home Ministry to disseminate orthodox nationalist ideology. Despite the great diversity of these programs, they were all intended to help realize the overriding goal of domestic mobilization for Japan's more effective participation at the international level.

One other scheme designed to stimulate nationalist loyalties and integrate those allegiances into a national administrative hierarchy was the shrine-merger program, initiated by the Home Ministry in 1906 and administered by the Shrine Bureau. Following the Russo-Japanese War, the Shrine Bureau actively pursued a policy of consolidating local shrines in conformity with the new national hierarchy of administrative towns and villages.

H

The integration of local shrines corresponded to the government's increasing public sponsorship of Japan's Shinto traditions. In this period, Shinto was deliberately promoted as Japan's national religion, in an attempt to unify the people in reverence for the emperor. Local Shinto shrines became transformed into centers for the practice of State Shinto rites, which served as the outward manifestation of Japan's eternal *kokutai* (national polity). These shrines were natural settings for the dissemination of nationalist symbols associated with the emperor and with *tennōsei* ideology. The Home Ministry played a leading role in reinforcing the connection among local worship, State Shinto, and the people's responsibility for maintaining Japan's sacred *kokutai*.

The Home Ministry also played a major role in enforcing numerous laws and ordinances designed to ensure loyalty and inspire nationalism. From the 1870s onward, it engaged in vigorous censorship of the press, proscribing materials that besmirched the imperial family, incited social disorder, divulged military secrets, or corrupted public morals. Ministry officers supervised elections and enforced laws aimed at curtailing political dissent, and, after 1925, they used the Peace Preservation Law to suppress socialist and other left-wing thought, engaging in numerous, often brutal roundups of "dangerous elements." The ministry's Thought Police (*tokkō*) became notorious in the 1920s and 1930s for strong-arm tactics and rigid suppression of unorthodox ideas.

It would be erroneous to suggest that the Home Ministry and other bureaucratic agencies were solely responsible for the proliferation of *tennōsei* ideology in prewar Japan. The nationalist ideology was the product of many sources, including grass-roots traditions, Western ideas, military propaganda, and the general international environment in which modern Japan was forged. It is undeniable, however, that central ministries such as the Naimushō played an active—often pivotal—role in stimulating the nationalism that shaped much of Japan's early-twentieth-century destiny.

Crayne Horton

Bibliography

Gluck, Carol. *Japan's Modern Myths: Ideology in the Late Meiji Period*. Princeton, NJ: Princeton University Press, 1985.

Pyle, Kenneth B. "Advantages of Followership: German Economics and Japanese Bureaucrats, 1890–1925." *Journal of Japanese Studies*. Vol. 1, No. 1 (Autumn 1974), 127–64.

———. "The Technology of Japanese Nationalism: The Local Improvement Movement, 1900–1918." *Journal of Asian Studies*. Vol. 3, No. 1 (November 1973), 51–65.

Hozumi Yatsuka (1860–1912)

Born to an Ehime Prefecture family long involved in the scholarship of national learning (*kokugaku*), Hozumi, from undergraduate days, was an active polemicist in support of the authoritarian constitution makers, especially in the debates of 1882. He returned in 1888 from nearly five years of study in Germany to begin a teaching career in constitutional law at Tokyo Imperial University just as the Meiji Constitution went into effect in 1889. His influential role in the academy and with the higher bureaucracy was cut short by death at the beginning of the Taishō era (1912–26).

The importance of Hozumi lay in the answers he gave to problems confronting conservatives wanting to preserve traditional values in a modernizing Japan. He offered a dogmatic and traditional move away from the state-centered theory then in fashion among those who studied in Germany, advocating in its place the emperor-centered familial-state ideas of conservative nationalism. The Hozumi school of constitutional theory did not prevail after 1910 at the university nor in elite quarters, but it continued in high favor elsewhere, most significantly among public-school authorities, who shaped the education received by most Japanese young people.

Frank O. Miller

Bibliography

Minear, Richard H. *Japanese Tradition and Western Law: Emperor, State and Law in the Thought of Hozumi Yatsuka*. Cambridge: Harvard University Press, 1970.

I

Ichikawa Fusae (1893–1981)

Born to an Aichi Prefecture farm family, feminist politician Ichikawa Fusae gave her early years to schoolteaching, journalism, and labor reform. In 1919, she took up her lifework, the struggle for women's political rights, when she joined Oku Mumeo and Hiratsuka Raichō in founding the Shin Fujin Kyōkai (New Women's Association). Ideological and personal differences as well as Ichikawa's departure for the United States, where she was inspired by her association with feminist Alice Paul, led to that group's dissolution in 1922.

Sharing Paul's focus on women's political rights, Ichikawa helped establish the Fusen Kakutoku Dōmei (Women's Suffrage League) in 1924. The league lobbied Diet (legislature) politicians and aided in the election campaigns of supporters of women's rights. Although many suffragists joined proletarian feminists in supporting social reform, and the two sides joined in All-Japan Women's Suffrage Conventions in the 1930s, the suffragists were often viewed as bourgeois supporters of established political parties. For Ichikawa, women's involvement in all forms of political activities took precedence over considerations of political alliances.

Ichikawa's hopes for women's suffrage were dashed after the 1931 Manchurian Incident, when Japan began its takeover of northeast China. She changed her tactics, making suffrage a tool for other social issues rather than an end in itself: In 1931, she wrote that suffrage would enhance prospects for peace; in 1934, she advocated suffrage as a way of promoting the welfare of mothers and children; and, in 1935, she formally cooperated with the government, for the first time, in the Women's Coalition to Purify Elections (Senkyo Shukusei Fujin Renmei.) Although distressed by the rise of militarism, she

began to call on her sisters to cooperate with Japan's war efforts in the late 1930s. The Women's Suffrage League was disbanded in 1940, and, in 1942, all women's organizations were merged into the Dainihon Fujinkai (Greater Japan Women's Association), of which Ichikawa was a director. She was also appointed to the government-sponsored Dainihon Genron Hōkokukai (Greater Japan Patriotic Speech Association) in 1942. Although Ichikawa had opposed escalation of Japan's war in Asia before 1938, she cooperated with Japan's wartime government insofar as it gave political opportunities and responsibilities to women.

Following her three-year purge (1947–50) during the American Occupation (1945–52), Ichikawa reentered politics, founding the League of Women Voters and serving in the upper house of the Diet from 1953 to 1971 and again from 1974 until her death. She chose to remain an independent without party affiliation and was the leader of the 1970s movement against political corruption among elected officials and business interests. She viewed her political independence and her anticorruption stance as ways of serving the whole Japanese nation.

Barbara Molony

Bibliography

Vavich, Dee Ann. "The Japanese Woman's Movement: Ichikawa Fusae—A Pioneer in Women's Suffrage." *Monumenta Nipponica.* Vol. 22, No. 3–4 (1967), 402–36.

Ideological Recanting (*Tenkō*)

The popular usage derives from a highly publicized 1933 defection from the Japanese Communist Party (JCP) by two imprisoned party leaders, Sano Manabu (1892–1953) and Nabeyama Sadachika (1901–79).

Although in colonial societies the Communist movement frequently encompasses nationalistic desires for independence, in prewar Japan the party's target was an independent state that had already developed a powerful ideology of emperor-centered nationalism. The JCP thus opposed the emperor system, but with considerable uneasiness.

The JCP was the target of the 1925 Peace Preservation Law (PPL), which outlawed organizational activity that aimed to alter either the capitalist economic system or the *kokutai* (national polity). Following mass arrests of several thousand people on March 15, 1929, and April 16, 1929, the government tracked down the JCP's underground leadership. Sano and Nabeyama had figured prominently in the mass trial of the party leadership in 1931–32, and both had received life sentences.

The impetus for their *tenkō* was a combination of their growing sense of national loyalty following the 1931 Manchurian Incident, which marked the beginning of Japanese aggression on the Asian mainland, and their frustration with the erratic political direction the JCP was receiving from the Communist leadership in Moscow. Their *tenkō* statement acknowledged the special position of the emperor and the *kokutai* in Japan. Although their *tenkō* was spontaneous, prison authorities encouraged the development of their joint statement, circulated the document widely, and pressured others to reject the party. Many quickly agreed, often for reasons unrelated to the arguments of Sano and Nabeyama.

Emboldened by their initial success, police and prison authorities quickly turned *tenkō* into an organized campaign. All persons arrested for violating the Peace Preservation Law were subjected to heavy pressure to make a *tenkō*, degrees of *tenkō* were classified, and bureaucratic procedures were developed to manage *tenkōsha* (recanters).

By 1943, of 2,440 persons prosecuted under the Peace Preservation Law, 51.1 percent had made a complete *tenkō*, 47.4 percent had made a partial *tenkō*, and only 1.5 percent had completely resisted (*hitenkō*). Although fewer than 3,000 persons were ever convicted of thought crimes under the Peace Preservation Law, from 1936 to 1938 more than 13,000 persons were subjected to special probation and rehabilitation services for *tenkōsha*. Most had made a *tenkō* before trial, sometimes after torture by the security police (*tokkō*).

Yet, many were never tortured, and *tenkō* generally involved genuine internal change. The inability to reconcile JCP doctrine with feelings of nationalism led some to *tenkō*, but for others the link to nationalism was indirect. The party had attracted many creative intellectuals who in prison discovered that they were unwilling to die for the party. Some found new identity in traditional Japanese religion and culture and, after *tenkō*, became proponents of cultural nationalism. The majority of *tenkōsha* were probably motivated by family pressures, but in the nationalism of the 1930s a *tenkō* based on family love and duty was simultaneously a patriotic act and a form of devotion to the emperor.

To the state authorities, the renunciation of ideology through *tenkō* was a logical resolution for crimes of thought. *Tenkō* was consistent with a nationalist ideology that considered every Japanese to be linked by indissoluble bonds to the imperial family and thus ultimately redeemable. Within the Left, *tenkō* was regarded as a betrayal of the party, one's comrades, and one's own ideals. *Tenkōsha* were despised as weaklings.

By the late 1930s, the Communist movement had been destroyed, but, in the increasingly nationalistic political atmosphere, the demands for ideological conformity escalated. A spontaneous *tenkō* expressing one's commitment to the emperor and the nation became a loyalty oath through which individuals and organizations could allay suspicion.

After World War II ended in 1945, a dozen *hitenkōsha* were released from Japanese prisons by the Allied Occupation to become the nucleus of the postwar Japan Communist Party. The reestablished JCP initially enjoyed considerable public respect because its leaders had clear records of having opposed Japanese nationalism, had been imprisoned for their beliefs, and had resisted all pressure to make a *tenkō*. The party was soon confronted with former members who claimed to have made a *tenkō* under duress or to have made a sham (*gisō*) *tenkō* to get out of prison. The party accepted them back but continued to condemn *tenkō* as a betrayal and emphasized the element of state coercion in *tenkō*.

The three elements of (1) renunciation of party affiliation, (2) state pressure to betray ideological commitment, and (3) sudden change in belief that characterized *tenkō* from 1933 to 1945 have led in postwar Japan to three different applications of the term *tenkō*. One postwar usage of *tenkō* applies to the act of leaving a Marxist-based political organization or of abandoning Marxism as a political theory. A second usage, often found in literary biography and intellectual history, labels any sudden, spontaneous shift in intellectual perspective a *tenkō*, regardless of the content. The third usage, found in the New Left since the 1960s, associates *tenkō* with capitulation to pressure from the authorities after an arrest. None of the three usages has a direct association with postwar nationalism, but the term *tenkō* still resonates with its original historical associations.

Patricia G. Steinhoff

Bibliography
Hoston, G. "Emperor, Nation, and the Transformation of Marxism to National Socialism in Prewar Japan: The Case of Sano Manabu." *Studies in Comparative Communism.* Vol. 18, No. 1 (1985), 25–47.
Mitchell, R. *Thought Control in Prewar Japan.* Ithaca, NY: Cornell University Press, 1976.
Steinhoff, P. *Tenkō: Ideology and Societal Integration in Prewar Japan.* New York: Garland, 1991.

Ienaga Saburō (1913–)

Historian and critic of Japanese imperialism. A professor at Tokyo University of Education from 1949 to 1977, Ienaga devoted his career to the study of Japanese thought and to urging Japan to take responsibility for its aggression in World War II. During the 1960s and 1970s, he gained wide attention for opposing the country's textbook-approval system, under which the Ministry of Education controls the content of all public-school texts.

In 1965 and 1967, Ienaga brought suits against the Education Ministry for its refusal to approve new editions of his high-school text, *Shin nihonshi* (A New History of Japan), unless he made hundreds of revisions. He claimed that the system, under which school texts could not be published without ministry approval, violated constitutional guarantees of freedom of expression and created unacceptable control of the educational process. Although the Tokyo District Court ruled in his favor in 1970, the decision was reversed by the

Ienaga Saburō. Asahi Shimbun Photo.

Supreme Court, and even the lower courts held against Ienaga in subsequent cases. His persistent struggle was effective in raising public consciousness about prewar militarism and the textbook-approval system. Although most of his 50 books were academic and uncontroversial, his reputation as a fighter against ultranationalism came from polemical antiwar works such as *Taiheiyō sensō,* published in an English translation as *The Pacific War.* His antiwar campaign continued into the late 1990s.

James L. Huffman

Bibliography
Ienaga, Saburō. *The Pacific War.* New York: Pantheon, 1968.

Ii Naosuke (1815–1860)

Powerful daimyo of Hikone (now Shiga Prefecture) and Tokugawa government regent (*tairō*) from 1858 to 1860, Ii was realistic in foreign policy, finding compromise necessary with the West. He was responsible for signing Japan's first commercial treaty (1858, with the United States), against the wishes of the imperial court. His decision to have Tokugawa Yoshitomi of Kii (shogunal name Iemochi) succeed shogun Tokugawa Iesada in 1858 caused hostility among rival factions. That same year, Ii began the Ansei Purge, punishing daimyo, officials, and samurai in the other factions for undermining the power of the *bakufu* (military government). He believed that increased central authority was essential to Japan's survival. Ii was assassinated outside the Sakurada Gate of Edo Castle on March 24, 1860, by samurai, all but one from the rival domain of Mito, in retaliation for the Ansei Purge (1858–59).

Ann M. Harrington

Bibliography

Beasley, W.G. *The Meiji Restoration*. Stanford, CA: Stanford University Press, 1972.

Ikeda Hayato (1899–1965)

Prime minister (1960–64). A native of Hiroshima Prefecture and a 1925 graduate of Kyoto University, he was a middle-level bureaucrat before World War II. He became finance minister under Yoshida Shigeru in 1949 and spent much of the 1950s developing a strong political base, serving once more as finance minister (1956–57) and twice as minister of international trade and industry (1952, 1959–60). Ikeda's tenure as prime minister, which began with the collapse of the Kishi Nobusuke government in 1960, was characterized by a widely-proclaimed, successful policy aimed at doubling Japan's gross national product within a decade. Internationally, Ikeda adopted a low profile even while pushing for the expansion of Japanese trade; at home, he worked on behalf of big business. His crowning moment came in 1964, when Japan's success in hosting the Summer Olympics was perceived widely as a symbol of the country's reentry into the community of nations. Forced to resign for health reasons shortly after the Olympics, he died of cancer the following year.

James L. Huffman

Bibliography

Johnson, Chalmers. *MITI and the Japanese Miracle*. Stanford, CA: Stanford University Press, 1982.

Imperial Household Ministry (*Kunaishō*)

The Kunaishō was established in 1869, immediately after the Meiji Restoration, in 1869, and restructured in 1886 in line with the overall revision of the administrative system. It remained in existence until the end of World War II in 1945, when it was replaced by the Imperial Household Agency. The Kunaishō was independent of the government, its chief functions being to maintain the autonomy of the imperial court, shield it from the turbulent political arena, and preserve the image of the emperor as a sacred being and a transcendent political authority. During the Meiji years (1868–1912), when the oligarchs maintained tight political control, they made the political decisions and presented their policies to the public as the imperial will.

After most of the Meiji oligarchs passed away in the 1910s and 1920s, there was a period of uncertainty as bureaucratic influence increased and diverse political forces sought to gain the upper hand politically. But the last of the oligarchs (*genrō*), Prince Saionji Kinmochi (1849–1940), became the chief watchdog of the imperial court, and the court officials in general followed his direction. In the 1920s, the influence of the constitutional monarchists, with the backing of Saionji, came to dominate the key imperial-court positions.

There were four key officials in the Kunaishō: the minister of imperial household affairs, the lord keeper of the privy seal, the grand chamberlain, and the chief aide-de-camp to the emperor.

The most important office in terms of the emperor's links to the political world, and the most prestigious, was that of the privy seal, a largely ceremonial post with ancient roots that became important early in the twentieth century because of the influential men who held it. Until the end of the Meiji era in 1912, the privy seal did not get deeply involved in political affairs: There was no conflict among the wielders of political power, the *genrō*, and the imperial court because the court officials were all part of the power elite. As the Meiji oligarchs gradually faded away from the political scene, diverse groups sought to influence the court in their favor. Hence, the position of the privy seal tended to become highly sensitive politically. Makino

Nobuaki became privy seal in 1925 and remained in office until 1935. He was a constitutional monarchist whose views tended to conflict with the ascending military and civilian radicals who began to condemn what they called the "evil advisers" to the emperor. An attempt was made on Makino's life, and Admiral Saitō Makoto, who succeeded Makino as privy seal, was assassinated in the military coup attempt of February 26, 1936.

The duties of the minister of imperial household affairs were not in the political realm. His chief function was to keep the political elements out of the court. How vigorous a role the minister played depended on the holder of that position.

The grand chamberlain did not equal the above two officials in official standing, but, because his duties were ill-defined, he could play a significant role, particularly because he could control access to the emperor. Early in the 1930s, for example, Grand Chamberlain Suzuki Kantarō was accused of blocking Admiral Katō Kanji, who opposed the London Naval Treaty, from having an audience with the emperor to present his views. This, in part, led to Suzuki being attacked during the 1936 coup attempt.

The chief aide-de-camp was the military's representative at the court. Again, when the Meiji oligarchs were in control and there were no serious conflicts between the civil and military authorities, the chief aide-de-camp and the other court officials worked in harmony. But as the divisions between the more militant military leaders and the civilian leaders grew, the function of the chief aide-de-camp as an arbitrator grew in importance.

The place of the Kunaishō in the ascendancy of nationalism in modern Japan depended on the *jisei* (trend of the times)— the internal and external political circumstances and developments in any given period. The court officials endeavored to prevent the court from getting embroiled in factional political strifes, but this became an increasingly difficult task during the stormy years of the 1930s and 1940s. The court certainly was not a motive force that pushed the country into an increasingly nationalistic direction, but, as the constitutional monarchists at the court came to be replaced by the more traditionalist elements who sought to keep it in tune with the trend of the times, the court went along with the policies favored by the militant nationalists. The official who played the crucial role in this area in those years was Kido Kōichi, who became privy seal in 1940.

Mikiso Hane

Bibliography

Hane, Mikiso, trans. *Emperor Hirohito and His Chief Aide-de-Camp: The Honjo Diary, 1933–36*. Tokyo: University of Tokyo Press, 1982.

Titus, David Anson. *Palace and Politics in Prewar Japan*. New York: Columbia University Press, 1974.

Imperial Military Reservist Association (*Teikoku Zaigō Gunjinkai*)

Organization of former servicemen, founded on November 3, 1910. The primary movers in the formation of the association, Field Marshal Yamagata Aritomo and his protégés, Army Minister General Terauchi Masatake and Colonel (later General) Tanaka Giichi, saw it as a means of mobilizing reservists in time of war and, more important, of achieving Yamagata's ideal that "all citizens are soldiers" by spreading patriotic military values to the public.

The Reservist Association quickly established branches and subbranches in every city, town, village, and hamlet in Japan; it also organized urban branches in factories, department stores, and other places of employment, as well as in neighborhoods. Under Tanaka's continuing leadership, the Reservist Association broadened its membership to include men who had passed the conscription physical examination but had not served on active duty. By 1920, more than half of the association's members had never served in the army or the navy. Because, as late as the outbreak of war with China in 1937, only 15–20 percent of those old enough to be in the military forces actually served, the policy of recruiting reservists who were not former servicemen greatly expanded the army's and navy's ability to spread martial values in the countryside and the factory.

The Reservist Association, which had its highest-level regional commander in the army's regimental district headquarters, was especially successful in rural areas, because it used long-standing village custom and organization as a basis for spreading military and patriotic values. Local branches served as age-group organizations for 20–40-year-old men, helping families of young villagers on active duty by carrying out duties such as firefighting, public works, and assistance at rice-transplanting and harvest times; they also made up a paramilitary organization, leading members of youth associations, youth training centers, and defense women's groups in military drill and sponsoring patriotic lectures and rallies. In both cases, reservists used their authority as hardworking members of the rural community to instill military-centered partiotism. Factory branches often functioned similarly, even serving as the pro-management backbone of their workplace; in 1917 in Muroran and again in 1920 in Yawata, for example, reservists aided their companies in breaking strikes.

In the 1930s, the 3-million-member Reservist Association was active as Japan's largest nationalistic political-pressure organization. It organized mass rallies, sent petitions, and made small-group visitations to officials to support the army during the Manchurian Incident in 1931–32, to encourage the government to leave the League of Nations in 1933, and to arouse opposition in 1934–35 to Minobe Tatsukichi and his theory that the emperor is an organ of the state. Officials of the Allied Occupation (1945–52) abolished the organization and purged all wartime reservist-branch chiefs as militarists after World War II.

Richard J. Smethurst

Bibliography

Smethurst, Richard J. *A Social Basis for Prewar Japanese Militarism.* Berkeley: University of California Press, 1974.

Imperial Rescript on Education
(*Kyōiku ni Kansuru Chokugo*)

A rescript issued in the name of the Meiji Emperor on October 30, 1890, defining the guiding principles of education in Japan. It made clear that public education and national goals were linked, that education was to serve the interests of the state, not the individual. Although ostensibly a statement on moral education, the document extended its importance beyond schools to society at large. By drawing on widely accepted traditions, it redefined the responsibilities of citizenship in a modern state and provided the moral basis for a prewar nationalism that defined service to the state in terms of loyalty to the emperor. The imperial rescript remained definitive until October 1946, when it was replaced by Allied Occupation authorities as part of sweeping democratic reforms of postwar Japanese education.

The need for such a document arose from great confusion over national values that had characterized the two decades since the establishment of a national school system in 1872. Conflict developed among Confucian moralists

seeking a return to the past, Westernizers intent on civilization and enlightenment (*bunmei kaika*) and politicians seeking guidance on the limits of public authority. The desire to create a public consensus concerning national values led Prime Minister Yamagata Aritomo to order the minister of education to draw up a document defining the basis of national education.

Although the rescript is often described as a triumph by Confucian reactionaries over Westernizing reformers, it actually represented a broad spectrum of Japanese political opinion. It satisfied a variety of concerns in a language so sweeping and general that proponents of all sides could claim it as their own. In the short space of 315 words it linked Confucian notions of loyalty and filial piety, Shinto ideas of a unique national essence (*kokutai*) with the emperor as the source of morality, and Western traditions of civil obedience, respect for law, and sacrifice for the national good.

The rescript was distributed to every school and displayed along with the imperial portrait. Principals read to students from it daily, and it was memorized in state ethics-training (*shūshin*) classes. Consequently, it became the basis for political indoctrination in schools for more than half a century.

Journalists, educators, and politicians praised the document for ending the confusion over values that had characterized the 1870s and 1880s. It inspired interpretive comment from all sides of the political spectrum. By 1940, just less than 600 books of commentary, along with hundreds of official directives and guidelines, had been issued. The broad conceptual sweep and ambiguity of language made it susceptible to interpretation by ideologues of any persuasion. As such, it was used in the first half of the twentieth century to support a particularly strident form of nationalism that focused increasingly narrowly on devotion to a mythical imperial cause.

Richard Rubinger

Bibliography

Gluck, Carol. *Japan's Modern Myths: Ideology in the Late Meiji Period.* Princeton, NJ: Princeton University Press, 1985.

Imperial Rescript to Soldiers and Sailors
(*Gunjin Chokuyu*)

The preeminent pronouncement defining the ideals and obligations of servicemen in the pre-World War II armed forces. Personally presented by the Meiji Emperor to the war minister on July 4,

1882, at a palace ceremony, the rescript, often coupled with the Imperial Rescript on Education of 1890, became a major pillar of nationalism by elevating previously enunciated codes of conduct needed for a disciplined military to a sacred obligation of absolute loyalty to the emperor.

In 2,500 words, the rescript enjoined servicemen to execute their duties according to five principles—loyalty, propriety, valor, righteousness, and simplicity—and explained how each should be fulfilled. Loyalty, for example, meant absolute obedience to the emperor and avoidance of political activity; righteousness called for honesty and faithfulness in personal relations; simplicity adjured soldiers and sailors to avoid luxury and cultivate frugality. The rescript was memorized by officers, recited by the rank and file, and disseminated throughout the populace by former servicemen and patriotic organizations. Its primary injunctions of loyalty and duty to the emperor embodied a central feature of the national ideology of prewar Japan.

Roger F. Hackett

Bibliography

Tiedemann, Arthur E. *Modern Japan: A Brief History*. New York: D. Van Nostrand, 1955, 107–12 (rescript translation).

Imperial Rule Assistance Association (*Taisei Yokusankai*)

World War II association designed to mobilize Japan's masses. The brainchild of Prime Minister Konoe Fumimaro, the IRAA was launched on October 12, 1940, to reform Japan's governmental system and to bring the masses into politics so that they would spontaneously challenge old elites, who were thought to be impeding strong national policies. Every Japanese citizen was to be a member. Almost as soon as Konoe set up a 37-person committee to create the IRAA in the summer of 1940, however, things became complicated. Members, chosen from diverse backgrounds, had trouble reaching consensus, and the resulting structure was neither strong nor reformist. The IRAA became, instead, an organization through which fairly traditional groups were able to control popular sentiment during World War II.

Under the IRAA, the old political parties were dissolved, and the new mass organization was controlled by five bureaus and 23 divisions in Tokyo, working through branches at the prefectural and local levels. Though various groups (particularly the army) attempted to influence appointments to IRAA offices, they were frustrated in most cases by the Home Ministry and traditional power holders. Within a few weeks of its October inauguration, Konoe himself, discouraged by developments, discontinued his own efforts to make the IRAA a reform organization and appointed enough nonreformists to top positions to thwart most of the IRAA's original goals.

As a result, the main function of the IRAA was its use of wartime agencies to control the popular will: to whip up enthusiasm for the war, stimulate production, encourage frugality, and encourage civil-defense efforts. It was also used as a means of controlling dissent. Although it never emulated the illegal, terror-oriented tactics of the German Nazi Party, neither did it in any way provide a voice for the masses. The IRAA was disbanded on June 13, 1945.

James L. Huffman

Bibliography

Berger, Gordon. *Parties out of Power in Japan, 1931–1941*. Princeton, NJ: Princeton University Press, 1977.

Kasza, Gregory. *The State and the Mass Media in Japan, 1918–1945*. Berkeley: University of California Press, 1988.

Imperial Way Faction (*Kōdōha*)

The Kōdōha was an ultranationalist military faction headed by Generals Araki Sadao and Mazaki Jinzaburō, which in the 1930s promoted the idea of revolution at home and aggression abroad, with Russia as Japan's foremost enemy. Its members were largely lower-middle-class junior officers who had an almost spiritual devotion to the emperor. They blamed corrupt, bureaucratic advisers for the ills of society and advocated the use of direct action to restore the emperor as the direct ruler of the people.

During the period 1931–34, with Araki as war minister, the Kōdōha shaped national military policy. In 1934, the faction's influence abruptly terminated when Hayashi Senjūrō, a leader of the rival Tōseiha (Control Faction), became war minister. Hayashi canceled Araki's policy of preparing for war with the Soviet Union and purged upper-level military positions of Kōdōha members. Only Mazaki managed to retain his former post as inspector-general of military education, but at the end of 1935 he was forced to resign.

The younger members of the Kōdōha blamed Nagata Tetsuzan, chief of the Bureau of Military Affairs and adviser to Hayashi, for the military's departure from Kōdōha ideals and for Mazaki's removal from the War Ministry. On August 12, 1935, Kōdōha member Lieutenant Aizawa Saburō assassinated Nagata. Throughout the ensuing highly-publicized trial, the defense emphasized Aizawa's devotion to the emperor. During the trial, on February 26, 1936, several hundred Kōdōha members attempted to overthrow the government and restore the emperor to direct power. They were convinced that the public's sympathy for Aizawa's case would lead to a general uprising in support of their cause. The public, however, did not respond, and the rebels were quickly subdued, sentenced to death, and executed. Aizawa too was found guilty and executed. The February 26 Incident marked the end of Kōdōha influence in the military establishment and the ascendancy of the rival Control Faction.

James L. Huffman
Tracy Pollard

Bibliography

Crowley, James B. "Japanese Army Factionalism in the Early 1930s." *Journal of Asian Studies*. Vol. 21, No. 3 (May 1962), 309–26.

Information Society (*Jōhōka Shakai*)

The term "information society" (*jōhōka shakai*) has been used widely in Japan since the late 1960s to refer to that stage of social development after the "industrial society," when information rather than material goods and energy becomes the basic resource, setting value and driving the development of the economy and social life. It is similar to "knowledge society," used more often in the United States, and is seen in Japan as having many of the same characteristics as sociologist Daniel Bell's "postindustrial society" (*datsukōgyōka shakai*) and the futurist Alvin Toffler's "third wave" (*daisan nami*). The information society is said to grow out of industrial society as the latter enters a high stage of development and complexity. Revolutions in computer and electronic communications technologies provide the means to manage the increased flow of information, which becomes the central force in transforming the economy and the society.

The Japanese concept of "information society" owes a good deal to Bell's conception of the "postindustrial society" and economist Walter Rostow's "stages of economic development," which inspired Japanese thinkers such as Kyoto University Professor Umesao Tadao, who, in the early 1960s, originated the theory of an information industry (*jōhō sangyōron*) as something distinct from traditional categories of industrial classification. Umesao's work led to an effort in the late 1960s by the Industrial Structure Advisory Council (Sangyō Kōzō Shingikai) of the Ministry of International Trade and Industry (MITI) to formulate a plan for stimulating the development of information technologies. By the start of the 1970s, even before the first oil crisis, MITI issued a long-term outline for the transformation of Japan's economy away from one based on the heavy-industry and chemical sectors toward one in which information industries would be the driving force of development.

The government's Economic Planning Agency developed documents that saw the information society emerging in three steps: (1) automation, including OA (office automation) and FA (factory automation); (2) knowledge creation, which brings about the diffusion of information infrastructure, such as INS (information network systems); and (3) social reform, in which people's lives are characterized by growth in the amount and importance of free time, work for self-realization, and community life based on the creative applications of processed information. Similarly, MITI reports characterized the information society as "a society that brings about the general flowering of mankind's intellectual creativity."

Japan moved smoothly through the first stage of office and factory automation in the 1970s and 1980s, as a result of social factors (e.g., limited labor resistance) and technical capabilities (e.g., rapid progress in electronics, communications, and computers). From teleconferencing to robotics and flexible manufacturing systems, the development and diffusion of OA and FA were unprecedented. By the mid-1990s, Japan had made significant progress in knowledge creation too, in developing INS's, which bring together telephone, data transmission, and facsimile services into a single network, and sophisticated value-added networks (VAN's), which transmitted data, thereby increasing their value.

Typical of official Japanese visions of the third stage is the Ministry of Posts and Telecommunication's *teretopia*—the use of telecommunications technology for the realization of the ideal society (utopia). Originally unveiled in 1983 and entering the planning stage in about 100 communities by the end of the 1990s, this vision proposes the diffusion of telecommunications technologies and creation of distinctive regional communities by using those technologies to establish research centers and high-technology industries, develop mature health and welfare programs, and find solutions to urban problems. Particularly important is MITI's 1987 *Jōhōka mirai toshi kōzō* (Vision of Future Cities in the Information Age), which concentrates on developing the facilities for information industries and an information-based lifestyle in eight model districts within the major metropolis, including an international financial focus for Tokyo and a research-development one for Kawasaki.

Progress toward a total information society has given rise to new problems, including information control, privacy, information security, intellectual property rights, transborder data flows, and intense competition in the development and marketing of the processes, products, and services of the emerging information society. Japan , having become a world leader along with the United States in the technologies of the information age, frequently finds itself at the center of controversies involving these matters; but the country is also a critical link in the more interdependent world that is emerging as a result of the information revolution.

Terry MacDougall

Bibliography

Christopher, Robert. *The Japanese Mind: The Goliath Explained*. New York: Linden Press/Simon and Schuster, 1983.

Inoue Junnosuke (1869–1932)

President of the Bank of Japan, three-time finance minister. Inoue became finance minister in the Hamaguchi Osachi government in 1929 to take Japan back on the gold standard. Japan, like the other powers, had banned the export of gold during World War I inflation, but it did not follow them back to the gold standard in the 1920s. The Rikken Minseitō (Constitutional Democratic Party) came to power in July 1929 with the aim of stabilizing foreign-exchange rates and thus encouraging exports by returning to gold, a policy it carried out in January 1930. This step required a significant upward valuation of the yen, which weakened Japan's international competitiveness and intensified the already deflationary impact of the world Depression. Unemployment, lower wages, bankruptcies, and falling farm prices ensued, and these trends, together

with the patriotic fervor stirred up by the advance into Asia after the 1931 Manchurian Incident, led to the downfall of the Minseitō government in December of that year, the end of party governments half a year later, and the beginnings of militarism. On February 9, 1932, Inoue was murdered by a member of the Ketsumeidan (League of Blood).

Richard J. Smethurst

Bibliography

Berger, Gordon. *Parties out of Power in Japan, 1931–1941*. Princeton, NJ: Princeton University Press, 1977.

Inoue Kaoru (1835–1915)

Meiji statesman. As a young man, he was active in the anti-Tokugawa *sonnō jōi* (revere the emperor and expel the barbarians) movement in Chōshū, though study in Great Britain (1863–64) made him less xenophobic than many of his colleagues. In the new Meiji government (1868–1912), he held numerous cabinet posts, including those of home, finance, and foreign minister. He was repeatedly called on to conduct negotiations with Korea after diplomatic and military clashes, and he was known throughout his career for close ties to the leading oligarch Itō Hirobumi and to the Mitsui clique's business interests. Inoue was most keenly associated in the public mind with his efforts as foreign minister (1879–85, 1887–88) to secure revision of the unequal treaties that had put Japan at a disadvantage in dealing with the Western powers. His negotiation of a system to allow foreign judges to sit in certain Japanese court cases in exchange for the abrogation of extraterritoriality evoked highly charged, often chauvinistic, public opposition, forcing Inoue to resign in 1888. After 1901, he became one of the *genrō* (original elder statesmen) and played a major role in selecting cabinets throughout the remainder of his life.

James L. Huffman

Bibliography

Akita, George. *The Foundations of Constitutional Government in Modern Japan, 1868–1900*. Cambridge: Harvard University Press, 1967.

Inoue Kowashi (1843–1895)

Official, governmental theorist. A native of Kumamoto Prefecture, Inoue joined the imperial side in the Meiji Restoration (1868) and quickly moved into prominence in the Ministry of Justice as a protégé of Restoration leader Ōkubo Toshimichi. He studied foreign constitutions in France and Germany early in the 1870s and held important posts in the Home Ministry, the Executive Council, the Privy Council, and the Ministry of Education, which he headed in 1893–94. He was close politically to the leading officials Itō Hirobumi and Iwakura Tomomi.

Inoue is best known for his work on numerous political documents, particularly the 1889 Meiji Constitution and the 1890 Imperial Rescript on Education, as well as the imperial household laws. Consulting with the German legal scholar, Hermann Roesler, he assisted Itō in the 1880s in drafting a constitution that emphasized imperial sovereignty as the essence of Japan's national polity (*kokutai*). His work with imperial councillor Motoda Eifu on the imperial rescript followed the Tokugawa nativist tradition, making the education document a personal, moral statement rather than a law. His consistent focus on the dual nature of the emperor—as both constitutional monarch and Shinto, or moral, leader—had a profound impact on prewar Japan's political institutions and on the increasing public veneration of the emperor.

James L. Huffman

Bibliography

Pittau, Joseph. "Inoue Kowashi, 1843–1895, and the Formation of Modern Japan." *Monumenta Nipponica*. Vol. 20, No. 3–4 (1965), 253–82.

Inoue Nisshō (1866–1967)

Right-wing activist and ideologue of agrarian nationalism (*nōhonshugi*). A native of Gumma Prefecture, he traveled to China and Manchuria during the early 1910s to gather intelligence for the Japanese army. Later, he became a militant Buddhist, converted to the Nichiren sect, and, in 1928, founded a school in Ibaraki Prefecture as a base from which to preach agrarian nationalism among the young people of rural Japan. Thereafter, reasoning that the reforms he sought for Japan could legitimately be achieved through coercive and violent measures, he began nurturing a following among young ultranationalist military officers. After some of them participated in an abortive coup attempt in October 1931, he became even more radical and formed the Ketsumeidan (League of Blood). Through it, he plotted and carried out the 1932 League of Blood Incident, in which the chairman of the Mitsui Holding Company, Baron Dan Takuma, and a former minister of finance, Inoue Junnosuke, were assassinated. He then surrendered to the authorities and was imprisoned from 1934 until 1940. Following World War II, he continued his right-wing activism but had relatively little influence.

J. Wayne Sabey

Bibliography

Havens, Thomas R.H. *Farm and Nation in Modern Japan*. Princeton, NJ: Princeton University Press, 1974.

Institute of the Golden Pheasant (*Kinkei Gakuin*)

Nationalist study group. The scholar Yasuoka Masaatsu began in 1926 to lecture on Confucianism at the Kinkeien (Golden Pheasant Garden) of Count Sakai Tadamasa, and the sessions eventually were given the name Kinkei Gakuin. His lectures, which drew leading officials and army officers, focused on the relationship between Confucianism and Japan's *kokutai* (national polity), emphasizing the close links between filial piety and loyalty to Japan's imperial household.

Though never ultranationalist in tone, the Kinkei Gakuin lectures introduced nationalist ideas to many rising bureaucrats in the Home and Education ministries. Yasuoka himself maintained ties to the right wing of the 1930s yet eschewed the more extreme forms of nationalism. He also helped create in 1932 the Kokuikai (Society for Maintaining National Prestige), a nationalist group with such powerful members as Konoe Fumimaro, Hirota Kōki, and Yoshida Shigeru, each of whom later became prime minister.

James L. Huffman

Bibliography

Storry, Richard. *The Double Patriots: A Study of Japanese Nationalism*. Westport, CT: Greenwood Press, 1973.

International News Agency (*Kokusai Tsūshinsha*)

Early-twentieth-century Japanese businessmen were concerned about Japan's international image in the wake of the 1914 Siemens Incident, in which the German company bribed Japanese government officials, and racial discrimination against Japanese in California. To counter

Japan's perceived lack of a national voice in the international press, Shibusawa Eiichi and other business leaders formed Kokusai Tsūshinsha in 1914 and hired Associated Press (AP) Tokyo agent John Russell Kennedy as general manager.

The founders of Kokusai hoped to sign a contract to exchange news with the AP. When Kennedy met in New York with AP General Manager Melville Stone, he was told that an agreement with the British agency Reuter prohibited the AP from distributing news in Japan. The Japanese had to acquiesce to Reuter's domination of Asian news, and Kokusai became a part of the British agency's news empire.

In 1923, Iwanaga Yūkichi replaced Kennedy as Kokusai's general manager and immediately tried to strengthen the agency's news-gathering operation. He sent a Kokusai agent to London to supervise the news Reuter sent to Japan and negotiated with Reuter the right for his agency to use only "Kokusai" as the credit for news it distributed in Japan. He also took advantage of the changes following World War I to sign a contract with Russia's Rosta, the forerunner of TASS. In 1926 Iwanaga reorganized Kokusai as Nihon Shimbun Rengōsha (Associated Press of Japan), a nonprofit newspaper cooperative modeled after the AP.

Roger W. Purdy

Bibliography

Purdy, Roger W. "The Ears and Voice of the Nation: The Dōmei News Agency and Japan's News Network, 1936–1945." Unpublished doctoral dissertation, University of California, Santa Barbara, 1987.

Internationalization (*Kokusaika*)

One of Japan's defining characteristics and major challenges in the last quarter of the twentieth century. *Kokusaika* gained currency in the 1980s in reference to the challenge for Japan to accommodate itself to the rapid increase in the flow of people, goods, money, and information across national borders, the need to make greater and more diverse international contributions, the difficult psychological and cultural adjustments needed for dealing with foreigners and foreign enterprises within Japanese society, and the imperative to address issues such as the environment on a global basis. Use of the term *kokusaika* generally involves the assumption that Japan must become more open to, and active in, the world if it is to manage frictions with other countries,

avoid isolation, and become a leading country in the twenty-first century.

Kokusaika is understood as an irreversible trend, brought on by the accelerating rate of the transnational flow of goods, services, money, people, and information and resulting in a high degree of interdependence among countries. Although interdependence has brought increased material prosperity, it has also caused significant frictions, by subjecting domestic enterprises and institutions to international standards and foreign competition and by necessitating wrenching structural adjustments in countries that are less competitive or less open than others.

Kokusaika is a particularly acute challenge for Japan because the country's rapid rise to economic predominance in many fields and its cultural and structural differences from major competitors cause international frictions and criticism of Japanese behavior. Hence, foreign pressure (*gaiatsu*), particularly from the United States, has led Japanese business and government to push market opening (*shijō kaihō*), financial liberalization (*kin'yū no jiyūka*), and transformation of the nation's economic structure (*keizai kōzō kaikaku*). The country's rapid liberalization of trade and capital flows and transition from an economy driven by heavy and chemical industrial development to one based on knowledge-intensive industries in the 1970s and 1980s indicate significant progress in economic internationalization. Japan's dialogue with the United States in the early 1990s over so-called "structural impediments" that restrict access to each other's markets reflects persistent differences in patterns of business operations and cultural or social priorities.

Kokusaika also entails the political expectation that Japan will increase its international contributions in light of its economic power. Since Japan's economic rise has occurred coincidentally with the relative decline of its postwar beneficiary and chief ally, the United States, this issue has been played out most frequently in bilateral Japan-U.S. relations. In the 1970s and 1980s, it was focused primarily on burden sharing with the United States, especially increased Japanese support for the international trading system, international monetary stability, Third World development, and defense. Large-scale budget increases for foreign aid and national defense during a period of budget stringency in domestic affairs in the 1980s suggest the high priority Japanese authorities put on their partnership with the United States while developing Japan's leading role in international economic development.

With Iraq's 1991 invasion of Kuwait, the issue of Japan's contribution of personnel (*jinteki na kōken*) as well as funds to maintain international order arose. This brought into focus the question of whether the legacy of World War II and the country's constitution negated any type of international military role, or whether foreign expectations of more positive Japanese support for international order might open the door to a limited overseas role for the Self-Defense Forces. More fundamental, it raised the issue of what Japan represented internationally and how to relate this to its history and sense of identity as a nation (*nihonjinron*).

Kokusaika also involves intimate psychological and cultural adjustments by Japanese as individuals, groups, and institutions to having foreigners and foreign enterprises within Japanese society. *Uchi naru kokusaika* (domestic internationalization) expresses a realization that Japan's highly structured and inward-looking society must change to accommodate the reintegration of the large numbers of Japanese returning from work or study abroad; to ameliorate the discriminatory conditions faced by Korean residents of Japan; to make room for more foreigners who come as students, trainees, or workers; and to provide reciprocal access to foreign enterprises doing business in Japan. *Kokusaika* at the intimate level of the household, neighborhood, and workplace may be difficult for a society traditionally protective of those within (*uchi*) and suspicious of the "outside" (*soto*), but the country's labor force needs foreign pressure for access and fair treatment, and the extent to which individual Japanese in the late 1990s are exposed to the outside world may ease adjustments at this level.

Finally, *kokusaika* also involves the belief that interdependence has reached a critical stage at which global survival necessitates greater efforts to live together in harmony (*tomo ni ikiru*) and to address the issues of human rights (*jinken*), environment (*kankyō*), economic development (*keizai hatten*), and peace (*heiwa*) on a universal basis. Japan has earmarked funds for environmental research, established procedures for assessing environmental impact, and explored the use of human-rights criteria in allocating its foreign aid.

Terry MacDougall

Bibliography

Higashi, Chikara, and G. Peter Lauter. *The Internationalization of the Japanese Economy*. Boston: Kluwer Academic Publishers, 1987.

Mannari, Hiroshi, and Befu Harumi, eds. *The Challenge of Japan's Internationalization*. New York: Kodansha International, 1983.

Inukai Tsuyoshi (1855–1932)

Party politician, prime minister. Born in Okayama Prefecture, he studied at the modernizer Fukuzawa Yukichi's school, Keiō Gijuku, in the late 1870s and spent his early years as a reporter or editor for four newspapers, including the prominent *Yūbin Hōchi Shimbun* and *Chōya Shimbun*. With former Finance Minister Ōkuma Shigenobu, he helped found the progressive political party Rikken Kaishintō (Constitutional Reform Party) in 1882 and commenced a political career in which he consistently fought against domination of the government by factions (especially the longstanding Satsuma and Chōshū cliques). He was elected to the first Diet (legislature) in 1890, then reelected in each of the 17 subsequent elections until his death. Playing a leading role in the succession of parties that came from the Kenseitō (Constitutional Party), he helped topple Katsura Tarō's government in a 1913 constitutional crisis and supported universal male suffrage. He was elected president of the Rikken Seiyūkai (Friends of Constitutional Government Party) in 1929 and became prime minister in December 1931. Faced with the worldwide depression and the army's recent aggression in the Manchurian Incident (September 18, 1931), he reembargoed gold and attempted to place strict restrictions on the army, while vigorously defending party rule. His efforts to control the army angered the rising ultranationalist movement, and, on May 15, 1932, he was assassinated.

James L. Huffman

Bibliography

Oka, Yoshitake. *Five Political Leaders of Modern Japan*. Tokyo: University of Tokyo Press, 1986.

Ise Shrine

See GRAND SHRINES OF ISE

Ishibashi Tanzan (1884–1973)

Journalist, politician. Born in Tokyo and graduated in 1907 from Waseda University, he became a reporter for the newspaper *Tokyo Mainichi Shimbun* in 1907. During the pre–World War II years, he was associated primarily with the economic journal *Tōyō Keizai Shimpō*, first as a writer, then as editor (1925–46), and finally as president (1941–46). Known for liberal, antimilitary views into the 1930s, he later became a supporter of the war effort. He entered politics after the war and became finance minister under Yoshida Shigeru. The Allied Occupation authorities purged him from 1947 to 1951, partly because of his opposition to their economic policies. He reentered the political world in 1951, serving three times as minister of international trade and industry and in 1956 becoming prime minister. He had to resign in less than two months, due to ill health, and spent his remaining years pushing for normalization of relations between Japan and the People's Republic of China.

James L. Huffman

Bibliography

Nolte, Sharon H. *Liberalism in Modern Japan: Ishibashi Tanzan and His Teachers, 1905–1960.* Berkeley: University of California Press, 1987.

Ishihara Shintarō (1932–)

Politician, novelist. Born in Kobe, he gained early prominence as a novelist, then moved into the world of politics, where he became one of Japan's most controversial nationalists. Ishihara graduated from Hitotsubashi University and won acclaim for his 1955 novel *Taiyō no kisetsu* (Season of Violence), which described the alienation and hedonism of postwar young people. After publishing several other novels, he entered politics and won a seat in the upper house of the Diet (legislature) in 1968. He was elected to the lower house four years later, lost the Tokyo gubernatorial election in 1975, then was reelected continuously to the lower house of the Diet from 1976 to the late 1990s.

His outspoken nationalism gained Ishihara international notoriety in the 1980s. In particular, his 1991 book *The Japan That Can Say No* called for Japan to stand up more forcefully against foreign pressure. He argued that "Japan bashing" in the United States was stimulated more by racism than by unfair Japanese practices and that America's need for technology gave Japan an advantage that it should use more effectively.

James L. Huffman

Bibliography

Ishihara, Shintarō. *The Japan That Can Say No.* New York: Simon and Schuster, 1991.

Ishiwara Kanji (1889–1949)

General and military theorist. Born to a police officer's family in Yamagata Prefecture, he is best known for his nonconformist military theories and his central role in the Manchurian Incident of 1931. After graduating from the Army Academy (1909) and the Army War College (1918), he became a student of military history and of the thirteenth-century Buddhist priest Nichiren's views of humankind's "last days." He developed a "final war" theory, arguing that the world was heading toward a culminating conflict in which Japan must defeat the United States and create an era of universal peace. The theory gained considerable popularity among young men at the War College, where he lectured from 1922 to 1928.

Assigned as an operations officer in the Guandong army in 1929, he advocated increased activism in Manchuria and helped mastermind the army's takeover there following the Manchurian Incident, which precipitated Japan's advance into Asia in 1931. In 1932, he was reassigned to the city of Sendai in the north, and in 1935 he was posted to the Operations Division of the general staff in Tokyo, where he began pushing for the creation of a "national defense state" that would focus all of Japan's policies on military mobilization. When the mutinous February 26 Incident threatened to topple the government in 1936, he won widespread praise for his key role in crushing the rebels, whom he saw as a disruptive force likely to undermine the national defense state.

The influence of Ishiwara declined after mid-1936, due partly to his continuing backstage political maneuvering and partly to his unorthodox ideas. In particular, he argued for greater cooperation with China even after the outbreak of war there in 1937. He was forced to resign from the army in 1941 and retired to Yamagata, where he wrote about his theories and worked with an agricultural community. Ishiwara spoke out publicly again following

Ishiwara Kanji. Asahi Shimbun Photo.

World War II, this time advocating the creation of a new Japan, but the Allied Occupation authorities purged him.

James L. Huffman

Bibliography

Peattie, Mark. *Ishiwara Kanji and Japan's Confrontation with the West*. Princeton, NJ: Princeton University Press, 1975.

Itagaki Seishirō (1885–1948)

Army general. Born in Iwate Prefecture, Itagaki graduated from Sendai Military Preparatory School in 1904 and from the Army War College in 1916. In June 1929, he was assigned to Manchuria as an officer in the Guandong army. Seeing Manchuria as vital to Japan's interests, Itagaki helped fellow officer Ishiwara Kanji formulate a plan for the Japanese occupation of that region. Initiated in 1931 with the Manchurian Incident, in which a section of the South Manchurian Railway was blown up, their plan enabled Japan to seize Manchuria and create the puppet state of Manchukuo. Itagaki was promoted to major-general in 1932 and, five years later with the onset of the second Sino-Japanese War, he became commander of the Fifth Division. He was named minister of war in 1938 and was promoted to general in 1941. Itagaki was convicted as a war criminal by the International Military Tribunal for the Far East and executed in 1948.

James L. Huffman

Bibliography
Ogata, Sadako N. *Defiance in Man-
churia: The Making of Japanese
Foreign Policy 1931–1932*. Los
Angeles: University of California
Press, 1964.

Itagaki Taisuke (1837–1919)

Popular-rights leader. Born to a leading samurai family in Tosa domain (Kōchi Prefecture),
Itagaki was an early opponent of the Tokugawa
government and led a battalion in the pro-im-
perial army following the 1868 Meiji Restoration. He took posts in the new government in
1869 and 1871 but resigned in protest in 1873
when his friend, the Restoration hero Saigō Takamori, was rebuffed in efforts to push through
an aggressive policy toward Korea. Though he
entered government service again briefly in
1875, he gave most of the 1870s and 1880s to
leadership of the antigovernment popular-rights
(*jiyū minken* movement).

Itagaki and others sparked the first national
debate over "people's rights" early in 1874, with
a memorial to the emperor calling for the creation
of a popular assembly. He also created several of
Japan's first political associations in the middle
1870s, and in 1881 he founded Japan's first political party, the Jiyūtō (Liberal Party). That party
folded in 1884, partly because of controversy over
a government-sponsored trip Itagaki took to investigate politics in Europe. It was revived, however, when the creation of the Diet (legislature) approached in 1890. Itagaki served twice as home
minister late in the 1890s, then retired from politics in 1900 and gave his last years to social work.
Though central to the activities of the early popular-rights movement, he remained an elitist, limiting his definition of "the people" to members of
the traditional ruling classes.

James L. Huffman

Bibliography
Akita, George. *Foundations of Constitutional
Government in Modern Japan, 1868–1900*.
Cambridge: Harvard University Press, 1967.

Itō Hirobumi (1841–1909)

Meiji statesman. Born in a farm family in Chōshū
domain (Yamaguchi Prefecture), he was made a
samurai by his fief in 1863 for his activities against
the ruling Tokugawa regime. During the next four
decades, he became Japan's foremost politician,

Itō Hirobumi. Asahi Shimbun Photo.

supervising the drafting of the 1889 Meiji Constitution, serving four times each as prime minister
and head of the Privy Council, and forming one
of Japan's first political parties.

When he was 16 years old, Itō entered the
school of the well-known anti-Tokugawa,
antiforeign activist Yoshida Shōin and soon
became a leader in that movement. A stint in
Great Britain (1863) impressed him with the
strength of Europe, and, when he came back,
his focus was on overthrowing the Tokugawa
regime rather than driving out the foreigners.

After the Meiji Restoration (1868), Itō
moved up quickly in the new government. Twice
he went to the West, first to study the American
financial system early in 1871 and later as one
of the leaders on the 50-member Iwakura Mission (1871–73), which studied modern institutions in Europe and America. In 1873, he was
named minister of public works and, by 1881,
he had emerged as one of the country's two or
three foremost officials, a man who hewed an increasingly conservative, pragmatic course in contrast to men such as Finance Minister Ōkuma
Shigenobu, who wanted to move more rapidly
toward representative government.

Itō's main task in the 1880s was supervis-
ing the drafting of the constitution. An 1882
European trip to study constitutional systems left
Itō convinced that sovereignty must be placed

wholly in the emperor. He created a peerage system in 1884, was named Japan's first prime minister in 1885, and saw the constitution promulgated in 1889. During the 1890s, he became a *genrō* (elder statesman), serving twice as prime minister, negotiating the end of the Sino-Japanese War in 1895 and fighting tumultuous battles in the Diet (legislature) for more taxes and stronger government. He formed his own political organization, Rikken Seiyūkai (Friends of Constitutional Government Party), in 1900, convinced that the clique-based oligarchs needed their own party to fend off liberal attacks.

Itō's last activities centered on Korea. After the Russo-Japanese War (1904–05), he became ambassador to Korea; in 1906 he was named Japan's first resident-general there, developing policies that led eventually to Korea's annexation, a move he opposed. In 1909, he was assassinated in Harbin, Manchuria, by a Korean nationalist.

Itō was one of the Meiji Emperor's closest confidants. He was arrogant and loved accolades, but he also read widely, wrote Chinese poetry, and eschewed personal wealth. His policies were among the most important in shaping the Meiji political system.

James L. Huffman

Bibliography

Akita, George. *Foundations of Constitutional Government in Modern Japan, 1868–1900.* Cambridge: Harvard University Press, 1967.

Oka, Yoshitake. *Five Political Leaders of Modern Japan.* Tokyo: University of Tokyo Press, 1986.

Itō Miyoji (1857–1934)

A protégé of leading oligarch Itō Hirobumi who made a career as a behind-the-scenes political manipulator (*kuromaku;* literally, "black curtain"). As Itō's chief cabinet secretary (1892–98), he became a power broker and intermediary between the oligarchy (*hambatsu*) and the political parties in the Diet (legislature).

A political ally of Itō and later of military leader and Home Minister Yamagata Aritomo and Prime Minister Katsura Tarō, he articulated the *hambatsu* political philosophy of an emperor-centered elitist government by writing many of the imperial edicts, rescripts, and national laws, including (with the conservative scholar Inoue Kowashi) the Meiji Constitution of 1889. He was also the publisher of the government-apologist newspaper *Tokyo Nichi Nichi Shimbun.* Increas-

ingly more conservative in his later years, he became a watchdog and defender of the constitution in his role as a privy councillor (1899–1934).

Louis G. Perez

Bibliography

Akita, George. "The Other Itō: A Political Failure." *Personality in Japanese History.* Ed. Albert Craig and Donald Shively. Berkeley: University of California Press, 1970.

Itō Noe (1895–1923)

Socialist and feminist. Born in Fukuoka Prefecture, Itō attended Ueno Girls' High School in Tokyo. Upon graduation, she returned home and was forced into an arranged marriage. A few days later, she escaped to Tokyo, where, at age 17, she began writing for *Seitō* (Bluestocking), journal of the Seitōsha (Bluestocking Society). Originally a literary society for women, the Seitōsha gradually became more involved in social issues and, under Itō's editorship, an open forum for the debate of women's issues. By publishing translations in *Seitō* of works by Emma Goldman, P.A. Kropotkin, and other feminists and anarchists, she helped connect the literary Seitōsha members with political-activist groups. Itō also acted as an adviser to the Sekirankai (Red Wave Society), a socialist women's group. After leaving the Seitōsha, she became involved with anarchist Ōsugi Sakae, and together they worked on labor reform and organization. On September 16, 1923, Itō, Ōsugi, and Ōsugi's nephew were murdered by nation-

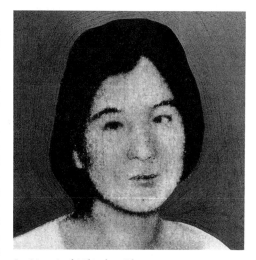

Itō Noe. Asahi Shimbun Photo.

alistic military police during the tumultuous aftermath of the Great Kantō Earthquake.

James L. Huffman

Bibliography
Sievers, Sharon L. *Flowers in Salt: The Beginnings of Feminist Consciousness in Modern Japan.* Stanford, CA: Stanford University Press, 1983.

Iwakura Tomomi (1825–83)

Court noble, political leader. Born to a low-ranking Kyoto family and adopted into the high-ranking Iwakura family, he was the most influential member of the nobility during Japan's transition from the feudal era to modern statehood. He helped persuade Emperor Kōmei in 1858 to refuse to give his approval to Japan's first commercial treaty with the United States, even though approval had been requested by the Tokugawa shogun; yet, Iwakura was exiled from the court from 1862 to 1867 for being too moderate in his view of the shogunal government. After release from exile, however, he served as a secret liaison between the court and leaders of the anti-Tokugawa movement.

In the new Meiji government, formed in 1868, Iwakura played a pivotal role, helping shape the system that replaced daimyo domains with prefectures and opposing aggressive policies in Korea in 1873. Because of his position on Korea, extremists made an attempt on his life in 1874. He is best known for leading the 50-member Iwakura Mission, in which many of Japan's most influential leaders spent 18 months (1871–73) in America and Europe, studying modern institutions and discussing treaty relationships. He fought consistently for a strong imperial system based on a Western-style constitution; he also worked to create financial institutions and structures, including the Daijūgo Ginko (Fifteenth Bank), which provided for the welfare of the imperial family and the former noble classes.

James L. Huffman

Bibliography
Beasley, W.G. *The Meiji Restoration.* Stanford, CA: Stanford University Press, 1972.

Iwakura Tomomi. Asahi Shimbun Photo.

Iwanaga Yūkichi (1883–1939)

News agency director. Born in Tokyo and graduated from Kyoto University, Iwanaga attended the Paris Peace Conference (1919) and the Washington Naval Conference (1921) and concluded that a lack of influence in world news operations hurt Japan's international image. Deciding to change that situation, he founded his own Iwanaga News Agency in 1920, then became director of Kokusai Tsūshinsha (International News Agency) in 1923. Three years later, he helped create Nihon Shimbun Rengōsha (Japan Newspaper Association), Japan's first newspaper cooperative. Iwanaga's most important contribution was the breaking of Reuter's monopoly on the flow of news from Japan to the rest of the world by negotiating an agreement with America's Associated Press in 1933. Three years later, he brought together Japan's news agencies to form Dōmei Tsūshinsha (Dōmei News Agency), a single national news agency intended to affect positively the world's understanding of Japan. Dōmei became an instrument of the central government for controlling information during World War II.

James L. Huffman

Bibliography

Purdy, Roger W. "The Ears and Voice of the Nation: The Dōmei News Agency and Japan's News Network, 1936–1945." Unpublished doctoral dissertation, University of California, Santa Barbara, 1987.

J

Japan Telegraphic News Agency
(*Nippon Denpō Tsūshinsha Dentsū*)

Nippon Denpō Tsūshinsha, known by its credit as Dentsū, was founded in 1901 by journalist Mitsunaga Hoshirō. It owed its success to dual activities: Its profitable advertising brokerage subsidized its news gathering and dissemination operation. In 1907, Dentsū contracted to exchange news with the American news agency United Press (UP). Although the exchange of news remained minimal until communication technology improved, the contract was significant because, for the first time, a Japanese news agency had exchanged news with a non-Japanese agency as an equal.

In the late 1920s, the Nihon Shimbun Rengōsha news agency challenged Dentsū. Following the Manchurian Incident (1931), which triggered Japan's expansion on the Asian mainland, Rengō's general manager, Iwanaga Yūkichi, urged the merger of Rengō and Dentsū to create a national news agency in Japan. Mitsunaga resisted the suggestion because it would necessitate the dissolution of Dentsū, the stronger of the two agencies. His clients protested the potential loss of their profitable advertising arrangements. In 1936, however, as a compromise, Dentsū retained its advertising brokerage, but its news operations merged with Rengō to form the Dōmei News Agency (Dōmei Tsūshinsha).

In 1955, the advertising agency officially changed its name to Dentsū; into the late 1990s, it is one of the world's most powerful mass-media forces. It represents most of the major companies in Japan and manages nearly one-quarter of all Japanese advertising.

Roger W. Purdy

Bibliography

Purdy, Roger W. "The Ears and Voice of the Nation: The Dōmei News Agency and Japan's News Network, 1936–1945." Unpublished doctoral dissertation, University of California, Santa Barbara, 1987.

Japan–U.S. Security Treaties
(*Nichibei Anzen Hoshō Jōyaku*)

Treaties establishing the post–World War II relationship between Japan and the United States; they provide for an American promise to defend Japan from outside attack in return for the right to maintain U.S. military bases in Japan. Japanese government policy in negotiating the treaties—the 1951 Japan–U.S. Security Treaty and the revised 1960 Treaty of Mutual Cooperation and Security—was strongly influenced by nationalism.

Since the term "nationalism" carries so much historical and emotional baggage, it is useful to explain what it means here. It is not being used in a pejorative sense as an atavistic, essentially violent instinct, nor is it being glorified in the Hegelian sense as the world-historical force leading to the highest stage of human development. Nationalism is used here to refer to the psychological phenomenon in which a group of people identifies itself as the bearer of certain cultural qualities that give it the right to govern itself and play an independent role in world history.

Modern Japan was born in response to the nineteenth-century threat of British, French, Russian, and, finally, American imperialism. Despite the deep, centuries-old conflicts that divided the numerous feudal *kuni* (literally, countries), many members of the Japanese ruling military class were quick to see that the Europeans and the Americans who threatened to take over the country were organized into nation–states and that this form of organization was somehow connected with their military strength, their powerful technology and manufactures, and their steamships, cannon, and telegraph. The Meiji oligarchs used their education system, military training, and the imperial institution to overcome local and class differences and to create a cohesive, independent Japan, capable of surviving in the global community of countries. The first Sino-Japanese War (1894–95), the Russo-Japanese War (1904–05), and even the disastrous defeat in World War II—all taught the Japanese that they are a nation, in their own minds and in the eyes of the world. Consequently, a deeply ingrained sense of nationalism permeated every level of Japanese society and extended from the relatively conservative former bureaucrats who negotiated the security treaties to the socialists and the Communists who opposed the 1951 and the 1960 treaties.

In 1951, the socialist parties and the Communists opposed the San Francisco Peace Treaty and the Japan–U.S. Security Treaty on nationalist grounds, arguing that the Security Treaty, in particular, was a device for perpetuating American military occupation and control of Japan. In 1960, the socialists and the Communists revived this same nationalist theme in opposing the ratification of the revised Treaty of Mutual Cooperation and Security and in organizing and leading demonstrations against it all over Japan. Their rallying cry was that Prime Minister Kishi Nobusuke, who had been a cabinet minister in wartime Japan, was a running dog of the American capitalist-militarist-imperialists—that he and his treaty violated the fundamental independence of the Japanese nation.

The ruling conservatives who negotiated the 1951 and 1960 treaties were also imbued with a sense of nationalism. Prime Ministers Yoshida Shigeru and Kishi were determined to preserve Japan as a nation and to protect its national interests as they understood them. As political leaders, they were also keenly aware of the importance of countering the nationalist arguments and appeals of the opposition parties. Prime Minister Yoshida governed Japan in the years 1946–47 and 1948–54. For more than half of his tenure, until the spring of 1952, Japan was under Allied Occupation control and was legally not a sovereign, independent state. Most historians of this period agree that a basic element in Yoshida's electoral strength and political power was the belief held by most Japanese voters that, while Yoshida worked effectively with the Occupation, he stubbornly protected Japan's vital national interests and its national pride.

Until the Korean War broke out in 1950, Yoshida was deeply concerned that a punitive peace treaty might be imposed on Japan and that Japan might have to live under Allied or United Nations control for many years. From his perspective, the San Francisco Peace Treaty fully restored Japan's sovereignty, and the signing of the Japan–U.S. Security Treaty with the United States several hours after the peace treaty was concluded, on September 8, 1951, was an exercise of Japan's independence. He believed that, in the aftermath of the destruction and suffering of World War II, the Japanese people had neither the will nor the means to defend themselves militarily against the Soviet Union or the Chinese Communists, who, in 1951, were waging war in Korea against the United States and the United Nations. Although Yoshida was not enthusiastic about having American military bases in Japan, he believed that the Japan–U.S. Security Treaty and the American bases were necessary as long as Japan remained unable to defend itself. On this point, the prime minister had a better understanding of the voters than the opposition did. Although the 1951 Security Treaty was never popular, it was accepted by most Japanese as an unpleasant necessity. The treaty offended their nationalism, but the alternatives of rearmament or neutrality looked even worse.

In negotiating the 1960 Treaty of Mutual Cooperation and Security, Prime Minister Kishi was successful in revising those portions of the 1951 treaty that had been most offensive to Japanese nationalist feeling. The revised treaty deleted the provision for American intervention "to put down large-scale riots and disturbances in Japan. . . . " It was agreed that the treaty was for a fixed period of 10 years, after which it could be terminated by either party giving one-year notice of intent to terminate. The 1951 treaty could have been terminated only by agreement of both parties, which was generally viewed as a way of ensuring that even if the opposition parties came to power in Japan, they would not be able to abrogate the treaty. In notes appended to the 1960 treaty, the United

States agreed not to bring nuclear weapons into Japan without first getting Japanese approval and explicitly stated that Japan had residual sovereignty over Okinawa and the Bonin Islands.

Although Prime Minister Kishi successfully addressed the sensitive nationalist issues raised by the 1951 treaty, his lack of firm support in his own party, his personal unpopularity with the voters, large-scale riots against the 1960 treaty, and a planned visit to Japan by U.S. President Dwight D. Eisenhower—all led to Kishi's resignation in July of that year. According to opposition and numerous foreign observers, Kishi's political demise meant that the opposition parties had captured the nationalist issue in Japan and would soon come to power and abrogate the treaty. However, the conservatives called and won a general election in the fall of 1960, demonstrating that it was Kishi much more than the treaty that had incited the disturbances of the summer.

The history of the security treaties suggests that, since 1945, nationalism in Japan has been deeply colored by pacifism and by a sophisticated understanding by the voters that national sovereignty and independence are not absolutes in a world of nuclear missiles and increasing economic interdependence.

Martin E. Weinstein

Bibliography
Packard, George R., III. *Protest in Tokyo.* Princeton, NJ: Princeton University Press, 1966.
Weinstein, Martin E. *Japan's Postwar Defense Policy, 1947–1968.* New York: Columbia University Press, 1970.

The Japanese (Nihonjin)

Opinion journal. Miyake Setsurei and Shiga Shigetaka, founders of the Seikyōsha (Society for Political Education), started *Nihonjin* in 1888 to oppose the intense Western orientation of the early Meiji years. Though small in circulation, with a peak distribution of only a few thousand copies, it exerted substantial influence on nationalist thought in the 1890s. The journal was clear in what it opposed—slavish Westernization, unequal treaties, clique government—and was suspended several times for criticizing government policies. It was less clear about what it supported. As the name indicated, its writers favored a kind of cultural Japanism.

Shiga often used the phrases *kokusui hozon* (preservation of nationality) and *kokusui kenshō* (promotion of nationality), and the journal supported progressive reforms aimed at increasing participation in public life. But its writers never developed a clear policy. In concert with Kuga Katsunan's newspaper, *Nihon,* they espoused increased Japanese involvement in Asia, twice changing *Nihonjin*'s name to *Ajia* (Asia) while the journal was under government suspension. The lack of a clear program, however, enabled conservative nationalists to oversimplify and distort the magazine's central theme. Partly to counteract that problem, *Nihonjin* began using more liberal writers, including socialists and Christians, after the mid-1890s.

Nihonjin merged with *Nihon* in 1907 to become *Nihon oyobi Nihonjin* (Japan and the Japanese), which functioned until 1923 as a moderately nationalist journal. Its offices were destroyed that year in the Great Kantō Earthquake, but it resumed publication in 1924, independent from Miyake and the old Seikyōsha forces; it continued until 1944, when it died of financial difficulties.

James L. Huffman

Bibliography
Pyle, Kenneth. *The New Generation in Meiji Japan.* Stanford, CA: Stanford University Press, 1969.

Kuga Katsunan. Courtesy Asahi Shimbun.

Japanese Language (*Nihongo*)

Considered to belong to the Altaic family of languages, Japanese is one of the most important languages of the world on the eve of the twenty-first century in terms of the number of users and the quality of its linguistic culture. It is regarded by many Japanese as a defining characteristic of national culture, a language whose linguistic features help create and explain many Japanese behavior patterns.

Japanese pronunciation is relatively easy and simple. Phonetically, it is one of the simplest languages after Polynesian. All sounds, except vowels and "n," have a combination of a consonant plus a vowel, and consonants do not occur by themselves, in clusters, or at the end of a syllable (except for "n"). Japanese has five standard vowels, namely, a, i, u, e, and o, which resemble those in Spanish, Italian, and German.

Japanese has approximately 114 syllables consisting of voiced, half-voiced, and contracted sounds. It does not have trill sounds as in the French "r." The language has a limited number of sound combinations and, thus, has more homonyms than other major languages do. Unlike Chinese or English, Japanese does not depend on tones or stressed accent.

The principles of Japanese grammar are reasonably straightforward and are close to Korean and Mongolian. Japanese does not distinguish between singular and plural, nor does it use the articles "a" and "the" or grammatical gender. It is an agglutinative language, highly inflected by a variety of syllables attached to the stem in order to designate grammatical relationships such as voice, number, mood, tense, negative and positive, and such. In order to make plural forms, for example, the same word may be repeated as in *ie* (house) and *ieie* (houses), or suffixes such as *tachi* may be added. However, there often is no grammatical distinction between singular and plural form: *inu* thus may mean either "dog" or "dogs." Prepositions or particles follow nouns and pronouns to indicate their function in a sentence, and verbs come at the end of the sentence.

Japanese abounds in the first- and second-person pronouns. Words used for "I" and "you" vary depending on the sex, age, social status, and mood of both the speaker and the listener. The Japanese language is highly contextual, and subjects are often omitted. Verb forms and endings, as well as honorific language, often indicate who the subject is.

Japanese has a complicated system of *keigo* (polite or honorific language) that indicates distinctions between social status and personal relationships; that is, degree of respect, politeness, humbleness, and intimacy, as well as the nature of previous interactions. That the Japanese are keenly aware of their social status is shown by the careful attention they pay to the use of proper verb endings and socially appropriate prefixes and suffixes.

The Japanese also use different verbs and nouns according to one's occupation, social status, age, or sex. There also are a number of different dialects, as well as differences between colloquial and written forms. Some dialects are so different that they sound like "foreign languages" to the speakers of other dialects.

Written Japanese reflects a history of interaction with other countries. The spoken language was not transcribed at all until Chinese characters were adopted in the fifth century A.D. As a result, the Japanese writing system utilizes four different systems: *hiragana* and *katakana* (46-symbol phonetic alphabets, using simplified forms of Chinese characters developed around the ninth century), *kanji* (Chinese characters), and *romaji* (the Latin alphabet, which is less widely used).

About 2,000 Chinese characters (*kanji*) are used in most adult-level readings. An additional 4,000 characters are used frequently enough to deserve attention. The most extensive Japanese *kanji* dictionaries list nearly 50,000 characters.

Throughout history, the Japanese have shown a proclivity for adapting foreign words: first from China, then from the Portuguese and the Dutch in the sixteenth and seventeenth centuries, and more recently from the Germans, British, French, and Americans. While nationalism caused the government to prohibit such adaptations during the 1930s and early 1940s, loan words from Europe and the United States have become highly fashionable, preferable sometimes to native words. The Western influence also has prompted some publishers, particularly in math and the sciences, to print Japanese horizontally, though vertical writing, moving from right to left, remains the norm for the written language.

Several characteristics of the spoken language are regarded by most Japanese as unique, giving rise to an ethos that sometimes equates language proficiency with "Japaneseness" itself.

The language is oriented, for example, to indirect and imprecise expressions rather than straightforward, explicit, clear, logical, or concise communication. People generally take it for granted that they share many common assumptions due to their racial homogeneity and almost identical cultural and social backgrounds. *Haragei* (belly talk or visceral communication) characterizes Japanese communication that is based on tacit understanding and abounds in ambiguous expressions. The word *haragei* is composed of two Chinese characters: *hara* (belly, abdomen, stomach) and *gei* (art, talent). *Hara* also means womb, mind, and clan. Idioms that contain the word *hara* express anger, timidity, frustration, impudence, laughter, cooperation, honesty, and decision.

Haragei originally comes from the theatrical vocabulary referring to an actor's ability to represent the feelings and emotions of the person being played without using language or action. *Haragei*, in everyday Japanese usage, is the art of saying what one means and hearing what others say without explicit or elaborate messages. Many Japanese continue to think that cultural and racial homogeneity plays a significant role in the Japanese *haragei* communication. Artful silence, tone of voice, facial expressions, eye movement, grunts, and other contextual cues are important factors in Japanese.

Many Japanese also make much of the idea that their language is different from other languages. Unlike English or French, which have become international languages, the Japanese language is not widely spoken or used except in Japan, an island nation where the people do not have many everyday contacts with different peoples or languages. Such Japanese thus have a keen sense of both their distinctiveness as a people and the uniqueness of their language, some going so far as to believe that only Japanese born in Japan can truly master the different, complex, and thus "superior" language. This sense of uniqueness declined somewhat after the 1980s, but its vestiges can be seen at all levels of society.

Kinko Ito

Bibliography
Christopher, Robert. *The Japanese Mind: The Goliath Explained*. New York: Linden Press/Simon Schuster, 1984.
Reischauer, Edwin O. *The Japanese*. Tokyo: Charles E. Tuttle, 1980.

Japanese Monroe Doctrine

Slogan used in Japan from World War I to 1945, especially by the journalist Tokutomi Sohō, along with the slogan, "Asia for Asiatics." Also known as the "Asiatic Monroe Doctrine," the slogan connoted expulsion of the West from Asia and establishment of independent Asian states under Japanese stewardship. Japanese officials attempted its implementation after 1931, through creation of the state of Manchukuo out of Manchuria and development of the Greater East Asia Coprosperity Sphere.

The term sparked an uproar in April 1934 when Amō Eijirō, chief of the Foreign Ministry Information Bureau, spoke informally to a group of journalists, criticizing Western assistance to China after the 1931 Manchurian Incident that propelled Japan onto the colonial scene in China, and stressing Japan's claim to exclusive responsibility for maintaining peace in East Asia. His disclosure of a policy dispatch from Foreign Minister Hirota Kōki to Japan's envoy to China, expressing support for peace on Japanese terms and calling for destruction of all anti-Japanese movements in China, evoked sharp American and British protests. The result was that Japan officially retracted Amō's remarks and made statements supporting China's independence and equal economic opportunity there for all. A year later, however, Japan abrogated the 1922 Nine Power Treaty, which had guaranteed Chinese independence, and the Japanese Monroe Doctrine eventually became government policy; it remained policy until the end of World War II.

Jacob Kovalio

Bibliography
Crowley, James B. *Japan's Quest for Autonomy*. Princeton, NJ: Princeton University Press, 1966.

Japanese Romantic School
(*Nihon Rōmanha*)

A literary association led by literary critic Yasuda Yojurō (1910–81) that promoted the thought, movement, and influence of a group of nationalistic writers who flourished in Japan from the 1930s to the end of World War II in 1945. The group published a literary magazine of the same title (1935–38). It insisted that the Japanese must return to the Japan of the ancient period, when gods and humans intermingled as one, and urged the Japanese to appreciate their classics. Its writings consisted of impassioned critical essays, persuasive essays praising Japanese heroes in myths and legends, and Romantic novels. The group functioned in a society that witnessed the rise of proletarian literature, its suppression by the government, the appearance of many *tenkōsha* (writers who renounced their belief in Communism), and modernist experimental literature. The Nihon Rōmanha opposed Japan's continued acceptance of Western standards and the country's modernization processes. Calling for the establishment of a Japanese national identity, it was fundamentally nationalistic, often irrational and fanatical, and usually pedantic.

The group and the magazine attracted many young authors and *tenkō* writers with far reaching influence who sought new ideological ground. As a young man, the novelist Mishima Yukio (1925–70) expressed his admiration for the emperor and for patriotic death. After World War II broke out, some of these writers became more vocal, and the military welcomed their writings. Military officials saw their calls for classicism as a means of arousing the Japanese spirit and promoting patriotism. Principal members of the Rōmanha included Nakatani Takao (1901–) and Jimbo Kōtarō (1905–), both students of German Romanticism, and literary critic and essayist Kamei Katsuichirō (1907–66).

James R. Morita

Bibliography
Doak, Kevin M. *Dreams of Difference: The Japanese Romantic School and the Crisis of Modernity.* Berkeley: University of California Press, 1994.

Jimmu Society (*Jimmukai*)

Right-wing organization. The activist Ōkawa Shūmei founded the Jimmukai on February 11, 1932, to promote patriotism and militarism based on national socialism. The society's platform called for the liberation of the nonwhite races, the moral unification of all peoples, the destruction of the political parties (though its members campaigned actively for national-socialist candidates in the 1932 Diet election), and direct imperial government. The most important activity of the 30,000-member society was its members' participation in the planning of the May 15 (1932) Incident, providing arms and advice to the extremists who assassinated Prime Minister Inukai Tsuyoshi and attempted to destroy business, political, and power centers in Tokyo. The society declined precipitously after Ōkawa was arrested in June in connection with the incident, though it did not disband until 1935.

James L. Huffman

Bibliography
Storry, Richard. *The Double Patriots: A Study of Japanese Nationalism.* Westport, CT: Greenwood Press, 1973.

K

Kagawa Toyohiko (1888–1960)

Japanese Christian evangelist and social reformer. Born to a wealthy former samurai and his mistress, Kagawa converted to Christianity at age 15 through the influence of Presbyterian missionaries. His reputation for selfless character, which was spread by his popular autobiographical writings and accounts by missionaries, began early in the 1910s during his time at Kōbe Theological Seminary, when he moved into the Shinkawa slum in Kobe to share life with social outcasts. Recognizing after study at Princeton University in the United States (1915–17) that charity alone would not raise the lot of the poor, he engaged in labor activism and farm-cooperative organization in the post–World War I period. In both movements, he was eventually edged aside by more left-wing organizers.

Though his activities as a nationalist in the 1930s and 1940s were not influential in their own right, Kagawa's utterances favorable to Japanese expansion on the Asian continent stirred alarm in the West because of the unwarranted presumptions there that Kagawa was the leading Christian of Japan and that he was a solid pacifist. He was arrested in August 1940 for antiwar activities, but a subsequent public apology to the government blunted in Japan the potential impact of the affair for peace. He is known to have praised Japan's colonial policies in Manchuria. In his writings during the war, he exonerated the 1941 Japanese attack on American naval ships and personnel at Pearl Harbor and condemned British Prime Minister Winston Churchill and U.S. President Franklin D. Roosevelt. As the end of the conflict neared, he gave anti-American radio talks directed overseas. Kagawa justified his nationalism as obedience to a Christian imperative to identify fully with his people. Scholars critical of Kagawa have suggested that his actions reflected his psychological need for approval and affirmation.

Thomas W. Burkman

Bibliography

Ota, Yuzo. "Kagawa Toyohiko: A Pacifist?" *Pacifism in Japan: The Christian and Socialist Tradition.* Ed. N. Bamba and J. Howes. Kyoto: Minerva Press, 1978, 91–122.

Schildgen, Robert D. *Toyohiko Kagawa: An Apostle of Love and Social Justice.* Berkeley, CA: Centenary Books, 1988.

Kamikaze (Divine Wind)

A general term applied to Japanese air and naval units and personnel that crashed intentionally into enemy ships or planes in World War II. "Kamikaze" originally referred to the typhoons that hampered Mongol invasions in the thirteenth century and, thus, became associated with divine protection of the Japanese nation.

The decision to use suicide tactics in World War II grew out of the worsening war situation. Both enlisted personnel and civilians in isolated areas had been ordered to fight to the death and to kill themselves rather than surrender. By 1944, shortages of trained pilots and fuel that would enable recruits to be trained led to decisions to form special attack units using conventional aircraft or rocket-powered gliding bombs, operated by young, hastily trained pilots. This strategy proved highly destructive of U.S. shipping in the devastating Okinawa campaign that began on April 1, 1945. The objective was not so much a Japanese victory as to ensure the survival of the Japanese nation and imperial government. Officials hoped that, rather than face unacceptable losses, the Allies would make last-ditch exceptions to unconditional-surrender terms and offer concessions that would safeguard Japanese sovereignty. While that hope proved illusory, the damage inflicted by the Kamikaze was considerable.

David G. Egler

Bibliography
Aitō, Hatsuho. *Thunder Gods: The Kamikaze Pilots Tell Their Story*. Tokyo: Kodansha International, 1989.
Hoyt, Edwin P. *The Kamikazes*. New York: Arbor House, 1983.

Kaneko Fumiko (1903–26)

Nihilist, activist. Born to impoverished parents in Yokohama, Kaneko was transferred from relative to relative as a child, then sent to live for seven years with a cruel grandmother in Korea. At age 17, she moved to Tokyo, where she spent several years scraping for jobs and studying. She flirted briefly with Christianity, then became involved with a group of young socialists and anarchists. Finding most of them shallow and hypocritical, she became a nihilist, advocating equality and better conditions for the poor and sympathizing with Korean nationalists. In 1923, she joined Korean anarchist Pak Yeol in a plot to assassinate the Japanese emperor with a bomb to demonstrate that he was not divine. She was convicted of high treason and sentenced to death. When the sentence was reduced to life imprisonment, Kaneko defiantly tore up the commutation order, then committed suicide in prison.

James L. Huffman

Bibliography
Hane, Mikiso. *Reflections on the Way to the Gallows: Voices of Japanese Rebel Women*. Berkeley: University of California Press, 1988.

Kanno Suga (also Sugako) (1881–1911)

Anarchist and women's rights activist. Born in Osaka to a mining family, Kanno became interested in socialism at age 15 after reading essays by socialist Sakai Toshihiko. Forced into marriage at age 17, she left her husband three years later to become a journalist. In 1903, she became affiliated with Fujin Kyōfūkai (Women's Moral Reform Society), which called for the banning of brothels. Active in various movements that opposed the Russo-Japanese War (1904–05), Kanno became a member, in 1904, of Heiminsha (Society of Commoners), an anarchist and socialist antiwar group.

In 1906, she returned to Tokyo with her common-law husband, socialist Arahata Kanson; they both were involved in the Red Flag Incident (1908), a socialist-anarchist rally that triggered a government crackdown on the socialist movement. Kanno was arrested following the incident and spent two months in jail. After her release, she became romantically involved with Kōtoku Shūsui, an anarchist, and, in 1909, they began publishing a journal, *Jiyū Shisō* (Free Thought). Kanno served a three-month prison term for espousing anarchy at the journal. During her incarceration, government officials uncovered her involvement in an alleged plot, known as the Great Treason Incident, to assassinate the emperor. Twenty-six people were arrested and put on trial on December 10, 1910, for their suspected involvement. On January 25, 1911, Kanno was hanged for her role as a leader.

James L. Huffman
Tracy Pollard

Bibliography
Hane, Mikiso. *Reflections on the Way to the Gallows: Voices of Japanese Rebel Women*. Berkeley: University of California Press, 1988.
Sievers, Sharon L. *Flowers in Salt: The Beginnings of Feminist Consciousness in Modern Japan*. Stanford, CA: Stanford University Press, 1983.

Katō Hiroharu (also known as Kanji) (1870–1939)

Admiral. A Fukui Prefecture native and graduate of the Navy War College, he became one of the navy's most outspoken advocates of military strength. As a member of Japan's delegation to the 1921 Washington Conference, he vigorously opposed the decision to accept a 5:5:3 capital tonnage ratio for the British, American, and Japanese navies, arguing unsuccessfully for a 10:10:7 ratio. In 1930, as chief of the naval general staff, he appealed directly to the emperor against the cabinet's acceptance of the same ratio at the London Naval Conference, then resigned in protest when his appeal was rejected. He remained active politically and was supported by right wingers for the prime ministership when Saitō Makoto stepped down in 1934. After resigning from the navy in 1935, he actively supported several ultranationalist organizations, including the Kokuhonsha (National Foundations Society).

James L. Huffman

Bibliography

Howarth, Stephen. *Morning Glory: A History of the Imperial Japanese Navy.* New York: Atheneum, 1983.

Katō Hiroyuki (1836–1916)

Educator and author who gave direction to the newly established system of higher education during the first three decades of the Meiji era (1868–1912). Accepted while still a young man as an instruction assistant at the Tokugawa government's Western Studies Institute in Edo, Katō rose rapidly in the estimation of his supervisors and, by 1860, had become the first Japanese intellectual proficient in German, a language he used to engage in his lifelong passion, the study of European intellectual history, political theory, law, and theory of state. He became a member of the *Yōgaku* (braintrusters)—specialists in Western studies—who advised Tokugawa Keiki, the last Tokugawa shogun, from 1866 to 1868.

Katō's influential writing career began in 1861. The corpus of writings totaled 50 or more items in published and manuscript form. A characteristic Meiji era enlightener, from 1866 to 1874 Katō introduced the Japanese public to constitutionalism, Western parliamentary institutions, and the history of Western political thought. He literally created the vocabulary that Japanese and later Chinese were to use to deal with the modern polity, and his works served as the foundation for Japan's first modern popular political movement, the campaign for "freedom and people's rights."

Early in 1874, however, when Katō modified the natural-rights theories that had served as the basis for his political and governmental theory, he assailed the former official Itagaki Taisuke's call for the government to create a popular legislature immediately. By 1882, he had published *Jinken shinsetsu* (New Theory of the Rights of Man), a repudiation of natural-rights doctrine, and he removed his earlier works from circulation, explaining that they were inconsistent with the views he now held.

Katō now incisively argued against the theory of natural rights, becoming a strong supporter of the governmental oligarchy in one of the earliest examples of what was later to be called *tenkō*, a "change of direction" or a reversal from long-held principles. From 1882 to 1893, in such works as *Kyōsha no kenri no kyosō* (The Struggle for the Rights of the Stronger), Katō provided a new basis for the authoritarian Meiji Constitution the government promulgated in 1889. More ominous still, he made what he called a "scientific case" for Japan's "right to hegemony" in East Asia.

Katō offered those advocating or seeking Japanese hegemony in East Asia a social-Darwinist rationale in addition to the traditionalist one that had long informed their thought. The Japanese sociopolitical organism was demonstrating it was fittest in the struggle for survival, or, as Katō wrote, "The strong eat, the weak are eaten." His scientific rationale lent itself to the mood of nationalism and expansionism that gripped ever wider strata of the public in the last decade of the nineteenth century and the first decades of the twentieth. His *Struggle for the Rights of the Stronger* was published in German in 1893, and, from this point on, his nationalist fervor grew ever more strident. He made virulent attacks, for example, against Christianity for its deleterious effect on the unique Japanese *kokutai* (national polity). To the end of his life, Katō continued also to shore up the scientific basis for Japanese nationalism/imperialism, drawing particularly on the tenets of social Darwinism.

From 1881 to 1893, Katō served as the first chancellor of the new Tokyo Imperial University, after having served several years as tutor in Western topics to the Meiji Emperor. As an educator, he introduced the German undergraduate curriculum in humanities and social sciences to Japan, and it was one of Katō's students, Aoki Shuzō, who, from his post as ambassador at Berlin, brokered the relationship between Prime Minister Itō Hirobumi and German Chancellor Otto von Bismarck when Itō visited Germany while drafting the Meiji Constitution. The result was a highly German flavor in the constitution.

For his services to the Meiji government, Katō was raised to the House of Peers, granted the rank of baron, and named imperial court councillor. He was named adviser to the Privy

K

Council (1906–16), awarded the Junior Grade Second Court Rank, and given the Grand Cordon of the Rising Sun.

David Abosch

Bibliography
Kōsaka, Masaaki, ed. *Japanese Thought in the Meiji Era*. Tokyo: Pan-Pacific Press, 1958.

Katō Takaaki
(also known as Kōmei) (1860–1926)

Bureaucrat and politician. A native of Aichi Prefecture, he graduated from Tokyo Imperial University in 1881, spent five years working for the Mitsubishi business enterprises and in 1886 married Mitsubishi founder Iwasaki Yatarō's oldest daughter. In 1887, he entered the foreign ministry, where he served four times as foreign minister and twice as minister to Great Britain. He played a key role in developing, then revising, the Anglo-Japanese Alliance of 1902. He also stirred up considerable controversy in 1914–15 by leading Japan into World War I, then issuing the imperialistic Twenty-One Demands to China. His Diet career began in 1902; in 1913, he joined Katsura Tarō's Rikken Dōshikai (Constitutional Association of Friends). When it merged into the Kenseikai (Constitutional Association) in 1916, Katō became president, using the Kenseikai to fight the established oligarchy. He was selected prime minister in 1924. Progressives hailed him for securing the passage of universal male suffrage in 1925. His administration also was responsible for passage the same year of the Peace Preservation Law (*chian iji hō*), which proscribed unpatriotic thought and thus provided a legal basis for the ultranationalism of the 1930s. Katō died in office on January 28, 1926.

James L. Huffman

Bibliography
Duus, Peter. *Party Rivalry and Change in Taishō Japan*. Cambridge: Harvard University Press, 1968.

Katsu Kaishū (1823–99)

Late-Tokugawa-Meiji statesman who played a prominent role in the development of Japan's first modern navy. Born the eldest son of a low-level *bakufu* retainer in Edo (now Tokyo),

Katsu studied Western learning and military techniques from an early age. After American Commodore Matthew Perry's squadron forced Japan to open its ports in 1854, Katsu's skills were in great demand, and, in 1855, he was appointed *bakufu* translator, an inspector of coastal defenses, and a student at the government's Dutch-operated naval school in Nagasaki.

In 1860, he sailed the first modern Japanese warship to America as part of the mission to ratify the 1858 U.S.–Japan Commercial Treaty, which opened trade between the two countries. Two years later, he was appointed commissioner of warships and, in this capacity, established a naval training center at Hyōgo. He was removed from office in 1864 over his criticism of *bakufu* leadership, but he regained the position in 1866, when the need for his services grew critical.

Katsu attempted to negotiate a settlement with Saigō Takamori, an official in Satsuma domain, to end the hostilities of the Meiji Restoration in 1868, but the compromise collapsed, and he was forced to follow the shogun into exile. From 1873 to 1875, he served as the Meiji government's minister of the navy, after which he retired to pursue scholarly activities.

Lane R. Earns

Bibliography
Jansen, Marius. *Sakamoto Ryōma and the Meiji Restoration*. Princeton, NJ: Princeton University Press, 1961.

Katsura Tarō (1848–1913)

Prime minister. With his patron, the oligarch Yamagata Aritomo, Katsura was one of Meiji (1868–1912) Japan's foremost advocates of emperor-centered nationalism. He argued that the government must remain studiously aloof ("transcendent") from political influences and that the military must be totally independent of civilian control. Believing that Japan's destiny was economic and political dominance in Asia, he advocated constantly higher military budgets and the untrammeled right of the military to extend Japanese influence into northeast Asia.

Educated in Germany, Katsura helped Yamagata establish German-style military conscription and an independent army general staff. The Anglo-Japanese Alliance (1902), the Russo-Japanese War (1904–05), the Taft-Katsura Agreement (1905) and the annexation of Korea (1910) expanded Japanese influence into Asia during his three terms as prime minister (1901–06, 1908–11, and 1912–13).

Because he held that the interests of the nation superseded any individual rights, he utilized peace-preservation laws to repress political dissent, culminating in the 1910 High Treason Incident in which his government used an alleged socialist conspiracy designed to assassinate the emperor to destroy the socialist movement in Japan. Until 1905, his policy toward the political parties was that of assaulting the center to divide and conquer through factionalism. After 1905, however, he cooperated with the Rikken Seiyūkai (Friends of Constitutional Government Party), and in 1912 he attempted to create his own "transcendental" party, precipitating the watershed Taishō Political Crisis of 1912–13 when he used an imperial rescript to force a recalcitrant navy to cooperate in forming a government. His government was toppled by the crisis, and he died not long after stepping down from the prime ministership.

Louis G. Perez

Bibliography

Hackett, Roger F. *Yamagata Aritomo*. Cambridge: Harvard University Press, 1971.
Najita, Tetsuo. *Hara Kei and the Politics of Compromise*. Cambridge: Harvard University Press, 1967.

Kawabata Yasunari (1899–1972)

Nobel Prize-winning novelist whose main concern was "Japaneseness." His works manifested his love of old Japan. Accepting the Nobel Prize in 1968, he discussed Japanese aesthetics, referring to Zen poems of the medieval period. He had stated that he would write only about Japan's beauty and sadness.

Kawabata usually published his novels in installments, leaving many unfinished. His major works included *Snow Country* (Knopf, 1956), *The Master of Go* (Knopf, 1972), *Thousand Cranes* (Knopf, 1959), and *Sound of the Mountain* (Knopf, 1970). His manner of writing and the resulting works reveal his belief in the art of *renga* (linked verse) and his inclination to accept all matters as in a state of flux. His characters are fragile, blending into nature. When he started his writing career at the magazine *Bungei jidai* (Age of Literary Art) (1924–27), he defined his action as moving "from the age of religions into the age of literary art." His religions included the contemporary leftist writers' movements. He was conscious of new nov-

Kawabata Yasunari at awards ceremony for Nobel Prize in Literature. Courtesy Consulate General of Japan, N.Y.

elistic techniques from the West but apparently considered them uncongenial, preferring instead to maintain the Japanese lyrical tradition.

Kawabata held only a few public positions, chiefly the presidency of the Japan Pen Club. His Nobel Prize gave Japanese pride, and he was much sought after. But he was more concerned with pursuing ideas of death and decay, coexisting with the beauty that he cherished. He committed suicide on April 16, 1972.

James R. Morita

Bibliography

Keene, Donald. *Dawn to the West: Japanese Literature in the Modern Era—Fiction.* New York: Henry Holt, 1984.

Kawai Eijirō (1891–1944)

Student of industrial policy. A native of Tokyo and a graduate of Tokyo University, he worked while a young man as a factory inspector for the Ministry of Agriculture and Commerce, developing there a sense of outrage over working conditions that would motivate his entire career. He joined the economics faculty at Tokyo University in 1920 and became a vocal, widely published advocate of social reform.

Kawai became particularly well known for his insistence on solving problems through a middle course between state authoritarianism and Communism. He called for cooperation of all groups against Japan's state to achieve social reform. Though students criticized him early for his opposition to Marxism, by the mid-1930s his spirited attacks on violence had made him a target of ultranationalists. Following the February 26, 1936, coup attempt that resulted in the deaths of several top officials, he wrote in a highly controversial article: "Even if force dominates the world for a time, it will inevitably destroy itself" (Hashikawa, 90). His statements led to his arrest in 1938. He was dismissed from his university post the next year and subjected to a six-year trial, which ended in his conviction for disseminating dangerous ideas. He died shortly thereafter.

James L. Huffman

Bibliography

Hashikawa, Bunsō. "Antiwar Values—The Resistance in Japan." *Japan Interpreter.* Vol. 9, No. 1 (Spring 1974), 86–97.

Kawakami Hajime (1879–1946)

Marxist theoretician. Born in Yamaguchi Prefecture, he devoted his life to the struggle for economic justice. After he graduated from Tokyo University in 1902, a brief teaching stint and a period in the Mugaen Buddhist sect led him to proclaim that he would give his life to the pursuit of personal selflessness and improvement of society. The bulk of his career was spent at Kyoto University, where he taught economics and introduced Marxism to Japan. He achieved fame in 1916–17 for *Bimbō monogatari* (Tale of Poverty), a study of the plight of the poor in advanced nations, and expounded his moralistic brand of Marxism after 1919 in his journal *Shakai Mondai Kenkyū* (Research in Social Problems). Criticized for a lack of Marxist orthodoxy, Kawakami shifted to a more radical stance and was forced to resign from the university in the government's antisocialist drive of 1928. Kawakami then became more active politically and joined the Communist Party in 1932; a year later, he was arrested as a party leader and sentenced to five years in prison. He spent the wartime era in relative seclusion, writing his autobiography and other works.

James L. Huffman

Bibliography

Bernstein, Gail. *Japanese Marxist: A Portrait of Kawakami Hajime.* Cambridge: Harvard University Press, 1976.

Kido Kōichi (1889–1977)

Government leader. A grandson of Kido Kōin and one of the architects of the Meiji Restoration (1868), he ascended the bureaucratic ladder easily and held top posts through much of his adult career. His diary, which records his activities from 1930 on, is essentially a log of meetings with elitist friends and political contacts.

An association with the Imperial Household Ministry commenced when Kido became secretary to Privy Seal Makino Nobuaki in 1930. From 1933 to 1937, he was director of peerage affairs. In 1937, he became minister of education in the Konoe Fumimaro cabinet and in 1938–39 he served as welfare minister. He was in the Konoe cabinet when the second Sino-Japanese War (1937–45) started. In 1939, he served in the Hiranuma Kiichirō cabinet as home minister. His associations with Konoe, who was acceptable to the military and civilian ultranationalists, and with Hiranuma, a fervent believer in Japan's national essence, as well as his cooperation with Konoe in establishing a new order and a one-party system, indicate that Kido clearly was not a liberal constitutional monarchist.

In 1940, Kido became privy seal. With the old oligarch Saionji Kinmochi's death that same year, he became the chief adviser to the emperor in selecting prime ministers and the person linking the emperor, government officials, and political leaders. He also kept in touch with the militant radical nationalists, considering it his duty to read the trend of the times (*jisei*), forge a consensus, and maintain unity among diverse forces. In July 1940, he was instrumental in the reappointment of Konoe as prime minister.

When Konoe resigned that post just before the outbreak of the Pacific War, Kido advised the emperor to appoint General Tōjō Hideki prime minister. In forging the consensus, he seemed to give greater consideration to the views of the ultranationalists and expansionists than those of the constitutional monarchists and moderates. Kido thus would have to be included among the right-of-center nationalists. He favored accepting the Potsdam Declaration to end the war in 1945 because he saw it as the only way to preserve the emperor system and the *kokutai* (national polity)—that is, Japan's national essence. He was charged, tried, and convicted as a Class A war criminal after the war and was sentenced to life imprisonment but was released by the government due to his failing health in 1955.

Mikiso Hane

Bibliography
Titus, David Anson. *Palace and Politics in Prewar Japan*. New York: Columbia University Press, 1974.

Kido Takayoshi (1833–77)
Leader in the Meiji Restoration (1868), the nationalist revolution that gave birth to modern Japan. Born in a Chōshū family of samurai, Kido traveled to Edo (now Tokyo) in 1852 to study swordsmanship and to enter the conspiratorial world of emperor loyalists. His patriotism intensified through his membership in coastal defense forces, which faced the steam vessels of the American navy under Commodore Matthew Perry as Japan was opened in 1854. A coup by new model rifle units in Chōshū in 1865 brought Kido to power in his domain, and he used its armies to fight the temporizing shogun to a standstill in 1865–66; he also formed a secret alliance with Satsuma domain in 1866 and helped restore the emperor to direct rule in 1868.

Kido worked to abolish Japanese feudalism in 1871 and, after directing a formal study of foreign governments during the Iwakura Mission (1871–73), wrote the memorial that determined the shape of the German-inspired Meiji Constitution of 1889. In his last years, Kido promoted domestic reform, presided over an appointed legislature, and supervised the moral education of the young Meiji Emperor. Kido died in 1877 from tuberculosis.

Sidney DeVere Brown

Bibliography
Brown, Sidney D., and Akiko Hirota, trans. *The Diary of Kido Takayoshi, 1868–1877*. 3 Vols. Tokyo: University of Tokyo Press, 1983–86.

Craig, Albert M. "Kido Kōin and Ōkubo Toshimichi: A Psychohistorical Analysis." *Personality in Japanese History*. Ed. Craig Shively and Donald H. Shively. Berkeley: University of California Press, 1970.

Kinoshita Naoe (1869–1937)
Socialist-pacifist writer. Born in Nagano Prefecture, he spent his early years as a journalist in Matsumoto, attacking established politicians and adopting Christianity and socialist ideas. He moved to Tokyo in 1898 (initially as a prisoner, for overly aggressive reporting at Matsumoto's progressive newspaper *Shin'yō Nippō*) and was hired by Shimada Saburō at the Tokyo daily *Mainichi Shimbun*, where he wrote forcefully at the turn of the century on pacifism and on the Ashio copper-mine-pollution struggle, Japan's first environmental dispute. He helped found Japan's first socialist party, the Shakai Minshūtō (Socialist People's Party), in 1900 and published a successful antiwar novel, *Hi no hashira* (Pillar of Fire), in 1904. Kinoshita was one of Japan's earliest pacifists, agitating against the Sino-Japanese War (1894–95), then continuing his antiwar writings at the socialist newspaper *Heimin Shimbun* during the Russo-Japanese War one decade later. Not long after that war, he abandoned public life, taking up Buddhist meditation and spending his last decades in contemplation, though he continued to write on political issues occasionally.

James L. Huffman

Bibliography

Nishida, Takeshi. "Kinoshita Naoe: Pacifism and Religious Withdrawal." *Pacifism in Japan: The Christian and Socialist Tradition.* Ed. N. Bamba and J. Howes. Vancouver: University of British Columbia Press, 1978.

Kiryū Yūyū (1873–1941)

Antiwar journalist. Born in Ishikawa Prefecture and graduated in 1899 from Tokyo University law department, he spent his life advocating and writing about liberal causes for several newspapers, including *Mainichi* and *Asahi* in Osaka. He vociferously criticized fascism as editor of *Shinano Mainichi Shimbun* early in the 1930s. Forced to resign following a 1933 attack on what he called the army's "ridiculous air-defense strategy," he pioneered a form of resistance in which liberal thinkers expressed themselves freely (despite continued official harassment) in private publications addressed to friends. Beginning in 1934, he published 163 issues of a private magazine, *Tazan no ishi* (Stones from Other Mountains), in Nagoya, recalling the liberal spirit of the Meiji era (1868–1912) and decrying Japan's descent into militarism. He saw the world heading toward bestiality but said shortly before his death that he regretted only that he would not live to see the demilitarized postwar era.

James L. Huffman

Bibliography

Hashikawa, Bunsō. "Antiwar Values—The Resistance in Japan." *Japan Interpreter.* Vol. 9, No. 1 (1974), 86–97.

Kishi Nobusuke (1896–1987)

Prime minister and key figure in Japan's policy-making from the 1930s to the 1980s. Influenced by such ideologues as Yoshida Shōin and Kita Ikki and nurtured in the political culture of Chōshū domain (Yamaguchi Prefecture), Kishi was a nationalist reformer who became increasingly conservative after the war.

After graduating from the law faculty of Tokyo Imperial University in 1920, Kishi entered the Ministry of Agriculture and Commerce. In the 1930s, he worked with the architect of Japan's increasingly promilitary industrial policy, Shinji Yoshino. Sympathetic to the national socialists' ideas, Kishi became a leader of the "new bureaucrats." During the period 1935–39, he was responsible for the implementation of Japan's Five-Year Plan for industrializing the puppet state of Manchukuo and exploiting its resources. From 1939 to 1944, during the Konoe Fumimaro and Tōjō Hideki cabinets, Kishi orchestrated the wartime economic mobilization program. His opposition to war policy was instrumental in the fall of the Tōjō cabinet in 1944.

Kishi was imprisoned as a suspected Class A war criminal in 1945 but was not indicted and consequently was released in 1948. He was elected to the lower house of the Diet as a Liberal Party candidate in 1953, and he contributed importantly to the 1955 unification of the conservative parties into the Liberal Democratic Party (LDP).

During his term as prime minister (February 1957–July 1960), Kishi "reversed course" in education and police-administration initiatives, rekindling public fear of a return to prewar policies. He provoked widespread public debate and protest for his aborted attempt to revise the Police Duties Law, and for his high-handed tactics in introducing ethics courses into the school curriculum and in revising the 1951 Japan–U.S. Security Treaty. Left-wing critics branded these moves as reactionary attempts to undo democratization and return Japan to prewar militarism and authoritarianism. Demonstrations over the security treaty forced him from office in July 1960, but he remained influential in LDP affairs until his death.

Shigeko Fukai

Bibliography

Fukui, Haruhiro. "Postwar Politics, 1945–1973." *Cambridge History of Japan.* Vol. 6. *The Twentieth Century.* Ed. Peter Duus. Cambridge: Cambridge University Press, 1988.

Kita Ikki (1883–1937)

Soldier of fortune and author of revolutionary nationalist tracts in Meiji-Taishō Japan. Born on the island of Sado facing Russia across the Sea of Japan, Kita detested Communism and advocated a process of nationalist revolution applicable to every Asian nation according to the dictates of its own historical experience. He wrote a book on socialism in Japan (*Kokutairon oyobi junsei shakaishugi,* or *National Essence and Pure Socialism,* 1906) arguing that the

Kita Ikki. Asahi Shimbun Photo.

Japanese national essence (*kokutai*) already conformed to the requirements of a correctly interpreted socialism. When the authorities banned the book, Kita went to China in 1911 as an adventurer in the revolutionary movement of Sun Yatsen and Song Jiaoren. He wrote a book attacking Japan's imperialistic China policy (*Shina kakumei gaishi,* or *Unofficial History of the Chinese Revolution,* 1916), and in 1919 he went home to join Ōkawa Shūmei's new patriotic society, the Yūzonsha (Endure Society), in the hope of promoting a revolution in his own country. To this end, Kita distributed a pamphlet embodying an incisive action program for putting Japan back together again. Called *Nihon kaizō hōan taikō* (*A Plan to Reorganize Japan* [1919]), it advocated a military coup d'état and the authoritarian restructuring of the whole society under the aegis of the emperor. Thus, Kita meant to rule out capitalism and Communism alike in the interest of total national development. This pamphlet became a favorite of the young army officers who staged the famous mutiny of February 26, 1936, that nearly brought down the government. An avid Nichiren Buddhist, Kita lived as a recluse after 1925 while receiving an allowance from Mitsui business interests who supported his nationalistic ideas. In 1936, he was arrested and tried

in camera by a military court, then executed the next year as a "Red" for his part (though he had not participated) in the unsuccessful February 26 insurrection.

George M. Wilson

Bibliography

Wilson, George. *Radical Nationalist in Japan: Kita Ikki, 1883–1937.* Cambridge: Harvard University Press, 1969.

Kiyoura Keigo (1850–1942)

Prime minister. A native of Kumamoto, he entered the Justice Ministry in the early years of the Meiji era (1868–1912) and, as a protégé of Home Minister and conservative oligarch Yamagata Aritomo, served in several cabinets. In 1914, he was Yamagata's choice for prime minister, but the nomination was opposed by the navy, and instead Ōkuma Shigenobu formed a cabinet. In January 1924, when an attempt on the life of the crown prince forced the Yamamoto Gonnohyōe cabinet to resign, Kiyoura formed a cabinet with the support of only one party, the Seiyū Hontō (True Friends of Government Party). His was the third consecutive "transcendental," or nonparty, cabinet, which violated the pattern of party cabinets that had begun in 1918 with the appointment of Hara Takashi as prime minister. The parties that opposed Kiyoura in 1924 won such a substantial victory in the election that followed that he was forced to resign in June. Kiyoura, then, represented the oligarchic opposition to party cabinets responsible to the lower house of the Diet (legislature), and his resignation ushered in the era of party rule, which lasted until 1932. He spent his remaining years largely as a private citizen, influencing politics from behind the scenes.

Sally A. Hastings

Bibliography

Duus, Peter. *Party Rivalry and Political Change in Taishō Japan.* Cambridge: Harvard University Press, 1968.

Kodama Yoshio (1911–84)

Political power broker. A native of Fukushima Prefecture, he spent a lifetime promoting right-wing causes and people. During the 1930s, Kodama spent six years in jail for his ultranationalist activities, including founding the Independence Youth Society (Dokuritsu Seinensha) and plotting to assassinate Prime Minister Saitō Makoto. He was active in the puppet state of Manchukuo and in China during the World War II years, first in intelligence and fact-finding work for the Foreign Ministry, later in securing military materials for the naval air force through his own Kodama Agency. His agency made a fortune in the latter tasks, largely by securing looted supplies cheaply. He was imprisoned early in 1946 as a suspected war criminal, then released in late 1948 with no formal charges ever having been brought. The reason for the dropping of charges was rumored to lie in a deal with Occupation authorities whereby he would supply information to American intelligence forces. He became a behind-the-scenes power in conservative politics, bankrolling favorite politicians and influencing policies, even while maintaining close ties to prewar extremists such as Akao Bin and Nemoto Hiroshi of the Sakurakai (Cherry Blossom Society). He was prosecuted for bribery in connection with the 1976 Lockheed scandal and was charged in 1977 with tax evasion by Tokyo authorities. He died following a stroke in 1984, before the trials had run their course.

James L. Huffman

Bibliography
Dubro, Alec, and David E. Kaplan. *Yakuza*. London: Futura, 1986.

Koiso Kuniaki (1880–1950)

Army general and prime minister (1944–45), who died while serving a life sentence as a war criminal. During the 1910s he promoted efforts to stimulate local Manchurian and Mongolian movements to gain independence from China and to tie those areas more closely to Japan. In March 1931, as chief of the Military Affairs Bureau, he was a key participant in the aborted plot to organize a coup d'état at home to facilitate military action abroad. He served as minister of colonial affairs (1939–41) and as governor-general of Korea (1942–44). He both acceded to and fell from the leadership of government with a smoothness unique among Axis leaders, taking over when Prime Minister Tōjō Hideki's support evaporated (July 1944), then resigning the next year when the army refused to initiate peace negotiations with China as a first step in extrica-

tion from disaster. Ironically, Koiso may be remembered less as an exemplar of militant Japanese nationalism than as the voice of the Koiso Declaration (September 7, 1944), which announced "the future independence of all Indonesian peoples." Sukarno's response as leader of Indonesian nationalists was equally opportunistic, in the context of Allied advances in the Pacific: "Life or death with Dai Nippon until we are independent . . . [and] when we are independent."

Theodore Friend

Bibliography
Shillony, Ben-Ami. *Politics and Culture in Wartime Japan*. New York: Oxford University Press, 1981.

Kokumin Shimbun

Daily newspaper. Tokutomi Sohō launched *Kokumin Shimbun* on February 1, 1890, as a politically oriented mouthpiece for his anti-government, "commonerism" (*heiminshugi*) views. The paper's nature and reputation mirrored Tokutomi's stormy personal career during the next four decades. Following a healthy beginning, the publication declined in popularity when Tokutomi moved closer to the government after the Sino-Japanese War (1894–95) and entered the Matsukata Masayoshi government in 1897. The paper revived somewhat at the beginning of the 1900s, but it became the focus for bitter riots and firebombings in September 1905 because of Tokutomi's support of the government in the Russo-Japanese War (1904–05) negotiations and again in February 1913 for his ties to Prime Minister Katsura Tarō during a cabinet-felling dispute over military influence in the government. The *Kokumin* offices were destroyed by the Great Kantō Earthquake in 1923, and, although the paper remained influential, it was devastated financially. Tokutomi resigned in 1929, unwilling to adopt a purely commercial approach to journalism. *Kokumin* continued to publish until 1942, when a wartime press consolidation forced it out of existence.

James L. Huffman

Bibliography
Pierson, John. *Tokutomi Sohō, 1863– 1957*. Princeton, NJ: Princeton University Press, 1980.

Komura Jutarō (1855–1911)

Meiji-era (1868–1912) diplomat and foreign minister. Komura was born in Miyazaki Prefecture and educated at Daigaku Nankō (now Tokyo University) and Harvard Law School in Cambridge, Massachusetts; in 1884, he entered the Ministry of Foreign Affairs, where he devoted his life to advocating a strong foreign policy. As ministry first secretary in Beijing in 1893, he urged Japan to take the initiative in its conflicts with China. In 1900, he called on Japan to help the Western powers suppress the Boxer Rebellion there. As foreign minister (1901–05), he pushed a hard line against the Russians, concluded the 1902 Anglo-Japanese Alliance as a check on Russian aggression, and signed the 1905 Portsmouth Treaty ending the Russo-Japanese War (1904–05), even though he would have preferred that Japan demand additional concessions from the Russians. He became foreign minister again in 1908, following a brief time on the Privy Council and a term as ambassador to England. During this tenure, Japan annexed Korea (1910) and signed treaties with the Western powers in 1911 securing tariff autonomy. Komura also served as ambassador to Korea (1895–96), the United States (1898–1900), Russia (1900), and China (1901).

James L. Huffman

Bibliography

Okamoto, Shumpei. *The Japanese Oligarchy and the Russo-Japanese War*. New York: Columbia University Press, 1970.

Konoe Fumimaro (1891–1945)

Prime minister. Born in an aristocratic family descended from the twelfth-century Fujiwara regents, he was one of the most prominent—and enigmatic—leaders in the years before World War II. He entered the upper house of the Diet (legislature) in 1916, a year before graduating from Kyoto University and three years before becoming a member of Japan's delegation to the Paris Peace Conference that brought World War I to an end. During the next two decades, he became one of the most influential peers, advocating a strong role for Japan as leader of Asia and opposing Western imperialism.

Effective at maintaining the support of politicians and significant elements in the military, he was asked to form a cabinet after the unsuccessful February 26, 1936, military coup, but he de-

clined. A year and a half later (June 4, 1937), he accepted the prime ministership. During this tenure (1937–39), the second Sino-Japanese War (1937–45) began and military spending increased markedly. Konoe served again as prime minister from July 1940 to October 1941, this time encouraging the formation of the Imperial Rule Assistance Association to unify all parties and factions in support of national goals; he also advocated Japanese leadership of Asia through the Greater East Asia Coprosperity Sphere and approved the 1940 Tripartite Pact with Germany and Italy to pressure the Americans and the British to curtail their demands that Japan withdraw from China.

When these policies seemed to be failing, Konoe turned over the prime ministership to Tōjō Hideki. In the later war years, he endeavored to bring hostilities to an end, and immediately after the war he worked on the revision of Japan's constitution. He committed suicide on December 12, 1945, after he was indicted as a war criminal.

Mainly as a result of Konoe's wide popularity and the emphasis he placed in his memoirs on his antiwar sentiments, interpretations of his role vary. His long-term goals, however, supported Japanese expansion in China and Asia, and his policies clearly moved Japan toward war.

James L. Huffman

Bibliography

Berger, Gordon M. *Parties out of Power in Japan, 1931–1941*. Princeton, NJ: Princeton University Press, 1977.

Oka, Yoshitake. *Konoe Fumimaro*. Tokyo: University of Tokyo Press, 1983.

Korea

A popular perception of contemporary Koreans is that they are nationalistic. This modern-day label is accurate enough but masks two key ingredients. First, Korean nationalism is not new but is rather the result of several centuries of accumulated historical forces. Second, Korean nationalism is a complex phenomenon in which interaction with Japan is a necessary, but not a sufficient, component.

Korea entered the sixteenth century with a strong sense of nationhood. It had successfully integrated elements of Chinese civilization with Korea's own indigenous features to create a high level of culture. As a political unit, the country had been unified since the seventh century, and its government at the time, the Yi Dynasty (1392–1910), had achieved a notable level of technological development and political stability. It is probably fair to say that Koreans viewed Japan condescendingly as a less-civilized Johnny-come-lately in East Asia.

Japanese unifier Toyotomi Hideyoshi's invasion of Korea in 1592 profoundly affected Korea and its attitude toward Japan. The sheer totality of destruction visited upon Korea sent the Yi Dynasty into a long decline from which it never recovered. It also inclined Korea to adopt an isolationist policy, which earned it the sobriquet "Hermit Kingdom." But most important, the Koreans came to distrust and fear the Japanese as an aggressive power that wanted to dominate or destroy Korea. It is noteworthy that Korea's greatest military hero, Admiral Yi Sun-sin, gained his reputation in Korea's resistance to Japanese invaders.

After the Meiji Restoration (1868), Japan once again looked to Korea in a way that Koreans found aggressive. Reactionaries such as Saigō Takamori, believing that Japan needed to expand its empire, almost succeeded in launching an invasion of Korea in 1873. Liberals such as Fukuzawa Yukichi believed that Japan had a duty to rescue Korea from China's stultifying influence. Conservatives in the government such as Itō Hirobumi tended to view Korea's weakness as a threat to Japan's security since the nearby peninsula presented an inviting target for potential enemies of Japan. Despite their differing goals, all three groups agreed that interference in Korea's affairs was necessary. And, as Japan's modernizing armed forces grew larger and more proficient, the means by which such interference might be carried out became more feasible.

During these last decades of the nineteenth century, Koreans were of two minds about Japan. Many, recalling the Hideyoshi invasion and the near-invasion of 1873, rejected Japan out of hand as a predator. Other Koreans, while acknowledging the potential threat from Japan, admired Japan's rapid modernization along Western lines and believed that Japan could serve as a model for their own country, weakened by centuries of tradition. In this sense, the internal debate was similar to that experienced by Japan several decades earlier. Thus, nationalism came to include not only defending the nation from Japan, but also finding the most useful model for nation building. Unlike in Japan, where the admirers of the threatening outside powers captured the reins of power, in Korea this group never came to power, and, as a result, Korea did not undertake significant steps to strengthen itself.

As Korea remained weak and Japan grew stronger, Japan's Meiji government moved to enhance its security by fighting and defeating first the Chinese (1894–95) and then the Russians (1904–05) over who would dominate Korea. Vowing not to fight yet another war over Korea, Japan established a protectorate in 1905 and, in 1910, annexed Korea. Koreans reacted viscerally to the extinction of the independence of their country (now referred to as Chōsen), the forcible ending of the Yi Dynasty, and the establishment of the Japanese governor-general as the paramount political authority. Some former soldiers launched an ill-fated guerrilla war against the Japanese occupiers. Any illusion of Korean acquiescence that Japan might have had was rudely shattered by the nationwide protests of March 1, 1919, enshrined in Korean history as the March First Movement (*Samil Undong*).

During this period, Korean nationalism took several forms inside and outside of Korea. Some, such as later president Syngman Rhee, advocated diplomatic efforts aimed primarily at the United States to rally support for Korean independence. One step in this process involved the formation of a Korean provisional government in exile in 1919 in Shanghai. Others, also outside Korea, resorted to armed struggle to force Japan out of Korea. Pak Yong-man and Kim Il-sung represented practitioners of this approach. That nationalism was concerned not only with reestablishing Korean independence but also with nation building was indicated through the activities of men such as An Ch'ang-ho and Kim Sŏng-su. They took the position that Koreans needed a modern education, an entrepreneurial and modernizing spirit, and Western political values to attain the prerequisites for the foundation of a modern nation–state. This implied an evolutionary model that would need to be developed within the parameters of Japanese colonial rule. More radical nationalists rejected this evolutionary, work-within-the-system approach and advocated grass-roots organization of workers and peasants in a class struggle against not only Japanese but also those more moderate upper-class Korean reformers. This disagreement over the appropriate nation-building model would be replicated in postwar Korea with the erection of two separate regimes on the peninsula.

During this colonial period (1910–45), the Japanese attempted to erase all traces of Korean nationhood and culture while discriminating, sometimes severely and brutally, against the Korean people. Books on Korean history were suppressed, Korean newspapers were closed, Korean businesses had difficulty receiving bank loans, Shinto worship of the Japanese emperor was required, Korean land was confiscated, Koreans were forced to take Japanese names, and the Japanese language became the only official language. By the end of this period, most Koreans understandably detested Japan. And this anti-Japan stance was the key ingredient in Korean nationalism up to 1945.

How to evaluate this aspect of Korean nationalism up to 1945? On the one hand, Korean nationalism failed either to provide a consensus for nation building (witness the continued existence of two separate regimes in the north and the south) or to win the independence of Korea from Japan (liberation was due primarily to Japan's military defeat in 1945 by Soviet and American military forces). On the other hand, Korean nationalism succeeded in giving the Korean people a renewed sense of distinctiveness as a culture and a heightened desire never to be dominated by a foreign power again.

As Korea moved into the post–World War II era, the focus of nationalism necessarily changed to reflect the desire to reunify the now-divided country, while the anti-Japan focus receded now that Korea was finally independent. Nonetheless, this anti-Japanese legacy of Korean nationalism has continued to color much of postwar Korea. Issues of postwar political legitimacy are often determined by what one did during the colonial period. The massive influx of Japanese capital and technology is sometimes viewed with alarm as presaging an attempt to dominate Korea economically. Textbook revisions in Japan are watched closely for signs of rationalization of the takeover of Korea. And discrimination against Koreans in Japan continues to evoke an emotional response. While the anti-Japanese component of Korean nationalism has been muted by time and events since 1945, it would be erroneous to dismiss it entirely.

Wayne Patterson

Bibliography

Conroy, Hilary. *The Japanese Seizure of Korea, 1868–1910: A Study of Realism and Idealism in International Relations*. Philadelphia: University of Pennsylvania Press, 1960.

Lee, Chong-Sik. *The Politics of Korean Nationalism*. Berkeley: University of California Press, 1965.

Robinson, Michael Edson. *Cultural Nationalism in Colonial Korea, 1920–1925*. Seattle: University of Washington Press, 1988.

Korean Minority in Japan

The 680,000 Koreans living in Japan in the mid-1990s fall into primarily two groups: (1) individuals conscripted to help Japan build the World War II fighting machine during the 1930s and 1940s when Korea was a Japanese colony; and (2) the descendants of those conscripts. Those originally brought to Japan worked under severe conditions as mine workers, dam builders and laborers in the military industry.

At the end of World War II in 1945, Korea was released from Japanese control, and the Koreans in Japan gained the status of liberated peoples. Of the 2.3 million Koreans then in Japan, all but 500,000 were repatriated to Korea. But the sympathetic policy of the U.S.-led Occupation government (nicknamed SCAP, for Supreme Commander of the Allied Powers) toward these Koreans quickly changed.

The transformation came about, in part, because of altered conditions in the Korean community itself. At the end of the war, the victors partitioned Korea into two countries—North Korea and South Korea—in which competing political ideologies emerged, resulting eventually in the Korean War (1950–53). This situation split the Korean community in Japan, dividing it into two groups: Communist pro-North and capitalist pro-South. The pro-North group actively opposed many of SCAP's Occupation policies. SCAP, consequently, developed a new policy regarding Koreans in Japan. Originally, the Japanese government tried to return all Koreans to Korea, but SCAP encouraged Japan to introduce the Alien Registration Law; enacted in 1947, it in effect placed the Koreans outside the Japanese Constitution and excluded them from the new Japanese national structure. The San Francisco Peace Treaty, which formally ended World War II hostilities and the Allied Occupation in 1952, deprived Koreans of Japanese citizenship and officially made them outsiders.

Gerhard Gohl, a German sociologist, has called the Korean minority in Japan unique because the Koreans have become a "political minority" perpetually linked to the political situations in their divided motherland. This group is political and nationalistic because it maintains a vertical relationship to the homeland rather than a horizontal relationship with the people in Japan.

In addition to the official Korean residents in Japan, some Koreans have become naturalized Japanese citizens, and some are the issue of Korean/Japanese marriages. Until the early 1990s, Koreans were subjected to legally sanctioned discrimination in a variety of circumstances, including the Alien Registration Law provision that all Koreans be fingerprinted annually. While modest legal reforms did away with the annual fingerprinting and slightly improved the Koreans' lot in these years, discrimination itself continued. Koreans still experience prejudice in employment and housing and, at times, suffer harassment by Japanese residents. Even naturalized Koreans are not completely accepted as Japanese because of the operative myth that the Japanese are a monocultural people. Koreans in Japan, therefore, are forced to struggle constantly with the issue of national identity.

In-ha Lee

Bibliography

Lee, Changsoo, and George deVos, eds. *Koreans in Japan: Ethnic Conflict and Accommodation.* Berkeley: University of California Press, 1981.

Kōtoku Shūsui (left) and Kanno Suga. Asahi Shimbun Photo.

Kōtoku Shūsui (1871–1911)

Socialist and anarchist. Kōtoku was born in Nakamura, a small town in Kochi Prefecture. Despite his Confucian education, after completing middle school he went to Tokyo to study English and participate in the popular-rights movement. His studies were interrupted temporarily when the 1887 peace regulations forced him to leave Tokyo as a dangerous person, but he graduated from a Tokyo school of English in 1893 and became a journalist for various newspapers, including *Jiyū Shimbun* and *Yorozu Chōhō.* In 1898, Kōtoku joined the Shakaishugi Kenkyūkai (Society for the Study of Socialism); in 1901, he helped establish the Shakai Minshūtō (Socialist People's Party), Japan's first socialist party, which was disbanded by the government just two days after its creation. In 1903, in opposition to rising prowar sentiment against Russia, Kōtoku and other socialists created the Heiminsha (Society of Commoners), which published the newspaper *Heimin Shim-* *bun.* Kōtoku was sentenced to five months in jail two years later for publishing in the *Heimin Shimbun* the first Japanese translation of Karl Marx's *Communist Manifesto.*

Following his release, he spent six months in San Francisco, California, where he became a confirmed anarchist and advocate of the use of direct action to speed social and political reform. At the second convention of a revived Socialist Party, in 1907, his call for direct action split the party and caused its dissolution. In 1909, he became acquainted with Kanno Suga, a socialist and a feminist, and together they started the journal *Jiyū Shisō* (Free Thought), which published a mere two issues before being banned. Though only marginally involved with the Great Treason Incident, a 1910 anarchist plot to assassinate the emperor, he was found guilty of treason and executed on January 24, 1911.

James L. Huffman
Tracy Pollard

Bibliography

Notehelfer, F.G. *Kōtoku Shūsui: Portrait of a Japanese Radical.* Cambridge: Cambridge University Press, 1971.

Kuroiwa Shūroku
(pen name Ruikō) (1862–1920)

Journalist. Born in Kochi Prefecture, he studied at Keiō University and spent his early years writing literary works and reporting and editing at small newspapers. In 1892, he founded the newspaper *Yorozu Chōhō* in Tokyo. His sensational approach and crusades against social ills helped transform Japanese journalism, heralding the age of commercial journalism and making *Yorozu* one of Japan's largest newspapers. He exhibited unusual sensitivity to the early socialist movement and sparked considerable criticism for his ambivalent stance toward war with Russia during most of 1903. When he finally adopted a prowar stance in October of that year, he created a sensation, and three of his leading reporters—Uchimura Kanzō, Kōtoku Shūsui, and Sakai Toshihiko—resigned. Kuroiwa became more directly involved in politics in the 1910s, aggressively supporting the Ōkuma Shigenobu cabinet even when it lost its popularity. He also was active as a novelist, a translator, and an essayist.

James L. Huffman

Bibliography

Huffman, James L. *Creating a Public:*

Kuroiwa Shūroku. Courtesy Asahi Shimbun.

People and Press in Meiji Japan. Honolulu: University of Hawaii Press, 1997.

Notehelfer, F.G. *Kōtoku Shūsui: Portrait of a Japanese Radical.* Cambridge: Cambridge University Press, 1971.

L

Labor-Farmer Faction (*Rōnōha*)

A group of intellectuals broke away from the mainstream of the clandestine Japan Communist Party, which was formed in 1922, and published a periodical, *Rōnō* (Laborers and Farmers), beginning in 1927. In 1932–33, the mainstream Communist intellectuals released a multivolume *Nihon shihonshugi hattatsushi kōza* (Lectures on the History of the Development of Japanese Capitalism). This group, the Kōsaha, claimed that the still largely feudal contemporary Japanese political economy was in need of a bourgeois revolution. The Rōnōha argued that Japan was already a bourgeois capitalist state. The controversy was suspended by the arrest and imprisonment of its leading participants in 1936–38. By the time the Rōnōha resumed operations after World War II, the Occupation (1945–52) reforms had rendered much of its concerns obsolete.

Koji Taira

Bibliography

Hoston, Germaine A. *Marxism and the Crisis of Development in Prewar Japan*. Princeton, NJ: Princeton University Press, 1986.

Sumiya, Mikio, and Koji Taira. *An Outline of Japanese Economic History 1603–1940*. Tokyo: University of Tokyo Press, 1979.

Labor Movement (Postwar)

Since World War II, the Japanese labor movement has been animated by the goals of peace, democracy, and a better life rather than national glory. The contrast with pre-1945 Japan, in which the movement came under the sway of an "emperor-system (*tennōsei*) nationalism," seems very sharp. Yet, even before the war, *tennōsei* nationalism had gained its vitality not from working-class wellsprings, but from state indoctrination and hierarchical social control in a context of agrarian poverty and active social support from the middle and upper classes. The rank-and-file labor movement was never fully committed to the nationalist cause, even though right-wing labor leaders in the 1930s willingly led their unions into the embrace of business and the state with the organization of Sanpō (Movement for Industrial Service to the Nation) in 1938. The costs of imperial aggrandizement as experienced in privations in the workplace, in daily life, and on the battlefield contrasted too starkly with the hollowness of national claims of greatness and strength. After Japan's catastrophic defeat, Japanese workers demanded an accounting of the elite and sought to democratize their society even as they struggled to rebuild their shattered economy and personal lives.

The conservative leaders of postwar Japan—even right-wing prime ministers such as Kishi Nobusuke and Nakasone Yasuhiro—have found it perilous to strike the full chord of nationalism again for fear of losing power through the ballot box to the leftist opposition. Indeed, in the postwar democratic order, the conservative elite is vulnerable to rejection on two counts.

On the one hand, as the leftist critique has made abundantly clear, the conservative lineage and ideology resonate with the discredited authoritarianism and *tennōsei* nationalism of the past. On the other, the Right and the Left both make the telling point that this same elite has compromised Japan's national sovereignty for the economic rewards flowing from a postwar treaty system that binds Japan to the United

States in political and strategic dependence. Thus, despite the elite's evident desire to return to a more overtly authoritarian political and social order, the reality of strong popular support for the democratic 1947 Constitution and dependence upon markets and the Pax America have left it only the two notes of economic nationalism and mass consumerism to sound in its search for a national consensus behind its continuation in power.

The conjunction of democracy and nationalism poses troublesome problems, not only in respect to postwar Japan. There is a clear contradiction between nationalism and democracy, as an expression of the related ideas of national equality between states and of rights of the individual (postwar Japan), and nationalism and imperialism, as a denial of equality of states and of rights of individuals (prewar Japan). This contradiction is apparent in countries as disparate as Indonesia and France and suggests that the term "nationalism" itself may be of limited explanatory use, a residual category convenient for lumping together all of the ideological ambiguities and conflicting practices of nation–states having quite different histories and relations of power among classes. Nationalism as a concept is inadequate if it is viewed merely as arising from a deep-seated popular need for community and identity, and if it is treated as a vessel into which virtually any ideology or national essence can be poured. On the contrary, it might be best conceived as a countervalue to democracy in the era of capitalist nation–states—democracy taken to mean real, as opposed to symbolic, participation in decisions that affect one's life.

Democracy and nationalism were intertwined in Europe when a rising bourgeoisie backed a limited extension of democratic rights to the people as leverage for its own ascension to rule in place of aristocrats and priests. But whenever business and bureaucratic elites (civil or military) firmly grasped power for themselves in industrialized countries such as Japan, democracy and nationalism parted ways, the former becoming a primary value of new but subordinate wage-earning classes, the latter becoming central to the ideologies of elites eager to deflect the revolutionary implications of democracy into more easily controlled populist notions of national destiny and elite representation of the popular will. It was in the colonized world that the link between nationalism and democracy maintained its vitality, in the national-liberation struggles of the mid-twentieth century to overthrow European, American, and Japanese overlords and their domestic allies in the name of national independence and a wider sharing of power within.

In short, the touchstone for assessing the role of nationalism in the postwar world is democracy. Two practical questions need to be asked: What stratum in society is the primary bearer of the nationalist cause? Does nationalism as an ideology in any given society or era further or retard democracy within, as well as between, nation–states?

Seen from this perspective, the Japanese labor movement has drifted away from its intense postwar concern with democracy and pulled toward a vague economic nationalism as the postwar elite has, step-by-step, revived aspects of prewar emperor-system nationalism. Three stages can be seen in this journey: (1) participatory democracy and rejection of nationalism (1945–60); (2) peace, democracy, and consumerism (1960–82); and (3) economic nationalism and corporatism (1982–).

The first period—participatory democracy and rejection of nationalism—witnessed a mass movement from below aimed at sweeping the old elites from power and carrying out a radical reconstruction that would achieve economic, social, and political democracy. The initial framework for Japan's democratization was established by the U.S. Occupation (1945–52), which dismantled the mechanism of authoritarian rule and began to establish from above a U.S.–style liberal democracy that fell short in respect to the aspirations of the mass movement. The labor movement took a leading part in the push for a radical reconstruction, under the umbrella of Sanbetsu (Japan Congress of Industrial Unions), the Marxist-led mainstream national center. Industrial democracy and worker participation in management became central tenets of the vision of a democratic and socialist Japan articulated by Sanbetsu and the leftist parties during the years 1945–49, much to the dismay of the Japanese elite.

Socialism was never part of the U.S. design for postwar Japan, and when U.S. policymakers made it clear in 1948 that Japan was to become the anti-Communist "workshop of Asia," U.S. authorities joined hands with the Japanese elite to initiate a "reverse course" against the gains of the radical approach to democratization that would not lose its momentum until the fall of the Kishi cabinet in 1960. From 1948, the powerful reaction of the labor movement against Japanese nationalism was increasingly complemented by a current of opposition to U.S. imperialism that momentarily resembled the anti-imperialist national-liberation movements then occurring in the old colonial empires.

The labor movement's rejection of Japanese nationalism and its commitment to participatory democracy as essential to national independence and a better life frayed under the impact of such events. The "reverse course" and "Red" purges, the Korean War (1950–53) and subsequent economic recovery, the U.S.-imposed security-treaty system, the big-business offensive to regain what it called the "right to manage" and to confine unions within enterprise walls, the conservative political unification in 1955 in the Liberal Democratic Party (LDP), and the enshrinement of the ideology of economic growth by the Ikeda Hayato cabinet in 1960—all were signposts on the way back to the conservative dominance of the national agenda. The destruction of Sanbetsu in 1949 and the rise of Sōhyō (General Council of Trade Unions) in its place in the 1950s symbolized the labor movement's turn away from socialist concerns and toward economically oriented business unionism. Although Sōhyō made its accommodation to business unionism with the inauguration of an annual spring wage offensive (*shuntō*) in 1955, it nevertheless continued to defend the principles of pacifism and internationalism abroad.

The second period—peace, democracy, and consumerism—was distinguished by the labor movement's readiness in the 1960s to accept the political status quo under the 1947 Constitution as the essence of peace and democracy and the narrowing of the unions' concerns to concentrate on raising their members' standard of living. The key underlying trend of the first part of this period was the high-speed economic growth of the 1960s generated by consumerism and a push into foreign markets. Economism was accorded the status of Japan's national mission by the Ikeda cabinet's plan to double the national economy in the 1960s, a shift in policy complemented by the conservatives' tactical acceptance as well of peace and democracy under the 1947 Constitution as necessary to their continued hold on power in the Diet (legislature). The combination of economic growth, low-profile politics, and old-fashioned gerrymandering and machine politics kept the LDP in power until 1993.

The onset of political peace and consumerism in the 1960s made the values of peace and democracy increasingly abstract for a rank and file no longer involved in defending postwar democracy either in the workplace or in political battles. The gradual political disengagement of organized labor was, in part, the product of the management strategy of installing enterprise unions and fostering an enterprise consciousness that undermined labor-movement solidarity. Insofar as feelings akin to nationalism existed, they took the anti-U.S. form of neutralism in the Cold War and opposition to the Vietnam War.

When the phase of high-speed economic growth and consumerism began to unravel in the 1970s—as a result of the Nixon and oil "shocks," the end of the Vietnam War and its stimulus to the economy, environmental degradation and citizens' movements, and a rising yen and protectionism—the result was increasing uneasiness about the future and a siege mentality that fed into economic nationalism. Though it can hardly be said that labor's rank and file had come around to economic nationalism to the exclusion of peace and democracy, the growing strength of Dōmei (Japanese Confederation of Labor, Sōhyō's competitor for the lead of labor's mainstream) and of the IMF–JC (International Metalworkers' Federation–Japan Council) testified to the rising influence of labor's right wing. These were the standard-bearers of economic nationalism in the labor movement because of their narrow business unionism and their base in Japan's export industries, such as automobiles, textiles, shipbuilding, and metals; on the other side were the internationalist leaders of the main Sōhyō unions based in public enterprises, such as railways, communications, and postal services. Even as Dōmei and the IMF–JC supplanted Sōhyō in the second half of the 1970s as the labor-movement mainstream, the Japanese elite was responding to the troubles of the decade by turning decisively to the export industries as the engine of future economic growth.

The third period—economic nationalism and corporatism—began in 1982 with the inauguration of the Nakasone cabinet. Sōhyō's fate as the organizational focus for peace and democracy was sealed in the early 1980s by two circumstances. One was the Nakasone agenda of settling accounts with peace and democracy by rehabilitating values central to *tennōsei* nationalism and by rationalizing government activities through administrative reform. The latter involved a privatization of public enterprises such as the railways that, not incidentally, broke the back of Sōhyō's largest and most militant unions. The second was the joint Dōmei and IMF–JC establishment of Zenmin Rōkyō (Japan Council of Private-Sector Labor Unions) in 1982 as the nucleus of a national center dedicated to working cooperatively with business and state to further Japan's continued expansion into foreign markets and thereby sustain trickle-down prosperity for organized labor.

The labor movement thereby came under the leadership of men who wanted to unify it behind the unions in the major export industries. These would-be men of power hoped to gain entry to the inner circles of the Japanese elite by representing the corporate interests of organized labor. Once organized labor was united as a corporate body and in harness with business and government, this troika would achieve a mutually satisfactory solution to the problems brought on by Japan's rise to economic dominance in world markets by a policy of constant technological innovation plus perpetual but harmonious labor-management cooperation in striving for ever higher productivity. In contrast to the Sōhyō stress on the economic interests of labor vis-à-vis business and the state, the new ideology of labor-management-government harmony in exploiting foreign markets bore the imprint of the economic nationalism and corporatism of Sanpō. The metamorphosis early in the 1990s of Zenmin Rōkyō into Rengō (Japanese Trade Union Confederation) and the dissolution of Sōhyō and Dōmei represented an advanced stage of the incorporation of organized labor at the national level parallel to the incorporation of labor unions at the enterprise level during the Sōhyō era.

In an ideological sense, the nationalistic emphasis on economic competition now endorsed by labor's right-wing leaders transferred crude social-Darwinist ideas of survival of the fittest to economic relations between states. Although social Darwinism has not been a respectable theme in individual relationships in Japan, it has found expression within and between enterprises and in the international economy. It lies at the heart of the idea that the jobs and prosperity of unionized workers in Japan are best safeguarded by all-out competition with workers in other countries for productivity, rather than by obtaining a larger share of the profits of Japanese industry. The inevitable results of export-oriented growth have been international tensions and accusations that Japan practices adversarial trade or worse— charges that have been rebuffed by right-wing elements within Japan, exemplified so well by the LDP's Ishihara Shintarō with his charges of American racism against Japan and crude extension of economic nationalism to the cultural and political spheres.

Thus, the 1980s saw the waning of peace and prosperity as the stated values of organized labor and the waxing of corporatism and economic nationalism by labor's now-dominant right-wing. Whether this trend will lead to complete erosion of rank-and-file commitment to postwar democracy and the reappearance of a virulent form of nationalism from above is uncertain. The outcome may well depend upon whether there will be a serious international economic breakdown of the magnitude of the 1930s that pits the major industrial powers against one another. One thing is certain. There has been no rank-and-file conversion to nationalism despite the other changes taking place in the labor movement and in Japanese society. Judging from past experience, it will be no easy task to mobilize Japanese workers behind aggressive nationalist ventures without first destroying democracy within Japan.

Joe B. Moore

Bibliography

Hidaka, Rokurō. *The Price of Affluence: Dilemmas of Contemporary Japan.* Tokyo: Kodansha International, 1984.

Kawanishi, Hirosuke. *Enterprise Unionism in Japan.* London: Kegan Paul, 1992.

Moore, Joe B. *Japanese Workers and the Struggle for Power, 1945–1947.* Madison: University of Wisconsin Press, 1983.

Muto, Ichiyo. "Class Struggle in Postwar Japan," Parts 1–3. *AMPO: Japan-Asia Quarterly Review.* Vol. 13, No. 4 (1981), 21–33; Vol. 14, No. 1 (1982), 16–21, 35; Vol. 14, No. 3 (1982), 19–27.

———. "Class Struggle on the Shopfloor— The Japanese Case (1945–84)," *AMPO. Japan-Asia Quarterly Review.* Vol. 16, No. 3 (1984), 38–49.

Labor Movement (Prewar)

Since the earliest days of labor organizing in Japan, nationalism has been a significant force.

At times, it powerfully stimulated laborers to protest; more often, it served to diminish the force of their actions.

The first large group of factory workers were young women in the textile industry. These teenage girls were often told by their bosses to spin and obey for the sake of family and nation. During prewar times, they mounted relatively few large-scale strikes compared to other workers, and while the reasons for this are numerous, the appeal to national and paternal symbols is part of the explanation. On the other hand, when female mill hands did engage in a number of fierce strikes in the late 1920s, at major producers such as Kanebō, Fujibō, and Tōyō Muslin, the workers claimed that precisely because the companies earned huge amounts of foreign exchange and profited the country immensely, the workers had the right to expect decent wages and treatment.

Among the first workers to form unions were the skilled machinists and metalworkers who joined the Iron Workers' Union between 1897 and 1900. The union's position was moderate. In the vision of one union leader, Katayama Sen, if workers and owners cooperated they could each claim a fair share in building Japan into a great nation; one factor motivating the members, who worked in strategic industries such as the arsenals and the shipyards, seems to have been a concern to win the respect and status due them as builders of the nation.

Despite initial success, the Iron Workers' Union collapsed by 1900. In the years immediately following, Japan's first generation of socialists became active. As internationalists and pacifists, the socialists opposed empire. Their appeal appears to have been ill-suited to win the allegiance of men such as the Iron Workers or of the broad mass of lower-class city dwellers who rioted between 1905 and 1918 to demand international respect for Japan's imperialist aspiration. In campaigns against increased streetcar fares and taxes, the socialists sought to enlist the support of the city dwellers, but they faced intensive repression from the state, and their anti-imperialism won little approval among workers.

The next surge of disputes and organizing came during World War I. The major organization founded in these years was the Yūaikai (Friendly Society), which developed into the major Japanese union federation of the interwar era. In the Yūaikai's early years, a sort of popu-list nationalism was of great importance in attracting members. The Yūaikai's message, articulated by the founder, Suzuki Bunji, and by impassioned advocates, such as the worker and playwright Hirasawa Keishichi, was that workers deserved, and could legitimately demand, the dignified treatment owed to human beings and *kokumin*. This latter term, a neologism of the early Meiji era (1868–1912), quickly gained currency and sunk deep roots as the Japanese word for "people" or "nation." When Japanese laboring men and women first organized in the early twentieth century, they spoke primarily of improving their status as "people of the nation," a formulation that supported, even as it derived from, the nineteenth-century program to build national strength and nationalism. They implicitly (sometimes explicitly) denied that workers as a class were locked in battle with another stratum of the Japanese nation.

By the early 1920s, the stance of activist workers had changed considerably. Important segments of the labor movement turned against imperialism and favored internationalism of the working class. Most unions during the 1920s supported international cooperation to limit naval arms, even though this cost jobs in shipbuilding and in related machine industries. The Sōdōmei (Japan Federation of Labor; successor to the Yūaikai) also championed native workers and independence movements in Japan's colonies. By the mid-1920s, the labor movement had fragmented into rightist, centrist, and leftist streams, with considerable variety in the extent of their nationalism. The Sōdōmei, on the right, most respected the fundamental symbols and structure of Japanese nationalism. The centrists were more ambiguous in their attitude toward the emperor and the nation. Only the Communists and related unions unambiguously opposed the emperor system, a position that won them fierce repression. Yet, all three streams assailed Japanese imperialism and defended the integrity or sovereignty of China. At least rhetorically, each claimed that the global interests of the working class must transcend those of any one nation.

The advocates of the internationalist position either transformed their own views or were overwhelmed in the maelstrom of economic Depression and continental military expansion of the late 1920s and the early 1930s. As early as 1927, the prominent intellectual and Sōdōmei leader Akamatsu Katsumarō established contact with radical young army officers and modified his view of the state. In the spring of 1931, he collaborated with the officers and with civilian rightists in an abortive coup attempt, in which a number of violent labor demonstrations would serve as the pretext for a declaration of martial law and military rule in the name of "national renovation." The fall of 1931 and early 1932 witnessed a number of ruptures in the labor movement, as major figures suddenly converted to the support of military action in Manchuria. They typically rationalized this transformation as a policy to help workers find jobs (as immigrants to the new puppet state) in the Depression. A surge of support among workers and the populace at large for the Manchurian action overwhelmed the small minority that still opposed Japanese expansionism.

Two additional factors contributed to the nationalistic reorientation of the labor movement: the government's ongoing repression of Communists, which became especially intense with mass arrests in March 1928, and the emergence of an ultranationalist stream of what were called "Japanist" unions. These groups advocated the fusion of the efforts of workers and capitalists, who were to abandon the selfish pursuit of self-interest and material gain and to work on behalf of the nation. The Japanists condemned as traitors all mainstream unions, conservative groups such as Sōdōmei, as much as the left-wing Hyōgikai (Labor Unions Council). Beginning with a major victory at the Ishikawajima Shipyard, the workplace of Kamino Shin'ichi, a godfather of the Japanist movement, the Japanists ousted mainstream unions at a number of factories during the Depression of the early 1930s. By 1936, 47,000 workers had joined a national federation of patriotic unions, but the Japanist drive petered out thereafter.

Ironically, however, by this time the mainstream unions had themselves turned enthusiastically nationalistic and increasingly statist. In 1933, the Sōdōmei formally adopted a program of industrial cooperation with management designed to build the country's industry while improving labor's position. In practice, this meant that, while the union disavowed the strike as a tactic, it gained relatively little in return. In general, the unions and the proletarian political parties that relied on labor support returned to the rhetoric of populist nationalism in the mid-1930s. They claimed once again to be seeking rights and benefits for all *kokumin*,

rather than raising what they now described as narrow "working-class" demands. In the aftermath of the outbreak of war in China in 1937, virtually all unions endorsed the "holy war" with enthusiasm. Throughout the 1930s, the military and the government bureaucracy paid increasingly close attention to the nationalism of the labor movement and aggressively repressed the few dissenting voices. The transformation of the labor movement was certainly the result of coercion in some measure. However, the idea that workers could and should secure their dignity and welfare through service to the nation and the empire was deeply rooted and found ready assent.

As the union movement retreated from strikes and embraced nationalism, it failed to grow in numbers. Bureaucrats and military leaders worried about keeping social peace and mobilizing production as the war economy expanded and nonunion strikes became numerous and costly to resolve. Taking the Nazi German Labor Front as their model, they came to promote Sangyō Hōkoku Undō (Sanpō) (Movement for Industrial Service to the Nation). They also drew on ideas first articulated by the Japanist unions. By 1938, the Industrial Patriotic Service Federation functioned as a semiofficial unit, and authorities vigorously encouraged firms to create labor-management discussion councils in all factories, to be linked to a national organization via local and regional umbrella councils.

In November 1940, the federation became Dainihon Sangyō Hōkokukai (Greater Japan Industrial Patriotic Service Association) by government fiat, and membership became mandatory. In short order, councils formed at virtually all of the country's workplaces, enrolling 4.6 million employees at 54,000 locations. The councils originally intended to promote labor-management harmony; during the Pacific War they reportedly became vehicles to stimulate production for the war effort. In practice, they were usually moribund. Managers, who feared that the councils might develop into oppositional groups, rarely gave them significant responsibility, and workers did not take the councils seriously. Some scholars have suggested that the Sanpō councils were forerunners of Japan's post–World War II enterprise unions, but evidence of a direct link between the Sanpō organizations and unions formed after the war is weak.

In the early postwar years, unions, enjoying American support for labor reform, gained a new legitimacy and enlisted millions of members. They demanded the prosecution of wartime executives as war criminals, and they quickly returned to a vocabulary and a vision that placed the interests of the working-class over those of an all-encompassing nation. The leading federation of the 1950s was Sōhyō (General Council of Trade Unions). The group supported socialist internationalism, opposed the military alliance with the United States as well as Japanese rearmament, and won broad popular support for its pacifism. In 1960, the labor movement was a major force in the massive demonstrations against the renewal of the 1951 Japan-U.S. Security Treaty. Through the 1960s, the mainstream labor movement saw the special mission of the Japanese people, shaped by the bitter experience of war, to be that of advocating peace. A strong pacifist and internationalist strain remained part of the labor movement through the 1970s and 1980s. In addition, during these decades, the conservative wing of the labor movement, centered on the private-sector unions of Dōmei (Japanese Confederation of Labor), articulated a new cultural nationalism celebrating the special cooperative and productive nature of Japan's labor relations.

Andrew G. Gordon

Bibliography

Garon, Sheldon. *State and Labor in Modern Japan.* Berkeley: University of California Press, 1987.

Gordon, Andrew. *Labor and Imperial Democracy in Prewar Japan.* Berkeley: University of California Press, 1991.

Large, Stephen. *Organized Workers and Socialist Politics in Interwar Japan.* New York: Cambridge University Press, 1981.

Tsurumi, E. Patricia. *Factory Girls: Women in the Thread Mills of Meiji Japan.* Princeton, NJ: Princeton University Press, 1990.

League for Establishing a National Assembly (*Kokkai Kisei Dōmei*)

Political association. In March 1880, the Aikokusha (Society of Patriots) decided to change its name to Kokkai Kisei Dōmei and press more directly for the creation of a national legislature. Thus, 114 delegates from 24 prefectures and two metropolitan districts met in Osaka and launched a petition drive for a national assembly. Their platform decried the arbitrary ways of officials and called for a representative assembly to better develop the "patriotic hearts of the people." Significantly, the central aim, even for this liberal group, was to satisfy the imperial will. Though they garnered nearly 97,000 signatures within a month and 130,000 by November, the government refused to accept the petitions. On October 29, 1881, shortly after the first imperial rescript promising a constitution, the league gave way to the Jiyūtō (Liberal Party), Japan's first political party.

James L. Huffman

Bibliography

Scalapino, Robert. *Democracy and the Party Movement in Prewar Japan.* Berkeley: University of California Press, 1967.

League for the Study of Government (*Keirin Gakumei*)

Nationalist organization. In 1923, Tokyo University Law Professor Uesugi Shinkichi and national-socialist writer Takabatake Motoyuki joined to form this short-lived forerunner of several right-wing organizations. Its purpose was to assail liberal students and professors, especially at Tokyo University. The league broke up in 1924 as a result of the founders' philosophical and personality differences: Uesugi was a scholarly proponent of expansive nationalism; Takabatake, a populist opponent of capitalism. For Uesugi's followers, the Keirin Gakumei became a precursor of the Kokuhonsha (National Foundations Society) and the Kenkokukai (State Foundation Society); on the Takabatake side, it helped spawn the Kyūshin Aikokutō (Radical Patriots' Party) and the Nihon Kokka Shakaitō (Japan National Socialist Party). All of these groups helped fan the flames of ultranationalism in the 1930s.

James L. Huffman

Bibliography

Storry, Richard. *The Double Patriots: A Study of Japanese Nationalism.* Westport, CT: Greenwood Press, 1973.

League of Blood Incident
(*Ketsumeidan Jiken*)

A series of assassinations planned and carried out against high-ranking government and business elites early in 1932 by members of the Ketsumeidan (League of Blood). The Ketsumeidan assassinated Inoue Junnosuke, a former finance minister, in February and Baron Dan Takuma, then head of the Mitsui Holding Company, in March. The May 15 Incident of the same year, when right-wing extremists murdered Prime Minister Inukai Tsuyoshi, was part of the same plot. The Ketsumeidan had formed in 1931 as a group of right-wing youth opposed to the outcome of the London Naval Conference (1930) and to the deterioration of living conditions in rural Japan. Led by agrarian nationalist Inoue Nisshō, the group drew plans to assassinate members of the Japanese elite whom it believed to be responsible for the suffering of rural Japan. Due to their seeming sincerity and patriotism, the young members of the Ketsumeidan captured the sympathy of the Japanese public and received light sentences.

Guy Yasko

Bibliography

Storry, Richard. *The Double Patriots: A Study of Japanese Nationalism.* Westport, CT: Greenwood Press, 1973.

League of Nations

Amidst a wave of liberal internationalism in the wake of the destructive World War I, the leading powers established an international peacekeeping organization in Geneva in 1920 as part of the postwar settlement. At the center of the League of Nations' structure were an assembly and a council, where international disputes were to be debated and sanctions against aggressors were to be recommended. The league also encompassed subsidiary organizations to deal with such human-welfare issues as labor, health, and education. Colonies stripped from Germany in the war were held by the league and assigned to the custody of specific members. The council first met in 1920, and the league continued to function at its Geneva headquarters until the outbreak of World War II in Europe in 1939. At one time or another, nearly every major sovereign state in the world, except the United States, was a member of the League of Nations. Its roster included the Asian countries of China, Siam, Persia, the Soviet Union (after 1934), and Japan.

Though Japan was a charter member of the league and one of the elite, permanent members of the council, it adhered to the organization with misgivings and amid acrid debate. Japanese realists perceived the league as a device designed by the leading Western powers to prevent violent change in the international status quo and preserve their own prerogatives won in the Great War. The organization, they complained, would hinder the elevation of latecomer countries such as Japan and would facilitate the meddling of Euro-American powers in East Asia's interstate affairs. Japanese sensibilities were deeply offended when the Paris Peace Conference of 1919, which drafted the league's charter, refused to incorporate in the document the principle of racial equality.

Japan nevertheless acted as an upstanding member of the league throughout the 1920s. Japanese representatives, such as Ishii Kikujirō, helped mediate thorny disputes involving European and South American members. Nitobe Inazō, an internationally known educator, and Sugimura Yōtarō, a respected diplomat, enhanced Japan's reputation in Geneva through distinguished service in the league secretariat. The league-related Permanent Court of International Justice usually included a Japanese jurist among its judges. Japan administered former German archipelagoes as league mandates in the Pacific Ocean north of the equator.

Japan became disillusioned with the Western powers at the 1921 Washington Naval Conference and began fortifying its islands in the Pacific, even while maintaining its cooperative international stance. Japanese confidence in the league as a security asset waned in the late 1920s as it became clear that the major powers were not willing to submit to the league's jurisdiction in matters of vital national interest. When, to Japan's surprise, the league strongly opposed the invasion of Manchuria (1931–32) and the establishment of the puppet state of Manchukuo in 1932, Japan accused the league of misjudgment and its members of hypocrisy. After an assembly vote in February 1933 condemned Japanese policy, Japan withdrew from the League of Nations. Nonetheless, the country continued to participate in the humanitarian and judicial activities of the league until 1938.

The saga of Japan's connection with the League of Nations parallels the shift in Japanese diplomacy from international accommodationism in the 1920s to autonomy and heightened nationalism after the Manchurian Incident.

Thomas W. Burkman

Bibliography
Burkman, Thomas W. "Nitobe Inazō: From World Order to Regional Order." *Culture and Identity: Japanese Intellectuals During the Interwar Years.* Ed. J. Thomas Rimer. Princeton, NJ: Princeton University Press, 1992, 191–216.
Thorne, Christopher. *The Limits of Foreign Policy: The West, the League and the Far Eastern Crisis of 1931–1933.* New York: Putnam, 1973.

League of the Divine Wind (*Shimpūren*)

Early-Meiji reactionary society. An organization of lower-level samurai and Shinto loyalists in Kumamoto Prefecture, this league typified the nationalistic, antimodernist reactions of many provincial Japanese to the young Meiji (1868–1912) government and its modernizing policies. Its members fought change of all kinds, refusing to surrender their swords, opposing the local School for Western Learning (Yōgakkō), and cutting down telegraph lines. On October 24, 1876, 700 Shimpūren supporters rebelled against the local government, attacked the Kumamoto garrison, killed its commander and the prefectural governor, and inflicted more than 200 casualties, including scores of deaths. They were quickly put down by official troops, but their story helped inspire other provincial uprisings and served as an inspiration for Mishima Yukio's nationalistic novel about the 1930s, *Runaway Horses* (Homba).

James L. Huffman

Bibliography
Mishima, Yukio. *Runaway Horses.* New York: Alfred A. Knopf, 1973.

Levellers Society (*Suiheisha*)

The Suiheisha movement was founded on March 3, 1922, with the aims of stimulating and organizing the Burakumin (outcastes) of Japan to liberate themselves from the discrimination and oppression that remained even after their formal liberation in 1871. Attempts had been made since the 1890s to create a national movement, but they lacked an aggressive ideology and a sympathetic social climate. The movement blossomed at a time when organized social-movement activity burgeoned in rural and urban areas and benefited considerably from its external support. By 1928, the Suiheisha had more than 400 groups with more than 50,000 followers. Its principal strategy was *kyūdan*, the denunciation of acts of discrimination.

Minor ideological division troubled the movement during its initial growth, but from 1925 onward the annual conferences became the arenas for major debates among the Bolshevik, anarchist, and moderate groupings. As a result of government pressure on leftists in the latter 1920s, anarchist influence soon faded within the Suiheisha as it did in the other social movements, and the mass arrests of socialists in 1928 and 1929 undermined the power of the Marxists. During the 1930s, social democrats led by Matsumoto Jiichirō (1887–1966) took charge of the Burakumin movement.

The Suiheisha was one of the few social movements that was able to regroup and grow in the repressive climate of the 1930s. Following a successful national *kyūdan* campaign against an instance of discrimination that occurred in 1933 in the Takamatsu regional court, when a judge ruled that the mere failure to disclose Burakumin origins was illegal, the movement claimed as many members in 1936 as it had 10 years earlier. A small nationalist element grew within the Suiheisha, during the pre-World War II years, as it had within the social democratic movement generally, but it never exerted much influence.

When the Suiheisha capitulated to the pressure to cooperate with the government-controlled Yūwa (conciliation) movement in the late 1930s, it had little to do with nationalist feeling or support for the war effort. Most who continued to be active believed that, even within the new structures that were being created, it was important for them to defend the rights of the Burakumin. The organization's leaders kept the movement in existence until the early 1940s and did not finally agree to disband it until wartime pressures made it necessary in March 1942.

Ian Neary

Bibliography
Yoshino, I. Roger, and Sueo Murakoshi. *The Invisible Visible Minority: Japan's Burakumin.* Osaka: Buraku Liberation Research Institute, 1977.

Lockheed Scandal (*Rokkiido Jiken*)

The 1976 corruption scandal in which the Lockheed Corporation paid bribes to Japanese officials of Marubeni Trading Company, All Nippon Airways, and the Liberal Democratic Party (LDP). In February 1976, a U.S. Senate subcommittee chaired by Senator Frank Church revealed that Lockheed paid bribes to ensure sales of its Tristar aircraft. Among Japanese politicians implicated, the most noted was former LDP Prime Minister Tanaka Kakuei, who had resigned following earlier corruption charges in December 1974. In 1976, the Lockheed investigations further alleged that, through contacts with right-wing leader Kodama Yoshio, various business and party leaders had accepted the bribes.

The Lockheed scandal involved charges of foreign intervention, economic corruption, and personal political gains that disrupted Japan's party politics. Tanaka was especially powerful because of the use of money in politics, which he distributed to opposition, as well as ruling-party, supporters. The corruption, fueled by such money politics and the international link to receiving foreign bribes, made Tanaka a symbol of the need for political reform. The opposition had only recently won regional elections and inaugurated what it called "progressive local governments" that challenged ruling LDP dominance; in June 1976, the New Liberal Club began as a splinter party, and divisiveness within the ruling party had been barely overcome by the compromise choice of Miki Takeo to succeed Tanaka as prime minister. The close ties to bribery from a foreign business added a dimension of nationalist backlash to the Lockheed scandal and caused the 1976 fall of the Miki government as well. Several of the principals in the case, including Tanaka, were eventually convicted and sent to jail.

Stephen J. Anderson

Bibliography

Baerwald, Hans H. "Lockheed and Japanese Politics." *Asian Survey*. Vol. 16, No. 9 (September 1976), 817–29.

Curtis, Gerald L. "Campaigning, Financing, and the Modern Party." *The Japanese Way of Politics*. New York: Columbia University Press, 1988, chap. 5.

Johnson, Chalmers. "Tanaka Kakuei, Structural Corruption, and the Advent of Machine Politics in Japan." *Journal of Japanese Studies*. Vol. 12, No. 1 (Winter 1986), 1–28.

London Naval Treaty

A product of the London Naval Conference (January 21–April 22, 1930), the treaty formally went into effect on January 1, 1931, after vigorous debates in Great Britain, the United States, and, especially, Japan. The treaty represented the peak of interwar naval limitations and, in Japan, the beginning of the rapid erosion of the civilian authority that negotiated it.

The conference wrestled with the difficult problem of capital ship ratios and parity of noncapital ships among the British, American, and Japanese fleets and, in effect, perpetuated the 1921 Washington Conference agreement, continuing to allow Japan just 60 percent of the capital ship tonnage maintained by the British and the Americans and extending that 10:10:6 ratio to noncapital ships.

Although Prime Minister Hamaguchi Osachi had earlier demanded a 10:10:7 ratio, he supported the new treaty limitations because they would limit military spending and would also enhance Japan's cooperation with Great Britain and the United States.

In Japan, widespread and bitter opposition erupted to the terms of the treaty and to the tactics Hamaguchi employed to secure its ratification. Naval authorities argued that the treaty undermined key agreements of the Washington Conference that had guaranteed Japanese naval hegemony in the western Pacific and had protected the security of the empire. Hamaguchi's argument that the Diet (legislature) had no legal means of challenging the government on the treaty angered members of the legislature. Admiral Katō Kanji, chief of the naval general staff, protested directly to the Emperor because Article 11 of the Meiji Constitution vested the "right of supreme command" in the navy rather than in the civilian government. The Supreme War Council opposed the treaty. Patriotic and nationalistic clubs, the popular press, and the opposition Rikken Seiyūkai (Friends of Constitutional Government Party) made its rejection a matter of national honor.

The emperor formally ratified the treaty on October 2, 1930, although this did not end the controversy or the series of constitutional confrontations over the right of supreme command and the role of the Diet in foreign policy. In November, Hamaguchi was shot by a radical youth who argued that the prime minister had violated the right of supreme command.

The London Naval Treaty contributed to the further polarization of Japanese politics and added to the already serious domestic political problems and tensions between civilian and military elements. It reduced popular support for civilian government and its control of foreign policy and alienated large and important groups in the press, the military, and the general public from the West. It enhanced the proponents of nationalistic chauvinism, territorial expansion, and radical social and political reform and rallied them in opposition to those who supported naval limitations and the democratic order. It contributed to the establishment of militarist government under Admiral Saitō Makoto in 1932. It led the Seiyūkai to reject cooperation with Great Britain and the United States over naval policy.

Thus, the London Naval Treaty, which had aimed at the reduction of naval armaments and the extension of international cooperation, had precisely the opposite impact. The changed course could be observed in the growth of military influence in the government and the expansion of Japan on the mainland, as well as the country's withdrawal from the Second London Naval Conference in January 1935 and resultant abandonment of naval limitations.

Robert D. Fiala

Bibliography

Crowley, James B. *Japan's Quest for Autonomy: National Security and Foreign Policy, 1930–1938*. Princeton, NJ: Princeton University Press, 1966.

Hall, Christopher. *Britain, America and Arms Control, 1921–37*. London: Macmillan, 1987.

Morley, James William, ed. *Japan's Road to the Pacific War: Japan Erupts: The London Naval Conference and the Manchurian Incident, 1928–1932. Selected translations from the* Taiheiyō sensō e no michi: kaisen gaikō shi. New York: Columbia University Press, 1984.

Lytton Commission

When Japan moved into Manchuria following the Manchurian Incident of September 1931, the League of Nations agreed, at Japan's suggestion, to create a commission to investigate the origins of the conflict between Japan and China. It was headed by Lord Lytton of Great Britain and included representatives from France, Germany, Italy, and the United States. The commission spent six weeks in the spring of 1932 conducting its investigation in Manchuria and reported to the League in October, condemning Japan as the aggressor but calling on China to respect Japanese rights. In the meantime, Japan had established the puppet state of Manchukuo in March and had recognized it officially in September. The Lytton report evoked a wave of indignation in Japan; when the League adopted the report in February 1933 (by a vote of 42–1, with only Japan opposing), Japan's delegate, Matsuoka Yōsuke, walked out, and the following month Japan withdrew from the League. The episode stimulated rising nationalism in Japan and further isolated the country from the international community.

James L. Huffman

Bibliography

Thorne, Christopher. *The Limits of Foreign Policy: The West, the League, and the Far Eastern Crisis of 1931–1933*. New York: Putnam, 1973.

M

MacArthur, Douglas (1880–1964)

Most lists of American experts on East Asian nationalism would place the name of Douglas MacArthur in a place of prominence. He spent the bulk of his career in Asia, and, before U.S. President Harry S Truman recalled him from Korea in April 1951, the general had not left the Pacific for 14 years. Despite all of this experience, MacArthur's understanding of nationalism in the region was flawed because he never had close relations with the Asian masses. In 1935, he became military adviser to the government of the Philippines and devoted the next six years to organizing Filipino defense forces, then accepted a vast personal financial gift from the Philippine president for his services. During World War II, MacArthur supervised Allied military operations in the Southwest Pacific Theater, liberating the Philippines primarily to fulfill his pledge of "I shall return!" As Supreme Commander of the Allied Powers (SCAP) from 1945 to 1951, he was in charge of the Allied Occupation of Japan and efficiently implemented a series of sweeping political, economic, and social reforms. His dictatorial behavior alienated many Japanese officials, but MacArthur gained heroic stature among the general populace.

MacArthur's misunderstanding of the relationship between Communism and nationalism in Asia led to his obsession with destroying Mao Zedong's regime in China. Any Asian leader who embraced Communist ideology, he thought, was a Soviet puppet acting in compliance with the Kremlin's plan for world conquest. During the Korean War (1950–53), MacArthur regularly lectured military and civilian leaders about East Asian affairs, but he failed to grasp the role that nationalism played in the conflict. He had no contact with average Koreans and was indifferent to popular desires because he viewed the war only as an opportunity to defeat Moscow's global ambitions. "The Oriental follows a winner," MacArthur insisted, and if "we win, the Chinese will not follow the U.S.S.R." Thinking that Asians lacked an independent spirit and initiative, he dismissed the possibility of Chinese military intervention in Korea. MacArthur then tried to exploit his reputation as an expert on Asia, build popular support for a war against China, and advance his presidential ambitions. He failed in all three efforts, but many Americans still endorse his simplistic and ethnocentric concept of East Asian nationalism.

James I. Matray

Bibliography

Schaller, Michael. *Douglas MacArthur: The Far Eastern General*. New York: Oxford University Press, 1989.

Manchukuo (*Manshūkoku*)

Japan's puppet state in Manchuria (1932–45). This region had been under indirect Japanese control since the end of the Russo-Japanese War in 1905, when Russian leases were taken over by Japan. As a result, the South Manchurian Railway Company developed vast industrial operations in Manchuria, while the Japanese Guandong army occupied territories around the railway and exerted wide influence in national life.

When the Guandong army attacked Mukden, the largest city in Manchuria, during the Manchurian Incident of September 18, 1931, Japan initiated active plans to create a formal puppet state. The Western powers opposed these plans, and even Inukai Tsuyoshi's civilian government in Tokyo attempted to delay them in order to combat the army's growing independence. But Inukai's assassination on May 15, 1932, crushed government resistance, and, on September 15 of that year, the Saitō Makoto administration recognized Manchukuo as a sovereign state, with Japan assuming responsibility for its internal security and defense.

Under the agreement, Pu Yi, the last emperor of China's Qing Dynasty (1644–1912) was made regent, and actual control of the country was placed under the General Affairs Board of the Guandong army, which had responsibility for approving laws and policies proposed by the nominal (Chinese) ministers of state. The General Affairs Board, in turn, worked under the Tokyo government's Manchurian Affairs Board. In 1934, Pu Yi was named emperor of Manchukuo.

The Manchukuo state consisted of the three Chinese provinces (Liaoning, Jilin, and Heilongjiang) that traditionally had made up Manchuria, plus Jehol Province in Inner Mongolia. It had a wartime population of more than 40 million, including 20,000 Japanese immigrant families and 2 million Koreans. From the mid-1930s onward, even its economy was dominated by the military, with the South Manchurian Railway Company losing its interests to the army-backed Manchuria Heavy Industry Company, and metals, minerals, and agricultural products being exported to assist in Japan's war effort. The Soviet Union invaded Manchukuo on September 9, 1945, and Pu Yi abdicated on September 18.

James L. Huffman

Bibliography

Duus, Peter, Ramon H. Myers, and Mark R. Peattie, eds. *The Japanese Informal Empire in China, 1895–1937*. Princeton, NJ: Princeton University Press, 1989.

Manchurian Incident (*Manshū Jihen*)

The Manchurian Incident, which took place on September 18, 1931, was the single act that enabled Japanese troops to occupy all of Manchuria. It placed the initiative for Japanese expansion into China in the hands of the Japanese military and thereby marked the end of cooperation between military and nonmilitary bureaucrats in Tokyo as equal partners in determining foreign policy. From this time until 1945, the military and its supporters in the government directed Japan's affairs.

Officially, Manchuria (Liaoning, Jilin, and Heilongjiang) belonged to China. Japan had a colony at the southern tip of the Liaodong Peninsula and maintained extraterritorial enclaves in several key cities along the South Manchurian Railway line. Armed Japanese railway guards also rode the trains and patrolled the tracks along this line. But the Japanese military was frustrated with its restricted freedom of action in the region. From its point of view, Manchuria was overrun with bandits, warlords, and inefficient local Chinese governments. Japan, the military believed, could bring modern government and industry to Manchuria if permitted, but most Japanese found it impossible to form smooth-working relationships with the Chinese business, governmental, and military people there.

The Japanese were proudly nationalistic in their conviction that they had a mission to bring Manchuria into the modern world, and they saw the Chinese as stubbornly nationalistic in refusing to allow the Japanese to claim any greater prerogatives than they already enjoyed.

On the night of September 18, 1931, an explosion occurred on the tracks of the South Manchurian Railway just outside Mukden, the largest and most important city in Manchuria. The blast was engineered by three Japanese military officers, Lieutenant-Colonel Ishiwara Kanji, Colonel Itagaki Seishirō, and Colonel Doihara Kenji. The Japanese claimed that it was caused by Chinese troops, and, asserting that they had to act to protect Japanese citizens and property in the region, Japanese troops of the Guandong army poured out of their barracks to occupy the city and the land along the tracks. Within four days after the incident, Guandong army units also occupied the two trading and administrative cities of Jilin and Changchun north of Mukden. To reinforce their units and consolidate their occupation of these key areas, additional Japanese troops arrived from Korea. These reinforcements were ordered into Manchuria by the Guandong commanders in the field without the permission of the government in Tokyo and in violation of standing orders.

To quell international concern, the Japanese government announced that its policy was to contain the incident and the conflict. But Japanese forces continued to take over key transportation links and population centers in Manchuria so that, by January 1932, the entire region was effectively under Japanese occupation. In February 1932, Japan established the puppet state of Manchukuo to create the illusion that power was being handed back to the Chinese and that the Chinese in Manchuria had decided to create a state independent of the Chinese government in Beijing and friendly to the Japanese.

During this time, members of the Lytton Commission dispatched by the League of Nations were touring Manchuria to investigate the facts of the explosion and appraise subsequent Japanese actions. The four-man commission headed by Lord Lytton of Great Britain, which had been appointed in December 1931, submitted the report of its findings in October 1932. The report criticized both the Chinese and the Japanese in the region but did not accept the Japanese version of the events that had transpired. When the league officially accepted the commission's report in February 1933 and it became clear that the state of Manchukuo would not be widely recognized internationally, Japan withdrew from the league. Early in 1933, Japanese troops moved westward and occupied Jehol Province in Inner Mongolia next to Manchuria, which meant that all of China north of the Shanhaikuan Pass, the psychologically important corridor between China and Manchuria, was under Japanese control.

Throughout the conflict between China and Japan during the 1930s and 1940s, the Manchurian Incident became a rallying cry for Chinese students and nationalists as a symbol of how brazen and internationally irresponsible the Japanese military had become.

Ronald Suleski

Bibliography

Ogata, Sadako. *Defiance in Manchuria: The Making of Japanese Foreign Policy, 1931–1932.* Berkeley: University of California Press, 1964.

Peattie, Mark. *Ishiwara Kanji and Japan's Confrontation with the West.* Princeton, NJ: Princeton University Press, 1975.

Yoshihashi, Takehiko. *Conspiracy at Mukden.* New Haven, CT: Yale University Press, 1963.

March 15 Incident (*San'ichigo Jiken*)

First mass arrest of suspected Communists under the 1925 Peace Preservation Law. After a lengthy investigation by the Justice Ministry and a marked increase in Japan Communist Party activity early in 1928, a decision was made to crack down. At 5:00 A.M., March 15, thousands of agents began a raid of 120 leftist centers, including party headquarters, publishing offices, and private residences, and by evening they had arrested 1,600 individuals and seized thousands of documents and membership lists. Though just one-third of those arrested were prosecuted, the arrests resulted in a sharp tightening of controls on leftist groups. Several organizations, including the Labor-Farmer Party (Rōdō Nōmintō), were banned; educational restrictions were increased; thought prosecutors (*shisō kenji*) were assigned to key courts; a death-penalty provision was added to the Peace Preservation Law; and additional mass arrests were carried out, including those of another 600 or 700 suspected Communists on April 16, 1929.

James L. Huffman

Bibliography

Mitchell, Richard. *Thought Control in Prewar Japan.* Ithaca, NY: Cornell University Press, 1976.

March Incident (*Sangatsu Jiken*)

Aborted military coup d'état in March 1931. This was the first among many efforts by right-wing military officers to change the government by force in the 1930s. Drawn up by senior military officers, as well as middle-grade officers in Hashimoto Kingorō's Sakurakai (Cherry Blossom Society) and leading civilians such as Ōkawa Shūmei, the plot called for armed demonstrators to attack the political parties' headquarters, the prime minister's residence, and the Diet (legislature) on March 20. The goal was to provoke the army to declare martial law, force the resignation of the Hamaguchi Osachi cabinet, and have War Minister Ugaki Kazushige named prime minister. The plot fizzled when Ugaki ultimately refused to go along with it. The incident was kept from the public until the end of World War II, and no reprisals were taken against the conspirators, except to reassign some officers to Manchuria, where they took part in the September 18, 1931, Manchurian Incident, which led to Japan's takeover of that region.

James L. Huffman

Bibliography
Crowley, James. *Japan's Quest for Autonomy,*
1930–1938. Princeton, NJ: Princeton
University Press, 1966.

Marco Polo Bridge Incident
(*Rokōkyō Jiken*)

Episode that sparked the second Sino-Japanese
War (1937–45). The Chinese call the bridge
Lukouchiao (Rokōkyō in Japanese), but Westerners named it the Marco Polo Bridge because
the thirteenth-century Venetian traveler com-
mented on the handsome stone carvings of li-
ons that grace the bridge's balustrades. It is located about 12 miles southwest of Beijing near
a strategic rail junction. On the night of July 7,
1937, a small detachment of Japanese troops,
permitted there by the terms of the Boxer Protocol of 1901, were conducting maneuvers.
Shots were heard, and a skirmish with troops
of General Song Zheyuan followed. Efforts by
Japanese and Chinese to settle the matter failed.
The incident veered out of control, and by August both countries had mobilized for war.
What followed was the eight-year-long Sino-
Japanese War, which in turn became a part of
World War II with Japan's attack on Pearl Harbor on December 7, 1941.

Many observers have succumbed to the
temptation to liken the Marco Polo Bridge Incident to the Manchurian Incident six years
earlier—that is, to imagine that the 1937 incident was the work of local imperial army officers, acting on their own and staging an incident,
which they then blamed on the Chinese and
used as a pretext to expand on the China mainland and present the government in Tokyo with
a fait accompli. That notion, however, has been
widely rejected by historians. For one thing,
Lieutenant-Colonel Ishiwara Kanji, responsible
for masterminding the earlier incident in Manchuria, had, by 1937, come to believe that Japan
should not be seeking to aggrandize itself at the
expense of China. He and many other military
strategists had concluded that expanding Soviet
Communism represented far more of a threat to
Japan than nationalist China. Indeed, the imperial army troops at the Marco Polo Bridge on
the fateful night in July 1937 were conducting
tactical maneuvers in preparation for a hypo-
thetical war with the Russians.

Hata Ikuhito, an expert on Japanese military
history, concedes that the details surrounding the
Marco Polo Bridge Incident remain clouded. He
constructs, however, a list of four hypotheses to
explain the incident. In descending order of prob-
ability, they are: (1) the "accidental shot" hypothesis, that it was a low-ranking Chinese soldier who
shot in an unplanned moment of fear; (2) the
"Communist plot" hypothesis, that the incident
was a conspiracy by Chinese Communist Party
soldiers; (3) the "warlord plot" theory, that the
clash was planned by Chinese warlords; and (4)
least likely, that the first shot was part of a private
plot by special intelligence organs of the Japanese
army or those connected with it.

Whatever caused the disturbance, the results
were awesome. As an example of a small, apparently manageable incident triggering a large, out-
of-control war, it is not out of order to liken the
Marco Polo Bridge Incident to the 1914 assassination of the Archduke Franz Ferdinand at
Sarajevo, which sparked World War I. After the
1937 incident, the Japanese army divided into two
groups. An expansionist faction, associated with
Tōjō Hideki, favored taking advantage of the incident to press China to allow Japan to expand its
rights in north China. An anti-imperialist faction,
associated with Ishiwara, argued that Japan
should reconcile its differences with China. Fate-
fully for Japan, the expansionists won.

John H. Boyle

Bibliography
Boyle, John H. *Modern Japan: The American*
Nexus. New York: Harcourt Brace
Jovanovich, 1993.
Crowley, James. "A Reconsideration of the
Marco Polo Bridge Incident." *Journal of*
Asian Studies. Vol. 22, No. 3 (May
1963), 261–87.
Hata, Ikuhito. "The Pacific War." *Cambridge*
History of Japan. Vol. 6, *The Twentieth*
Century. Ed. Peter Duus. Cambridge:
Cambridge University Press, 1989.

Maria Luz Incident (*Maria Rusugō Jiken*)

On July 7, 1872, bad weather forced the *Maria*
Luz, a Peruvian coolie ship with more than 200
Chinese forced laborers aboard, to take shelter
in Yokohama harbor. During the first day in
port, one of the Chinese escaped to the *Iron*
Duke, a British ship, and others followed. Fearing that the Chinese were being ill-treated, the
British charge d'affaires urged Japanese authorities to investigate. On July 14, an inquiry determined that the Chinese were indeed being
abused. The Chinese were moved ashore under

the care of the Japanese while the *Maria Luz's* captain, Ricardo Herrera, stood trial in a Japanese court in Kanagawa Prefecture. on August 26, 1872, Herrera was found guilty of cruel treatment of the Chinese, but he was pardoned and permitted to sail his ship back to Peru without the Chinese on board.

The Peruvian government, which had no diplomatic relations with Japan, protested and sent a mission to Japan to demand apologies and compensation and to establish diplomatic ties. The mission arrived in Yokohama on February 27, 1873; when no agreement had been reached by June, the two countries solicited arbitration by the czar of Russia. He decided Japan had acted properly in handling the affair, whereupon the two counties established diplomatic relations.

James L. Huffman

Bibliography

Gardiner, C. Harvey. *The Japanese and Peru, 1873–1973.* Albuquerque: University of New Mexico Press, 1975.

Maruyama Masao (1914–96)

The foremost historian of Japanese political thought and an important political thinker in his own right. His relation to Japanese nationalism can be approached on two levels. The first is his analysis of the phenomenon itself; the second is his mode of embodying it.

Maruyama's analysis of Japanese nationalism has been enormously influential inside and outside of Japan. This is probably because Maruyama has framed it in terms of a general narrative of modernity in which differing modes of nationalism (or national integration) play a prominent role. He regards Japanese nationalism in a specifically East Asian context as the only successful application of what he calls the formula of "differential usage" to meet the threat of Western imperialism during the nineteenth century. "Differential usage" refers to the separation of national essence (spirit) from Western means (technique). Having achieved this success, however, Japan was compelled to perpetuate the sense of crisis in which it took place; Japan's patriotism was to be one of "national emergency." As a result, bourgeois (popular) nationalism, which in Maruyama's view had driven the paradigmatic French Revolution, was suppressed or sublimated into statism.

Statism, in turn, took a uniquely Japanese form, that of the "family state," with its central notion of an emperor-centered *kokutai* (national polity). This concept, Maruyama asserts, involved the "full-scale mobilization of irrational attachment to the primary group." In a famous essay written immediately after Japan's World War II defeat, Maruyama exposed and dissected the consequences of what he termed "ultranationalism"—that is, the identification of state power with (familistic) morality. He saw a people robbed of the ability to act individually or collectively upon an autonomous moral sense, people who had been deceived and bludgeoned into looking to the emperor (via his officials) for values. In his role as "pathologist," Maruyama sought to excise this mentality of dependence: Unless this was done, Japan could not develop its own healthy, democratic nationalism.

In assuming the role of democratic enlightener, Maruyama clearly acted out of a profound national concern. Indeed, as a thinker, he sought to create the intellectual foundations for democratic political integration at the national level rather than to promote social solidarity. In this sense, Maruyama may be considered a critical nationalist and, as such, the representative of a modern tradition of elite public service in Japan.

Andrew E. Barshay

Bibliography

Maruyama, Masao. *Thought and Behaviour in Modern Japanese Politics.* Oxford: Oxford University Press, 1963.

Masterless Samurai (*Rōnin*)

Peasants who moved away from their land were called *rōnin* as early as the Nara period (710–84). By the Middle Ages, however, the term had come to denote warriors whose employment and income had ended with the loss of their master, as shown in the movie *Seven Samurai.* A samurai might become masterless in one of three ways: extinction of his lord's family, release from his lord's service, or renunciation of his vows of loyalty.

By the beginning of the Tokugawa period (1600–1868), the nationwide number of *rōnin* was estimated at 40,000, and what to do about them had become a political problem. The last revolt of the *rōnin* against a stable order in which they had no place was led by Yui Shosetsu (1605–51) in 1651. At the end of the Tokugawa period, antishogunal loyalists (*shishi*) frequently renounced their vows of loyalty in order to shed the constraints imposed by service to their lords while acting in what they perceived as the national interest. Their lords, or daimyo, were often amenable to this type of behavior because it isolated them from any short-term trouble their former retainers might encounter while still giving the daimyo at least a source of knowledge and sometimes an in–direct voice in the activities of antishogunal groups. In the domain of Mito, the entire imperialist party became *rōnin* (they were also known as *roshi*, masterless gentlemen) when they rebelled in 1864 against the policies of those who were acting in the name of the daimyo.

In the 1930s, young military officers took these *rōnin* as their model when they dedicated themselves to an ultranationalist vision of the national interest. The term has come to refer most commonly to students who are unaffiliated with any degree-granting educational institution or who try repeatedly to pass the entrance examinations required by the universities they wish to attend.

Anne Walthall

Bibliography

Koschmann, J. Victor. *The Mito Ideology: Discourse, Reform, and Insurrection in Late Tokugawa Japan, 1790–1864.* Berkeley: University of California Press, 1987.

Shimazaki, Toson. *Before the Dawn.* Honolulu: University of Hawaii Press, 1987.

Matsumoto Shigeharu (1899–1989)

Journalist, internationalist. Born in Osaka, he graduated from the University of Tokyo and studied in the mid-1920s at Yale University in the United States and Oxford University in England prior to becoming a journalist. In 1933, he was appointed bureau chief in Shanghai for the Nihon Shimbun Rengōsha (Associated Press of Japan). There, he built a growing reputation as an internationalist by making wide contacts among the Chinese people and speaking out against Japan's military activities in China. In 1936, he won an international scoop in reporting the kidnapping of China's President Chiang Kaishek. During World War II, he served as managing editor of the quasi-official Dōmei News Agency.

After the war, Matsumoto called for the Japanese to cooperate with the rest of the world without losing their national identity. He published an opinion journal, *Minpō*, for a few years, then, in 1952, created the International House of Japan, an institution that fosters international understanding through exchange programs for scholars, journalists, and opinion leaders. A close adviser to prominent politicians, he was asked at various times to serve as ambassador to the United States, Great Britain, and the United Nations, but he always refused, saying that he preferred to work privately.

James L. Huffman

Bibliography

Jansen, Marius B. *Japan and Its World: Two Centuries of Change.* Princeton, NJ: Princeton University Press, 1980.

Matsuoka Yōsuke (1880–1946)

Diplomat and businessman. Born in Chōshū domain, Matsuoka left Japan at age 13 for the United States, where he worked at various part-time jobs to finance his education. He attended school in Oregon and, at age 20, graduated from the University of Oregon law school. In 1902, Matsuoka returned to Japan and studied for a few months at Meiji University, then began his career as a diplomat, with strong ties to leaders in the Chōshū faction, the army, and big business. In 1921, Matsuoka left the Foreign Service to become a director of the South Manchurian Railway Company (SMRC); in 1927, he became SMRC vice president.

Following the fall of the Tanaka Giichi cabinet in 1929, he returned to Japan, where he became active in national politics as a member of the Rikken Seiyūkai (Friends of Constitutional Government Party). Throughout 1929, he openly supported expansion in Manchuria to acquire natural resources; in 1930, he was elected to the Diet (legislature). Matsuoka led Japan's withdrawal from the League of Nations on February 24, 1933. The same year, he withdrew from the Seiyūkai, resigned from the Diet, and founded the Seitō Kaisho Renmei (League to Dissolve the Parties), a movement to enhance national unity by eliminating all political parties and creating a non-partisan Diet. In 1935, he became president of the SMRC, but, by 1938, the Guandong army had acquired all SMRC enterprises, excepting the railway industry. Matsuoka returned to Japan in 1939 and became foreign minister in the Konoe Fumimaro cabinet in 1940. Because he handled foreign affairs according to his own agenda, disregarding the wishes of the cabinet, he was maneuvered out of office in 1941. Widely considered insane, Matsuoka died during the Tokyo War Crimes Trials in June 1946.

James L. Huffman

Bibliography
Burns, Richard Dean, and Edward M. Bennett, eds. *Diplomats in Crisis: United States-Chinese-Japanese Relations, 1919–1941.* Santa Barbara, CA: ABC-Clio, 1974.

May Day Incident (*Mēdē Jiken*)

"Bloody May Day" refers to the clashes involving workers, students, Koreans, and the police that swept Japan on May Day 1952, just after Japan had regained its independence from the U.S.-led Occupation government. The most serious incident took place in Tokyo following a rally of 200,000 labor unionists and 10,000 students at Meiji Park. The causes of the Tokyo confrontation were the implementation of the Japan-U.S. Security Treaty and accompanying administrative agreement allowing the stationing of U.S. troops in Japan, government submission of the Subversive Activities Prevention Bill to the Diet and government denial of permission to use the Imperial Plaza for the rally, and the stationing of 5,000 armed police to enforce the ban.

Zengakuren (All-Japan Student Federation) students played a prominent part, chanting "down with the Yoshida government," "Yankee, go home," and "On to the People's [Imperial] Plaza." After the scheduled rallies dispersed, approximately 6,000 workers, Koreans, and students marched to the Imperial Plaza, where bloody fighting broke out. Police used tear gas and pistols against them. In the course of restoring order, they killed two protesters (a worker and a student), arrested more than 1,200, and injured many more.

The protesters strongly objected to the U.S.-imposed treaty system as compromising Japan's national independence, but they focused their anger on the Yoshida Shigeru government, which they regarded as leading a drive to cripple the labor movement, reverse postwar democratic reforms, revive the military, and return the country to authoritarian rule. A similar five-hour battle took place in Kyoto.

Joe B. Moore

Bibliography
Battistini, Lawrence H. *The Postwar Student Struggle in Japan.* Tokyo: Charles E. Tuttle, 1956.

May 15 Incident (*Go Ichi Go Jiken*)

A failed coup in 1932, led by young naval officers. Following the 1930 London Naval Treaty, in which Japan failed to achieve its goals for an enlarged navy, radical elements in the military and civilian ultranationalists conspired against the government, calling for a Shōwa Restoration. They were frustrated by the political parties' weak military posture, alleged collusion with big business, and inability to solve Japan's social and economic problems. In October 1931, the Sakurakai (Cherry Blossom Society) planned a coup against the Wakatsuki Reijirō cabinet, but it was uncovered and stopped by senior army officials. Early in 1932, young radical naval officers planned their own coup, but worldwide commotion over unexpected military skirmishes in Shanghai forced them to postpone their plans.

Later, in the spring, the young naval officers, with support from the remnants of the ultranationalist Ketsumeidan (League of Blood), planned another coup. The targets for the May 15 Incident included Prime Minister Inukai Tsuyoshi, Privy Seal Makino Nobuaki, the headquarters of the Tokyo metropolitan police force, the offices of Seiyūkai (Friends of Constitutional Government Party), and Mitsubishi Bank. Other conspirators were to blow up six electrical substations to black out Tokyo. The resulting chaos would provide the military with the opportunity to declare martial law and begin restructuring Japanese society and government.

The conspirators' plans were vague, and they lacked a backup scheme. The bomb attempts at Makino's house, at the police headquarters, and at Mitsubishi and Seiyūkai offices did little damage; the conspirators also failed to destroy the substations, giving the military no reason to declare martial law. They did assassinate Inukai, who was the last party prime minister until after World War II. The conspirators' light sentences—and emotional, patriotic rhetoric during their trials—stimulated a rising nationalistic mood among the general public.

Roger W. Purdy

Bibliography
Shillony, Ben-Ami. *Revolt in Japan: The Young Officers and the February 26,*

1936, Incident. Princeton, NJ: Princeton University Press, 1973.

Storry, Richard. *The Double Patriots: A Study of Japanese Nationalism*. Westport, CT: Greenwood Press, 1973.

Mazaki (Masaki) Jinzaburō (1876–1956)

Army general. A native of Saga Prefecture, he held numerous significant posts, including service on the Supreme War Council (1935–36). He was a member of the ultranationalist Kokuhonsha (National Foundations Society), a leader in the army's Imperial Way Faction (Kōdōha), and an influential confidant to such political leaders as Konoe Fumimaro.

As commander of the Army Academy (1923–26), Mazaki promoted what he called "absolute reverence to imperial Japanism" (*sonnō zettai nihonshugi*) in ideological training sessions. In the mid-1930s, as inspector-general of military education, he reinforced nationalistic interpretations of *kokutai* (national essence), opposing the scholar Minobe Tatsukichi's long-standard view that the emperor was simply an organ of the state. Mazaki's 1935 ouster as inspector-general helped trigger the assassination of his political foe and head of the Military Affairs Bureau, Nagata Tetsuzan, by Aizawa Saburō, one of Mazaki's minions. Suspected of collusion in the massive, though abortive, military coup on February 26, 1936, Mazaki was deactivated, court-martialed, and found innocent. Following World War II, he was incarcerated for two years as a war criminal, then became a member of the rightist New Life Japan People's League (Shinsei Nihon Kokumin Dōmei).

Jacob Kovalio

Bibliography

Crowley, James. *Japan's Quest for Autonomy: 1930–1938*. Princeton, NJ: Princeton University Press, 1966.

Meiji Constitution
(Constitution of the Empire of Japan)
(*Dai Nihon Teikoku Kempō*)

Promulgated on February 11, 1889, the Meiji Constitution represented a climactic point in the effort to create a modern political system that would balance the emperor-centered, autocratic approach of Japanese tradition with the new era's demands for popular participation in government. Though traditional and conservative in its provision for imperial sovereignty and cabinets that remained aloof from partisan or Diet (legislature) politics, it had the potential for supporting democratic government through a parliamentary system and an independent judiciary.

The kind of constitution appropriate to Japan's unique polity was the subject of intense debate throughout the early years of the Meiji era (1868–1912). Almost from the first, officials such as the progressive junior councillor Kido Takayoshi asserted the necessity of adopting a constitution, partly out of a desire to gain standing with Western powers and partly from a belief in the inherent need for a rational governmental foundation to provide a basis for wider participation. As early as 1874, political outsider Itagaki Taisuke and others touched off an intense discussion in Japan's newspapers and opinion journals with a memorial to the throne, calling for the early creation of a national popular assembly. All sides agreed that an assembly—and a constitution undergirding it—were needed, but the debate on their nature and timing was heated. Following an 1878 Genrōin (Chamber of Elders) draft constitution that Prince Iwakura Tomomi and other leading officials found too liberal, a call went out for a group of top officials to submit constitutional opinions; they all did so between December 1879 and March 1881.

Most of them advocated a relatively conservative document, focusing on the central role of the emperor and on the importance of allowing adequate time to prepare the way for effective constitutional government. Several, including Itō Hirobumi and Inoue Kaoru, called for limited popular participation. And one, Ōkuma Shigenobu, shocked many of his colleagues by demanding a British-style constitution, with a cabinet headed by the majority party in the Diet; he also demanded the immediate creation of this constitutional system. Draft constitutions also were published and discussed, often heatedly, in the press. The progovernment journalist Fukuchi Gen'ichirō, for example, sparked considerable debate with a series of editorials at his newspaper *Tokyo Nichi Nichi Shimbun* early in 1882 that placed sovereignty squarely (and solely) in the emperor, while the rival newspaper *Tokyo-Yokohama Mainichi Shimbun* countered that sovereignty should be shared by the emperor and the people. Popular-rights leaders Ueki Emori and Nakae Chōmin went so far as to posit sovereignty in the Japanese people alone and to advocate sharp limits on the emperor's powers. Important in the debate were the frequent references to Japan's *kokutai* (national essence), with many writers declaring that the imperial line, "unbroken for ages eternal," was what made Japan unique, and that, because of that, the emperor should be at the center of Japan's constitutional system.

Concrete work on the constitution began after October 1881, when the progressive Ōkuma was ousted from the government, and an imperial decree promised a constitution within a decade. A special drafting bureau with Itō as chair, created on October 21, was asked to lead a mission to Europe to study constitutional systems. By way of preparation for the constitution, in the middle of the 1880s new administrative structures, including a peerage and a modern cabinet, were created. Foreign advisers (particularly the German scholar Hermann Roesler) assisted in the drafting process. And from 1886 to 1888, a number of central officials, including Inoue Kowashi, Itō Miyoji, and Kaneko Kentarō, prepared a succession of drafts, with an ad hoc Privy Council (*sūmitsuin*) ratifying the final draft in January 1889. The promulgation on February 11 (the constitution actually took effect in 1890) was heralded across the country by celebrations and a sense of national pride. Indeed, the nationalist intellectual Kuga Katsunan chose this day as the occasion to launch his influential nationalistic newspaper, *Nihon*.

The highly traditionalist preamble of the constitution referred to the "glories" of the imperial ancestors and described the document as a gift to "our beloved subjects," while the first 17 articles made the "sacred and inviolable" emperor "head of the Empire." He was given the right to exercise legislative power, with the consent of the Diet, and the ministers of state were made responsible to him alone, as was the military. Thus, the power of the cabinet and the military was placed beyond the sanctions of the legislature, in a system referred to as transcendentalism, with sovereignty residing solely in the emperor.

At the same time, imperial sovereignty was balanced by the creation of an independent judiciary and a Diet of limited, though real, powers. The legislature's approval was required for all laws, and it was given the right to initiate laws, receive petitions and present memorials to the throne, and approve budgets.

The constitution guaranteed numerous popular rights, including freedom of speech, publication, religion, abode, and assembly, though all of these freedoms were circumscribed by the phrase "within the limits of the law."

The Meiji Constitution was regarded in its day as a conservative but moderate document, a relatively effective balancing of Japan's own traditions with the norms of a new era and the demands of public opinion. While the prerogatives of the legislature and the rights of citizens were clearly circumscribed, and while there was no provision for responsible cabinets or party governments, the very fact of creating a legislature—combined with the acceptance now of the basic principle of rule by law—was seen by most as sufficient to assure increasing popular participation in the government. The future would prove this analysis correct: By the end of the 1910s, the politicians had used the leverage provided by the Diet to create a system in which majority-party cabinets became the norm. The fact that democracy eventually succumbed to the ultranationalism of the 1930s may have been facilitated by certain provisions in the Meiji Constitution, but popular government's demise resulted more from the times and the people than from the nature of the constitution.

James L. Huffman

Bibliography

Akita, George. *Foundations of Constitutional Government in Modern Japan, 1868–1900.* Cambridge: Harvard University Press, 1967.

Pittau, Joseph. *Political Thought in Early Meiji Japan.* Cambridge: Harvard University Press, 1967.

Meiji Emperor (*Meiji Tennō*) (1852–1912)

The 122nd emperor, according to the traditional count, of Japan and prime focus of Japanese nationalism during his 1867–1912 reign. Son of Emperor Kōmei, he was known by his personal name Mutsuhito. He, or rather the imperial institution, was the rallying point for activists who sought to overthrow the Tokugawa feudal regime and succeeded in restoring direct imperial rule in the Meiji Restoration of January 3, 1868.

In the spring of 1868, a Charter Oath, issued in the emperor's name, defined the character of the new regime. It promised the establishment of deliberative assemblies, freedom of residence and occupation, abolition of hereditary classes, and a new openness to the West. In 1869, the young emperor took up residence in Tokyo, which became firmly established as Japan's national capital. The leaders of the new regime used

Newspaper announcement of Meiji Emperor's death, July 30, 1912. Courtesy Meiji Shimbun Zasshi Bunkō.

the imperial symbol to realize programs of national political and economic centralization. In 1871, the government abolished the former feudal domains and established a prefectural system. In similar fashion, Emperor Meiji created land-tax laws and a national conscription system in 1873, and a new national educational system in 1874. The emperor also promoted Westernization by appearing in public wearing Western clothes. Newspapers informed the Japanese people that the emperor favored a Western-style diet of meat and milk.

As proof of Japan's most obvious symbol of political unity, Mutsuhito made more than 100 official visits outside the capital, including nearly every area in Japan from Hokkaido to Kyushu, to establish a personal bond with the Japanese people. Particularly significant were the Six Great Circuits accomplished between 1872 and 1885.

In the latter half of his reign, Mutsuhito made fewer public appearances. The 1889 Meiji Constitution declared the throne "sacred and inviolable" and sought to place the monarchy above politics. While sovereignty rested with the emperor, not with the people, the constitution did limit the emperor from pursuing independent action. The emperor gradually assumed a dual character as a constitutional monarch and as the high priest of a national ideology that stressed the uniqueness, if not superiority, of the Japanese nation, its people, and its emperor.

By the 1890s, Japan appeared as a *kazoku kokka* (family state), in which the emperor served as the national patriarch. The 1890 Imperial Rescript on Education demanded that Japan's educational institutions produce "good and faithful subjects" who would "guard and maintain the prosperity of Our Imperial Throne coeval with heaven and earth." Portraits of the emperor and empress were displayed and venerated in all public offices and schools. An official cult of State Shinto, organized to inculcate patriotism and loyalty to the throne, referred to the emperor as a "living god" to be respected and worshiped.

The Meiji emperor also became closely associated with the expansion of the Japanese empire. The 1889 Constitution made the emperor the commander in chief of Japanese military forces and granted him powers to initiate war and conclude treaties of peace. During the Sino-Japanese War (1894–95), Mutsuhito established his residence in Hiroshima to be nearer to the front. Again, during the Russo-Japanese War (1904–05) the emperor's concern for the fighting men became almost legendary. At the end of his reign, the emperor represented Japanese power and progress and commanded the absolute loyalty of his people.

During the 45 years of Mutsuhito's reign, Japan became transformed from a feudal agrarian polity to a bureaucratic and parliamentary state; indeed, into one of the great military and industrial powers of the world. While it is questionable how much personal involvement the Meiji emperor had in this process, his role as the embodiment of Japanese national unity was indispensable for Japan's remarkable development during these years.

M. *William Steele*

Bibliography

Gluck, Carol. *Japan's Modern Myths: Ideology in the Late Meiji Period.* Princeton, NJ: Princeton University Press, 1985.

Hall, John W. "A Monarch for Modern Japan." *Political Development in Modern Japan.* Ed. Robert E. Ward. Princeton, NJ: Princeton University Press, 1968.

Jansen, Marius B. "Monarch and Modernization in Japan." *Journal of Asian Studies.* Vol. 36, No. 4 (August 1977), 611–22.

Meiji Era (1868–1912)

The Meiji era was the formative period of modern Japanese nationalism. Not until the late nineteenth and early twentieth centuries did nearly all of the people living in "Japan" realize that it was commonsensical and natural to possess a national identity and to feel a sense of responsibility to the national collectivity. While a consciousness of national identity rests upon a subjective belief in a collective destiny and the possession of a shared national culture, the samurai elite of the Tokugawa period (1600–1868) governed through a system that fostered status rather than a national consciousness, and that countenanced cultural disintegration regionally and among the various social estates. To be sure, the term signifying Japan, *nippon,* has existed since at least the early eighth century; and historians have pointed out that some commoners might have begun to acquire a faint sense of national consciousness in the cities of the Kyoto/Osaka region as early as the late seventeenth century. All of this, however, serves merely to highlight the fact that, prior to the Meiji era, national identity at the popular level existed only in an emergent and geographically restricted way.

The Meiji state's most important social policy regarding the creation of mass nationalism was the abolition of the hierarchically ordered Tokugawa social-status system, since the leveling of society enabled the masses to feel themselves more fully a part of, and responsible to, one national community. This major historical revolution in the social assumptions of rule took concrete form from 1869, when the government placed peasants, artisans and merchants under the single category of *heimin* (commoner). The de facto declassing of the samurai proceeded over the next few years through the removal of their special privileges and the granting to commoners of prerogatives formerly limited to the samurai class. The latter included the right of all Japanese to take surnames. Such specific measures as legal abolition of outcast statuses, formal recognition of intermarriage among the people, and freedom to choose their occupation also contributed to the formal leveling of society, captured in the phrase *ikkun banmin* (the equality of all under one ruler), even though discrimination certainly persisted in practice.

At the same time, the state sought to limit regionalism. The most dramatic steps in this spatial centralization of the national community came with the abolition in 1871 of the largely autonomous Tokugawa-period domains (*haihan chiken*) and with the invention of a national culture. However, this centralization could not have been accomplished without the aid of rapid developments in the country's transportation and communications network. The removal of road barriers in 1869, the beginnings of telegraphic communications, the centralization of postal services, the development of inexpensive newspapers in the second half of the Meiji era, the inauguration of the Shinbashi-Yokohama railway line in 1872, and the elaboration of a nationwide railway network by the turn of the century—all of these technological developments, which facilitated communication among members of the national community who previously could not have had face-to-face contact, were necessary material preconditions for the emergence of mass nationalism.

The Meiji political elite and the state bureaucracy also took the lead in the creation of the culture of Japanese nationalism—that is they invented or reproduced a countless array of national symbols, rites, practices, and ideas, an entire system of meaning through which the people might imagine the nation.

The most important national symbol of the modern era has been the monarchy, but popular recognition of it as such is a Meiji product. Although there is no doubt that the imperial institution is of ancient vintage, popular consciousness of the emperor during the Tokugawa period did not exist in many areas and was weak or fused with folk beliefs about wandering sacred beings (*marebito*) in others. To make the imperial institution Japan's central national symbol, the Meiji rulers had to aggressively introduce the imperial household to the people.

During the first few Meiji years, officials posted notices throughout the country informing the people about their ruler. One such pronouncement at the Nagasaki Courthouse explained: "In this land called Japan there is one called the Emperor, who is descended from the Sun Deity. This has not changed a bit from long ago and just like the Sun being up in the heavens He is the Master." More spectacular and effective, however, were a variety of public pageants. During the first two decades, the emperor set out on a number of what were called "progresses," a stylized state ritual in which the emperor traveled throughout the country watching and being watched by the people. From the late 1880s, however, the state adopted new kinds of ceremonies much influenced by the public pageants of European royalty. These included imperial weddings, wedding anniversaries, funerals, and celebrations of victories in war and of national political accomplishments. Just as important was the widespread distribution of the imperial portrait from the 1890s onward, made possible by a revolutionary technological innovation: photographic reproduction.

Other important national symbols that the populace at large came to share during the Meiji era included the *hinomaru* (Rising Sun) flag, the "kimi ga yo" (The Imperial Reign) anthem, the national capital city, the Imperial Palace, the *banzai* cheer hailing the monarch, the palace's Nijūbashi bridge, and a large number of national shrines. Some of these cultural artifacts, such as the anthem and the Yasukuni Shrine (founded in 1869), Japan's pantheon to the war dead, were complete fabrications of the Meiji era. Others, such as the flag, the *banzai* cheer, the Ise Shrine, the new Imperial Palace, and the Nijūbashi bridge (the latter two date from 1889), had existed in earlier forms; but they only now acquired a national significance, through propaganda, education, and a significant manipulation of the physical appearance of these sites.

As some of the above descriptions would suggest, the dominant culture of Japan included a religious dimension conventionally called State Shinto (*kokka shintō*). Through this political religion, the state attempted to bring the country's localized and enormously varied popular religious practices into one overarching religious system centering on the cult of emperor and nation.

While no rigid intellectual orthodoxy marked the Meiji era, key texts and ideas that ought to be considered a part of the dominant discourse on the nation certainly existed. No idea was more important to this dominant discourse than that of the imperial institution's centrality in the past, present, and future of the national community. The central meaning of the critically important term *kokutai* (national essence or national polity), was that the nation's and the people's fundamental and exceptional character lay precisely in the imperial household's continuity. Important texts, such as the Imperial Rescript on Education (1890), stressed that the nation itself had been founded by the imperial ancestors; *Kigensetsu,* prewar Japan's most important national holiday, emphasized the historical contemporaneity of the nation and the emperorship by celebrating the mythical first emperor Jimmu's accession as Empire Day. The centrality of the emperor in the national history was an idea also made explicit in prewar Japan's most important legal document, the Meiji Constitution (1889). Accordingly, loyalty to emperor and nation, summed up in the slogan *chukun aikoku* (loyalty to ruler and patriotism), were considered to be the citizen's highest virtues.

The view of Japan as a family state (*kazoku kokka*), with the emperor as parent, or head, of the nation's main family, was a particularly important intellectual justification for emperor-centered nationalism. Widely disseminated throughout Japan's primary schools from the 1890s onward, this ideology systematically articulated an organismic interpretation of the individual's and the family's relationship to the nation–state and imperial household.

Official culture was most effectively disseminated to the people through schools and the military barracks. Compulsory schooling for boys and girls, beginning in 1872, was the state's most effective means of nationalizing the masses. While there would be shifts in what the national leaders deemed should be specific emphases in educational curricula—from practical learning for national wealth and strength to a greater concentration on ethical instruction in putatively traditional morals from the early 1880s—the central objective of Meiji educational policies remained constant: the production of a skilled, literate, and patriotic citizenry, equipped with a common body of knowledge, whose energies could be tapped for the realization of national objectives. Central control over curriculum content increased from the 1880s, especially with the 1883 requirement that all textbooks be certified by the Ministry of Education and even more so from 1903, when the ministry assumed full control over the compilation and distribution of primary-school textbooks. The Ministry of Education and the schools also played a central role in the unification and development of a standard Japanese language.

The introduction of universal male conscription in 1873 had widespread consequences for the development of mass nationalism. Not only did it help equalize the former samurai (*shizoku*) class and the commoners by eliminating the special military prerogatives of the former, it also led to the institutionalization of a new and highly efficient mechanism for the uniform socialization of young men into a national way of life. In the barracks, commoners might learn to communicate in the standard Japanese language. They were taught that the highest values were loyalty to the emperor and the nation, and they could begin to feel the commonality that bound them to one another, despite differences in their local cultures.

While the Meiji political elite, the state bureaucracy, and state apparatuses such as schools and the military barracks took the lead in propagating the culture and ideas of nationalism, the massive contribution of people outside of government and the bureaucracy—intellectuals, journalists, oppositional political leaders, the rural elite, and the middle classes—must also be recognized. The fact that such a range of people existed who produced and circulated discourses on the nation ensured a variety of national narratives—stories about the nation—and that they would often be in competition.

M

Those active in the Meiji period's first sustained opposition political group, the Freedom and People's Rights Movement (Jiyū Minken Undō), did not challenge the legitimacy of the nation-state or the emperor. Whether of former samurai (*shizoku*) or of wealthy peasant (*gōnō*) background, most shared with the oligarchs a revulsion against the unequal treaties with the Western powers and a desire to preserve national independence. Indeed, *aikoku* (patriotism) was a term they often invoked, and the political organization founded by one of the movement's early leaders, Itagaki Taisuke, was called the Aikokusha (Society of Patriots). The popular-rights activists differed with the government only over the extent to which they would have permitted broader participation in government and the establishment of a national assembly. In short, they fought about access to power within the nation, not about the validity of the nation-state's existence or the necessity of nationalism. Theirs was a liberal nationalism that challenged the more statist model of the Meiji oligarchs.

Particularly after the late 1880s, many others outside the government contributed to the production of a huge (and still growing) body of knowledge that expounded on the unique history and cultural characteristics of Japan and its people. In arts and architecture, men such as Ōkakura Tenshin (1862–1913) and Itō Chūta (1867–1954) promoted a new appreciation of native aesthetics. Yanagita Kunio (1875–1962), the founder of folklore studies (*minzokugaku*) in Japan, gave life to the modern belief in an authentic Japanese culture by attempting to locate its pristine forms and traces in the countryside. Anthropologists, especially after the founding of the *Tokyo Jinruigaku Zasshi* (Tokyo Journal of Anthropology) in 1886, constructed cultural and racial "others," against whom the "Japanese" could be defined. In language and literature, such literary scholars as Mozume Takami (1847–1928) argued for the refinement of a national language that would unify the literary and oral languages (*genbun itchi*), while novelists such as Yamada Bimyō (1868–1910) and Futabatei Shimei (1864–1909) wrote in a style close to the colloquial.

Intellectuals such as Shiga Shigetaka (1863–1927), Miyake Setsurei (1860–1945), and Kuga Katsunan (1857–1907) likewise turned their knowledge of European thought toward a new brand of cultural exceptionalism. In 1888, Shiga and Miyake founded the Seikyōsha (Society for Political Education). The society's members published the journal *Nihonjin* (The Japanese) and pressed for what they called the "preservation of the national essence" (*kokusui hozon*). The most radical nationalist thought of the Meiji era was produced by those associated with the Gen'yōsha (Black Sea Society, founded in 1881) and the Kokuryūkai (Amur River Society, founded in 1901). However, from the 1890s onward, many nonofficial associations, such as the Oriental Society (Tōhō Kyōkai), promoted the idea of expansionism in Asia as a means of preserving national independence.

Moreover, around the turn of the century, and especially from the Russo-Japanese War (1904–05) onward, semiofficial patriotic organizations such as the Red Cross, the Patriotic Women's Society (Aikoku Fujinkai), young men's associations (*seinendan*), and military reservists associations (*zaigō gunjinkai*) helped spread the culture of nationalism through what were becoming nationwide networks.

The production of nationalism during the Meiji era was thus the result of a complex interplay and transformation of state, society, culture, and knowledge. Although nationalism could not flourish under the Tokugawa period's system of fragmented rule, it began to do so in the late Meiji era, with consequences that continue to reverberate through national and global politics.

Takashi Fujitani

Bibliography

Fujitani, Takashi. *Splendid Monarchy: Power and Pageantry in Modern Japan.* Berkeley: University of California Press, 1996.

Gluck, Carol. *Japan's Modern Myths: Ideology in the Late Meiji Period.* Princeton, NJ: Princeton University Press, 1985.

Murthy, P.A. Narasimha. *The Rise of Modern Nationalism in Japan: A Historical Study of the Role of Education in the Making of Modern Japan.* New Delhi: Ashajanak Publications, 1973.

Pyle, Kenneth B. *The New Generation in Meiji Japan: Problems of Cultural Identity, 1885–1895.* Stanford, CA: Stanford University Press, 1969.

Meiji Restoration (*Meiji Ishin*)

The 1868 coup d'état, named after the young emperor who had assumed the throne the previous year, that marked Japan's shift from feudalism to modernity. By the second-third of the nineteenth century, the ruling Tokugawa regime was experiencing unprecedented problems in governing: serious financial difficulties, foreign challenges, intellectual attacks, and increasing restiveness in the domains. The problems were exacerbated in the 1850s, when the Americans forced Japan to end its two-century-old exclusion policy and open up to international exchange.

As a result, an active opposition began to grow. Though hardly a unified movement, it found intellectual underpinnings in the *kokugaku* (national learning) schools of domains like Mito that emphasized the centrality of the emperor system in Japanese history (and, by implication, the "illegal" nature of Tokugawa rule). Much of the movement's passion came from the *sonnō jōi* (revere the emperor and expel the barbarians) slogans of hundreds of *shishi* (antishogunal loyalists) who carried out anti-Tokugawa, antiforeign acts of terrorism in the streets of Tokyo and Kyoto.

Most devastating to the Tokugawa, however, was the spread of active anti-Tokugawa sentiments to the leadership of powerful domains such as Satsuma, in southern Kyushu, and Chōshū, on the western tip of Honshu. By the mid-1860s, anti-Tokugawa zealots were firmly in control of Chōshū, and Satsuma leaders were secretly assisting them. Recognizing the difficulty of the Tokugawa position after a disastrous attempt to punish Chōshū militarily, Shogun Tokugawa Keiki announced in November 1867 that he was returning political power to the emperor. The meaning of his announcement was ambiguous, however, since his family still held a quarter of Japan's land.

As a result, on January 3, 1868, a group from Satsuma, Tosa, and Chōshū fiefs joined several court nobles in seizing the palace and securing an imperial announcement that the Tokugawa government had been abolished and that government power and the Tokugawa lands had been returned to the throne. Keiki put up a brief military resistance, then ordered his followers to surrender early in February. Not all did so, and the Boshin War that ensued lasted until June 1869. While the war resulted in more than 13,000 casualties, the bloodshed and disruption were so much less than they might have been had Keiki resisted that the Restoration often is referred to as bloodless.

Though the Restoration leaders—most of them relatively young samurai from Satsuma and Chōshū—seem to have had rather vague and limited ideas of governmental reform in January 1868, the harsh reality of the international system quickly turned them into visionaries. Concluding that Japan must modernize if it were to avoid the humiliations that an imperialistic West had visited on China and other Asian countries, they committed themselves to studying, and working with, the powerful Western states and to creating a workable, centralized, modern national system. Their goals were captured in such phrases as *bunmei kaika* (civilization and enlightenment) and *fukoku kyōhei* (rich country, strong army). The result was a modernization program that within a generation turned Japan into a constitutional monarchy, with a growing economy, a spreading school system based on the idea of universal education, and a modern military establishment capable of defeating China and Russia. So remarkable were the changes that historians often refer to the restoration as the Meiji revolution.

James L. Huffman

Bibliography

Beasley, W.B. *The Meiji Restoration.* Stanford, CA: Stanford University Press, 1972.

Nagai, Michio, and Miguel Urrutia, eds. *Meiji Ishin: Restoration and Revolution.* Tokyo: United Nations University, 1985.

Meiji Shrine (*Meiji Jingū*)

The Meiji Shrine, located in Shibuya Ward, Tokyo, encompassed the spirit of the Meiji Emperor (r. 1867–1912) as its deity (*kami*). It was completed in 1920 through an unprecedented mobilization of youth groups and other civic associations from all over Japan, who contributed labor and funds to the building of the shrine as a national project. The Meiji Emperor presided over a period of truly revolutionary change in Japanese history. He was the first Japanese emperor to be made visible to the populace through a series of nationwide imperial progresses (tours), and he was genuinely beloved by the people, thousands of whom came to kneel on the palace grounds when he lay near death. It was inevitable that he would be deified and worshiped in a great shrine; along with other shrines built in the modern period, such as the Yasukuni Shrine, the name for the national shrine of the war dead, the Meiji Shrine became a symbolic center for the

Meiji Shrine. Courtesy Consulate General of Japan, N.Y.

religious expression of national sentiment. Construction began in 1915, but because of a great rise in construction costs after World War I and a severe labor shortage, the project nearly faltered. Only the mobilization of youth and civic groups brought it to completion. Provincial branches of the shrine enabled Japanese to worship the Meiji Emperor at cult centers all over Japan.

Helen Hardacre

Bibliography

Murakami, Shigeyoshi. *Japanese Religion in the Modern Century.* Trans. Byron Earhart. Tokyo: University of Tokyo Press, 1980.

Meiji Six Society (*Meirokusha*)

Intellectual society. After returning in 1873 from two years as ambassador to the United States, Mori Arinori proposed to several colleagues that they found a society to discuss the issues facing Japan as it moved into the modern era. The society began operations the following February 1, with 33 members meeting biweekly to talk about issues as broadranging as language reform, state religion, educational systems, and national morality.

The society included a number of Japan's most influential, mostly junior, opinion leaders—officials, journalists, merchants, and physicians—along with one American, the missionary educator William Elliot Griffis. Among the most prominent were Nishimura Shigeki, Katō Hiroyuki, Nishi Amane, Tsuda Sen, Maejima Hisoka, Mitsukuri Rinshō, and Fukuzawa Yukichi. Most of the members had studied European languages, and nearly half had traveled abroad. All of them were dedicated to the progressive idea of "civilization and enlightenment" (*bunmei kaika*), and all were committed to Japan's entry into the community of powerful countries.

The discussions of the Meirokusha proved unusually influential, partly because of the stature of its members and partly because the society published a journal, *Meiroku Zasshi,* until a new Press Law in June 1875 threatened to restrict the freedom with which views could be expressed. Mori argued that the journal should be continued despite the risks of the law, but Fukuzawa carried the day with the argument that the threat of censorship would stifle members and that the journal should, for that reason, be terminated. The society continued to hold meetings for another quarter of a century, but its influence waned.

James L. Huffman

Bibliography

Braisted, William R., trans. *Meiroku Zasshi: Journal of the Japanese Enlightenment.* Tokyo: University of Tokyo Press, 1976.

Miki Kiyoshi (1895–1945)

Prominent philosopher and writer who first became well known as an interpreter of Marxism. The police arrested him in 1930 because of alleged ties to the Japan Communist Party. He died of illness after his second imprisonment, again for alleged Communist sympathies.

Confronting increased authoritarianism in the early 1930s, Miki defended intellectual liberty and rejected what he called irrational nationalism that sought to exclude Western influence. At the same time, he believed in the special quality of Asian thought, arguing for a new Oriental ideology that would surpass Western liberalism.

In 1938, the Cultural Problems Committee that Miki directed in the Shōwa Kenkyūkai (Shōwa Research Society) issued a report, *Principles of Thought for a New Japan,* that affirmed Japan's quest to lead Asia by outlining a moral mission to create an East Asian Cooperative Body based on the principles of a new ideology, cooperativism. Superior to liberalism and socialism, cooperativism would resolve class conflict and emphasize the welfare of the whole. It would bind Japan and China in the task of building a regional bloc. Though naive in suggesting the possibility of genuine Chinese-Japanese cooperation, Miki's approach illustrated the variety and subtle sophistication of some nationalist thought in the 1930s.

William Miles Fletcher III

Bibliography

Fletcher, William Miles, III. *The Search for a New Order: Intellectuals and Fascism in Prewar Japan.* Chapel Hill: University of North Carolina Press, 1982.

Piovesana, Gino K. "Miki Kiyoshi: Representative Thinker for an Anguished Generation." *Studies of Japanese Culture.* Ed. Joseph Roggendorff. Tokyo: Sophia University Press, 1963.

Military Police (*Kenpeitai*)

The *kenpeitai* was formed in 1881 by the Meiji government to enforce order among members of the armed forces and civilians attached to the military. Initially a strictly military body, it gradually expanded its activities to assist in maintaining order and ideological purity among the general public; in 1906, the establishment of the *kenpeitai* in Korea resulted in widespread Japanese legal and administrative authority there over matters with no direct relationship to the military. During the 1930s and World War II, the military police involved themselves in every phase of Japanese life, often using gestapolike tactics to ensure not only order but widespread fear. Controlled by the Army, Navy, Justice and Home Ministries, the *kenpeitai* was known for intimidating tactics intended to ensure "correct thought," including thorough interrogations, breaking into homes and conducting sweeping investigations of individuals whose patriotism was suspected, and harassing alleged Marxists, Christians, and pacifists. The *kenpeitai* also exercised wide control over the civilian populations in Manchukuo, Japan's puppet state in Manchuria, where it was headed during the mid-1930s by Tōjō Hideki, who would be Japan's prime minister in World War II. The organization was disbanded in 1945.

James L. Huffman

Bibliography

Ienaga, Saburō. *The Pacific War.* New York: Pantheon Books, 1978.

M

Ministry of Education (*Mombushō*)

Treatments of the Mombushō by American authors typically lead to two conclusions: (1) Education has been a more vital concern in modern Japan than in the United States; and (2) the organization directly responsible for policy formulation and administration of education, the Mombushō, is a far more powerful and centralized institution than the federal Department of Education in the United States. The American colonial experience caused a revulsion against centralized government; consequently, the U.S. Constitution gives direct control over education to the individual states, which have generally set minimum standards, then surrendered the operation and policy formulation of education to local school districts. The Japanese, by contrast, have seen centralization as a means to achieve efficiency, high standards, consistency, uniformity, and control.

Given Japan's need in the late 1800s to catch up with the West, to modernize, and to maintain Japanese independence, the Meiji leaders determined within three years of the Meiji Restoration (1868) the need for a strong centralized government. Accordingly, in June 1871, they established a Department of Education, Mombushō, which became a ministry in 1885, when the Itō Hirobumi cabinet created Japan's first ministerial system of government. To control, supervise, and finance Japan's schools, Mombushō officials created a Bureau of Superintendence in November 1872, giving it the responsibility of inspecting and supervising the country's schools. The ministry received appropriations from the central government's taxation revenues to make annual distributions of funds to local governments to assist elementary schools. The Mombushō continues to be the main source of revenue for the compulsory elementary and junior-high schools and provides 50 percent of high-school teachers' salaries.

From Mombushō's inception, its officials were ambitious. The Educational Code of 1872, influenced largely by France's centralized education system, attempted to introduce a comprehensive nationwide plan that divided Japan into eight university districts. Each comprised 32 secondary-school districts, divided again into 210 elementary-school districts, one for every area with a population of at least 600 people. That meant the establishment of 256 secondary and 53,760 elementary schools. Education became compulsory for the first four years, and eight-year elementary schools and six-year middle schools were to be established.

This plan proved too expensive and premature to be implemented successfully. Japan lacked the revenues or the personnel to maintain and superintend such a costly program. Local inhabitants decried the military conscription levy and the education taxes as "blood taxes." In practice, by 1879 only 41.2 percent of Japanese children attended elementary school, and many among them attended for only 18 months. Given these obstacles, Minister of Education Tanaka Fujimaro, who had been sent to the United States to study its educational system, attempted a thorough decentralization in 1879 that established elected local school boards. The new system proved to be even more ineffective and had to be scrapped within one year. Local districts lacked experience in educational matters and abused their new autonomy by neglecting to support the schools adequately. Japan's first experiment in decentralization had failed. Japanese authorities used that experience repeatedly during the Allied Occupation of Japan (1945–52) as an argument to substantiate the Mombushō view that American decentralization of education would not succeed in Japan.

In 1885, Mori Arinori became Japan's first minister of education. He left a permanent mark on the Mombushō and on Japanese education, through an Elementary-School Education Law, a Middle School Law, a Normal School Law and an Imperial University Law, which produced a comprehensive, national system of education characterized by mass education, elitism, and nationalism. He created a mass elementary-education system that would produce obedient, loyal, competent, and diligent workers, farmers, and soldiers; a teacher-training system for producing Spartan, nationalistic, and loyal teachers; and an academic track from middle schools to Tokyo Imperial University to produce the elite military officers, bureaucrats, and businessmen Japan needed to achieve its goal of *fukoku kyōhei* (rich country, strong army).

These national ambitions are illustrated by Mori's frequent comment that Japan must move from a third, to a second, and then to a first ranking in international power politics. Subsequent years saw the establishment of vocational schools and a Higher School. Japan, like European countries, had a multitrack system until the end of World War II, with separate courses of study for girls, teachers, and others. The American Occupation forces in 1947 implemented a unitrack 6–3–3–4 educational-ladder system, with six years of elementary school, three each of middle and high school, and four of college.

Although the Mombushō has exercised enormous power over education, it was considered the weakest and least desirable ministry by Tokyo Imperial University's Law School graduates in the prewar period. The best and brightest students sought employment in the Ministry of Finance, the Home Ministry, and the Ministry of Foreign Affairs. Less prominent and less powerful individuals often became ministers of education, and the ministry was staffed largely by noneducators. The Mombushō was often referred to contemptuously as the Home Ministry's errand boy, since Home Ministry officials sometimes became ministers or held other important posts in the Mombushō and since the Home Ministry appointed prefectural governors who served as the Mombushō's legal educational officials. The Mombushō also had to kowtow to the Ministry of Finance, which controlled the public budget and distributed the general tax revenues and educational subsidies. The Ministry of War exerted much influence from 1925 onward by appointing military officers to direct Japan's middle schools.

The Mombushō played an important role in promoting *seishin kyōiku* (moral education) and nationalism in the pre-World War II period. Although *seishin kyōiku* originally meant inculcating Confucian virtues, by the 1930s it had become saturated with nationalistic thought. The ministry could reach nationalistic objectives through imperial rescripts and ordinances, by appointing school inspectors, educating normal-school teachers, authoring teachers' manuals (and, after 1871, textbooks), licensing textbooks through 1903, and by actually writing the textbooks from that date until 1948.

The Mombushō's use of the Imperial Rescript on Education (1890) as an instrument to produce loyal, obedient, and diligent nationalists became more intense with the passage of each decade. During the 1930s, the Mombushō's bureaucrats worked hand in hand with ultranationalists, State Shintoists, and militarists, such as General Araki Sadao, who in 1937 became minister of education, and it cooperated in establishing Shinto shrines in occupied areas. In 1935, a Mombushō Bureau of Thought Control was established and divided into two sections, the Section of Thought Problems and the Investigation Section. The former was responsible for "guidance and control of thought problems in schools and social educational institutes, and control of thought problems in other directions" (Hall, 236–37). It worked actively with the National Spiritual Culture Research Institute to promote propaganda within Japan and occupied areas. The Investigation Section was mandated to "investigate thought problems in schools and social educational institutes . . . at home and abroad . . . and in books" (Hall, 236–37). The Bureau of Thought Control was responsible for producing such ultranationalistic books as *Kokutai no hongi* (Cardinal Principles of the National Polity) and *Shimmin no michi* (The Way of the Subject).

The Allied Occupation forces in Japan attempted to decentralize education and to eradicate State Shinto, ultranationalism, and militarism. The U.S. educational missions to Japan and Occupation forces conceived of the Mombushō as merely a professional and advisory organ. As a result, the Mombushō underwent a number of reorganizations and was renamed the Ministry of Education, Science, and Culture. The Home Ministry and the Mombushō's Bureau of Thought Control and Bureau of Religious Affairs were abolished; local, elected boards of education were established; the ministry's authorship of textbooks was prohibited, and control of education temporarily became largely a prefectural and local matter.

The Mombushō has proved to be amazingly resilient. This is a testimony to the ruling Liberal Democratic Party's commitment to conservative educational policies, centralization, and academic competence, as well as to the Japanese citizenry's lack of experience with administering an educational system. If anything, Mombushō's power is greater than before the war, though it is staffed and advised by more professional educators. The Mombushō must be given a large degree of the credit for the prevailing high academic standards of Japan. It has been responsive—some think too responsive—to promoting a Japanese educational system that meets the needs of Japanese industries.

In the 1990s, it reflects the ambiguity characteristic of the Japanese public—namely, a predisposition to reflect both nationalistic and internationalistic trends. The Mombushō reintroduced moral education in 1957 at the elementary- and junior-high-school levels, and in 1990 it made mandatory the singing of the national anthem and the hoisting of the Japanese

M

flag on important school occasions. It prohibits the hiring of foreigners as full-time elementary and secondary teachers but actively encourages hiring more of them at the university level. The Mombushō has been working, with varying degrees of success, to internationalize the curriculum at all levels, to facilitate Japanese students' foreign study, to increase the number of foreign students at the university level, to make greater use of returning students from abroad, to promote international conferences and exchange, and to foster studies designed to promote internationalization.

Harry Wray

Bibliography

Hall, Robert King. *Education for a New Japan*. New Haven, CT: Yale University Press, 1949.

Passin, Herbert. *Society and Education in Japan*. New York: Teacher's College, Columbia University, 1965.

Wray, Harry. "Decentralization of Education in the Allied Occupation of Japan, 1945–1952." *The Occupation of Japan: Educational and Social Reform*. Ed. Thomas W. Burkman. Norfolk, VA: Gatling, 1982.

Ministry of Education (1872–77) (*Kyōbushō*)

The organ of government responsible in the mid-1870s for the management of temples and shrines. The Kyōbushō was preceded by the Bureau of Rites (Jingikan) established in 1868 as the highest organ of government, even surpassing the Council of State (Dajōkan). In August 1871, the Department of Divinity was demoted to the status of a ministry and renamed the Ministry of Divinity (Jingishō). In the following year, the Ministry of Divinity was abolished, and its functions reconstituted in the Kyōbushō.

The confusing bureaucratic maneuvers resulting in the creation of the Kyōbushō represented a demotion of Shinto affairs within the Meiji government (1868–1912). The original establishment of the Department of Divinity had been a victory for Shinto nationalists, who believed in the unity of rites and government (*saisei itchi*). These Shinto ideologues, exemplified by such activists of the Meiji Restoration (1868) as Fukuba Bisei (1831–1907), were unable, however, to impose unity upon shrine priests and to control the conduct of imperial rites, with the result that they did not prove to be as useful to the state in the desired ideological unification of the populace as had been hoped originally. Politicians, for their part, were increasingly preoccupied with such matters of realpolitik as treaty revision and decreasingly sympathetic with the claims of Shinto bureaucrats, who worried instead about such arcane matters as whether the imperial dignity would be impugned if the court were moved from Kyoto to Edo (later, Tokyo). For these reasons, the bureaucratic status given to Shinto affairs was successively lowered, as registered in the establishment of the Kyōbushō. From 1872 until its abolition in 1877, the Kyōbushō assumed responsibility for the ultimately unsuccessful Great Promulgation Campaign, in which the government attempted to write, and gain popular support for, Shinto doctrine.

Helen Hardacre

Bibliography

Hardacre, Helen. *Shinto and the State, 1868–1988*. Princeton, NJ: Princeton University Press, 1989, chap. 2.

Ministry of International Trade and Industry (MITI)

The foundation of Japan's "economic miracles"—the first occurring during the Meiji period (1868–1912) and the second after World War II (1950–1970)—was well established during the Tokugawa period (1600–1868), especially by the presence of a highly competent bureaucracy within a well-structured and culturally attune central government. In fact, the two economic miracles were both orchestrated by the governments of the respective eras, assisted by well-educated bureaucrats who usually were graduates of such leading academic institutions as Tokyo University and Kyoto University.

The Ministry of Finance and MITI, working together through the Economic Planning Agency, have coordinated the economic planning at the heart of Japan's "guided capitalism" since the war. With cleverly institutionalized "administrative guidance" (the term appeared during fiscal 1962), MITI would often target a potentially growing industry and implement an industrial policy that would enhance productivity in that industry and ultimately improve its competitiveness in the global market through coordinated efforts by the government and business leaders. This administrative guidance, based on a national propensity for centralized decision making and cooperation with central authority, is the main weapon MITI uses to guide and support trade; the institution is uniquely Japanese in nature.

MITI was created in 1949 through the merger of the Trade Agency and the Ministry of Commerce and Industry as part of Detroit banker Joseph Dodge's plan, under the American-led Occupation (1945–52), to stimulate the struggling postwar economy. Its influence grew steadily until it had near-total control of imports and exports by the 1960s. A reorganization in 1973 shifted the ministry's emphasis toward the encouragement of high-tech, non-polluting industries.

With the power to license industries and to approve loans and investments for large organizations such as the Japan Development Bank, MITI has maintained its influence through close ties to both big business and Japan's elite political circles. Nearly half of the postwar prime ministers have been MITI officials. It also holds authority over many of the government's mixed public-private enterprises and controls nearly two-dozen advisory commissions, which communicate MITI politics to private industry. It operates the powerful Japan External Trade Organization (JETRO), which promotes Japanese trade around the world.

Organizationally, MITI consists of three divisions: an agency of Natural Resources and Energy, the Patent Office, and the Small and Medium Enterprise Agency. It has eight internal divisions, including the Secretariat, an Industrial Policy Bureau, an International Trade Policy Bureau, and a Bureau for Consumer Goods, and it operates 17 regional branches. In contrast to its image as a behemoth, it has the smallest staff and budget of any of the five government ministries in the economic area.

As Japan evolves into an economic superpower, MITI is undergoing a rapid change in its industrial and trade policies to meet the conditions of the dynamic economic environment domestically and abroad. Since the late 1980s, its policies have moved in the direction of greater sensitivity toward, and cooperation with, trading partners.

Masato Yamazaki

Bibliography

Johnson, Chalmers. *MITI and the Japanese Miracle.* Stanford, CA: Stanford University Press, 1982.

Minobe Tatsukichi (1873–1948)

Liberal constitutional theorist in the era of Taishō (1912–26) democracy. His career from his 1902 accession to the chair of public law at Tokyo University to his resignation from the House of Peers in 1935 spanned and echoed the rise and demise of normal constitutional government. A native of Hyogo Prefecture, he entered Tokyo Imperial University in the mid-1890s when Western learning had already driven into eclipse those who explained the constitutional order in Japan on the basis of native or Confucianist tradition. His heroes were bright, young bureaucratic-academic stars, and, like they did, he went to study in Europe, mainly Germany.

Minobe's voice was heard at the apex of higher bureaucratic training and selection. The considerable official preference he enjoyed indicates the extent to which the post-Meiji establishment tolerated the idea that Japan's constitutional development should be understood as part of a universal drive toward constitutional democracy. Minobe called for the parliamentary cabinet system; he argued for universal suffrage, civilian control of the military, and intellectual freedom; and he espoused what was known as the "organ theory," maintaining that the emperor was merely an organ of the state, albeit the central organ. He also opposed irresponsible bureaucratic power as displayed in the Privy Council and the upper house of the Diet.

Failures of policy and the siege mentality that grew in Japan after 1931 put the establishment generally on the defensive, and most officials were ill-disposed to stand by Minobe when he came under noisy attack by ultranationalists and militarists for what they considered his "un-Japanese" theories. A Diet-instigated Campaign to Clarify National Polity in 1935–36 resulted in a thorough purging of his offending theories. Restored to public life and honors in 1945, Minobe spent the last years of his life in a failed attempt to bring about a Japanese-inspired revision of the Meiji Constitution.

Frank O. Miller

Bibliography

Miller, Frank O. *Minobe Tatsukichi: Interpreter of Constitutionalism in Japan.* Berkeley: University of California Press, 1965.

Mishima Yukio (1925–70)

One of Japan's prominent postwar novelists. His life and literature made Mishima a prominent symbol of extreme nationalism. He turned to rightist politics after witnessing the Left-inspired mass demonstrations directed against the Japan-U.S. Security Treaty in 1960. In that year, he wrote a short story, "Patriotism," that eulogized the ritual suicide of a soldier involved in the February 26, 1936, Incident. This was a mutiny engineered by junior officers who, while swearing allegiance to the emperor, assassinated several top state officials. Mishima later enacted the role of the protagonist in a film version of the incident. He also described the incident in a play, *Tōka no kiku* (Tenth-Day Chrysanthemum), and memorialized it in an inflammatory 1966 political essay, *Eirei no koe* (The Voices of the Heroic Dead).

Another event that conveyed Mishima's political ideals was the Shinpūren Rebellion of 1877, an abortive samurai uprising in opposition to the Meiji government's modernizing reforms. Mishima praised the selfless spirit of the rebels in a nonfiction essay and in his political novel *Runaway Horses*.

In 1968, Mishima organized a private militia comprising approximately 80 rightist university students. The founding members mingled their blood, signed their names in it, and then drank the residue. The group's name, Tatenokai (Shield Society), indicated an intention to protect, or shield, the emperor.

The government failed to take Mishima's politics seriously until he committed ritual suicide in November 1970 at the Ichigaya headquarters of the Army Self-Defense Force (SDF). In a well-rehearsed plot, he and several members of his militia took a general of the armed forces hostage and demanded that the SDF troops be assembled to hear Mishima speak. The soldiers mustered to listen to Mishima jeered his demand that they overthrow the constitution in the emperor's name. He then berated them as "American mercenaries" and withdrew to the general's office, where he and one of his companions committed hara kiri. This action coincided with the completion of Mishima's literary masterpiece, the tetralogy *The Sea of Fertility*.

Most Japanese probably view Mishima as having been a literary genius but a political crackpot. He spoke of restoring the sword to Japan and of abolishing the postwar constitution. He criticized Emperor Hirohito for having renounced his divinity, berated postwar materialism, and revered the purity of samurai ideals. Beyond this, he offered few specifics.

Into the late 1990s, Mishima remains the most exalted postwar intellectual connected with the extreme Right. The proclamation he released on the day of his suicide concluded: "We will show you a value which is greater than respect for life. Not liberty, not democracy. It is Nippon! Nippon, the land of history and tradition. The Japan we love."

Gregory J. Kasza

Bibliography

Scott-Stokes, Henry. *The Life and Death of Yukio Mishima.* New York: Farrar, Straus and Giroux, 1974.

Mito Domain (*Mito Han*)

One of three houses collateral to the line of Tokugawa shoguns who ruled Japan from 1600 to 1868. Mito han was formed early in the 1600s when Tokugawa Ieyasu granted Tokugawa Yorifusa, his eleventh son, a domain of about 280,000 *koku* in size (later construed as 350,000 *koku*) in a strategic location on the coast north of Edo (later, Tokyo). (Note: A *koku,* the standard unit of Tokugawa measurement, equaled about five bushels of rice, and the size of a domain was calculated by the number of *koku* it could be expected to produce.) In 1657, the second Mito daimyo, Tokugawa Mitsukuni, initiated the major task of assembling a historiographical compilation that eventually resulted in the *Dainihonshi* (History of Great Japan). The project extended over 250 years before its completion in 1906, and was partly responsible for the high level of scholarship, emperor-centered loyalism, and national consciousness that came to be associated with the Mito house. Especially in the late Tokugawa period, from the 1780s to 1864, when violent factional strife escalated to pose a major military challenge to the Tokugawa government (*bakufu*), Mito han was a focal point of thought and action associated with the ideology of *sonnō jōi* (revere the emperor and expel the barbarians).

Many of the individuals who led the anti-*bakufu* movement in the 1850s and 1860s received their inspiration in Mito. However, the emperor-centered, restorationist ideology—often called *mitogaku* (Mito learning)—that was produced in Mito han in the early nineteenth century was not overtly anti-*bakufu*. Major Mito texts, such as Aizawa Seishisai's 1825 *Shinron* (New Theses), creatively sought to defend and to revitalize the existing system, not to overthrow it. Nevertheless, in the course of conceiving remedies to counteract external threat and internal decay, they developed concepts and initiated reforms that, in effect, weakened the legitimacy of the old regime. One of the concepts developed by Aizawa, *kokutai* (national essence, national polity) was to become a staple element of the post-Meiji Restoration (1868) discourse on national identity and the rise of ultranationalism.

J. Victor Koschmann

Bibliography

Koschmann, J. Victor. *The Mito Ideology.* Berkeley: University of California Press, 1987.
Wakabayashi, Bob Tadashi. *Anti-Foreignism and Western Learning in Early-Modern Japan: The New Theses of 1825.* Cambridge: Harvard University Press, 1986.

Mito Learning (*Mitogaku*)

Mitogaku, together with *kokugaku* (native, or national, learning), inspired the movement to "revere the emperor and expel the barbarians" in the late-Tokugawa era, which culminated in the Meiji Restoration (1868). *Mitogaku*, which thus helped create Japanese nationalism in the nineteenth century, may be divided into early and later schools.

Early *mitogaku* evolved from the compilation of the *Dainihonshi* (*History of Great Japan*), begun in 1657 by Mito domain. This work was unprecedented in Japanese scholarship because it was modeled directly on Chinese dynastic histories, which were based on the Confucian principle of dynastic change. History had a didactic role in China; each new dynastic house chronicled the history of the previous dynasty in order to learn about the misrule or moral turpitude that had caused its fall. Because the *Dainihonshi* followed this Chinese format, its premises and implications contradicted nativist political ideas. For example, the work interpreted the imperial family in Kyoto as a fallen dynasty that had been deposed and replaced by the Edo *bakufu* (Tokugawa government). This displacement was unacceptable to the nativists, since they saw the Japanese imperial family as a divinely descended ruling

house that could never be overthrown. Early *mitogaku*, then, was prenationalistic in nature; it would undergo revision as later *mitogaku*.

Later *mitogaku* scholars, such as Fujita Yūkoku (1774–1826), Aizawa Seishisai (1781–1863), and Fujita Tōko (1806–55) borrowed a great deal from *kokugaku* and rejected much of the moralistic universalism in Confucian historical thought. They eschewed criticism of past emperors for moral turpitude, a key feature of the *Dainihonshi*. Instead, they emphasized the divine origins of Japan's imperial house, to which all Japanese owed reverence, and they portrayed Japan as the land of the gods possessing a unique national essence (*kokutai*), that made it different from, and superior to, foreign countries. They believed that nineteenth-century Japan was vulnerable to Western encroachment because of internal weakness. To overcome this dual crisis, they called for invigoration of the daimyo and the samurai classes and promoted pro-*bakufu* political reforms.

One of the most controversial reforms in Aizawa's *Shinron* (New Theses), published in 1825, derived from Western learning. Aizawa believed that Western states were powerful because their rulers used Christianity as a state religion to instill patriotism in their subjects, so he suggested that the emperor in Kyoto use Shinto as a similar state cult—a proposal implemented by the Meiji regime. Meanwhile, Fujita Tōko inspired samurai activists throughout the country in the 1840s with works such as *Seiki no uta* (The Moral Spirit of Our Divine Land).

After 1853, when Japan was forced open to foreign trade and diplomacy and suffered semicolonial domination at the hand of the Western powers, later Mito learning became a potent force inspiring reverence for the emperor and the recovery of national sovereign rights. Men such as Fujita Tōko did not intend to overthrow, or even to criticize, the *bakufu*; but their ideas were adopted by revolutionaries who destroyed the Tokugawa regime and established a modern nation–state. Later, particularly in the 1930s and 1940s, men such as Fujita were worshiped as national heroes and paragons of "the Japanese spirit"; some continue to be revered—and influential. In 1990, a member of the right-wing Seikijuku (School of the Spirit), named after Fujita's tract, attempted unsuccessfully to assassinate the mayor of Nagasaki for suggesting that the emperor bore some guilt for Japan's actions in World War II.

Bob Tadashi Wakabayashi

Bibliography

Harrotunian, Harry. *Before Restoration*. Berkeley: University of California Press, 1970.

Nakai, Kate W. "Tokugawa Confucian Historiography." *Confucianism and Tokugawa Culture*. Ed. Peter Nosco. Princeton, NJ: Princeton University Press, 1984.

Wakabayashi, Bob Tadashi. *Anti-Foreignism and Western Learning in Early-Modern Japan: The New Theses of 1825*. Cambridge: Harvard University Press, 1986.

Miura Gorō (1846–1926)

Japanese army general, appointed minister to Korea in September 1895. After its victory in the Sino-Japanese War (1894–95), Japan attempted to reform and modernize Korea. These efforts seemed to be getting nowhere due, the Japanese had come to believe, to the behind-the-scenes machinations of Korea's Queen Min. Miura, probably without express authorization from higher authority in Tokyo, decided to hatch a plot to restore the longtime power-holder, the Taewongun, as a Japanese puppet. He authorized Kunrentai (Japanese-trained Korean troops) under their Japanese officers to attack the royal palace in Seoul and kill the queen, which they did in a bloody massacre on October 8, 1895. Amidst foreign protests, the Japanese government recalled Miura to Japan, where he was tried for conspiracy but not convicted. The incident was one of many that helped poison Japanese-Korean relations in the Meiji era (1868–1912).

Hilary Conroy

Bibliography

Conroy, Hilary. *The Japanese Seizure of Korea*. Philadelphia: University of Pennsylvania Press, 1974.

Miyake Setsurei (real name Yujiro) (1860–1945)

Historian and social philosopher. Born in Ishikawa Prefecture and graduated in 1883 from Tokyo University, Miyake dedicated his life to the study of Japanese culture. After brief stints at teaching in several places and studying the history of Japanese Buddhism, he joined others to form the Seikyōsha (Society for Political Edu-

cation) in 1888 to oppose the national tone of subservience toward the West that had marked the early Meiji years. The group published a journal, *Nihonjin* (The Japanese), to spread their views. In the 1890s, Miyake declaimed against Japan's unequal treaties, and he consistently opposed oligarchic domination of the government by cliques from the southwest (*hambatsu*) and official complicity in modern Japan's first major pollution episode, the Ashio copper-mine-pollution scandal of the 1890s. His mature works, which included the six-volume *Dōjidai shi* (History of These Times, 1949–54) and *Uchu* (The Universe, 1908), called for Japan to exert more independence in dealing with other countries and attempted to formulate a universal philosophy that placed Japanese culture in a world context. He and his wife, Miyake Kaho, published the magazine *Josei Nihonjin* (Japanese Women) for several years after 1920.

James L. Huffman

Bibliography

Pyle, Kenneth. *The New Generation in Meiji Japan*. Stanford, CA: Stanford University Press, 1969.

Moral Education (*Seishin Kyōiku*)

Seishin kyōiku has a long history in Japan. Throughout the history of Japanese education, character formation has received priority over scholarship. This predisposition comes from native Shinto, Confucianism, Zen Buddhism, and *bushidō* (the way of the warrior). Although Shinto possessed no written principles or theology, its values strongly influenced Japanese thought, teaching a respect for nature, a love of the simple, a situational ethics dependent on time, place, and situation, and a concern for the immanent world. Since Shinto is largely secular, and unconcerned about issues such as sin or the next life, however, it remained for Confucianism to sketch out the major framework of moral education.

The Japanese aristocracy introduced Confucian thought in the seventh century, but its system deeply pervaded Japanese society only during the Tokugawa period (1600–1868), when the Tokugawa shogunate found its conservative teachings conducive to maintaining order and stability. The importance of *seishin kyōiku* reflects the importation of Confucian thought from China. Confucius believed that education made virtuous men, who were essential because they advised the emperor and provided an example of "the Way." Knowledge of "the Way" was essential to produce the good—orderly and harmonious—society. In Confucian thought, education that taught knowledge but ignored the cultivation of good character was worthless. One acquired good character by learning such Confucian virtues as sincerity, loyalty, knowledge, benevolence, propriety, and filial piety. Study taught the superiority of an agricultural society and the necessity to observe the five relationships: ruler to ruled, father to son, husband to wife, elder brother to younger brother, and friend to friend. In Confucian thinking, the good life is synonymous with fulfilling the roles given to one by birth and occupation. It says nothing about rights; people have only duties. The superior person observes them at all costs, even when it is necessary to sacrifice family pleasures. Confucius said, "The man who hankers after family life is not much of a man."

In Confucian thought in China, leadership was relegated to the scholar-gentry, but Japan's long feudal period led the samurai to co-opt the teachings and the role ascribed to the scholar-gentry and to arrogate to themselves the role of moral leadership. The samurai emphasized the *seishin kyōiku*, which included courage, frugality, perseverance, endurance of pain, self-sacrifice, selfless behavior, and will. Under samurai influence, loyalty and harmony were altered somewhat to fit Japanese indigenous values. Loyalty to lord superseded loyalty to family. The observance of harmony meant even greater selflessness and conformity to the group than it did in China. Zen Buddhism added to the Japanese emphasis on character formation by its stress on nature, self-discipline, concentration, willpower, and the intuitive. During the 268-year period of Tokugawa rule, education spread throughout Japan, and literacy rates reached 40 percent for males and 17 percent for females. Even though the education of artisans, wealthy farmers, and merchants took a more practical bent than that of the samurai class, moral education was stressed for all classes.

When the Tokugawa shogunate was overthrown, a struggle developed among three groups—the Westernizers, the Confucianists, and the *kokugakusha* (national-learning-scholars)—for the control of Japan's modern educational system. That struggle has continued to some extent into the 1990s. Victory meant control over the young students' minds and determining the kind of Japan that would emerge. Westernizers wanted the new education to emphasize knowledge and Western values, such as individualism, independence, equality, and rights. Confucianists wanted moral education to receive priority over knowledge, believing that adoption of Western values would achieve modernization at the expense of order, stability, and harmony. Western science, they complained, paid too much attention to outer forms and neglected the inner and, ultimately, unchanging moral essence; it bypassed distinctions, roles, and forms pertinent to the smooth functioning of society. The *kokugaku* school thought that Western values offended the Japanese gods and the national way of life. Its proponents extolled Japan's uniqueness, the imperial household, traditional values, and the study of the national literature. They advocated the teaching of the worship of Shinto in the schools.

The Westernizers won a short-lived victory between 1872 and 1879, but from 1880 through 1885, and again from 1890 to the end of World War II in 1945, the Confucianists gained control over Japanese education. In 1881, they succeeded in placing moral education at the top of the school curriculum, and they wrote textbooks that taught Confucian virtues. They hailed submissiveness and humility as important civic virtues. A *Shūshin* (national ethics training) primer admonished pupils to doff their hats, to bow low before the emperor, to treat government officials with respect, and to refrain from insulting policemen "who protect us all and help us at times of hardship and disaster." When Mori Arinori became minister of education in 1885, he replaced Confucian virtues with nationalistic and modern moral teachings because he thought Confucian values inappropriate to promote Japan's modernization drive. But, following his premature death in 1889 at the hands of a right-wing fanatic, the Confucianists joined with the *kokugaku* group to obtain the most important ideological instrument for forming prewar Japanese education, the Imperial Rescript on Education of 1890 (IRE).

The rescript was a brief statement of Confucian and State Shinto thought, which exhorted students to be filial, obedient, loyal, and respectful of the national polity (*kokutai*); to serve the country diligently and unselfishly in their respective vocations during peacetime; and to throw "away their bodies" by dying for the emperor, if necessary, during wartime. The IRE was accompanied by the mandate that history

M

education must henceforth clarify the *kokutai* as the first priority. On the surface a harmless and noncontroversial document, the IRE came to play a major ideological role. Each textbook edition after 1910 interpreted the IRE more narrowly and nationalistically. The IRE could be found in the beginning of most elementary-school textbooks, and its ideas completely saturated the content of the *Shushin* texts. The study of moral education introduced the students to men and women who epitomized the virtues enunciated in the IRE. Gradually, those heroes became ever more fanatical nationalists and militarists who sought to clarify the *kokutai*, expand the national honor and empire, and drive the Western imperialists from Asia. Moral education after 1931 became a matter of indoctrinating young Japanese minds with the contents of the IRE and, after 1937, the newly published *Kokutai no hongi* (Cardinal Principles of the National Polity), a much more explicit and detailed piece of wartime propaganda.

Allied Occupation (1945–52) forces abolished ultranationalistic, Shintoistic, and militaristic teachings and the *Shushin* course. With the cooperation of the national Diet (legislature), the IRE was rescinded. The Occupation substituted democratic education, progressive educational methodology, and a new course, social studies. The depth of indigenous values and behavior patterns was too great, however, and the conservative Liberal Democratic Party government reintroduced moral education in 1957 at the elementary and junior-high levels. *Seishin kyōiku,* stressing traditional virtues, came once again to be emphasized in the schools.

In today's schools, from kindergarten through college, students constantly hear the value of virtues such as perseverance, responsibility, effort, sincerity, loyalty, meticulousness, and subordination of self to the group. Teachers foster these qualities at the kindergarten and elementary level to such an extent that they seem almost a fetish, but the fact that they are followed up with reinforcement at every grade level helps make Japanese classrooms orderly and disciplined. That condition translates into the ability to teach and learn more subject matter. Emphasis on character formation thus deserves at least a part of the credit for Japan's high academic standards. Many see the teaching of this *seishin kyōiku* as fundamental to Japan's rapid modernization, high industrial performance, and orderly society.

Harry Wray

Bibliography
Dore, Ronald. *Education in Tokugawa Japan.* Berkeley: University of California Press, 1965.
Rohlen, Thomas P. *Japan's High Schools.* Berkeley: University of California Press, 1983.

Mori Arinori (1847–89)

Meiji statesman. Born in Kagoshima Prefecture (Satsuma domain), he devoted his life to modernization and national strength, spending most of his career in the foreign and education ministries. In 1865, Mori was sent by his domain to England to study the sciences and naval surveying. After an additional year in America, he returned and entered the new Meiji government (1868–1912). He spent the first decade and a half of the Meiji era working for the Foreign Ministry, serving as ambassador to the United States (1871–73), China (1876–77), and England (1880–84). During those years, he became an ardent nationalist and an advocate of enlightenment. He helped found the Meirokusha (Meiji Six Society), an influential debating society in 1874, as well as Japan's first commercial college, the Shōhō Kōshūjo, which later became Hitotsubahi University. While maintaining close ties to the West and to such mentors as the British parliamentarian Laur-

Mori Arinori. Asahi Shimbun Photo.

ence Oliphant and the social Darwinist philosopher Herbert Spencer, he rejected British- and American-style democratic systems and argued for imperial sovereignty and a strong central state.

Such views prompted Itō Hirobumi to appoint Mori minister of education in the first cabinet (1885–89), where he set his mark indelibly on prewar Japan's educational system. He regarded service to the state as the primary role of education, emphasizing a hierarchical system, with utilitarian schooling for the lower classes and higher schools for the elite. He did not, however, advocate the kind of narrow, emperor-centered nationalism that took over the educational system in later decades. Indeed, his strong support for modernization and ties with the West won him many foes, and he was assassinated on February 11, 1889 (the day the Meiji Constitution was promulgated) by a nationalist assailant.

James L. Huffman

Bibliography
Hall, Ivan. *Mori Arinori*. Cambridge: Harvard University Press, 1973.

Motoda Eifu (1818–91)

Educator and tutor to the emperor. Born in Kumamoto, he studied in Yokoi Shōnan's *jitsugaku* (pragmatic) school of Confucianism prior to the 1868 Meiji Restoration, then became a tutor to the Meiji Emperor in 1871. Later, he became court adviser and a member of the Privy Council.

Motoda was a highly conservative scholar, who believed deeply in the importance of a strong emperor system and advocated training in the values and ways of traditional Japan. Education, he believed, should center on reverence for the emperor. In addition to writing widely about Japan's unique ethical system, he was a major force in the drafting of the 1890 Imperial Rescript on Education, a conservative document that served as the foundation of Japan's educational system until 1945.

James L. Huffman

Bibliography
Gluck, Carol. *Japan's Modern Myths: Ideology in the Late Meiji Period*. Princeton, NJ: Princeton University Press, 1985.
Shively, Donald. "Motoda Eifu: Confucian Lecturer to the Meiji Emperor." *Confucianism in Action*. Ed. S.S. Nivison and A.F. Wright. Stanford, CA: Stanford University Press, 1959.

Mutō Akira (1892–1948)

Lieutenant-general and imperial strategist. Mutō became chief of operations, general staff (1937–39), in which post he helped formulate the army's Manchurian policies. As director of the Military Affairs Bureau, he schemed in 1940 to force the resignation of Hata Shunroku as minister of war, precipitating the resignation of the Yonai Mitsumasa cabinet. From command of the imperial guard division in Sumatra (1942–44), he proceeded to chief of staff, 14th Area Army, in the Philippines (1944–45).

Mutō, like his commander, General Yamashita Tomoyuki, was hanged for crimes against humanity. These sentences weighed insufficiently the diffusion in Japanese military, naval, and air commands, which enabled subordinate officers to reach independent decisions in a desperate situation. Mutō consistently advocated Japanese imperial expansion and favored military administration policies based heavily on Japanese needs, rather than on accommodation to local and national interests. He believed steadfastly in the importance of basing military power on spiritual preparedness but acknowledged the need for maintaining reasonable limits, especially after the losses Japan suffered at Leyte late in 1944. Highly intelligent, frank to the point of bluntness, Mutō was moved by others' simplicity, sincerity, and devotion to duty. He composed haiku in retreat and encouraged subordinates to regenerate the fatherland and the empire.

Theodore Friend

Bibliography
Butow, Robert. *Tōjō and the Coming of War*. Stanford, CA: Stanford University Press, 1961.

Mutsu Munemitsu (1844–97)

Meiji statesman and diplomat. Mutsu represented the transitional political leadership of Meiji Japan. Born in Wakayama domain, scion of a samurai family in the service of the domain government, Mutsu renounced his samurai status and joined the Restoration movement as a youth, enlisting with a group called the Kaientai (Naval Auxiliary Force), a semipublic maritime force organized by the anti-Tokugawa strategist

Sakamoto Ryōma to support the opening of the country. He early cast his lot with the adherents of change and modernization. A moderate nationalist, keenly aware of Japan's vulnerability in the late nineteenth century, he developed superb skills as a politician-diplomat and was the practical architect of a successful policy to establish Japan's diplomatic equality with the West through revision of Japan's unequal treaties with Western nations.

Immediately after the Meiji Restoration (1868), he was appointed to the Gaikoku Jimukyoku (Foreign Affairs Bureau). In 1872, he became chief of the Land Tax Revision Bureau. He was imprisoned in the aftermath of the unsuccessful 1877 Satsuma Rebellion for having worked with antigovernment people to raise private troops. After his release from prison in 1884, he traveled abroad for two years. In 1888, Mutsu became minister to the United States, and his career as a diplomat began in earnest. He carried out successful negotiations the same year for a commercial treaty of equality with Mexico, which became the precedent for the revision of the whole unequal-treaty structure.

In the 1890s, he served as minister of agriculture in the first Yamagata Aritomo cabinet; in 1894, he became foreign minister in the first Itō Hirobumi cabinet. In that post, he successfully negotiated the 1894 revision of the commercial treaty with Great Britain, which confirmed the treaty-revision process he had initiated with Mexico in 1888. He was the key negotiator in 1895 in the talks to end the first Sino-Japanese War, and he was caught up that same spring in the discussions over the Triple Intervention, in which Russia, Germany, and France forced Japan to return some of the land it had won in the war.

Mutsu's diplomatic memoir, *Kenkenroku* (A Record of Suffering), provides one of the finest sources of firsthand information about the functionings of the Japanese political process in the 1890s.

Jackson H. Bailey

Bibliography

Hagihara, Hobutoshi. "Mutsu Munemitsu: A Portrait." *Themes and Theories in Modern Japanese History.* Ed. Sue Henny. London: Athlone Press, 1988.

Mutsu, Munemitsu. *Kenkenroku.* Trans. Gordon Berger. Princeton, NJ: Princeton University Press, 1982.

Mutual Friendship Society (*Sōaikai*)

Government-supported organization for the promotion of harmony between Japanese and Koreans. The Korean organizer was Pak Ch'un-kum (1891–1973), a construction foreman for Korean laborers in Tokyo, who used his own funds to form a society in 1921 to provide food and shelter for jobless Koreans. After the Great Kantō Earthquake of 1923, when Japanese vigilante bands massacred hundreds of Koreans, the Sōaikai cooperated with the Tokyo police in a well-publicized effort to organize Korean work crews to assist in the cleanup.

By 1924, the Sōaikai, with branches in six prefectures as well as Pusan, was the primary instrument for cooperation between Koreans who were resigned to Japanese rule and government officials determined to prevent the rise of a leftist movement among Korean workers. The Sōaikai provided shelter and employment for Korean workers and mediation in housing and labor disputes. It sponsored memorial services for the Koreans massacred in 1923 and rallied Korean support for Japanese national holidays, such as Kigensetsu (Empire Day). The Sōaikai also assisted the Japanese police in their surveillance of potentially subversive Korean activists.

Prominent among the Japanese advisers to the society were Maruyama Tsurukichi (1883–1956) and Akaike Atsushi (1879–1945), both of whom had served as director-general of the Police Bureau in Korea. The society was moderately successful in providing a showcase for those Koreans willing to collaborate with the Japanese. In the 1930s, Pak Ch'un-kum was twice elected to the Japanese Diet (legislature) from the district where the Sōaikai welfare facilities were located. The society was, however, the embodiment of Japanese enthusiasm for incorporating Koreans into Japan and, as such, was antithetical to Korean nationalism.

Sally A. Hastings

Bibliography

Lee, Changsoo, and George deVos, eds. *Koreans in Japan: Ethnic Conflict and Accommodation.* Berkeley: University of California Press, 1981.

Weiner, Michael. *The Origins of the Korean Community in Japan, 1910–1923.* Atlantic Highlands, NJ: Humanities Press, 1989.

N

Nagai Ryūtarō (1881–1944)

Politician. The career of this Kanazawa City native reflected the changing public mood of the 1920s and 1930s. Nagai was educated at Waseda University, where the famous Meiji political leader Ōkuma Shigenobu became his mentor, and at Oxford University in England where overt anti-Japanese prejudice affected him personally, and became a popular Waseda lecturer on social and colonial policy in the 1910s. He entered politics in 1917; throughout the 1920s, he was reelected to the Diet (legislature), gaining a reputation as a champion of the masses for his dynamic oratory in support of democratic positions. Nagai became a leader in the Rikken Minseitō (Constitutional Democratic Party), but, in the 1930s, he grew more nationalistic, disillusioned with party politics and with Japan's relationships with Great Britain and the United States. He held four cabinet posts, including director of the colonial and the communications ministries, and became a supporter of Japan's wartime goals and structures, advocating pan-Asianism and the abolition of the multiparty system. He died of cancer on December 5, 1944, remorseful about his role in leading Japan toward war.

James L. Huffman

Bibliography

Minichiello, Sharon. *Retreat from Reform.* Honolulu: University of Hawaii Press, 1984.

Nagasaki Flag Incident (*Nagasaki Kokki Jiken*) (1958)

In 1958, when Japan had not yet recognized the government of the People's Republic of China (PRC), China's national flag, a symbol of Chinese nationalism, became the focal point of a serious diplomatic issue between China and Japan. Prior to this event, questions concerning the rights of the PRC's representatives to hoist the national flag at their headquarters in Japan had caused bitter disputes involving not only Japan and the PRC but also the nationalist Chinese in Taiwan. The Japanese government stated that since Japan had no formal diplomatic relations with the PRC, the Chinese flag was not protected by Japanese law.

On May 2, 1958, a Japanese man hauled down the national flag of the PRC at an exhibition of Chinese postage stamps and paper cuttings sponsored by the Japan-China Friendship Association at the Hamaya department store in Nagasaki. The man was arrested but soon released. The incident dramatized the fact that Japan had not yet officially recognized the PRC. After the incident, the Chinese terminated trade negotiations, as well as cultural and friendship exchanges, and more than two years elapsed before another Chinese trade delegation visited Japan.

Noriko Kamachi

Bibliography

Kosaka, Masataka. *A History of Postwar Japan.* Tokyo: Kodansha International, 1972.

Nagata Tetsuzan (1884–1935)

Lieutenant-general in the army. A native of Nagano Prefecture, he developed a reputation as an effective strategist and became a leader in the Tōseiha (Control Faction), the less radical of the army's two leading pre-World War II factions. He became associated in the 1920s with Tōjō Hideki, later prime minister, in army groups committed to ending domination of the army by factions from the old Chōshū domain and to promoting a Japanese takeover of Manchuria and Mongolia. His 1926 plan for national mobilization generally is considered the first of many calls for a National Defense State. He also organized reservist seminars on the superiority of Japan's emperor ideology and compiled a memorandum in August 1931 suggesting the early seizure of Manchuria.

In 1933, Nagata advocated accommodation with the Soviet Union, and, in 1934, he was appointed chief of the Bureau of Military Affairs. There, he advocated cooperation with politicians, business leaders, and a group of "new bureaucrats" intent on creating a system of centralized national control led by the military. An army pamphlet that he inspired in 1934 called for national mobilization to put Japan on a war footing. When he plotted the removal of the more radical Kōdōha (Imperial Way Faction) leader Mazaki Jinzaburō as inspector-general of military education in 1935, Nagata was himself assassinated by Lieutenant-Colonel Aizawa Saburō, an ultranationalist officer in Mazaki's faction.

Jacob Kovalio

Bibliography

Crowley, James. *Japan's Quest for Autonomy, 1930–1938*. Princeton, NJ: Princeton University Press, 1966.

Nakano Seigō (1886–1943)

Politician and writer. A native of Fukuoka, he worked as a correspondent for the *Tokyo Asahi Shimbun* newspaper and also wrote for several prominent Japanese journals, joining Miyake Setsurei in 1923 in publishing *Gakan* (Our View). A close associate of the rightwing opinion leader Tōyama Mitsuru and a member of the Gen'yōsha (Black Sea Society), he propounded strong nationalistic views, which stressed the potential for contributions from common people and criticized the domination of Japanese politics by elite groups. His best-known work, *Meiji minken shi ron* (A Discourse on the History of Popular Rights in the Meiji Period), was published in 1913.

Shortly after this book was issued, Nakano became active in the political-party movement in an attempt to put his ideas into practice. He represented the city of Fukuoka for eight successive terms in the Diet (legislature), beginning in 1920, and became vice minister of communications in the Hamaguchi Osachi Cabinet (1929–31). However, his populist views gained little influence among mainstream politicians, and he eventually formed his own political organization, the Tōhōkai (East Asia Society), to spread them. As its president, Nakano criticized the Diet as totally debased, and eventually he sharply attacked the Tōjō Hideki cabinet, claiming it was bureaucratically corrupt and out of touch with the people. In 1943, he was charged with conspiring to overthrow Tōjō, arrested, and imprisoned. Shortly thereafter, he was released to house arrest and, despondent at being denied access to the public, committed suicide.

J. Wayne Sabey

Bibliography

Oates, Leslie R. *Populist Nationalism in Prewar Japan: A Biography of Nakano Seigō*. Boston: Allen and Unwin, 1985.

Nakasone Yasuhiro (1918–)

Conservative politician. As prime minister from November 1982 through November 1987, he sought to rehabilitate traditional symbols of nationalism and stimulate reconsideration of postwar Occupation reforms, many of which he considered corrosive to national pride and inimical to state interests. He favored revision of the constitution to remove military constraints. Although he did not press for constitutional revision while he was prime minister, he did succeed in scrapping the long-standing cabinet resolution limiting defense spending to 1 percent of the gross national product (GNP). He became the first postwar prime minister to visit Yasukuni, the national Shinto shrine dedicated to Japan's war dead and to participate in Empire Day (Kigensetsu) ceremonies in an official capacity.

Nakasone stressed respect for the emperor and favored the use of education to instill patriotism and respect for Japanese institutions. While he was prime minister, the Ministry of Education tightened controls on textbook authorization and moved to enforce the compulsory use of the "Rising Sun" flag (*Hinomaru*) and the singing of the "*Kimi ga yo*" anthem in the schools. He also encouraged discussion of reintroducing ethics courses, which critics re-

Nakasone Yasuhiro. Courtesy Consulate General of Japan, N.Y.

garded as a return to prewar and wartime education in nationalistic values.

Nakasone was prone to issue statements that lent support to the concepts of popular nationalism. He attracted controversy by attributing Japanese superiority to the supposed homogeneity of Japanese society and by endorsing a Japanese report to the United Nations early in the 1980s that denied the presence of ethnic minorities in the country.

Nakasone's high-profile forays into international affairs served to define an identity for Japan externally but also played to an internal audience in an effort to stimulate national pride. Nakasone used his activist persona to highlight the role of the state, and he deliberately broke various postwar political taboos in order to legitimize nationalist concerns and bring them closer to the mainstream of political discourse.

Ellen H. Hammond

Bibliography

Horsley, William, and Roger Buckley. *Nippon, New Superpower: Japan Since 1945.* London: BBC Books, 1990.

Nanjing Massacre (1937)

Having seized Manchuria in the Manchurian Incident in 1931, Japan continued to escalate her aggression against China with the objection of severing north China from the central government at Nanjing. Eventually, Japan launched a full-scale invasion following the Marco Polo Bridge Incident on July 7, 1937, and China was forced to muster an all-out resistance against Japan. One month later, Japan opened a second front at Shanghai in the August thirteenth Incident. The battle in Shanghai lasted until November 12, 1937.

The biggest prize for the Japanese army was the capture of Nanjing, the capital of China, which was defended by thirteen Chinese divisions comprising approximately 150,000 men, against the Japanese attacking force of seven-and-a-half divisions numbering nearly 200,000 men. The Shanghai Refugee Shelter had taken in 450,000 Chinese refugees during the battle. Trying to forestall a similar crisis, foreign residents at Nanjing established the International Committee for the Nanjing "safety zone" in mid-November 1937, and negotiated with the Chinese authorities and the Japanese embassy for support. On December 1, Ma Chaojun, mayor of Nanjing, turned over to the committee responsibility for the safety zone, which centered around the American embassy and the University of Nanjing, opposite the Japanese embassy. After the fall of the city, the population of the Safety Zone exceeded 290,000 people.

By December 8, Japanese forces had taken most of the strategic positions of the outer defense of Nanjing. On the morning of December 13, the Japanese took the west gate, followed by the fall of the other gates in quick succession. By 11 A.M., some Japanese soldiers had entered the safety zone. In the presence of George A. Fitcher, an American missionary who served as deputy secretary-general of the zone, they killed twenty refugees. Thus commenced the wanton massacre, rape, looting, and burning that did not abate until March 1938.

The postwar Tokyo Trial confirmed that in the first six weeks after the fall of Nanjing, over 200,000 Chinese civilians and disarmed soldiers were killed, and 20,000 women were raped. Subsequent investigations, including interviews with 1,700 survivors of the Nanjing Massacre, determined that the death toll was actually 340,000, including Chinese men and women of all ages. Apparently, 28 cases of large-scale mass murders had resulted in the deaths of 190,000 people, whereas individual murders had taken about 150,000 lives. Equally shocking was the raping. A recent study has shown that as many as 80,000 women had been raped, many of them then murdered, at Nanjing.

The Nanjing Massacre, also known in the West as the "Rape of Nanking," provoked worldwide condemnation at the time and ranks among the worst wartime atrocities in human history. One of the first reports on the massacre was filed by Tillman Durdin for the *The New York Times* on December 18, 1938. In China, the Japanese brutalities enraged the whole population, which now was more than ever determined to continue the war of resistance.

After World War II, little attention has been given to this tragedy by historians writing outside of China. Since the 1970s, the Japanese government has made several attempts, officially or unofficially, to deny the veracity of this occurrence. Despite Chinese protest of these denials the Western countries have been guided in their reactions by the economic success of postwar Japan and by the strategic importance of Japan in the Cold War. Consequently, they have generally tolerated Japanese attempts to whitewash the incident. The Nanjing Massacre has turned into an "alleged" incident in the minds of many Japanese, especially those of the younger generation.

In 1990, a 190-page document prepared by Nazi Germany's embassy in Nanjing was discovered in the Potsdam archives in the reunified Germany. The document confirmed the occurrence and extent of the Nanjing Massacre. The discovery was followed by the release in 1991 of photographs taken by an American witness, a Mr. Fitcher, and film footages shot by Reverend John Magee, another American. Meanwhile, the Chinese government has completed the construction of a memorial museum dedicated to the victims of the massacre at Nanjing.

Tien-wei Wu

References
Timperley, H. J. *Japanese Terror in China.* New York: Modern Age Books, Inc., 1938.

Narita Airport Dispute
The government's decision to use several farms in the Narita area northeast of Tokyo as the site of the New Tokyo International Airport sparked major clashes between the government and radical citizens' movements throughout the 1970s and into the 1980s. The government set up an authority in 1966 to create a new airport in this region, which was part of Chiba Prefecture, to relieve crowding at Haneda, Tokyo's earlier international airport. Construction began in 1969, but when farmers in the area objected to having their land confiscated at much less than market value, a major dispute ensued.

The farmers soon were joined by members of the radical student group Zengakuren (All-Japan Student Federation) and other antigovernment organizations. Their protests included the construction of towers, tunnels, and bunkers to prevent the building of the runways, and many farmers refused to leave their lands. The struggle eventually turned violent, and at least six people were killed in battles between riot police and the airport opponents. As a result, the opening of the airport was delayed seven years, until 1978. Even in the 1980s, some farmers continued to resist the confiscation of their land, and protesters delayed the construction of additional runways.

From the outset, a significant segment of the Japanese public supported the protests, regarding them as steps in either a legitimate struggle by ordinary citizens against the power of big government or a fight against the exploitation of rural areas by city-oriented politicians and bureaucrats. Well into the 1990s, the airport remained a semi-fortress, ringed by electric fences, watchtowers, and searchlights and guarded by more than 1,000 police.

James L. Huffman

Bibliography
Apter, David, and Nagayo Sawa. *Against the State: Politics and Social Protest in Japan.* Cambridge: Harvard University Press, 1984.

National Defense State (*Kokubō Kokka*)
Goal of some members of the army's Tōseiha (Control Faction) before World War II, through which industrial production was to be coordinated by a totalitarian regime for the purpose of a gradual but massive military buildup. The first advocate of the National Defense State was Nagata Tetsuzan, who designed a plan for national mobilization in 1926. Nagata and his followers were most concerned with the possibility of war with the Soviet Union; accordingly, their plans were modeled after the first Soviet

Five-Year Plan. Urging that all governmental bodies come under the control of a central state board, which would replace the cabinet and the prime minister, military educator Ishiwara Kanji and nationalist bureaucrat Miyazaki Masayoshi proposed the abolition of parliamentary government. Believing that a market economy could not meet Japan's military needs, Ishiwara proposed a central-planning organ, the General Affairs Office, to supervise Japanese industry. At the same time, advocates of the National Defense State urged caution in foreign affairs, fearing that war could detract from a carefully planned military buildup. Though escalation in China made a gradual military buildup impossible, the nationalization of the electric-power industry and the National Mobilization Law of 1938 brought into effect the authoritarian politics and economic planning favored by advocates of the National Defense State.

Guy Yasko

Bibliography

Crowley, James. *Japan's Quest for Autonomy: National Security and Foreign Policy, 1930–1938*. Princeton, NJ: Princeton University Press, 1966.

Peattie, Mark. *Ishiwara Kanji and Japan's Confrontation with the West*. Princeton, NJ: Princeton University Press, 1975.

National Essence; National Polity (*Kokutai*)

Japan's most comprehensive national ideology in the critical Westernizing era of 1868–1945. It represented, for Japan's leaders, a superlative commitment (above the religions) for rallying all true subjects to the great task of modern nation building.

The word *kokutai* is the Japanese rendering of the ancient Chinese expression *kuo t'i* (organ of state or organization of the state). The term came into Japanese usage in the late years of the Tokugawa era (1600–1868), especially among scholars of the Mito school of emperor-centered historians. Literally translated "nation body" or "national body," *kokutai* can be described as the Japanese national structure, polity, or essence. More broadly, it refers to the basic principles on which the Japanese nation was founded and to Japan's much-vaunted unique national character.

Kokutai was a rich amalgam of indigenized Chinese Confucian and native Shinto elements. From its basically Confucian nature, it derived its primary emphasis on ethics in social relations. According to the Confucian model, filial piety is learned in the home, where parents train their children to express gratitude toward them and family ancestors for all blessings received. Once internalized in the home, this ethic is extended upward to all superiors and ultimately to the emperor himself, who was the sacred, patriarchal father figure of the entire national family, and all his little ones (subjects) were bound to him in reverent gratitude.

According to *kokutai*, life is to be lived according to the two basic virtues: filial piety in the home and emperor loyalty in the nation. Together, these were known as the national ethic (*kokumin dōtoku*).

The importance of Shinto for *kokutai* was that it provided ultimate sanctification for the emperor. The Meiji Constitution (1889) declared that the imperial dynasty derived from "an unbroken line of descent for ages past" (Article 1) and that the emperor was "sacred and inviolable" (Article 3). With such exalted credentials, there was no problem in generating reverence for him as the highest living object of patriotic commitment.

Itō Hirobumi, a leading Meiji official, observed from extensive travels abroad that, whereas in the West religion served to unify nations as the axis of the state, in Japan the religions fragmented people's loyalties. He saw no single Japanese religious tradition that could unite the people's hearts, so he concluded that Japan's best unifying force as it moved toward modernity was reverence for the emperor and the throne. For this reason, he gave strong support to *kokutai* as a unifying power.

Along with the primary values of filial piety and emperor loyalty, *kokutai* was enshrined in the highly influential Imperial Rescript on Education (1890). It declared that Japanese subjects had been united over many years in loyalty and filial piety: the "glory of the fundamental character [*kokutai*] of Our Empire . . . and the source of Our education."

The Imperial Rescript on Education was skillfully promoted through an impressive school ritual. Principals periodically read the rescript in a solemn assembly in which the document was virtually elevated to the status of a sacred scripture. For schoolteachers, correct formal bowing before the rescript and pictures of the emperor and the empress became a kind of litmus test of patriotic commitment. More than mere etiquette, this public ritual took on the nature of religious reverence before the most sacred symbols of Japanese national life.

In 1891, at the first rescript ceremony in a prestigious feeder school to Tokyo Imperial University, a young Christian instructor named Uchimura Kanzō refused to bow, and this "Uchimura incident" hit the press with great impact. Inoue Tetsujirō, philosophy professor at Tokyo Imperial University and expert on the education rescript, wrote widely about the fundamental incompatibility between Japanese nationalism and Christian universalism. The impact of this incident on Japanese Christians was profound and rendered most of them timid about their deviant faith.

Throughout the early twentieth century, state authorities persistently worked to filter out or downplay any Shinto religious elements, such as seasonal festivals and *kami* worship at the shrines, in the composition of *kokutai*. The intent was to present the shrines as essentially ethical in nature—that is, nonreligious.

Government officials felt the need to do this because of a provision in the 1889 Meiji Constitution that guaranteed freedom of religious belief. Although somewhat qualified, this statement was sufficient to protect the right of a person to make his or her own decisions about religious commitment or association.

However, government officials were adamant that *kokutai* and the national ethic (*kokumin dōtoku*) were too important to be left to individual choice: They comprised a nonreligious ethical system that must be elevated to a special position above the religions so that freedom of choice would not apply. This ethical system was, in the words of the sociologist Peter Berger, a veritable "sacred canopy" overarching the entirety of Japanese life.

In 1891, the year after the promulgation of the Imperial Rescript on Education, the Education Ministry began to experiment with ethics textbooks; in 1903, it produced a set of texts that, with minor revisions, continued in use until the close of the Pacific War in 1945. In language that children could understand, these books spelled out the fundamental components of *kokutai*: filial piety and emperor loyalty; familism (*kazokushugi*) as the prototype for national life; and the national ethic (*kokumin dōtoku*) as the transcendent moral law of the land. All editions of the ethics texts over the years, as well as textbooks in fields as diverse as language, history, and math, were saturated with military allusions glorifying the Japa-

nese nation's military adventures—with China (1894–95), Russia (1904–05), Manchuria (1931), French Indochina (1940), and, America and its allies (1941–45). Throughout long years of warfare, *kokutai* was exalted as a kind of shining Holy Grail to inspire Japanese subjects in their country's ultranationalistic campaigns.

Minobe Tatsukichi, professor of constitutional law at Tokyo Imperial University, held a more rational, less mystical view of the emperor, and, during much of the early twentieth century, his thought had been the standard for scholars. But with the outbreak of nationalistic enthusiasm following Japan's advance into Manchuria in 1931, these views were challenged by intellectual conservatives, who charged Minobe with lèse majesté, had his writings proscribed, and secured his dismissal from his professorship at Tokyo Imperial University and his seat in the House of Peers. In the face of this ultranationalistic attack, Minobe's balanced view of *kokutai* became a casualty of the times.

Shaken by the Minobe affair, officials of the Ministry of Education determined to produce an authoritative statement on national ideology for the guidance of the people. In 1937, they published and widely distributed a work called "Cardinal Principles of the National Polity" (*Kokutai no hongi*). This soon took its place alongside the Imperial Rescript on Education as a sacred scripture of Japanese nationalism, and it became the chief ideological instrument for thought control.

The book's basic message is that the Japanese people must reject Western self-centered individualism, which did much to promote the evils of socialism, anarchism, and Communism, all of which had gained influence in Japan during the liberal years of Taishō democracy (1912–26). In place of these, the people must cling to the selfless communal harmony of *kokutai*. The *Kokutai no Hongi* presents an essentially religious attitude toward *kokutai*, in that it is exalted as an object of veneration for every good Japanese. This national devotion finds its highest expression in reverence for the unbroken line of sacred emperors and in grateful obedience to the state.

The politicians and educators of pre-1945 Japan promoted *kokutai* among the people with the dual purpose of instructing their minds and capturing their hearts. As they instinctively understood, while nationalism carries ideological content it derives its great power from the emotional commitment it generates: More than reason, mystery, and reverence draw people and enrich their lives.

When American bombs wiped out cities and people in 1945, the ideal of *kokutai* was destroyed. But the Japanese are forever seeking clarity in their own minds as to what it means to "be Japanese" in the new age; so, without reference to *kokutai* as such, they continue to dig below the many Western ways they have adopted to find and affirm their essential "Japaneseness." In this sense, the search for the national essence goes on.

Wilbur M. Fridell

Bibliography
Gluck, Carol. *Japan's Modern Myths: Ideology in the Late Meiji Period*. Princeton, NJ: Princeton University Press, 1985.
Kokutai no Hongi (Cardinal Principles of the National Entity of Japan). Trans. John Owen Gauntlett. Belmont, MA: Crofton, 1974.
Ienaga, Saburō. *The Pacific War, 1931–45*. New York: Pantheon, 1978.

National Foundations Society (*Kokuhonsha*)

Conservative, nationalist society founded by Hiranuma Kiichirō in 1924. The name Kokuhon (nation-based) indicated an organization opposed to democracy (*minpon* or *minshu*). Alarmed by the prevalence after World War I of foreign-inspired political movements such as democracy and Marxism, Hiranuma and Kokuhonsha leaders attempted to revive the spirit of national unity that they believed had served the Japanese people well during the Meiji era (1868–1912).

They regarded democracy as alien and, therefore, disruptive to a harmonious, emperor-centered Japan. Kokuhonsha propaganda accused party politicians and party governments of undermining the unique moral relationships inherent in the traditional Japanese polity. The Kokuhonsha movement was popular during the early 1930s, and the organization claimed 80,000 members by 1936, including such prominent figures as Generals Araki Sadao and Mazaki Jinzaburō and Admiral Tōgō Heihachirō. Hiranuma also used the Kokuhonsha as a forum from which to advance his own political career. Embarrassed by links to radical revolutionary nationalists, he disbanded the Kokuhonsha shortly after the unsuccessful February 26, 1936, coup d'état by right-wing troops.

Richard Yasko

Bibliography
Yasko, Richard. "Hiranuma Kiichirō and Conservative Politics in Pre-War Japan." Unpublished doctoral dissertation, University of Chicago, 1973.

National Mobilization Law (*Kokka Sōdōin Hō*) (1938)

Law creating the means to mobilize Japan's people and resources for World War II. The 50-article National Mobilization Bill, proposed by the first Konoe Fumimaro cabinet, passed the Diet on March 24, 1938, following intense debate over its appropriateness and the sweeping power it gave national officials. Prewar measures required that businesses train people for national-defense work, that war reserves be developed, and that incentives be provided for production and stockpiling of certain goods and supplies such as petroleum and steel. The wartime measures included a much broader range of activities, including creating business associations; drafting labor; controlling profits and wages; setting work hours; supervising production, transportation, and trade; and forcing banks to offer loans.

To secure Diet (legislature) approval, the government agreed to create a 50-member General Mobilization Council (30 of them Diet members), whose approval would be required before mobilization decisions could be carried out. It also promised that the law would not be applied during the second Sino-Japanese War, then underway, although a number of its measures were put into effect anyway as that conflict grew more intense. The bill was revised and broadened in 1941, shortly before the bombing of American operations at Pearl Harbor, and its most extensive use came during the years 1942–45, when every effort was made to bend the national economy to war needs, despite constant coordination problems and resource shortages. The law was rescinded on September 29, 1945.

James L. Huffman

Bibliography
Berger, Gordon. *Parties out of Power in Japan, 1931–1941*. Princeton, NJ: Princeton University Press, 1977.

N

National Seclusion (*Sakoku*)

Edo government policy, the main elements of which included the exclusion of Catholic missionaries and traders, the proscription of Christianity, and the prohibition of foreign travel by Japanese during much of the Tokugawa era (1600–1868). The seclusion was not total, because of Dutch, Chinese, and Korean access to Japan; moreover, designated officials and traders from Satsuma and Tsushima were allowed to go to the Ryūkyū Islands and to Korea, respectively.

The seclusion policy was enunciated in five *bakufu* (military government) directives issued between 1633 and 1639. The term *sakoku* (literally, closed country) did not originate, however, until the early nineteenth century. Contrary to the image fostered by the term, the directives of the 1630s were not simply attempts by the *bakufu* to close Japan to the outside world, but were rather continuing efforts to eliminate Christianity and control the direction of, and participation in, foreign trade.

The first *sakoku* edict placed restrictions on Japanese travel overseas, outlined search procedures for Christians; and detailed the regulation of foreign trade. The second and third edicts absolutely prohibited the dispatching of ships abroad and ordered the execution of all Japanese caught trying to leave or return to Japan. The fourth edict deported the offspring of Portuguese and Spanish origins and all Japanese who had adopted such offspring. The last *sakoku* edict, issued in the aftermath of northern Kyushu's 1637–38 Shimabara Rebellion in which more than 35,000 peasant rebels, many of them Christian, were killed by government troops, stated that, in light of continued Portuguese violations of the anti-Christian prohibition, Portuguese ships would no longer be allowed to enter Japanese ports. Any ship disobeying this order was to be destroyed, and its crew and passengers executed.

In 1641, the *bakufu* transferred the Dutch from Hirado Island off western Kyushu to the man-made island of Dejima in Nagasaki Harbor. After that, apart from the Ryūkyūan and Korean trade, the only foreign trade permitted was that of the Dutch and the Chinese at Nagasaki.

Over the next two centuries, the Portuguese, British, Russians, and Americans attempted unsuccessfully to alter the *sakoku* policy. The policy, which in the 1630s had been a rational attempt to legitimize and strengthen shogunate authority, had by the early nineteenth century become more of a burden than an asset. The *Phaeton* Incident of 1808, in which a British warship sailed into Nagasaki Harbor in defiance of *bakufu* orders, demonstrated that enforcement of regulations had become lax. Although the *bakufu* temporarily attempted to strengthen *sakoku* in 1825, it relaxed the policy again in 1842. On the theoretical level, scholars of the nationalistic Mito school continued to champion the policy and make it an issue of national debate, but, with the arrival of Commodore Matthew Perry and his fleet from the United States in 1853 to open relations with Japan, the *bakufu* was forced to rethink the practical aspects of enforcing its seclusion policy. *Sakoku* was formally ended by the Kanagawa Treaty of 1854 with the United States and the Ansei commercial treaties of 1858 signed with the United States and other Western countries.

Lane R. Earns

Bibliography

Toby, Ronald P. *State and Diplomacy in Early Modern Japan.* Princeton, NJ: Princeton University Press, 1984.

Wakabayashi, Bob Tadashi. *Anti-Foreignism and Western Learning in Early-Modern Japan: The New Theses of 1825.* Cambridge: Harvard University Press, 1986.

National Socialism Movement (*Kokka Shakaishugi Undō*)

Revolutionary nationalist movement in the 1920s and 1930s that urged a complete restructuring of Japanese society under direct imperial rule. In 1919, traditional right-wing nationalist Uesugi Shinkichi joined with socialist Takabatake Motoyuki in forming the Keirin Gakumei (League for the Study of Government) to oppose left-wing academicians and propound a system that would abolish capitalism and place Japan under the emperor's control. The organization did not last long because Uesugi and traditional nationalists had little genuine interest in the revolutionary proposals of Takabatake, but a significant number of ultranationalists continued to be influenced by the ideas of state socialism and Italian fascism throughout the 1920s and 1930s.

The most influential leader of the national-socialism movement was Kita Ikki, who advocated socialism and liberation of Asian nations from Western colonialism. His plan for reorganizing Japan called for nationalizing nearly all business, industry, and private property, and for the military to assist the emperor in taking direct control of the country. Once Japan was restructured, he argued, it should take the lead in driving out the West and stimulating Asian nationalism.

Though the movement dissipated much of its energy in fights with more traditional nationalists, its impact was substantial. It had wide support among junior officers in the Imperial Way Faction (Kōdōha) of the army, and its adherents played major roles in many of the assassinations and violent incidents of the early 1930s. In 1932, thousands of its adherents joined together politically in Akamatsu Katsumaro's Nihon Kokka Shakaitō (Japan National Socialist Party), though divisions between economic reformers and traditional nationalists caused the party's demise two years later. National-socialist ideologues also briefly asserted control of the Taisei Yokusankai (Imperial Rule Assistance Association) that replaced the political parties in 1940. Prime Minister Konoe Fumimaro quickly countered their moves, however, and maneuvered more traditional conservatives into the IRAA leadership.

James L. Huffman

Bibliography

Storry, Richard. *The Double Patriots: A Study of Japanese Nationalism*. Westport, CT: Greenwood Press, 1973.

Wilson, George. *Radical Nationalist in Japan: Kita Ikki*. Cambridge: Harvard University Press, 1969.

Nativism, National Learning (*Kokugaku*)

An intellectual, religious, and political movement of the mid- to late-Tokugawa period (1600–1868) emphasizing the existence of, and ideological commitment to, a "Japanese Way" distinct from Confucianism and Buddhism. A key impetus for the appearance of *kokugaku* was the rise of the *kogaku* (ancient learning) school of Japanese Confucianism represented by figures such as Ogyū Sorai (1666–1728), who, through philologically based reinterpretations of the ancient Chinese classical texts, challenged the preeminence of the metaphysically oriented Song neo-Confucianism. The *kogaku* scholars' acclamation of the centrality of the Chinese tradition spurred a counter affirmation of Japan as the source of cultural value, which became one of the

rallying cries of the *kokugaku* movement. At the same time, *kokugaku* scholars found in Sorai's philological methodology and call for recuperation of an unadulterated archaic tradition an intellectual mode they could readily adapt to the study of Japan.

These trends were already visible in the work of Kamo no Mabuchi (1697–1769), who wrote commentaries on the *Manyōshū*, an eighth-century collection of native poetry, and advocated a revival of its fresh, manly spirit, uncorrupted by later foreign influences, as the true spirit of Japan. They reached a peak of development in the writings of Motoori Norinaga (1730–1801), who concentrated his interpretative efforts on the *Kojiki*, an early eighth-century compilation of legendary accounts of the origins of Japan and its ruling line. Norinaga took a rigorously literalist approach to the account of the "age of the gods" in the *Kojiki*, disavowing the syncretistic efforts of medieval and early-Tokugawa commentators to give them a deeper or more sophisticated meaning as evidence of a "Chinese mind" (*karagokoro*). His successors, such as Hirata Atsutane (1776–1843), were inspired by the emphasis on the centrality of Japan and the divine origin of its ruling line resulting from this literalist reading. While he was often xenophobic in his efforts to provide *kokugaku* with stronger theological underpinnings, by declaring the superiority of Japan and condemning the corrupting influence of Buddhism and Confucianism, Atsutane in fact reverted to syncretistic interpretations that drew not only from those traditions but also the prohibited Christian religion. The teachings of Atsutane and his followers, often referred to as *ukko* (restoration) *shintō* to distinguish them from earlier forms of *kokugaku*, reached a substantial audience in late-Tokugawa Japan and were an important element in the formation of modern State Shinto.

Kate Wildman Nakai

Bibliography

Maruyama, Masao. *Studies in the Intellectual History of Tokugawa Japan*. Trans. Mikiso Hane. Princeton, NJ: Princeton University Press, 1974.

Natsume Sōseki (1867–1916)

Hailed unanimously as Meiji (1868–1912) Japan's preeminent writer, Natsume Sōseki began his brief but productive career in 1905, in

Natsume Sōseki. Asahi Shimbun Photo.

a climate charged with nationalistic sentiments accompanying Japan's victories in the Russo-Japanese War (1904–05). He was skeptical of all ideologies, including nationalism, that imposed an outlook founded on absolute terms.

Sōseki despised not only the jingoists in his own country but also the imperialistic designs of Western countries. Especially during his sojourn in England (1900–03), he observed firsthand the cultural imperialism of the West. His *Bungakuron* (On Literature, 1907), first delivered as a series of lectures between 1903 and 1905 during his stint as a professor of literature at Tokyo Imperial University, may be read as an attempt to construct a theory of literature that would discover what is universal in a literary work while honoring the respective culture's unique qualities. Sōseki championed an ethnicity that would be the source, not of nationalism, but of creative potential.

Scattered throughout Sōseki's writings are notions that oppose the ideas underlying nationalism. *Wagahai wa neko de aru* (1905; English translation *I Am a Cat,* Tokyo: Tuttle, 1975), a work that satirizes all manner of social practices during Meiji times, lampoons those who make a fetish of *yamato-damashii*

(Japanese spirit). *Nowaki* (*Autumn Wind,* 1907) presents a main character who subscribes to socialist views. In *Sore kara* (1909; English translation *And Then,* Baton Rouge: Louisiana State University Press, 1978) the protagonist, Daisuke, voices his dismay at the unscrupulousness of those with money and power who, under the guise of national service, carry out selfish deeds that undermine the people's liberties.

Sōseki's pluralistic outlook, which challenged the monism of nationalism, is perhaps best expressed in a lecture entitled "Watakushi no kojinshugi" (My Individualism) that he delivered in 1914, two years before his early death. In it, he unequivocally asserts that "a nationalistic morality comes out a very poor second when compared with an individualistic morality," and he urges his audience to develop a sense of responsible individualism that could become the basis for independent judgment.

Yoshio Iwamoto

Bibliography

Yu, Beongcheon. *Natsume Sōseki.* New York: Twayne, 1969.

Naturalism (*Shizenshugi*)

A literary movement that flourished from 1906 to 1910 (although writers bearing the naturalist label went on writing into the 1940s), *shizenshugi* may be viewed as the point at which Japanese literature turned decisively away from its 1,000-year-old conventions to adopt the modern novel, inspired by Western models, as the preferred mode of expression. When writers ceased to be facile manipulators of well-worn tropes and adopted the posture of dispassionate observers of the "real world," they became for the first time a threat to the orthodoxy of the Meiji state. It was the naturalist movement that first attracted the systematic attention of the Home Ministry's police censors to fiction devoid of political polemic, casting in high relief the conflict between the nationalistic, self-sacrificing, puritanical neo-Confucianism of the aging Meiji establishment and the Western-inspired individualism of a new, Meiji-educated generation.

At the same time, naturalism is often viewed as the point at which modern Japanese fiction abandoned an incipient interest in large social questions to devote itself exclusively to the limited sphere of the autobiographical author's sense experiences, which rendered the modern Japanese novel a political irrelevance. The writer most often blamed for having single-handedly accomplished this change is Tayama Katai (1871–1930), whose novella *Futon* (1907, in English *The Quilt*, Tokyo: University of Tokyo Press, 1981), portrays the frustrated longings of a writer in his mid-thirties for the lovely young woman he has taken on as his disciple. So successful was Katai at painting his confessional self-portrait, goes the argument, that he distracted several generations of writers from the more admirable path that had been laid down for them the year before by Shimazaki Tōson (1872–1943), whose novel *Hakai* (in English, *The Broken Commandment*, Tokyo: University of Tokyo Press, 1974) had focused not on mere sexual hunger but on the larger question of the suffering of Japan's pariah caste.

The proposition seems doubtful that a single short work such as *Futon* could have diverted a country's writers from the pursuit of lofty causes. Nor in the case of *Hakai* was the novel's social consciousness what most appealed to its youthful readers. Rather, it was the secret anguish of Tōson's sensitive young protagonist, estranged from his father's generation, that moved them so profoundly. "The controversy between the naturalist school and its opponents is, finally, a struggle between the fathers and the sons," a major spokesman for naturalism, Hasegawa Tenkei, would declare in 1908 (Rubin, 61). *Futon*'s tortured protagonist must also be seen as an embodiment of the struggle between the old and the new.

Having been exhorted by the Meiji government to devote their lives to the national mission of establishing Japan on a par with the Western countries, many Japanese thought that the mission had been accomplished with the defeat of a Caucasian country in the Russo-Japanese War (1904–05). Disillusionment with the fact that the Treaty of Portsmouth gave Japan no indemnity also turned many away from the national focus and led to a widespread belief that the time had come for individuals to live for themselves. A great influx of translations from contemporary European literature did much to undermine high-minded Confucian values of loyalty and filial piety in the eyes of the young and turned them, instead, to an appreciation of the raw, gutsy side of real life.

The new writers saw themselves as casting aside the old, unscientific view of man as noble in spirit but base in his physicality. Almost inevitably, their determination to study life for its truth rather than beauty led to a far bolder depiction of sexual—and other normally hidden—matters than many traditional minds were willing to countenance. Conservative commentators (not to be confused with anti-naturalist writers and critics who opposed naturalism on literary grounds) began to grumble about "unwholesome" ideas, and the clash between old and new crystallized quickly.

Soon the government decided to step into the fray. Not only did police censors ban the February 1908 issue of *Bungei kurabu*, an important literary journal, for carrying the allegedly obscene story "Tokai" (The City) by Ikuta Kizan (1876–1945), but the Procurator's Office took the unprecedented step of putting on trial the author of the story and Ishibashi Shian, the editor/publisher of the journal. Their conviction and the resulting notoriety convinced many that what were called "flesh-lust novels" were corrupting the young on a vast scale and that naturalism was simply a synonym for pornography, so much so that a sensational thwarted love suicide and a rape-murder that occurred just three weeks after the end of the trial were seen as further proof of the evil power of naturalism.

This trial against naturalism occurred under the government of the relatively liberal Saionji Kinmochi, but, when the reactionary Katsura Tarō came to power in July 1908, serious literature became one of the targets of a new, more pervasive "campaign of national mobilization" designed to "stem the evil tide of extravagance and frivolity." Vice minister of education Okada Ryōhei declared in 1908 that the campaign was prompted by a decline in the spirit of national unity caused by "many undesirable phenomena . . . such as naturalism and extreme individualism (Rubin, 109)."

Under Katsura, Japanese children were taught Shinto myth as historical fact, and filial piety for the head of the individual family was seen as the same as loyalty to the warm, loving father of the national family, the emperor, and the latter became synonymous with patriotism. Literature stood in direct opposition to the state's official philosophy whenever it questioned the sanctity of the family, or implied a change in the family structure by portraying liberated women, or suggested that an individual might live for himself and not for his family as part of the family state, or that the fulfillment of his own sexual drive was a legitimate end in itself, quite apart from the maintenance of the family line. It was precisely all of the family-centered values that naturalism questioned, and the emergence of the new literature was taken by the government as simply another sign of a moral breakdown that had to be reversed.

Liberal critics of naturalism have taxed the movement for failing to elucidate a consistent critical program, but if naturalist writers contributed anything to modern Japanese literature, it was not an a priori program to be imposed on their fictional worlds; rather, it was the legitimization of that inductive vision that has been central to the development of all modern fiction. With naturalism came the death of convention, that element in traditional Japanese literature that, since the ninth century, had required all poems of travel to describe travel *away* from the capital, or all poems about the cuckoo to allude to the lover's nightlong wait for a few lovely notes (no matter that the bird may have kept the whole household awake with its chirping). With naturalism came not only open reference to sex, but also unflattering portraits of parents and other authority figures.

As a movement, naturalism was all but played out by 1910, but the major authors who had been associated with the school—Tōson, Katai, Tokuda Shūsei (1871–1943), and Masamune Hakuchō (1879–1962)—went on to develop their original visions, contributing a quotidian, often autobiographical, realism to mainstream Japanese literature that has continued to inspire and frustrate subsequent generations of critics and writers. Antinaturalists promoted greater intellectualism or romanticism or fantasy or eroticism than the austere naturalists were willing or able to embrace, but they never advocated turning the clock back to the cherry blossoms and the moon at the center of the imperial court's aesthetic orthodoxy.

Jay Rubin

Bibliography

Rubin, Jay. *Injurious to Public Morals: Writers and the Meiji State*. Seattle: University of Washington Press, 1984.

Sibley, William F. "Naturalism in Japanese Literature." *Harvard Journal of Asiatic Studies*. Vol. 28 (1968), 157–69.

Shimazaki, Tōson. *The Broken Commandment*. Trans. Kenneth Strong. Tokyo: University of Tokyo Press, 1974.

Tayama, Katai. *The Quilt and Other Stories*. Trans. Kenneth Henshall. Tokyo: University of Tokyo Press, 1981.

New Nationalism
(*Shin-Kokkashugi, Neo-Nashonarizumu*)

Term used to refer to the agenda of a diverse group of politicians, bureaucrats, businessmen, academics, and critics who advocate full remilitarization and an independent role for Japan in foreign affairs and defense, revision of the 1947 Constitution and other legacies of the Occupation era (1945–52), and the rehabilitation of the state as a legitimate focus for popular loyalty. More generally, it refers to trends evident since the late 1970s of popular pride in Japan's postwar social and economic achievements, feelings of superiority and self-confidence as Japanese, and resentment of outside criticism of Japan over trade and other economic and political issues.

The new-nationalism program resembles to some extent that of traditional nationalists, conservatives who would also revise the constitution in a conservative manner, legitimize the Self-Defense Forces, and stimulate patriotism and allegiance to the state. The new nationalists, however, actively reject accommodation to U.S. interests, alignment with the Western democracies, and anti-Communism in favor of a broadly based diplomacy of realpolitik in which international cooperation would be subordinated to the promotion of Japanese interests. They tend to eschew the manipulation of traditional symbols of national polity (*kokutai*) and spiritual reliance on the emperor system (*tennōsei*) in favor of a secular, material rationale for Japan's superiority—the hard, physical work and superior technology they see as underpinning Japan's economic resurgence. They advocate a Japan free to maneuver in international affairs, uninhibited by fetters on the use of military force or by what they view as unfair economic restrictions, which, they argue are little more than attempts by less competitive trading partners to hobble Japan's economy or, at worst, racist attempts to deny Japan preeminence. Their writings posit a Japan emasculated by Occupation-era reforms, hamstrung by the 1960 Japan-U.S. Treaty of Mutual Cooperation and Security, and denied a truly independent, sovereign existence.

The new nationalism has its roots in the 1970s, when a series of economic and political shocks led to a heightened sense of vulnerability and greater uneasiness about the U.S.-Japan relationship and stimulated a national debate on security issues. In this context, Shimizu Ikutarō, formerly a prominent member of the progressive camp, began issuing public calls in 1980 for the revision of the 1947 Constitution to allow Japan the right to use arms in international disputes. Violating an informal postwar taboo, he went so far as to declare Japan's right to maintain nuclear weapons.

About the same time, renewed debate began about "Japaneseness" and the nature of Japanese social institutions, a debate fed by Western commentators who lavishly praised such features of Japanese society as the high educational achievements, the lack of crime, and the impressive savings rates. On the other hand, some Japanese commentators were starting to bemoan the loss of the work ethic, especially among the young. The new nationalism may be seen as one effort to stimulate feelings of separateness and superiority even as, at the same time, it provides a catharsis for anxiety about Japan's future. As such, it is meant as much for internal as external consumption.

In the 1980s, new nationalists increased their profile. Intensified trade friction with the United States, revisionist criticism of Japan as a state with only neo-mercantilist policies, and various instances of alleged Japan bashing led to an often aggressive response from new nationalists. Liberal Democratic Party (LDP) politician Ishihara Shintarō, for example, has attacked the United States for its perceived failings and urged Japan to use its economic and technological power to stand up to the Americans. Although they are often sensationalistic and anti-American, Ishihara's writings also reflect the emotional, defensive, inward-looking tone, the hierarchical view of international relations, and the lack of any coherent national mission beyond aggressive pursuit of self-interest common to the new nationalism.

Ellen H. Hammond

Bibliography
Ishihara, Shintarō. *The Japan That Can Say No.* New York: Simon and Schuster, 1991.
Pyle, Kenneth B. "Japan, the World, and the Twenty-First Century." *The Political Economy of Japan.* Vol. 2. Ed. Inoguchi Takahashi and Daniel Okimoto. Stanford, CA: Stanford University Press, 1988.

New Order in East Asia
(*Tōa Shinchitsujo*)

This phrase originated in a radio broadcast by Prime Minister Konoe Fumimaro on November 3, 1938. Hoping to induce the Nationalist government of China to surrender after almost one year and a half of fighting with Japan, he declared the need to create a new order of international relations in East Asia. Japan and China would cooperate in resisting Communism and Western imperialism. If the Nationalists reformed appropriately, Japan would accept their participation in this project.

The declaration presented Japan's mission in the second Sino-Japanese War (1937–45) as mandated by the progress of history. The concept of a new Asian order reflected widely held beliefs by Japanese intellectuals and officials that the great powers were dividing the world into regional blocs and that Japan deserved one of its own. Konoe urged Japan to start a new era by eschewing the exploitation of Western-style imperialism, rising above parochial nationalism, and emphasizing mutual aid in order to strengthen the Orient as a whole. The Nationalists quickly spurned Konoe's offer and continued their resistance.

The ideal of a new order in East Asia captured the imagination of Japanese writers. Many directed their energies toward devising policies to enhance confederation with China and to fortify Japan for this momentous project. Foreign Minister Matsuoka Yōsuke expanded the new-order concept in the summer of 1940 when he announced that Japan wanted to create a Greater East Asia Coprosperity Sphere. This became the country's official goal during the Pacific War.

William Miles Fletcher III

Bibliography
Crowley, James B. "Intellectuals as Visionaries of the New Asian Order." *Dilemmas of Growth in Prewar Japan.* Ed. James W. Morley. Princeton, NJ: Princeton University Press, 1971.
Fletcher, William Miles, III. *The Search for a New Order: Intellectuals and Fascism in Prewar Japan.* Chapel Hill: University of North Carolina Press, 1982.

New Order Movement (*Shin Taisei Undō*)

Loose term for a political-reorganization movement of the early 1940s designed to ensure that Japan's major institutions would better serve the country's economic and military needs. Though the term was vaguely applied to organizations in numerous spheres, most "new order" talk focused on politics. In particular, by the late 1930s, many groups—including established political parties and partisan associations outside the political mainstream, as well as leading bureaucrats and military officials—were frustrated by a perceived loss of influence during the nationalistic upheavals. As a result, they began talking widely about a new order that would ostensibly serve national interests but that also would increase their own power.

Former Prime Minister Konoe Fumimaro announced his support for the *shin taisei undō* idea in June 1940, and when he became prime minister the next month, it became official national policy. He wanted to secure national unity, develop a mechanism for getting all of the country's competing groups to support the economic and military policies deemed necessary for carrying out the country's mission, and improve communications between the government and the masses. Amid considerable enthusiasm, the major parties dissolved themselves, and, in October 1940, the Imperial Rule Assistance Association (Taisei Yokusankai) was launched as the single party through which the new order would be realized.

Despite the initial optimism, the movement never realized its potential. Once it became clear that the individual factions likely would have even less influence under the new system, many leaders criticized it and struggled for their own objectives. The movement became little more than a tool for stimulating popular support for government policies, and most decisions continued to be made by the old elites who long had held sway under the Meiji constitutional system.

James L. Huffman

Bibliography

Berger, Gordon. *Parties out of Power in Japan, 1931–1941*. Princeton, NJ: Princeton University Press, 1977.

Nichiren Sect

One of the popular Buddhist sects that grew out of Tendai Buddhism in the Kamakura period (1185–1333), Nichiren has inspired more nationalistic writers and movements over the centuries than has any other Buddhist group. Founded by the priest Nichiren (1222–82), it focused on belief in the Lotus Sutra and repetition of the phrase, *Namu myōhō renge kyō* (I take refuge in the Lotus Sutra). The distinctive features of Nichirenism were its aggressive denunciations of other sects and its contention that Japan was to be the center of a Buddhist revival in humankind's last, degenerate days (*mappō*).

Nichiren Buddhism was subject to innumerable schisms throughout the centuries after the prophet's death, giving rise to positions supportive of nearly every philosophical and political doctrine. The largest number of followers, however, has been of a conservative, often nationalist, bent. Indeed, several leading untranationalists of the 1920s and 1930s, such as Ishiwara Kanji and Kita Ikki, grounded their right-wing rhetoric at least partly in Nichiren's ideas. Some favored the emperor as the faith's central worship object (*honzon*). Since World War II, Nichiren has been most widely visible through one of its lay organizations, Sōka Gakkai (Value Creation Society), which by the late 1960s had become a major force in Japanese politics.

James L. Huffman

Bibliography

Rodd, Laurel. *Nichiren: Selected Writings*. Honolulu: University of Hawaii Press, 1980.

Saunders, E. Dale. *Buddhism in Japan*. Philadelphia: University of Pennsylvania Press, 1964.

Nihon Hōsō Kyōkai (NHK)

Japan's public broadcasting agency. NHK was founded in August 1926 to function as the sole transmitter of radio broadcasts in Japan. Although some local groups hoped to establish private stations, the prewar Ministry of Communications, recognizing the new medium's importance and potential mass influence, induced the establishment of a public-interest national monopoly under government supervision. Politicians and bureaucrats conceived of broadcasting as an important force for the setting and maintenance of cultural standards and homogeneity. The prewar NHK collected receivers' fees directly from the public and thus was not dependent on state subsidies; however, many of its top personnel were former government bureaucrats. Its budgetary plans, receivers'-fee structure, and definition of executives' roles required Ministry of Communication approval, and programming was subject to prior government censorship.

The nationalism of the prewar emperor-centered state and the development of NHK radio were closely linked. For example, government and broadcast officials cooperated on a crash program to rush the completion of NHK's radio network in time for the live broadcast of the new Shōwa Emperor's coronation ceremonies in November 1928. In turn, the broadcast of the enthronement ceremonies was a tremendous boost to the sales of radio receiver sets. With the increasing military influence in government and nationalism during the 1930s, even the limited autonomy that NHK had possessed was curtailed. More and more, people saw the network as a surrogate or agent for the government. After the mobilization for war with China began in 1937, NHK became a simple propaganda arm of the state, and official state policy was to support the diffusion of radios to every household to promote the state's nationalist goals.

The American Occupation of Japan (1945–52) thoroughly changed NHK in the process of its democratization programs. Since then, NHK has been formally autonomous from government, with the latter legally forbidden from interference in programming. NHK continues to collect its receivers' fees directly from the public and is a public broadcasting agency, not a state-owned one. The national Diet (legislature), however, approves the overall yearly budget of NHK and any increases in receivers' fees. NHK's board of governors is appointed by the government, and the board selects the chief executive officer, the president. Most important, NHK no longer has a monopoly on broadcasting: It faces competition in television broadcasting, for example, from private commercial stations, including several loose nationwide networks centered on major Tokyo stations with connections to the major national newspapers.

In the mid-1990s, NHK was the second-largest broadcasting agency in the world, after the BBC (British Broadcasting Corporation) in England, with more than 16,000 employees and an annual budget of about $3 billion. It operates two over-the-air television networks—general and educational—as well as radio stations, an overseas broadcast service, and an extensive book-publishing enterprise. Its general television network emphasizes news and information and high-quality historical dramas, both of which are popular with the public. NHK also pioneered in the development of new media in Japan in the 1980s, establishing the world's first direct satellite broadcast network and 24-hour satellite broadcasting and developing high-definition television. These activities continue to make it a major force in creating a homogeneous public culture and maintaining high cultural standards in Japan, but now within a broader democratic context.

NHK's contribution to nationalism in the postwar era is primarily indirect. For example, its coverage in 1959 of the marriage of the then-crown prince Akihito and in 1964 of the Tokyo Olympics gave a major stimulus to the nationwide distribution of television sets and also reinforced a shared national identity through media culture. Its extensive coverage of the Shōwa Emperor's funeral in 1989 had a similar effect. Many of its frequent major news programs, known for their reliability and objective coverage, continued into the 1990s to focus on governmental, particularly bureaucratic, activities and on domestic rather than international news.

As the twenty-first century nears, NHK faces increasing competition in news and entertainment programming from the commercial networks. Further, as in all advanced industrialized societies, the proliferation and internationalization of types of media present the challenge of increasing diversification of information, segmentation of the audience, and, thus, fragmentation of culture. NHK's extensive resources, reputation for quality programming, and continued telecommunications leadership likely will enable it to continue to serve as the core of Japan's broadcasting system—and, therefore, as a homogenizing influence on public culture and an agent of national identity.

Ellis S. Krauss

Bibliography

Kasza, Gregory J. *The State and the Mass Media in Japan, 1918–1945*. Berkeley: University of California Press, 1988.

Krauss, Ellis S. "Portraying the State in Japan: NHK Television News and Politics." *Media and Politics in Japan*. Ed. Susan J. Pharr and Ellis Krauss. Honolulu: University of Hawaii Press, 1996.

Tracey, Michael. "Japan: Broadcasting in a New Democracy." *The Politics of Broadcasting*. Ed. Raymond Kuhn. New York: St. Martin's Press, 1985.

Nihonjinron

A genre of discourse concerned with establishing Japan's cultural and national identity. All peoples around the world are interested in defining who they are. Few, however, make cultural introspection their favorite parlor game as much as the Japanese. Indeed, 82 percent of those questioned in a survey conducted in Nishinomiya, Japan, in 1987 expressed keen interest in this topic and claimed to monitor it in newspapers and other media. All major bookstores in Japan maintain a large section devoted to *Nihonjinron* topics. Some works in this genre, such as those of contemporary scholars like social anthropologist Nakane Chie (which characterize Japanese society as being organized into small, intimate, hierarchically aligned groups) and of sociologist Doi Takeo (which emphasize the Japanese tendency for mutual emotional dependency among close kinsmen, friends, and colleagues) have achieved best-seller status and gone through scores of printings.

Authors in this category unanimously claim Japanese uniqueness in some form or another—from the presumed special impact of the monsoon climate on the culture, wet rice agriculture, and tight-knit consensus-oriented community structure to affectively dependent interpersonal relationships. They also find uniqueness in the language, which expresses the inner mystery of the culture, reveals the philosophy of endurance, characterizes the esthetics of subdued beauty, and even lends itself to the business management style that presumably integrates many of these other qualities, which have made Japan's "economic miracle" possible.

Explanations vary as to why the Japanese are so concerned with their uniqueness. Some believe that the Japanese search for cultural identity may be ascribed to excessive Western influence, which commenced in 1868, when Japan opened its ports to foreign trade. The average, modern-day middle-class Japanese have minimal contact with traditional conationals in their daily life. Their food, shelter, and clothing are basically Western-style; they work in concrete buildings, use desks and chairs, computers and telephones, and thus are removed from the traditional environment. Language is about the only traditional element they have retained, and even that is replete with Western loan words.

Added to this intrusion of materialistic Western culture is the rapidly increasing personal contact of Japanese with Westerners and their culture domestically. Also Japanese are traveling abroad increasingly; their number reached 1 million in 1990. Confronted with cultures and languages that are totally alien to them, they are being forced to contemplate the nature and essence of their own cultural identity.

The identity that emerges, regardless of its objective validity, is largely based on a comparison between Japan and the West. Japanese are group oriented; Westerners are individualistic. Japanese often rely on nonverbal, indirect communication; Westerners favor direct verbal contact. Japanese society is hierarchically organized; Western society is relatively egalitarian. In surveying these contrasts, Japanese all but ignore the non-Western cultures of Islam, Africa, and Southeast Asia, thus demonstrating Japan's basically Western orientation. The West is seen as Japan's reference group, the standard to be emulated, caught up with, and overtaken. Inherent in this effort is the widespread Japanese feeling of inferiority compared to the West, a drawback that Japanese have been desperately trying to overcome. The obverse side of the feeling of inferiority is an arrogance directed against the non-Western world, which was expressed in World War II through Japan's attempt to colonize Southeast Asia; since then, the arrogance has shown up more subtly in economic efforts at domination.

Nihonjinron should not be construed as emerging entirely from the "rice roots" of Japan's people. The political leadership since the Meiji era (1868–1912) has manipulated traditional values to influence the construction of Japan's national identity. This task was accomplished in the early modern period through blatant means of dominance: dictating school curricula, controlling the press, and creating institutions to disseminate government-approved versions of *Nihonjinron*. In the constitutionally enshrined postwar environment characterized by a free press, the method of control has become covert and more sophisticated, as in the government's censorship of textbooks. Prime Minister Ohira Masayoshi (1978–80), for example, placed his stamp of approval on the report of an advisory committee that regarded traditional Japanese values as the foundation of Japan's economic success. And Prime Minister Nakasone Yasuhiro (1982–87) tended to cloak his highly nationalistic views in calls for the expansion of Japan's international role. These approaches are firmly grounded in *Nihonjinron*.

Nihonjinron has evolved as modern Japan's political ideology, which fosters cultural nationalism. It is Japan's ultimate response to Japan bashing abroad. Foreigners may criticize Japan, but, armed with Nihonjinron, Japanese can proudly refute any criticism leveled against them: The Japanese people are what they are because they are the proud possessors of a unique cultural heritage that is responsible for their nation's success.

Harumi Befu

Bibliography

Ben-Dasan, Isaiah (pseud.). *The Japanese and the Jews.* Tokyo: Weatherhill, 1972.
Dale, Peter. *The Myth of Japanese Uniqueness.* New York: St. Martin's Press, 1986.

1980s

Defeat in World War II discredited much of Japan's historical and traditional culture. In its place, the Allied Occupation (1945–52) offered a new vision of a peace-loving and democratic people dedicated to economic recovery and eventual prosperity. The early postwar years *were* dedicated to recovery and the pursuit of economic security. Early postwar leaders tended to join their American critics in repudiating prewar culture and affirming the new democratic order. Some nostalgia for prewar culture and institutions reappeared in the 1950s and 1960s, but by the time the author Mishima Yukio committed his dramatic suicide in an appeal for a return to prewar values in 1970, his cause already was regarded by the general public as a historical anachronism. The Mishima incident made it clear that extremist nationalism would be relegated in time to nothing more than a political sideshow, where it remains, reappearing now and again in the form of tiny demonstrations by right-wing groups.

But Japanese nationalism itself was by no means being pushed to the sidelines of Japanese political consciousness after the 1970s. If anything, in the 1980s the Japanese people began to search in earnest for a mode of national self-understanding that would allow them to affirm *independently* some combination of present-day economic achievements and historical culture.

By 1980, Japan's economic growth had become too prodigious and globally consequential to be contained within the shell of political passivity and dependency imposed by the U.S. Occupation. The West had cast Japan as a diplomatically and militarily passive "merchant nation" (*chōnin kokka*), but the reality of its global economic ascendancy, set against the relative decline of American economic and political might in the world, invited the Japanese to reexamine the roots of their postwar achievements.

Earlier self-assessments had assigned much of the credit for Japan's growth to the reforming and helping hand of the United States. National pride in the new economy had been muted by a sense that it could not have been achieved without that help. But by the late 1970s, Japan's global economic power was achieving such stand-alone integrity that the Americans themselves began to search the story of Japan's postwar success for lessons that would help America catch up to the emerging Japanese superstate. (See Herman Kahn's 1970 book by that title.)

It was Ezra Vogel's *Japan As Number One: Lessons for America*, published in 1979, that seemed to bring the new view of Japan as an economic pacesetter into sharp focus for Japanese as well as Americans. It suggested that Japanese methods of organizing modern society, especially business, might well set the global standard for national excellence in the twenty-first century. Many Japanese felt romanced by this new image of themselves. Similar lines of argument began to appear in Japanese-language publications. Opinion polls reflected a new confidence in Japan's international position. A wave of what has been called "GNP (gross national product) Nationalism" began to take shape in the early 1980s. The term was coined to identify a widespread recovery of confidence in Japanese culture and society, organized around pride in the business and technological prowess of the Japanese economy, particularly its *kaisha* (companies).

But not every Japanese citizen agreed with this new form of self-understanding. Many critics who comprise Japan's "watchdog opposition" took exception to the relatively uncritical celebration of Japan's "unique society" that was released along with this new economic achievement–based confidence. They feared that an unbridled economic pride might gradually revive illusions about the moral superiority of various prewar native cultural traditions.

The new mood of economic nationalism seemed to release the Japanese people from restraints on proposals to (1) revise the Occupation-imposed Constitution (particularly Article 9, forbidding war and military forces); (2) rewrite textbook descriptions of Japanese aggression in Asia during World War II (conservatives wanted a more neutral description inserted to replace words such as "aggression" and "invasion"); and (3) revive Yasukuni Shrine in Tokyo as the national memorial site for Japan's war dead (Yasukuni had been a centerpiece in the prewar system of ultranationalist State Shinto). It also was possible in the 1980s to detect increasing affirmations of Japanese cultural uniqueness and racial superiority. Some of the former found expression in serious new philosophical treatises on Shinto, while the latter manifested itself in occasional racist gaffs by Japanese politicians drawing unfavorable comparisons between American diversity and Japanese homogeneity.

But none of this search for a more native and independent source of self-understanding would have acquired the aggressive and even arrogant tone that characterized it by the end of 1970s had it not been for what has been termed "pressure nationalism," emerging from the increasingly contentious trade relationship with the United States over the course of the decade. The U.S. economy had been sliding into the red since 1970, in almost direct proportion to the growth of Japanese import penetration in the American market. America responded to this loss of competitive edge by externalizing most of the blame in Japan's direction.

Japan conceded the accuracy of some of the U.S. criticism of its business practices and proceeded, from 1985 onward, to move more production facilities to the United States and to offer market concessions and incentives to U.S. businesses dealing in the Japanese market. But the U.S. trade deficit and the damage to U.S. industries through sectoral unemployment continued without much abatement. American criticism of Japan's economic nationalism grew virulent, and Japanese critics grew indignant. U.S. demands to reopen markets encountered grudging Japanese concessions coupled with the protest that the United States was using Japan as a scapegoat to conceal its own problems of domestic economic decline.

Indignation over unjust outside pressure finally found its way to publication in *The Japan That Can Say No* (1989, English translation, 1991) by Morita Akio and Ishihara Shintarō. If Vogel's book had enabled Japan to say yes to itself about the world-class value of its economic achievements, Ishihara's book, published just 10 years later, marked the advent of Japan's ability to say no to American trade pressure and, more generally, to resist American attempts to limit Japanese foreign policy. Ishihara's views have been characterized by many Japanese as extreme, but others have acknowledged privately that he said what many had been thinking but were hesitant to say publicly: "that Japan is getting tired of being pushed around."

Just days before the publication of the Ishihara book, the longest reign in the world's oldest continuing monarchy ended with the death of Emperor Hirohito. If the Ishihara book reflected Japan's new-found independence born of anger over U.S. economic demands, the public reaction to the changing of the imperial guard also affirmed a strong continuation of public support for Japan's most ancient of all nationalisms. Public opinion polls suggested a marginal increase in the already strong public support for the institution of monarchy and a strong increase in the degree of public identification with the new emperor.

But this trend seemed to have little connection to the more indignant forms of nationalism expressed by the likes of Ishihara. The emperor remained above the politics of GNP pressure nationalism, secure in his role as benevolent symbol of Japanese unity. In fact, the attitude and behavior of the Heisei Emperor (Akihito) and his generation of the royal family are more in harmony with an emerging liberal and cosmopolitan Japan than with any of the more conservative versions publicized by the more vocal nationalists on the scene.

The course of events in the 1980s seemed to bring the postwar development of Japanese nationalism to a kind of crossroads by the early 1990s, indicated by a detectable rise in the respectability of nativist philosophical and aesthetic research. Some young Japanese, at times classified by the Japanese themselves as a new breed (*shinjinrui*), had taken even stronger anti-American nationalist positions than Ishihara had. Greatly increased was the belief that Japan's strength lay in the racial and cultural homogeneity of its community as compared with the United States, which many Japanese perceived to be in decline because of its racial and cultural diversity. All of this meant that pressure nationalism could conceivably drive Japan defensively inward in its search for self-understanding and, to some extent, away from the early 1980s belief in Japan as a model for other countries.

Yet there was always the brute reality for Japan of what has been called "outward dependency." It cannot afford, nor do most of its people seek, retreat into a purely Japanese world. Its economy and society are perennially drawn out into the world of other countries, which continue to whittle away at the all-Japanese home base through migration and business initiatives in Japan.

Japanese nationalism in the early 1990s had a high side that was not fueled by indignation but that saw Japan as a proud, generous creator of unprecedented triumphs in nonmilitary technology. It was hoped that this technology would help developing countries and that it would achieve such distinctions in design and function that technological prowess would come to be regarded as Japan's world-class contribution to international culture and to the global economy.

Despite its defensiveness and a residual tendency to sink into xenophobia, Japan has moved beyond narrowly traditional or economic forms of self-understanding to a more cosmopolitan confidence in its national style and a more thorough domestic acceptance of its moral obligations to the rest of the world. GNP nationalism was being refined and superseded in the last decade of the twentieth century by a more philosophically and morally complete formula. The pressure nationalism of the 1980s might continue to produce some distortions of national identity in the direction of prewar xenophobia, but, in the long run, the secularizing forces of global economic interdependency are more likely to carry Japan in a cosmopolitan direction.

Bradford L. Simcock

Bibliography

Ishihara, Shintarō. *The Japan That Can Say No.* New York: Simon and Schuster, 1991.

Kahn, Herman. *The Emerging Japanese Superstate: Challenge and Response.* Englewood-Cliffs, NJ: Prentice-Hall, 1970.

Katō, Shūichi. "GNP Nationalism on the Upswing." *Japan Quarterly* (January–March 1988), 2–7.

Vogel, Ezra F. *Japan As No. 1: Lessons for America.* Cambridge: Harvard University Press, 1979.

N

Nishida Kitarō (1870–1945)

Philosopher and teacher. Born in Ishikawa Prefecture and reared in Kanazawa, he earned a degree in philosophy from Tokyo University in 1894. After a year of unemployment, he married and began his teaching career on the Noto Peninsula. In 1896, Nishida began teaching at the Fourth Higher School in Kanazawa.

Overwhelmed by family problems and the responsibilities of family life, Nishida took a teaching position in Yamaguchi, away from his family. While there, he developed an interest in Zen and began visiting Zen temples regularly to meditate. In 1899, he returned to Kanazawa, made peace with his family, and resumed his teaching position at the Fourth Higher School. In 1910, Nishida became an assistant professor of philosophy at Kyoto University; in 1911, he published his first major work, *Zen no kenkyū* (A Study of Good), which established the foundation for his philosophy of "pure experience," a category that undergirds all other human characteristics.

Even after his retirement in 1928, Nishida continued to publish works that refined his philosophy and applied a logical system of thought to Japan's Buddhist-influenced intellectual traditions. Nishida's school has been recognized as the first system of Japanese philosophy to develop independently from Western thought, and, as such, it has influenced many of Japan's contemporary philosophers.

James L. Huffman

Bibliography

Viglielmo, Valdo Humbert. "Nishida Kitarō: The Early Years." *Tradition and Modernization in Japanese Culture.* Princeton, NJ: Princeton University Press, 1971.

Nishida Mitsugi (also Zei, Mitsugu) (1901–37)

Right-wing activist. Born in Tottori Prefecture, he joined the military as a youth, and, early in the 1920s, organized his own secret political discussion group while studying at the Army Academy in Tokyo. After three years as a cavalry officer, he resigned from the army in 1925 and spent his remaining years agitating on behalf of nationalist causes. A follower of Kita Ikki and a zealous propagandist rather than a theoretician, he worked most actively among young soldiers, helping in the late 1920s to form the Young Officers' Movement (Seinen Shōkō

Undō), an informal association of like-minded army patriots. Nishida formed or joined numerous organizations, including the terrorist Hakurōkai (Society of the White Wolf) and the Nihon Kokumintō (National People's Party of Japan). He refused to support the May 15, 1932, uprising in which Prime Minister Inukai Tsuyoshi was assassinated (and was the object of a rightist assassination attempt as a result), but he helped defend Aizawa Saburō, the ultranationalist who assassinated General Nagata Tetsuzan in 1935, and he played an active supportive role in the young army officers' unsuccessful February 26, 1936, coup d'état. Along with Kita, he was convicted and executed on August 19, 1937, for his role in that uprising.

James L. Huffman

Bibliography

Storry, Richard. *The Double Patriots: A Study of Japanese Nationalism.* Westport, CT: Greenwood Press, 1973.

Nishimura Shigeki (1828–1902)

Moral philosopher, enlightener. A native of Chiba Prefecture, he published more than 300 books and articles in the Meiji era (1868–1912) calling for modernization and enlightenment based on a Confucian moral foundation. He was born into a samurai family that served Hotta Masayoshi, a leading late-Tokugawa official. In the early 1850s, he studied Western learning under Sakuma Shōzan and became an advocate of a strong national-defense policy. He opposed the Meiji Restoration in 1868, but quickly concluded that the new government was permanent and must be supported. He wrote prolifically on such subjects as moral science and Western history, economics and education. He also became one of the more articulate members of the Meirokusha (Meiji Six Society), which joined some of the country's most influential young officials to discuss Japan's development and response to the West.

Nishimura entered the Education Ministry in 1873, and two years later, began giving lectures to the emperor on Western writings, a task he continued informally for more than a decade. In 1887, he published two well-received books, *Nihon dōtoku ron* (On Japanese Morality) and *Fujo kagami* (Mirror for Women), and the following year he became president of Joshi Gakushuin, an institution that eventually became Gakushuin University. He was made a peer in 1890.

More than most men of the Meiji era, Nishimura combined enlightenment zeal with a profound respect for Confucian values. He advocated personal freedom, democracy, and human rights, calling for a constitution and the early creation of a popular assembly. At the same time, he maintained that, unless education and politics were grounded in traditional Confucian values such as loyalty and public-mindedness, progress would come to naught. His Nihon Kōdōkai (Japan Society for Expansion of the Way), founded in 1887 to promote ethical training, eventually had more than 10,000 members.

James L. Huffman

Bibliography

Shively, Donald H. "Nishimura Shigeki: A Confucian View of Modernization." *Changing Japanese Attitudes Toward Modernization.* Ed. Marius B. Jansen. Princeton, NJ: Princeton University Press, 1965.

Nitobe Inazō (1862–1933)

Educator, author, and public servant. Born into a high-ranking samurai family of the Nambu domain in Morioka, Nitobe entered the Sapporo Agricultural School in 1877, where he became influenced by Christianity. In 1884, he left for studies at Johns Hopkins University in the United States and at several universities (1887–89) in Germany; he received a doctorate at Halle University, in agricultural economics. In Philadelphia, he married a Quaker, Mary Elkington, which strengthened his ties to America. His later career was varied. Nitobe won international acclaim with his best-selling book in English, *Bushidō, the Soul of Japan,* in which he explained Japanese progress by an examination of traditional samurai values. He later held positions as a colonial administrator in Taiwan (1901–03); headmaster at the prestigious First Higher School, formerly Tokyo University Preparatory School (1906–13); professor of colonial policy at Tokyo Imperial University (1913–18); first president of Tokyo Women's College (1918–23); undersecretary-general in the League of Nations (1920–26); member of the House of Peers (1926–33); and Japanese chairman of the Institute of Pacific Relations (IPR; 1929–33), an organization created to improve relationships among nations bordering the Pacific Ocean.

Nitobe Inazō. Asahi Shimbun Photo.

As an educator, Nitobe exerted a strong moral influence on youth who later became prominent leaders in different sectors of Japanese society. He is remembered for his attempts to serve as an intercultural mediator, what he called a "bridge over the Pacific." A staunch supporter of internationalism, Nitobe saw his later years marred by changing political circumstances in Asia. After the outbreak of Japan's aggression in Manchuria in September 1931, Nitobe lectured in the United States. Although he advocated international cooperation and mutual understanding, he also supported the Japanese position in China, a stance that tarnished his subsequent reputation as an internationalist. He died in Victoria, British Columbia, while heading the Japanese delegation to the 5th Conference of the Institute of Pacific Relations.

George M. Oshiro

Bibliography

Howes, John F., ed. *Nitobe Inazō: Japan's Bridge Across the Pacific.* Boulder, CO: Westview Press, 1995.

Nitobe, Inazō. *Bushidō: The Soul of Japan.* Rutland, VT: Charles E. Tuttle, 1969.

Uchikawa, Eiichirō. *Nitobe, Inazō: The Twilight Years.* Tokyo: Kyōbunkan, 1985.

Nixon Shocks (*Nikuson Shokku*)

Series of episodes in 1971, in which U.S. President Richard Nixon shocked the Japanese by taking unilateral actions on matters affecting both countries. The result was a sharp rise in tensions, leaving many Japanese with the impression that their country was no longer central to U.S. Asian policies, and pushing Japan toward a more independent foreign policy.

The first shock came on July 15, when Nixon announced his impending Beijing trip, ending a long period of U.S.-Chinese estrangement. The announcement created a sensation in Japan, because Nixon had not consulted the Japanese, even though Japan had, for two decades, reluctantly followed the U.S. lead on Chinese relations—and even though the Americans had always promised close coordination of the two countries' China policies. In many ways, Nixon's move had a positive effect, by freeing the Japanese to develop a long-desired closer relationship with the People's Republic of China; indeed, Japan resumed full diplomatic relations with China one year later. But a new sense of estrangement from the United States was undeniable.

That sense was heightened by a second shock, in August, when Nixon announced a temporary 10 percent surcharge, aimed primarily at Japan, on many U.S. imports and ended the gold exchange, in effect allowing the yen exchange rate to rise against the dollar. Once again, the decisions were made without serious consultations with Tokyo, and the economic impact was considerable. Many of the trade issues were settled following a meeting between Nixon and Prime Minister Satō Eisaku that fall, but the value of the yen, which had been held artificially at 360 to the dollar ever since the end of World War II in 1945, now increased precipitously, rising by nearly 17 percent to 300 yen per dollar immediately and to 230 yen per dollar in February 1973.

Since 30 percent of Japan's trade volume was with the United States, the economic effect on Japan was significant. Even more important was the psychological impact. Nixon's unilateral moves may have helped initiate needed movement toward a more independent foreign policy in Japan, but they also raised questions about Japan's importance to the United States and thus became a touch point for the tensions that would plague U.S.-Japanese relations over the next decades.

James L. Huffman

Bibliography

Welfield, John. *An Empire in Eclipse: Japan in the Postwar American Alliance System*. London: Athlone Press, 1988.

Nogi Maresuke (1849–1912)

Military hero. A native of Chōshū domain, Nogi spent almost his entire career in the military, winning the adulation of the Japanese people for his personification of old-time samurai values. His record on the battlefield was mixed. In the unsuccessful Satsuma Rebellion of 1877, the regiment under his command lost its standard to the rebel forces, and his poorly executed attacks on Port Arthur during the Russo-Japanese War (1904–05) resulted in 56,000 casualties before General Kodama Gentarō was sent in to assist him. At the same time, he received widespread acclaim for his leadership of the 1st Infantry Brigade that captured the Liaodong Peninsula and Port Arthur during the Sino-Japanese War (1894–95).

Mistakes notwithstanding, Nogi moved constantly upward in his army career. In 1885, he was promoted to major-general; in 1895, he was named lieutenant-general and baron; in 1904, he became a general. He served (rather ineffectively) as governor-general of Taiwan from 1896 to 1898, and, in 1907, he was appointed director of the prestigious Peers School, a position that he used to instill patriotism and spartan values in the country's young elite.

Nogi was loved by the public primarily for his values. When his two sons were killed in the Russo-Japanese War, he remained stoic because they had given their lives for the emperor. And when the Meiji Emperor died in 1912, he and his wife committed suicide to follow their leader to his grave. The act created a national sensation, exerting a powerful impact not only on the masses but on the country's intellectuals, many of whom were prompted by the suicide to examine more openly questions about what "Japaneseness" meant.

James L. Huffman

Bibliography

Peattie, Mark. "The Last Samurai: The Military Career of Nogi Maresuke." *Princeton Papers on East Asian Studies: Japan*. Vol. 1 (1972).

Nomura Bōtōni (1806–67)

Poet and restoration leader. Born in Fukuoka Prefecture, she and her husband, Nomura Sadatsura, spent a major portion of their lives in a mountain villa, writing prose and poetry. Bōtōni was a student of the prominent five-line *waka*-style poet Ōkuma Kotomichi (1798–1868). Her poetry was both concrete and philosophical, and in her later years it reflected an intense, nativist love of the emperor and Japan, which led her into active support for the anti-Tokugawa, antiforeign forces in the 1860s. A high moment came when she was able to visit the imperial capital of Kyoto in 1861 to make obeisance to her emperor.

Bōtōni developed close relationships with such activists for the Meiji Restoration as Sanjō Sanetomi, Saigō Takamori, and Takasugi Shinsaku, who hid in her mountain home in 1864. She was captured, placed under house arrest, then banished to a small cell on Himeshima island in 1865 for her restorationist activities. Rescued from prison in October 1866, she died one year later.

James L. Huffman

Bibliography

Huber, Thomas. *Revolutionary Origins of Modern Japan*. Stanford, CA: Stanford University Press, 1981.

Nonchurch Christian Movement (*Mukyōkai*)

A Japanese group, attributed to the early Christian leader Uchimura Kanzō (1861–1930), whose name adds to the word *kyōkai* (church) the negative prefix *mu* (without or lacking). Uchimura coined the term to describe his own disillusionment with institutional Christianity ("I became a man without a church"), then later used it to describe his own and his followers' attitude toward ecclesiasticism.

Followers consider Mukyōkai particularly appropriate to Japanese sensibilities. It consists of individuals organized around a *sensei* (teacher) who conducts Sunday meetings featuring interpretations of a biblical passage and ending with exhortations that followers incorporate the lesson of the passage in their own lives. The movement's followers identify themselves as Christians for attempting to follow the teachings of the Bible. No group maintains a formal relation with or to any other group, nor do any sacraments, creeds, or confessions join them. Uchimura considered organizational elements of Christianity to be products of Western custom rather than of biblical instruction. Japanese Christianity, in his view, could embrace only Japanese individuals, with their native ethics, who prayerfully linked themselves to God and Jesus through the study of the Bible.

The assertion that Christian salvation did not necessarily require affiliation with the Western church offended many missionaries linked to specific denominations. Uchimura's claims seemed both presumptuous and nationalistic. His leading disciple, Yanaihara Tadao, orchestrated Mukyōkai's nationalistic overtones in the late 1930s in opposition to the jingoism generated by the Pacific War (1941–45). In the mid-1990s, the movement had about 35,000 adherents.

John F. Howes

Bibliography
Caldarola, Carlo. *Christianity, the Japanese Way.* Leiden: Brill, 1979.

Normanton Incident
(*Norumanton Gō Jiken*)
On October 21, 1886, the British cargo ship Normanton sank off the Kii Peninsula. The captain, John William Drake, and his 26 crew members were rescued, but the 23 Japanese passengers, unable to get into the lifeboats, all drowned. On November 9, the British consular court in Kobe found the captain and crew innocent of wrongdoing. The story, which was reported widely in the Japanese press, raised an outcry against extraterritoriality and the system of unequal treaties, which deprived the Japanese of jurisdiction in legal issues involving foreigners. The British consulate in Yokohama thereupon reopened the case and announced on December 8 that Drake would have to serve a three-month jail sentence. The crew members were found innocent once again. The new verdict temporarily muted the clamor, but the episode stimulated a growing antitreaty movement, which led to increasingly widespread attacks on the Japanese government for not acting more forcefully in its dealings with the Western powers.

James L. Huffman

Bibliography
Jones, F.C. *Extraterritoriality in Japan.* New Haven, CT: Yale University Press, 1931.

N

O

Obata Toshirō (1884–1947)

Army officer and minister of state, a native of Kochi Prefecture. He was a Russian-affairs expert who in the 1920s advocated the occupation of Manchuria and the curtailment of the Chōshū region's influence in the army. He was close to reformist leaders such as Mori Kaku and Prime Minster Konoe Fumimaro and played an important role in the War Ministry during the early 1930s. From 1934 to 1935, he served as commander of the Army War College; in the late 1930s, he urged Japan to confront the Soviet threat by strengthening its military forces and improving relations with China and the West.

Although considered a member of the army's more extreme Kōdōha (Imperial Way Faction), Obata opposed the political activism of young Kōdōha officers in the 1930s, including the unsuccessful February 26 uprising that paralyzed Tokyo for several days in 1936. He left military service that year, consistently opposed the war with China; in 1944, he participated in the ouster of Prime Minister Tōjō Hideki. He served for two months (August–October 1945) as minister of state in Higashikuni Naruhiko's "surrender cabinet" at the end of World War II.

Jacob Kovalio

Bibliography

Kovalio, Jacob. "Personnel Policy of Army Minister Araki Sadao." *Tradition and Modern Japan.* Ed. P.G. O'Neill. Kent, UK: Paul Norbury, 1981.

Occupation (Allied)

The Allied Occupation of Japan, which lasted six-and-a-half years (September 2, 1945–April 28, 1952) following Japan's surrender in World War II, was a major watershed in Japanese history, in which the victorious Allies tried to restructure Japanese political life and society in accordance with the principles of liberal democracy. That their efforts bore significant fruit may be attributed in large part to latent and newly kindled Japanese aspirations for reform. As Japan's first experience of subjugation to a foreign conqueror, the Occupation was naturally a challenge to nationalism.

Occupation policies were drawn up in Washington, D.C., and issued in Japan by the Supreme Commander for the Allied Powers (SCAP), General Douglas MacArthur. Although an international Far Eastern Commission was theoretically responsible for overall direction, the Occupation was, in reality, a U.S.-dominated enterprise. The decision to conduct an indirect Occupation left the Japanese government (unlike Occupied Germany) largely intact to manage the day-to-day affairs of state and to enforce Occupation directives. The imperial institution remained intact when the victors perceived its usefulness in securing public support for reform. Nonetheless, in a massive purge, SCAP barred more than 200,000 military, government, and business leaders from occupying positions of influence. Organizations and publications deemed ultranationalist and/ or feudal were banned. Even the martial arts, classical *kabuki* plays, and the Japanese written language offered initial targets for rectification. The controversial Tokyo War Crimes Trial of 1946–48 indicted 28 officials for having conspired to wage war. Seven defendants, including former Prime Minister Tōjō Hideki, were executed; others served prison terms. Separate military tribunals sentenced about 700 less-prominent war criminals to death.

The Occupation period may be divided into three phases. The first, covering the fall of 1945, saw the dismantling of the overseas Japanese empire, the disarming of troops, and the destruction of Japanese war potential. At this time, the repatriation of more than 6 million troops and civilians to their Japanese homeland was begun. Expressions of Japanese militarism and nationalism—evinced in school textbooks, music, cinema, and other areas—were censored. Shinto rites were dissociated from affairs of state, and prewar rituals of nationalism, such as the public reading of the 1890 Imperial Rescript on Education, were proscribed. Use of the Rising Sun flag (*hinomaru*) was prohibited until New Year's Day 1949, and the meager products of Japanese cottage industry were sold abroad under the label "Made in Occupation Japan."

The second phase, a time of intense reform, extended from late 1945 to early 1947. The constitution, rewritten on the basis of a draft prepared by SCAP's Government Section, placed the locus of sovereignty in the people rather than the emperor. The cabinet, in imitation of British parliamentary practice, was made responsible to the Diet (legislature). The electorate was enlarged by lowering the voting age to 20 and including women for the first time. Revised marriage, labor, and welfare laws initiated new patterns of rights for individuals. Ownership of farmland passed to the tiller, while owners of large land holdings suffered confiscatory settlements.

Not all reforms initiated by the idealistically motivated Occupation authorities took hold in Japanese society. Noteworthy failures were programs to decentralize education and establish a U.S.-style civil service. The prewar *zaibatsu* (financial cliques) were broken up and ceased to function as family corporations, but powerful informal ties among units of formerly unitary enterprises moderated the effectiveness of economic deconcentration.

The new 1947 Constitution toppled many of the edifices of prewar and wartime nationalism. Article 9 renounced Japan's right to wage war and banned the military services. The emperor was relegated to the position of a state symbol, and his actions were made subject to the advice and approval of the cabinet. The constitutional preamble imposed on Japan peaceful cooperation with all countries and ensured Japan's obedience to universal "laws of political morality."

Much scholarly controversy surrounds the third phase, a time of economic rehabilitation and remilitarization from early 1947 to the end of the Occupation in 1952. While leftists enjoyed unprecedented freedom in the first two years of the Occupation, many became subjected to a "Red Purge" in 1947. Labor's right to strike was compromised, and the pacifist Article 9 of the constitution was interpreted loosely to allow the introduction of the Self-Defense Force. Missions of economic experts from the United States (such as a commission led by Detroit banker Joseph Dodge in 1948) offered sweeping recommendations for economic stabilization and reconstruction. Some historians view this proceeding as an abrupt "reverse course" in Occupation policy generated by the Cold War; others see it as consistent with strategy established at the beginning of the Occupation. Relief programs in the early Occupation years did help stave off starvation and epidemics, but genuine industrial recovery came about only as a byproduct of the Korean War, which began in June 1950.

The Occupation formally ended when the San Francisco Peace Treaty was implemented in May 1952. Most Japanese credit the Occupation with forcing needed changes that Japanese society, bound by privilege and tradition, was incapable of implementing of its own volition. Others, however, criticize the forcible measures, purges, censorship, and indoctrination employed by the sponsors of democracy. In any case, the postwar period opened the door to an influx of new culture, much of it sponsored by the Occupiers, that permanently altered Japan.

The Occupation is a common target for nationalistic revisionists, who view it as a forced ordeal in which Japan was stripped of essential elements of its sovereignty and indigenous cultural expression. Particularly irate are the literary conservatives who decry the destruction of a generation of postwar literary creativity at the hands of SCAP censors. Right-wing spokesmen urge the writing of a new Japanese constitution, cleansed of alien concepts and wording and assertive of the sovereign right of armed self-defense. Most Japanese, however, are conscious of the ways in which they have directly benefited from Occupation reforms and are reluctant to tamper with the constitution and Occupation-era legislation for fear of sacrificing some valued self-interest.

Thomas W. Burkman

Bibliography
Burkman, Thomas W., ed. *The Occupation of Japan: Arts and Culture.* Norfolk, VA: MacArthur Memorial, 1988.

Cohen, Theodore. *Remaking Japan: The American Occupation As New Deal.* New York: Free Press, 1987.

Inoue, Kyoko. *MacArthur's Japanese Constitution: A Linguistic and Cultural Study of Its Making.* Chicago: University of Chicago Press, 1991.

Ward, Robert E., and Sakamoto Yoshikazu, eds. *Democratizing Japan: The Allied Occupation.* Honolulu: University of Hawaii Press, 1987.

October Incident (*Jūgatsu Jiken*)

Attempted military coup; also called the Imperial Flag Revolution (Kinki Kakumei). After the Manchurian Incident in September 1931, right-wing officers in the Sakurakai (Cherry Blossom Society), led by Colonel Hashimoto Kingorō and civilian extremists such as Ōkawa Shūmei, decided to carry out a coup d'état on October 21. They intended to bomb key locations by air, assassinate the prime minister and other top officials, capture metropolitan police headquarters, declare martial law—and force the military establishment under General Araki Sadao to seize the reins of government, thus bringing the party-cabinet system to an end. Araki refused to cooperate, however, and the plot was uncovered on October 17. The leaders were arrested, but the incident was kept from the public. Hashimoto was sentenced to a mere 20-day house arrest, and the other leaders were left unpunished, due to what were called their sincere, patriotic motives. The authorities endeavored to break up the planning group, and the Sakurakai itself disbanded shortly thereafter. The incident encouraged increased military involvement in politics, particularly when Araki was appointed minister of war that December.

James L. Huffman

Bibliography
Yoshihashi, Takehiko. *Conspiracy at Mukden.* New Haven, CT: Yale University Press, 1963.

Ōe Kenzaburō (1935–)

Novelist, winner of the 1994 Nobel Prize in Literature. Born in Ehime on the island of Shikoku, Ōe came to maturity under the impact of major transforming influences, including the world's first atomic bombings, of Hiroshima and Nagasaki, in 1945; the promulgation of the 1947 Constitution; and the writings of existential philosophers like France's Jean Paul Sartre. Ōe's work had already begun to attract notice in prominent literary circles by the time of his graduation from Tokyo University in 1959.

A string of works critiquing the shallowness of society and espousing liberal causes early in the 1960s made Ōe a target of the intellectual mainstream and drew special fire from right-wing nationalists. He was married in 1960, and the birth, in 1963, of a disabled son, Hikaru, produced *A Personal Matter*, the story of a father's bitter struggle with personal tragedy, which won the 1964 Shinchō Literary Prize. By the 1970s, Ōe was focusing on such angst-ridden issues as the atomic-bomb victims in Hiroshima and Nagasaki, the denial of power and respect to the Okinawans, and the increasingly oppressive nature of Japan's political system. His 1974 novel *The Silent Cry* won the prestigious Tanizaki Jun'ichirō Prize. His Nobel Prize speech, "Japan the Ambiguous—and Me," criticized his homeland for its failure to achieve genuine democracy.

James L. Huffman

Bibliography
Ōe, Kenzaburō. *A Personal Matter*. Tokyo: Charles Tuttle, 1969.

Ōi Kentarō (1843–1922)

Political leader in the mid-Meiji popular-rights movement. Born a samurai in Buzen domain (modern-day Oita Prefecture), Ōi pursued Western studies during the 1860s at Nagasaki and Edo (now Tokyo), where he became particularly influenced by French political thought. As a young man, Ōi held minor positions in government but resigned in 1876 to participate in the budding popular-rights movement. In the newly formed Jiyūtō (Liberal Party), he led the radical faction; as a lawyer, he defended political activists in the popular uprisings of the early 1880s at Takada, Fukushima, and Kabasan.

Ōi was imprisoned for his deep involvement in the unsuccessful 1885 Osaka Incident, in which some liberal civilians plotted a military uprising in Korea; after his release in 1889, he rejoined the Jiyūtō but departed when party leader Itagaki Taisuke began to compromise with the government. In 1892, Ōi founded and became president of the Tōyō Jiyūtō (Asian Liberal Party), which advocated universal suffrage, land-tax reform, and help for tenants. A forceful critic of the Meiji government, he continued assisting the underprivileged. Although his influence in public movements decreased after 1898 when he shifted his focus from politics to direct work among the lower classes, he maintained his support of democratic tendencies. In foreign affairs, he advocated an activist international policy. An avid writer, Ōi published many works on politics and economics.

George M. Oshiro

Bibliography
Jansen, Marius. "Ōi Kentarō: Radicalism and Chauvinism." *Far Eastern Quarterly.* Vol. 2, No. 3 (May 1952), pp. 305–16.

Oil Crisis (Sekiyu Kiki)

Rising prices and a resultant political-economic crisis that followed the 1973 oil embargo imposed by the Organization of Petroleum Exporting Countries (OPEC). Dependence on oil imports in the early 1970s left the Japanese manufacturing sector vulnerable to embargo-induced price increases. When rapid inflation followed an increase of 31.6 percent in 1974 wholesale oil prices, Japanese leaders initiated national policies for comprehensive security and sought diversified energy resources that assured adequate supplies and stockpiles and stable oil prices.

Japanese responses to the oil crisis were belated but deliberate attempts to safeguard national goals of economic growth. At first, internal political divisions hampered the achievement of a unified national strategy. The ruling Liberal Democratic Party of Prime Minister Tanaka Kakuei was committed to the Archipelago Plan, a government spending initiative begun in 1972–73 to revive the prosperity of the Japanese islands through public works, education, and welfare programs. Such public spending combined with the wage demands of labor unions to intensify inflation. The crisis, which soon threatened to eliminate the past consensus on Japanese economic goals, necessitated a reassessment of national objectives.

By the later 1970s, the national response had produced a qualified success. Labor unions modified their wage demands in exchange for employment guarantees and slower rising prices. The era of double-digit Japanese growth ended, but the economy expanded in the 3–5 percent range, and a national accommodation followed. By 1979 and the second OPEC oil embargo, Japanese policy sheltered the economy from severe impacts, and the term *sekiyu kiki* was hardly applicable. Japanese response to the first oil crisis, while delayed and disorganized in the early 1970s, proved more effective in assuring economic growth and recovery than the response of other oil-consuming countries.

Stephen J. Anderson

Bibliography
Dore, Ronald, et al. *Structural Adjustment in Japan, 1970–1982.* Geneva: International Labour Office, 1986.
Samuels, Richard J. *The Business of the Japanese State.* Ithaca, NY: Cornell University Press, 1988.

Okada Keisuke (1868–1952)

Admiral and prime minister. Born in Fukui Prefecture and an 1889 graduate of the Naval War College, he was promoted to admiral in 1924 and became navy minister three years later in the Tanaka Giichi cabinet (1927–29). In 1930, Okada won the admiration of government moderates for his role in bringing key naval officials to support Japan's conciliatory stance at the London Naval Conference. After two more years as navy minister (1932–34), he became prime minister in 1934. Always a moderate within the military establishment, Okada was selected to curb the military extremists. He was unsuccessful, however, particularly when the rightists forced scholar Minobe Tatsukichi out of the Diet (legislature) in 1935 for having formulated his theory that the emperor is an organ of the state. Rebel young military officers thought they had assassinated Okada during the unsuccessful February 26, 1936, uprising. In fact, they had mistakenly murdered his brother-in-law. Okada and his entire cabinet resigned as a result of the incident. Okada remained a critic of army tactics and played a key role in toppling the Tōjō Hideki cabinet in 1944.

James L. Huffman

Bibliography
Shillony, Ben-Ami. *Revolt in Japan: The Young Officers and the February, 26, 1936, Incident.* Princeton, NJ: Princeton University Press, 1973.

Okakura Kakuzō (pen name Tenshin) (1862–1914)

Art critic and philosopher whom the novelist Shimazaki Tōson regarded as one of the archetypal romantics of the Meiji era (1868–1912). An objective explication of his family background, personality traits, command of English, and rapport with foreigners has yet to be extracted from the prevailing tales of his ancestry and youth in Yokohama and Tokyo. Despite an early interest in literature, art, and music, he acquiesced, on graduation from Tokyo University in 1880, to enter the Ministry of Education. He spent 10 years there as a bureaucrat and then eight more as principal of the newly established Tokyo Art School (Tokyo Bijutsu Gakkō), which originally catered exclusively to the traditional arts. Throughout this period, his career waxed and waned with those of his mentors, the educators Hamao Arata and Kuku Ryūichi. While he was the principal at the Art School, neither his program nor his pupils could compete with those of the other traditional schools, nor could he thwart the establishment in 1896 of a Department of Western Art headed by Kuroda Kiyoteru, who two years later helped engineer his ouster from the school.

It was principally his post-1900 travels, his position after 1905 as curator of Chinese and Japanese art at the Boston Museum of Fine Arts, and the publication, originally in English, of his non-fiction works *The Book of Tea* (1906), *The Ideals of the East* (1903), and *The Awakening of Japan* (1904) that gained him recognition at home and abroad. Hamao secured his reinstatement into the Japanese art world by facilitating his reappointment to numerous committees of the Ministry of Education during the late-Meiji years. He spent much of his last half decade traveling back and forth between assignments in Tokyo and the United States. His reputation was enhanced by the many memorials and publications that appeared following his death, which coincided with the reorganization of the Japan Fine Arts Academy (Nihon Bijutsuin) in 1914 and the growing popularity of his pupils during the period between the World Wars. The Japanese government's endorsement during World War II of his tenet, "Asia is One" and Japan is its treasure house, assured him a new audience that was enlarged by his romantic appeal to a sympathetic postwar audience eager to foster better understanding between East and West.

Ellen T. Conant

Bibliography

Maruyama, Masao. "Fukuzawa, Uchimura, and Okakura." *Developing Economies.* Vol. 4, No. 4 (December 1966), 594–611.

Ōkawa Shūmei (1886–1957)

Right-wing activist and ideologue. Born in Yamagata Prefecture, he studied Confucianism and Western religions at Tokyo Imperial University, graduating in 1911. Contact with Tokyo-based activists in the Indian independence movement induced him to adopt a strong stance against Western colonialism in the 1910s; by the end of the decade, he had begun to find in Japan's own traditional values solutions to contemporary problems. Moving even further to the right, in 1919 Ōkawa joined Kita Ikki and others in forming the Yūzonsha (Endure Society), which called for a reorganization of Japanese society along traditional lines.

During the 1920s, Ōkawa broke with the radical Kita but lectured and wrote widely on behalf of nationalist ideas. He helped found several right-wing societies, including the Kōchisha (Activist Society), and wrote the influential *Nihon oyobi nihonjin no michi* (Japan and the Way of the Japanese), which was published in 1926.

Ōkawa served two years in prison for his behind-the-scenes role in the May 15, 1932, plot against the government. In the years just before World War II, he joined the Research Department of the South Manchurian Railway; served on the faculty of, and lectured at, Hōsei University; and wrote prolifically, advocating a leadership role for Japan in Asia. One of only two civilians charged with war crimes after World War II, he was declared insane and his case was dismissed. He continued to write and lecture for another decade.

James L. Huffman

Bibliography

Takeuchi, Yoshimi. "Profile of Asian Minded Man X: Ōkawa Shūmei." *Developing Economies.* Vol. 7, No. 3 (1969), 367–79.

Ōkubo Toshimichi (1830–78)

The 1868 Meiji Restoration hero who dominated the new government's modernization policies, which protected Japan from the challenge of European imperialism. Born a lower samurai in Kagoshima, the castle town of Satsuma domain, Ōkubo rose to be chief adviser to the domain's regent in 1862, as Satsuma moved from

Ōkubo Toshimichi. Asahi Shimbun Photo.

Ōkuma Shigenobu. Asahi Shimbun Photo.

cautious support of the ruling Tokugawa government to secret alliance with the anti-Tokugawa domain of Chōshū. His efforts helped to bring about the 1868 Restoration.

As an active councillor in the new Meiji government, Ōkubo helped terminate the feudal system in 1871, joined the Iwakura Mission to America and Europe (1871–73), guided the domestic-reform faction to victory in the cabinet quarrels of 1873, and promoted state-sponsored industrialization to counter the economic challenge of the West. He was assassinated in 1878 by samurai deprived of status through his policies.

This cold and reserved leader was long a pariah in his native Satsuma for his firm suppression of the rebellion of declassed samurai there in the summer of 1877; but, at the centennial of his death, Ōkubo was given belated recognition for his economic policies by the erection of a splendid Ōkubo statue in Kagoshima.

Sidney DeVere Brown

Bibliography

Brown, Sidney D. "Ōkubo Toshimichi: His Political and Economic Policies in Early Meiji Japan." *Journal of Asian Studies*. Vol. 21, No. 2 (February 1962), 183–97.

Iwata, Masakazu. *Ōkubo Toshimichi: The Bismarck of Japan*. Berkeley: University of California Press, 1964.

Ōkuma Shigenobu (1838–1922)

Politician and educator. A native of Saga Prefecture (Hizen domain), he was an early advocate of emperor-centered nationalism and of Japan's special interests and destiny in northeast Asia. Because he distrusted any loyalties that impinged on imperial nationalism, Ōkuma spent his life building nationalist coalitions that transcended social, economic, religious, and regional loyalties. Suspicious of all religions, he advocated a moral system focused on loyalty to the emperor and the nation.

Ōkuma was an early supporter of a British-style constitutional monarchy, believing that such a system would best enable patriotism to filter down to the masses. Throughout most of his career, he envisioned himself as the "loyal opposition" to the government. As the founder of several political parties, he used his influence to move in and out of the government, serving twice as prime minister (1898 and 1914–16) and three times as foreign minister (1888, 1896–97, and 1898).

Ōkuma generally promoted Japanese political, economic, and, ultimately, military expansionism into China. He was a member of the Gunjin Kōenkai (Army Supporters' Association) and the Tōhō Kyōkai (Oriental Society), both of which supported the military's wish to expand into northeast Asia. He supported larger military budgets, and, as prime minister, he proposed a Pan-Asian Ōkuma Doctrine of a Japanese-dominated economic cooperative of Asian peoples. During his second cabinet, Japan entered World War I and foisted the imperialistic Twenty-One Demands on the Chinese government.

Ōkuma was immensely popular with the press (he introduced the practice of the prime minister's press conference in Japan and was the publisher of several newspapers) and with the public at large. An early advocate of Western-style education, he founded Waseda University and was the author of works on education.

Louis G. Perez

Bibliography
Lebra, Joyce. *Ōkuma Shigenobu.* Canberra: Australian National University Press, 1973.

Okumura Ioko (1845–1907)

Founder of the Aikoku Fujinkai (Patriotic Women's Society). Born in Saga Prefecture, into a priestly household of the Higashi Honganji branch of True Pure Land Buddhism, she married, was widowed, remarried, and divorced before returning to her family of birth in 1887. In the 1860s, Okumura and her brother joined Takasugi Gensaku (1839–67) and others to support the imperial cause against the failing Tokugawa regime. After the Meiji Restoration of 1868, Okumura sided with disillusioned former samurai such as Etō Shimpei (1833–74) and Saigō Takamori (1827–77), who left the new government. She favored Japanese involvement in Korea and founded a girls' school there, in Kwangju. In 1900, she joined a Buddhist mission to the Japanese soldiers in China in connection with that summer's Boxer Rebellion; upon her return, she founded the Aikoku Fujinkai to care for wounded soldiers and bereaved families. She recruited support from the imperial family, courtiers, and others who reflected her own romantic vision of the Meiji Restoration and thus staked out a space for female participation in imperial Japan.

Sally A. Hastings

Bibliography
Sievers, Sharon L. *Flowers in Salt: The Beginnings of Feminist Consciousness in Modern Japan.* Stanford, CA: Stanford University Press, 1983.

Olympic Games (1964)

First Olympic Games held in Tokyo, regarded as a symbol of Japan's successful recovery from World War II. The torch for the 1964 Summer

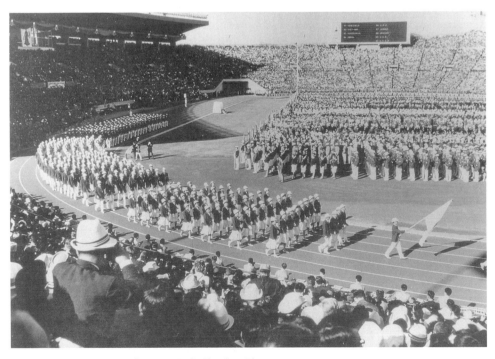

Opening ceremony, 1964 Olympics. Asahi Shimbun Photo.

Olympic Games was lighted by a teenager born in Hiroshima on August 6, 1945, the day the first atomic bomb was dropped. The 1940 Games had been scheduled to be held in Japan but were canceled due to the war in Europe. Now, with Japan awarded the Games again, officials decided to create a showcase. Preparations included the erection of $40 million worth of new sports centers, including a new National Stadium; the construction of Tokyo International Airport; the training of 41,000 workers, including 14,000 flag hoisters; and the building of the world's first bullet train, the Shinkansen connecting Tokyo and Osaka, which was completed 10 days before the opening ceremonies—at a combined cost of $3 billion.

The Games themselves were generally recognized as having been the best managed to that date. A total of 100,000 youths carried the Olympic torch from Mt. Olympus in Greece to Tokyo; more than 6,000 athletes from 94 countries competed; 2 million spectators bought $40 million worth of tickets; and 4,500 reporters covered the games. Japan won gold medals in a record (for Japan) 16 sports, including women's volleyball. The efficient, well-orchestrated conduct of the Games prompted International Olympic Commission President Avery Brundage to say that Japan now ranked first among Olympic nations. For the people of Japan, the widely covered Games were a source of unusual pride, a symbol to the world of Japan's reemergence as a powerful, peace-loving country.

James L. Huffman

Bibliography
Lucas, John. *The Modern Olympic Games.* New York: A.S. Barnes, 1980.

Ono Azusa (1852–86)

Meiji intellectual, political reformer, and educator. Born in Tosa domain, he early broke with the fief and studied from 1871 to 1874 in the United States and England, where he embraced the utilitarian theories of Jeremy Bentham and John Stuart Mill and became an advocate of parliamentary government and civil rights. He served in the Japanese government from 1876 to 1881, first as an official in the Ministry of Justice and then on the Board of Audit. During this time, he became a supporter of Finance Minister Ōkuma Shigenobu and was a key figure in revealing the Hokkaido Colonization Commission Incident, a corruption scandal that caused a split in the government in 1881. He left the government and became the key organizer and theorist of the Rikken Kaishintō (Constitutional Reform Party), which was founded in 1882, and then organized Tokyo Senmon Gakkō, the predecessor of Waseda University, at Ōkuma's request.

Ono was an advocate of increased popular participation in government through representative institutions and British-style political parties. He called for selective modernization that would enable Japan to survive as a unified, independent country while preserving its own traditions and institutions.

His *Kokken hanron* (Outline of the National Constitution, 1882–85) provided the theoretical basis for a new parliamentary institution, political parties, the role of the emperor in the modern Japanese state, and the rights and duties of the people. The work represents a synthesis of Western political theories and traditional Japanese and Chinese concepts of government and was written to provide the theoretical basis for party government and the Kaishintō. It was the most detailed work on modern political theory written in Japan prior to the promulgation of the Meiji Constitution in 1889.

Loyalism, to Ono, was an expression of nationalism, since the emperor was a living symbol of the cultural continuity of the Japanese people and state. Nationalism implied unity, an end to clan rivalries and localism, and a truly national leadership. National unity was essential to rid the country of the unequal treaties that the Western powers had imposed on Japan in the 1850s, in order to maintain national independence and regain tariff autonomy so that Japan could progress economically. National unity and a sense of nationhood were essential prerequisites for progress and national survival. Ono saw Japan as the only Oriental country capable of providing leadership against Western imperialism and called for a unified Japanese, Chinese, and Korean stand in the face of foreign aggression.

Sandra T.W. Davis

Bibliography
Davis, Sandra T.W. *Intellectual Change and Political Development in Early Modern Japan: Ono Azusa, A Case Study.* Cranbury, NJ: Associated University Presses, 1980.

Organ Theory (*Kikan Setsu*)

A corollary of the "state personality–state sovereignty theory" and the basic construct underlying the controversial "emperor-organ" theory propounded by the scholar Minobe Tatsukichi (1873–1948) early in the twentieth century. The state-personality theory was a concept developed in the state-law theory of the German legal positivists of the late nineteenth century, most influentially in the work of Paul Laband (1838–1918) and, with particular reference to the sources of Minobe's thought, in the work of Georg Jellinek (1851–1911). Introduced at Tokyo Imperial University at the turn of the twentieth century, it was well established by 1920 among Japan's academic elite concerned with constitutional theory.

As Minobe explained it, the state is a corporate entity endowed with powers of government. Like other corporate bodies, it is, in theory, a legal person with a will and purpose of its own (*kokka hōjin setsu*). The will of the state is exhibited in the acts of those who constitute its organs. In their official capacities, such persons are exercising not their own will and purpose, but those of the state. Minobe asserted that the organ theory described the way governments *actually* worked as well as the way they *should* work juristically.

From 1908 to 1935, Minobe set forth the organ theory in his major theoretical works, but it had no place in the more voluminous polemical and analytical literature on the current constitutional issues. Indeed, the organ theory had little audience outside of high academic and other intellectual circles. Nevertheless, it was the theory that identified the emperor as the organ of the state that brought Minobe to grief. In the minds of some, to designate the emperor as an organ of the state was tantamount to an absurdity, if not a blasphemy. To endow the parliament with independent status alongside the emperor and to assign a lesser, dependent status to such prestigious authoritarian agencies as the Supreme Command, the Privy Council, and the House of Peers, with which the imperial prerogative was girded against democratic encroachment; to suggest that the day might come when advice and assistance to the emperor would derive from a cabinet based on a parliamentary majority; indeed, to submit the Constitution of the Empire of Japan to measurement against the template of alien models in the West—these were all grounds for charges of lèse majesté and subversion of the national polity. Purging all traces of the organ theory and related doctrine from any academic or political publication was one of the salient objectives of the National Polity Clarification Campaign of 1935.

Frank O. Miller

Bibliography

Miller, Frank O. *Minobe Tatsukichi: Interpreter of Constitutionalism in Japan.* Berkeley: University of California Press, 1965.

Original Elder Statesmen (*Genrō*)

The *genrō* as an institution came into being in the 1890s as part of the evolution of the Japanese political process in the wake of the promulgation of the Meiji Constitution in 1889. The *genrō* was an extraconstitutional structure (as were political parties) that played a determinative role in Japanese politics in the period 1895–1920. It served as the formal locus for political negotiation and decision making by the senior political leaders of Japan in that period.

The *genrō* was not related institutionally to the Genrōin (Senate), which was established in 1875 and abolished in 1890. Rather, it was an informal group that appeared in the 1890s as a result of two developments associated with the emerging political process. One was a series of formal letters that were sent by the Meiji Emperor to various leaders of the 1868 Restoration asking each to continue to serve the throne in an advisory capacity. The other was the establishment of the term *genrō* in clearly defined usage in newspapers and journals in the period 1892–96.

The clearest early definition appeared in the *Tokyo Nichi Nichi Shimbun* newspaper for November 5, 1898.

Since the establishment of the Meiji Constitution it has almost without exception become the settled practice for the veteran politicians known as *genrō* or *genkun* to be summoned for questioning by the Emperor whenever a cabinet crisis occurs. When this happens it is more common for these men to consult together and report jointly than for them to present their view individually. Occasionally their conference takes place as an imperial audience [*gozen kaigi*] as, for instance, in June of this year when Marqui Itō resigned. Therefore the *genrō* actually carry responsibility as [political] advisers of the highest rank although they do not have any status in the administrative system, nor is such an organization provided for in the Constitution. This status has been conferred only through natural evolvement and convention (quoted in Yamada Shikazo. *Seiji Kenkyū*. Tokyo: Iwanami, 1926).

The composition of the *genrō* was determined by the fact of the receipt by an individual of a formal letter from the Meiji Emperor addressing him and designating him as *genkun*. By 1900, eight people had been so designated (Itō Hirabumi, Yamagata Aritomo, Inoue Kaoru, Ōyama Iwao, Kuroda Kiyotaka, Matsukata Masayoshi, Saigō Tsugumichi, and Yamada Akiyoshi). In later years, two more names were associated with the *genrō*, Katsura Tarō and Saionji Kinmochi. Only Saionji, however, received a formal letter designating him a *genkun*. The fact that Katsura died in 1912 makes it problematic to include him, but Saionji clearly became an important member of the *genrō* and, after Matsukata's death in 1924, was the only *genrō*.

The *genrō* was created by the need for a formal structure to deal with the crisis created whenever a cabinet fell. While it was dominated by Satsuma and Chōshū people, by 1900 it had come to provide a unifying way to deal with decision making at the highest level of national politics, given the fact that the emperor reigned but did not rule. In the 1880s and early 1890s, leaders intended that the cabinet or the Privy Council would be the forum for this process. When this did not work, the *genrō* emerged as the alternative. The members of the *genrō* were the men closest to the emperor. They were people who had served the throne from the time of the Restoration and were devoted to it above and beyond partisan politics.

Jackson H. Bailey

Bibliography

Bailey, J.H. "The Origin and Nature of the Genrō." *Studies on Asia*. Vol. 6. Ed. Robert Sakai. Lincoln: University of Nebraska Press, 1965, 125–41.

Hackett, Roger. "Political Modernization and the Meiji *Genrō*." *Political Development in Modern Japan*. Ed. Robert Ward. Princeton, NJ: Princeton University Press, 1968.

Ōsugi Sakae (1885–1923)

Anarchist and activist. Born in Kagawa Prefecture, he pursued a military career until he was about 20 years old, then came under the influence of young leftists, and in 1906 was jailed for demonstrating against Tokyo trolley-fare increases. From that point, he became increasingly radical, spending several terms in jail during the last of the Meiji era (1868–1912). In the 1910s, he shifted from activism to writing and gained recognition as Japan's leading anarchist with discussions of Russian revolutionary P.A. Kropotkin and others in *Kindai shisō* (Modern Thought) and other journals. He also scandalized the leftist world by having concurrent affairs with two leading social activist women, Kamichika Ichiko and Itō Noe, even while he was married. The 1920s found him becoming more politically active again, working with anarchist and Communist movements in Europe and the Soviet Union.

Ōsugi's anarchism focused on the potential of the working class to destroy the hierarchical social order and on the need for what he called "individualistic anarchism." He castigated intellectuals for their lack of social conscience and asserted that "blind action" was needed to effect change, but he offered few concrete proposals for social reconstruction. On September 16, 1923, following the Great Kantō Earthquake, he was arrested (along with Itō and his nephew), then was murdered in jail by a military police captain, apparently with the secret approval of higher officials.

James L. Huffman

Bibliography

Ōsugi, Sakae. *The Autobiography of Ōsugi Sakae*. Trans. Byron K. Marshall. Berkeley: University of California Press, 1992.

Stanley, Thomas. *Ōsugi Sakae: Anarchist in Taishō Japan*. Cambridge: Harvard University Press, 1982.

Overcoming the Modern (*Kindai No Chōkoku*)

The slogan and guiding theme of a conference held in Kyoto during July 1942 and the title of the transcript and series of papers subsequently published in the sponsoring journal, *Bungakukai*. More broadly, the phrase denotes Japan's emergent wartime critique of Western society and thought and of the post-Meiji order, which together were held to constitute the "modern." As the volume subtitle, *Conference on Intellectual Cooperation*, indicates, the idea also refers to the related effort to transform that critique into an ideology supporting Japan's wars in Asia and against the Western powers.

The opening of hostilities against the Anglo-American powers in December 1941 produced, according to the conference moderator, "intellectual shock" in Japan. It had apparently resolved the tension between "our Japanese blood, which is the true motive force for our intellectual activity," and the "clumsily systematized Western intelligence" that had been at the core of education since the late 1800s. December 8, 1941, Pearl Harbor Day in Japan, thus swept away lingering doubts about the Japanese cause and provoked questions about the deeper historical and intellectual significance of the conflict. The gathering was a direct and self-conscious response to the new situation.

Many of the participants were associated, although in varying degrees, with the Japanese Romantic School. Most prominent among those were Kawakami Tetsutarō, the moderator; Kobayashi Hideo; Hayashi Fusao; and Kamei Katsuichirō. The ideas of Yasuda Yojurō were strongly influential, though he himself was absent. As with many European thinkers, conference participants shared a rejection of materialism and rationalism, especially in its cruder, mass-market American variety. In its place, they sought, following the poet Hagiwara Sakutarō, to "return to Japan,"—to a whole rather than a fragmented, specialized world, a world not in the grip of linear temporality and utilitarian thinking.

It is significant that many "overcomers," particularly Kamei, were bitterly critical of the post-Meiji order, which they saw as an artificial bureaucratic construct at odds with a truly Japanese culture. This position highlights the element of intellectual evasion and self-deception running through the conference and its milieu: Only the modern could overcome the modern. Only a strong, modern state such as Japan, it was thought, could attempt to drive Western imperialism from Asia. Although this would seem to require methods all too similar to those of imperialism itself, somehow Japan's spirit would overcome this contradiction and produce harmony among the Japanese-led peoples of Asia.

This was the central claim of the other major group of participants in the conference: the disciples of the Kyoto school of philosophy, including Suzuki Shigetaka and Nishitani Keiji, with the ideas of Kōyama Iwao and Kōsaka Masaaki close at hand. Their concern was to put the philosophy of Japan's world historical position into ideological practice. Such thinkers saw the war in terms of a historical dialectic in which the West—capitalist, rationalist, materialist, and democratic—was to be superseded by a Japan that had synthesized the values of East and West. In this sense, Japan as a state and culture represented "absolute negativity," denying and sublimating the forms of an earlier history.

At one level, therefore, "overcoming the modern" was little more than an opportunistic exposition or commentary on the war; its appeal was tied strictly to Japan's early and dramatic successes. At another level, one admittedly difficult to separate from the first, the notion resonates with the profound yet typical dilemmas that have faced Japan's intellectuals since the late nineteenth century. In this sense, as Takeuchi Yoshimi put it, "overcoming the modern presented in condensed form the aporia of Japan's modern history" (quoted in Kawakami, 338).

Andrew E. Barshay

Bibliography

Harootunian, Harry, and Tetsuo Najiita. "Japanese Revolt Against the West: Political and Cultural Criticism in the Twentieth Century." *Cambridge History of Japan: The Twentieth Century*. Vol. 6. Ed. Peter Duus. Cambridge: Cambridge University Press, 1988.

Kawakami Tetsutarō, et al., eds. *Kindai no Chōkoku* (Overcoming the Modern). Tokyo: Fuzanbō, 1979, 338.

Ōyama Ikuo (1880–1955)

Teacher, journalist, and politician. Born in Hyogo Prefecture, Ōyama devoted his career to fighting autocratic government policies and supporting the expansion of democracy and peace. He taught at Waseda University in three different periods of his life, from 1914 to 1917, when he resigned to protest the firing of a faculty colleague; from 1920 to 1927, when he was dismissed for his involvement in leftist politics (students struck to protest his dismissal), and once again after 1947. He wrote for the newspaper *Osaka Asahi Shimbun*, until he was forced out for criticizing government measures during the 1918 rice riots. He joined the Marxist intellectual Kawakami Hajime and others in launching the democratically-oriented magazine *Warera* (We) in 1919, and he played a major role in the formation of the proletarian Labor-Farmer Party (Rōdō Nōmintō) in 1926, then again in 1929 after it had been disbanded by the government. He was elected to the Diet (legislature) in 1930.

Early in the 1930s, nationalist organizations frequently harassed and threatened Ōyama; in 1932, he and his wife immigrated to the United States, where he worked in the library and the Political Science Department at Northwestern University in Evanston, Illinois, until October 1947. He returned to Japan then and in 1950 was elected to the upper house of the Diet and became active in international peace movements.

James L. Huffman

Bibliography

Totten, George. *The Social Democratic Movement in Prewar Japan.* New Haven, CT: Yale University Press, 1966.

Ozaki Yukio (1859–1954)

Politician. During a career that spanned more than half a century, this liberal politician moved from unqualified advocacy of Japanese continental aims in the first Sino-Japanese War (1894–95) to unqualified opposition to Japan's military expansion during the 1930s and 1940s. After Japan's defeat in 1945, he continued to be actively involved in pro-democracy and antiwar causes until his death at age 96. At the end of his life, Ozaki, known as a "god of constitutional government," had become a critic of the individual nation–state and a champion of world federalism.

Ozaki entered electoral politics by winning a seat in the lower house in the first Diet election (1890). Thereafter, he was elected to 25 terms; in 1953, he was made an honorary Diet member. His remarkable career in national affairs, however, predated his election to national office. Ozaki, a protégé of Ōkuma Shigenobu, worked in the Freedom and People's Rights (Jiyū Minken) movement as a co-organizer of the Rikken Kaishintō (Constitutional Reform Party) and as a journalist for newspapers sympathetic to the Jiyū Minken cause. His involvement in the Coalition (Daidō Danketsu) movement, which attacked government policies on treaty revision, brought him afoul of the Peace Regulations, and he was banished from Tokyo in 1887. Osaki used the enforced recess for a study trip to the United States and Europe.

Although he strongly opposed the domination of politics by oligarchs from the Satsuma and Chōshū regions, Ozaki also found it difficult to work within the Japanese party system. Inimical to factions and bosses, he joined, quit, or was expelled from virtually every major prewar Japanese political party. Despite his iconoclasm, he nevertheless attained such high posts as minister of education (1898), mayor of Tokyo (1903–12), and minister of justice (1914). From the mid-1920s until the postwar period, however, he tended to be alienated from mainstream party politics. His isolation resulted partly from an unbending advocacy of expanded suffrage for men *and* women during the 1920s, and partly from his antimilitarism during the 1930s and 1940s.

Michael Lewis

Bibliography

Mendel, D. "Ozaki Yukio: Political Conscience of Modern Japan." *Far Eastern Quarterly.* Vol. 15, No. 3 (May 1956), 343–56.

P

Pacifism

Although unbridled violence characterized much of Japanese history in the early twentieth century, pacifism developed parallel to it. The rulers of Japan's new Meiji government (1868–1912) formed a state modeled after what they perceived were the best countries in the world. They sought military strength to prevent invasion by Western colonial powers. They achieved, after considerable fighting, an empire like those of the leading Western powers. The opposite trend—against war and empire—triumphed after World War II.

Both the imperialism and its opposite reflected Japanese responses to changes in the advanced countries themselves. Nineteenth-century conflicts convinced many Westerners that war fails to achieve its ends, even while it cruelly wastes material and human resources. During the Napoleonic Wars and the American Civil War, persuasive movements to outlaw war developed.

Japan's military strength grew from institutions modeled on contemporary Western strategy. Almost no Japanese individuals disagreed with militaristic national policies. The very few who emulated the growing peace movement in Europe and North America early in the twentieth century defied the overwhelming power of their own state. They shared their government's desire for national greatness, but they did not agree that military strength would achieve this end. Consequently, they remained an almost insignificant minority until the end of the Pacific War, in 1945.

The 1947 Constitution embraced what had been the opinions of a tiny minority as government policy. Under this new dispensation, the road to national preeminence lay in the preservation of the pacifist clause (Article 9) in the constitution. In this way, pacifism in Japan developed as part of the desire for national might, resting first on assumptions of military power and then on opposing assumptions of carefully restrained armed capability.

The idea of pacifism was initially a novelty to the Japanese of the Meiji era. Centuries of peace juxtaposed against an earlier tradition of hand-to-hand combat hampered understanding of the high cost of modern warfare. Western missionaries introduced pacifist assumptions along with a whole new worldview that stressed obedience to foreign ideas and, to a lesser extent, to foreign spiritual authority. As a result, Christianity and pacifism seemed to threaten Japanese national independence. Christians and pacifists appeared traitorous.

Geographic isolation, government regulation, and family solidarity precluded alternatives to nationalism. Those who adopted Christianity or its concomitant pacifism faced ostracism by nonbelievers, who had lived through three decades when militancy appeared to achieve national goals. Victory in the first Sino-Japanese War (1894–95) and the Russo-Japanese War (1904–05), service alongside Western troops in the Boxer Rebellion (1900) and World War I (1914–18), and, finally, an executive role in the League of Nations—these symbols of recognition were generally regarded as having resulted from Japan's military strength. The vast majority of Japanese shared the national pride it engendered. Those who disagreed were regarded as abnormal and faced self-doubt and criticism from others.

Although the list of prewar pacifists includes perhaps 10 names, two typify the problems faced by Japanese who loved their country but hated war: writer and religious thinker Uchimura Kanzō and his spiritual successor, Yanaihara Tadao. Very few Japanese in the late nineteenth century possessed the skill to defend their country in the English language. Uchimura did. His first article about war, written in 1894, defended Japan's military policy. With great eloquence, he assured dubious Westerners that, in the first Sino-Japanese War, Japan had acted to assist the Chinese and the Koreans. Japan, he insisted, would help them develop institutions that resembled its own so that they might prevent Western encroachments and invasion. When Prime Minister Itō Hirobumi's imperialistic war-ending demands for Chinese territory and massive indemnities proved Uchimura wrong, he attacked the government in numerous newspaper and magazine articles that elicited considerable support. He argued that political leaders' promises to assist could not be trusted. For about a decade, he sought public support for his views until the government decided in 1904 to evict Russia from Manchuria and began the Russo-Japanese War. Dismayed and convinced now that secular efforts could not effect a change in ethics, he abandoned journalism. For the rest of his days, Uchimura lectured and wrote about Bible study, convinced that pacifism was the touchstone by which to judge Christian faith. He died one year prior to the Manchurian Incident of 1931, which launched Japan's aggression in China.

His student Yanaihara served as professor of colonial policy (*shokumin seisaku*) at Tokyo University. As a university professor, Yanaihara was a government official; his duty was to develop policy to manage Japan's colonies. With the seizure of Manchuria, Yanaihara's professional responsibility required that he discover exactly what had triggered the incident. Military officials claimed that they had acted only to restore peace after responding to Chinese violence. An inspection trip to Manchuria convinced Yanaihara that army officers had, in fact, planned the takeover. He decried their action. When the army moved farther into China in 1937 and so started the second Sino-Japanese War (1937–1945), he shifted from criticism to denunciation. Echoing the Old Testament prophet Jeremiah, Yanaihara proclaimed that Japan's sins would lead to its destruction. Although a nationalist, he reviled his own government on the basis of his personal Christian convictions. Forced to resign, he, like Uchimura before him,

became a full-time evangelist. The devastation at the end of World War II vindicated him in the public view, and in 1951 he was named president of Tokyo University, a post he held for six years.

By losing World War II, the army thoroughly discredited militarism. The new 1947 Constitution, drafted by Allied Occupation authorities but welcomed by many Japanese, renounced war. The idea of becoming the world's first pacifist country appealed to a people desperate again for international recognition. Since then, everyday politics and international relations have frequently focused on Japan's pacifism. The meaning of this pacifism has not, however, been without debate; indeed few issues have fueled public discourse more constantly than the question of whether Japan's pacifism should be armed or unarmed and, if armed, to what degree.

At the heart of the debate was a shift in American policy during the Occupation (1945–52). In 1948, Communist victories in China anticipated the eventual takeover of that country. The outbreak of the Korean War in 1950 promoted immediate anti-Communist intervention. American involvement in the Vietnam War 15 years later emphasized the vulnerability of the United States. In each case, the U.S. government encouraged Japan to strengthen its military forces for increased cooperation. Japanese opposition to remilitarization at first centered on the Japan-U.S. Security Treaty of 1951 that permitted the United States to maintain forces in Japan in exchange for the protection ensured under its nuclear umbrella.

When the United States reintroduced military force into Japan, the former hero of those who opposed government remilitarization became the enemy. Reaction against American policies became a major domestic political issue in 1960, when demonstrators estimated in the tens of millions tried (but failed) to prevent the revision of the Security Treaty. The peace activists did, however, prevent the abrogation of the peace clause in the constitution.

While the government failed to change the constitution, it gradually enlarged the role and the scope of Japan's military forces. They increasingly trained with those of the United States. Military budgets grew more rapidly than civilian ones. In the 1980s, for instance, the military budget increased 58 percent, compared to increases of 23 percent for social services and 7 percent for education. These administrative changes did not attract the attention that earlier attempts to amend the constitution did, but they nevertheless represented a substantial departure from the ideal of pacifism.

Underlying the arguments regarding Japan's responsibilities and the piecemeal changes were the huge increases in the Japanese economy during those years. What seemed a reasonable share of gross national product to spend on national defense after the war, first 2 percent and then 1 percent, has resulted in a Japanese defense budget that equals that of any major Western European state. The achievement of Japan's original nineteenth-century ambition to become a rich country means near the dawn of the twenty-first-century, that a slight percentage increase in military spending creates considerable concern among Japan's East Asian neighbors.

Possessed of such potential, the Japanese find it increasingly difficult to sit smugly on the sidelines of international relations behind their constitutional rejection of force. Furtherance of the pacifism enshrined in their constitution would require them to divest themselves of American influence and use their economic power to develop new ways to ensure peace. Drifts in policy in the 1980s and 1990s indicated that most Japanese favored incremental increases in their responsibility and capability for armed defense. Observers in Japan late in 1990 viewed on television the national debate that resulted from Iraq's invasion of Kuwait. They knew that a large percentage of the oil that fuels Japanese prosperity came from Kuwait. The attack, therefore, threatened Japan's well-being. The United States moved to defend Kuwait, then required assistance from its allies. Parliamentary opposition forced the Japanese government to refuse to send troops. When the United States asked Japan to advance funds to ease its own financial burden, the Japanese government argued for days over whether to offer the United States $9 billion and whether Japan could find the money in the last four months of the fiscal year so that the country would not have to end the year with a deficit. Their national desire for recognition as a great power goaded the Japanese to provide liberal assistance, while their pride in their pacifist tradition and fiscal prudence made them hesitate. In the end, Japan gave the Americans the funds, but the heat of the debate demonstrated how deeply success in its major desire for wealth and glo-

bal position has complicated Japan's concomitant desire for the moral ascendancy of a national pacifist policy.

John F. Howes

Bibliography

Bamba, Nobuya, and John F. Howes, eds. *Pacifism in Japan: The Christian and Socialist Tradition.* Vancouver: University of British Columbia Press, 1978.

Hook, Glenn D., ed. "Peace Ideas in Postwar Japan." *Peace and Change.* Vol. 12, No. 3–4 (1987), 1–49.

Panay Incident (*Pane Gō Jiken*)

On December 12, 1937, as Japanese troops were about to capture Nanjing, China, Japanese military planes bombed and sank the American ship *Panay*, even though the ship was flying the American flag. The *Panay* was on the Yangtze River to evacuate Americans threatened by the hostilities in Nanjing and to maintain communications with the American ambassador to China. Several other ships also were shelled (as the British gunboat *Ladybird* had been a few days earlier). The bombings, ordered by officers on the scene who said that they thought the *Panay* was carrying Chinese weapons and military personnel, seriously embarrassed the Japanese government, which immediately apologized and paid the United States an indemnity of more than $2 million. Japan's prompt response mollified Western officials, but the event moved U.S. President Franklin D. Roosevelt to initiate quiet talks with the British government regarding the possibility of eventual hostilities with Japan.

James L. Huffman

Bibliography

Spector, Ronald. *Eagle Against the Sun: The American War with Japan.* New York: Vintage Books, 1985.

Patriotic Women's Society (*Aikoku Fujinkai*)

The first and, until the 1930s, the largest mass organization for women in Japan. Okumura Ioko, on her return from observing Japanese soldiers in China to suppress the 1990 Boxer Rebellion, enlisted aristocratic women and female educators to found the society in 1901. With army and home ministry support, membership increased steadily, reaching 560,000 by 1906 and 1 million by 1919. As a government-sponsored organization, the Aikoku Fujinkai supported participation by women in patriotic activities. Members saw enlisted men off to war, welcomed them home, visited hospitals, and raised money for the relief of bereaved families. In the 1920s, the society established its own social-work facilities, and local chapters participated in women's suffrage activities and supported government savings and patriotic campaigns. In the 1930s, the society sponsored the empress's birthday celebrations, solicited donations for airplanes, and organized mass rallies. In 1942, it combined with the army-sponsored Dainihon Kokubō Fujinkai (Women's Society for the Defense of Japan) and other organizations to form the Dainihon Fujinkai (Greater Japan Women's Association), which lasted until the end of World War II (1937–45).

Sally A. Hastings

Bibliography

Sievers, Sharon L. *Flowers in Salt: The Beginnings of Consciousness in Modern Japan.* Stanford, CA: Stanford University Press, 1983.

Peace Preservation Law (*Chian Iji Hō*) (1925)

Legal basis for the suppression of left-wing activism prior to World War II. Many members of Japan's governing elite grew apprehensive in the early 1920s over the growth of radical leftist dissent. In particular, they reacted to a 1923 attempt on the life of the crown prince by devising legal means to curb the spread of what were called "dangerous elements." Led by Hiranuma Kiichirō of the Justice Ministry, they succeeded in enacting the far-reaching Chian Iji Hō on May 12, 1925, shortly after passage of the more liberal Universal Male-Suffrage Act. The new Peace Preservation Law laid the groundwork for increasingly oppressive thought-control policies over the next two decades.

The law, passed with little protest, provided for sentences of up to 10 years' hard labor for advocating changes in the country's *kokutai* (national polity) or for "denying the system of private property." It made it illegal even to discuss such proposals or to provide assistance to those who advocated them. Aimed originally at anarchists and Communists, the

law was used eventually to prosecute extremists on the Left and the Right. It was revised in 1928 to provide for the death penalty and expanded in 1941 to make enforcement easier and still broader.

Authorities began almost immediately to put the law into effect. It was first applied to the pro-Communist Student Social Science Federation (Gakuren) in the Kyoto area in 1925. Then, in March 1928, 1,600 suspected leftists around the country were rounded up on a single day for alleged ties to Communism. The Justice Ministry established a Thought Section, and, by mid-1927, the Tokyo District Court had created its own special section for "thought offenses." Under the Tanaka Giichi cabinet (1927–29), a Student Section also emerged, with agents assigned to individual campuses to ferret out illegal groups; other agents were dispatched abroad, and the government began appointing thought prosecutors to treat appropriate cases. A special feature of enforcement was the use of a *tenkō* (conversion) system, under which offenders were pressured to recant and be forgiven.

In all, nearly 66,000 individuals were apprehended under the law between 1928 and 1941, though fewer than 6,000 were charged with crimes. One person was executed under the Chian Iji Hō. The law was abolished on October 15, 1945.

James L. Huffman

Bibliography

Mitchell, Richard H. *Thought Control in Prewar Japan.* Ithaca, NY: Cornell University Press, 1976.

Peace Regulations (*Hoan Jōrei*) (1887)

Name given to politically repressive regulations issued on December 26, 1887, with the intention of suppressing political dissent. The regulations were specifically aimed at putting an end to mass demonstrations by the liberal political parties against government policies. The most vociferous party, Daidō Danketsu Undō (Coalition Movement), led by Gotō Shōjirō, had mounted a series of mass political demonstrations especially opposed to Foreign Minister Inoue Kaoru's attempt that same year at revising Japan's unequal treaties with the Western countries by allowing foreigners to continue to be under their own judicial systems while in Japan.

A month after the *hoan jōrei*, in January 1888, the government would manipulate another of the liberal opposition leaders, Ōkuma Shigenobu, into joining the cabinet as foreign minister in the hope of silencing a substantial faction of the dissenters. But in December 1887, Prime Minister Itō Hirobumi, Home Minister Yamagata Aritomo, and the government attempted to suppress the radical political-party faction by force. Accordingly, an imperial regulation was issued that (1) forbade the existence of secret societies and secret assemblies; (2) allowed the police to break up any open-air meetings; (3) forbade the publication of any printed material "designed to disturb public tranquillity"; (4) allowed the creation of districts wherein the police could abridge civil rights; and (5) permitted police to remove to a distance of 3 *ri* (about 7.6 miles) from the imperial palace in Tokyo whoever "is judged to be scheming something detrimental to public tranquillity."

A total of 570 persons were rounded up by the police, escorted out of Tokyo, and placed under constant surveillance, in some cases for almost two years. Among those were a future speaker of the lower house of the Diet (legislature) and ambassador to Washington, Hoshi Tōru; a future minister of justice, mayor of Tokyo, and Diet representative, Ozaki Yukio; and such future Diet representatives as Nakae Chōmin, Hayashi Yuzō, and Kataoka Kenkichi.

The regulations cast a chilling and repressive pall on domestic politics that was not lifted until 1889, when the Meiji Constitution was promulgated, allowing the formation of legitimate political parties in preparation for the opening of Japan's legislature.

Louis G. Perez

Bibliography

Ike, Nobutaka. *The Beginnings of Political Democracy in Japan.* Baltimore, MD: Johns Hopkins University Press, 1950.

Perry, Matthew Calbraith (1794–1858)

U.S. naval commodore; brother of Oliver Hazard Perry. Following a distinguished naval career in which he gained the name "father of the steam navy," he was appointed in 1852 by President Millard Fillmore to head a mission to open relations with Japan. His fleet arrived at Uraga on Edo Bay on July 8, 1853, following the establishment of a base in Okinawa, and

Perry presented a set of American demands. After giving Tokugawa officials time to consider the terms, Perry returned to Japan with nine ships on February 12, 1854, and, on March 31, signed the Kanagawa Treaty, which assured safe harbor for shipwrecked American vessels, open ports at Shimoda and Hakodate, the posting of an American consular official within 18 months of the signing, and most-favored-nation treatment. Perry returned to widespread acclaim in America. In Japan, the treaty ended more than two centuries of seclusion and gave rise to the *sonnō jōi* (revere the emperor and expel the barbarians) movement that helped topple the Tokugawa regime in 1868.

James L. Huffman

Bibliography

Perry, Matthew. *Narrative of the Expedition of an American Squadron to the China Seas and Japan.* New York: Coward-McCann, 1952.

Political Crisis of 1881
(*Meiji Jūyon'nen No Seihen*)

In the fall of 1881, two political crises converged to produce a major change in the government, moving Japan closer to constitutional rule and more sharply defining the emerging group of oligarchs in control of the government. For more than one year, leading officials had been submitting opinions on the form an eventual constitution should take. When Finance Minister Ōkuma Shigenobu, a native of Saga Prefecture, submitted his opinion in March 1881, it proved to be far more liberal than that of the others. His plan called for a British-style parliamentary system and rapid movement toward the establishment of a legislature.

Just as this break in ranks was causing consternation within the leadership circle, a financial scandal erupted. In late July, the press reported details—apparently leaked by colleagues of Ōkuma—regarding plans of the Hokkaido Colonization Office (Kaitakushi) to sell lands and equipment in which it had invested millions of yen for a mere 380,000 yen to Godai Tomoatsu, a friend of commission Director Kuroda Kiyotaka. Moreover, the loans were to be repaid over 30 years at no interest. The revelations created a sensation, and, for one month, writers and speakers across Japan censured the government, calling for a constitutional system to check abuses. Nearly 5,000

P

attended a lecture meeting at Tokyo's well-known Shintomiza theater featuring a blistering attack by *Tokyo Nichi Nichi Shimbun* editor Fukuchi Gen'ichirō, long known as a staunch government ally.

Bitterly stung, the Meiji officials announced on October 12 that the Hokkaido sale had been rescinded and that a constitution would be presented within 10 years. At the same time, Ōkuma was dismissed from the government. The clamor died down, but an important result of the episode was a revitalization of the Jiyū Minken (Freedom and People's Rights) movement that had fought the government regarding various issues over the previous half-decade. Also in October 1881, Jiyū Minken leader Itagaki Taisuke launched Japan's first political party, the Jiyūtō (Liberal Party), and Ōkuma created the Rikken Kaishintō (Constitutional Reform Party) shortly after that. Within the government, however, the conservative ruling group became more cohesive. The Meiji Constitution was promulgated on February 11, 1889.

James L. Huffman

Bibliography

Akita, George. *The Foundations of Constitutional Government in Modern Japan.* Cambridge: Harvard University Press, 1967.

Popular Front Incident
(*Jimmin Sensen Jiken*) (1937–38)

Three-month crackdown on leftist leaders following the outbreak of the second Sino-Japanese War (1937–45). The episode began in mid-December, when 400 well-known socialists were arrested on charges of impeding Japan's war activities. It continued in late December with the banning of two leftist groups, the Nihon Musantō (Japan Proletarian Party) and the Nihon Rōdō Kumiai Zenkoku Hōgikai (All-Japan Council of Labor Unions). It concluded in February with arrests of nearly 50 well-known intellectuals.

The impact of this series of apprehensions was significant, especially in the intellectual world. Included were many of the Left's leading writers, a number of whom were regarded as relatively moderate liberals, such as Yamakawa Hitoshi (who had written nearly 200 essays in the respected general-interest opinion journal *Kaizō*), the political theorist

Minobe Ryōkichi, the social democrat Arahata Kanson, and the Marxist educator Ouchi Hyōe. The arrested individuals were prosecuted under the Peace Preservation Law of 1925, and the press was forbidden henceforth from publishing anything written by any of them. The result was that left-leaning comment largely vanished from the public scene. Many of those rounded up in this series of episodes were not released from prison until World War II ended in 1945.

James L. Huffman

Bibliography

Kasza, Gregory J. *The State and the Mass Media in Japan, 1918–1945.* Berkeley: University of California Press, 1988.

Portsmouth Treaty
(*Pōtsumasu Jōyaku*) (1905)

Treaty ending the Russo-Japanese War (1904–05). Despite surprisingly easy early victories, Japan's war-making resources were seriously depleted by 1905; following victory in the naval battle off Tsushima on May 28, Japan asked the United States to mediate peace talks. These began on August 9, at Portsmouth, New Hampshire, and a treaty was signed by Japan's Foreign Minister Komura Jutarō and Russia's chief delegate Sergei Witte on September 5.

The Japanese initially demanded the cession of Sakhalin Island and an indemnity, but when the Russians refused to budge on either issue, the Japanese cabinet, pressured by France and aware of the scarcity of its own war materials, decided, over Komura's objections, to compromise. The treaty, which still highly favored the Japanese, gave Japan the southern half of Sakhalin, dominant interests in Korea, and control of Russia's holdings in Manchuria, including the South Manchurian Railway and its leases in the Liaodong Peninsula. It also called for Russian troops to leave Manchuria.

Despite the favorable terms, the treaty, particularly the lack of an indemnity, sparked a wave of protest in Japan, where wartime propaganda had led people to believe that Japanese troops were on the verge of total victory. Newspapers deplored the settlement, and three days of antigovernment riots, which began in Tokyo's Hibiya Park on September 5, resulted in more than 1,000 casualties and the destruction of 350 police boxes.

Many scholars perceive a new, more aggressive kind of nationalism in the patriotic enthusiasm fueled by the Russo-Japanese War—and in the reaction to the treaty. The removal of Russia from the East Asian political scene left Japan and the United States as primary international rivals in the western Pacific.

James L. Huffman

Bibliography

Okamoto, Shumpei. *The Japanese Oligarchy and the Russo-Japanese War*. New York: Columbia University Press, 1970.

Potsdam Declaration (*Potsudamu Sengen*)

Document issued July 26, 1945, by China, Great Britain, and the United States, outlining World War II surrender terms for Japan. The Soviet Union, which also participated in the Potsdam Conference, did not formally endorse the declaration until after its declaration of war with Japan on August 8. Threatening "prompt and utter destruction" if Japan did not surrender unconditionally, the document asserted that Japan would be occupied until all military, authoritarian influences had been eliminated and a "new order of peace, security, and justice" had been created. It called for Japan's territory to be limited to its four main islands and "such minor islands as we determine," for the military to be disarmed, for war criminals to be punished, and for "fundamental human rights" to be established. The declaration also promised that the Allied Occupation would be aimed at rebuilding Japan and that occupying forces would be withdrawn once a peaceful, responsible government, created by "the freely expressed will of the Japanese people," was solidly in place.

Japanese leaders initially issued no official response to the Potsdam Declaration, though they engaged in intense discussions. Prime Minister Suzuki Kantarō, however, was quoted in the Japanese press as saying that the government would "take no notice of it" (*mokusatsu suru*), a comment interpreted abroad as a rejection. Japan's lack of response was one of the things that prompted the U.S. decision to drop the atomic bomb on Hiroshima on August 6 and the announcement by the Soviet Union that it was entering the war against Japan on August 8. The Japanese government essentially agreed to the Potsdam terms on August 10 and formally did so on August 14, one day before surrender was announced.

James L. Huffman

Bibliography

Butow, Robert. *Japan's Decision to Surrender*. Stanford, CA: Stanford University Press, 1954.

Power of Supreme Command (*Tōsuiken*)

Under Article 11 of the Meiji Constitution, the emperor was given "supreme command of the Army and Navy;" under Article 12, he was given charge of the "peace standing" of the military forces. Though capable of various interpretations, these clauses generally were taken before 1945 to mean that neither the cabinet nor the Diet (legislature) had the right to interfere in military decisions—the military was independent of civilian control.

Although the military and the civilian bureaucracies usually cooperated through the end of the Meiji era in 1912, the standard interpretation of *tōsuiken* created frequent clashes between the government and the military during the 1920s and 1930s, as the general staff offices of the army and the navy claimed again and again that the cabinet was overstepping its bounds. In 1926 the Katō Takaaki government touched off protests when it cut the army by four divisions. In 1930, when the Hamaguchi Osachi cabinet decided to sign the London Naval Treaty, which set limits on Japan's naval construction, the navy fought vigorously to force a reversal. The Privy Council eventually sided with the cabinet on this issue, but the acrimony created by the dispute remained for years. Prime Minister Hamaguchi was shot in November 1930 (he never recovered from the wound and died in August 1931) in the aftermath of the London Naval Treaty dispute, and many see the disagreements over *tōsuiken* as centrally responsible for the extreme violence of ultranationalist militarists that poisoned domestic politics in the 1930s. The *tōsuiken* debate also played an obvious role in the increasing control the military exerted over the cabinets as the 1930s progressed.

James L. Huffman

Bibliography

Butow, Robert. *Tōjō and the Coming of the War*. Stanford, CA: Stanford University Press, 1961.

Privy Council (*Sūmitsu In*)

Established on April 28, 1888, and abolished on May 2, 1947, the Privy Council was designed by the conservative political leader Itō

P

Hirobumi as a major bulwark against changes in the Meiji (1868–1912) political system, what he called "the palladium of the constitution and of the law." In deciding whether the emperor should sign a law, a treaty, or an imperial ordinance, the Privy Council exercised the emperor's absolute veto power.

Privy Council membership was fixed at 14 in 1888, raised to 27 in 1890, and increased to 30 in 1903 before being stabilized at 26 in 1913. Selected by the cabinet, council members held lifetime appointments. Vacancies were never sufficiently numerous to enable any cabinet after 1888 to appoint more than a small minority of council members. Between 1888 and Japan's World War II surrender in 1945, a total of 163 men served on the council. Nearly three-quarters (72 percent) were former civilian bureaucrats. Another 20 percent were generals or admirals. Many had served in the appointive upper house of the Diet, but only six of the 163 had been in the elective lower house.

Always dominated by career bureaucrats committed to the Meiji system, the council proved to be reliably resistant to changes advocated by political parties. The chief limitation on the council's power was that it could act only when consulted; it did not review all statutes but only those the cabinet chose to refer to it.

Itō thought that the council would act primarily as a restraint on the party-dominated House of Representatives. Another of the Meiji era's leading government leaders, Yamagata Aritomo, foresaw more acutely than Itō that a political party might eventually control not only the House of Representatives but even the cabinet. Yamagata, therefore, greatly strengthened the council's authority by having the Meiji emperor sign an imperial message (*gosatasho*) in 1900 requiring the cabinet to obtain Privy Council approval of 10 categories of most important ordinances, including any change in civil-service rules.

Yamagata's shrewd move enabled the council in the 1920s to be a formidable combatant against party cabinets, disputing not only constitutional issues, such as imperial sovereignty in the 1928 Kellogg–Briand Treaty, in which Japan joined 14 other nations in outlawing war, but also policy issues, as in the 1927 financial crisis, when 37 debt-ridden banks folded and council opposition forced a cabinet to resign. However, the council was far less successful in resisting military demands after Japan began moving aggressively into China in 1931 and played no significant role in the 1941 and 1945 decisions on war and peace.

Robert M. Spaulding

Bibliography
Spaulding, Robert M. *Imperial Japan's Higher Civil Service Examinations*. Princeton, NJ: Princeton University Press, 1967.
Titus, David. *Palace and Politics in Prewar Japan*. New York: Columbia University Press, 1974.

Professors' Group Affair (*Kyōju Gurupu Jiken*)

Also translated as "the Academicians' Group Incident." It was the label given by the press to the February 1938 arrest of professors suspected of connections to the Popular Front, the antifascist movement alleged to be part of a Communist strategy to undermine Japan's military effort in China. A crackdown on antiwar protest, begun the previous December, already had netted 400 arrests. Spurred by self-appointed nationalist witch-hunters, the government intensified pressure on the universities by jailing left-wing academics, including Ouchi Hyōe and Arisawa Hiromi, from the Economics Department of Tokyo Imperial University, and Minobe Ryōkichi of Hosei University.

The defendants claimed to be merely "academic Marxists and took no part in these political activities," and, in the first trial, all but two were acquitted of subversive acts. Because Japanese law permitted appeals by the prosecution as well as the defense, they were retried and convicted. Ultimately, however, the case ended in an unusual instance of wartime justice: In September 1944, the High Court reversed the earlier convictions of all but two of the Professors' Group. Of course, by this time, the group members had paid heavily in terms of their professional careers and the loss of personal liberty during their detention, and the government had achieved its aim of silencing dissent, because the university professors had been banned from lecturing or publishing even when they were free on bail. Many of these academics reemerged in the political arena of the postwar era.

Byron K. Marshall

Bibliography
Marshall, Byron K. *Academic Freedom and the Japanese Imperial University*. New York: Peter Lang, 1990.

Public Party of Patriots (*Aikoku Kōtō*)

Japan's first private political association. Founded by Itagaki Taisuke and several allies early in 1874, it called for the creation of a limited representative national assembly composed of samurai and other members of the old elite. The actual aim of the group was to challenge the growing power of the Meiji regime. The Aikoku Kōtō disbanded just a month after its founding, due to fear of government suppression after one of its founders, Etō Shimpei, helped instigate the abortive Saga Rebellion. Itagaki revived the party briefly in 1890 to assist in the founding of the Rikken Jiyūtō (Constitutional Liberal Party).

James L. Huffman

Bibliography

Scalapino, Robert. *Democracy and the Party Movement in Prewar Japan.* Berkeley: University of California Press, 1967.

Public Peace Police Law
(*Chian Keisatsu Hō*)

Law enacted in March 1900 to control anti-government activities. The Yamagata Aritomo cabinet drew up the Public Peace Police Law in an effort to ensure public order and strengthen state control; in the process, it set the early-twentieth-century standard for strictly controlling all public expression and political organization. Among other provisions, the law required that political groups receive police permission before holding meetings, allowed the home minister to ban any group deemed a threat to the social order, proscribed secret associations, forbade organization or strikes by workers, and gave police the right to attend and dissolve political meetings or to disband the sponsoring group if deemed necessary. The law also prohibited police, priests, minors, military personnel, and women from joining political groups, with violators fined or jailed for up to one year.

The ban on women's political participation was removed in 1922, and the prohibition on labor organization was deleted in 1926. By that time, however, the repressive 1925 Peace Preservation Law had replaced the Chian Keisatsu Hō as the government's primary tool in controlling dissent. The law was abolished by Occupation authorities in November 1945.

James L. Huffman

Bibliography

Crump, John. *The Origins of Socialist Thought in Japan.* New York: St. Martin's Press, 1983.

Purges During the Allied Occupation (1945–52)

The U.S. Initial Post-Surrender Policy for Japan used purges to remove "persons who have been active exponents of militarism and militant nationalism . . . from public office and from any other position of public or substantial private responsibility" in order to facilitate Japan's democratization and prevent Japan from becoming "a menace . . . to the peace and security of the world." Advocacy of militarism and nationalism was equated after World War II with aggressive war and opposition to democracy.

The terms of the purge directive went far beyond the military to all those in key positions of authority during the period 1937–45, such as politicians, bureaucrats, businessmen, and leaders of right-wing organizations, on the assumption that they were active supporters of militarism and nationalism. The actual purge did not approach the scope of the directive, for only 210,000 were removed and excluded from office. The vast majority (96.1 percent) of these were military personnel (79.6 percent) or political figures (16.5 percent); the other two wings of Japan's ruling elite, businessmen and bureaucrats, were virtually untouched, accounting for less than 1 percent each of the total.

Most of those purged (201,000)—even Tōjō Hideki's wartime cabinet minister Kishi Nobusuke, who had been charged as a Class A war criminal—were restored to full political rights during the "reverse course" of the Occupation (1945–52). At the same time, the purge was redirected, contrary to original intent, into a Red Purge against leftists that brought dismissal of tens of thousands of public and private employees, especially labor-union militants and schoolteachers.

These events undermined the effort to root out militarism and nationalism and lent legitimacy to nationalistic attacks on Japan's new democratic institutions as shameful evidence of foreign domination and, above all, on the 1947 Constitution with its reduction of the emperor to a symbol of the state and its renunciation of war in Article 9. After the purge had run its course, nationalism in Japan continued, as before, to inspire and drive conservatives and the right wing, although militarism lost its prestige from the country's defeat in World War II.

However, a popular upsurge of nationalism did not occur. The mass movements of the 1950s sought to defend the new postwar era of peace and democracy against resurgent right-wing nationalists such as Kishi, who returned to positions of power throughout society. More effective than the purges against nationalism were people's memories of suffering at the hands of militarists and nationalists before and during the war.

Joe B. Moore

Bibliography

Baerwald, Hans H. *The Purge of Japanese Leaders under the Occupation*. Berkeley: University of California Press, 1959.

Ward, Robert E. and Sakamoto Yoshikazu, eds. *Democratizing Japan: The Allied Occupation*. Honolulu: University of Hawaii Press, 1987.

R

Red Flag Incident (*Akahata Jiken*)
Episode in 1908 marking a government shift toward harsh repression of the socialist movement. On June 22, a group representing the parliamentary and the direct-action socialist camps met at Kanda's Kinkikan hall in Tokyo to celebrate the release of fellow activist Yamaguchi Gizō from prison. During the meeting, radicals hoisted red flags bearing the slogans "anarchism" and "anarcho-Communism," in defiance of the moderates' call for a quiet celebration, then continued to carry the flags and shout "anarchy" when they left the hall. A fight with police ensued, and 16 people were arrested. Controversy over the episode helped topple the Saionji Kinmochi cabinet. Its successor government, headed by Katsura Tarō, handed down unusually harsh sentences at the August 15 trial, finding two of those charged innocent, giving suspended sentences to two more, and imposing prison terms exceeding one year on 12. Leading socialist Ōsugi Sakae received two and one half years; Sakai Toshihiko and Yamakawa Hitoshi, two each.

James L. Huffman

Bibliography

Notehelfer, F.G. *Kōtoku Shūsui: Portrait of a Japanese Radical*. Cambridge: Cambridge University Press, 1971.

Revere the Emperor and Expel the Barbarians (*Sonnō Jōi*)
The goal of anti-*bakufu* activists in the mid-nineteenth century, when Japan succumbed to Western semicolonial domination. *Sonnō jōi* combined two elements crucial to modern Japanese nationalism: the desire to create popular solidarity through allegiance to the emperor as sovereign head of a unified nation–state, and a consciousness of the need to defend that state from foreign territorial encroachment. Although *sonnō jōi* supported the existing Tokugawa feudal order at first, it helped destroy that order and create a centralized nation–state after 1853.

Jōi must be seen in historical relation to Tokugawa Japan's foreign policy of *sakoku* (seclusion). The Edo *bakufu* (military government, 1600–1868) had always assumed responsibility for conducting Japan's foreign trade and diplomacy with Korea and China. For most of the 1600s and 1700s, Western intercourse with Japan was extremely limited because of natural causes: Europe was far away, navigation was primitive, and Russian and American expansion had not yet reached the Pacific. So the only Western peoples who came to Japan in the first half of the Edo period were the English, the Portuguese, the Spanish, and the Dutch. The English left voluntarily in 1623, and the *bakufu* expelled the Portuguese and the Spanish in the 1640s; that left the Dutch as the only Westerners in Japan. The Dutch navy forcibly prevented small Southeast Asian countries, such as Siam, Annam, and Cambodia, as well as other European states from reaching Japan from the early seventeenth to the late-eighteenth centuries.

Seclusion evolved mainly because of geographic accident and Dutch naval supremacy in the Far East. But, during these first 200 years of Tokugawa rule, most Japanese came to believe that seclusion was good for their country; and it had become official *bakufu* policy by 1825, when the government issued its No Two Thoughts Expulsion Edict, ordering any non-Dutch Western ships to be fired on and driven away. Thus began "*jōi*," the expulsion of Westerners.

This concept soon became associated with *sonnō* (reverence for the emperor). *Sonnō* had historical roots in earlier Tokugawa Confucian and *kokugaku* (national learning) thinkers who sought to legitimize warrior supremacy and *bakufu* rule in Japan vis-à-vis the imperial court. Their logic was as follows. Japan's imperial family, descended from the Sun Goddess, had lost ruling power in the realm to warrior houses such as the Tokugawa, who had set up *bakufu*. But unlike hegemons in China, who overthrew and slew the sovereigns whom they served, omnipotent Tokugawa shoguns respectfully deferred to powerless but sacred emperors. The shogun accepted vassal status and assumed administrative burdens on behalf of his imperial sovereign. This shogunal virtue of loyal "reverence for the emperor," the *bakufu* claimed, accorded with Japan's *kokutai* (national essence), which required that the country be ruled eternally by the divine imperial house. By the late eighteenth century, *kokugaku* and other thinkers were declaring—with no basis in historical fact—that the *bakufu* had received an imperial mandate: The emperor had entrusted the shogun with responsibility for ruling Japan and conducting foreign relations.

By 1825, then, the political imperatives of *sonnō* and *jōi* converged and functioned to bolster *bakufu* authority. The shogun, though not himself sovereign, enjoyed imperial sanction to wield sovereign power. True, shogunal legitimacy was theoretically subject to two conditions: submission to the imperial will and the ability to expel Westerners other than the Dutch. But, in reality, the emperor could not express any will contrary to that of the *bakufu* because his court was impotent, and no Western power, not even Russia or the United States (which had now reached the Pacific), was strong enough to defeat the *bakufu*. By the 1840s and 1850s, though, world conditions changed—with dire consequences for the *bakufu*. The major Western powers had an overwhelming edge in military technology because of the Industrial Revolution, and they mobilized popular and fiscal resources effectively in pursuit of state goals in view of their nationalism and efforts at national consolidation. Western might was demonstrated against China in the Opium War (1840–42) and against Japan when Commodore Matthew Perry visited Edo Bay with one-fourth of the U.S. navy in 1853–54.

Perry forced the *bakufu* to sign a treaty that would open two ports; faced with this unprecedented crisis, Tokugawa officials made the mistake of asking for advice from the imperial court and the daimyos. This blunder had crucial implications for nationalism in Japan. First, it opened political decision-making to broader popular participation by including hitherto excluded groups. More important, the government was repudiating its own authority. The *bakufu* already enjoyed imperial sanction to conduct foreign affairs as it saw fit; so why ask for advice from the court? In 1856, Edo committed a worse blunder. In that year, U.S. Consul Townsend Harris demanded a shogunal audience, at which he proposed a new treaty that would open Japan to foreign residence and more ports to foreign trade. This time, the *bakufu* requested imperial ratification of the treaty, which was denied. Thereafter, other Western countries extracted from Edo still more concessions that reduced Japan to semicolonial status. In this way, the Tokugawa government appeared unwilling to "revere the emperor" by carrying out his explicit desire to "expel the barbarians." Indeed, Edo seemed to be abusing the imperial mandate to maintain its own supremacy without regard for the national welfare. This was the pretext that the forces of Satsuma and Chōshū domains used to justify replacing the *bakufu*-led feudal order with a nation-state in the Meiji era (1868–1912). A centralized government under imperial aegis, they claimed, would be better able to reclaim sovereign rights lost to foreigners.

Bob Tadashi Wakabayashi

Bibliography

Hane, Mikiso. *Studies in the Intellectual History of Tokugawa Japan.* Tokyo: Tokyo University Press, 1974, 323–67.

Wakabayashi, Bob T. *Anti-Foreignism and Western Learning in Early-Modern Japan: The New Theses of 1825.* Cambridge: Harvard University Press, 1986.

Reverse Course

Term used to denote a reversal in the democratization and demilitarization policies of Occupied Japan (1945–52) by the Supreme Commander for the Allied Powers (SCAP), leading to its reconstruction as an industrial and military base in the struggle against Communism.

First manifested in SCAP's prohibition of a general strike in early 1947, this reversal was the Allies' response to the unfolding Cold War and to the rise of militant labor unions and left-wing parties that sprang up in postwar Japan as a result of SCAP's own early liberal reform policy.

"Reverse course" also refers to policies implemented throughout the 1950s to rectify what conservative governments regarded as the excesses of SCAP-directed reforms. The term was popularized by a special series in the fall of 1951 in the newspaper *Yomiuri Shimbun* that reported a revival of the right wing, the renewed popularity of samurai movies, rearmament, and the reformation of financial cliques (*zaibatsu*). Provoked by the rise of militant leftist forces, these "reverse course" tendencies were essentially a nationalist reaction to foreign-imposed values and institutions. "Reverse course" in this sense embodied first the reexamination and revision of Japan's relationship with the United States, and second the restoration of Japan's prewar, or traditional, values and institutions. Major issues were rearmament and the 1951 Japan-U.S. Security Treaty, police administration, labor unions, educational administration and curriculum, and revision of the postwar Constitution.

The debate on reverse course policies began during the administrations of Yoshida Shigeru (1948–54) and Hatoyama Ichirō (1954–56), and climaxed during the Kishi Nobusuke government of 1957–60. Kishi provoked a widespread public debate and protest for his aborted attempt to revise the Police Duties Law and expand law enforcers' pre-crime investigatory powers, and for his high-handed tactics in introducing ethics courses into school curricula and revising the Japan-U.S. Security Treaty. Left-wing critics branded these moves reactionary attempts to undo democratization and return Japan to prewar militarism and authoritarianism.

Shigeko Fukai

Bibliography

Dower, John W., *Empire and Its Aftermath: Yoshida Shigeru and the Japanese*. Cambridge: Harvard University Press, 1979.

Fukui, Haruhiro. "Postwar Politics, 1945–1973." *Cambridge History of Japan: The Twentieth Century*. Vol. 6. Ed. Peter Duus. Cambridge: Cambridge University Press, 1988, 154–213.

Rice (*Kome*)

A staple of the Japanese diet for two millennia, rice in more recent generations has assumed an almost mystical quality in national lore. Though affordable in quantity only by the upper classes until the Meiji era (1868–1912), it consumed more than half of Japan's cultivated land for centuries and came to be seen as tied to the very soul of the country. This attitude significantly influenced government economic policies in the 1980s and 1990s.

Rice first was grown in Japan 2,000 years ago. Intensive cultivation techniques similar to those used today date to the late Nara era (710–84). Though productivity always was high for its time, only in the twentieth century have improved techniques made rice affordable by all classes. Rice production peaked at more than 13 million metric tons in 1962 and since then has declined by a third, even though productivity has continued to rise, primarily because people now also eat other grains and meat products.

One reason for the mystique surrounding rice is that its cultivation methods have had a profound effect on Japanese village society. The intense, heavy work required in its cultivation, the seasonal nature of each rice-growing activity, and the communal efforts necessary for water allocation and use have created villages where cooperation is essential. The *ie* (traditional family structure) also developed around rice-growing activities, and a large number of traditional religious festivals center on rice: from January prayers for the coming season, through *kaze matsuri* (wind festivals) to avert typhoons, to thankful harvest festivals in the fall. Even the emperor observes the ritual importance by offering rice to Amaterasu, the Sun Goddess, in the *daijōsai* (great new food festival), one of the three important rites when he ascends the throne, and then repeating the ceremony on a smaller scale each November.

Partly for this reason and partly because of the political influence of rural interest groups, the ruling Liberal Democratic Party artificially supported the price of rice after World War II, leading Japanese consumers to pay the highest rice prices in the world and creating large government debts. The government began modifying this practice and allowing some rice imports early in the 1990s, but it has remained a contentious issue at home and in international trade discussions.

James L. Huffman

Bibliography
Ohnuki-Tierney, Emiko. *Rice As Self.*
 Princeton, NJ: Princeton University
 Press, 1993.

Rice Riots (*Kome Sōdō*) (1918)

The rice riots began in July 1918, when a small band of fishermen's wives in Toyama Prefecture mounted nonviolent protests to bring down the cost of locally produced rice. Following the Toyama unrest, a series of mass demonstrations, labor strikes, and armed clashes continued for eight weeks throughout Japan on a scale unprecedented in the country's modern history. The rioters' targets varied according to local conditions and grievances, but rice merchants, local officials, nouveau riche (*narikin*) companies, and the Terauchi Masatake cabinet were commonly marked for criticism or attack. The central government, which had been unable to control wartime inflation or the corresponding fall in real wages, resorted to drastic measures to contain the breakdown of civil order. As local police proved incapable of controlling urban protests, which some observers believed were a signal of the onset of a second "Russian Revolution," the government mobilized 92,000 troops in 120 localities to suppress the rioting. In restoring order, soldiers turned their guns on some crowds, killing more than 30 civilians and wounding many more.

Although of enormous scale, the riots did not produce lower market prices for rice. Rice prices, which in some regions had doubled between 1917 and 1918, continued at high levels for nearly one year after the riots. The imperial system, which the protesters never seriously challenged, remained intact and unaltered, as did the basic structure of the Meiji constitutional order. Indeed, the robust health of state authority appeared confirmed by the swift and usually uncontested conviction of more than 5,000 individuals for riot-related crimes.

Nevertheless, the riots did change long-term social policy and national politics. In their wake, officials initiated new laws affecting commodity trading, social welfare, police control, and labor relations. The unrest also brought an intensification of mass participation in political movements, although the expansion was matched by the introduction of repressive police laws and the growth of rightist movements for the protection of the country's farmers. The immediate political repercussions of the riots caused the downfall of the Terauchi government. The breakdown of civil order thus played an important role in the rise of Hara Takashi, the first nonpeer prime minister, and the routinization of cabinet formation by majority parties in the Diet (legislature).

The riots were not the sole cause of the turn from aloof, transcendent political-party governments, but they were symptomatic of deeper changes that had begun before, and continued after, the protests. The transformation altered public attitudes toward governmental and corporate policies, whether such policies were explicit, as in the legal prohibition of strikes, or implied, as in the gulf separating company profits from worker wages.

The protests demonstrated that the Meiji oligarchs' aim of creating a new ideologically unified citizenry consistently supportive of national goals was still a work in progress. The unrest also made clear that local politics and the maintenance of "moral" economic relations still preoccupied citizens in many regions of Japan. In city rioting or in protests between management and workers, however, "rational" collective bargaining by riot seemed to replace any popular desire to reinstate traditional social norms. In major cities where tens of thousands joined citizens' meetings, protesters demanded full rights for citizens, including the right to political participation and an equitable share in the fruits of Japan's economic successes. Despite such demands, the riots did not signify the polarization of Japanese society into opposing camps, the people on one side, the state on the other.

Michael Lewis

Bibliography
Lewis, Michael. *Rioters and Citizens: Mass
 Protest in Imperial Japan.* Berkeley: University of California Press, 1990.

Rich Country, Strong Army (*Fukoku Kyōhei*)

Slogan, encapsulating the major features of government political policy during the Meiji era (1868–1912). Drawing on an ancient Chinese slogan as well as the ideas of several early nineteenth-century scholars, the Meiji leaders began almost immediately after the 1868 Meiji Restoration to use the phrase to denote the policies necessary to meet the challenge of Western imperialism and colonialism. Essentially, *fukoku kyōhei* aimed at the development of an industrial economic base strong enough to undergird a strong military. At the core of this Westernizing policy was the idea of making Japan strong enough to compete economically and militarily on an equal footing with the major Western powers.

Several ministries—particularly home, public works, and military affairs—actively encouraged the expansion of military, communication, and textile industries and mining in the 1870s. At the same time, the government in 1873 enacted a law mandating universal military conscription for men and initiated a significant buildup of the army and the navy. Military spending nearly doubled in the 1880s despite the period's general economic retrenchment, while the number of servicemen increased to 75,000. New consumption and business taxes also were levied to support the expanding military.

Though a vocal minority questioned government priorities at this time—with individuals such as the young essayist Tokutomi Sohō and people's-rights leaders expressing doubts about whether Japan could have national wealth and a sizable military simultaneously—most Japanese were supportive. With the rapid spread of nationalistic thought after the late 1880s, the ideas of *fukoku kyōhei* grew even more popular. Japan's victories in the first Sino-Japanese War (1894–95) and the Russo-Japanese War (1904–05) convinced most doubters of the wisdom of the policy, as did Japan's success in gaining treaty equality with the Western powers by the early 1910s.

James L. Huffman

Bibliography
Hane, Mikiso. *Modern Japan: A Historical Survey*. Boulder, CO: Westview Press, 1986.

Root-Takahira Agreement (*Rūto-Takahira Kyōtei*)

A 1908 agreement aimed at reducing tensions between Japan and the United States. The previous two years had produced numerous disputes: over American immigration restrictions, President Theodore Roosevelt's dispatch of the U.S. naval fleet to Japanese waters, and press rumors of potential war. To calm passions, on November 30, U.S. Secretary of State Elihu Root and Japan's U.S. Ambassador Takahira

Kogorō signed an agreement pledging the mutual peaceful maintenance of the status quo.

The document bound both countries to "respect the territorial possessions belonging to each other," maintain the open door in China, support China's "independence and integrity," and consult with each other if the status quo "or the principle of equal opportunity" in China were threatened. The primary aim of the agreement lay in public relations, because neither country's legislature ratified it, and, therefore, it was not binding. It did, however, improve the bilateral relationship.

James L. Huffman

Bibliography
Esthus, Raymond. *Theodore Roosevelt and Japan*. Seattle: University of Washington Press, 1966.

Russo-Japanese War (*Nichiro Senso*) (1904–05)

After Japan's victory in the first Sino-Japanese War (1894–95), Russia and Japan struggled for heightened influence in the northeast Asia region. Russia forced Japan to restore Manchuria's Liaodong Peninsula to China in the Triple Intervention (Russia, Germany, and France) of 1895, then gained control over that region by forcing unequal treaties on China in 1898. Meanwhile, Japan was increasing its influence in Korea. When Russian troops failed to leave Manchuria following the 1900 Boxer Rebellion, tensions mounted between Japan and Russia. When talks between the two countries failed to improve the situation, the Japanese army, under heavy pressure from the Japanese public, launched a surprise attack on the Russian ships at Port Arthur on February 8, 1904. Japan declared war two days later.

On land, the first major battle was fought for Port Arthur, Russia's chief Far Eastern naval base, which was heavily fortified within a 95-foot-high wall. After more than six months of fighting and 56,000 Japanese casualties, the Japanese army took the city on January 1, 1905. Next, the Japanese turned north to Mukden, an even more difficult obstacle. Again Japan won—but only after committing 250,000 troops against Russia's 320,000. The casualties were staggering: 70,000 for the Japanese, 90,000 for the Russians. By the end of this 10-day battle, Japan's resources for extending the war further were largely gone.

The war's decisive victory came at sea. Having defeated Russia's Pacific fleet early in the war, the Japanese also wiped out its European navy on May 27, 1905, at the Battle of Tsushima, when Admiral Tōgō Heihachirō's ships pounced on the Russian fleet as it sailed through the narrow straits between Kyushu and Korea on its way to Vladivostok.

Recognizing that the resource situation was grave, the Japanese already had decided to negotiate. They asked U.S. President Theodore Roosevelt to mediate, and the peace talks, held in Portsmouth, New Hampshire, gave Japan Russia's Manchurian holdings, as well as the southern half of Sakhalin Island. The treaty also recognized Japan's "paramount interest" in Korea and provided for the withdrawal of foreign troops from Manchuria, except for the Japanese forces needed to guard the South Manchurian Railway. The omission of an indemnity from the peace treaty sparked violent demonstrations in Japan, where censorship had kept a passionately prowar public from knowing the critical military situation.

The war provoked Japan's first pacifist movement as a few Christians and socialists spoke out openly against aggression. For most Japanese, however, the war was the most glorious incident of the Meiji era (1868–1912), proof positive that Japan had joined the top ranks among the world's great powers. In practical terms, it changed the Asian power balance, moving Japan to the center, and it set the stage for even more Japanese advances in mainland Asia and the Pacific Ocean.

James L. Huffman

Bibliography
Okamoto, Shumpei. *The Japanese Oligarchy and the Russo-Japanese War*. New York: Columbia University Press, 1970.
White, John. *The Diplomacy of the Russo-Japanese War*. Princeton, NJ: Princeton University Press, 1964.

Ryūkyū, Disposition of (*Ryūkyū Shobun*)

In 1866, the emperor of China delegated his envoys in Okinawa to appoint Sho Tai (1843–1901) king of Ryūkyū. In 1879, eleven years after the Meiji Restoration, Japan seized the Ryūkyū kingdom and established Okinawa Prefecture in its place. Sho Tai, the last king of Ryūkyū, was transferred to Tokyo.

Ryūkyū shobun is the term used to describe Japan's coup de grâce. More broadly, it includes a series of strategic Japanese moves between 1871 and the establishment of Okinawa Prefecture in 1879 to justify the annexation of Ryūkyū. China's refusal to countenance these Japanese moves and Ryūkyūan resistance challenged Japan's sovereignty over the kingdom. How Ryūkyū became a Japanese prefecture requires a degree of familiarity with the history of the Ryūkyū kingdom.

Three kingdoms ruling the northern, central, and southern provinces of Okinawa Island became tributary states of Ming China in the fourteenth century. The central kingdom of Zhonshan eventually unified the entire Ryūkyū archipelago. In the fourteenth and fifteenth centuries, the Ryūkyū kingdom prospered through long-distance trade with East and Southeast Asian countries.

Dependence on trade became a disadvantage for Ryūkyū when the weakening of the Ming dynasty disrupted peace in Asia. In the 1590s, Japan's national overlord Toyotomi Hideyoshi invaded Korea. When Ryūkyū refused to heed Hideyoshi's order to contribute troops and resources to his cause, the daimyo of Satsuma fief in southern Japan interceded in Ryūkyū's favor and appeased Hideyoshi.

But Satsuma had its own designs on Ryūkyū, and, in 1609, it invaded the kingdom. As conditions of the peace, Ryūkyū agreed to cede the northern Ryūkyū Islands (the Amami group) and to pay an annual tax to Satsuma. The kingdom remained a tributary state of China, because Satsuma desired to share in the profits of the China trade. This began Ryūkyū's dual subordination, to China and Satsuma. Within Japan's general system of centralized feudalism, Ryūkyū was a region of the Satsuma domain, and the Ryūkyū king was regarded as merely a subdomain governor, subordinate to a daimyo, or feudal lord.

In the Chinese hierarchy, however, the Ryūkyū king was equivalent to the king of a province (*jun-wang*), a rank one step below that of prince-king, a nonheir son of the emperor. In a family metaphor, the Ryūkyū king was a grandson of the emperor of China. The crown, the robe, and other paraphernalia of the Ryūkyū king were designed to show this rank and the respective privileges. The functions and ranking of the king's officials followed the *jun-wang* government's pattern.

Ryūkyūans generally found the Chinese world order congenial and satisfactory.

After 1609, the Ryūkyū economy in part became transformed into a Japanese type of agrarian feudal system (*kokudakasei*) for taxation purposes. The Japanese government's attempts to recast Ryūkyū's socioeconomic structure according to Japan's feudal class system remained uncompleted. Instead, the Ryūkyūan ruling class and literati drew closer to China. To the Japanese, Ryūkyūans became as foreign as Chinese and Koreans.

When Japan signed the unequal treaties with Western countries in the 1850s, it was ignorant of Western concepts of national sovereignty and international law; the treaties provided a bitter lesson. Having acquired the knowledge of Western international relations, Japan was eager to use it vis-à-vis its Asian neighbors, China, Korea, and Ryūkyū.

The latter was already half Japanese, as implied by its dual subordination. A major obstacle to Japan's full sovereignty over Ryūkyū was China's traditional suzerainty over it. Thus arose Sino-Japanese conflicts rooted in different concepts of state and world order. The Ryūkyūan objection was only a minor matter to Japan. To Ryūkyūans, Japan simply made a high-handed, unilateral declaration that their kingdom was a part of Japan and sought to enforce its dominance regardless of their feelings about it. However, Ryūkyūans were not totally helpless. On the one hand, they were determined to engage the Japanese in an endless debate about the history and principles of the Ryūkyūan state. On the other hand, they launched a diplomatic campaign to turn the world against Japan's plans to annex Ryūkyū, albeit Japanese maneuvers proved much more sophisticated.

In 1872, Satsuma (modern-day Kagoshima Prefecture) informed the Ryūkyūans of political changes in Japan. Kagoshima also instructed the Ryūkyū king to send a congratulatory mission to Tokyo to honor the new government. The Meiji Emperor seized the opportunity and issued a rescript making Sho Tai "king of the Ryūkyū *han* (fief)," even though the *han* system had been abolished in Japan itself the previous year. Ryūkyū then was to be abolished and replaced by a prefecture, according to the new Japanese political formula. This was the beginning of *Ryūkyū shobun.*

The Ryūkyūan mission, which failed to grasp the Japanese logic, accepted the rescript on the assumption that it merely symbolized the investiture of the Ryūkyū king by the new Japanese emperor. The ulterior motive behind the rescript emerged when the Meiji government announced to the Western diplomatic community that Ryūkyū had been made a Japanese *han* and that Ryūkyū's international relations were henceforth under the jurisdiction of Japan's foreign office. No serious protests arose from the West, and China had no embassy in Japan at the time.

In 1874, Japan undertook a military expedition to Taiwan to punish aboriginal tribesmen for having killed 54 shipwrecked "Japanese subjects" off the Taiwan coast in 1871. These "Japanese subjects" were actually Ryūkyūans, and Chinese officials made it clear that they saw them as Ryūkyūans under Chinese control and the perpetrators as savages. The Japanese government officially claimed the Ryūkyūans as Japanese subjects under the above-mentioned 1872 rescript. The Chinese government disputed this claim, as well as the matter of Ryūkyū reverting to Japan. The Ryūkyū government also objected to the Japanese idea that wrongs suffered by Ryūkyūans ought to be avenged by Japanese authorities.

The language of the terms of settlement for the termination of the Taiwan expedition is extremely nuanced. The document does not explicitly refer to Ryūkyūans. China merely agreed not to object to the Japanese claim that it was right for Japan to take action to protect its people. Nevertheless, the received understanding of the implications of the agreement was that China recognized Ryūkyūans as Japanese and that the Japanese government had the right to protect them from harm.

Encouraged by the results of the Taiwan expedition, the Meiji government greatly intensified intervention in the internal affairs of Ryūkyū. In 1875, Japan ordered Ryūkyū to terminate its tributary relations with China, to use the era title of Meiji, to shut down the Ryūkyūan office in Fuzhou, China, and to send the king to Tokyo. In March 1879, Japanese troops occupied the Ryūkyū royal palace and evicted the king. In April, Japan proclaimed the establishment of the Okinawa Prefecture.

Ryūkyūan protests persisted. However, Western diplomats and the press were generally cool toward to the Ryūkyūan cause. China offered the only hope for Ryūkyūans, who exiled themselves to China in droves and lobbied the Chinese government for the restoration of the Ryūkyū kingdom. Post–1879 Sino-Japanese negotiations produced a tentative compromise to the effect that the Okinawa group of islands belonged to Japan and that the southern Ryūkyūan islands (Miyako and Yaeyama) belonged to China. China wished to maintain the Ryūkyū kingdom in these islands, but Sho Tai doubted that it would make a viable state, and China finally failed to sign the compromise agreement. Thereafter, Sino-Japanese talks ceased over Ryūkyū. Ryūkyūan exile movements for the restoration of the kingdom continued, though in increasing disarray, until the first Sino-Japanese War (1894–95).

Koji Taira

Bibliography

Kobata, Atsushi, and Mitsugu Matsuda. *Ryūkyūan Relations with Korea and Southsea Countries*. Kyoto: University of Kyoto Press, 1969.

Leung, Edwin Pak-Wah. "The Quasi-War in East Asia: Japan's Expedition to Taiwan and the Ryūkyū Controversy." *Modern Asian Studies*. Vol. 17, No. 2 (1969), 257–81.

S

Saga Rebellion (1874)

The first armed insurrection against the Japanese government after the Meiji imperial Restoration (1868) occurred in the wake of the *seikanron*, or 1873 crisis over whether Japan should go to war against Korea. When the conservative council of state leader Saigō Takamori's plan for sparking a war with Korea was rescinded in October 1873 widespread discontent arose among the *shizoku* (former samurai) class. Many of them, like Saigō, regarded war against Korea as necessary to defend Japan's honor and as a means to preserve the samurai as the country's exclusive warrior class. Etō Shimpei and Soejima Taneomi, the leading representatives of the Saga Prefecture in the Meiji government, were among the government leaders who sided with Saigō and resigned their government posts in protest after his Korea plan was refused.

In Saga, located in Japan across Tsushima Strait from Korea, discontent mounted, and, by January 1874, the *shizoku* organized their own army to carry out an attack against Korea. Upon hearing of this, Etō hastened back from Tokyo to lead the growing insurrection. Violence erupted in early February, and the Meiji government, fearing that the rebellion might spread, moved quickly to suppress the revolt. Within two weeks, the hastily organized rebel force of about 5,000 men suffered defeat by a better equipped Meiji army more than twice its size.

Wayne M. McWilliams

Bibliography

McWilliams, Wayne M. "Etō Shimpei and the Saga Rebellion." *Proceedings of the First International Symposium on Asian Studies, 1979.* Hong Kong: Asian Research Service, 1979.

Saigō Takamori (1827–77)

Meiji-era warrior and statesman. A low-ranking samurai from the domain of Satsuma (modern-day Kagoshima Prefecture) in southern Kyushu, Saigō rose to prominence in the 1860s and played a key role in the Meiji Restoration (1868) coup d'état. As a government councillor (*sangi*) between 1871 and 1873, he helped create a conscript army, a Tokyo metropolitan police force, and other early Meiji institutions. He left the government in 1873 after he

Saigō Takamori. Asahi Shimbun Photo.

was denied permission to go to Korea to resolve tensions between that country and Japan, and he died in the 1877 Satsuma Rebellion (*Seinan Sensō*).

Saigō's comprehension of politics was simple and formulaic: he espoused such traditional Confucian values as loyalty, obedience, righteousness, and benevolence, and he understood all social interactions to be determined by them. Political space, for him, was ideal and conceptual. The polity consisted of a hierarchy of relationships among servants, each loyal to his immediate superior and benevolent toward inferiors, and all supremely loyal to the emperor, whose authority came from Heaven, the final arbiter of all actions.

There is no evidence in Saigō's extant writings that he had any specific idea of Japan as a distinct and coherent political entity, or of the Japanese as a people united by a shared sense of nationhood. For him, there was an irreducible difference between *kokka* (nation), by which he meant the land, the people, and the institutions of the early modern feudal lord, or daimyo, and *tenka* (realm), by which he meant an ideal social hierarchy informed normatively by Heaven and centered on the emperor.

Charles Yates

Bibliography

Morris, Ivan. "The Apotheosis of Saigō the Great." *The Nobility of Failure*. New York: New American Library, 1975, 217–75.

Yates, Charles L. *Saigō Takamori: The Man Behind the Myth*. London, Kegan Paul, 1995.

Saigō Tsugumichi (1843–1902)

A Meiji leader from Satsuma domain (modern-day Kagoshima Prefecture) who was first a general then an admiral while serving in various bureaucratic posts. A younger brother of Saigō Takamori, he participated in the political and military actions that ended the Tokugawa shogunate in 1868; as a member of the new Meiji military department, he accompanied Meiji Restoration leader Yamagata Aritomo to Europe in 1869 to study military organization there and worked for the adoption of a conscription system. In 1874, he commanded Japan's expedition to Formosa; three years later, in a dramatic split with his better-known brother, he commanded the imperial guard in the defeat of the Takamori-led Satsuma rebels.

Thereafter, his career was distinguished by almost continuous service in a variety of ministerial posts. As a state councillor, he was, successively, minister of education (1878), war (1878–80), and agriculture and commerce (1881–85). After 1885, he became affiliated with the navy, serving as navy minister (1885–90, 1893–98); he also served twice as home minister (1890–91, 1898–1900). His Sutsuma background, seniority, and dependable bureaucratic service placed him among the Meiji *genrō* (elder statesmen), the nonlegal but highly influential group that advised the emperor from the early 1890s on.

Roger F. Hackett

Bibliography

Hackett, Roger. *Yamagata Aritomo in the Rise of Modern Japan*. Cambridge: Harvard University Press, 1971.

Saionji Kinmochi (1849–1940)

Statesman. Saionji's career spanned more than 70 years, from the late 1860s to 1940. He represented the best of the Meiji political leadership in his ability to learn and adapt to new circumstances and new challenges, and he was the last major voice raised against rising mili-

Saionji Kinmochi. Asahi Shimbun Photo.

tarism in the late 1930s. Yet, in his later years, he, too, was overwhelmed by the forces of extremism as Japan lurched onto the disastrous road to all-out war and military defeat from 1935 on.

Born in Kyoto in 1849 as the second son of a court noble family, the Tokudaiji, he was given for adoption in 1851 as son and heir to another court noble family, the Saionji. As a member of the court nobility, he was thrust into a leadership role in the Meiji Restoration (1868) at the age of 19, serving as titular commander of imperial forces in military expeditions to assert the new government's authority in the provinces to the north and west of Kyoto.

Saionji joined the government's Iwakura Mission to America and Europe in 1871 and stayed on at the Sorbonne in Paris to study, spending nearly 10 years absorbing Western liberal thought and immersing himself in the life of Paris. On his return to Japan in 1880, he joined two other Francophiles, Matsuda Masahisa and Nakae Chōmin, to establish a radical newspaper, the *Tōyō Jiyū Shimbun*. He was also instrumental in 1881 in founding the Meiji Hōritsu Gakkō (Meiji School of Law), which became the Ritsumeikan University in the twentieth century.

The older Meiji leaders found his political stance and his editorials too radical and urged him to resign from the presidency of the paper just weeks after its founding. He refused, only to be served with a formal imperial letter ordering his resignation. Reluctantly, but obediently, he withdrew from the paper. In 1882, he joined Itō Hirobumi's mission to study constitutional systems in Europe. His loyalty to the emperor and his aristocratic background provide threads of continuity in his career. In 1913, he resigned the presidency of the Rikken Seiyūkai (Friends of Constitutional Government Party) in response to another imperial letter. He sought always to move Japan in the direction of a more open polity, but he was never a twentieth-century egalitarian. He believed that Japanese politics should evolve toward a full-fledged parliamentary system, in which politics would operate much as the British system did, with the head of the majority party in the Diet (legislature) automatically becoming prime minister.

As an active politician, Saionji worked with Itō on the Meiji Constitution (1889) and in the founding in 1900 of the Seiyūkai, succeeding to the presidency of the party in 1903 when Itō left the office to become president of the Privy Council. In the 1890s, Saionji had served as minister of education in the second and third Itō cabinets, and he became prime minister himself in 1906 and again in 1911. His resignation in 1912 precipitated the Taishō political crisis, in which civilian politicians loudly opposed an increasingly military-dominated government. Behind the scenes, he encouraged his followers to push through the reforms that ended the crisis in 1913 with a victory for the parties and civilian government, a triumph that established a pattern of civilian control that lasted for nearly 20 years and ushered in the era known as the Taishō democracy (1912–26).

When worldwide Depression, Chinese nationalism, and the structural prerogatives of the military leaders in the Meiji state combined to destroy that fragile evolutionary movement toward full democracy for Japan, Saionji carried on a lonely rear-guard defense of civilian rule and an open society, giving ground inch by inch throughout the 1930s. His protégé, Prince Konoe Fumimaro, failed him, and his own failing physical powers and influence were overwhelmed by the march toward full-scale war that the Japanese military launched in July 1937.

Jackson H. Bailey

Bibliography

Bailey, Jackson. "Prince Saionji and the Popular Rights Movement." *Journal of Asian Studies* Vol. 21, No. 1 (November 1961), 49–63.

Connors, L. *The Emperor's Advisor*. London: Croom Helm, 1987.

Oka, Yoshitake. *Five Political Leaders of Modern Japan*. Tokyo: University of Tokyo Press, 1986.

Saitō Makoto (1858–1936)

Admiral and statesman. Born in Iwate Prefecture, Saitō graduated from the Naval Academy, then spent most of his life in government posts, consistently following a moderate military approach. A champion of naval modernization, he was navy minister for eight years (1906–14), resigning when the Yamamoto Gonnohyōe cabinet fell in the Siemens bribery scandal over naval purchases. He spent the years 1919–27 and 1929–31 as governor-general of Korea, where he attempted to replace military with civilian rule and to pursue less exploitative policies. When Prime Minister Inukai Tsuyoshi was assassinated in May 1932, Saitō was named prime minister, heading the national unity cabinet that brought rule by political parties to an end. Though his government recognized the Japan-dominated puppet state of Manchukuo in Manchuria and led Japan out of the League of Nations in 1933, Saitō was too moderate for the right wing; his efforts to assist Depression-plagued farmers angered advocates of greater military spending. His cabinet fell in 1934 during a corruption scandal in which leading members of his government were implicated in the manipulation of the stock of the Teijin rayon manufacturing firm, and he was assassinated by ultranationalists during the February 26, 1936, coup d'état by young military officers.

James L. Huffman

Bibliography

Young, Arthur. *Imperial Japan, 1926–1938.* William Morrow, 1938.

Saitō Takao (1870–1949)

Antiwar politician. Saitō first won election to the national Diet (legislature) in 1912 and served 13 terms. As a member of the Rikken Minseitō (Constitutional Democratic Party), he gained attention in the 1930s for his persistent and sharp criticism of the military. He openly denounced the army rebellion of February 26, 1936, bemoaned rising military interference in politics, and led the opposition to the National Mobilization Law of 1938.

In February 1940, Saitō delivered his most famous speech, in which he offered a scathing critique of the second Sino-Japanese War (1937–45) that had begun three years before. Ordinary citizens, he argued, did not know why Japan was waging the war. Justifying it as a holy war for ethical principles or the creation of an Asian new order was hypocritical, because all wars were struggles for power. The burden of sacrifice fell unevenly on the people; some suffered greatly while others profited. The government had no plan for resolving the conflict.

Saitō's solitary stance of forthright opposition to the war highlighted the dominant nationalistic mood at the time. When the army demanded that Saitō be punished for his comments in 1940, the Diet, including members of his own party, obliged by voting overwhelmingly to eject him.

William Miles Fletcher III

Bibliography

Berger, Gordon M. *Parties out of Power in Japan, 1931–1941.* Princeton, NJ: Princeton University Press, 1977.

Sakai Toshihiko (1870–1933)

Socialist and Communist activist. Born in Fukuoka Prefecture, Sakai left the First Higher School in 1889 to become a writer. In 1899, he became a journalist for the *Yorozu Chōhō* newspaper and developed an interest in socialism from his fellow journalists Kōtoku Shūsui and Uchimura Kanzō. When *Yorozu Chōhō* began advocating war with Russia in October 1903, Sakai resigned with considerable fanfare and helped organize the Heiminsha (Society of Commoners), a socialist organization that openly criticized the war through its newspaper, the *Heimin Shimbun.* In January 1905, the government shut down the paper for publishing a translation of Karl Marx's *Communist Manifesto,* and Sakai, Kōtoku, and other leaders were arrested.

Also in 1905, Sakai helped found the Japan Socialist Party. He was a leader of the 1908 Red Flag Incident, a socialist-anarchist rally that triggered a government crackdown on socialism and resulted in two-year prison terms for Sakai and others. Sakai was arrested in 1922 for illegally organizing the Nihon Kyōsantō (Japanese Communist Party). Two years later, he parted ways with the Moscow-influenced Communist Party, joined the socialists, and began promoting social-democratic ideas through the magazine *Rōnō* (Labor-Farmer). Sakai also helped organize numerous non-Communist leftist groups under the Nihon Taishūtō (Japanese Masses Party).

In 1929, he was elected to the Tokyo Metropolitan Assembly, and, in 1931, he returned to Fukuoka to open a school for farmers and laborers. With the threat of confrontation between China and Japan, he became the chairman of the antiwar Committee of the Zenkoku Rōnō Taishūtō (National Labor-Farmer Party).

James L. Huffman
Tracy Pollard

Bibliography

Hane, Mikiso. *Reflections on the Way to the Gallows: Japanese Rebel Women.* New York: Pantheon, 1988.

Notehelfer, F.G. *Kōtoku Shūsui: Portrait of a Japanese Radical.* Cambridge: Cambridge University Press, 1971.

Sake (Rice "Wine")

An alcoholic beverage (about 30 proof) made from rice. Tasting like dry sherry although brewed more like beer than wine, *sake* is richly evocative of Japanese social life and is symbolically the national beverage of Japan. It is central to Shinto as sacrament, offering to the *kami* (spirits), and purifier of the profane. The beverage's link to the national identity is expressed by the fact that the Japanese use the terms *nihonshū* (Japanese liquor) and *osake* (honorable liquor) to designate the specific beverage. The word *sake* is the generic Japanese term for alcoholic beverages.

Stephen R. Smith

Sakuma Shōzan (also Zōzan) (1811–64)

Tokugawa-era scholar who favored ending Japan's seclusion policy. An early advocate of coastal defense against foreign threat, Sakuma was a samurai administrator and adviser to the lord of Matsuhiro, Shinano Province (modern-day Nagano Prefecture). In 1844, he began Rangaku (Dutch studies), leading to his compilation of a Japanese-Dutch dictionary, construction of a camera, and experimentation with casting cannon. Though critical of Tokugawa Japan's weakness in response to U.S. Navy Commodore Matthew Perry's forced opening of the country in 1853–54, Sakuma was concerned about Japan's ability to compete with the West. This compelled him to favor *kaikoku* (open-country) policies. He greatly influenced his famous pupil Yoshida Shōin, along with thousands of others, through his school in Edo. To make Japan strong yet retain what was unique, he advocated *tōyō dōtoku, seiyō gei* (Eastern Ethics, Western Science) and was a proponent of *kōbugattai* (unity of court and *bakufu*). In 1864, the emperor appointed him naval and military adviser to the court. That same year, he was killed by an antiforeign fanatic for mediating between the court and the *bakufu* (military government).

Ann M. Harrington

Bibliography

Beasley, W.G. *The Meiji Restoration.* Stanford, CA: Stanford University Press, 1972.

Harootunian, H.D. *Toward Restoration: The Growth of Political Consciousness in Tokugawa Japan.* Berkeley: University of California Press, 1970.

San Francisco Peace Treaty (*Sanfuranshisuku Kōwa Jōyaku*)

Treaty signed September 8, 1951, that formally ended World War II hostilities. In March 1947, U.S. General Douglas MacArthur, head of the Allied Occupation in Japan, called for negotiations toward a peace treaty. The U.S. State Department began discussions in the fall of 1950, under the direction of Secretary of State John Foster Dulles. From the outset, disputes abounded. Many countries, including Great Britain, wanted a restrictive treaty that would keep postwar Japan under international controls, while the Americans desired a more benevolent agreement that would make Japan a strong Cold War ally. The Soviets and the Americans disagreed on the role of U.S. bases after the Occupation. Questions of who would participate in the peace conference also proved nettlesome.

Ultimately, the United States dominated the process. The formal conference, convened in San Francisco, included 51 countries plus Japan. Three (Burma, India, and Yugoslavia) refused to attend, and three others (Czechoslovakia, Poland, and the U.S.S.R.) walked out during the conference. The treaty was relatively lenient, granting Japan full sovereignty. It deprived Japan of its wartime territories, including Korea, Taiwan, the Kuriles, Pescadores, and Sakhalin; provided for Japanese payment of reparations even while calling for consideration of Japan's weak economic situation; and advocated Japanese membership in the United Nations. Immediately after the signing, Japan and the United States also concluded the Japan-U.S. Security Treaty, providing for the continuation of U.S. bases in Japan.

The treaty took effect on April 28, 1952, ending the Occupation and restoring sovereignty to Japan. The Japanese government reached separate agreements with the Communist countries later in the 1950s. It restored diplomatic relations but signed no peace treaties with them, due to continuing disputes over ownership of the Kuril Islands, called the "northern territories." It also concluded a peace treaty with the Nationalist government on Taiwan in April 1952, in response to American pressures to avoid relations with the People's Republic of China. The San Francisco treaty made Japan a central part of America's security system in Asia, tying the two countries closely to each other even while laying the groundwork for ongoing tensions between them.

James L. Huffman

Bibliography
Finn, Richard. *Winners in Peace: MacArthur, Yoshida and Postwar Japan*. Berkeley: University of California Press, 1992.

Sasagawa Ryōichi (1899–1995)

Prewar fascist leader, postwar businessman and right-wing leader. A worshiper of the fascist Italian dictator Benito Mussolini, Sasagawa kicked off his right-wing extremist career in 1925. In 1931, he became president of the Kokusui Taishūtō (Mass Party Representing Japan's National Essence), which claimed a membership of 110,000 by 1941. In 1933, he and party members plotted to kill the moderate political leader Wakatsuki Reijirō; in 1935, they took part in a campaign of terror against the scholar Minobe Tatsukichi during the National Polity Clarification Campaign (1935–36). That same year, Sasagawa and 22 other party members were arrested for extortion in a series of incidents dating from 1932. Six members, Sasagawa included, were imprisoned until July 1937, but, in 1938, they were cleared of the charges. By 1941, Sasagawa was pressing for continued aggression in China, sponsoring mass rallies to whip up hatred toward Great Britain and the United States, and launching a Southern Advance Campaign to win public support for military leaders who wanted to extend the war to the Pacific.

After Japan's surrender in World War II (1937–45), Sasagawa reorganized his old National Essence Party into new right-wing organizations, but both were outlawed. In December 1945, he was arrested as a major war criminal on the basis of his prewar, wartime, and post-surrender activities, which the United States deemed inimical to democracy in Japan. After serving three years in Sugamo Prison, he was released without trial for reasons that remain mysterious (many said he struck a deal with American officials). Through much of the postwar era, Sasagawa served as an adviser to the Zen-Nippon Aikokusha Dantai Kaigi (National Council of Patriotic Societies), which represented more than 800 Japanese right-wing and gangster groups analogous to white supremacists or neo-Nazis in the West. In 1960, it recruited and coordinated members for large-scale attacks, condoned by the Kishi Nobusuke government, on students protesting the renewal and revision of the 1951 Japan-U.S. Security Treaty. Although the revised treaty eventually was ratified, the heavy handedness of the attacks inspired wide public revulsion and brought down the Kishi government. Into the 1990s the Council maintained intimate relations with a Nagasaki-based group that publicly praised the attempt by one of its members to kill Motoshima Hitoshi, mayor of Nagasaki, in 1990 for raising questions about the Shōwa Emperor's war guilt.

In 1974, *Time* quoted Sasagawa as proclaiming himself "the world's wealthiest fascist." At that time, he boasted that he commanded 8 million ultranationalist followers. He was an important force behind remilitarization and the revival of emperor worship in postwar Japan, and he enjoyed close ties with prominent political leaders, such as former Prime Minister Kishi Nobusuke (1896–1987), and with right-wing gangster bosses, such as Kodama Yoshio (1911–84)—both of whom were fellow Class A war-crimes suspects and cell mates in Sugamo. The Shōwa Emperor (1901–89) decorated Sasagawa twice, with the First Order of the Sacred Treasure in 1978 and with the First Order of Merit with the Grand Cordon of the Rising Sun in 1987.

Bob Tadashi Wakabayashi

Bibliography
Kaplan, David, and Alec Dubro. *Yakuza*. New York: Macmillan, 1987.

Satchō

Abbreviation for Satsuma and Chōshū, the two Tokugawa domains that predominated in overthrowing the Tokugawa shogunate and establishing the Meiji government. The two large domains had been rivals of the Tokugawa before the establishment of the Tokugawa shogunate in 1600. As the Tokugawa regime faltered under pressure from the Western powers in the 1850s and early 1860s, each domain sought a larger role for itself in national affairs. For some time, their mutual rivalry and the Tokugawa policy of isolating its potential enemies from each other kept Satsuma and Chōshū from collaborating, but, in 1867, activists from the two domains forged an alliance that in 1868 ousted the Tokugawa shogun in the name of restoring direct imperial rule. Having seized the initiative, Satsuma and Chōshū retainers continued to dominate the new Meiji government (1868–1912) for the next several decades.

Kate Wildman Nakai

Bibliography
Beasley, W.G. *The Meiji Restoration.*
Stanford, CA: Stanford University Press,
1972.

Satō Eisaku (1901–75)

Prime Minister. Born in Yamaguchi Prefecture to a leading political family, he graduated from the University of Tokyo in 1924, spent his entire adult life in government, and served more consecutive years as prime minister (1964–72) than any other individual. Most of his pre–World War II work was in the Ministry of Railways. After the war, he resumed this activity, then became director of the cabinet secretariat in 1948 and entered the lower house of the Diet (legislature) in 1949. His career was tainted in 1954 by a shipbuilding scandal when he was reported to have accepted bribes, but he survived politically and served as cabinet minister four times after 1951. He won the prime ministership when Ikeda Hayato was forced to resign that position for health reasons in 1964.

As prime minister, Satō continued Japan's emphasis on economic growth led by big business, though, by the late 1960s, he was encountering considerable criticism for the country's increasing problems with pollution, urban crowding, and student disputes. His chief foreign successes lay in the normalization of relations with Korea (1965) and America's return

Satō Eisaku. Courtesy Consulate General of Japan, N.Y.

of the Ryūkyū Islands to Japan (1972). Japan's relations with the United States were cordial during the 1960s but then turned sour over textile disputes and U.S. President Richard Nixon's failure to consult Japan on issues such as the 1972 resumption of contacts with the People's Republic of China. Satō was a highly controversial recipient of the Nobel Peace Prize in 1974, for his role in keeping nuclear weapons out of Japan. His tenure was known more for stability than for innovation.

James L. Huffman

Bibliography
Curtis, Gerald L. *The Japanese Way of Politics.* New York: Columbia University Press, 1988.

Satō Nobuhiro (1769–1850)

Major exponent of a variety of national absolutism in the late Tokugawa period (1600–1868). Late in life, Satō wrote a number of treatises outlining his plan to consolidate all of Japan into a single political unit and to unify the world as part of Japan. He proposed a centralized administrative structure with three departments, six ministries, and five bureaus. He also envisioned that the existing class structure would be completely replaced by eight categories of people, based on their specialization: plant cultivation, forestry, mining, manufacture, trade, miscellaneous labor, shipping, and fishing. He planned to retain the *han* (feudal domains) but to limit their size and place them under the control of governors appointed by the ruler. Satō's use of terms such as *kōkyo* (imperial court) and *kōkoku* (imperial country) to describe this structure suggests that he envisioned an imperial rule.

Satō was born in Dewa Province (now Akita Prefecture) to a family of scholars and introduced early by his father to social research, focused especially on agriculture. He traveled widely across Japan, initially with his father and later on his own. Besides agronomy and mining, he learned astronomy, geography, and surveying from Rangaku (Dutch studies) scholars and became deeply interested in Shinto. Around the turn of the nineteenth century, he became a disciple of the *kokugaku* (national learning) iconoclast Hirata Atsutane. Satō advised several daimyo and wrote a major text advocating direct government control over agricultural production, commerce, and transportation.

In his classic essays on the development of Tokugawa thought, Maruyama Masao associated the works of Satō and others with a premodern nationalist discourse on the need for *fukoku kyōhei* (rich country, strong army). This discourse was in large part a response to European pressure and eventually merged with the nationalist ideology of *sonnō jōi* (revere the emperor and expel the barbarians).

J. Victor Koschmann

Bibliography

Maruyama, Masao. *Studies in the Intellectual History of Tokugawa Japan*. Tokyo: University of Tokyo Press, 1974.

Satsuma Rebellion (*Seinan Sensō*) (1877)

The last of a series of armed uprisings initiated between 1873 and 1877 by former samurai who opposed the institutional and social policies of the young Meiji government. The rebellion began in February 1877, when young samurai seized government arsenals in the city of Kagoshima. Unstoppable at first, the rebels dissipated their strength in a pointless attempt to reduce the government garrison at Kumamoto. By autumn they were in retreat, and their remnants were overwhelmed in Kagoshima in late September 1877.

The causes of the rebellion were complex but had little to do with Saigō Takamori, the warrior and statesman who died in the uprising and is generally held to have fomented it. Rather, it arose from the reluctance of Kagoshima officials to surrender their local autonomy to the Meiji government. Their stubborn resistance to centralization steadily isolated Kagoshima from Tokyo and created the atmosphere of mutual suspicion in which the rebellion finally erupted.

The avowed aim of the rebel army was to march on Tokyo and use the threat of force to alter government policy; the goal was not to overthrow the government but to modify it. Some scholars believe that the rebels rose up because of conflicting views regarding what features should characterize the newly emerging Japanese polity, but this view grants them more political sophistication and vision than most of them had. Their aims were modest and conservative.

At stake for the rebels was the familiar world of the Tokugawa institutional order, particularly the social relationships and values it embodied. They fought to preserve a world in which inherited status and the behavior it entailed were the primary determinants of social interaction. The chief importance of the rebellion, however, was to serve as a watershed in the formation of centralized national government. It was the last significant military challenge to centralization, and its suppression silenced the last significant armed opponents of the Meiji government.

Charles Yates

Bibliography

Buck, James. "The Satsuma Rebellion of 1877: An Enquiry into Some of Its Military and Political Aspects." Unpublished doctoral dissertation, American University, 1959.

Mounsey, Augustus. *The Satsuma Rebellion*. London: John Murray, 1879.

Self-Defense Forces (SDF) (*Jieitai*)

Japan's ground (GSDF), maritime (MSDF), and air (ASDF) services under the control of the prime minister, via the civilian Defense Agency. The primary mission of the SDF is to protect Japanese territory in cooperation with the U.S. armed forces. Despite its relatively small size, the SDF is equipped with a large number of state-of-the-art weapons systems. The Japanese defense budget is among the largest in the world, even though it is held to about 1 percent of gross national product.

Following its defeat in World War II, Japan was stripped of its armed forces and defense industries to ensure that it never again posed a threat to peace. The Allied powers believed that dismantling the imperial army and navy was the surest way to prevent a resurgence of militarism. This view is embodied in Article 9 of the Japanese Constitution, which states that Japan will not maintain war potential for the purpose of settling international disputes. In the immediate postwar period, many Japanese were persuaded that national security could be guaranteed by the United Nations or by a declaration of neutrality in accordance with the Swiss model.

The onset of the Cold War in East Asia forced a reassessment of Japan's defense. In June 1950, the outbreak of the Korean War led U.S. General Douglas MacArthur, head of the Occupation, to order the formation of a National Police Reserve (NPR), which was made responsible for defending Japan; that allowed

U.S. forces to be dispatched to Korea. Under subsequent pressure from the United States, the Japanese government increased the size of the NPR (later the National Safety Forces) to assist the United States in its regional defense efforts. In 1954, a pair of laws passed by the Diet (legislature) established the Defense Agency and the SDF. The name "Self Defense Forces" stresses that its existence did not infringe on Article 9.

Since its inception, the SDF has labored under numerous constraints, a legacy of Japan's militarist past. The principle of civilian control ensures that the SDF has little political influence; the National Defense Program Outline (1976) places ceilings on the number of SDF personnel and the number of weapons it may acquire, and government refusal to dispatch the SDF abroad has limited its mission to national defense. Moreover, a number of political groups, citing Article 9, have disputed the constitutionality of the SDF and have consistently opposed government efforts to expand its capabilities. Public opinion surveys continued in the latter 1990s to record tepid support for the SDF.

This distrust of the military has thwarted efforts to exploit the SDF as a patriotic symbol. The most notorious incident occurred in 1970, when author Mishima Yukio and his Shield Society took control of GSDF headquarters in Tokyo. Calling for a rebirth of the Japanese martial spirit and an end to political corruption, Mishima hoped to incite SDF officers to launch a coup d'état. Although the entreaties found little support and Mishima subsequently committed suicide, the incident revealed a stratum of SDF officers deeply troubled by the absence of a patriotic spirit in postwar Japanese society. Such incidents have, however, been few.

In the 1970s, external pressure on Japan to expand its defense efforts began to erode domestic constraints on the SDF. Recognition of Japanese economic strength and the emergence of a potent Soviet naval threat in the Pacific prompted U.S. demands on Japan for sharing the defense burden. As a result, the SDF was permitted to participate in regional military exercises and to defend Japanese sea lanes to a distance of 1,000 nautical miles. With the end of the Cold War in 1989, Japan was urged by many of its allies to shift from regional to global responsibilities.

In 1990–91, U.S. criticism of Japan during the Persian Gulf crisis triggered domestic controversy over whether the SDF should be permitted a role in U.N. collective security operations. In a major policy shift, the Diet passed the International Peace Cooperation bill in June 1992, allowing the SDF to participate in U.N. peacekeeping and humanitarian operations. By the middle of the 1990s, SDF contingents had been sent to U.N. operations in Cambodia, Mozambique and Zaire.

Bill Heinrich

Bibliography

Katzenstein, Peter, and Nobuo Okawara. *Japan's National Security: Structures, Norms and Policy Responses in a Changing World.* Ithaca, NY: Cornell University Press, 1993.

Welfield, John. *An Empire in Eclipse: Japan in the Postwar American Alliance System.* London: Athlone Press, 1988.

Senior Statesmen (*Jūshin*)

The Japanese preference for group decisions is evident throughout history and even in prehistoric legends about Shinto deities. The chief variable has been the composition of the deciding group. To define and propagate the official nationalism of the Meiji era (1868–1912) a small, self-appointed group eventually called the *genrō* (elder statesmen) made major decisions in the name of the theoretically autocratic emperor.

By the 1930s, only one *genrō* survived, the octogenarian Saionji Kinmochi (1849–1940), and civilian and military leaders had become sharply divided. Before advising the emperor on major decisions, Saionji consulted widely, and, in 1934, convened the first meeting of *jūshin* (senior statesmen), comprising all former prime ministers, the current lord keeper of the privy seal, and the current president of the Privy Council.

After Saionji's death in 1940, *jūshin* meetings were called by Kido Kōichi (1889–1977), lord keeper of the privy seal, but *jūshin* authority was always feeble by comparison with *genrō* power before the 1930s. The *jūshin* chose prime ministers from 1934 to 1945 but were overshadowed by other groups in making major decisions on war and peace. For both Saionji and Kido, the prime duty of the *jūshin* was not to shape policy but to protect the throne.

Robert M. Spaulding

Bibliography

Berger, Gordon. *Parties out of Power in Japan, 1931–1941.* Princeton, NJ: Princeton University Press, 1977.

S

Seven Professors Incident (*Shichi Hakase Jiken*)

Most accurately translated as the Affair of the Seven Ph.D.'s but also known as the Tomizu affair, this 1905 confrontation between the Katsura Tarō cabinet and nationalists on the faculty of Tokyo University climaxed five years of heated public debate over foreign policy regarding Korea and Manchuria. Membership in the "group of seven" fluctuated, but over time it included some of the most prominent academics of the era, including Kanai Noburu, Onozuka Kiheiji, Terao Tōru, and Tomii Masaaki. Collectively, they used the prestige of their doctoral (*hakase*) degrees to champion the cause of Japanese expansion.

The most outspoken scholar was Tomizu Hirondo (1861–1935), given the sobriquet "Dr. Baikal" for his extreme view that Russia should be forced to withdraw from all of its territories east of that Siberian lake. The government, pursuing a diplomatic compromise to secure hegemony over Korea, was embarrassed by the attention paid to the professors' group in the foreign and domestic press. Prior to the Russo-Japanese War (1904–05), it unsuccessfully pressured the group to tone down its public statements. When, in August 1905, the professors' vehement denunciation of the terms of the Portsmouth Treaty ending the war threatened to inflame popular discontent, Prime Minister Katsura retaliated by suspending Tomizu from his faculty post. This transformed the affair into a confrontation over academic freedom, and the faculties at Tokyo and Kyoto Imperial Universities threatened mass resignations to support the principle of academic autonomy. The government finally capitulated and reinstated Tomizu in January 1906.

Byron K. Marshall

Bibliography

Marshall, Byron. *Academic Freedom and the Japanese Imperial University*. Berkeley: University of California Press, 1992.

Shanghai Incident (*Shanhai Jihen*)

On January 8, 1932, nearly four months after the Manchurian Incident, a Chinese mob attacked some Japanese Buddhist priests in Shanghai, killing one. This incident, apparently instigated by local Japanese army officers against the desire of higher Japanese authorities, provoked anti-Japanese demonstrations, counterdemonstrations, then relatively heavy fighting between Japanese and Chinese troops throughout February. China invoked the League of Nations to act against the Japanese. Though the Chinese army called for a halt to the engagement on March 3, and a May 5 truce provided for the withdrawal of Japanese forces from Shanghai and an end to the Chinese boycott of Japanese goods, the episode greatly heightened international opposition to Japan's military moves in Asia. It also played a significant role in undermining civilian rule in Tokyo. When Prime Minister Inukai Tsuyoshi was assassinated 10 days after the truce, political-party government terminated in Japan.

James L. Huffman

Bibliography

Crowley, James. *Japan's Quest for Autonomy*: Princeton, NJ: Princeton University Press, 1966.

Shibusawa Eiichi (1840–1931)

Business leader. Born to a wealthy farmer in modern-day Saitama Prefecture, Shibusawa ranked among prewar Japan's wealthiest and most influential men, making major contributions to modern banking, business, and industrial practices. Shibusawa received an unorthodox Confucian education and thus developed a fondness for the Confucian *Analects,* to which he referred frequently. As a young man, he participated in anti-Tokugawa movements and joined a wild, unsuccessful scheme to drive the foreigners out of Yokohama. At age 24, after a change of heart, he became a samurai retainer of the Tokugawa-branch family Hitotsubashi, and, in 1867–68, he accompanied Akitake, the shogun's younger brother, to Paris. This period abroad shaped Shibusawa's worldview, convincing him of Japan's need to modernize. Back in Japan, he served in the Finance Ministry from 1869 to 1873 and helped lay the foundations for the new Meiji government's tax system.

After leaving government service in 1872, Shibusawa devoted the rest of his working life to private enterprise. He built and supported hundreds of business organizations, using methods, such as the joint-stock company, he had learned abroad. Among his noteworthy accomplishments were the founding of the Ōji Paper Company and the Osaka Spinning Company. At his retirement from the business world in 1907, Shibusawa had been involved in more than 500 different business organizations. He continued his social and humanitarian projects and activities until the end of his life.

George M. Oshiro

Bibliography
Obata, Kyukorō. *An Interpretation of the Life of Viscount Shibusawa*. Tokyo: Tokyo Insatsu Kabushiki Kaisha, 1937.

Shidehara Kijūrō (1872–1951)

Statesman. Born in Osaka, graduated in 1895 from the Tokyo University law department, and married to a daughter of Mitsubishi founder Iwasaki Yatarō, he served two terms as foreign minister and became known in prewar Japan for "Shidehara diplomacy," a term that symbolized conciliatory international policies. Following diplomatic postings in Korea, the United States, and several European countries, he was named foreign minister in the Katō Takaaki cabinet in 1924. In contrast to his expansionist predecessor, Tanaka Giichi, he opposed the use of force in China and worked for international cooperation. During his second term as foreign minister (1929–31), he won the enmity of ultranationalists by advocating the approval of the 1930 London Naval Treaty, which continued American and British supremacy on the seas. He served for four months as acting prime minister after the shooting of Prime Minister Hamaguchi Osachi in November 1930 and then resigned, along with the rest of the cabinet, in the wake of the Manchurian Incident, late in 1931.

Although Shidehara largely retired from public life then, he was summoned to become prime minister in October 1945 as a result of his reputation for internationalism and his Anglo-American orientation. He fought during his seven months in office to maintain the emperor system, agreeing only reluctantly to many Occupation reforms. He was speaker of the lower house of the Diet (legislature) when he died.

James L. Huffman

Bibliography
Bamba, Nobuya. *Japanese Diplomacy in a Dilemma*. Vancouver: University of British Columbia Press, 1972.

Shiga Shigetaka (1863–1927)

Nationalist writer and geographer. A native of Aichi Prefecture, he gained prominence in 1887 for his account of life in the South Pacific, *Nan'yō jiji* (Conditions in the South Seas), which urged the Japanese to develop industry and trade as a source of national strength. He helped form the Seikyōsha (Society for Political Education) in 1888 and became editor of its publication, *Nihonjin* (The Japanese). There, he popularized the phrase *kokusui hozon* (preservation of national essence), arguing that Japan must counter thoughtless Westernization by reviving its own roots and culture. As a student of geography, he emphasized the unique beauty of Japan's physical setting. He held posts in the Foreign Ministry and the Agriculture and Commerce Ministry late in the 1890s and served in the Diet (legislature) from 1902 to 1904, advocating a forceful foreign policy. During his last 20 years, he took three trips around the world, wrote widely, and lectured at Waseda University.

James L. Huffman

Bibliography
Pyle, Kenneth B. *The New Generation in Meiji Japan*. Stanford, CA: Stanford University Press, 1969.

Shigemitsu Mamoru (1887–1957)

Politician and foreign minister. Born in Oita Prefecture and a 1911 graduate of the University of Tokyo, he spent most of his career in the Foreign Ministry, first in European posts, then in Asia. He was minister to China at the time of the Manchurian Incident (September 1931). In 1933, he became vice minister of foreign affairs and aligned himself with the Asia faction, which favored a strong China policy but opposed the ultranationalists. After terms as minister to the U.S.S.R. (1936–38), Great Britain (1938–41), and China (1941–43), he served as foreign minister under Tōjō Hideki (1943–45). In that post, he worked actively to moderate Japan's World War II policies and hasten peace. Following the war, Shigemitsu was indicted as a war criminal, despite wide opposition; he was found guilty and given a seven-year prison sentence, the lightest of any of those tried.

After an early release from prison for good behavior in November 1950, he entered party politics and became president of the Nihon Kaishintō (Japan Reform Party). In 1954, he was named foreign minister again, this time under Hatoyama Ichirō. He now worked for rapprochement with the Soviet Union and represented Japan when it entered the United Nations in 1956. He resigned with Hatoyama in December of that year, after normalizing relations with the Soviets.

James L. Huffman

Bibliography
Coox, Alvin. "Shigemitsu Mamoru: The Diplomacy of Crisis." *Diplomats in Crisis: United States-Chinese-Japanese Relations, 1919–1941.* Ed. Richard Burns and Edward Bennet. Santa Barbara: University of California Press, 1974.

Shimanaka Incident (*Shimanaka Jiken*)

Events surrounding the 1960 attempted assassination of Shimanaka Hōji, president of the Chūō Kōronsha publishing firm by a right-wing nationalist youth. In December 1960, the firm's monthly journal, *Chūō Kōron* (Central Review), published an excerpt of Fukazawa Shichirō's fiction, in which the imperial couple are beheaded. Right-wing groups and even the Imperial Household Agency immediately leveled charges of lèse majesté, and Shimanaka became involved in negotiations to quiet the furor. However, before these negotiations bore fruit, a young former member of Akao Bin's Dainihon Aikokutō (Greater Japan Patriots Party) broke into the Shimanaka residence looking for Shimanaka Hōji, who was not at home. The youth did succeed in murdering a household maid and seriously wounding Shimanaka's wife. In response to the attack, and to forestall further incidents, officials at the Chūō Kōronsha firm apologized—in various newspapers in early February 1961 and in the March issue of *Chūō Kōron*—for running the story.

The Shimanaka attack and the parallel assassination of the socialist leader Asanuma Inejirō are often interpreted as elements of a right-wing nationalist reaction to the widespread protests led by the left wing earlier in 1960 against the Japan-U.S. Security Treaty. The incident made Chūō Kōronsha extremely sensitive to criticism from the Right and is said to have caused a lasting conservative editorial turn at *Chūō Kōron*, which continued to be a leading opinion journal throughout the remainder of the century. In 1962, the company canceled publication of the April issue of another magazine it published, *Shisōno Kagaku*

because the issue focused on the emperor system. Then, in 1963, *Chūō Kōron* began the serialization of Hayashi Fusao's nationalistic narration of the Pacific War (1937–45), the *Dai-Tōa sensō kōteiron* (Affirmation of the Greater East Asia War).

J. Victor Koschmann

Bibliography
Koschmann, J. Victor. "Intellectuals and Politics." *Postwar Japan as History.* Ed. Andrew Gordon. Berkeley: University of California Press, 1993, 395–423.

Shimazu Hisamitsu (1817–87)

Late-Tokugawa leader from Satsuma domain. A supporter of *kōbugattai* (union of court and *bakufu*) policies in the late 1850s designed to broaden government participation, he became de facto ruler of Satsuma in 1858 when his half-brother Nariakira died and his own son became daimyo.

Shimazu favored the opening of Japan to the West and daimyo participation in government affairs. In 1862, he suppressed antiforeign radicals in Kyoto, then proceeded to Edo to advocate the *kōbugattai* policy, in which he would serve as a major link between the imperial court and the *bakufu* (military government). On the return trip to Satsuma, his escort troops killed an English merchant named Charles Richardson, resulting in British military reprisals against his domain.

Shimazu returned to Kyoto in 1863 and became a member of the daimyo council, but, disillusioned by the lack of daimyo influence in the Tokugawa government and faced with increasingly powerful anti-*bakufu* sentiment, he once again returned to Satsuma. Thereafter, his influence waned, and the *kōbugattai* movement steadily lost credibility.

After the Meiji Restoration (1868), Shimazu became minister of the left, but he remained a conservative opponent of Meiji reform programs until his resignation and retirement in 1876.

Lane R. Earns

Bibliography
Totman, Conrad. *The Collapse of the Tokugawa Bakufu.* Honolulu: University of Hawaii Press, 1980.

Shimizu Ikutarō (1907–88)

Intellectual. Shimizu's relation to Japanese nationalism is complex. His prolific intellectual career has been a series of conscious, skillfully rationalized recanting (*tenkō*) made in consideration of the fluid political and social situation of Japan between the 1930s and the 1990s. Each *tenkō* placed Shimizu at what he took to be the forefront of national life; in these reorientations, nationalism has been at one (explicit) level a phase and at another (implicit) level a motivation in itself.

Shimizu graduated from Tokyo Imperial University in 1931 and began his career as a Marxist critic of "bourgeois sociology." Although not a party member, Shimizu carried out his first *tenkō* following the mass defections from the Japan Communist Party in 1933. Inspired by American philosopher and educator John Dewey, Shimizu adopted a highly self-conscious pragmatism, maintaining an independent, though transitional, leftist position.

In 1937, Shimizu joined Prime Minister Konoe Fumimaro's Shōwa Kenkyūkai (Shōwa Research Association). He wrote for the *Asahi* and *Yomiuri* newspapers (1938–41, 1941–45, respectively) and traveled to Southeast Asia as an army correspondent. He grew interested in Japanese culture and in social psychology. Shimizu especially wanted science to illuminate the problems of everyday life, and he demonstrated what he meant in a brilliant study of the social function of false rumor, *Ryūgen higo* (False Rumor, 1937).

Shimizu was never a mere propagandist for the new order; his writing was politically, but not aesthetically, vague. Declaring, nevertheless, that the nation constituted basic society, Shimizu did take a nationalist position and contributed to the intellectual mobilization for war.

Following Japan's defeat in World War II (1937–45), Shimizu performed a third *tenkō*. As a self-designated democratic enlightener, Shimizu took a modernist position, insisting on the need to circumscribe the deeply rooted irrationalities within Japanese society by applying rational ideas and means introduced from outside. He also campaigned passionately for a comprehensive, rather than a bilateral, peace treaty. As proponent of citizens' democracy (*shimin minshu-shugi*), Shimizu was influential in the movement against revision of the 1951 Japan-U.S. Security Treaty, which felled the Kishi Nobusuke government in 1960.

After the treaty was ratified, Shimizu performed a pessimistic, and extreme, fourth *tenkō*. His nationalist realism produced a bitter denunciation of Japan's postwar 1947 Constitution, particularly Article 9, the no-war clause; this, Shimizu claimed, had emasculated Japan, which had ceased to be a true state. To recover its proper position, Shimizu urged Japan to produce nuclear weapons as part of a general policy of bolstering its military to a level commensurate with the country's economic power.

Andrew E. Barshay

Bibliography

Pyle, Kenneth B. "Japan, the World, and the Twenty-First Century." *The Political Economy of Japan.* Vol. 2. Ed. Inoguchi Takahashi, et al. Stanford, CA: Stanford University Press, 1988, 446–86.

Shimoda Utako (1854–1936)

Educator and club woman. The daughter of a loyalist samurai of Iwamura domain, she went to serve at the imperial court in 1872, then left seven years later to marry. Soon widowed, she returned to imperial service and participated in the 1885 founding of the Peeresses' School (which became the girls' section of the Peers'

Shimoda Utako. Asahi Shimbun Photo.

School in 1896). From 1893 to 1895, she made a tour of the United States and Europe to study women's education there and was received by Queen Victoria. In 1898, she founded the Imperial Women's Society (Teikoku Fujinkyōkai) to extend women's education to the middle and lower classes. The society sponsored Jissen Girls' School, which in 1901 admitted the first overseas Chinese women students. Although Shimoda sought to inculcate traditional East Asian feminine virtues and respect for Japan, some of her Chinese students became revolutionaries, including Qiu Jin, who was executed in China in 1907. Shimoda served as principal of Jissen and as head of the girls' section of the Peers' School. She was a founding member of the Aikoku Fujinkai (Patriotic Women's Society) and its president in the 1920s.

Sally A. Hastings

Bibliography
Sievers, Sharon L. *Flowers in Salt: The Beginnings of Feminist Consciousness in Japan.* Stanford, CA: Stanford University Press, 1983.

Shimonoseki Treaty (*Shimonoseki Jōyaku*)

Concluded on April 17, 1895, at the Japanese city of Shimonoseki, between Li Hongzhang representing China and Itō Hirobumi, prime minister of Japan, this treaty brought to an end the first Sino-Japanese War (1894–95).

Defeated on land and sea, China had at first sent Chang Yin-huan as envoy of peace to the Japanese war command headquarters at Hiroshima, but the Japanese refused to deal with him for his lack of full plenipotentiary credentials. After that, Li Hongzhang, China's senior diplomat and holder of the title "High Commissioner for the Northern Ocean," came to seek peace. The Japanese terms were harsh, including an end to all Chinese claims to suzerainty over Korea; cession of the Liaodong Peninsula (southern Manchuria), Formosa, and the Pescadores Islands; most-favored-nation treatment (Western style) for Japanese subjects in China; an indemnity to pay the costs of the war; and Japanese military occupation of the Chinese port of Weihaiwei in Shandong to guarantee Chinese compliance with the treaty.

Representing a defeated country, Li had no options but to accept, although an ill-timed attempt on his life by a Japanese extremist during the peace negotiations gave China a temporary armistice and a Japanese imperial apology. Rumors that European powers, notably Russia, might not allow the Japanese terms to stand also gave the Japanese some pause. In the end, however, Itō and Foreign Minister Mutsu Munemitsu stood by the harsh terms, deciding that they would have their terms from China first and then negotiate with the European powers if such proved necessary. It did, just six days after the treaty was concluded, with a Triple Intervention by Russia, France, and Germany demanding that Japan return the Liaodong Peninsula to China. However, Japan was allowed to retain Formosa and the Pescadores as consolation. In 1898, Russia received Liaodong, and Germany and France obtained other Chinese territories as their reward.

Hilary Conroy
George C.C. Chang

Bibliography
Lensen, George. *Balance of Intrigue: International Rivalry in Korea and Manchuria, 1884–1899.* Tallahassee: University Presses of Florida, 1982.

Shimpeitai Incident (*Shimpeitai Jiken*)

Divine Soldiers Incident, 1933. Abortive plan to create a military government in Japan. In 1933, a group of ultranationalist civilian activists collaborated with right-wing military officers led by Commander Yamaguchi Saburō of the navy and Suzuki Zen'ichi of the Dainippon Seisantō (Great Japan Production Party) to overthrow the cabinet of Admiral Saitō Makoto, contending that it was too moderate and objecting to the fact that military representatives constituted only one-third of its membership. In addition to help from their own organizations, they also had strong support from the Aikoku Kinrōtō (Patriotic Labor Party) and fairly large numbers of young military officers. They planned to form squads to assassinate the prime minister and other important politicians and to storm and occupy the metropolitan police headquarters and the offices of liberal political parties.

Moreover, they intended to attack and bomb the Diet (legislature) building, the residence of the prime minister, and other key locations to create general chaos in the heart of Tokyo. They hoped this would force a declaration of martial law and the creation of a cabinet composed solely of the military and its strongest civilian allies. However, because a similar incident had occurred on May 15, 1932, police surveillance of known ultranationalist radicals had become intense; their plot was discovered, and key conspirators arrested in July 1933. The mild sentences they received symbolized growing government leniency toward the violent acts of ultranationalist radicals, due to the rising public insistence on more aggressive foreign policies.

J. Wayne Sabey

Bibliography

Byas, Hugh. *Government by Assassination.* New York: Knopf, 1942.

Shinto

Shinto, frequently described as the indigenous religion of the Japanese people, has had a substantive connection with nationalism only since the 1868 Meiji Restoration. It was systematically—if erratically—patronized by the state from 1868 to 1945 and, during that time, provided the rites of state that served as the country's symbolic legitimation. State patronage officially ended in 1945, but governments have sometimes appealed to nationalistic sentiment by seeking to reestablish state support for Shinto shrines.

In its earliest history, Shinto was a cult of native deities called *kami*, including spirits of nature (waterfalls, mountains, strangely shaped or very large trees and boulders), deified emperors and heroes, and mythological deities. Because many of the *kami* are identified with particular places, sometimes originating as their guardian or tutelary deities, Shinto has been highly localized for most of its history. *Kami* are worshiped to ensure the well-being of a community and the fertility of its crops, domestic animals, and people, and to ward off natural disasters. Shinto has been united more by the type of deity worshiped (*kami*, as opposed to Buddhas or other deities) and by the type of ritual involved (generally, offerings of food and *sake* presented as a communal meal uniting communities with their gods) than by any common creed.

Except for its sectarian varieties and under state patronage, Shinto does not emphasize or promulgate any doctrine, nor, except in the colonies of imperial Japan, has it sought to convert non-Japanese people. It is an ethnic religion, containing the essence of Japanese ethnic identity alone and not relevant to others.

Shinto is conventionally divided into imperial Shinto, folk Shinto, sect Shinto, and State Shinto; only the first and last bear any inherent relation to nationalism, but all types have been appropriated for nationalist aims in the modern period.

Imperial Shinto refers to the ritual practice of the imperial court, in which the emperor presides over rites of the harvest, the equinoxes, worship of the four directions, and other observances. One type of enthronement rite (*daijōsai*) consists of the new emperor offering first fruits to, and symbolically sharing a meal with, the ancestors of the imperial house. Worship of the imperial ancestors, ultimately dating to Amaterasu Omikami, the Sun Goddess enshrined in the Grand Shrines of Ise, is a regular feature of imperial Shinto.

Folk Shinto represents the continuation of the localized worship of communal tutelary deities, a tradition that persists in contemporary Japan. Local men without specialized ordination of any kind have generally acted as officiants, or priests. Added to purely localized *kami* and their shrines were cults of transregional deities that had grown up over a long history, including the cult of Hachiman, god of war; Inari, the fox god and messenger of the rice god; Tenjin, god of learning; and others. The priesthoods of these shrines formed sacerdotal lineages with esoterically transmitted teachings. Beyond these lineages, there was no comprehensive organizational structure, no organization of all shrine priests, no head shrine over all the rest, and no central figure analogous to a pope. Shrines were often attached to Buddhist temples, and, within these temple-shrine complexes, it was generally the Buddhist priests who held the higher position, owing to the prestige accruing to ordination. Shrine priests in the Tokugawa period (1600–1868) were consistently frustrated in their efforts to establish their institutional and doctrinal independence from Buddhism.

Sectarian Shinto refers to a loosely connected group of 13 organizations that had adopted specific doctrines beyond the local practice of communities or the esoteric teachings of the sacerdotal lineages of priests of transregional *kami*. Early in the Meiji period (1868–1912), the state required that each religious organization be joined to a recognized association; those organizations that did not comply could not proselytize freely, and their membership would be open to harassment and suppression. A number of groups thereupon adopted the label "Shinto," sometimes more to escape persecution than because of any inherent connection of their teaching to Shinto. The label "sectarian Shinto" masks much variety; some sects, such as Kurozumikyō (founded 1814), originated in a revelation from the *kami* to a charismatic founder; others, also originating in revelation, had no intrinsic connection to shrine cults but took the title Shinto so its members could avoid persecution. Tenrikyō, founded in 1838, is an example of this type, as is Konkōkyō, founded in 1858. Other sects of Shinto, such as Jingukyō, originated in a state-sponsored attempt to promulgate a Shinto-based doctrine as a means to prevent the spread of Christianity after the Meiji Restoration (1868) and had no basis in a popular cult or in a founder's religious experience.

State Shinto is a term subject to a variety of usages. Shinto scholars have argued that it applies only after the establishment of a Shrine Office (Jinja Kyoku) within the Home Ministry in 1900, and they have restricted its use to administrative measures regulating Shinto shrines and priests. Because state supervision and patronage of Shinto officially ended in 1945, so did State Shinto.

Historians and historians of religions, on the other hand, use the term more broadly. They refer to State Shinto as a systemic phenomenon that arose early in the Meiji period and encompassed government support and regulation of shrines, the emperor's sacerdotal roles, state creation and sponsorship of Shinto rites, construction of Shinto shrines in Japan and in overseas colonies, education of schoolchildren in Shinto mythology, plus their compulsory participation in Shinto rituals, and persecution of other religious groups for exhibiting disrespect for some aspect of authorized mythology. These scholars are likely to mean by State Shinto a pervasive nationalistic coloration of the thought and beliefs of the people by state-authored Shinto ideology—and to speak of a resurgence of State Shinto after 1945.

The modern period has witnessed a variety of relations between Shinto and the state. The period 1868–1880 was a time of experimentation. A forcible separation of Shinto from Buddhism (*shinbutsu bunri*) in 1868 was an occasion for the state to abandon its former patronage of Buddhism in favor of Shinto. As part of the state-sponsored Great Promulgation Campaign (Taikyū Senpu Undō, 1870–84), state officials wrote doctrine and empowered a bureaucracy

headed by Shinto priests to promulgate it. When the campaign failed to gain popular support, however, state support declined, and the bureaucratic organs in which Shinto priests held office were demoted.

From 1880 to 1905, state support for Shinto declined, but many important shrines were constructed, nevertheless, and linked in a national hierarchy. The cult of the war dead, centering on the Yasukuni Shrine in Tokyo, gained popular support, and the populace as a whole was drawn into the cult and into shrine life generally by conscription and by an alliance at the local level between the educational system and shrine priests. The first national association of shrine priests was formed in 1900.

The years 1905–1930 witnessed expansion and increased influence for Shinto, beginning with the tide of patriotism engendered by the Russo-Japanese War (1904–05). The war, the annexation of Korea (1910), and the colonization of Manchuria produced a heightened mood of patriotism that the priesthood enthusiastically supported. Shrines and their priests were expected to serve the country in fostering patriotism, and the state proved willing to pay for their services. From around 1910, the state underwrote a program for the training of Shinto priests. The priesthood increased its influence in the educational system, as graduates of Shinto schools such as Kokugakuin University and Kōgakkan University, and those holding even a second-class rank as a priest, were automatically qualified to teach in the public schools. Priests assisted the state in universalizing such practices as formal veneration of the imperial portrait and the Imperial Rescript on Education (1890), as well as periodic visits to shrines by schoolchildren for labor and formal worship.

State Shinto reached its optimum influence between 1930 and 1945. State subsidy continued at a high level, and, in a separate development, religious movements whose teachings or symbolism were believed contrary to Shinto were suppressed. It became a nearly universal custom to enshrine a paper talisman from the Grand Shrines of Ise in the home, and millions of persons visited the shrines on pilgrimages.

The decades since 1945 have seen first, as a result of the Allied Occupation (1945–52), a complete dismantling of state support for Shinto, as Article 89 of the 1947 Constitution prohibits state support for any religion, and Article 20 grants freedom of religion and prohibits the state from engaging in religious education. Various covert forms of state support for Shinto have been quietly reinstated, however, such as provision of official information about the death of World War II combatants to the Yasukuni Shrine on an exclusive basis, while denying the same service to other religious groups requesting it. The Supreme Court has gradually expanded the scope of religious activity deemed permissible to the state. The Yasukuni Shrine has been the center of controversy, and the state has lost much prestige from five failed efforts to reestablish state support for it. The general populace remains largely unaware of these developments. Those who protest are a vigorous, if small, minority, consisting mostly of Christians, members of religions persecuted before 1945, and the academic intelligentsia. Shinto-related issues continue to provide a symbolic focus for discussions of the national identity, though their significance for generations educated after 1945 seemed by the 1990s to be waning.

Helen Hardacre

Shōwa Emperor (Hirohito). Courtesy Consulate General of Japan, N.Y.

Bibliography

Hardacre, Helen. *Shintō and the State, 1868–1988*. Princeton, NJ: Princeton University Press, 1989.

Holtom, Daniel C. *Modern Japan and Shintō Nationalism*. Chicago: University of Chicago Press, 1947.

Shōwa Era (1926–89)

The Taishō years (1912–26) witnessed militant nationalism, which had ebbed and flowed during the Meiji years (1868–1912), reach its low tide. Cultural nationalism, which had been on the rise since the 1880s, had subsided and Western standards, especially American, were in vogue. Hollywood movies, dance halls, cafe bars, jazz, music halls, baseball, Western apparel, and the permanent wave—all were the rage in the big cities. In the intellectual realm, scholars perused the works of Western philosophers and social theorists, including Marxist literature. Translations of the literary works of Western writers were widely read. The government, dominated now by the political parties, was moving in a more democratic direction, and makers of foreign policy were aiming at cooperation with the Western powers. The rich sent their sons to study in England or the United States. Japan seemed to be on the verge of becoming truly cosmopolitan.

Then, in the mid-1920s, the emergence of the Chinese Nationalist Party and its drive for Chinese unification alarmed the militarists. The Great Depression caused serious economic strains throughout Japan after 1929, and the tide shifted away from Westernism and democracy. This coincided with the early reign years of the Shōwa Emperor (more commonly known in the West as Hirohito). Thus, Hirohito sat on the throne during the two decades when militant nationalism swept across the island country.

Almost immediately after he mounted the throne, Japan suffered a bank crisis in April 1927. One month later, General Tanaka Giichi, who had just assumed the premiership as head of the Rikken Seiyūkai (Friends of Constitutional Government Party), dispatched Japanese troops to the Shandong Peninsula in northeastern China. In May of the following year, Japanese and Chinese forces clashed at Tsinan. In June, Japanese officers stationed in Manchuria assassinated Zhang Zolin, the Manchurian warlord, by blowing up the train on which he was riding on his way back to Manchuria after conferring with Chinese Nationalist government officials. This was the precursor to radical Japanese military officers' efforts to bring Manchuria under direct Japanese rule. The result was the Manchurian Incident in 1931,

S

which militant nationalists used to whip up a frenzied nationalist climate among the people, with military and naval songs replacing popular Western tunes such as "My Blue Heaven."

The advent of the Great Depression in 1929 caused severe economic hardships among Japanese peasants and led agrarian nationalists to rouse public opinion against big-business tycoons and government leaders. Among the agrarian nationalists were Gondō Seikyō and Tachibana Kōzaburō, who linked up with embittered army and navy officers in opposition to the arms-limitation policy pursued by the Taishō and early Shōwa leaders, as well as with radical civilian nationalists such as Inoue Nisshō, who organized the Ketsumeidan (League of Blood) to restructure Japan on the basis of the vague idea of "Japanese spirit." They set out to assassinate greedy capitalists and evil advisers to the emperor who were leading the country astray.

Some right-wing political leaders deplored the direction taken by liberal political parties in Japan. In 1924, Hiranuma Kiichirō, who became prime minister in 1939, organized the Kokuhonsha (National Foundations Society) to redirect Japan to its historical moral and religious roots and clarify the principles of kokutai (national polity). By the 1930s, it had a membership of nearly 200,000, and its roster included right-wing admirals, generals, and political leaders.

Among the right-wing organizations was the Aikokusha (Society of Patriots) which was linked to the right-wing guru Tōyama Mitsuru's Gen'yōsha (Black Sea Society). One of the Aikokusha members attempted in 1931 to assassinate Prime Minister Hamaguchi Osachi, who later died of his wound. Another group was the Sakurakai (Cherry Blossom Society), organized by a group of disgruntled army officers in 1930. Their object was to enhance the role of the military at home and expand Japan's imperialistic activities abroad. Sakurakai members, bent on staging a coup, vowed to arouse themselves and thoroughly destroy what they regarded as the wholly decadent politicians.

In early 1932, members of the Ketsumeidan assassinated two prominent business leaders, Inoue Junnosuke, a former finance minister, and Dan Takuma, director of the Mitsui Holding Company. In May 1932, Prime Minister Inukai Tsuyoshi fell victim to militant nationalists consisting of Ketsumeidan members and disgruntled young army and naval officers who were incensed at his policy of limiting the 1931–32 Manchurian campaign. When he was leader of the opposition party (the Seiyūkai), Inukai himself had attacked the government for not pursuing a hard line policy. His assassination spelled an end to the era of parliamentary government. Japan entered the heyday of militant nationalism. Anybody critical of the army's policies on the Asian continent or in favor of liberal policies at home became a target.

The rising tide of ultranationalism swept through the political and intellectual arenas at a frenzied pace. Organizations designed to arouse nationalistic spirit and strengthen the kokutai intensified their activities. The defense of the kokutai became the litmus test of one's patriotism and loyalty to the emperor. In this respect, the emperor system came to constitute the emblem of nationalism. The army and the ultranationalists made themselves the guardians of the kokutai.

Besides the Kokuhonsha, there were other, more militant groups bent on clarifying the essence of the national polity. In 1930, the Kokuryūkai (Amur River Society), which had been organized at the turn of the twentieth century to further the imperial mission in East Asia, commemorated its 30th anniversary. It called for the defense of the kokutai against dangerous thought and advocated strengthening the armed forces to carry out the imperial mission. Kita Ikki, an advocate of national socialism who had loyal followers among the rebel military officers, called for the radical transformation of Japan to fulfill its mission of forging a union of "resurgent Asiatic peoples." His chief targets were the zaibatsu (financial, industrial cliques), the corrupt politicians, and the imperial-court advisers. Ōkawa Shūmei, Kita's colleague, called for the transformation of the existing order. He held Japan to be heaven's choice to be the champion of Asia.

In the military forces, the radicals looked to General Araki Sadao, the leader of the army faction known as the Kōdōha (Imperial Way Faction). He believed that the Japanese had been corrupted by frivolous foreign ideologies and were pursuing materialistic goals. To cleanse Japan of foreign ideologies, the Japanese must, he insisted, get back to their roots and recognize their own uniqueness as Japanese. The fundamental principles of the Japanese system of government, he held, consist in the unity between the emperor and the people. In the thinking of this Shōwa nationalist, Japanese nationalism was intimately intertwined with the emperor system.

The enhancement of the Japanese nation meant defense of the emperor system and the extension of the imperial virtue over "eight corners of the world." Thus the right-wing nationalists set out to purge the land of dangerous, un-Japanese thought.

The first target of the militant nationalists in their move to rid the universities of such thought was Takigawa Yukitoki, a liberal professor of constitutional law at Kyoto University. In May 1933, under pressure from right-wing nationalists, the minister of education overrode the objections of the university president, faculty, and students and removed Takigawa from his position at the university. Prior to this, professors had been dismissed for being Communists or Communist sympathizers, but Takigawa's only fault was that he was a liberal constitutional law scholar. This affair seriously undermined academic freedom and tended to make the academic community excessively cautious.

Among the accusers of Takigawa was a right-wing constitutional law scholar, Minoda Muneki, who had backers in the House of Peers. In 1935, Minoda launched an attack on Minobe Tatsukichi, a prominent constitutional law professor at the University of Tokyo. Since 1903, Minobe had been widely respected for his view of the constitution, which held that the emperor was an organ of the state, a part of the corporate state, and that Japan's system was similar to Europe's constitutional monarchies. Uesugi Shinkichi, another constitutional scholar, joined in the challenge to Minobe's interpretation, arguing that Minobe was denying the validity of Japan's national polity and was turning Japan into a democratic state. Minobe's interpretation, Uesugi added, makes the emperor a servant of the people or a functionary of the state.

The debate between the two scholars had subsided in the years of Taishō democracy, but in the late 1920s and early 1930s the emperor-organ theory was made the object of attack by the right-wing nationalists to discredit the constitutional monarchists. A member of the House of Peers and director of the Kokuhonsha, Kikuchi Takeo, charged Minobe with being "a traitor, rebel, and academic bandit." The army, led by General Mazaki Jinazburō, called on the Imperial Military Reservist Association to rally public opinion against Minobe. Compelled in 1935 to resign from the House of Peers, Minobe also was dismissed from his position at the University of Tokyo, and his books were banned.

Education had been regulated stringently by the Ministry of Education since the Meiji years (1868–1912), but, in the 1930s, greater emphasis came to be placed on loyalty to the emperor and the state. In 1937, the Ministry of Education published a booklet titled *Kokutai no Hongi* (Cardinal Principles of the National Polity), which condemned Western ideologies based on individualism and emphasized loyalty and patriotism. In the booklet, the ministry said that loyalty to the emperor "means to reverence the emperor as [our] pivot and to follow him implicitly." It also emphasized filial piety, which, it stated, was identical with loyalty since Japan was "a great family nation, and the Imperial Household is the head family." It also stressed the importance of the martial spirit.

The instructions in the public schools followed the principles promulgated in the *Kokutai no Hongi*. For example, one-fifth to one-third of the lessons in the ethics textbooks emphasized these values. Every morning in all schools, the principal read the Imperial Rescript on Education (1890) to the student assembly, then the students sang the national anthem and marched off to their respective classrooms. The boys were told that the persons they should emulate were the three heroic soldiers who carried a live bomb through enemy lines to enable the Japanese army to charge through during the Shanghai Incident in which Japanese troops clashed with Chinese forces early in 1932. The girls were told to learn from the old peasant woman who walked miles from the countryside to send her son off to serve in the Russo-Japanese War (1904–05). To die while serving the nation and be returned to Japan to be enshrined among the war dead at Yasukuni Shrine in Tokyo, the youths were told, was the greatest honor anyone could hope for.

While the intellectual community was being targeted for purging, in the political arena the radical military officers of the *Kōdōha* circle decided to take direct action. They were not satisfied with the elimination of party government following the 1932 assassination of Prime Minister Inukai. The *Kōdōha* officers were convinced that evil advisers at the imperial court were preventing the transformation necessary for the purification of the land of corrupt officials and foreign ideologies, the enhancement of the welfare of the common people, and the defense of the national polity.

On February 26, 1936, these young officers attempted a major coup d'état. They assassinated and wounded many imperial advisers and occupied strategic areas of Tokyo, but, because the emperor was determined to have the insurgency quashed, the coup failed. Still, the army dominated the government and the political arena through to the end of World War II (1937–45). Militarism and ultranationalism swept over the land following the outbreak of war with China in 1937, and, as Japan rushed headlong toward the Pacific War, the suppression of any sign of nonconformity became ever more stringent. Women often were forced to shear off Western-style hairdos, and Western-style apparel came to be replaced by baggy trousers called *mompei*, while words adopted from English were condemned.

Since nationalism and patriotism sweeps across all countries engaged in "do or die" wartime struggles, Japan's fanatical nationalism should come as no surprise, but it led to a rude awakening at the end of the war in 1945, when Japan was plunged instantly from the height of self-aggrandizement to the depth of self-denigration. The stunning defeat seemed to make all Japanese values worthless. The emperor claimed that he was not a divine being. The men who had died for him had died in vain. Superhuman war heroes turned out to be men with feet of clay. The superior Japanese race had become a nation of sheep, misled by the military. All blame was heaped on Prime Minister Tōjō Hideki and his fellow generals.

The American-led Occupation (1945–52) reforms in education sought to cleanse the textbooks of nationalistic, militaristic, and fascistic lessons. Freedom, democracy, and peace replaced patriotism, militarism, and loyalty. The inferiority complex that lurked beneath the surface, even during the years when the Japanese flag was being waved throughout East Asia, seemed to overwhelm the land. All Japanese objects were forsaken for Western ones again, much as they had been in the early Meiji years, but with even greater force this time.

This situation gradually changed as Japan recovered from the depths of its collapse and disarray. As the country emerged as a major economic power in the 1960s, the sense of Japanese uniqueness revived. A sense of exultation swept the country when Harvard sociologist Ezra Vogel published a book entitled *Japan As Number One* in 1979. By the 1970s and 1980s, there was growing talk of Japaneseness, and an effort to define this uniqueness in terms of the language, culture, psychology, and national character began to surface.

This trend may not necessarily be a sign of the revival of Japanese nationalism. It may sim-

ply reflect the tradition of Japanese insularity. Despite the extension of Japanese economic activities throughout the world, the Japanese still have not developed a truly cosmopolitan outlook. There remains the notion that the Japanese are a distinctive people, that one cannot become a Japanese, but is Japanese only by birth and blood. Many an observer, both Japanese and foreign, has noted a prevailing sense of Japaneseness that appears to stem not simply from insularity but from a belief in racial uniqueness. The sense that one is Japanese by birth and ancestry alone is emphasized by the Japanese unwillingness to allow Korean residents who have lived in Japan for many generations to become Japanese citizens.

Japan's growing self-confidence also is seen in the willingness to speak out more forcefully in criticizing the United States, a country it had accorded deference since the Occupation years. A notable example of this trend, which incensed many Americans, was the publication in 1989 of the book *The Japan That Can Say No*, by Isihara Shintarō. He said, "There is no need for our country to follow the United States slavishly. . . . I hardly think that possessing ideals of our own means being overconfident or lapsing into an arrogant, dangerous sort of nationalism" (quoted in Hane, 414–15). Some critics see the Ministry of Education's textbook certification policy as fostering nationalistic sentiments in the students. Also, the ministry's instruction to the schools in 1992 to have students sing the national anthem and hoist the national flag on special occasions has been seen as another indication of the officials' nationalistic inclination.

As the Shōwa years came to a close with the death of the Shōwa Emperor, the turbulent cycle of ups and downs in nationalistic sentiments ended in an upward swing, but, into the late 1990s, it did not appear that the kind of militant and fanatical nationalism that swept the land in the 1930s and 1940s would visit the country in the near future.

Mikiso Hane

Bibliography
Gluck, Carol, and Stephen Graubard, eds. *Shōwa: The Japan of Hirohito*. New York: Norton, 1992.

Hane, Mikiso. *Modern Japan: A Historical Survey*. Boulder, CO: Westview Press, 1992.

Ishihara, Shintaro. *The Japan That Can Say No*. English language edition. New York: Simon and Schuster, 1991.

Maruyama, Masao. *Thought and Behaviour in Modern Japanese Politics*. Oxford: Oxford University Press, 1963.
Vogel, Ezra F. *Japan As No. 1: Lessons for America*. Cambridge: Harvard University Press, 1979.

Bibliography
Fletcher III, William Miles. *The Search for a New Order: Intellectuals and Fascism in Prewar Japan*. Chapel Hill: University of North Carolina Press, 1982.

Shōwa Research Association (*Shōwa Kenkyūkai*)

The Shōwa Kenkyūkai (Shōwa Research Association) encompassed more than 300 prominent intellectuals and officials in Japan in the 1930s. Prince Konoe Fumimaro, prime minister from 1937 to 1938 and 1940 to 1941, encouraged the creation of the association in 1933, and one of his close confidants, Gotō Ryūnosuke, administered it. Because of the connection to Konoe and the participation of government officials, other members hoped to influence government policies. A firm grounding in socialism or Marxism predisposed many participants toward advancing basic political and economic reforms as they tried to define new policies for the country.

The start of the second Sino-Japanese War in July 1937 prompted a surge of activity by the association's numerous committees. In September 1938, one group proposed a new order, in which Japan would guide the formation of a regional bloc with China and guide its economic development. Two months later, Konoe announced Japan's new ambitious goal of forging a new East Asian order. National mobilization provided an opportunity to achieve reforms through the power of the state. Influenced by the Nazi-controlled economy, Ryū Shintarō's Economics Section devised plans for a national-defense state that would implement comprehensive industrial planning and strictly control profits. Liberated from the demands of greedy stockholders, management could concentrate on productivity. The Politics Section, under the guidance of men such as political scientist Yabe Teiji, envisioned nationwide mass organization of occupational groups that would create direct links between the cabinet and the people. This would bypass the elected Diet (legislature), guarantee what Yabe called "organic unity," and form a "Japanese form of one nation, one party." Konoe tried to enact these changes with his new order movement in 1940 but failed. Late that year, the association disbanded.

William Miles Fletcher III

Shōwa Restoration (*Shōwa Ishin*)

A hazy concept, popular among ultranationalist groups in the 1930s, using the analogy of the Meiji Restoration (1868) to promote radical state renovation (*kokka kaizō*). The goal of supporters of Shōwa Restoration was to eliminate corrupt elements at the court—that is, to remove incumbent party and business leaders, as well as moderate military and civilian advisers to the throne—in order to inaugurate a military-based spiritual revival and promote direct imperial rule of Japan and the rest of Asia. The phrase is usually regarded as a euphemism for military dictatorship and foreign expansion.

Supporters of this concept instigated eight coups between 1931 and 1936, culminating in the massive February 26 Incident in which 1,400 extremists assassinated several leading citizens, including Finance Minister Takahashi Korekiyo and Privy Seal Saitō Makoto, in an unsuccessful attempt to take over the government. Many of these extremists were stirred into action by developments in the 1920s and early 1930s, including economic hardships, widespread political-party corruption, growing Chinese nationalism, emerging Bolshevism, and Japan's dependence on the Anglo-Saxon powers. Their specific ideas grew from the writings of right-wing and left-wing nationalist extremists, such as Kita Ikki, who advocated state national socialism, Ōkawa Shūmei, who called for ideological rightism, and Gondō Seikyō, a proponent of peasant nationalism.

The movement was hurt by the inability of the various nationalist organizations to unite and by the uneven support their zeal elicited even from the more nationalistic officers in the army, many of whom paid lip service to their cause but failed to cooperate with their activities. After 1938, the "Shōwa Restoration" slogan was replaced by Prime Minister Konoe Fumimaro's new order movement (*shin taisei undō*). More extreme members of the right-wing revived calls for a Shōwa (or, after 1989, Heisei) Restoration in the post–World War II era.

Jacob Kovalio

Bibliography

Shillony, Ben-Ami. *Revolt in Japan: The Young Officers and the February 26, 1936, Incident*. Princeton, NJ: Princeton University Press, 1973.

Shrine of the Peaceful Country (*Yasukuni Jinja*)

Located on Kudan heights in central Tokyo, the shrine was established in 1869 by order of the imperial government. Dedicated to the celebration and consolation of the spirits of all those who had died to defend the emperor and the empire, it was given the name Yasukuni and a special rank among all Shinto shrines in 1879. Through the years, it enjoyed the favor of the government as well as the sentimental and patriotic regard of much of the citizenry. Starting with imperial loyalist martyrs of 1853, some 2.4 million war dead had been enshrined at Yasukuni by the 1990s. Through successive changes in official policy on the role of religion in the government of the empire, Yasukuni stood throughout the prewar era as a conspicuous example of the official formula that shrine Shinto, funded and regulated by the government, was not a religion but a civic cult, with the corollary that official support for the festivals and ceremonies of these shrines was not an encroachment on the religious freedom guaranteed by the imperial constitution.

With the surrender and Allied Occupation (1945–52) at the end of World War II (1937–45) came a sharp reversal in Yasukuni's situation. A number of factors combined to deter a restoration of Yasukuni to its prewar prominence, among them the directives of the U.S.-led occupation authorities; the secular, liberal rhetoric, and substance of the Shōwa Constitution of 1947; the muted voice of the military; and the resistance of most of the new elite to anything military. Since 1946, Yasukuni has been registered as a privately funded religious corporation. Although customary Shinto ceremonies occur there, public officials who attend usually do so in a private, personal capacity. Even so, such activity draws critical notice from opposition parties and from Buddhist, Christian, and sect Shinto organizations. On the other hand, the Japan Bereaved Families Association and the powerful Liberal Democratic Party have pressed steadily, though in vain, for government funding of Yasukuni. By the late 1980s, this issue had sparked annual rallies for and against the reestablishment of Yasukuni. In August 1985, Prime Minister Nakasone Yasuhiro and his cabinet officially attended memorial services at Yasukuni, sparking strong protests from Beijing and other Asian capitals, as well as from groups within Japan. He did not repeat the official visit the next year. The issue of whether prime ministers would visit the shrine in an official capacity continued to spark controversy into the latter 1990s.

Frank O. Miller

Bibliography

Garon, Sheldon. "State and Religion in Imperial Japan, 1912–1945." *Journal of Japanese Studies*. Vol. 12, No. 2 (Summer 1986).
Holtom Daniel C. *Modern Japan and Shintō Nationalism*. Chicago: University of Chicago Press, 1947.

Siberian Intervention (*Shiberia Shuppei*) (1918–22)

A struggle for Japanese control of the northeastern Asia region, waged between foreign and domestic forces and among elements within each of these groups. Japan, a principal foreign contestant, was already Russia's competitor for mastery in northeastern Asia and continued this pursuit in the chaos of World War I (1914–18) and the Russian Revolution (1917), announcing in August 1918 that it would send 12,000 troops to aid Czechoslovak forces in Siberia.

The United States, a prerevolutionary opponent of these continental aspirations, was for the same reason opposed to Japan's objectives in the intervention. U.S. President Woodrow Wilson, however, agreed to sanction and participate in the intervention in view of the expressed desire of the European Allies for such a move and in an effort to exercise a restraining hand upon Japan, which clearly wanted to take as full an advantage as possible of the present opportunity. In an *aide memoire* of July 17, 1918, Wilson approved the operation, citing the need to guard the military stores at Vladivostok, to aid the Czechoslovak forces stranded in Siberia, and to steady the efforts of Russia to achieve a stable government.

The most promising domestic contender for power in postrevolutionary Siberia was the government headed by Admiral Aleksandr Vasilievich Kolchak, who had the title of "Supreme Ruler." Kolchak assumed political power and command of the military forces in November 1918 in the Volga-Ural region with the expectation of wielding authority not only in Siberia but also in the rest of Russia. But Kolchak's undertaking was opposed by Cossack leaders, by Japan, and by the Soviet forces approaching from the west. By the spring of 1919, his army was suffering defeat; by the following February, his effort collapsed and he was executed. The American forces under General William S. Graves withdrew from Siberia in April 1920 and, under pressure from the 1927 Washington Conference, which set international arms limits, the Japanese forces departed on October 25, 1922. This day was commemorated at the end of World War II in 1945, the year when the Soviet Union finally shared a victory over the rising challenger of 40 years before.

John A. White

Bibliography

Morley, J.S. *The Japanese Thrust into Siberia, 1918.* New York: Columbia University Press, 1957.

Siemens Incident (*Shimensu Jiken*)

Naval scandal. In the decade following the Russo-Japanese War (1904–05), public demonstrations erupted frequently over such issues as clique politics, high taxes, and cozy cabinet-military relationships. One of the larger of these, the Siemens Incident in 1914, brought down the Yamamoto Gonnohyōe government. In January of that year, the *London Telegram* reported the accusations of a former employee of the German firm Siemens that his company had provided 15 percent kickbacks to Japanese naval officials to secure contracts. The Japanese press pursued the charges vigorously, also reporting on similar bribes made by the British firm Vickers. The result was a series of massive, sometimes violent demonstrations in mid-February, with the public and the opposition party demanding the government's resignation. Yamamoto resisted the public pressure for a time but resigned on March 24, when the upper house of the Diet refused to pass his cabinet's budget. A number of naval officials also were dismissed from office.

James L. Huffman

Bibliography

Najita, Tetsuo. *Hara Kei in the Politics of Compromise.* Cambridge: Harvard University Press, 1967.

Sino-Japanese War (1894–95) (*Nitchū Sensō*)

China's and Japan's responses to Western imperialism were expressed in the Tongzhi and the Meiji Restorations, which occurred in 1861 and 1868, respectively, but by the time of the Sino-Japanese War (1894–95) Japan's strengthening had far outstripped that of China. As a result, Japan soundly defeated China, gaining territory, indemnities, and international recognition as a burgeoning power. The Japanese victory could, of course, be construed negatively as well as positively, as the Chinese peace negotiator warned his Japanese counterparts—namely, Japan's harsh demands for the peace settlement could lead to an era of bad relations with China. It can even be argued in retrospect that Japan's victory initiated an imperialist course that led finally to Pearl Harbor, the Pacific War, defeat, and Occupation.

In the immediate sense, however, the Sino-Japanese War was a short and glorious one for Japan. It began with disputes over Korea, dating to the early 1880s, when Japan began to intrude there into what had long been a tributary state of China after a Japanese naval expedition brought Korea to accept a treaty of friendship and commerce (Kanghwa Treaty) in 1876. With this move, Japan undercut China's position and rendered Korea theoretically independent—as a country that could make treaties with other states. Most Western countries, including the United States, had treaties with Korea by the mid-1880s.

However, at that point China awakened to the situation, or at least Li Hongzhang, who held the title "High Commissioner for the Northern Ocean," did, and he sent his protégé, Yuan Shikai, to Seoul to guide the Korean king and court back into the Chinese fold. Japan was not ready for a showdown on the issue, and its envoy and subsequent premier, Itō Hirobumi, went to China to see Li and negotiate the Tientsin Treaty in 1885, by which Korea would be allowed to develop on its own, although, in the event of emergencies, either Chinese or Japanese troops might intervene to help, but only after notifying the other country. In effect, this kept Japanese troops out of Korea, while China, through Yuan, directed affairs at the Korean court from 1885 to 1894—utilizing traditional Chinese nonmilitary techniques of persuasion. Meanwhile, "progressive" Koreans went to Japan or the United States, where many became dissatisfied with Korea's lack of progress toward modernization. In addition, some elements within Korea, embodied in the Taewongun (Father of the King) Movement and a Tong Hak (Eastern Learning) Movement, began to resent the modernization that Western and Japanese influences were bringing to Korea and, to some extent, the increased Yuan-Chinese direction of affairs at court.

As a result, in 1894 a double flareup occurred: the murder of Japanese-connected progressive Kim Ok-kyun in Shanghai and a Tong Hak uprising in Korea itself. This double emergency provided sufficient reason (or excuse) for either China or Japan to send in troops. Both did, and they were soon fighting—with the Japanese winning. It could be argued that the Japanese government had been waiting for just such an opportunity, but the story is more complicated than that. The men in power in 1894, the Meiji oligarchs, as they later became known, had rejected an opportunity to conquer Korea in 1873, when Japan's great Meiji Restoration general, Saigō Takamori, was ready to lead the conquest to avenge the Korean king's insult in refusing to recognize the restoration of the Japanese emperor, which had ended the Tokugawa shogunate and introduced the Meiji era (1868–1912) of progress and reform. At that time, the more practical, less militant forces in the government had defeated and ousted Saigō, and those same forces still controlled the government in 1894. They had been and still were cautious about Japan's relations with Western powers and wanted to avoid actions that could not be justified in the broader international setting.

There were, however, pressures on them, from liberal and reactionary political elements in Japan, to become more patriotic, and there were signs that the international community viewed Japan's role in Korea as positive. Moreover, Japan's top foreign-policy priority had long been Western acceptance of Japan as an equal, so that the country could be relieved forever of the unequal treaties that had been forced on it in the aftermath of U.S. naval Commodore Matthew Perry's visit in 1853–54. Release from these obligations was promised by Great Britain that very year of 1894 (which may have been taken to indicate the prospect of an Anglo-Japanese alliance in the future), and other Western powers seemed unconcerned about, or even supportive of, Japan's interest in removing Korea from the Chinese sphere. Hence, war was approved in high circles in Tokyo, and an offer by China to remove troops from Korea if Japan would do the same was rejected.

While tension remained high despite half-hearted urgings by Russian, British, and American embassies in Beijing and Tokyo that war should be avoided, the Japanese fleet was taking control of the Yellow Sea and, on July 25, sank the *Kowshing,* a Chinese troopship en route to Korea. The *Kowshing,* was a former British merchant ship that had been converted into a troopship, and it still had an English captain. Europeans aboard the sinking vessel were rescued by the Japanese, but Chinese were allowed to drown and/or were fired upon as they struggled in the water. Peace feelers then collapsed, and all-out fighting found Japanese forces quickly driving the Chinese from Korea and moving into Manchuria. Soon, Japan controlled the Yellow Sea and its ports, including Port Arthur and Weihaiwei, and its ground forces were in a position to threaten Beijing. Then the Chinese, seeking and obtaining Western (especially American) advice, sued for peace, which was concluded in the Shimonoseki Treaty.

The war had shown Chinese defenses to be monstrously disordered. Even though its Beiyang (Northern Ocean) fleet had many ships and its armies had millions of men, they were hopelessly outfought. The Chinese had neither the training nor the will to fight effectively. They had many flags, costumes, and ceremonies, but no real organization for fighting against modern weapons; rather, their tactics might have been more appropriate fending off nomadic tribesmen from the north, in keeping with China's historical tradition. The Japanese, on the other hand, had mastered the art of modern warfare.

Hilary Conroy
George C.C. Chang

Bibliography

Conroy, Hilary. *The Japanese Seizure of Korea*. Philadelphia: University of Pennsylvania Press, 1974.

Conroy, Hilary, et al. *Japan in Transition*. Toronto: Associated University Press, 1984, chaps. 3–4.

Lensen, George A. *Balance of Intrigue*. Tallahassee: University Presses of Florida, 1982.

Social Masses Party (*Shakai Taishūtō*)

A proletarian party formed by the merger of the Zenkoku Rōnō Taishūtō (National Labor-

Farmer Party) and the Shakai Minshūtō (Social-ist People's Party) on July 24, 1932. Abe Isoo was the first party president, and Asō Hisashi served as party secretary. During its eight-year existence, the party sought, with considerable success, to unify Japan's non-Communist work-ing-class political forces. After poor showings in the elections of 1932–34, the party improved its fortunes in the prefectural and national elec-toral contests of 1935–37. By the April 1937 lower-house election, the party elected 37 mem-bers of parliament nationwide, winning 10 per-cent of the total vote. The party won more than 20 percent of the vote and at least one seat in every district in Tokyo.

During these years, the party's ideology and policy followed a steady trajectory away from an initial emphasis on class struggle and opposition to the government, toward a stat-ist domestic program and support for expan-sion and war in Asia. The transformation be-gan in 1932, when the party opposed calls for Japan to withdraw from the League of Nations but recognized the country's "independent" puppet state of Manchukuo in Manchuria. The party made its shift clear with a new Policy for Japan in Transition adopted in 1933 and a decision to support the military pam-phlet of 1934 that posited war as the father of creativity and the mother of culture and called for total mobilization across the political, eco-nomic, and cultural spectrum. In 1934, it be-came a people's party (*kokuminnotō*) rather than a class party. From 1935 to 1937, the party rejected the antifascist United Front movement; after the outbreak of war in China in July 1937, the mainstream overrode a reluc-tant Abe Isoo and his supporters to embrace the holy war in China. By November, the re-vised party platform called for totalitarianism. In 1939, the party entered merger negotiations with Nakano Seigō's national socialist Tō-hōkai (East Asia Society), though these col-lapsed because of opposition from Abe's fac-tion rooted in the old Shakai Minshūtō. In February 1940, the party expelled Abe, Nishio Suehiro, and Katayama Tetsu for opposing its decision to support Saitō Takao's ouster from the Diet (legislature) for an antiwar speech there. In its enthusiasm to join Konoe Fumi-maro's new order (*shin taisei*) movement, the Imperial Rule Assistance Association, the party dissolved itself ahead of the other major parties in July 1940.

Andrew G. Gordon

Bibliography
Totten, George O. *Studies on Japan's Social Democratic Parties*. New Haven, CT: Yale University Press, 1966.

Society for Political Education (*Seikyōsha*)

Founded in 1888 by such leading young and basically conservative critics as Miyake Setsurei, Shiga Shigetaka, and Sugiura Jūgō, the Seikyō-sha promoted an ideology of cultural relativism, whereby "the preservation of national essence" (*kokusui hozon*) accompanied the drive for national strength and development. The early Seikyōsha members, along with intellectual fellow travelers such as the journalist Kuga Katsunan, attempted to steer a middle course between the atavism of diehard traditionalists and the iconoclasm of *bunmei kaika* (civiliza-tion and enlightenment) liberals. Their insis-tence that particularistic cultures strengthened, rather than subverted, the nation–state also resonated with the widely held view of cultural nationalists in nineteenth-century Europe.

After the first Sino-Japanese War (1894–95), the architects of the Seikyōsha found themselves in the awkward position of distinguishing their ideology of cultural preservation from the more aggressive nationalism of a new empire in the Pa-cific. Miyake, in particular, decried the misuse of the "national essence" as a pretext to attack any-thing of foreign provenance. Still, despite Miyake's vision of an inclusive national character, the Seikyōsha, under new leadership after 1923, in-evitably drifted into the grasp of a more militant chauvinism until its final dissolution in 1945.

Donald Roden

Bibliography
Pyle, Kenneth B. *The New Generation in Meiji Japan*. Stanford, CA: Stanford Uni-versity Press, 1969.

Society of Patriots (Aikokusha)

One of Japan's first political associations. Formed in Osaka in February 1875 by Itagaki Taisuke, it sought to foster ties between the lo-cal Risshisha (Self-Help Society) and other anti-government groups advocating a popular assem-bly and a constitution. The tiny organization, disbanded when Itagaki took a government post in March 1875, was reformed in 1878 when he and other members of the rising *jiyū minken* (popular rights) movement grew impatient with the halting moves toward constitutionalism. By its fourth assembly, in 1880, the Aikokusa claimed nearly 100,000 members nationwide. It yielded that year to the more broadly based Kokkai Kisei Dōmei (League for Establishing a National Assembly), which, in turn, helped create the Jiyūtō (Liberal Party) in 1881. The Aikokusha leaders' insistence on national rather than local solutions to problems encouraged a spreading sense of nationhood.

James L. Huffman

Bibliography

Akita, George. *Foundations of Constitutional Government in Modern Japan, 1868–1900.* Cambridge: Harvard University Press, 1967.

Society of the People's Friends (*Min'yūsha*)

Publishing company and literary society. When Tokutomi Sohō launched his journal *Kokumin no Tomo* (The Nation's Friend) in 1887, he founded Min'yūsha to publish it, his newspaper *Kokumin Shimbun*, and most of his voluminous subsequent publications. The company disbanded in 1929. The term Min'yūsha also came to denote Tokutomi's associates, who revitalized the Meiji intellectual world. They included Tokutomi's brother Roka, as well as Yamaji Aizan, Kunikida Doppo, and Uchida Roan, who espoused Westernization and youthful progressivism. Since the Meiji leaders had lost their intellectual vigor, they maintained, a new generation would have to promote Japan's strength and progress. Their philosophy, *heiminshugi* (commonerism), pertained more to the abolition of status and rank than to the adoption of parliamentary democracy. In the mid-1890s, the group joined the more nationalistic Seikyōsha (Society for Political Education) of Miyake Setsurei to demand speedy revision of Japan's unequal treaties with the Western powers. After the first Sino-Japanese War (1894–95), Tokutomi shifted his support to the government, whereupon the Min'yūsha group lost its unifying bond.

James L. Huffman

Bibliography

Pierson, John D. *Tokutomi Sohō, 1863–1957.* Princeton, NJ: Princeton University Press, 1980.

Soejima Taneomi (1828–1905)

Former samurai and leader of early-Meiji government. Prior to his emergence as a national leader, Soejima distinguished himself in his native Saga (Hizen) domain as a scholar of the Chinese classics, an imperial loyalist, and an advocate of imperial restoration. In the 1868–73 period, he held several posts in the central government, promoted modern reform and representative government, and served as foreign minister (1871–73). In the latter capacity, he is noted for his national-rights diplomacy (the endeavor to recover and protect Japan's sovereignty against infringements by the Western powers); for his action against the "coolie trade" in the 1872 *Maria Luz* case, when the crew of a Peruvian ship that docked at Yokohama was found to be mistreating some 230 Chinese aboard; for his diplomatic mission to China, where he won acclaim for settling the issue of audiences with the emperor; for his expansionist foreign policy designed to extend Japanese sovereignty or influence over the Ryūkyū Islands, Taiwan, and Korea; and for siding with Council of State leader Saigō Takamori in an unsuccessful bid to implement a plan for the conquest of Korea. As a consequence of being on the losing side of the cabinet clash over Korean policy, Soejima left the government in October 1873, cutting short his career as a Japanese statesman.

Wayne M. McWilliams

Bibliography

McWilliams, Wayne M. "East Meets East: The Soejima Mission to China, 1873." *Monumenta Nipponica.* Vol. 30, No. 3 (Autumn 1975), 230–75.
———. "Soejima Taneomi: Statesman of Early Meiji Japan, 1868–1874." Unpublished doctoral dissertation, University of Kansas, 1973.

Sōmagahara Incident (*Sōmagahara Jiken*)

A 1957 case regarding legal jurisdiction over U.S. troops on duty in Japan. William S. Girard, an active-duty guard at Gumma Prefecture's Sōmagahara range, fired at and killed Nakai Saka, a woman collecting empty shells, on January 30. The case sparked an international dispute when the U.S. government ruled that since his action had not occurred while he was on duty, he could be tried by Japanese courts. Residents of Girard's hometown, Aurora, Illinois, appealed to the emperor for a pardon; the Illinois legislature protested the granting of jurisdiction to Japan, and, on July 11, 1957, the U.S. Supreme Court announced that the U.S. government ruling had been correct.

The Japanese court then found Girard guilty of causing bodily injury resulting in death and gave him a suspended three-year sentence, whereupon he returned home. The court decisions, as much political as judicial, quieted passions on both sides and allayed some of the Japanese public's concerns about American bases in Japan.

James L. Huffman

Bibliography

Kataoka, Tetsuya. *The Price of a Constitution: The Origin of Japan's Postwar Politics*. New York: Crane Russak, 1991.

Sorge Incident (*Zoruge Jiken*)

Spy case. German journalist Richard Sorge and several associates were arrested in Tokyo on October 18, 1941, for espionage against Japan. As it turned out, Sorge, who prepared daily news reports at the German Embassy, had been doing intelligence work for the Soviet government since 1933. He had maintained close relationships during that time with leading German diplomats in Japan, while his top associate, Ozaki Hotsumi, had been a member of the influential Shōwa Kenkyūkai (Shōwa Research Association) with intimate ties to top officials in the Konoe Fumimaro cabinet (1937–39); indeed, during 1938, Sorge had served as a cabinet consultant, with access to cabinet papers. Among other information, the Sorge ring uncovered Japan's plans not to attack the Soviet Union in 1941.

The case shocked the official world because of Sorge's and Ozaki's high-ranking ties and the long period in which they had operated undetected. Sentenced to death in September 1943, both men were executed in November 1944. Associates were given life sentences. Sorge and Ozaki became public heroes following the war, as resisters against Japan's war effort.

James L. Huffman

Bibliography

Deakin, F.W., and F.R. Storry. *The Case of Richard Sorge*. London: Chatto and Windus, 1966.

South Manchurian Railway

The principal line of this rail network was the track that led from Changchun in the heart of northeast China south to the port city of Dairen. In 1906, this main track and a few feeder lines in south Manchuria were under the control of the Japanese, while the Russians operated the other rail lines in north Manchuria, and the Chinese managed the others in south Manchuria.

For the Chinese, their lines represented an attempt to use Chinese capital and entrepreneurial skill to make modern transportation technology available in bringing the rich resources of the region to Chinese markets. Although in 1917 the Russians experienced a revolution that condemned imperialism, even after the revolution they preserved their influence in north Manchuria by continuing to operate their own Chinese Eastern Railway.

The Japanese, bolstered by their growing sense of mission to advance the Asian races, used the rail lines as instruments of economic and political development, military expansion, and modernization. They exploited the South Manchurian Railway and the proceeds from its operations to bring in medical doctors and agricultural researchers, to give employment to Chinese and Japanese citizens, and to provide rapid and efficient transportation at competitive prices.

During the first 50 years of the twentieth century, the rail lines in Manchuria were one focus for the sense of nationalism that each of these three countries cultivated. They were flashpoints for the anger any one of them felt against the others, but the confrontations were most often economic rather than military. An exception was the September 18, 1931, explosion along this railway line, engineered by Japanese military officers and known to the world as the Manchurian Incident, which helped launch Japan along the road that led to World War II (1937–45).

After 1949, the Chinese government tried to preserve the South Manchurian Railway and its smooth functioning, initially by employing many of the Japanese engineers who had managed it during the war. But since then, the Chinese have not significantly improved what the Japanese had built during the 1930s. In its heyday, the South Manchurian Railway was a model of the latest and the best in rail transportation. As the twentieth century draws to a close, it is just another regional Chinese rail line.

Ronald Suleski

Bibliography

Ito, Takeo. *Life Along the South Manchurian Railway: The Memoirs of Itō Takeo.* Trans. Joshua A. Fogel. Armonk, NY: M.E. Sharpe, 1988.

"Sovereign's Reign," The (*Kimi Ga Yo*)

Unofficial national anthem. Japan has never adopted a national anthem, but this Heian-era work generally is regarded as the national song. Based on a poem in the tenth-century *Kokinshū* anthology, which calls for the sovereign to rule until the pebbles grow into moss-covered rocks, it became popular in medieval *biwa* (lute) and *jōruri* (ballad-drama) songs. When an 1870 tune composed for it by John Fenton, a British music teacher in Satsuma, proved unacceptable, the Imperial Household Ministry in 1880 selected a score by Hayashi Hiromori (with Western-style harmony added by the German Franz von Eckert) and had it performed for the emperor. In 1893, the Education Ministry required that it be sung at elementary schools on national holidays, and, from that time, it became the de facto national anthem. "Kimi ga yo" was used incessantly at public gatherings during the World War II era and is still sung at sports gatherings. The Education Ministry created considerable controversy in 1989 by ordering that it be sung at public primary-school ceremonies. In contrast to most national anthems, "Kimi ga yo" contains no references to war or fighting.

James L. Huffman

Bibliography

Harich-Schneider, Eta. *A History of Japanese Music.* London: Oxford University Press, 1973.

Special Higher Police (*Tokkō Keisatsu*) (1911–45)

The Home Ministry's Special Higher Police (*tokubetsu kōtō keisatsu,* or *tokkō* for short) were launched in 1911 to combat socialism and anarchism. The Peace Preservation Law of 1925 greatly expanded their operations. This law forbade agitation against private property and the national polity (*kokutai*), which included the emperor system and basic political structure, and the *tokkō* were its enforcers. They arrested more than 65,000 people under this law from 1928 to 1942, over 10,000 per year during the peak period of 1931–33.

The Peace Preservation Law drew a vague boundary between nationalist orthodoxy and criminal heresy, and police and justice officials had considerable latitude in its implementation.

Until 1935, most of the *tokkō's* victims were leftists, who comprised over 95 percent of all people arrested for violating the Peace Preservation Law. They included members of the proletarian political parties, labor and tenant farmers' unions and university groups. Advocates of independence for Japan's colonies and supporters of the *burakumin* (outcaste) liberation organization, the Levellers Society (Suiheisha), were also targeted. The *tokkō* engineered mass arrests of leftists in 1923, 1925, 1928, 1929, 1931, and 1932. Since few radicals engaged in violence, most were collared for spreading dangerous ideas, earning the *tokkō* the nickname of "thought police" (*shisō keisatsu*).

By 1935, the radical left had been thoroughly routed, and the *tokkō* turned its attention elsewhere. It harassed religious organizations such as the Jehovah's Witnesses, splinter Shinto groups, and the Buddhist sects of Tenritsu and Ōmotokyō, whose doctrines regarding the emperor departed from official dogma. More than 1,700 religious people were eventually arrested under the Peace Preservation Law.

Less well known is the *tokkō's* concern with the radical right. In 1936, a separate *tokkō* section was formed to monitor religious elements and those rightists whose doctrines leaned toward national socialism or who threatened violent action. Its staff soon outnumbered that of the *tokkō's* first section, which dealt with the left. Although extreme rightists did not fear the Peace Preservation Law (they accepted the emperor system and private property in some form), they were liable to arrest under the press and criminal laws.

Among opponents of the state, the *tokkō* became synonymous with the abuse of police power. Law enforcement was often arbitrary, owing to the politicization of the police and the lack of judicial oversight. The top police officials were replaced by each new cabinet, and police behavior thus often reflected the mood of the government rather than the letter of the law. The application of the same statute could change dramatically with the political context.

Moreover, the average subject was defenseless against police brutality, because the regular courts had no jurisdiction over the administrative arms of government. The beating of suspects to extract a confession was standard practice in the prewar era, and although other police branches were also guilty of this, the *tokkō's* treatment of jailed leftists stands out. It was rare for even the Special Higher Police to kill a prisoner, but when this happened, as it did in Tsukiji in 1933 and in Yokohama late in the war, no police officer ever answered for the crime.

Gregory J. Kasza

Bibliography
Mitchell, Richard H. *Thought Control in Prewar Japan*. Ithaca, NY: Cornell University Press, 1976.

Spencer, Herbert (1820–1903)

Philosopher. Few Western thinkers had more impact on nineteenth-century Japan than this British exponent of social Darwinism. A native of Derby, he exerted worldwide influence with his universal system of philosophy, which emphasized individualistic utilitarianism and evolution. In works such as *Social Statics* (1850), *Synthetic Philosophy* (10 volumes, 1860–96), and *The Study of Sociology* (1873), he argued that societies progress on the basis of unbending universal principles. He foreshadowed Charles Darwin in coining the phrase "survival of the fittest," contending that creatures not energetic enough to succeed in the natural struggle must necessarily die.

Spencer's theories helped shape the thought of such influential Meiji writers as Katō Hiroyuki, Fukuzawa Yukichi, Miyake Setsurei, Itagaki Taisuke, and Tokutomi Sohō. By the 1880s, the natural-rights ideas that had appealed to many intellectuals in the 1870s were largely supplanted by Spencer's ideas of social evolution and the concomitant necessity for national strength. The young Tokutomi, in particular, used Spencer's belief that societies evolve from the militant to the industrial stage as a basis for his best-selling 1886 book, *The Future Japan* (Shōrai no Nihon).

James L. Huffman

Bibliography
Nagai, Michio. "Herbert Spencer in Early Meiji Japan." *Far Eastern Quarterly*. Vol. 14, No. 1 (1954), 55–64.

Spirit of Japan (*Yamato Damashii*)

Nationalistic expression of World War II era, based on the word *Yamato,* the earliest name for the Japanese land and people. The phrase first appeared in the *Genji monogatari* (Tale of Genji) and other literature of the Heian era (794–1185) as an indication of the cultural and behavioral norms that distinguished Japan from China. Without *Yamato damashii*, the writers suggested, one could not adequately exert leadership or show civilized sensitivity. After centuries of disuse, the concept was picked up by late-Tokugawa (1600–1868) *kokugaku* (national learning) scholars who were pursuing the sources of Japan's heritage. Some detected in the phrase the aesthetic sensitivities of Heian court literature; others, the martial loyalty and discipline of the warrior eras. Nationalists and militarists of the 1930s adopted this latter sense of the phrase, which they used constantly in the prewar and war years as a code for those qualities—purity, discipline, *bushidō* (the way of the warrior), and, above all, loyalty to the emperor.

James L. Huffman

Bibliography
Brown, Delmer. *Nationalism in Japan*. Berkeley: University of California Press, 1955.

State Foundation Society (*Kenkokukai*)

Ultranationalist organization. A group of nationalist leaders, including Hiranuma Kiichirō, Uesugi Shinkichi, and Tōyama Mitsuru, created the Kenkokukai in 1926 to espouse imperial rule and pan-Asianism and to oppose political parties, socialism, labor unions, and the *zaibatsu* (financial cliques). When former anarchist Akao Bin moved the society in an openly activist, violent direction at the beginning of the 1930s, most of its more respectable founders left, and the Kenkokukai became primarily Akao's organization. Though its membership was small, its militant tactics created considerable fear on the Left. It was particularly active following the 1931 Manchurian Incident, when Japan began its aggression in China, and again in widespread anti-British agitato in 1939. Akao disbanded the Kenkokukai in 1940, creating the Dainihon Kōdōkai (Greater Japan Imperial Way Association) in its stead.

James L. Huffman

Bibliography

Storry, Richard. *The Double Patriots: A Study of Japanese Nationalism.* Westport, CT: Greenwood Press, 1973.

State Shinto (*Kokka Shintō*)

State Shinto (*kokka shintō*) was the powerfully nationalistic, religio-ideological cult that Japan's ruling clique created after 1868 to unify the country and appropriate for themselves the emperor-sanctified authority necessary to implement a remarkable period of sustained modern nationbuilding. It lasted until 1945 and Japan's defeat in the Pacific War (1937–45).

Shinto is Japan's oldest indigenous religious tradition, going back to prehistory. Throughout Japanese history, until the fundamental changes made under the postwar American-led Occupation (1945–52), Shinto shrines were closely linked with the Japanese state in the ancient pattern of *saisei-itchi* (oneness of *kami* worship and government). The effect of this symbiosis of government and the indigenous Shinto *kami* (spirits) was to force the shrines to become the sanctifiers of whatever political administration with which they were linked. In this pattern lay the roots of latter-day State Shinto.

Toward the end of the Tokugawa period, in the mid-nineteenth century when Japan was weak, powerful Western countries sent superior warships to Japanese shores to demand that Japan end its two-and-a-half centuries of "closed door" isolation and enter into mutual trade relations. Fearful that these barbarians might colonize them as they recently had other Asian lands, Japan's young samurai leaders launched a crash program of sweeping modernization, adapting Western ideas and institutions to protect themselves against the West.

As the country proceeded with widespread modernization, many feared that rapid change could destroy those precious indigenous values that made Japan uniquely "Japanese." There followed a conservative reaction, in which many of the country's leaders turned away from Western models to embrace indigenous patterns, including the distinctive native Shinto shrines, as useful for buttressing such old values as reverence, duty, national devotion, hierarchy, and obedience. Shrine elements were increasingly placed under state supervision, with the intent of systematically enlisting shrine worship as a spiritual force for mobilizing imperial loyalties on behalf of modern nation building. Over succeeding years, government promotion (and partial support) of the shrines led to their control, which produced the phenomenon of *kokka shintō*.

Existing as it did only in the 1868–1945 era, State Shinto was a relatively brief overlay on the country's great mass of traditional shrines, which, taken together, have for ages constituted what we have come to call Shrine Shinto. The shrines continue and are deeply rooted in local custom. They are basically grassroots "people's shrines."

During the critical 1868–1945 modernizing era, the state simply took these ubiquitous people's shrines and bent them to national-imperial purposes. Each of the shrines simultaneously performed a double role: As a local guardian shrine, it served its parishioners' needs (its shrine Shinto role); as an arm of the state, it served the country's needs (its State Shinto role).

It was national policy to treat the shrines as nonreligious, ethical institutions for promoting patriotism among Japanese subjects. From the government's point of view, if the shrines could be treated as *ethical* in nature, the provision in Chapter 3, Article 28 of the Meiji Constitution for freedom of *religious* belief would not apply, and Shinto observances could be made obligatory for every Japanese subject, regardless of individual religious preferences. In this way, the state demanded of every Japanese a suprareligious, transcendent patriotic commitment to the single overarching national ethic (*kokumin dōtoku*) as the great unifier of all the people.

In the half century between 1894 and 1945, Japan used its modern armed forces to fight several wars—on the Asian mainland, in Southeast Asia, and in the Pacific Theater after its attack on U.S. operations at Pearl Harbor in 1941. Although this ultimately led to disastrous consequences for Japan, throughout the 15 years of continuous conflict the shrines faithfully played their designated role, sanctifying Japan's military aggressions with the blessing of the *kami*.

After Japan's defeat, the Allied Occupation under U.S. General Douglas MacArthur instituted sweeping changes that had a fundamental impact on the shrines and their role in Japanese life. The Occupation wrote into the 1947 Constitution the disestablishment of the shrines and a guarantee of religious freedom. Shinto was reduced to the status of "a religion among religions," with no connection to, or privileges from, the state. The emperor readily disavowed the divinity attributed to him in the prewar Meiji Constitution, and he was officially transmuted from sacred head of state to what Chapter 1, Article 1 of the 1947 Constitution calls "the symbol of the State and of the unity of the people, with whom resides sovereign power."

One of the most far-reaching of the many basic postwar changes in Japanese national life was the termination of the ancient pattern of *saisei-itchi*, the unity of shrines and government that had powerfully marked the modern, nationalistic era. When *saisei-itchi* ended with the close of the Pacific War, the shrines, finally released from state control, were free to return to their true historic role as simply people's shrines.

Wilbur M. Fridell

Bibliography

Hardacre, Helen. *Shinto and the State, 1868–1988.* Princeton, NJ: Princeton University Press, 1989.

Student Movements

For nearly three-quarters of a century, the Japanese student movement has been closely linked with Marxism and activism. The movement began when students, responding to the ferment of socialist revolution and Wilsonian democracy during the era of World War I (1914–18), established groups in Higher Schools and universities to study reformist and radical social thought. In 1922, Gakuren (Student Social Science Federation) was established to coordinate the burgeoning movement. In the 1920s, students engaged not only in intense study of Marxism and campus issues such as compulsory military education, but also in the labor movement and politics. Gakuren members became intimately involved in the 1922 formation of the Japanese Communist Party (JCP). Between 1928 and 1931, government suppression destroyed both organizations, though clandestine student study of Marxism and resistance continued through the next 15 years of war.

Student activists in Japan, unlike their counterparts in China and colonial Southeast Asia, generally were repelled by the nationalist cause because Japan's elite had long before appropriated emperor-system (*tennōsei*) nationalism as the ideological prop for authoritarian rule and imperial expansion. Thus, internationalism, anti-imperialism, and antimilitarism became key tenets of the student movement, alongside an abiding concern with Marxism and democracy.

After World War II, the student movement seemed at first to be submerged in the larger mass movement that coalesced behind the JCP and the left wing of the Japan Socialist Party (JSP) in pursuit of the postwar promise of pacifism and democratic socialism. A national student movement appeared in September 1948 with the establishment of Zengakuren (All-Japan Student Federation). Zengakuren adopted an antiwar and antifascist stance that resonated with the postwar popular commitment to pacifism and participatory democracy. Originally intended to focus on educational problems such as high fees and university governance and structure, Zengakuren became increasingly politicized following the onset of the "reverse course" of the Occupation and Red Purges in education that same year.

The student movement became further radicalized early in the 1950s due to such factors as the JCP policy change (1950) from parliamentarianism to revolution, the Korean War (1950–53), the U.S. demand for Japan's rearmament and exaction of the 1951 Japan-U.S. Security Treaty as the price for a peace treaty and the return of sovereignty, and the anti-democratic policies of the Yoshida Shigeru cabinets (1946–47, 1948–54). The movement burst into prominence on "Bloody May Day" 1952 (the May Day Incident), when Zengakuren took to the streets, along with angry workers and Koreans, against the Yoshida government and U.S. imperialism.

The JCP's return to peaceful parliamentarianism in the mid-1950s disillusioned many in the student movement. The nonparty Left came to the fore within Zengakuren with the establishment in 1958 of the Bund (Communist League) as an organization standing for revolutionary Marxism purified of JCP opportunism. The spirit of the Bund was evident in the Zengakuren-led massive demonstrations and street battles with the police in 1960 to prevent renewal of the 1951 Japan-U.S. Security Treaty and to force the resignation of the reactionary Kishi Nobusuke cabinet.

The Bund failed to prevent the treaty's renewal, much less to turn the popular movement in defense of peace and democracy into a revolutionary struggle for power, and dissolved in disarray in 1961, while Zengakuren splintered into competing groups. The break with the now thoroughly reformist JCP became permanent, and the student movement's rejection of party-line authoritarianism opened the way for an innovative, but sectarian, blossoming of New Left Marxism in the 1960s. If the anti-American bent of the Security Treaty crisis of 1960 gave the impression that student protest was fundamentally nationalistic, that illusion was exploded in the 1960s as the movement assaulted the state in earnest and rejected the ruling elite's project of economic nationalism in favor of the transcendent values of participatory democracy and social justice.

From late 1966 onward, the Sampa (Three Faction) Zengakuren provided a rallying point as the Bund had done in the late 1950s. The student movement grew explosively and took aim at what were thought to be three weak points in the structure of Japanese capitalism: the 1960 Treaty of Mutual Cooperation and Security; Japan's collusion with the United States in waging aggressive war in Vietnam; and the commercialization of education that was turning schools and universities into diploma mills in service to business and government. The students' goals were to jolt a public addicted to mass consumerism out of its complacency over postwar Japan's peace and democracy and force it to confront the role of Japanese economic imperialism in Japan's postwar prosperity, thereby bringing sufficient force to bear to bring down the capitalist order and put in place new forms of radical, participatory democracy.

The student movement and the New Left forced the issue by street actions and university occupations until the government learned techniques for containing both. Demoralized by government successes in restoring order on the campuses—symbolized by the police victory in the battle for possession of the Tokyo University clock tower in January 1969—and in continuing the 1960 security treaty and the 1972 return of Okinawa to Japan by the United States, the student movement lost its momentum; in the 1970s and 1980s, it was supplanted by movements outside the university against environmental destruction and for minority and women's rights.

From the vantage point of the 1990s, it was clear that nationalism had never been a central value for the student movement. The state and the Japanese elite had been the bearers of that ideology, both before the war and after, when the imperial nationalism of the past was reduced to economic nationalism within the Pax Americana and rationalized by an ideology deifying growth and international competitiveness as the imperative for national survival. In contrast, the student movement responded to long-standing ideals of internationalism, democracy, and social justice in ways that placed it at the forefront of the opposition to Japanese nationalism, not among the ranks of its supporters.

Joe B. Moore

Bibliography

Bailey, Jackson H., ed. *Listening to Japan: A Japanese Anthology*. New York: Praeger, 1973. See essays by Oda Makoto, "Making Democracy on Our Own," 122–37, and Ōno Tsutomu, "Student Protest in Japan: What It Means to Society," 166–84.

Havens, Thomas R.H. *Fire Across the Sea: The Vietnam War and Japan, 1965– 1975*. Princeton, NJ: Princeton University Press, 1987.

Muto, Ichiyo, and Inoue Reiko. "Beyond the New Left." Parts 1–2. *AMPO: Japan-Asia Quarterly Review*. Vol. 17, No. 2–4 (1985), 20–35.

Smith, Henry DeWitt. *Japan's First Student Radicals*. Cambridge: Harvard University Press, 1972.

Tsurumi, Kazuko. "Student Movements in 1960 and 1969: Continuity and Change." *Postwar Trends in Japan*. Ed. Takayanagi Shunichi and Miwa Kimitada. Tokyo: University of Tokyo Press, 1975, 195–227.

Sugiura Shigetake (also Jūgō) (1855–1924)

Educator and journalist. Born in Shiga Prefecture, he studied Confucianism (under Takahashi Tandō, who was executed in 1865 for supporting an imperial restoration) and Western learning. After spending the 1870s at Daigaku Nankō (modern-day Tokyo University) and in England, he worked in education during the 1880s, at Tokyo Daigaku Yobimon (later, First Higher School), Kokugakuin University, and his own Tokyo English Institute. Sugiura's major contributions came as a nationalistic writer and lecturer. He helped Miyake Setsurei and Kuga Katsunan found, respectively, the journal *Nihonjin* (1888) and the newspaper *Nihon* (1889), both advocates of a strong Japanese foreign policy grounded in the preservation of national culture. He also helped organize the Nihon Kurabu (Japan Club) to agitate for the revision of Japan's unequal treaties with the

Western powers. During his later years, he spent most of his time teaching ethics to Crown Prince Hirohito, who became the Shōwa emperor.

James L. Huffman

Bibliography
Pyle, Kenneth. *The New Generation in Meiji Japan.* Stanford, CA: Stanford University Press, 1969.

Sumo

Japanese wrestling. With a 2,000-year history, sumo is more fully identified with the spirit of Japan than any other sport. Simple yet highly structured and rooted in ancient ceremonies, it brings two huge, nearly-naked men to an elevated ring (*dohyō*) for matches that rarely last more than one minute. Its six annual tournaments garner television audiences in the tens of millions and make national celebrities of the winners.

The first records of sumo appear in the *Nihon shoki* (Chronicle of Japan, A.D. 720) when two men fought in front of the Emperor Suinin; the sport has been practiced professionally since the late 1600s. The 700-plus wrestlers in Japan in the 1990s train in feudal-style institutions known as stables (*heya*), where younger trainees rise at 4:00 A.M. to practice and serve the needs of the senior wrestlers. At maturity, sumo wrestlers average more than 300 pounds; some exceed 400. In a match, their aim is to push the other wrestler out of the ring or to get any part of his body (other than his feet) to touch the ground.

The wrestlers are divided into six ranks, based on the number of victories in tournaments, with about three dozen of the best competing in the *makuuchi* (inside the tent) division. The highest rank in that division is called *yokozuna* (grand champion). A wrestler who reaches that rank cannot be demoted; instead, he must retire if he experiences a succession of mediocre tournaments. Tournaments, promotions, demotions, and all other sumo matters are controlled by the Japan Sumo Association, an organization composed in the mid-1990s of 105 former top-level wrestlers.

Despite its modern-day popularity, the sport is saturated with traditional, Shinto-based rituals. The *dohyō* sits under a roof that looks like a shrine; *yokozuna* enter the ring wearing thick white ropes from which hang strips of shrine-style, zigzagged paper; foot-stamping before each match is intended to drive away evil spirits; salt is thrown to purify the ring; and judges wear medieval court attire and hold war fans dating from the sixteenth century. Little wonder that the sport has been called present-day Japan's "most feudal activity."

Adding a touch of irony—and interest—is the increasing number of foreign wrestlers. By the early 1990s, several Hawaiians, along with men from mainland North and South America, had worked their way to the top ranks, and in 1992 the Hawaiian wrestler Akebono became a *yokozuna*, a fact that caused consternation among the more nationalistic sumo followers, although the majority of Japanese appear to be fans of the most successful foreigners.

James L. Huffman

Bibliography
Cuyler, Patricia L. *Sumo: History, Rites, Traditions.* New York, NY: Weatherhill, 1979.

Suzuki Bunji (1885–1946)

Labor leader. Born in Miyagi Prefecture, he became involved in Christian social reform as a University of Tokyo law student. After graduation in 1909, he worked at the newspaper *Asahi Shimbun*, then, in 1911, he entered social work as a secretary in the Unitarian Church. Concerned with the plight of Japan's workers, he and 14 others formed the early labor organization, Yūaikai (Friendly Society) in 1912. After Suzuki observed the American Federation of Labor in America in 1915–16, the Yūaikai evolved into a union and, in 1919, became the 30,000-member Sōdōmei (Japan Federation of Labor). Suzuki served four times as Japanese representative to the International Labor Organization. He entered politics late in the 1920s, thrice winning election to the Diet (legislature). He also ran for the Diet as a socialist in 1946 but died prior to the election. To the end, Suzuki remained a moderate socialist, opposing Communism and advocating worker self-help through education. He sought labor-management cooperation rather than confrontation.

James L. Huffman
David Hewitt

Bibliography
Large, Stephen. *The Rise of Labor in Japan: The Yūaikai, 1912–1919.* Tokyo: Sophia University, 1972.

S

Suzuki Kantarō (1867–1948)

Admiral and prime minister. Born in Osaka, he spent his first six decades in the navy, the rest of his life in politics. After serving successfully in the first (1894–95) Sino- and Russo-Japanese (1904–05) wars, he moved up steadily in the naval hierarchy, becoming admiral in 1923 and chief of the naval general staff in 1925. In 1929, he went into the reserves and moved to the Privy Council, where he was councillor (1929–40), vice president (1940–44), and president (1944–45); he also was grand chamberlain from 1929 until he was injured during the February 26, 1936, military uprising. Suzuki became prime minister on April 5, 1945. Though he openly supported the war, he was known privately to favor an early peace. He tried secretly (and unsuccessfully) to get the U.S.S.R. to intervene on behalf of peace. After the United States dropped the atomic bombs on Hiroshima and Nagasaki in August 1945, Suzuki's cabinet agreed to surrender terms on August 14 and resigned the following day. He presided over the Privy Council again in 1945–46.

James L. Huffman

Bibliography

Butow, Robert. *Japan's Decision to Surrender.* Stanford, CA: Stanford University Press, 1954.

Symposium Faction (*Kōzaha*)

Also known as the feudal school, the Kōzaha was a faction of Japanese Marxists that took its name from its seven-volume *Nihon shihonshugi hattatsu shi kōzo* (Symposium on the History of the Development of Japanese Capitalism) (Tokyo: Iwanami Shoten, 1932–33). Yamakawa Hitoshi, Sakai Toshihiko, and others seceded from the Japanese Communist Party (JCP) in December 1927 to protest the Comintern's 1927 Theses prescribing a two-stage (first bourgeois-democratic, then proletarian-socialist) revolution

for Japan. When the secessionists defended their own thesis of an immediate socialist revolution, in their journal *Rōnō* (Labor-Farmer), scholar-activists who remained loyal to the JCP and the Comintern's Theses contributed to the Kōzaha scholarly studies to undergird the two-stage-revolution formula. The most prominent Kōzaha members included Yamada Moritarō, Hirano Yoshitarō, Hani Gorō, and Hattori Shisō.

The Kōzaha position on the legitimacy of Japanese nationalism was complex, if not confused. On the one hand, as orthodox Marxists, the Kōzaha authors adhered to the Comintern's claim that the JCP must seek to abolish the emperor system (*tennōsei*). On the other hand, Japan's official *kokutai* (national polity) orthodoxy, which undergirded the imperial claim to power, was premised on Shinto mythology concerning the origin of the emperor, and made the imperial household the focal point of Japanese national identity. Even for many Marxists, the emperor was considered the divine patriarch of the extended Japanese family, so that the Confucian value of loyalty (*chu*) reinforced that of filial piety (*kō*). Thus, the Shinto mythology attributed to the Japanese imperial system a unique quality, one that conflicted with the need to interpret the imperial system in Marxist universalist terms. As a result, the Kōzaha's emphasis on Japan's semifeudal attributes involved a stress on the unique aspects of Japanese society, particularly in the countryside, that could be read to reinforce rather than vitiate the mythology surrounding the emperor system. Having neglected to confront these tensions, during the war, virtually all Kōzaha Marxists converted to the national cause.

Germaine A. Hoston

Bibliography

Hoston, Germaine A. *Marxism and the Crisis of Development in Prewar Japan.* Princeton, NJ: Princeton University Press, 1986.

T

Tachibana Kōzaburō (1893–1974)

Agrarian nationalist, political activist, and ideologist. A native of Ibaraki Prefecture, he founded a utopian rural commune in 1915 and a school called the Aikyō juku (Academy for the Love of One's Community) in 1931. He espoused a philosophy of rural utopianism and attributed Japan's problems to evils arising from urbanization, capitalism, and bureaucracy in government and industry. Some of his students joined with young military officers on May 15, 1932, in violent attacks against police, utilities installations, and government officials that resulted in the death of Prime Minister Inukai Tsuyoshi, among others. Tachibana was arrested for complicity, tried, and sentenced to six years in jail. Following World War II, he renounced political activism and devoted himself to writing philosophical treatises urging a return to the virtues of agrarian life. He is particularly noted for his criticism of the wealthy urban elite and his advocacy of progressive taxation to redistribute Japan's wealth.

J. Wayne Sabey

Bibliography

Havens, Thomas R.H. *Farm and Nation in Modern Japan*. Princeton, NJ: Princeton University Press, 1974.

Taft-Katsura Agreement
(*Katsura-Tafuto Kyōtei*)

July 1905 diplomatic agreement aimed at preserving the status quo in the Pacific. This confidential memorandum, based on conversations between Prime Minister Katsura Tarō and U.S. Secretary of War William Howard Taft, pledged American support for Japan's expansion in Korea and Japanese support of U.S. control of the Philippines. It also endorsed cooperation among Japan, the United States, and Great Britain to stabilize East Asia. First made public in 1924, the agreement appears never to have had the force of a formal pact but to have been merely an informal agreement between the two leaders. It presaged the similar but more detailed Root-Takahira Agreement of 1908.

James L. Huffman

Bibliography

Chay, Jongsuk. "The Taft-Katsura Memorandum Reconsidered." *Pacific Historical Review*. Vol. 37 (August 1958), 321–26.

Taishō Era (1912–26)

The period during which Emperor Yoshihito was sovereign of Japan was one of substantial economic and technological change. The rapid industrial expansion during World War I (1914–18) quickly gave way to recession and bank failures. The devastating earthquake that leveled Tokyo and Yokohama in 1923 accelerated the replacement of trolleys by buses, of wood by concrete. By the time Yoshihito died on Christmas Day 1926, automobiles and planes were coming into their own, movie theaters and cafes dotted the urban landscape, and radio and phonographs were changing the sounds of Japan.

The era is more or less synonymous with Taishō democracy, a postwar term that refers to two important developments of the period. The first is the growth of parliamentary government. In 1918, when Hara Kei (1856–1921) became prime minister, he did so as the head of the majority political party in the Diet (legislature).

Between then and 1932, the parties enjoyed a position of quasi-supremacy within the political system. The second facet of Taishō democracy was the increased participation of the masses in political activities, beginning with the 1905 Hibiya Riots, which protested the terms of the peace treaty with Russia that ended the Russo-Japanese War that same year. Urban demonstrators again took to the streets in the rice riots of 1918. Both aspects of Taishō democracy contributed to the passage of a 1925 law mandating universal manhood suffrage.

Parliamentary politics and mass participation were possible because of the accomplishments of the Meiji era (1868–1912). Under the 1889 Meiji Constitution, the early, idealistic political parties transformed themselves into pragmatic power brokers, linked with business, bureaucracy, and voters. The Rikken Seiyūkai (Friends of Constitutional Government Party), founded in 1900, was the first such party. Worthy rivals, known successively as the Dōshikai (Society of Friends), the Kenseikai (Constitutional Government Party), and the Rikken Minseitō (Constitutional Democratic Party), emerged from the Taishō Political Crisis of 1912–13.

Mass participation reflected the accomplishments of the educational system. By the beginning of the Taishō era, there was high compliance with the six years of compulsory education required of boys and girls. University intellectuals as well as elementary-school graduates could exchange ideas through the pages of journals and magazines. Newspapers flourished and created the climate of opinion that made such protests as the 1905 Hibiya Riots possible. Knowledge of Western political institutions combined with literacy and the maturation of the Japanese economy to produce labor and tenant unions.

The philosophical foundation for the parliamentary evolution and the mass participation had been established within the academic world. Minobe Tatsukichi (1873–1948), a constitutional scholar on the faculty of Tokyo University, argued that the Japanese government is composed of various organs, of which the emperor is only one, thus providing a modicum of legitimacy for other governmental organs such as the Diet (legislature) and the bureaucracy. Yoshino Sakuzō (1878–1933), another professor at Tokyo University, published a series of articles, beginning in 1915, in the magazine *Chūō Kōron*, in which he advocated democracy

(*minponshugi*), defined as government on behalf of the people. He argued that such democracy would be possible within the existing Japanese constitutional order, and he urged the establishment of universal manhood suffrage. Students whom he encouraged to join the labor movement introduced socialism and political activism to workers and peasants during and immediately after World War I.

Within the literary world, feminists and socialists launched new journals. Hiratsuka Raichō founded *Seitō* (Bluestocking) in 1911 as a journal of, by, and for women. One decade later, the magazine *Tane-maku Hito* (The Sower) gave expression to the struggling proletarian literary movement.

World War I, which followed rapidly upon the opening of the Taishō era, was to have been the war to end all wars. Japan, allied with Great Britain by the Anglo-Japanese Alliance of 1902, entered the war on the side of the Allies. Political-party prime ministers, feminism, socialism, and labor unions in Japan—all seemed to be echoes of the democracy sweeping the world. The war to end all wars sowed the seeds, of course, for the next war to come. It was during World War I that Japan seized the German holdings in China, issued the draconian Twenty-One Demands on the Chinese government, and provoked numerous boycotts of Japanese goods by Chinese nationalists. Increasing economic investment on the Asian continent provided the occasion for labor disputes between Japanese factory owners and Chinese workers and fueled the flame of Chinese patriotism with anti-Japanese sentiment.

The Hibiya Riots of 1905, which signaled the entrance of the masses onto the political stage and foreshadowed Taishō democracy, were equally a sign that the cabinet was losing its monopoly on policy-making. Japan was far more diverse at the end of the Taishō period than it had been at its beginning. In the Taishō Political Crisis of 1912–13, Prime Minister Katsura Tarō, who disputed with the armed services about the budget, was himself a general. By 1926, there were differences of opinion among civilians and military, army and navy, Home Ministry and Education Ministry, graduates of the imperial universities and those of private institutions such as Waseda and Keiō Universities, and competing business conglomerates such as Mitsubishi and Mitsui.

In the opening years of the Taishō era, bureaucrats, especially those of the Home Ministry, had perceived a need to maintain control over proliferating private interests and to foster behavior that would contribute to the national good. The ministry sponsored or cosponsored youth associations, the Patriotic Women's Society (Aikoku Fujinkai), a philanthropic organization for Koreans in Japan, and improvement groups for outcastes. The Army Ministry had similar motives for formally drawing together veterans' groups into the Imperial Military Reservist Association in 1910.

Bureaucrats educated abroad were ever wary that dangerous, perhaps even revolutionary, forces would develop within Japan, and they seized opportune moments to institute policies that would prevent alienation and revolution in Japan. The Taishō era began not long after the Great Treason Incident of 1911, in which anarchists plotted (and failed) to assassinate the emperor. The government responded by executing the plotters and a number of their associates and by setting up a private philanthropic society to provide medical care for the poor. The government responded to the rice riots that occurred in the summer of 1918 with a similar duality: calling out the army, censoring the press, and indicting the reported instigators, on the one hand, and establishing social-welfare measures and instituting mechanisms for mediation between management and labor, on the other.

Other dramatic events of the era gave expression to the conflicts that remained within the society. As the victor in two wars, Japan had acquired two colonies, Taiwan and Korea, but Japan's new subjects did not integrate smoothly into the empire, nor did the Japanese citizenry adjust well to the new diversity of its population. In the chaos resulting from the Great Kantō Earthquake of 1923, Japanese slaughtered thousands of innocent Koreans because of unfounded rumors that Koreans were poisoning wells. A few months later, a leftwing Japanese student tried, but failed, to kill the Crown Prince—in an effort to avenge the executions of anarchists convicted of high treason in 1910.

When the Taishō era ended in 1926, Japan was a great power, allied with Great Britain and the United States and a member in good standing of the League of Nations. The parliamentary government had passed a law mandating universal male suffrage in 1925, and women's suffrage was a possibility that seemed within reach. Intellectuals and labor leaders were cooperating in the founding of a proletarian political party in preparation for the first elections in which all males could vote. To be sure, rifts between leftists and moderates, Marxists and non-Marxists were beginning to appear within the reform forces.

Within a few short years, the Great Depression and the Manchurian Incident of September 1931 generated tensions that alienated Japan from its Anglo-American allies, ended political-party cabinets, and postponed the further development of liberalism and democracy in Japan until after 1945. Mass participation in the society, however, continued right through the war. The prosperous, democratic, international Japan of the late twentieth century is unquestionably heir to the Taishō era of the early 1900s.

Sally A. Hastings

Bibliography

Duus, Peter. "Yoshino Sakuzo: The Christian as Political Critic." *Journal of Japanese Studies*. Vol. 4, No. 2 (1978), 301–26.

Najita, Tetsuo, and J. Victor Koschmann, eds. *Conflict in Modern Japan: The Neglected Tradition*. Princeton, NJ: Princeton University Press, 1982.

Nolte, Sharon H. *Liberalism in Modern Japan: Ishibashi Tanzan and His Teachers, 1905–1960*. Berkeley: University of California Press, 1987.

Taishō Political Crisis (*Taishō Seihen*) (1912–13)

Popular movement that brought down the government in 1913. In December 1912, the army forced the collapse of the Saionji Kinmochi government by refusing to supply an army minister after Saionji denied its request for two new divisions. A public outcry ensued over military interference in the government. The outcry intensified when Katsura Tarō, the autocratic former prime minister who had retired from politics in 1911 to become lord keeper of the privy seal, was called on now, in December 1912, to form a new government, and it grew stronger still when he immediately used an imperial edict to bring the navy into line with his policies. The opposition, led by the Kensei Yōgo Undō (Movement to Protect Constitutional Government), included people in all walks of life: journalists, business leaders (who saw heavy military spending undermining the economy), and the opposition political party, the Rikken Seiyūkai (Friends of Constitutional Government Party).

At the beginning of 1913, Katsura formed his own party, the Rikken Dōshikai (Constitutional Society of Friends), to challenge his opponents. He also postponed, then suspended, the Diet (legislature) at this time. With each of Katsura's moves the public outrage grew more intense, however, and, on February 10, 1913, massive demonstrations led to attacks on progovernment newspaper offices and police stations across Tokyo. With government activity paralyzed, Katsura resigned on February 11 and was replaced by Yamamoto Gonnohyōe, an admiral who was acceptable to the Seiyūkai—but who was toppled by scandals one year later.

The significance of the Taishō Political Crisis lies in the fact that, for the first time, a popular uprising had forced a transfer of power from one administration to another.

James L. Huffman

Bibliography

Najita, Tetsuo. *Hara Kei in the Politics of Compromise, 1912–1913*. Cambridge: Harvard University Press, 1967.

Taiwan

Colony of Japan, 1895–1945. Taiwan was ceded to Japan following Japan's victory in the 1894–95 Sino-Japanese War, making Japan the world's first non-Western colonial power. For that reason, politicians in Tokyo and officials in Taipei (renamed Taihoku) felt that all eyes in the West were on them as they developed colonial policies. After three years of military campaigns against defiant aborigine and Chinese populations on the island, in 1898 the third governor-general, Kodama Gentarō (1852–1906), arrived with his chief civilian administrator, Gotō Shimpei (1857–1929). Speedily they began to lay the foundations for civil rule and economic exploitation of the island's resources.

Establishing civil rule meant erecting imposing public buildings and accommodations for Japanese residents in the capital to impress the native populations with the power and dignity of their Japanese rulers. It also meant fashioning a large, intrusive police network for control of the indigenous population. The network included the use of native auxiliary officers and the employment of the ancient Chinese system of self-policing for communities, the *bao-jia* system of making households mutually responsible for their members' activities. Kodama's and Gotō's policies regarding economic infra-

structure—education and health projects, transportation and communication facilities, and a streamlined landholding system—paved the way for future profits for the colonial government and private Japanese companies.

Taiwan's agricultural products, especially sugar, were soon feeding the home islands. The 1930s was a time of industrial expansion; among Taiwan's important industries, aluminum came to rank second only to sugar. Colonial capital formation also reaped benefits: The Bank of Taiwan loaned surplus funds to firms in Japan, and the governor-general sent reserve funds to Japan.

Although early administrators paid lip service to slow, evolutionary transformation of at least the ethnic Chinese (Taiwanese) population into Japanese, carefully maintained segregation between rulers and ruled in employment, education, housing, and marriage was official policy until 1922. In that year, under the island's first civil governor-general, Den Kenjirō, and the slogan "assimilation" (*dōka*), came promises to abolish the separatism in education and other aspects of colonial life that symbolized discrimination and disadvantage for the Chinese-Taiwanese and aborigines.

The change, however, was mostly on paper. The declared aim of educational revision was integration of Japanese and Taiwanese into identical schooling, but after 1922 only a tiny minority of Taiwanese actually gained access to the superior educational facilities open to all Japanese in the colony, while the best of the segregated schools for Taiwanese began filling up with Japanese students. As before, Taiwanese faced discrimination in employment and pay in relation to equally or less qualified Japanese. No serious attempts were ever made to integrate aborigines, who mainly lived in segregated villages.

By the 1920s, there was a militant anticolonial movement, the mainstream of which was led by Taiwanese who, outwardly at least, were assimilated enough to use institutions of the ruling country to skillfully publicize their case for home rule in the face of censorship and police persecution, in Japan as well as in the colony. Activism that demanded the independence of Taiwan from Japan was severely punished by the governor-general, but a remnant of the right wing of Taiwan's anticolonial movement was allowed to exist until 1936, by which time opposition politics of any kind was extremely difficult to mount.

In that year, military governors-general began to be appointed again, and official policy became one of the militant Japanization, or imperialization (*kōminka*) of natives. Again the change was one of rhetoric. Until the end of the colony's existence in 1945, Japanese residents kept their privileges; among other things, different and unequal wartime ration tickets were distributed to Japanese and Taiwanese.

E. Patricia Tsurumi

Bibliography
Ho, Samuel P. *Economic Development of Taiwan 1860–1970.* New Haven, CT: Yale University Press, 1978.
Tsurumi, E. Patricia. *Japanese Colonial Education in Taiwan, 1895–1945.* Cambridge: Harvard University Press, 1977.

Takabatake Motoyuki (1886–1928)
National socialist thinker. A native of Gumma Prefecture, he was a leading socialist in his early years, translating German philosopher Karl Marx's *Das Kapital* into Japanese and spending two months in prison for his writings. By the late 1910s, however, he had moved toward national socialism, a doctrine that called for all capitalists to turn their holdings over to the emperor, for capitalism and party politics to be abolished, and for an emperor-headed government to bring economic unity to Japan. He helped Uesugi Shinkichi, Kita Ikki, and others form several of Japan's influential nationalist societies, including the Rōsōkai (Old and Young Society, 1919) and the Keirin Gakumei (League for the Study of Government, 1923). As splits occurred in the ultranationalist movement between conservative advocates of "Japanism" and the more radical, revolutionary types, Takabatake gravitated toward the latter.

James L. Huffman

Bibliography
Storry, Richard. *The Double Patriots: A Study of Japanese Nationalism.* Westport, CT: Greenwood Press, 1973.

Takahashi Korekiyo (1854–1936)
Financial statesman, president of the Bank of Japan, seven-time finance minister, prime minister (1921–22), "Japan's Keynes." Takahashi, an English-language specialist, became a major governmental figure by raising more than 800 million yen abroad to finance Japan's war against Russia (1904–05). After Inoue Junnosuke's stringent fiscal policies intensified already severe economic distress during the Shōwa depression of the early 1930s, Takahashi became Inukai Tsuyoshi's finance minister in December 1931. He served also during the succeeding Saitō Makoto and Okada Keisuke cabinets and undertook what later would be called Keynesian policies: increased government spending through deficit financing, massive bond flotations, low interest rates, and the devaluation of the yen—all to stimulate domestic investment and encourage exports. His policies brought Japan out of the Depression by 1935. Because of political realities in 1932–33, much of his increased governmental spending went to the military, leading it to expect continuing larger budgets. In the years 1934–36, Takahashi, in a move to cool a now overheating economy, decided to rein in military spending, a decision that led to sharp confrontations with the army and the navy. He was assassinated in a massive (and unsuccessful) coup attempt on February 26, 1936.

Richard J. Smethurst

Bibliography
Duus, Peter. *Party Rivalry and Political Change in Taishō Japan.* Cambridge: Harvard University Press, 1968.

Takamure Itsue (1894–1964)
Born in a remote Kumamoto village, feminist Takamure arrived in Tokyo at age 26 to begin three successive, connected careers as a poet, an anarchist polemicist, and a historian. Although this utopian idealist, who demanded revolutionary change without accommodation to male structures, lived at a time when Japanese intellectuals were highly influenced by Western ideas and ideologies, she always sought solutions within a Japanese cultural context. Her most lasting achievement may be her historical research on Japanese women and the family. Takamure was initially ignored by most of the academic establishment and gained the enormous respect her work deserved only after her death. Her studies employed insights gained from the scholarship of an earlier nationalist thinker, Motoori Norinaga (1730–1801). Knowledge of Japanese women in past eras was to be ammunition with which to fight those who maintained that the Japanese patriarchy of

Takamure's day had always existed and, thus, must always exist.

E. Patricia Tsurumi

Bibliography
Tsurumi, E. Patricia. "Feminism and Anarchism in Japan: Takamure Itsue, 1894–1964." *Bulletin of Concerned Asian Scholars*. Vol. 17, No. 2 (April–June 1985), 2–29.

Takashima Shūhan (1798–1866)
The first advocate of Japanese military modernization along Western lines. Born into a powerful Nagasaki *machidoshiyori* (town magistrate) family, he studied Western military science and gunnery with his father following the challenge by the English warship *Phaeton* to Japan's national seclusion (*sakoku*) policy in 1808.

From his studies under Dutch scholars at Dejima in Nagasaki harbor and Japan's importation of Western artillery, Takashima came to recognize the inadequacy of Japan's defenses against Western weapons. His pleas for reform went unheeded, however, until the early British victories over China in the Opium War in 1840. In 1841, he was ordered to Edo (modern-day Tokyo) to demonstrate Western artillery, but conservative factions within the *bakufu* (military government) opposed to Western methods later had him charged with treason.

Exiled in 1846, Takashima was released only after U.S. naval Commodore Matthew Perry arrived in 1853 with four American military ships, and forced Japan to open its harbors, thus vindicating his earlier judgment of Japan's inadequate defenses. From 1855 to his death, he was an instructor at the *bakufu*'s military training school in Edo.

Lane R. Earns

Bibliography
Sansom, George. *The Western World and Japan*. New York: Knopf, 1973.

Takeuchi Yoshimi (1910–77)
Takeuchi was a professor of modern Chinese literature and a key figure in reviving nationalism as a legitimate topic for debate on the Japanese Left after World War II (1937–45). He also became a progressive intellectual leader in the 1960 opposition to revision and renewal of the 1951 Japan-U.S. Security Treaty.

Born in Nagano Prefecture and reared in Tokyo, Takeuchi attended Higher School in Osaka and, in 1931, entered Tokyo Imperial University, where he was the only student of modern literature in the Chinese Literature Department. A trip to Manchuria and north China in 1932 affected him profoundly, and, shortly after returning to Japan, he helped form the Chūgoku Bungaku Kenkyūkai (Chinese Literary Studies Society). The group published a small bulletin, *Chūgoku Bungaku Geppō*, starting in 1935. Takeuchi had been greatly impressed by the Chinese novelist-essayist Lu Xun's profound nationalism and social concern rooted in daily life and wrote his first major work on Lu Xun in 1943 while waiting to be called up for military service. Takeuchi's postwar call for a national literature (*kokumin bungaku*) generated from the folk as a vehicle for Japan's cultural independence was also modeled on Lu Xun's work.

In the immediate postwar period, Takeuchi vigorously pursued the issue of Japan's wartime responsibility, particularly the need to atone to the Chinese. For Takeuchi, the fundamental problem was that nationalist sentiment in Japan had been channeled into Western-style capitalist modernization and imperialism rather than social revolution, as was the case in China. Thus, Japan had to comprehend the difference between its nationalism and China's before it could settle its account with Asia. Takeuchi condemned the nationalism that had fueled Japan's aggressive war against Asia, but, at the same time, he searched for a justifiable nationalism that would be capable of resisting Western imperialism in Asia, as his 1959 article, "Kindai no Chōkoku" (Overcoming the Modern) indicates. His commentary on the 1942 Kyoto symposium of the same name shows his effort to recover a Japanese nationalism that eschews a developmental model of Western modernity while avoiding the ultranationalism of the prewar state. This stance informed his position on the Security Treaty issue.

Takeuchi opposed the treaty because it would bind Japan militarily to the Western bloc and hinder Japanese atonement to, and normalization of relations with, mainland China. He resigned his teaching post at Tokyo Municipal University on May 21, 1960, two days after Prime Minister Kishi Nobusuke had the opposition parties forcibly removed from the Diet (legislature) in order to achieve ratification of the treaty revisions. Takeuchi said that if he had continued teaching at a national university under a dictatorial government, he would be violating his conscience and his oath to respect and uphold the constitution as a public official. Through the protests, he worked to build an independent people's movement through which he hoped the Japanese would conquer what he called their slavishness to authority and to the West and, thus, legitimately join in common cause with Asian nationalism. He withdrew from political activism after 1960, although he continued to publish works on China and social issues until his death.

Wesley Sasaki-Uemura

Bibliography

Harootunian, H.D. "Visible Discourses/Invisible Ideologies." *South Atlantic Quarterly*. Vol. 87, No. 3 (Summer 1988), 445–74.

Kawakami Tetsutarō, et. al, eds. *Kindai no chōkoku* (Overcoming the Modern). Tokyo: Fuzanbō, 1979.

Sakai, Naoki. "Modernity and Its Critique: The Problem of Universalism and Particularism." *South Atlantic Quarterly*. Vol. 87, No. 3 (Summer 1988), 475–504.

Takigawa Affair (Takigawa Jiken)

Also known as the Kyōdai Jiken (Kyoto University Affair) of 1933. Professor Takigawa Yukitoki (1891–1962), along with one dozen colleagues, was forced from the law faculty at Kyoto University by right-wing nationalists because of his opposition to the takeover of Manchuria and to the suppression of leftists on campus. When his books were banned and the Education Ministry recommended his suspension, the entire law faculty tendered its resignation, and the campus was pitched into turmoil as self-styled patriotic student groups and others clashed with supporters of academic freedom. In the end, the university lost 12 of its 22 law faculty through resignation. This victory by the Right has been called by liberal and Marxist commentators a major turning point, and it was this affair rather than either the better-known 1935 ouster of Minobe Tatsukichi from the Diet (legislature) or the 1939 purge of Tokyo University economics professors by university president Hiraga Yuzuru that was the first full-scale confrontation of the 1930s between the government and the imperial universities.

Byron K. Marshall

Bibliography

Marshall, Byron K. *Academic Freedom and the Japanese Imperial University*. Berkeley: University of California Press, 1992.

Tanaka Giichi (1863–1929)

General and prime minister. Born in Chōshū domain, Tanaka was a protégé of Yamagata Aritomo. He served as army minister in the Hara Kei (1918–21) and second Yamamoto Gonnohyōe (1923–24) cabinets. While still a colonel, Tanaka played the key role in the formation of the Imperial Military Reservist Association in 1910. During World War I (1914–18), he worked to create a centrally controlled youth association. His goal was to use both groups to spread military values to the Japanese populace.

During the 1927–29 period, Tanaka served concurrently as prime minister and foreign minister. In foreign affairs, he pursued a positive policy of interference in mainland Asian affairs. In those same years, his government sent troops to the Shandong Peninsula in north China, ostensibly to protect Japanese residents there but, in fact, to intervene in the Nationalist revolution then underway in China. In the summer of 1927, Tanaka called the Far Eastern Conference, at which the Chinese alleged the existence of the Tanaka Memorandum, which they said was a Japanese blueprint for the conquest of Manchuria and Mongolia. Although the existence of a document of this scope has never been proved, claims about it played a role in wartime charges of a Japanese blueprint for aggressive expansionism. Domestically, Tanaka pursued a policy of repression of the Radical Left. On March 15, 1928, and April 16, 1929, his government ordered mass arrests of members of the Japan Communist Party, crushing that fledgling organization. His government fell in 1929 over Tanaka's inadequate handling of the aftermath of the assassination of Manchurian warlord Zhang Zolin by Japanese militarists.

Richard J. Smethurst

Bibliography

Morton, William F. *Tanaka Giichi and Japan's China Policy*. New York: St. Martin's Press, 1980.

Tanaka Memorandum
(*Tanaka Memorandamu*)

An alleged 1927 document outlining Japan's plans for conquering Mongolia and Manchuria. The document, first made public in 1928 in a Chinese-language journal in Nanjing, was purported to have been written by Prime Minister Tanaka Giichi. Translated subsequently into English, it triggered widespread anti-Japanese feelings in China and the United States, particularly after the Manchurian Incident (1931) and Japan's creation of the puppet state of Manchukuo in Manchuria (1932) seemed to bear out its authenticity. The Japanese government consistently denied the existence of such a document, and all of those who might have known about it repeatedly denied its authenticity during the War Crimes Trials of 1947 and later. Corroborative materials have never been found in archives. Authentic or not, the memorandum was important in fueling anti-Japanese sentiments in the prewar years.

James L. Huffman

Bibliography

Morton, William F. *Tanaka Giichi and Japan's China Policy*. New York: St. Martin's Press, 1980.

Tanigawa Gan (1923–)

A poet and critic, Tanigawa is most noted for his work in initiating local circle movements in Kyushu in the 1950s and 1960s and for cofounding *Saakurumura* (Circle Village) magazine in the fall of 1958.

Tanigawa sought a new understanding of nationalism that maintained the cultural particularity and autonomy of each local community. A number of prominent activists, as well as his own action corps at the Taishō coal mines, came out of the circle movement, and the Minamata anti-pollution movement of the late 1960s and early 1970s was ideologically influenced by its work. Tanigawa denied that "folk" and "nation" were isomorphic terms, claiming instead that local community and nation competed for people's loyalties, each at the expense of the other. He asserted the need for facilitators (*kōsakusha*) who, rather than work from elite theory to enlighten the masses, would translate the feelings and actions of local communities into terms understandable to elite intellectuals. He believed that the 1960 protest against revising the 1951 Japan-U.S. Security Treaty and the Miike coal miners' strike the same year showed that neither government leaders nor the Japan Communist Party understood the nature of resistance by local communities to state projects.

Wesley Sasaki-Uemura

Tanizaki Jun'ichirō (1886–1965)

After an early fascination with the West, Tanizaki, considered by many the preeminent novelist of modern Japan, espoused an allegiance to Japanese tradition. His self-proclaimed nativism grew especially conspicuous in the late 1920s and 1930s, when he produced essays such as *In'ei raisan* (In Praise of Shadows, 1933–34), which eloquently evokes a traditional aesthetics rooted in a uniquely Japanese appreciation of shadows. Tanizaki is sometimes regarded among those who underwent the conversion to national traditions commonly called *Nihon e no kaiki* (return to Japan). Such a characterization, however, fails to take account of the writer's playfulness, his deliberate theatricality, and his willful delight in bending tradition to accord with his powerfully distinct sensibility; in *In'ei raisan*, Tanizaki sardonically praises Japanese toilets as an example of shadowed beauty.

Seeing Tanizaki merely as a returned cultural prodigal, moreover, misses the penetrating irony that marks his fictional considerations of cultural aspiration. In *Chijin no ai* (Naomi, 1924–25), for example, a Japanese narrator obsessed with the West offers his own degradation as a warning to those who might be similarly inclined. Yet, this cautionary tale revels in its portrayal of the joyful, sensually intoxicating pursuit of the exotic.

Tanizaki's most incisive treatment of the attraction of tradition occurs in *Tade kuu mushi* (Some Prefer Nettles, 1928–29; in English, Knopf, 1955), in which the Westernized protagonist finds himself drawn to phenomena associated with the Japanese past. The allure of olden days is lyrically dramatized in this novel through scenes in which the protagonist visits a traditional puppet theater and discovers a strangely familiar, yet heretofore unrecognized, source of beauty. The very choice of the puppet theater as an instrument for the protagonist's cultural redemption, however, reveals the novel's deeper concern with a past that had become a dehumanized cultural abstraction, a past shaped by mediation and defined by the pursuit of disguises. Perhaps, then, Tanizaki's notable contribution to the consideration of nationalism was that he problematized cultural aspiration by locating it in the sphere of fantasy and desire. For Tanizaki, tradition, like everything else, existed in a world of fictions ruled by the individual human subjectivity.

Ken K. Ito

Bibliography

Ito, Ken K. *Visions of Desire: Tanizaki's Fictional Worlds.* Stanford, CA: Stanford University Press, 1991.

Tatekawa Yoshitsugu (1880–1945)

Tatekawa rose to the rank of lieutenant-general in the army, serving in numerous general staff and overseas military attaché posts. He was involved in much of the intrigue and factionalism that characterized Japanese military life in the 1920s and 1930s. He was regarded as a senior patron, for example, of the right-wing Sakurakai (Cherry Blossom Society), which attempted to overthrow the government in the aborted March Incident of 1931. In September 1931, he was dispatched to Manchuria to curb expansion-minded officers of the Guandong army, but his tacit support of their plans led directly to the Japanese takeover of Manchuria, which began in that month. Because of his indirect association with the plotters of the failed coup attempt by 1,400 soldiers and officers on February 26, 1936, Tatekawa was forced into the inactive reserves. In addition to his military service, Tatekawa also undertook several diplomatic missions. Most important, he served from 1940 to 1942 as ambassador in Moscow, where he negotiated the Japan-Soviet Neutrality Pact.

John H. Boyle

Bibliography

Storry, Richard. *The Double Patriots: A Study of Japanese Nationalism.* Westport, CT: Greenwood Press, 1973.

Terauchi Masatake (1852–1919)

Minister of war and prime minister who endeavored to center citizen loyalty on the national state and to limit popular participation in national politics. Born into a samurai family in Chōshū domain (Yamaguchi Prefecture), Terauchi was associated with military affairs throughout his career. He fought on the side of the Meiji Restoration government against Tokugawa loyalists (1869), headed the national military academy (1887), and systematized national military training during his tenure as the first inspector-general of military education (1898–90). After directing the annexation of Korea in 1910, he served as its first governor-general from 1910 to 1916, a period characterized by harsh military rule and the rigidly enforced "Japanization" of Korean education, language, and government.

Terauchi undertook the expansion of Japanese interests in China by supporting the regime of warlord Duan Qirui and by concluding the Lansing-Ishii Agreement (1917), which affirmed American recognition of Japan's special continental interests. He further cooperated with the Western powers in authorizing Japanese intervention to aid stranded Czechoslovak troops in the 1918–22 Siberian Expedition.

Terauchi followed his mentor, the powerful oligarch and prime minister Yamagata Aritomo, in opposing popular participation in domestic politics. As an advocate of "transcendent" governments composed of nonparty cabinet ministers, he opposed a major role in national affairs for party leaders or for the constituencies they represented. The Terauchi cabinet (1916–18) was brought down by widespread rioting in protest of high wartime inflation and soaring rice prices. Although economic mismanagement played a primary role in the collapse of his cabinet, public resentment of a national government that did not represent citizens' interests also contributed to its demise.

Michael Lewis

Bibliography

Mitchell, Richard. *Censorship in Imperial Japan.* Princeton, NJ: Princeton University Press, 1983.

Territorial Disputes

A number of islands surrounding Japan have been the subject of territorial disputes throughout the modern era, stimulating considerable nationalist sentiment. While most territorial issues have been settled, several disputes remained in the late 1990s. The more important sources of contention have been:

Kuril Islands. This chain of 30 islands extends northeast from eastern Hokkaido to the Russian peninsula of Kamchatka and has been a source of constant friction between Japan and

Russia. An 1855 treaty between the two countries divided control between the islands of Etorofu and Uruppu, approximately 180 miles from the Hokkaido mainland, and an 1875 treaty gave Japan all of the chain up to Shumushu, a small island immediately south of Kamchatka. At the conclusion of World War II (1937–45), the Kurils were ceded to the Soviet Union. Since that time, however, claims to the four southern groups—Kunashiri, Habomai, Shikotan, and Etorofu—have created bitter friction. Russia occupies the islands, but the Japanese contend that they are rightfully theirs, asserting that these islands, all within about 90 miles of Hokkaido, are not actually part of the Kuril chain to which Japan renounced its claims at the end of the war. Indeed, many sources published in Japan simply assume Japanese sovereignty, ignoring Russian claims. The dispute has been a continuing roadblock to improved relations between the two countries, with neither state willing to budge. Slight signs of Russian flexibility were shown after the late 1980s, but progress remained glacial.

Ryūkyū Islands. A group of islands extending southwest from Kyushu and centering on Okinawa. Island rulers gave tribute to the Chinese from the Ming dynasty (1368–1644) onward but also swore allegiance to the lord of Satsuma fief during the Tokugawa era (1600–1868). As a result, both Japan and China claimed the islands in the nineteenth century. The Meiji government (1868–1912) appointed a king of the Ryūkyūs in 1872, then two years later sent troops to Taiwan to punish islanders there for the murder of a group of shipwrecked Ryūkyūans, thus implicitly asserting Japan's sovereignty over Okinawa. In the settlement, the Chinese agreed to pay an indemnity to Japan, tacitly—though not necessarily intentionally—recognizing Japan's claim to Okinawa. Japan created Okinawa Prefecture in 1879; it lost the islands to the Americans in World War II but had them returned in 1971.

Sakhalin. Long a source of dispute because of forestry, fishing, and hunting, this large island north of Hokkaido was recognized as being under joint Russian and Japanese control in a treaty between the two countries in 1855. A subsequent treaty in 1875 gave sovereignty to Russia, in exchange for Japanese control of most of the Kuril islands. At the conclusion of the Russo-Japanese War in 1905, Russia ceded all of Sakhalin south of the 50th parallel to Japan, but at the end of World

War II, Japan renounced all claims to the island.

Senkaku Islands. An uninhabited group of islands about 100 miles north and west of the Ryūkyūs, they were included in Okinawa Prefecture by the Japanese government in 1896, lost in World War II, and returned by the United States in 1971, along with Okinawa. They contain rich fishing areas and undersea oil deposits and, since the late 1960s, have been claimed by both the People's Republic of China and the Republic of China (Taiwan). In the mid-1990s, their ownership became a source of major disputes and demonstrations by nationalistic groups in both Japan and China, as well as in Hong Kong.

Takeshima. A small island midway between Japan and Korea placed under Shimane Prefecture by the Meiji government in 1905, its nationality continues to be disputed. The South Koreans claim that Japan took it forcibly at a time when Korea was under Japanese control and thus unable to protest; the Japanese claim it is theirs. South Korea occupied the island in the mid-1990s.

James L. Huffman

Bibliography

Stephen, John J. *The Kuril Islands.* Oxford: Clarendon Press, 1974.

———. *Sakhalin: A History.* Oxford: Clarendon Press, 1971.

Rees, David. *The Soviet Seizure of the Kurils.* New York: Praeger, 1985.

Textbook Controversy

Public debate in 1982 over revisions in Japan's high-school textbooks. Because the content of Japan's public-school textbooks is controlled by the Education Ministry (Mombushō), many observers watch it carefully for shifts in official ideologies. The historian Ienaga Saburō, for example, has challenged the ministry since the 1960s over nationalistic restrictions that have been placed on his own textbook writing, and journalists since the early 1970s have written to complain about increasingly benign interpretations of Japan's role in World War II.

The textbook-revision issue flared up dramatically in mid-1982, when journalists reported that the ministry had made alterations in high-school history books that downplayed Japan's responsibility for World War II. References to massacres of Okinawan citizens, for example, had been removed, as had casualty figures from accounts of the 1937 rape of Nanjing, when Japanese troops went on a rampage of looting, killing, and raping after taking the Yangtze River city. Descriptions of Japan's 1937 invasion (*shinryaku*) of China were changed to an advance into (*shinshutsu*) China, and, conversely, Korean attempts to jettison Japanese colonialism in 1919 were changed from demonstrations to riots.

The Japanese press reacted vociferously to the revelations. Teachers' unions condemned the revisions, as did editorial writers, letters to the editor, and campus activists. While most citizens probably remained unconcerned about the changes, the lively press coverage made it appear otherwise. Perhaps the most remarkable development was the vocal reaction of Asian governments whose people had suffered at the hands of the Japanese before and during World War II (1937–45). China, South Korea, Taiwan, and other governments officially expressed their anger about the revisions. The Chinese sent representatives to Tokyo to protest the changes and published vivid pictures at home of Japan's wartime atrocities. In South Korea, the education minister met with top Japanese parliamentary officials and threatened dire consequences if the Japanese government did not make amends. The harsh foreign criticism touched off strong debates between Japan's own Foreign Ministry, where most favored a conciliatory approach, and the hard-line Education Ministry. In the end, the Mombushō agreed to make no further revisions when future texts were approved but made no changes in the material already approved. The issue was widely viewed as illustrating Japan's growing sensitivity to national image and the apprehensions with which other Asian countries still regarded Japan.

James L. Huffman

Bibliography
Asahi Shimbun Staff. "Teachers, Children, and School." *Japan Interpreter.* Vol. 9, No. 1 (Spring 1974), 13–14.

Textbooks

Japanese textbooks have reflected and stimulated the evolution in Japanese thinking, as well as changes in national and international conditions, since the inception of the Meiji government in 1868. Few mediums give a clearer picture of what the government, particularly the Ministry of Education (Mombushō), has considered important at any particular time. Textbooks from 1872 to 1879, the civilization and enlightenment (*bunmei kaika*) period, introduced Japan to advanced Western institutions and ways of thinking. They were sometimes merely translations of Western textbooks, sometimes the work of Westernizers such as Fukuzawa Yukichi. An American, W.W. Scott, who headed Japan's normal schools during these years, was responsible for teacher training and the translation and writing of school textbooks. During this period, world history was required while Japanese history was optional.

Textbooks of the 1879–84 period reflected a reaction against these extremes and the temporary triumph of Confucian values. Japanese history became required, Western history an option, and translated textbooks were forbidden. Moreover, textbooks could no longer be freely published and adopted by local schools. Under the direction of two Confucianists—Motoda Eifu, the emperor's tutor, and Nishimura Shigeki, director of the textbook-compilation board—ethics training (*shūshin*) gained priority in the curriculum.

With the appointment of Mori Arinori as minister of education from 1885 to 1889, however, textbooks began to inculcate more modern values and nationalistic sentiments. Mori expressed his nationalism by admonishing school administrators to remember that the aim of education was the good of the state, not of the students. He viewed education and textbooks as powerful instruments for creating a strong Japan.

Motoda, Yamagata Aritomo, and Inoue Kowashi believed that the promulgation of the modern Meiji Constitution in 1889 should be balanced by the fostering of an ideology that would put brakes on Westernization and place priority on traditional Confucian and samurai virtues. To that end they wrote the 1890 Imperial Rescript on Education (IRE), which stressed the obligation that all Japanese had to serve the emperor selflessly in peacetime by diligent work and in wartime by offering their lives. From the date of the IRE's promulgation, knowledge of the national polity (*kokutai*) received first priority in the teaching of history; cultivating constancy and skills came second and third, respectively. After 1910, the ethics of *shūshin* textbooks faithfully repeated at each grade level virtues mentioned in the IRE.

T

As a result of textbook scandals at the turn of the century involving bribery of government officials by textbook publishers and the desire of the Japanese government to achieve greater standardization, professionalization, and indoctrination, the Mombushō in 1903 assumed sole authorship of elementary-school textbooks (*kokutei kyōkasho*). Ministry editions of elementary national language, *shūshin*, history, and geography textbooks were published in 1903, 1910, 1918–1923, 1933–38, and 1941, and additional history and geography editions were produced in 1943–44.

These *kokutei kyōkasho* faithfully reflected domestic and international changes and views that the Mombushō wanted to inculcate. Those of the 1903 period were characterized by an open and subdued nationalism, pluralism, and pro-Western orientation, with Western heroes abounding and Confucius alone representing the Orient. From 1910 through 1945, the history and geography textbooks expressed strong nationalistic sentiments; Western heroes steadily declined in all but the 1918–23 textbooks. In reaction to the growth of anarchist, socialist, liberal, and Christian thought, all four 1910 textbooks expressed a conservative orthodoxy, along with rising nationalism and militarism. They linked traditional virtues of filial piety, loyalty, and ancestral will to patriotic and loyal service to the emperor, and they made a national hero of Saigō Takamori, the Meiji-era warrior and statesman who had led—and died in—the Satsuma Rebellion against the national government in 1877.

Ambiguity characterized the 1918–23 textbooks. The national language and *shūshin* textbooks reflected new pacifistic, international, and democratic trends. The theme of the former was "Make a Companion of the World." The last lesson of the sixth-grade *shūshin* textbook, entitled "Diplomacy," emphasized that Japan's well-being depended on international cooperation and multilateral diplomacy. In contrast, the history and geography textbooks proclaimed nationalistic and militaristic messages. The history textbook contained three times as many national and military heroes as the previous edition. The section on the "Age of the Gods" presented Japan's mythical origins as fact, and the expression "Kamikaze" (Divine Wind) was used for the first time as an explanation for the successful repulsion of the Mongolian invasions of the thirteenth century. A historical destiny in the Orient equivalent to that of the Monroe

Doctrine in the Western hemisphere was proclaimed.

The Manchurian Incident of September 18, 1931, when Japan launched its advance on the Asian mainland, led to wartime textbooks from which all moderate, internationalist themes were removed. Now, texts became blatantly militaristic and nationalistic. The opening pages of the 1934 first-grade reader contained pictures of cherry trees (associated with the life of samurai warriors) in blossom and the words *saita, saita, sakura ga saita* (they blossomed, they blossomed, the cherry trees have blossomed). The subsequent two pages pictured two soldiers with guns lined up in military formation. The accompanying script read: *susume, susume, heitai susume* (advance, advance, soldier advance). Students learned that Japan must "carry out and undertake the peace of the world in the Far East from an independent standpoint." Many stories on the Japanese army and navy and their exploits appeared; spartan values were strongly emphasized; and the call went out for the people "to fight with one mind and to mobilize all our natural resources to defend the country."

The new history and geography textbooks of 1943–44 made children more fully aware of Japan's new far-flung empire and of the organic nature of the relationship between Southeast Asian peoples and Japan. The Mombushō authors lifted up the sixteenth-century warriors Hamada Yahyoe, Yamada Nagamasa, and Tokutomi Hideyoshi as forerunners of Japan's wartime mission. Current Japanese, it declared, were reestablishing Yamada's influential role in Thailand, Hideyoshi's goal of a Greater East Asia centered on Japan, and Hamada's effort to protect Taiwan (and all Asia) from the Dutch and other Western imperialists.

As Japan became more militaristic, nationalistic, and imperialistic, textbooks became tools for blatant indoctrination. Consequently, during the Allied Occupation of Japan (1945–52), Occupation forces thoroughly purged them of ultranationalistic and militaristic content and abolished Mombushō authorship. In their place, the Occupation forces created a licensing system intended to ensure high standards of textbook style. They demanded that mythical history be replaced by facts based on archaeology and Chinese and Korean historical sources. Occupation forces also insisted on democratic, comprehensive textbooks covering the economic, social, and cultural life of the Japanese people in place of the old political histories centered on the emperors and loyalists.

The appearance of *Shinpen Nihonshi* (New Edition, Japanese History) in 1987 was the first partial retreat from that goal. Well written and illustrated, this nationalistic history textbook, written by a conservative group of scholars, emphasizes the history of Japanese emperors and justifies Japan's prewar foreign policy. By the mid-1990s, however, it had captured less than 5 percent of the high-school textbook market.

Harry Wray

Bibliography

Wray, Harold J. "Changes and Continuity in Japanese Images of the Kokutai and Attitudes and Roles Toward the Outside World: A Content Analysis of Japanese Textbooks, 1903–1945," Unpublished doctoral dissertation, University of Hawaii, 1971.

Wray, Harry. "A Study in Contrasts: Japanese School Textbooks of 1903 and 1941–45." *Monumentica Nipponica*. Vol. 28, No. 1 (Spring 1973).

Three Nonnuclear Principles (*Hikaku Sangensoku*)

Japan's policy on nuclear weapons. The atomic bombs dropped by the United States on Hiroshima and Nagasaki in 1945 have made nuclear weapons a sensitive issue in Japan. Operating under the U.S. defense umbrella through the 1960 Treaty of Mutual Cooperation and Security, and having signed the 1958 nuclear nonproliferation treaty, Japan has made the three nonnuclear principles its official policy since 1972. Prime Minister Satō Eisaku articulated that policy in 1968, saying, "Japan will not produce, possess, or let others bring in" nuclear weapons. The ruling Liberal Democratic Party responded by incorporating those principles into its party platform; then, in 1972, the Diet (legislature) adopted them unanimously. Though they do not have the force of law, they have been accepted as the basis for national military policy ever since.

The late 1980s brought increasing discussion of the *hikaku sangensoku*, with some raising questions about the wisdom of continued reliance on the United States for security, others advocating removal of the prohibition on letting others bring in nuclear weapons (in rec-ognition of the common practice of letting American ships with nuclear weapons call at Japanese ports), and still others calling for the Diet to make the principles law. There had, however, been no change in public policies by the late 1990s, at least in part because of the strong public opposition to any major change.

James L. Huffman

Bibliography

Okimoto, Daniel I. "Chrysanthemum Without the Sword: Japan's Non-Nuclear Policy." *Northeast Asian Security After Vietnam*. Ed. Martin Weinstein. Urbana: University of Illinois Press, 1982, 128–56.

Tōgō Heihachirō (1851–1934)

Commander of the Japanese fleet at the battle of Tsushima during the Russo-Japanese War (1904–05). Tōgō was born in Satsuma domain to a samurai family. During the 1868–69 Boshin War, he fought against the *bakufu* forces with the pro-Meiji Satsuma navy. After that war, he studied in England from 1871 to 1878.

Tōgō had risen to the rank of captain by the outbreak of the first Sino-Japanese War (1894–95). Just before that, as commander of the *Naniwa*, Tōgō gained notoriety when he fired upon and sank a British merchant ship, the *Kowshing*, which was ferrying Chinese troops to positions near Asan. The sinking of the *Kowshing* aroused indignation around the world, not only because the ship was flying the neutral British flag but also because Tōgō had struck before the formal opening of hostilities. Furthermore, Tōgō's crew opened fire at the Chinese troops and British sailors who had abandoned their sinking ship.

The outbreak of the Russo-Japanese War found Tōgō in command of the Japanese fleet. He was able to confine the Russian Pacific fleet in Port Arthur and destroy it piece by piece. When the Russian Baltic fleet reached the Tsushima Strait on May 27, 1905, Tōgō destroyed it despite the superior numbers of the Russians, by employing his tactical expertise and the training and discipline of Japanese sailors. He was hailed as a national hero and a naval genius in Japan and abroad.

Tōgō served as a role model for Japanese schoolchildren, who read in their textbooks of his unswerving loyalty to the state and his unsurpassed sense of duty. Later in his life (1914–

24), he was given responsibility for educating Crown Prince Hirohito. Under Tōgō's supervision Hirohito received an education that included the military arts and large doses of ethics. Tōgō also served as chief of the navy's general staff, fleet admiral, and military adviser to the emperor.

As a naval hero, Tōgō wielded considerable influence in matters of naval policy. A staunch opponent of limits on Japanese naval expansion, he urged rejection of the terms of the Washington (1921) and London (1930) naval conferences. During the latter, he argued that the Japanese delegation should walk out of the conference rather than endanger national objectives by accepting sharp limits on Japan's shipping tonnage.

By resisting naval disarmament, Tōgō added his authority and respectability to the side of the ultranationalists who also protested the naval treaties. Although publicly he rejected the introduction of politics into the military, his sympathies seem to have been with the right-wing militarists in the early 1930s. During the debate over the London Naval Treaty, he complained that the navy, rather than the civilian cabinet, should have the right to determine naval policy, and he suggested that it would be better if the military were to wrest control of the government from the parties and politicians. This was the reason for the vain hopes of the Sakurakai (Cherry Blossom Society) in October 1931 that Tōgō would persuade the emperor, if its coup attempt succeeded, to issue an imperial rescript dissolving the cabinet and providing for what it called "national renewal." The right-wing officers behind the May 15 Incident (1932) in which Prime Minister Inukai Tsuyoshi was assassinated also had hopes that, after a coup d'état, Tōgō would assist in directing the Japanese state along militarist lines.

Beset with numerous physical ailments, the elderly Tōgō retired from an active role in political and military affairs shortly after the London Naval Treaty debate. He died of cancer in 1934.

Guy Yasko

Bibliography

Blond, Georges. *Admiral Tōgō*. New York: Macmillan, 1960.

Tōgō Shigenori (1882–1950)

Diplomat. A native of Kagoshima Prefecture, Tōgō graduated from Tokyo University in 1908 with a degree in German literature. In 1913, he began a diplomatic career with the Foreign Ministry, serving in Asia, the United States, and Europe. He was ambassador to Germany from 1937 to 1938; in 1939, he became ambassador to the Soviet Union, where he was instrumental in resolving friction over fishing and territorial rights. Tōgō became foreign minister in 1941 in Tōjō Hideki's cabinet, where he voiced his opposition to the 1940 Tripartite Pact that brought Japan closer to Germany and Italy and was involved with prewar negotiations with the United States. He resigned in 1942 in opposition to the establishment of the Greater East Asia Ministry, but he remained politically active as a member of the House of Peers. In 1945, he once again took the position of foreign minister, in the Suzuki Kantarō cabinet. Tōgō was found guilty of conspiracy by the Tokyo War Crimes Trials in 1948 and sentenced to 20 years' imprisonment. He wrote *The Cause of Japan* while in prison, where he died of natural causes, on July 23, 1950.

James L. Huffman

Bibliography

Tōgō, Shigenori. *The Cause of Japan*. New York: Simon and Schuster, 1956.

Tōjō Hideki (1883–1948)

General and prime minister during World War II (1937–45). Born in Tokyo to a military family, he attended the Military Academy and the Army Staff College, then spent the early years of his army career in a variety of posts, at home and in Europe. He was promoted to major general in 1933. In the mid-1930s, he associated himself with the more moderate Tōseiha (Control Faction) of the army, in opposition to the ultranationalist Kōdōha (Imperial Way Faction) that dominated the ranks of the young officers.

Tōjō came to prominence in 1936 for his role in managing the arrests of the perpetrators of the massive, and abortive, February 26 coup attempt. He was assigned shortly after that to the Manchurian headquarters of the Guandong army, where his organizational skills came into full play. His success in assembling a clique of effective officials helped gain him the nickname "razor-sharp Tōjō"—and undergirded many of his efforts when he moved into the country's leadership elite in the 1940s.

Once war broke out with China in 1937, Tōjō advocated an aggressive policy and maneuvered the transfer back to Tokyo of one of his chief rivals, Ishiwara Kanji, who opposed escalation. Tōjō returned to Tokyo in May 1938, to serve first as vice minister of the War Ministry, then as army minister and head of the Manchuria Bureau in the second Konoe Fumimaro cabinet (1940). He called consistently for aggressive military policies in China, supporting the 1940 Tripartite Pact with Germany and Italy and advocating fuller government control of Japan's political processes.

Tōjō was named prime minister in October 1941, after an imperial conference had decided that Japan would commence hostilities with the United States if agreements could not be reached in the negotiations then under way. Throughout the war, he worked constantly—though not always successfully—to consolidate his power, holding several ministries simultaneously, suppressing political parties and opposition voices, and expanding the war effort rapidly. As Japan began to suffer losses, his influence declined; in July 1944, he was replaced as prime minister by Koiso Kuniaki. Tōjō tried, but failed, to kill himself following Japan's surrender in 1945; he was convicted as a Class A war criminal in December 1948 at the Tokyo War Crimes Trials. He experienced a change of heart while in prison and told a reporter not long before his execution that Japan's war actions had resulted from national greed, though he had considered military action a matter of national survival at the time.

James L. Huffman

Bibliography

Butow, Robert. *Tōjō and the Coming of War.* Princeton, NJ: Princeton University Press, 1961.

Tokutomi Sohō (1863–1957)

Pen name of Tokutomi Iichirō, born in Higo Province (modern-day Kumamoto Prefecture). A journalist, historian, critic, and essayist, Tokutomi was one of the foremost proponents of Japan's national ideals from the mid-1880s to 1945. He also was the founder of the leading publishing house, Min'yūsha (Society of the People's Friends), which distributed, among others, *Kokumin no Tomo* (The Nation's Friend, 1887–98), Japan's first general-interest magazine, and one of Japan's leading newspapers, *Kokumin Shimbun* (1890–1929). Besides contributing to his own periodicals, Tokutomi wrote more than 300 works, many of

Tokutomi Sohō. Courtesy Asahi Shimbun.

which enjoyed great popularity.

Although Tokutomi wrote about many subjects, from domestic and international affairs to history and literature, he paid utmost attention to the search for a respectable position for Japan in the world. This intense commitment to writing in the service of the nation (*bunshō hōkoku*) runs like a thread through his prolific and long career, which was otherwise marked by a notable shift in political principles from *heiminshugi* (commoner-ism), a concept derived from his reading of Western literature on liberal democracy, in the 1880s to militant nationalism and expansionism in the 1900s.

Tokutomi's principal works include *Shōrai no Nihon* (The Future Japan, 1886; in English, Edmonton: University of Alberta Press, 1989), a liberal, panoramic view of history's world trends, calling for Japan to transform itself into an industrial and democratic country; and the 100-volume *Kinsei Nihon Kokuminshi* (A History of the Modern Japanese Nation, 1918–52), which reflects his fervent faith in the emperor system in his later years but is, nevertheless, an exhaustive compendium of valuable materials related to Japanese history from the mid-sixteenth to the late nineteenth century.

Sinh Vinh

Bibliography

Pierson, John D. *Tokutomi Sohō, 1863–1957: A Journalist for Modern Japan*. Princeton, NJ: Princeton University Press, 1980.

Vinh, Sinh. *Tokutomi Sohō (1863–1957): The Later Career*. Toronto: University of Toronto-York University, 1986.

Tokyo War Crimes Trials (*Tōkyō Saiban*)

International trials of Class A, or major, war criminals following World War II (1937–45). In one of the more controversial moves of the American-led Occupation, the Allies decided to try Japan's leading government and military officials for "crimes against peace." In addition to conventional war crimes, they accused them of aggression and conspiracy to commit aggression, charges that had no legal precedent prior to the end of the war. For that reason, the trials sparked heated debate among officials at the time and considerable criticism from scholars— some of whom labeled the trials "victors' justice"—in the years that followed.

In all, 28 individuals were charged in the Tokyo trials. Of these, three either died before the proceedings or were ruled incapable of standing trial; the others, including 13 generals, three admirals, and four prime ministers, all were found guilty. The trial was presided over by William Webb, an Australian, and decisions were made by 11 judges representing India, the Philippines, and the nine Allied countries that signed the surrender. No judges came from neutral countries.

The defendants were tried simultaneously, though each was given an individual sentence based on a majority vote of the court. Of the 25 found guilty, seven were sentenced to death (six by a 7–4 vote and one, Prime Minister Hirota Kōki, by a 6–5 vote); 16 received a life sentence; one was given 20 years, and one seven years. They all appealed to U.S. General Douglas MacArthur, the leader of the Occupation forces, then to the U.S. Supreme Court, which ruled that it had no jurisdiction in the case. The seven were executed on December 23, 1948. The others were paroled after the 1951 signing of the San Francisco Peace Treaty, then unconditionally released in April 1958.

In addition, approximately 6,000 Japanese were tried for "minor" war crimes. Most of these trials were held away from Tokyo, often in the locality where the alleged crimes had occurred. Of those, 920 received death sentences, and the vast majority were sent to prison. The most controversial of these cases was the hurried trial of Yamashita Tomoyuki, who had been given command of the Japanese forces in the Philippines in October 1944, not long before MacArthur's invasion. Convicted of failing to keep those under him from committing atrocities, he was executed by hanging.

James L. Huffman

Bibliography

Hosoya, C., et al., eds. *The Tokyo War Crimes Trial: An International Symposium*. Tokyo: Kodansha International, 1986.

Minear, Richard. *Victors' Justice: The Tokyo War Crimes Trial*. Princeton, NJ: Princeton University Press, 1971.

Toranomon Incident (*Toranomon Jiken*)

Assassination attempt on Crown Prince Hirohito, December 27, 1923. While the prince was on his way to convene the Diet (legislature) that morning, Namba Daisuke, a young man from a political family in Yamaguchi Prefecture, shot at him at the Toranomon intersection in downtown Tokyo. Namba, a leftist, claimed that he was attempting to avenge Kōtoku Shūsui's death in 1911 for taking part in a plot against the Meiji Emperor; he also was angered by the widespread killing of socialists and Koreans following the Great Kantō Earthquake earlier that year.

Officials apprehensive about postearthquake social disruptions were already in the process of trying to curtail leftists. They said Namba was insane and tried him secretly. He was found guilty on November 13, 1924, and executed on November 15. The sensation caused by the assassination attempt brought down the Yamamoto Gonnohyōe cabinet and reportedly helped inspire the Peace Preservation Law, passed by the Diet in 1925 to control leftist ideas.

James L. Huffman

Bibliography

Mitchell, Richard. *Thought Control in Prewar Japan*. Ithaca, NY: Cornell University Press, 1976.

Toshiba Scandal (*Toshiba Jiken*)

April 1987 revelation that Toshiba Machine Company, a subsidiary of consumer electronics giant Toshiba Corporation, had sold computerized milling equipment for production of submarine propellers to the Soviet Union in violation of COCOM (Coordinating Committee for Export Control) regulations on exports to Communist countries. The incident led to harsh criticism of Japan in the U.S. Congress, which subsequently restricted Toshiba Corporation's sales to U.S. government agencies. The American reaction stimulated a nationalistic response from some circles in Japan, where the incident was seen as another case of Japan bashing.

Toshiba Machine's violation occurred in 1983–84 and was first reported to the Japanese government by the United States in 1985. Public disclosure in 1987 followed closely on the heels of another controversy: alleged violations by Japan of the terms of a bilateral agreement on trade in semiconductors that resulted in punitive tariffs levied on Japanese exports of certain electronics goods. In both incidents, the Japanese were criticized for ruthlessly pursuing economic advantage. Revisionist commentators used both affairs as evidence to support their allegations of Japanese neo-mercantilism. In the Toshiba case, since the machinery concerned was reportedly used to make Soviet submarines quieter and, thus, less susceptible to detection, Japan was accused of selling out its ally, the United States. American displeasure was symbolized by the much reprinted and televised image of U.S. legislators using sledgehammers to destroy a Toshiba electronic component.

The response from Japan included a strong, defensive condemnation of American scapegoating of Toshiba, seen as arising from trade friction and the loss of U.S. competitiveness in high technology. Although Toshiba Machine's actions in the case were not in dispute, some portrayed the incident as an unreasonable American attempt to deprive Japan of legitimate economic gains. As in the semiconductor affair, the punishment was seen as unfair and motivated by anti-Japan sentiment. This response was widespread, typical of writers in the new nationalist camp and of a cross section of leaders in government and industry. The incident thus added to the increasing strain in the U.S.-Japan relationship in the late 1980s and fueled the new nationalism seen in Japan in those years.

Ellen H. Hammond

Bibliography
Masuzoe, Yōichi. "Fallout from the Toshiba Affair." *Japan Echo*. Vol. 14, No. 4 (1987), 25–26.

Tōyama Mitsuru (1855–1944)

Right-wing theoretician, political organizer, and cofounder of the ultranationalist Gen'yōsha (Black Sea Society). Born into a samurai family in the Fukuoka area, Tōyama became involved in antigovernment activities in Kyushu during the years following the Meiji Restoration (1868) and was arrested and imprisoned in 1876. Consequently, although he strongly supported the objectives of the 1877 Satsuma Rebellion, he was in prison for its entirety and was frustrated at being unable to participate in it. Following its failure and his release, he concluded that the cause of Japanese expansion on the Asian continent (*dai-Ajia shugi*) could succeed better through political education, lobbying, and intimidation than through open rebellion. After creating the Gen'yōsha in 1881, he dedicated the remainder of his long life to being a spiritual leader of Japan's ultranationalists. Though his associates were responsible for such acts as the attempted assassination of Foreign Minister Ōkuma Shigenobu in 1889, Tōyama never directly participated in violence; in ultranationalist circles, he was widely regarded as the founder of the right-wing movement and a great leader and adviser.

J. Wayne Sabey

Bibliography
Sabey, J. Wayne. "The Gen'yōsha, the Kokuryūkai, and Japanese Expansionism." Unpublished doctoral dissertation, University of Michigan, 1972.

Trade and Economic Development

According to old theories of economic development, Japan should be a hopeless case simply because of its poor natural-resource endowment. However, postwar Japan has been a textbook example of the economic-growth model, utilizing a principle of comparative advantage for success in international trade, which, in turn, led the entire economy to Japan's "economic miracle."

Japan is hardly a newly industrialized country. Its main economic development began in the Meiji era (1868–1912), from roots established in the Tokugawa period (1600–1868). Among the early factors that contributed to economic success were internal peace, which promoted domestic commerce; carefully developed infrastructures, with highways, waterways, and seaports; high education levels; a sizable pool of human resources, readily available for modern economic development; and a stable, centralized bureaucratic government. The fact that the last shogun of the Tokugawa government, Tokugawa Keiki, managed a relatively peaceful transition of political power to the new Meiji rulers in 1868 also contributed significantly to laying a solid economic foundation.

From the very beginning of the Meiji period, the government was able to focus many of its modernizing efforts on economic development, under the slogan of *fukoku kyōhei* (rich country, strong army). Using the agricultural sector as its principal source for taxes and exports, the Meiji government successfully managed to finance all necessary expenses for industrialization, including the import of Western ships, munitions, and railway equipment, and the hiring of Western teachers and specialists.

The rise of an export industry became an important national goal from the outset of Japan's modern era. The export of raw silk and silk fabrics provided much of the capital needed

to enable Japan to adopt Western technology without depending heavily on foreign aid or accumulating a crushing burden of debt. Indeed, to understand the successful Japanese export trade of modern times, it is important to pay attention to a number of external economic factors during the Meiji years.

First, the fact that many Tokugawa-era scholars had begun studying the West even while Japan was closed to outsiders had helped prepare the scientific and technical bases needed for modern economic development. Moreover, the speed with which Japan's leaders grasped the imperialistic, Western-dominated nature of the nineteenth-century world order stimulated the kinds of economic nation-building policies that would be needed for a strong economy. The Western threat, in other words, served as an economic stimulus.

Second, in spite of unequal treaties, which limited Japanese import tariffs to 5 percent, Japan took full advantage of its comparative advantage in export trade, selling increasing volumes of silk and other products to European

Keihin Industrial Plant on Tokyo Bay. Asahi Shimbun Photo.

countries under the significant free-world trade movement that was spreading across Europe in the late nineteenth century.

Third, the increased import of cotton from the United States and India decreased domestic demands for silk, which, in turn, led to the expansion of the Japanese silk-export industry. During the critical mid-Meiji years, the Japanese silk industry was thereby given a golden opportunity to dominate the world silk market, while the competing silk industries of China, France, and Italy were temporarily incapacitated by blight and other problems.

The role of foreign trade in the Japanese economy continued to grow after the Meiji period, as the traditional semimanufactured exports, silk and tea, became a springboard for the development of modern Japanese industries. By the 1920s, Japanese exports of cotton textiles and other manufactured goods had increased Japan's share of the world market. This dynamic process of transformation in the industrial sector through foreign trade contributed more than anything else to the rapid continuing growth in Japan's GNP (gross national product).

The World War II years (1937–45) caused a dramatic setback in this growth process. At the end of the war in 1945, economic production had been reduced to only 10 percent of the prewar level. However, once peace was restored, the Japanese economy again demonstrated a significant capacity for growth, due partly to the demand for military supplies during the Korean War (1950–53) and partly to the policies of the American-dominated Occupation (1945–52).

During the 1950s and 1960s, known as the postwar high-growth period, the export-led growth was orchestrated carefully by the Japanese government, primarily by MITI (Ministry of International Trade and Industry). The success of Japan's postwar economic development is the result, many believe, of a government industrial policy in which MITI targeted certain private industries for indirect forms of assistance and thereby paved the way for dynamic, efficient private-sector growth.

Several other domestic factors also fueled the high growth rate. The low level of defense spending (less than 1 percent of the GNP annually) enabled the Japanese government to finance the expansion of industrial-production capacity. Low interest rates encouraged private investment. Increased labor productivity, induced by rapid capital formation, and a growing domestic market facilitated rising exports. And the Japanese economy demonstrated a high level of flexibility in terms of the structural transformation of industry.

On the external level, three related developments also helped fuel the high growth rate. First, the exchange rate, fixed in 1949 at 360 yen to the dollar, kept the yen undervalued for more than 20 years and thus stimulated exports. Second, the developed countries' commitment to the General Agreement on Tariffs and Trade (GATT) rules and employment policies created an expanding, relatively open world market. Third, Japan was able to procure, inexpensively, the new technology of the developed countries, a so-called "borrowed technology."

Since the early 1970s, the nature of Japanese economic growth has changed considerably, due to a number of other internal and external changes. Externally, a series of setbacks, sometimes called the "Nixon shocks," rocked Japan after the fall of 1971. For one thing, when the U.S. trade balance now began to encounter difficulties, the international monetary system felt the impact, and the fixed exchange rate of 360 yen to the dollar was replaced in 1971 by a new 308–1 rate; then in 1973, the yen moved to a floating exchange rate system. For another, the international economic environment gradually turned against Japanese exports. In particular, trade friction over prices Japan charged on textiles sold in the United States led to the onset of Japan bashing in the United States, and Japan, as a result, had to begin developing new policies to deal with a less friendly international trade environment.

The decade of the 1980s was an exciting period, which exhibited an economic-power transition. On the one hand, Japan became an economic superpower with a large production share in the world market. On the other hand, the United States appeared to be losing its economic strength while clinging to its military might. The sometimes emotional reaction by the U.S. government to the foreign-trade deficit with Japan, which grew progressively worse after 1981, seemed to symbolize the traumas of a declining economic superpower.

As Japan moved to the front rank of world economies, its leaders felt increasing pressure to take on more responsibilities in the international community, even as many Western leaders urged it to curtail its account surplus with other countries.

Masato Yamazaki

Bibliography

Higashi, Chileara, and G. Peter Lauther. *The Internationalization of the Japanese Economy*. Boston, MA: Kluwer Academic Publishers, 1987.

Newland, Kathleen, et al. *The International Relations of Japan*. New York: St. Martin's Press, 1991.

Sato, Ryuzo, and Paul Wachtel, eds. *Trade Friction and Economic Policy*. New York: Cambridge University Press, 1987.

Shinohara, Miyohei. *Industrial Growth, Trade, and Dynamic Patterns in the Japanese Economy*. Tokyo: University of Tokyo Press, 1982.

Treaty Revision (*Jōyaku Kaisei*)

Japanese efforts in the nineteenth century to obtain equitable treaties with Western countries. Japan's first comprehensive treaty with a foreign power, the Treaty of Amity and Commerce signed with the United States in 1858, provided a model for unequal treaties with 16 countries, which plagued Japan's international relations throughout much of the Meiji era (1868–1912). The treaties were unequal in two important respects: They deprived Japan of tariff autonomy, limiting duties on imports to an average of 5 percent, and they gave extraterritorial rights to foreigners, placing foreign residents in Japan under the jurisdiction of their own consular courts and thus denying Japan any legal control over foreigners residing there. The Meiji government announced its intention to secure revision of the treaties in February 1868, just one month after assuming power, and, for the next three decades, few issues had greater impact on either foreign or domestic politics.

Near the end of 1868, the fledgling government proposed revision to the ministers of the leading Western states in Tokyo. In 1871, it dispatched the Iwakura Mission to Europe and America to begin laying the groundwork for treaty revision, among other things, and mission members negotiated seriously, though unsuccessfully, in Washington for treaty changes. In 1878, the Japanese secured a treaty draft with the United States that restored tariff autonomy, but the refusal of other countries to follow suit doomed the agreement.

Informal, sometimes secret, efforts made in the late 1870s and early 1880s prepared the way for more favorable treaties. The bureaucrat Fukuchi Gen'ichirō went to Egypt in 1873 to study a mixed-court system in which resident foreigners were tried by a panel consisting of foreigners and Egyptians. American journalist Edward H. House went on a secret trip to England and France early in the 1880s to lobby officials there on behalf of treaty change. And many of Japan's Westernization efforts, including the erection in Tokyo in 1883 of the Rokumeikan, a Western-style social hall, had treaty revision as one of their major purposes.

All of the important foreign ministers in this period—especially Terashima Munenori (1873–79), Inoue Kaoru (1879–87), and Ōkuma Shigenobu (1888–89)—devoted major amounts of time to the treaty revision effort. Terashima and Inoue used a conference approach, assembling the major powers for joint negotiations. They achieved significant progress toward higher tariffs and a partial end to extraterritoriality until their efforts were blocked in the mid-1880s by opposition from the popular rights movement and nationalists, who found many of the proposed provisions demeaning to Japan. Ōkuma tried negotiating separately with individual countries, although when he secured agreements with the United States, Russia, and Germany, the British resisted. Terms of these proposed treaties, leaked to the *Times* of London, created an uproar in Japan, with one nationalist zealot throwing a bomb at Ōkuma's carriage in October 1889, causing the foreign minister to lose his leg and the cabinet to resign.

The nationalistic fervor stirred up by the unequal treaties proved a continuing problem for the government throughout the first half of the Meiji era. In 1879, for example, the press was outraged when the captain of the German ship *Hesperia* refused Japanese attempts to have his crew quarantined outside Yokohama harbor, even though there was cholera aboard; the extraterritoriality provisions of the treaty made the Japanese helpless in the face of his obstinacy. In 1886, the Normanton Incident caused a sensation, when a British captain was acquitted by a British consular court after all 23 Japanese passengers aboard were drowned, while all British crew members were saved, when his cargo ship sank off the Kii Peninsula. And one of the Meiji government's most draconian moves—the *hoan jōrei* (peace regulations) of 1887, prohibiting nearly 600 political opposition leaders from living within 7.6 miles of the imperial palace—was issued to curb the vociferous opposition to the perceived weakness of treaty-revision efforts. The treaties also became one of the major issues for opposition parties in the early years of the Diet (legislature).

International events probably played the most important role in finally bringing about revision in the 1890s. The British, in particular, began taking a more favorable stance toward Japan in that decade, largely because of their growing concerns about Russia's expansionist policies in East Asia. As a result, Foreign Minister Mutsu Munemitsu was able in July 1894 to conclude the Anglo-Japanese Commercial Treaty, which provided that extraterritoriality would cease in five years. All the other countries signed similar treaties by 1897. Additional treaties giving Japan tariff autonomy were concluded in 1911. Though treaty equality came more quickly for Japan than for other Asian countries, the long delay had a powerful, and generally negative, impact on its modern history. The delay shaped and propelled many of the country's Westernizing policies, stimulated widespread and bitter antiforeign sentiments, and kept alive questions about Japan's place in the Western-dominated world well into the twentieth century.

James L. Huffman

Bibliography

Jones, F. *Extraterritoriality in Japan and the Diplomatic Relations Resulting in Its Abolition, 1853–1899.* New Haven, CT: Yale University Press, 1931.

Morley, James. *Japan's Foreign Policy, 1868–1941: A Research Guide.* New York: Columbia University Press, 1974.

Tripartite Pact
(*Nichidokui Sangoku Dōmei*)

In 1940, Foreign Minister Matsuoka Yōsuke observed that, because Japan had become weak and isolated due to its war in China and U.S. economic pressure, it needed to enlist the power of another country. Germany was the logical choice; the devastating *blitzkrieg* in the spring of 1940 had convinced Japanese expansionists that the disintegration of the British Empire was inevitable. Accordingly, Matsuoka signed the Tripartite Pact with Germany and Italy on September 27, 1940, in Berlin. In it, Japan recognized the leadership of Germany and Italy in the creation of a new order in Europe, while Germany and Italy recognized Japan's designs on Asia. The chief goal of the alliance—to frighten the United States into passivity—was not fulfilled.

John H. Boyle

Bibliography

Schroeder, Paul W. *The Axis Alliance and Japanese-American Relations, 1941.* Ithaca, NY: Cornell University Press, 1958.

Triple Intervention (*Sangoku Kanshō*)

Diplomatic maneuver by Russia, Germany, and France, which forced Japan to return Manchuria's Liaodong Peninsula to China. Japan had won the peninsula on April 17, 1895, in the Treaty of Shimonoseki, which brought the first Sino-Japanese War (1894–95) to a conclusion. Less than one week later, on April 23, the three European countries advised Japan to return Liaodong and to seek a larger cash indemnity in exchange. They feared that Japan's acquisition of the peninsula would undermine the Manchu dynasty, potentially bring even greater instability to China, and precipitate a shift in the balance of power in East Asia; the Russians were afraid that Japan's acquisition of Manchurian territory would limit their own future activities in that region. The Japanese were shocked (though they had been warned earlier of Russia's apprehensions about the Shimonoseki Treaty), and turned to the Americans and the British for assistance. When those countries refused to involve themselves, the Japanese yielded on May 4, returned Liaodong to China, and settled for an increase in the indemnity from 200 million to 230 million taels (from about 3 billion to 3.45 billion yen).

The domestic impact of this episode could hardly be overestimated. Most Japanese felt deeply humiliated. Officials issued more than 200 temporary newspaper-publication bans in the weeks after the intervention to curb a furious press. The event convinced most Japanese that international relations hinged on power alone and that Japan would gain the respect of the Western countries only through the use of force. Many date Japan's decision to join the world of imperialist power politics from this point. When Russia seized Liaodong just three years later by leasing important parts of the peninsula from the Chinese, the seeds of the Russo-Japanese War (1904–05) began to sprout rapidly.

James L. Huffman

Bibliography

Mutsu Munemitsu. *Kenkenroku: A Diplomatic Record of the Sino-Japanese War, 1894–95*. Tokyo: University of Tokyo Press, 1982.

True Japan Society (*Genri Nihonsha*)

Founded in 1925 by right-wing agitator Minoda Muneki and others, this organization was the source of persistent and virulent anti-Communist, antiliberal, anti-internationalist, and anti-imperial-university propaganda focusing on the academic world. Although it lacked either intellectual or institutional prestige, the society did have access to funds and other expressions of approbation from sympathetic bureaucratic, military, business, and party circles. As a publishing vehicle, the Genri Nihonsha served Minoda in his pretense to be the heir of nationalist legal scholars Hozumi Yatsuka and Uesugi Shinkichi in carrying on the struggle against liberal constitutionalism at Tokyo Imperial University. Minoda and his associates contributed importantly to building up the attacks that silenced a number of liberal academicians, notably Tokyo Imperial University Professors Minobe Tatsukichi in 1935 and Nambara Shigeru in 1939. Although the Genri Nihonsha appealed to traditional values and symbols and specifically rejected Nazism as un-Japanese, Minoda's political thought had a strong national-socialist flavor.

Frank O. Miller

Bibliography

Barshay, Andrew C. *State and Intellectual in Imperial Japan*. Berkeley: University of California Press, 1988.

Twenty-One Demands (*Taika Nijūikkajō Yōkyū*)

Diplomatic attempt to expand Japanese influence in China during World War I (1914–18), when Japanese leaders thought the time was right to strengthen their position in that country. Some of their leases in Manchuria were scheduled to lapse in 1923, and the European powers were preoccupied with the war. After defeating the Germans in Shandong Province in November 1914, the Japanese tendered the Chinese Yuan Shikai government a set of 21 demands intended to substantially increase their own influence and holdings in China.

The demands were divided into five groups. The first demanded recognition of Japan's gains in Shandong; the second concerned the south Manchurian leases and would grant Japan new rights in Inner Mongolia; the third provided for joint ownership of the Hanyeping Iron Works; the fourth prohibited China from ceding any ports or islands to third parties; and the fifth, which essentially would have made China a Japanese protectorate, included such varied demands as placing Japanese advisers in China's key government ministries and requiring China to purchase armaments from Japan.

The Chinese attempted to stall the negotiations by seeking help from Great Britain and the United States. When neither was forthcoming, except in the form of expressions of disapproval, and after Japan had dropped the final group of demands, the Chinese government granted the remaining demands on May 25, 1915. The episode created universal resentment in China and increased worldwide criticism of Japan. Japan's material gains from the demands proved slight.

James L. Huffman

Bibliography

Jansen, Marius. *Japan and China: From War to Peace, 1894–1972*. Chicago: Rand McNally, 1975.

U

Uchida Ryōhei (1874–1937)

Ultranationalist, political activist and founder of the Kokuryūkai (Amur River Society). A native of Fukuoka Prefecture, he became a disciple of Tōyama Mitsuru, joined the Gen'yōsha (Black Sea Society), formed the Kokuryūkai in 1901, and actively supported Japanese expansion on the Asian continent (*dai-Ajia shugi*). Regarding Russia as the main threat to Japan, he wrote and published a series of virulently anti-Russian pamphlets and books, visited Vladivostok to gather intelligence on Russian activities in Asia, and advocated Japanese control of the Amur River Basin as a buffer against the Russian advance. He led antigovernment demonstrations in Tokyo when the 1905 Treaty of Portsmouth, which ended the Russo-Japanese War (1904–05), gained fewer concessions from Russia than the Kokuryūkai wanted. In 1906, he obtained an appointment to the staff of Itō Hirobumi, Japan's resident-general in Korea, and used his position there to help foment the unrest that resulted in Japan's annexation of Korea in 1910. Thereafter, he primarily attacked the political Left in Japan and published a huge volume of propaganda in support of *dai-Ajia shugi*.

J. Wayne Sabey

Bibliography

Sabey, J. Wayne. "The Gen'yōsha, the Kokuryūkai and Japanese Expansionism." Unpublished doctoral dissertation, University of Michigan, 1972.

Uchimura Kanzō (1861–1930)

Japanese writer and religious thinker known among Christians as the founder of the Mukyō-kai (Nonchurch Christian Movement). Uchimura matured in a Japan obsessed with becoming one of the world's leading countries. To promote this goal, Uchimura converted to Christianity at the age of 17. With close friends, such as the educator-diplomat Nitobe Inazō, he later championed Christianity, first through the secular press and then in his own magazine, *Seisho no Kenkyū* (Biblical study).

Graduate study in the United States alienated Uchimura from America, which he found lacking in spirituality, and from his fellow Japanese. At the same time, a heightened awareness of the need for public morality prevented him from agreeing with the Meiji government's growing statism. Two of his resultant acts appeared traitorous to most of his compatriots: In 1891, he hesitated to bow before the imperial signature on a copy of the 1890 Imperial Rescript on Education, and, in 1903, along with the entire editorial staff of Japan's largest newspaper, *Yorozu Chōhō*, he declared himself a pacifist as the country prepared to go to war against Russia. These acts symbolized to nationalists and conservatives the perfidy of Christians; since the Pacific War (1937–45), they have epitomized, for many, the loyal opposition.

Uchimura considered them acts of nationalism. As a Christian, he envisioned a benevolent and caring Japan. Japan's ethical tradition, which he, like Nitobe, called *bushidō* (the way of the warrior), seemed an apt preparation for Christianity, which, grafted onto this ethical stock, would make Japan virtuous. Christians, he maintained, were equipped to serve this refined nationalism.

John F. Howes

Bibliography
Howes, John F. "Uchimura Kanzo: Japanese Prophet." *Philosophers and Kings*. Ed. Dankwart A. Rostow. New York: G. Braziller, 1970, 180–207.

Uesugi Shinkichi (1878–1929)

Nationalist thinker. Born in Fukui Prefecture, he graduated in 1903 from the law department of Tokyo University and spent the years 1906–09 studying in Germany. The rest of his academic career he spent at his alma mater. An outspoken nationalist, Uesugi bitterly opposed leftism in the academic world. He also fought against moderately liberal scholars, such as Yoshino Sakuzō and Minobe Tatsukichi, whose description of the emperor as a state organ, he said, violated the concept of imperial sovereignty.

Uesugi helped found several active nationalist organizations in the late 1910s and 1920s. In 1919, he and Takabatake Motoyuki created the Keirin Kakumei (League for the Study of Statesmanship); when they feuded, he founded the Kokoku Dōshikai (Imperial Thinkers Society) in 1920, and, in 1926, he, Akao Bin, Hiranuma Kiichirō, Tōyama Mitsuru, and others started the Kenkokukai (State Foundation Society), which called for an emperor-centered state devoid of political parties. Within the nationalist community, Uesugi participated in those groups that advocated *nihonshugi* (Japanism), an expansive, warriorlike approach to national strength.

James L. Huffman

Bibliography
Storry, Richard. *The Double Patriots: A Study of Japanese Nationalism*. Westport, CT: Greenwood Press, 1973.

Ugaki Kazushige (1858–1956)

General and cabinet minister. Born in Okayama Prefecture, he graduated in 1900 from the Army Staff College and commenced a lifetime of military leadership. He became vice minister under Army Minister Tanaka Giichi in 1923 and army minister one year later. Ugaki held that post under four prime ministers (1924–27, 1930–31), for a total of nearly five years, and gained acclaim for cutting the army from 21 to 17 divisions, although he used the savings to modernize air and tank forces and had discharged troops offer paid military lectures in public schools. In 1931, as war minister, he refused to cooperate with the March Incident plotters, who schemed to topple the government and make him prime minister, but he did not have them punished. He also served as governor-general of Korea (1931–36), where he created an industrial base for Japan's expansion into China.

Ugaki was nominated for the post of prime minister early in 1937 but could not assemble a cabinet because of opposition from expansionist army rivals. Rivals also blocked him one year later, as foreign minister, from conducting peace negotiations with the Chinese. Moderates touted Ugaki several times during World War II (1937–45) as a possible candidate for prime minister. He was purged following the war, rehabilitated in 1952, and elected to the upper house of the Diet (legislature) the following year.

James L. Huffman

Bibliography
Storry, Richard. *The Double Patriots: A Study of Japanese Nationalism*. Westport, CT: Greenwood Press, 1973.

Ultranationalist Groups

In modern Japan, the term "ultranationalism" (*chō kokka shugi*) has been used to denote a wide variety of extreme forms of nationalism that supported, to one degree or another: (1) the use of military force to expand the Japanese empire; (2) reverence for the emperor and his will as a focus for domestic political activity; and (3) national regimentation in the cause of increasing Japan's power and prominence in the world. The diversity of views with respect to the proper means to achieve these extremely popular ends spawned a large number of groups and societies that the Japanese generally call *uyoku dantai* (right-wing groups).

Whereas emperor-centered nationalism has as long a history as Japan itself, the leaders of the ultranationalist groups during the Meiji period (1868–1912) saw their movement as having its origins in a number of armed insurrections against the Meiji government. The failure of the 1877 Satsuma Rebellion (Seinan Sensō), the last and most important of these uprisings, convinced most dissident samurai that open warfare could not succeed against the government's forces. They believed that other means to their desired ends must be found.

Consequently, the earliest of the *uyoku dantai*, the Gen'yōsha (Black Sea Society), was founded by Tōyama Mitsuru, Hiraoka Kōtarō, and others in 1881. Their objective was to further the cause of expansionism on the Asian continent (*dai-Ajia shugi*) through political education, propaganda, intimidation, lobbying, placing sympathetic individuals in important government positions, and occasional well-chosen acts of political violence and intimidation, including the attempted assassination of Foreign Minister Ōkuma Shigenobu in 1889. The Gen'yōsha was centered in the city of Fukuoka, which, as a consequence, became the early home of the right-wing movement in Japan. Moreover, many of Fukuoka's native sons, such as Tōyama, Uchida Ryōhei, Hirota Kōki, and Nakano Seigō, were always among the most prominent prewar ultranationalists despite a later shift of the bulk of right-wing activity to more highly populated areas, such as Tokyo.

After the founding of the Gen'yōsha, Tōyama eschewed personal participation in political activism and violence. Preferring the role of ideologist and spiritual leader, he sought to cultivate as many friendships and political relationships for his movement as possible. This preference helped initiate the proliferation of the *uyoku dantai*, when Tōyama encouraged Uchida in 1901 to form the Kokuryūkai (Amur River Society) as a tool designed to halt Russian expansion into East Asia so that Japan could move into the power vacuum that he feared might otherwise be filled by Russia. In his role as head of the Kokuryūkai, Uchida could thus engage in propagandizing, intelligence gathering, and political intimidation, while leaving public relations and ideological functions of the movement to Tōyama. Uchida, in turn, formed other organizations to serve different functions in the cause of the right-wing movement, and this precedent was followed by others, as additional groups were formed to pursue a variety of means to the ends that ultranationalists had identified.

Moreover, as Japan experienced the pull of widely varying worldwide ideologies which intensified in the aftermath of World War I (1914–18), social and economic strains resulted in disorders, demonstrations, riots, and conditions of great political flux. In response, critics of the government proliferated, while political philosophies and proposals for action multiplied. These, in turn, resulted in a crescendo of activity across the political spectrum that included an increasing number of groups oriented to the political Left—which served to intensify thought and activity among rightists and spawned philosophies such as Japanism (*nihonshugi*). Agrarian nationalism (*nōhonshugi*) rose to prominence alongside expansionism and emperorism and thus added to the growth, both in numbers of participating individuals and in numbers of groups, of the right-wing movement.

Another world development that served as a spur to the proliferation of ultranationalist groups in Japan was the Great Depression, which was precipitated by the stock market crash in the United States in 1929 and quickly spread throughout the rest of the industrialized world. As its effects were felt in Japan, the right wing seized upon its devastation of the Japanese economy as evidence that democracy and the economic system it had created had failed. It argued that Japan could be saved from further economic and political chaos only by a hard turn to the right. Furthermore, as impoverished farmers and shopkeepers sent their sons to serve in the Japanese military in the hope that their pay could help save their families at home from starvation, large numbers of these young men readily gravitated to the ultranationalists. Right-wing groups such as the Sakurakai (Cherry Blossom Society) were formed by young officers in an effort to use the power of the military establishment they served to spearhead national political and economic reform.

Hence, the early 1930s became the peak period for the development of ultranationalist societies and, although exact statistics are not available, at least 137 new groups emerged between 1931 and 1933. At the height of the right-wing movement prior to the outbreak of World War II (1937–45), at least 300 ultranationalist groups functioned in Japan, ranging in size from huge entities such as the Dainihon Kokusuikai (Great Japan National Essence Association), which had more than 500,000 members, to small local societies with only a handful of members.

Following the start of World War II, some Western observers believed that the ultranationalist groups in Japan exerted a major, if not determining, influence on the political and military developments that had led Japan into the war. However, a careful analysis of the political situation in Japan during the period between the Meiji Restoration (1868) and World War II suggests that their impact was by no means as important as that of the armed services or the country's political leaders. They did, to some degree, affect the direction, pace, and development of political policy, but it was not within their power to initiate major changes in national military and political developments.

Some observers have also regarded the use of violence and intimidation as a major source of power and influence for right-wing groups. However, the very samurai tradition out of which many of the ultranationalists arose made the Japanese some of the most physically courageous people in the world and meant that intimidation would have only a limited effect. It is much more accurate to say that most of the influence these groups wielded was due to the efforts of their members who held public office or had important connections in the bureaucracy, the military, and the political establishment.

After Japan's surrender at the end of World War II, the Allied Occupation forces officially purged large numbers of leaders and key members of the prewar ultranationalist groups, denying them the right to vote, to hold political office, or otherwise participate in the political process. However, as the Occupation (1945–52) drew to a close, a "depurge" restored these rights to almost all of those whose names originally had been placed on the purge lists. As a result, many of them reentered the political arena, some have become members of the Diet (legislature), and a few have served on the cabinets of various postwar prime ministers.

Postwar Japan has also experienced the establishment of several right-wing societies, some of which are considered by their members to be descended from prewar groups. The city of Fukuoka has seen the creation of a new society with an old name: the Gen'yōsha. Another group, the Kokuryū Club, views itself as a successor to the Kokuryūkai. Since the war, other new groups have come into existence, such as the Tatenokai (Shield Society), founded by the ultranationalist novelist Mishima Yukio. It gained notoriety through the participation of some of its leading members in Mishima's sensational 1970 suicide in the office of the commandant of the Eastern Division of the Army Self-Defense Force.

Nevertheless, these postwar ultranationalist activist groups have had significantly less influence than their prewar counterparts. Their frustrations in their quest for power are symbolized by the fact that one of Japan's best-known and most active postwar right-wing leaders, Akao Bin, never gained a large following, had relatively little influence, and was a failure as a politician. Much of the postwar right wing's lack of power is the result of Japan's crushing defeat in the war, which served to discredit ultranationalism in the eyes of many Japanese. In addition, postwar economic success has led the majority of Japan's citizens to perceive no need for the kinds of political changes sought by right-wing activists. Postwar ultranationalism also has been damaged by the support it has received from organized-crime gangs (*yakuza*) in Japan and by the eccentricities of some of its most famous advocates, such as Mishima and Akao.

It is also important to recognize that right-wingers in postwar Japan are generally more moderate than their prewar counterparts. Furthermore, despite the much publicized example of Mishima's suicide, they are considerably less prone to violence and overt intimidation. In fact, in the late 1990s, 50 years after the war, their greatest source of power in Japan lies, as it did before the war, in the personal influence of individual rightists who hold governmental and bureaucratic positions and serve as key personnel in Japanese corporations. Very few of these men, however, seek a return to militarism and/or territorial expansionism. They favor a more conservative political and economic agenda, more respect for the imperial household, and, in many cases, amendment of Article 9 of the Japanese Constitution to give Japan a stronger military role in the world. Their influence is limited, however, by the fact that even such a moderate move as amending or eliminating Article 9 is extremely unpopular among the overwhelming majority of the Japanese electorate.

J. Wayne Sabey

Bibliography

Morris, I.I. *Nationalism and the Right Wing in Japan*. New York: Oxford University Press, 1960.

Sabey, J. Wayne. "The Gen'yōsha, the Kokuryūkai, and Japanese Expansionism." Unpublished doctoral dissertation, University of Michigan, 1972.

Union of Court and *Bakufu* (*Kōbugattai*)

Proposals to unify the government of Japan to resist the foreign threat and overcome the political crisis that was created when the imperial court and the ruling Tokugawa *bakufu* government began to struggle over the commercial treaty with the United States signed in 1858. To overcome this division, an imperial princess, Kazunomiya (1846–77), was married to the shogun Tokugawa Iemochi (1846–66) in 1862, and, in return, the *bakufu* had to promise to expel the barbarians (all foreigners) in 1863. Still unappeased, radicals around the emperor pushed for greater imperial authority. At the same time, the domains of Chōshū and Satsuma proposed plans for governmental centralization that would bring their leaders into the national decision-making process, but conservative leaders on the *bakufu* side had no wish to share power. Fearful that civil war would enable the foreign powers to take over Japan, both sides proposed various forms of coalition government until 1866, when the *bakufu* sent a punitive expedition against Chōshū domain, which had rebelled against the entire *bakufu* system. *Kōbugattai* proponents eventually were overwhelmed by the anti-Tokugawa movement that resulted in the 1868 Meiji Restoration.

Anne Walthall

Bibliography

Totman, Conrad. *The Collapse of the Tokugawa Bakufu, 1862–1868.* Honolulu: University of Hawaii Press, 1980.
———. "Tokugawa Yoshinobu and *Kōbugattai*: A Study of Political Inadequacy." *Monumenta Nipponica.* Vol. 30, No. 4 (1975), 393–403.

United Church of Christ in Japan (*Nihon Kirisuto Kyōdan*)

A union of Protestant denominations whose formation in 1941 was influenced by government pressure and nationalist sentiment. After 1945, the Kyōdan worked steadily to establish itself as an independent and unified ecclesiastical structure, and in the late 1990s it is Japan's largest Protestant denomination.

The term *kyōdan* (religious body), in contrast to the more usual *kyōkai* (church), reflects the denomination's political and federational origins. Movements for church unity had existed since the early days of Japanese Christianity, often associated with a nationalistic desire to be free of missionary control. The Western ecumenical movement also led to the formation of the National Christian Council in 1936, the direct progenitor of the Kyōdan. But it took pressure from the prewar militarist government, which wanted to tighten control over all social organizations, to bring about the actual foundation. The Religious Bodies Law (*shūkyō dantai hō*) of 1939, which set a floor of 50 churches and 5,000 members for minimum qualification as an independent body, added impetus to the movement for unification.

On Jimmu Tennō Day (October 17, 1940), a daylong meeting of more than 30 Protestant denominations (Seventh Day Adventists were about the only nonattenders) issued a manifesto pledging the churches to greater support of the national war effort and agreeing to unite in one body. The Nihon Kirisuto Kyōdan held its founding General Assembly on June 24–25, 1941. In the end, the Anglican-Episcopal Church withdrew, though two of its bishops and a number of parishes in other dioceses remained. Following the end of the Pacific War in 1945, these Anglicans, as well as Baptists, Lutherans, and some Presbyterians, formed independent denominations.

Strong Japanese nationalism, which took the form of attempts to integrate Christianity with the emperor system (*tennōsei*), national polity (*kokutai*), and State Shinto, had characterized elements of Japanese Christianity for many years, and missionary influence had done little to counter such tendencies. Leaders with a nationalistic bent came to the fore in the wartime Kyōdan. Tomita Mitsuru, the first director (1941–46), was granted autocratic powers by the Ministry of Education and played a prominent role in urging members "to go beyond the range of duty in 'reverently promoting the Great Endeavour" (i.e., the War; quoted in Iglehart, 242)." Others, such as former Methodist Bishop Abe Yoshimune, traveled in China, Korea, and Southeast Asia to speak up in defense of the Japanese occupation of those countries and, where possible, to enlist the cooperation of local Christians. At home, the texts of hymns underwent alterations in a nationalistic vein, and special prayers for victory crept into the liturgy. Yet, as in so many aspects of Japanese nationalism, contradictions appeared because many pastors remained loyal to the universalistic aspects of their faith, which incurred police suspicions.

Following Japan's defeat in 1945, people of a more internationalist bent gradually replaced the nationalistic leadership. Churches paid more attention to structural and doctrinal unification—although, true to Japanese style, local and denominational allegiances remained tenacious. In 1967, more than two decades following the end of the war, the Kyōdan issued its noted *Confession of War Guilt* (*Sensō sekinin no kokuhaku*). In 1969, several conferences (regional divisions) separated over opposition to participation in the Osaka International Exposition (Expo '70), which some of the churches regarded as a new expression of Japanese economic expansion with an imperialistic bent. The Kyōdan had come full circle, and its nationalism became transmuted into social criticism.

Cyril H. Powles

Bibliography

Iglehart, Charles W. *A Century of Protestant Christianity in Japan.* Rutland, VT: Tuttle, 1959.

V

Value Creation Society (Sōka Gakkai)

A Japanese religious movement (commonly known as a "new religion"), founded in the 1930s by Makiguchi Tsunesaburō (1871–1944). Although, as an educator, Makiguchi based his ideas on pedagogical theory, he converted to Nichiren Buddhism and affiliated his small movement, Nichiren Shōshū, with the Nichiren denomination. Nichiren, the thirteenth-century prophet, is noted for having developed the most nationalistic form of Japanese Buddhism. Buddhism and the state have always been closely allied in Japan. Nichiren insisted, however, that the Lotus Sutra was the only true Buddhism, that the state should support only this form of Buddhism, and that it should abolish all other Buddhist sects as heretical. Nichiren did not succeed in attaining these goals, but he has been a continuing inspiration for nationalists who combine absolute trust in the Lotus Sutra with absolute loyalty to the state. In the troubled political times preceding World War II, some who used violence and assassination tactics claimed Nichiren as their religious authority.

Sōka Gakkai, only one of a number of new religious movements whose primary teachings and practices focus on the Lotus Sutra, has worked to revive the teachings and practices of Nichiren in contemporary Japan. During World War II, the government persecuted Sōka Gakkai for its refusal to allow members to install the talisman of the Ise Shrine in their homes, on the grounds that the talisman went against Nichiren's teaching of honoring only the Lotus Sutra. Makiguchi and his protégé Toda Jōsei (1900–58) were arrested in 1943; Makiguchi died in prison. Toda, the second leader of the movement (1951–58), emphasized Nichiren's religious teachings rather than Makiguchi's educational theory, and was responsible for the postwar expansion of the movement. Together with the third president, Ikeda Daisaku (1960–79), he made Sōka Gakkai Japan's largest voluntary organization, with claims of more than 15 million members.

During the 1950s, Sōka Gakkai became notorious for extremely aggressive proselytizing techniques; at that time, the authorities feared Sōka Gakkai because it took literally Nichiren's goal of uniting state and Buddhism. In the 1960s, Ikeda toned down the controversial techniques. The movement consolidated its organization, formulated its teaching, and established a high school and a university.

In 1964, members of Sōka Gakkai founded Kōmeitō (Clean Government Party), the only religiously based political party in Japan. In 1970, Kōmeitō formally separated from Sōka Gakkai, but the two groups retained their close relationship. The party developed an anti-Communist stance and favored a humanitarian socialism based on the religious principles of Buddhism. By the mid-1970s it had become a major political force in urban and national elections. Ikeda, who resigned as leader in 1979, remained active into the 1990s in promoting international peace. He traveled frequently to other countries, meeting various political, religious and philanthropic figures. Sōka Gakkai has recruited members and maintains branches throughout the world, but is usually known outside Japan as Nichiren Shōshū, emphasizing faith in the Lotus Sutra as a solution to personal problems and a key to international peace.

H. Byron Earhart

Bibliography

Palmer, Arvin. *Buddhist Politics: Japan's Clean Government Party*. The Hague: Martinus Nijhoff, 1971.

White, James W. *The Sokagakkai and Mass Society*. Stanford, CA: Stanford University Press, 1970.

Versailles Peace Treaty
(*Berusaiyu Heiwa Jōyaku*)

Treaty ending World War I. The peace conference convened in January 1919, amid high hopes in Japan and around the world. The Japanese delegation, led by Saionji Kinmochi, hoped to obtain Japanese control over the territories Japan had taken from Germany in China's Shandong Province, as well as over Germany's Pacific islands north of the equator. They also sought ratification of a racial-equality clause as an antidote to discrimination that Asian immigrants had experienced in Western countries. Despite U.S. President Woodrow Wilson's inspiring preconference rhetoric, the treaty itself disappointed the Japanese.

Japan gained a permanent seat in the League of Nations, had its Shandong holdings confirmed, and had Germany's Pacific islands (the Carolinas, Marshall, and Marianas) mandated. But, even though China, Italy, France, and Great Britain had earlier agreed to support Japan's territorial claims, Wilson resisted and went along only when Japan threatened not to sign the treaty. Moreover, China's government refused to ratify the treaty, in response to the anger that swept that country on May 4, 1919, in reaction to Japan's territorial acquisitions, among other things. Most distressing to many Japanese was the American and British opposition to the racial-equality clause. Although a clear majority favored it, the Americans and the British (joined by Poland, Romania, and Brazil) blocked it. A final disappointment was the American failure to join the League of Nations.

James L. Huffman

Bibliography

Murakami, Hyoe. *Japan: The Years of Trial, 1919–52*. Tokyo: Japan Culture Institute, 1982.

Nish, Ian. *Japanese Foreign Policy, 1869–1942*. London: Routledge and Kegan Paul, 1977.

Wang Jingwei Regime

The "National Government" established by Wang Jingwei, with Japanese support, during the second Sino-Japanese War.

Between 1940 and 1945, there were two Nationalist (Guomindang; GMD) governments in China, one in Chongqing, the other in Nanjing; each claimed to be the legitimate government of China. This was not the first time that such an event occurred; in 1927, 1930 and 1931, China briefly had more than one GMD government. However, the 1940 split of the GMD government was fundamentally different from the previous incidents. The GMD government in Nanjing was established in March 1940 under the aegis of the Japan, then engaged in an all-out invasion against China. In spite of itself, the Nanjing government was by definition a collaborationist regime, whose fate had been inextricably bound up since its inception with that of the Japanese imperialists.

The Wang Jingwei regime was launched on March 31, 1940, well over a year after Wang Jingwei fled Chongqing to embark on peace negotiations with the Japanese in response to the overtures of the then Japanese Prime Minister Konoe Fumimaro. The delay was mainly due to opposition within the Japanese leadership concerning the wisdom of supporting Wang, a yet unknown factor, lest this move forestall any chance of reconciliation with Chiang Kaishek in Chongqing. According to Wang, the establishment of a rival government to Chongqing was not part of his original plan either. He made the decision only after Zeng Zhongming, his confidential secretary and close friend, was assassinated by Chongqing secret agents in Hanoi on March 20, 1939.

Styled as a replica of its namesake in Chongqing, the GMD government in Nanjing retained all the symbolism pertaining to Chongqing, including the tri-color national flag but with a yellow triangular pennant attached, bearing the slogan "Peace, National Construction, and Anti-Communism." As far as its political organization was concerned, the Wang regime copied the Chongqing establishment with only minor revisions. A Central Political Council was created, allegedly superseding the old Central Political Committee in Chongqing as the main decision-making body, to which the five ministries were responsible. The regime dismissed the GMD and its government in Chongqing as illegal on the grounds that members of the Party leadership there had come under Chinese Communist control. It based its claim to political legitimacy on the Sixth National Congress held in Shanghai on August 28, 1939, a haphazard gathering of dubious party members and others. Through Japan's mediation, it received diplomatic recognition from nine Axis countries. Ironically, Japan did not extend its formal recognition to the regime until November 30, 1940.

The Wang regime incorporated the existing "Provisional Government" in Beijing and the "Reformed Government" in Nanjing, formerly set up by the Japanese North China Despatch Army and Central China Despatch Army, respectively. While the "Reformed government" was absorbed into Wang Jingwei's government, the "Provisional government" was transformed into the North China Political Council, and remained beyond the control of the Wang regime. The territory over which Nanjing had some measure of control was mainly confined to Southeast China. Even there, it had access only to cities, leaving large portions of the rural areas to guerrilla troops of Chongqing and the Communists.

Wang himself served as Acting Chairman and Premier of his regime, with Lin Sen, recognized Chairman of the Nationalist Government in Chongqing, as its top leader until Lin's death in 1943. After Wang's own demise in 1944, his positions were succeeded by Chen Gongbo. Chen announced the dissolution of the regime when Japan surrendered in August 1945.

Luo Jiu-jung

Bibliography

Boyle, John Hunter. *China and Japan at War, 1937–1945: The Politics of Collaboration.* Stanford: Stanford University Press, 1972.

Bunker, Gerald E. *The Peace Conspiracy: Wang Ching-wei and the China War, 1937–1941.* Cambridge, MA: Harvard University Press, 1972.

Morley, James W. ed. *The China Quagmire: Japan's Expansion on the Asian Continent, 1933–1941.* New York: Columbia University Press, 1983.

War Songs

From Emperor Jimmu's era (660–585 B.C.) to World War II, war songs contributed significantly to the shaping of Japanese culture. They did not become a vehicle of nationalism, however, until the 1860s and 1870s, when developments encouraged the birth of nationalistic, emperor-praising war songs. Among these were Japan's early contacts with an imperialistic West, the 1868 Meiji Restoration, and the government's Westernization policy, which promoted, among other things, militarism and modern music.

The first modern war song, "Miya san, miya san" (Your Highness, Your Highness, 1870), supported the *sonnō jōi* (revere the emperor and expel the barbarians) ideology by glorifying "the brocade banner commanding us to subdue the enemies of the imperial court." As the banner was raised again in anticipation of the first Sino- and the Russo-Japanese Wars (1894–95 and 1904–05, respectively), the military academies, staffed with Western composers, and the Office of Imperial Affairs created numerous war songs and ceremonial music, including the de facto national anthem, *"Kimi ga yo"* (The Sovereign's Reign, 1881), most of which were performed frequently until 1945. Music schools, too, produced military songs that stirred all segments of the public. War songs, or *heitai bushi* (soldiers' songs), reaffirming *akaki kokoro* (the red heart for sincerity) consequently reached the height of popularity in the 1890s and 1900s.

Written in ornate classical diction in the lengthy repetitions of the traditional 7- and 5-syllable lines and sung to the long-familiar *yonanuki* melody (the Western scale with the notes *fa* and *ti* omitted), these songs of war heroes, combat scenes, enemy bashing, and glorious victories held significant emotional appeal that stimulated the nationalist imagination of the public.

Most of these war songs were male-centered, with a few exceptions. "Fujin Jūgun ka" (The Song of Military Nurses, 1894), for instance, praised Japanese women who "not only to our soldiers / but to the enemies / whose language they know not / open their hearts and ease their pains / The women of sincerity, the nurses of the Red Cross." And "Sen'yū" (A Comrade in Arms, 1905), which captured a soldier's profound affection for his fallen comrade, could be interpreted as a subtle expression of an antiwar sentiment.

Increased songbook publications, the spread of phonographs, and the 1931 Manchurian Incident enhanced the war songs' hallucinatory effects. One of the most successful songs of the 1930s, "Manshū kōshin kyoku" (Manchurian Marching Song, 1932), began: "Raise your head and look / at the monument honoring our brave soldiers / in the war against Russia / Shining in the color of blood it stands tall / against the setting sun of this vast alien land." Another song, "Hawai daikaisen" (The Great Sea Battle of Hawaii, 1942) by Kitahara Hakushū, asserted: "Heaven permits not two suns to shine; / Seize the flag of the Stars and Stripes: / At His Majesty's command we rise / and traverse across the stormy sea / of the Pacific to Pearl Harbor."

Despite the government's public solicitation of war songs, relatively few new songs appeared after 1931, whereas Meiji songs, revitalized under new titles and with some of the lyrics changed, continued to boost the spirit of *ichioku isshin* (literally 10 million people, one mind; solidarity among all Japanese toward victory). At the end of the war, in 1945, the Allied Occupation forces suppressed all war songs, and they were heard no more, except for a few years in the 1960s, when war-song singing pubs sprang up in major cities and encouraged men to gather and indulge in the nostalgic recollections of the war years.

Yoshiko Yokochi Samuel

Washington Conference (*Washinton Kaigi*)

November 1921–February 1922. Through its three major treaties and associated resolutions, the Washington Conference reformulated international foreign policy in East Asia after World War I by bringing limited disarmament and a degree of multilateral cooperation among the major powers with interests in the western Pacific. It served as a basis for Japanese-Western relations until the London Naval Conference of 1930.

The Four Power Treaty confirmed Japan as the leading military power in East Asia by guaranteeing naval superiority in its home waters and by prohibiting the great powers from constructing new naval bases in the Western Pacific. The Five Power Treaty created a 5:5:3 ratio of capital ships for Great Britain, the United States, and Japan and limited the potential for a disastrously expensive naval race at a time when the Japanese economy was weakened. The Nine Power Treaty pledged respect for the sovereignty, independence, and territorial integrity of China. From the perspective of the United States, it also ended the Lansing-Ishii Agreement that had recognized Japan's special Manchurian interests.

Japan's actions at the conference culminated a struggle between military and diplomatic advocates and temporarily enhanced the position of the civilian leadership in foreign policy. The agreements confirmed cooperation with Western powers and demonstrated that national defense based on arms control and treaties could benefit Japan by providing security and by reducing military costs. They also increased economic ties and improved Japanese-American relations.

Yet, the Washington agreements also irritated many Japanese. Nationalists complained of the humiliating capitulation to London and Washington and objected to the limitations on capital ships, which compromised Japan's independence, and to the undermining of Japan's legitimate special mission on the Asian mainland.

After 1925, particularly as tensions increased in China, it became increasingly difficult for Japanese leaders to accept the Washington system of international cooperation, even though most argued that the agreements only slightly affected Japanese special interests and that Japan retained freedom of action in Manchuria. Tanaka Giichi of the Rikken Seiyūkai (Friends of Constitutional Government Party), in particular, called for a positive foreign policy to strengthen Japan's position in Manchuria. Yet, even Shidehara Kijūrō of the rival Rikken Minseitō (Constitutional Democratic Party), who preferred operating more within an international framework, could not appear to sacrifice Japanese national interests. By the end of the decade, advocates for a Japanese-dominated economic bloc, encompassing Manchuria, Mongolia, and China's Maritime Provinces, and advocates of territorial expansion were clearly challenging the international cooperation reflected in the Washington agreements.

Robert D. Fiala

Bibliography

Iriye, Akira. *After Imperialism: The Search for a New Order in the Far East, 1921–1931*. Cambridge: Harvard University Press, 1965.

Nish, Ian. "Japan and Naval Aspects of the Washington Conference." *Modern Japan: Aspects of History, Literature and Society*. Ed. W.G. Beasley. Berkeley: University of California Press, 1975.

Watsuji Tetsurō (1889–1960)

Philosopher. Born in Hyogo Prefecture and graduated from Tokyo University, he became one of the modern era's foremost philosophers of Japanese culture. Watsuji originally studied Western philosophy, but, during his 20s, he shifted to Japan's cultural origins, starting with seventh- and eighth-century Buddhism. He helped revive interest in the early Buddhist monk Dōgen and, in the 1930s, began publishing a multivolume systematic work on ethics. He taught at Kyoto University (1925–34) and Tokyo University (1934–49). Watsuji regarded Japan's tradition as superior because of its ability to balance the individual and society, unlike the Western tradition that overly emphasizes the individual. He found evidence of this balance in such classical arts as the tea ceremony. His published works total 20 volumes.

James L. Huffman

Bibliography
Bellah, Robert. "Japan's Cultural Identity:
Some Reflections on the Work of Watsuji
Tetsurō." *Journal of Asian Studies*. Vol.
24, No. 4 (1965).

Women's Movements

The Meiji transformation of Japan into a strong
and wealthy country modeled on the West stimulated women's movements. Westerners who
measured the level of foreign civilizations by the
treatment of women inspired Japanese officials,
eager to rid Japan of its unequal treaties, to
improve women's position in society and encourage their education. At the same time, some
Japanese credited representative political institutions for the military strength of the West and,
for that reason, advocated the introduction of
a number of human rights, including women's
rights, for Japan. Fukuzawa Yukichi (1835–
1901), Mori Arinori (1847–89), and Nakamura
Masanao (1832–91) criticized concubinage and
advocated equal marital rights for men and
women.

An articulate women's movement, founded
and led by women, took shape in 1911, when
Hiratsuka Raichō (1886–1971) and Yosano
Akiko (1878–1942) founded the literary journal *Seitō* (Bluestocking), which published articles on diverse topics, such as Norwegian dra-
matist Henrik Ibsen's *A Doll's House,* women's
suffrage, sexual mores, and Western feminists,
and thus sparked further discussion of these
issues in mainstream journals. The socially liberated "new women" of the Bluestocking Society drank alcohol and dared to visit the prostitution quarters. From this literary society came
some of the leadership for the suffrage movement in the 1920s.

Because it questioned the existing orthodoxy on gender roles and challenged the legal
exclusion of women from politics, the women's
movement that began with the publication of
Seitō has been considered one of the liberal
movements that constituted Taishō democracy
(1912–26). Both liberal and feminist historians
have sought its antecedents in the popular-rights movement, which Itagaki Taisuke
(1837–1919) and others launched when they resigned from their government posts in 1873–74
to protest what they saw as a narrowing base of
decision-making and formed opposition political parties. Among the participants in this movement, Ueki Emori (1857–92) was notable for his
advocacy of women's rights. A few women spoke
and acted on their own behalf, among them
Kishida (later Nakajima) Toshiko (1863–1901),
who made numerous public speeches. At one
point, she was arrested and spent eight days in
jail. As a political prisoner, she was a forerunner
of other women who defied the state. Among
these were Fukuda Hideko (1865–1927), who
was imprisoned for her participation in the 1885
Osaka Incident, in which popular rights activists
tried to foment an uprising in Korea, and the
anarchist Kanno Suga (1881–1911), who was
executed with Kōtoku Shūsui in 1911 for plotting the assassination of the emperor.

As internationalist critics of the status quo,
the women of the Bluestocking Society con-
signed to the ranks of conservatism women's organizations that had used more moderate
means to improve women's condition. Such
reformers included not only Christian opponents of prostitution and alcohol, but also a
number of women of samurai birth, educated
in the Confucian classics, who founded schools
and women's organizations, including the Imperial Women's Society and the Oriental Wom-
en's Society, both of which stressed Japan's ties
with Asia. Among the nationalist educators
were Atomi Kakei (1840–1926), Miwata Masa-
ko (1843–1927), Shimoda Utako (1854–1936),
Tanahashi Ayako (1839–1939), and Yamawaki
Fusako (1867–1935), all of whom were founding members in 1901 of the Aikoku Fujinkai
(Patriotic Women's Society). Christian women's
organizations included the Tokyo Moral Reform Society, founded in 1906 to work for tem-
perance and the abolition of prostitution, and
the Japan YWCA, founded in 1905.

The quintessential women's movement
of the 1920s was that for suffrage, which originated in 1920, when Hiratsuka Raichō, Ichikawa Fusae (1893–1981), and Oku Mumeo
(1895–) formed the New Women's Association
(Shin Fujin Kyōkai). The New Women's Association dissolved by the end of 1921, but the
movement to enfranchise women was spurred
on by the universal manhood-suffrage movement. By 1922, women had succeeded in winning repeal of Article 5 of the Peace Police Law,
which had barred women from participation in
political meetings, and, in 1924, a number of
women's organizations amalgamated to form
the Women's Suffrage League (Fusen Kakutoku
Dōmei). In the late 1920s, some Diet (legislature) members introduced women's-suffrage
bills. In 1931, the lower house passed a bill

sponsored by the cabinet, only to have it struck down by the House of Peers. In the atmosphere of crisis that the Manchurian Incident of 1931 generated in Japan, women's suffrage became a dead issue until the postwar period.

In the same period that women's suffrage was finding advocates within the Home Ministry, a few women struggled to bring about a radical transformation not simply of gender roles but of the entire society. In 1921, a group of women, most of them romantic partners of male socialists, organized the Red Wave Society (Sekirankai) as a socialist women's group. Although the society fell victim to the splintering of the socialist movement and dissolved in 1925, some women remained true to leftist principles. Kaneko Fumiko (1903–26) was convicted of plotting an attempt on the life of the emperor in 1923, and committed suicide in prison, while Yamashiro Tomoe served a prison term in the 1940s for attempting to revive the Communist Party.

In the 1930s, women joined organizations in unprecedented numbers. The Aikoku Fujinkai and the Dainihon Kokubō Fujinkai (Greater Japan National Defense Women's Association) each claimed a membership of millions. The women who had worked for suffrage did not disappear from public life; they just shifted their attention to more socially acceptable goals, such as improved social-welfare programs for women and children.

After the war, the Allied Occupation government (1945–52) granted suffrage to women and guaranteed their rights, in the 1947 Constitution. As in the 1930s, women continued to be highly organized. Although suffrage was no longer an issue, some leaders of the prewar suffrage movement formed new women's organizations to work for the betterment of society. The patriotic rhetoric of the 1930s disappeared, but the emphasis on motherhood and homemaking did not. Millions of women joined the National Federation of Regional Women's Organizations (Chifuren), founded in 1952 by Yamataka Shigeri (1899–1977) to elevate the status of women, reform home and society, and promote social welfare. Oku Mumeo founded the Housewives' Society (Shufuren) in 1948. Both organizations have actively promoted consumer issues.

Women's definition of themselves as housewives has not removed them from the political arena. Both Oku and Yamataka have served in the Diet. More important, women have used their responsibility as wives and mothers as a mandate to raise issues about product safety, the environment, and peace. In a series of political upheavals in 1989–90, Japanese women were outspoken critics of the sales tax, the prime minister's romantic relationships, and the Recruit Company's political corruption scandal; in the 1989 election to the upper house of the Diet and the 1990 election to the lower house, they won an unprecedented number of seats.

The Western-style "women's lib" movement has been relatively small. In the 1970s and 1980s, the philosopher and poet Tanaka Mitsu led considerable numbers of women in questioning the necessity of confining women's primary role to the home. One of the more colorful, explicitly feminist, organizations of postwar Japan has been the Pink Helmet Brigade of the 1970s. Wearing pink and blue helmets and waving pink flags, members demonstrated for legalization of birth-control pills and against proposed restrictions in the Eugenics Protection Law. They also picketed wayward husbands and men delinquent in alimony and child-support payments. The brigade was an outgrowth of Chūpiren (Women's Liberation League Against the Abortion Law and for the Pill), founded in 1972 by Enoki Misako. Although Enoki eventually retired from activism, into the late 1990s a small, articulate group of women continued to push for reforms, such as the right of women to keep their own names after marriage.

Sally A. Hastings

Bibliography

Hane, Mikiso. *Reflections on the Way to the Gallows: Voices of Japanese Rebel Women.* New York: Pantheon, 1988.

Nolte, Sharon H. "Women's Rights and Society's Needs: Japan's 1931 Suffrage Bill." *Comparative Studies in Society and History.* Vol. 28, No. 4 (1986), 690–714.

Robins-Mowry, Dorothy. *The Hidden Sun: Women of Modern Japan.* Boulder, CO: Westview Press, 1983.

Sievers, Sharon L. *Flowers in Salt: The Beginnings of Feminist Consciousness in Modern Japan.* Stanford, CA: Stanford University Press, 1983.

World War I (*Daiichiji Sekai Taisen*)

Japanese greeted the outbreak of World War I in Europe as a heaven-sent opportunity. Japan soon became a belligerent in that conflict and skillfully utilized the global state of war to extend its material and political influence on the Asian mainland and its territorial interests in Micronesia.

Acting in the spirit, though not the letter, of the 1902 Anglo-Japanese Alliance, the Japanese government, on August 15, 1914, issued an ultimatum to imperial Germany to turn over its leasehold in China's Shandong Peninsula to Japan for eventual restoration to China. After a week of no German response, 60,000 Japanese troops invaded the peninsula from the north and marched overland to dislodge a badly outnumbered German garrison from Qingdao. During the succeeding eight years, until Japan ceded its rights in Shandong to China in 1922, Japanese interests displaced German industrial, mining, and commercial operations in the region. After securing Qingdao, units of the Japanese navy sortied into the German-held Mariana, Marshall, Caroline, and Palau archipelagoes and easily captured them with the full intention of incorporating them into the Japanese Empire. Resisting Allied requests for the dispatch of Japanese troops to the European war, Japan restricted its military involvement outside of East Asia to the convoying of Allied merchant ships in the Indian Ocean and the Mediterranean Sea.

The preoccupation of major European powers with the fighting in Europe presented Japan with an unprecedented chance to expand its Asian markets and extend its influence and control in China and Siberia. By displacing European manufactured goods in Southeast Asian and Chinese ports and by becoming the major source of foreign war material for czarist Russia, Japan experienced a wartime economic boom that gave the country its first favorable trade balance since the Russo-Japanese War (1904–05) and transformed the country from a light- to a heavy-industrial power. Capitalizing upon Chinese disarray that followed the downfall of the Manchu or Qing dynasty (1644–1912), Japan in 1915 levied on its neighbor the onerous Twenty-One Demands—and, in the process, gained commercial privileges, extensions on its continental leaseholds, and the distrust of the Western powers. Japan exploited Russian disintegration in 1918 by joining an Allied incursion into Siberia. In the end, Japan held the Trans-Siberian rail line as far west as Lake Baikal and declined to remove its troops when the American and British forces withdrew from Siberia at the end of the war.

While World War I engendered a substantial internationalist movement in Japan, international reconstruction and intellectual ferment stimulated the formation of new ultranationalist and pan-Asianist societies. The print media published frequent references to "Asia for Asians" and warnings of an impending Euro-American war against yellow peoples. The voices of nationalist spokesmen such as Miyake Setsurei, Tokutomi Sohō, Itō Miyoji, and Konoe Fumimaro joined those of established right-wing activists, such as Tōyama Mitsuru and Uchida Ryōhei.

A prominent challenge to nationalists' convictions was the formation of the League of Nations. While, on the one hand, permanent membership in the league council offered Japan prestige, nationalistic-minded Japanese condemned the league as a device to perpetuate the secondary status of have-not countries such as Japan. When delegates at the Paris Peace Conference of 1919 refused to incorporate the principle of racial equality into the league covenant, nationalists warned that the organization could accomplish no good in Asia.

Many of the nationalist hopes foundered in the postwar period. The peace conference designated the Pacific islands as league-mandate territories and thereby denied Japan sovereignty over them. The Siberian incursion bore no fruits and lost public support. The Washington Conference of 1921–22 pressured Japan to vacate Qingdao and Siberia and accept an inferior naval ratio. Party cabinets after 1918 promoted harmony with the Western powers and endorsed the League of Nations. Racist sentiments in the United States and Canada brought about humiliating immigration restrictions aimed at Japanese. From a long-range perspective, the greatest blow to Japanese nationalism in the World War I period was the rise of lasting, modern nationalist movements in China and Korea.

Thomas W. Burkman

Bibliography

Burdick, Charles B. *The Japanese Siege of Tsingtao: World War I in Asia.* Hamden, CT: Archon Books, 1976.

Fifield, Russell H. *Woodrow Wilson and the Far East: The Diplomacy of the*

Shantung Question. Hamden, CT: Archon Books, 1952.

Morley, James W. *The Japanese Thrust into Siberia, 1918*. New York: Columbia University Press, 1957.

World War II (*Dainiji Sekai Taisen*)

Also known in Japan as the Pacific War (*Taiheiyō Sensō*). A few date the Asian portion of World War II from the Manchurian Incident on September 18, 1931, when Japan began the takeover of Manchuria. Japan's aggressive activities on the Asian continent surged forward after that event, as Japan quickly turned Manchuria into the puppet state of Manchukuo, then began aggression in Mongolia and in the northern sections of China proper. About this time, ultranationalist extremists at home began to disrupt the political process, brought down the system of political-party government, and stirred up chauvinist sentiments. By the middle of the 1930s, the government had committed itself to "correct" Western imperialism in Asia and stabilize the situation in East Asia.

Others would date the war from July 1937, when the second Sino-Japanese War (often called the China War) erupted at the Marco Polo Bridge near Beijing. Thereafter, Japanese troops engaged in full-scale and unremitting battle against China. Shanghai fell to the Japanese in November of that year, Nanjing in December, and, within a year, much of the coast. China itself never fell, however, partly because of its size, partly because of the intensity of Chinese resistance, and partly because of coordination and decision-making difficulties within Japan's own command structure.

Japan became bogged down and looked to Southeast Asia and the United States for supplies; Japanese leaders also signed the Tripartite Pact with Germany and Italy in September 1940 and a nonaggression pact with the Soviet Union in May 1941 to secure the northern front. At the same time, the Americans tightened the screws on Japan. They first curtailed supplies, then placed an embargo on goods destined for Japan, and, in July 1941, froze all Japanese assets in the United States. When negotiations between the two countries stalled late in November, Japan's leaders decided to launch a surprise attack on Pearl Harbor (linked with lesser attacks at several other Pacific harbors), reckoning that their best hope was to deal the United States an early knockout blow. With the bombing of Pearl Harbor on December 7, 1941, the European war became clearly linked to the fighting in eastern Asia; a world war had begun.

Japan won a dramatic series of victories in the months following Pearl Harbor and, by May 1942, had taken Guam, Wake, Hong Kong, the Malay Peninsula, Burma, Siam, the resource-rich Dutch East Indies, and the Philippines. Indeed, some observers have suggested that Japan caught the "victory disease" as a result of the surprisingly rapid triumphs. This caused the country's leaders to expand their vision of the empire and exacerbated squabbles between the northern-oriented army and the Pacific-oriented navy.

The war turned, however, in the spring and summer of 1942. Early in May, Japanese troops inflicted heavy losses on the American forces in the battle of the Coral Sea at Port Moresby in New Guinea but failed to take the port. Then, an American naval attack at Midway June 4–6 resulted in a disastrous loss for the Japanese, thanks, in part, to the fact that the Americans had cracked Japanese codes. From the late summer of 1942, the Allies launched three offensives: one in the Aleutian Islands of the north Pacific, another in the southwest Pacific, and a third in the central Pacific, with U.S. Admiral Chester Nimitz's forces leapfrogging from island to island in the Gilberts, the Marshalls, and the Marianas. The fighting was vicious; on Saipan, for example, only 1,000 of the 32,000 Japanese troops remained alive when the Allies finally took the island—and the Americans had suffered nearly 15,000 casualties themselves. The story, however, was consistently the same: steady progress by the Allies.

The Japanese lost Guam in August 1944, which placed the homeland within the range of Allied warplanes. In January 1945, U.S. General Douglas MacArthur invaded the Philippines and launched a six-month campaign that resulted in more than 250,000 Japanese deaths. The battle for Okinawa, begun on April 1, was particularly brutal, with estimates of up to 250,000 or one-quarter of the Okinawan population dying during the next three months. The early months of 1945 also saw the beginning of Allied bombings of Japan's homeland cities. On a single March night, bombers dropped 2,000 tons of artillery shells on Tokyo and left more than 80,000 dead. In all, nearly 100 Japanese cities were bombed, more than 2 million homes burned.

Although the Tōjō Hideki cabinet struggled monumentally to coordinate the mas-sive war effort, it never succeeded. Factionalism, army-navy rivalry, and coordination problems hampered the cabinet from the first. The populace, however, remained largely supportive, in part because of severe governmental control mechanisms, including heavy censorship of the media, and in part because of genuine patriotism. A courageous few resisted—for example, authors such as Tanizaki Jun'ichirō, who retreated into silence during the war, and holiness ministers who refused to recognize the emperor's divinity—but by and large, Japan's citizens remained dutiful and loyal. Their patience was stretched thin by 1944, however, as the use of resources for the war effort made food, clothing, and health care scarce. At the end of the war, people often scavanged for edible weeds and frequently simply went hungry.

By early 1945, former foreign minister Tōgō Shigenori and keeper of the Privy Seal Kido Kōichi quietly worked to hasten the end of the great disaster. Their influence in discussions behind the scenes was apparent in the selection of a moderate statesman without ties to the army, retired Admiral Suzuki Kantarō, as prime minister in April. In June, they secured an agreement among members of the Supreme War Council to seek Soviet mediation in the war, but that mediation came to naught because the Russians had no interest in such a role. On July 27, the Allies issued the Potsdam Declaration, which offered Japan the choice of "unconditional surrender" or "prompt and utter destruction." When the Japanese failed to respond, the United States dropped the world's first atomic bomb on Hiroshima on August 6, leaving more than 100,000 dead. An even greater shock came two days later, when the Russians revoked their nonaggression pact with the Japanese and entered the war. And one day after that, on August 9, the second atomic bomb fell on Nagasaki. The combined effect of these developments shifted the balance in the Supreme War Council to those who desired peace. When Emperor Hirohito himself spoke up in their favor, surrender was announced on August 15 in a scratchy radio recording in which the sovereign noted that the war situation had "developed not necessarily to Japan's advantage." Japan signed formal surrender documents on September 2.

The war costs were massive: an empire lost, millions left homeless by the Allied bombings, the economy ruined, more than 8 million casualties. Yet, the long-term aftermath was, in some ways, surprising. As scholars have noted, many of the institutions and structures created to carry out the war effort also proved effective in helping to drive Japan's economic resurgence in the 1950s and 1960s. At the same time, the war had seriously undermined the Western domination of Asia, to the point that, within one decade, colonialism was largely dead. And the Occupation (1945–52) reforms resulted in an exceptionally democratic constitution, as well as land reform and other measures that dramatically increased popular participation in the political system.

James L. Huffman

Bibliography

Butow, Robert. *Japan's Decision to Surrender.* Stanford, CA: Stanford University Press, 1954.

Cook, Haruko, and Theodore Cook. *Japan at War: An Oral History.* New York: New Press, 1992.

Havens, Thomas. *Valley of Darkness: The Japanese People and World War Two.* New York: Norton, 1978.

Inenaga, Saburō. *The Pacific War, 1931–45.* New York: Pantheon, 1978.

Spector, Ronald. *Eagle Against the Sun: The American War with Japan.* New York: Vintage Books, 1985.

Y

Yalta Agreement (*Yaruta Kyōtei*)

Discussions involving U.S. President Franklin D. Roosevelt, Soviet leader Joseph Stalin, and British Prime Minister Winston Churchill in February 1945. The three Allied leaders met at this Crimean city primarily to plan for the German surrender and postwar Europe. They also discussed Asia and secured Stalin's promise that the Soviets would enter the war against Japan within three months after the German surrender. In return, the Allies agreed to support Soviet demands for the return of southern Sakhalin and the Kuril Islands and for a significant Soviet presence in Manchuria, including a lease on Port Arthur.

On February 8, Roosevelt secretly discussed his vision of postwar Asia with Stalin, calling for combined American and Soviet influence in Korea, a diminished Asian role for Great Britain, and the removal of France from Indochina. He also proposed Communist participation in the government of China. His support of Stalin's claim to the Kurils created complications in territorial disputes between Japan and the Soviets for decades after the war.

James L. Huffman

Bibliography

Dallek, R. *Franklin D. Roosevelt and American Foreign Policy, 1932–1945*. New York: Oxford University Press, 1979.

Yamagata Aritomo (1838–1922)

Best known as the architect of the modern Japanese army. Yamagata was also influential in building the political institutions of Meiji (1868–1912) Japan and in shaping the course of Japan's rise as a major world power. As a young man, he participated, as a low-ranking samurai from Hagi, in Chōshū domain's loyalist movement, which played a key role in restoring the emperor to power in 1868. After the Meiji Restoration and following travel to Europe and the United States to observe military systems, he was instrumental in promoting military conscription as the basis for modern armed forces. He rose rapidly in the military bureaucracy, served as war minister from 1873 to 1878 (while also serving as state councillor from 1874 to 1885), led government forces to victory over Saigō Takamori's Satsuma Rebellion in 1877, and, the following year, adopted the Prussian-style general-staff system that separated command from administrative functions within the military establishment. As the first chief of staff of the army (1878–82 and 1884–85), he solidified the independence of the military directly under the emperor and fostered the loyalty of servicemen to the throne by promoting the Imperial Rescript to Soldiers and Sailors in 1882.

After 1881, Yamagata's rise in the civil bureaucracy paralleled his ascent to the apex of the military bureaucracy. As home minister (1883–89), he reorganized the ministry, the police system, and the local government system. He twice served as prime minister (1889–90, 1898–1900), held the post of justice minister (1892–93), and, for a total of 17 nonconsecutive years, he was president of the Privy Council. For three decades, until his death in 1922, he also served as a *genrō*, one of the small group of elder statesmen who informally advised the emperor on crucial domestic issues—most notably, the selection of prime ministers—and on foreign policy.

His more than half a century of civil and military service earned him the highest civil and military ranks of prince and field mar-

Yamagata Aritomo. Asahi Shimbun Photo.

Yamagata-Lobanov Convention
(*Yamagata-Robanofu Kyōtei*)

The Yamagata-Lobanov Convention, otherwise known as the Moscow Protocol, was signed on June 9, 1896, in Moscow. It was an attempt to alleviate serious antagonism between Japan and Russia that stemmed from Russia's participation in the 1895 Triple Intervention against Japan's Shimonoseki Treaty with China and from Russian interference in Korean affairs. After winning what it termed the "independence" of Korea from China in the 1894–95 Sino-Japanese War, the Japanese government had named distinguished statesman Count Inoue Kaoru, ambassador to Korea, with advisers and money (not enough, Inoue said) to "assist progressive Koreans" in Korea's modernization.

However, the Korean court, rife with intrigue, blocked Japan's moves, which frustrated Inoue so much that he aborted the mission and returned to Tokyo to be replaced as minister by General Miura Gorō, who arranged the murder of Korea's Queen Min. King Kojong retaliated by seeking and obtaining refuge in Russia's Seoul legation, which, after Miura's ignominious recall to Japan for his role in the assassination, gave Russia the chance to take charge of Seoul and begin to reap the benefits Japan had expected from its Sino-Japanese War victory. Thereupon Japan sent former Prime Minister Yamagata Aritomo to Russia, while lower-level talks with Russian embassy officials proceeded in Tokyo and Seoul. After long and delicate negotiations, the Waeber-Komura Agreement was reached in Seoul on May 14, 1896. It did not require King Kojong to leave the Russian Embassy as the Japanese had wanted. Under its terms, the number of Russian troops kept in Korea would not exceed the number of Japanese troops (which were os-tensibly guarding the Pusan-Seoul telegraph line), and further Russo-Japanese negotiations would be conducted in a "most friendly sense." This agreement set the tone for the more vague Yamagata-Labonov Moscow Protocol of June 9, which recognized Korean independence and pledged assistance from Japan and Russia for Korean reforms—all in the ostensible name of "removing financial difficulties of Korea."

Hilary Conroy

shal, respectively. Although he was a revolutionary in early manhood and a bold builder of new institutions in his early career, in full maturity he combined traditional tastes (he was an accomplished poet, landscape architect, and tea master) with conservative political views (he disliked parties and politicians who, he maintained, divided the country for narrow, selfish motives) and an autocratic style.

Yamagata was a key figure in the rise of Japan as a modern state. His guiding goal of a strong, unified country recognized as a major world power was in considerable measure accomplished by his legacy: a powerful, independent military and a dominant conservative bureaucracy.

Roger F. Hackett

Bibliography

Hackett, Roger. *Yamagata Aritomo in the Rise of Modern Japan.* Cambridge: Harvard University Press, 1971.

Bibliography

Conroy, Hilary. *The Japanese Seizure of Korea.* Philadelphia: University of Pennsylvania Press, 1974.

Duus, Peter. *The Abacus and the Sword: The Japanese Penetration of Korea, 1895–1910*. Berkeley: University of California Press, 1995.

Lensen, George A. *The Diplomacy of Intrigue*. Vol. 2. Tallahassee: University Presses of Florida, 1982.

Yamaji Aizan (1864–1917)

Nationalistic journalist. Born in Tokyo and educated at Tokyo Eiwa Gakkō, Yamaji converted early to Christianity and, in 1892, entered journalist Tokutomi Sohō's publishing firm, the Min'yūsha. He wrote for numerous journals over the years, including *Kokumin no Tomo*, *Shinano Mainichi Shimbun*, which he edited, and two of his own magazines, *Dokuritsu Hyōron* (founded 1903) and *Kokumin Zasshi* (1910). His often polemical writings focused on Japanese history and literature, and he frequently engaged literary critics, such as Takayama Chogyū and Kitamura Tōkoku, in fierce debate.

In 1904, Yamaji became an enthusiastic supporter of the Russo-Japanese War (1904–05) and temporarily renamed his journal *Nichiro Sensō Jikki* (Authentic Record of the Russo-Japanese War). In later years, he tended toward national socialism. He also began, but did not complete, a comprehensive history of the Japanese people.

James L. Huffman

Bibliography
Pyle, Kenneth. *The New Generation in Meiji Japan*. Stanford, CA: Stanford University Press, 1969.

Yamamoto Gonnohyōe (also Gonbei) (1852–1933)

Yamamoto's dual military and political career included elevation to central decision-making positions within the admiralty, service as navy minister in successive cabinets (1898–1904), and appointment to two terms as prime minister (1913–14 and 1923–24). In those roles, he consistently advocated two broad policies: naval expansion and appointment of talented government men to national office. In pursuit of these aims, he willingly collaborated with political-party leaders. During the Taishō Political Crisis (1912–13), Yamamoto cooperated with Rikken Seiyūkai (Friends of Constitutional Government Party) leaders Saionji Kinmochi and Hara Takashi in the creation of a reform-minded government. The first Yamamoto government abolished restrictions that permitted only active-duty officers to serve as war or navy ministers, improved government financial administration, and broadened the basis for civil-service appointments. The 1914 Siemens Incident over bribery for naval procurements, coupled with the cabinet's inability to establish a budget because of Diet (legislature) demands for cuts in naval expenditures, resulted in the collapse of the first Yamamoto government.

With his cabinet's fall, Yamamoto retired from politics and the navy. Nevertheless, in 1923 he complied with an imperial summons to form a second government, one charged with resurrecting Tokyo following the destruction wrought by the Great Kantō Earthquake. Although the press harshly criticized Yamamoto as a partisan leader of the Satsuma-domain military clique, the second Yamamoto cabinet included Inukai Tsuyoshi and other political-party liberals who advocated universal manhood suffrage and social reforms. Yamamoto resigned from public life for a second and final time following an attempt on the life of the Crown Prince Hirohito (Toranomon Incident, 1923). Between 1924 and his death in 1933, Yamamoto took no role in the increasing militarization of Japanese politics and society. On balance, his legacy is that of an enlightened nationalist, one who consistently placed Japan's interests first, but who also tolerated a modicum of popular rights and cooperation with political parties.

Michael Lewis

Bibliography
Najita, Tetsuo. *Hara Kei and the Politics of Compromise*. Cambridge: Harvard University Press, 1967.

Yamamoto Isoroku (1884–1943)

Fleet admiral. A native of Niigata Prefecture and graduate of the Naval Academy and the Naval War College, he directed Japan's naval war from the bombing of Pearl Harbor (December 7, 1941) until 1943. Early in his career, he spent more than four years in the United States, at Harvard University and the Japanese Embassy in Washington, D.C. He also served on the Japanese delegation to the 1930 London Naval Conference and negotiated arms reduction in London in the mid-1930s. As a result of these foreign contacts, by the time he became vice minister of the navy in 1936, he had decided that war with the United States or Great Britain would be a mistake. He also opposed the 1940 Tripartite Pact with Germany and Italy.

Despite this view, Yamamoto was named fleet commander in chief in 1939 and planned the Pearl Harbor attack, convinced now that Japan's only chance lay in a quick defeat of the United States. His forces won successive victories early in 1942, but then the Americans, having broken Japan's naval code, seriously wounded Yamamoto's fleet at Midway in June 1942. He was shot down by the Americans over the Solomon Islands in April 1943—a devastating loss to troops who depended heavily on his planning and personal inspiration.

James L. Huffman

Bibliography

Hoyt, Edwin. *Yamamoto: The Man Who Planned Pearl Harbor.* New York: McGraw-Hill, 1990.

Yamawaki Fusako (1867–1935)

Educator and club woman. The daughter of a Matsue samurai, she was educated in the Confucian classics before attending Shimane Prefectural Normal School in western Japan. As the widow of a military officer, she studied English in Sendai and Tokyo. In 1894, she married Yamawaki Gen (1849–1925), a legal scholar, former official, and member of the House of Peers. In 1903, she became principal of the Jisshu Girls' Higher School (which in 1908 became Yamawaki Girls' Higher School), a position that she held until her death. A founding member in 1901 of the Aikoku Fujinkai (Patriotic Women's Society), and an early member of the Dainihon Fujin Kyōikukai (Japanese Women's Educational Society), the Tōyō Fujinkai (Women of the East Society), and the Taishō Fujinkai (Taishō Women's Society), Yamawaki also helped organize the Fujin Dōshikai (Society of Like-Minded Women), a moderate suffrage group. When the Dainihon Rengō Joshi Seinendan (Greater Japan League of Girls' Clubs) was founded in 1927 under government direction, she became its first president. She was one of a handful of exceptionally well educated women who cooperated with the state in promoting women's education and women's participation in patriotic activities.

Sally A. Hastings

Yanagita Kunio (1875–1962)

Poet, bureaucrat, journalist, and founder of *minzokugaku* (folklore studies). Born in Hyogo Prefecture, he was the sixth son of a doctor, Confucian scholar, and later Shinto priest. Graduated from the political course in the Department of Law at Tokyo Imperial University in 1900 and married, in 1901, into the influential Yanagita family whose patriarch was a Supreme Court judge, he worked for two decades as a specialist in agricultural policy for the Agricultural Affairs Bureau of the Ministry of Agriculture and Commerce and later for the Legislative Bureau and the Imperial Household Ministry. He also taught agricultural policy at Waseda University. Yanagita was a chief secretary to the House of Peers between 1914 and 1919 and wrote for the newspaper *Asahi Shimbun* from 1919 to 1930.

Yanagita's *minzokugaku* focused on the search for the traditional elements of distinctively Japanese folkways: local folklore, oral traditions, thought patterns, popular customs and manners, beliefs, rituals, dialects, regional religious practices, and seasonal and religious festivals. Yanagita also explored the distinctive Japanese national character, especially the influence of the emperor system and rice cultivation; to that end, he diligently preserved indigenous rural culture, educated and enlightened rural youth, and advocated social reform.

Yanagita wanted to establish Japanese folklore studies as a distinct discipline, removed from the influences of Western ethnology. He studied

Yanagita Kunio. Asahi Shimbun Photo.

Japanese themes from within—the Japanese folk culture as it actually was lived by the *jomin* (abiding folk) in towns and villages. He studied the countryside folk Shinto rather than the national, or State, Shinto that the West criticized for promoting narrow-minded nationalism. Especially after World War II, Yanagita concentrated on Shinto and nativistic *kokugaku* (national learning), both of which rightists used to justify their ideologies. Fundamentally, *minzokugaku* revealed Yanagita's passionate love of Japan. After Japan's defeat in the war, he used it to boost the morale of the Japanese people and to lead them to the discovery of identity, self-knowledge, and self-renewal. He advocated a new society created from indigenous culture as an alternative to the modern, rational, industrial, Western capitalistic state based on central bureaucracy and technology.

Kinko Ito

Bibliography

Irokawa, Daikichi. *The Culture of the Meiji Period*. Princeton, NJ: Princeton University Press, 1985.

Yanaihara Tadao (1893–1961)

Economist, Christian evangelist, and educator, who continued the humanistic colonialism of his political mentor, the educator-diplomat Nitobe Inazō, and the biblical evangelism of his religious teacher, the essayist Uchimura Kanzō. Though both of his mentors died before Japanese forces drove deeply into China in 1937, Yanaihara used his own position as a professor of colonial policy at Tokyo University (1920–37) to decry the greed that motivated the invasion of China. He believed that Japan's Christians should follow the biblical prophet Jeremiah and oppose their unjust government. Driven from his university post in 1937, he continued, as a loyal nationalist, to criticize chauvinism. One university associate later recalled: "We felt that as long as Yanaihara lived, Japan would survive." In 1951, colleagues elected him president of Tokyo University, where he helped liberalize Japan's post-secondary education.

John F. Howes

Bibliography

Fujita, Wakao. "Yanaihara Tadao: Disciple of Uchimara Kanzō." *Pacifism in Japan: The Christian and Socialist Tradition*. Ed. N. Bamba and J. Howes. Vancouver: University of British Columbia Press, 1978, 199–219.

Yokohama Incident (*Yokohama Jiken*) (1943–45)

An extreme instance of police brutality during World War II. The Yokohama Special Higher Police arrested nearly three-dozen intellectuals between 1943 and 1945 on the spurious charge of trying to revive the Communist Party. The accused included editors of prestigious, relatively liberal magazines—*Chūō Kōron, Kaizō*, and *Nippon Hyōron*—and the allegation against them may have been fabricated to justify closing these journals. *Chūō Kōron* and *Kaizō* were dissolved in mid-1944.

Without solid evidence against their suspects, the police sought to coerce confessions. Thirty-two of those jailed claimed to have suffered serious beatings, 12 stated that they were knocked unconscious, and three died as a result of mistreatment. None were tried until immediately after Japan's surrender, when they all were summarily convicted in court. They were released shortly thereafter by the Occupation.

Considering that none of the accused was a Communist or had opposed the war effort, the Yokohama Incident indicates how extreme the state's nationalistic ideology became late in the war. It also illustrates vividly the arbitrary powers of the police, which enforced that ideology.

Gregory J. Kasza

Bibliography

Havens, Thomas. *Valley of Darkness*. New York: Norton, 1978.

Yonai Mitsumasa (1880–1948)

Admiral and prime minister. Born in Iwate Prefecture, he graduated from the Naval Academy and the Naval Staff College, then advanced steadily in the navy until he became commander in chief of the combined fleet in 1936; he became a full admiral the next year. Yonai served in seven administrations as navy minister (1937–39, 1944–45) and once as prime minister (January–July 1940). He favored cooperation with the United States and Great Britain and incurred the wrath of ultranationalists for his opposition to the 1940 Tripartite Pact, which tied Japan to Germany and Italy in World War II. He was forced to resign as prime minister when the army refused to name a war minister after Yonai had asked Hata Shunroku to resign from that post for advocating the expansionistic *shin taisei undō* (new order movement). Late in World War II, Yonai worked as naval minister to secure an early peace, and he oversaw the dismantling of the navy after the war ended in 1945.

James L. Huffman

Bibliography
Butow, Robert. *Japan's Decision to Surrender*. Stanford, CA: Stanford University Press, 1954.

Yosano Akiko (1878–1942)

In September 1904, Yosano Akiko, who was known for the frank sensuality of her romantic Japanese-style poetry (*waka*), published the poem "My Brother, You Must Not Die" (Kimi shinitamau koto nakare) in the arts journal *Myōjō* (Morning Star). The Russo-Japanese War (1904–05) was at its peak. In August, the Japanese army had suffered a reported 15,000 casualties in an attack on Port Arthur in Manchuria. Akiko had originally written her poem as a postscript to a letter to her younger brother, recently married and heir to the family confectionery business in Sakai, and the publication was preceded by the note that the poem was written while "grieving over my younger brother, who is taking part in the siege of Port Arthur."

Such a candid expression of concern for her brother's safety (My brother, you must not die. / Whether the fortress at Port Arthur falls or not—what does it matter? / Should it concern you? War is not the tradition of a merchant family. . . .) and her criticism of the emperor (Let the Emperor himself go off to war. / "Die like a beast, leaving pools of human blood. / In death is your glory." / If that majestic heart is truly wise, / he cannot have such thoughts. . . .) led to Akiko's denunciation in the press as a traitor. The following month, Akiko and her husband, Yosano Tekkan, published an "Open Letter" (Hirakibumi) in *Myōjō*, defending the artist's right and responsibility to express personal emotions and responses to the world ("the truth of my heart") in literary form and criticizing war literature, the only aim of which was to serve a public purpose.

Akiko devoted the remainder of her life to poetry and literature. She published more than 20 volumes of poems and twice translated Murasaki Shikibu's classic novel, *The Tale of Genji* into modern Japanese (1912, 1939). She also supported struggling young poets. Until her death of a stroke in 1942, she remained a critic of Japan's aggression abroad. Her work, ignored by the literary mainstream in the war era, became popular in subsequent years.

Laurel Rasplica Rodd

Bibliography
Keene, Donald. *Dawn to the West*. Vol. 2. New York: Henry Holt, 1984.
Rodd, Laurel Rasplica. "Yosano Akiko and the Taishō Debate over the 'New Woman.'" *Recreating Japanese Women, 1600–1945*. Ed. Gail Lee Bernstein. Berkeley: University of California Press, 1991.

Yosano Akiko. Asahi Shimbun Photo.

Yoshida Shigeru (1878–1967)

Prewar diplomat and postwar prime minister. Yoshida left a unique mark on the political history of twentieth-century Japan. As head of five cabinets that held power for 86 months between May 1946 and December 1954, he led the government during the turbulent years of transition from defeat and Occupation to Japan's reemergence as a sovereign country. Japan's post-Occupation policy of economic nationalism coupled with strategic dependency on the United States is often referred to as the Yoshida Legacy, or the Yoshida Doctrine.

Adopted shortly after birth by a former samurai from Fukui Prefecture, Yoshida was raised as a privileged young Meiji gentleman, and, in 1909, he arranged a strategically advantageous marriage with Makino Yukiko, the daughter of prominent diplomat Makino Nobuaki and granddaughter of the Meiji oligarch Ōkubo Toshimichi.

Yoshida entered the Ministry of Foreign Affairs in 1906, at the age of 34. Although he eventually held two ambassadorships, in Rome (1931–32) and London (1936–38), he later acknowledged that his diplomatic career as a whole was mediocre and unworthy of particular attention.

Following his retirement from the university in 1938, Yoshida moved in upper-class circles, including the imperial-court society. He criticized the trend toward war with the Anglo-American powers and cultivated personal relations with Western diplomats. During the Pacific War (1937–45), he sporadically criticized Prime Minister Tōjō Hideki and other military leaders. In February 1945, he helped draft the famous *Konoe Memorial* (*Konoe jōsōbun*), which warned that Japan faced the prospect of a Communist revolution if it did not surrender soon. Yoshida was arrested in April 1945 for his antiwar activities and imprisoned for more than two months.

Yoshida was almost 67 years old when the war ended, and no one anticipated that he had a serious political future. After serving as foreign minister in two cabinets (1945–46), however, he was unexpectedly elevated in May 1946 to the presidency of the Jiyūtō (Liberal Party), and with this the prime ministership, when Hatoyama Ichirō was purged in April 1946.

As a great admirer of the legacies of the Meiji (1868–1912) and Taishō (1912–26) periods, Yoshida explained the militarism of the 1930s as an aberration, and he opposed virtually every basic early policy of the American-led Allied Occupation (1945–52). At the same time, he espoused a philosophy of being a "good loser" and implemented required reforms in the belief that this would eliminate international distrust of Japan and hasten the restoration of the country's sovereignty. When the Cold War intensified in the 1950s and U.S. policy shifted from political reform to economic reconstruction, Yoshida's views became more popular among U.S. leaders. The second-through-fifth Yoshida cabinets (October 19, 1948–December 10, 1954) were thus able to pursue a "reverse course" against the early reformist policies while concentrating on economic reconstruction and Japan's reemergence as a sovereign country.

Yoshida's proudest accomplishment was the peace settlement that ended the Occupation in April 1952. His personal contribution to this was conspicuous in at least three respects: (1) As early as May 1950, he had secretly informed the United States that Japan was willing to accept U.S. military bases after regaining sovereignty. This became the basis of the bilateral Japan-U.S. Security Treaty in 1951. (2) At the same time, while agreeing to place Okinawa under U.S. military control, Yoshida successfully insisted that Japan retain residual sovereignty over the Ryūkyū Islands. This was the legal basis under which the Ryūkyūs reverted to Japan in 1970. (3) Yoshida successfully resisted immense U.S. pressure to rearm Japan more rapidly. After the outbreak of the Korean War in June 1950, the United States consistently demanded that Japan create a military force of 300,000 to 350,000 men; when the Yoshida era ended in 1954, however, the Japanese military establishment was half that number.

Yoshida was not a popular figure in 1954, when he was forced out of the prime ministership. As Japan became more prosperous in the years that followed, however, his image as a wise elder statesman grew. In 1964, three years before his death, Yoshida was awarded Japan's highest honor, the Supreme Order of the Chrysanthemum.

John W. Dower

Bibliography
Dower, John W. *Empire and Aftermath*. Cambridge: Harvard University Press, 1979.

Yoshida Shōin (1830–59)

Teacher and activist from the domain of Chōshū in western Japan, Yoshida typified the ideal of the *sonnō jōi* (revere the emperor and expel the barbarians) samurai on the eve of the Meiji Restoration (1868). He advocated opening Japan's feudal political system and taught his pupils that all members of the samurai status group deserved a chance to hold office and make policy at both the domain and the *bakufu* levels.

In 1854, Yoshida tried to stow away on U.S. Commodore Matthew Perry's flagship when his fleet was anchored off Shimoda, waiting for the signing of the first treaty between Japan and another country. He wanted to go to America and study the secrets of the West. Rebuffed, he spent several months in prison and under house arrest. Starting in 1856, his private academy, the Shōka Sonjuku in Chōshū, taught more than one dozen of Japan's future leaders and trained some of the most decisive and best-informed men of his age.

In 1858, when shogunal regent Ii Naosuke signed a commercial treaty with the United States without first obtaining the emperor's approval, Yoshida concluded that the *bakufu* had outlived its usefulness. He proposed direct action and offered to kill Ii's messenger in Kyoto. Jailed and taken to Edo by *bakufu* officials, Yoshida was executed late in 1859. His punishment was one of the harshest that Ii meted out as he tried to shore up *bakufu* rule in what came to be known as the Ansei Purge (1858–60).

Yoshida wanted Japan to reform its institutions and adopt Western learning; he studied Dutch texts. But he took a narrow view of *sonnō jōi* that ultimately repudiated foreigners and exalted an exclusive Japanese nationalism.

George M. Wilson

Bibliography
Harootunian, Harry. *Toward Restoration.* Berkeley: University of California Press, 1970.
Huber, Thomas M. *The Revolutionary Origins of the Meiji Restoration.* Stanford, CA: Stanford University Press, 1981.

Yoshimoto Takaaki (1924–)
Poet and literary critic. Yoshimoto was a major intellectual figure during the 1960 protests against the revisions and renewal of the 1951 Japan-U.S. Security Treaty. He was particularly popular with anti-Stalinist student radicals, in that he advocated a stance independent from the two opposing Cold War blocs. Yoshimoto reexamined nativist thought to evolve a concept of popular nationalism centered on nature and concrete existence, which he claimed that prewar Japanese intellectuals had abstracted and perverted into ultranationalism. Postwar intellectuals, he asserted, continued to devalue the thought of common people and sought to impose on them the values and political forms of Western moderniza-

tion or Marxism. He especially derogated the Japan Communist Party for depending on Comintern directives from Moscow and for claiming revolutionary leadership while failing to defend student protesters from police violence. His call for *jiritsu* (standing on one's own feet) implied the need for individual, as well as national, independence. Social change, Yoshimoto thought, originated from the masses and their indigenous thought and culture rather than from a foreign-influenced elite, and his subsequent work sought to define Japanese national identity.

Wesley Sasaki-Uemura

Bibliography
Olson, Lawrence. "Intellectuals and 'The People'; on Yoshimoto Takaaki." *Journal of Japanese Studies.* Vol. 4, No. 2 (Summer 1978), 327–57.

Yoshino Sakuzō (1878–1933)
Scholar. Born in Miyagi Prefecture and graduated in 1904 from the Tokyo University Law Faculty, he became the leading exponent of many practical, moderately liberal ideas considered typical of the Taishō era (1912–26). With the exception of two stints in China (1906–09), and Europe (1910–13) and as an editorialist at the newspaper *Osaka Asahi Shimbun* (1924), Yoshino spent his entire career teaching in the Law Faculty at Tokyo University. His willingness to write for popular journals such as *Chūō Kōron*, as well as for academic media, intensified Yoshino's influence.

An avowed Christian influenced by Christian socialists, Yoshino was committed to constitutionalism and human equality. He was best known for his advocacy of *minponshugi* (people as the base), which maintained that, while true democracy (*minshushugi*) would not work in Japan, where the emperor was sovereign, the government must act on behalf of the people, and the people must use elections to judge how effectively the government had performed.

A frequent target of the Right and the Left, Yoshino asked scholars to eschew pure theory and deal with practical problems. He advocated such causes as universal male suffrage, the removal of groups such as the Privy Council and the military from politics, legal acceptance of labor unions, and cabinet responsibility to the Diet (legislature). He created or worked with several organizations, including the student political group Shinjinkai (New Person Society) and the progressive intellectuals' Reimeikai (Dawn Society). He also helped in 1919 to form a consumers' cooperative union, the Family Purchasing Association (Katei Kōbai Kumiai) and did volunteer work in hospitals. In his latter years, he focused on the roots of democratic ideas in the Meiji years (1868–1912) and edited the widely used 24-volume collection of Meiji documents, *Meiji bunka zenshū* (Collected Works of Meiji Culture). He died of tuberculosis.

James L. Huffman

Bibliography
Duus, Peter. "Yoshino Sakuzō: The Christian as Political Critic." *Journal of Japanese Studies*. Vol. 4, No. 2 (Summer 1978), 301–26.

Yoshioka Yayoi (1881–1959)

Born in Shizuoka Prefecture, Yoshioka was one of Japan's first female physicians. In 1900, she founded Japan's first medical college for women, Tokyo Joigakkō (Tokyo Women's Medical School), renamed Tokyo Joshi Igaku Senmon Gakkō (Tokyo Women's Medical Professional School) in 1912. Though inspired as a girl by radical feminist Fukuda Hideko, she represented the conservative wing of the women's movement and publicly criticized "new women" such as Hiratsuka Raichō and Ichikawa Fusae for their feminist tactics and unconventional lifestyles. Nevertheless, she cooperated with a broad spectrum of women's groups in the Tokyo Rengō Fujinkai (Tokyo League of Women's Organizations) in the years after the Great Kantō Earthquake of 1923.

In 1928, Yoshioka accompanied nine other middle-class feminists as Japan's delegation to the Pan Pacific Women's Conference, and, in 1930, she joined a moderate women's suffrage group, Fujin Dōshikai (Society of Like-Minded Women). In 1937, she helped create the Federation of Women's Organizations that joined conservative women's groups with moderate women's-suffrage organizations. Yoshioka was purged by the postwar American-led Occupation (1945–52) for her progovernment wartime affiliations. These included the Education Ministry's Social Education Research Association, 1933; Women's Coalition to Purify Elections (chair), 1936; Tokyo City Association to Implement National Spiritual Mobilization, 1937; the cabinet's Education Deliberative Association, 1937; the Committee to Celebrate the 2600th Anniversary of Japan's Founding, 1937; and the National Spiritual Mobilization Central Committee (director), 1938.

Barbara Molony

Bibliography
Robins-Mowry, Dorothy. *The Hidden Sun: Women of Modern Japan*. Boulder, CO: Westview Press, 1983.

Young Officers' Movement (*Seinen Shōkō Undō*)

Extremist group of young military officers. This illegal, loosely formed movement (a few hundred strong) of chiefly low-ranking officers and cadets of the army and the navy, postured as descendants of the *shishi* (antishogunal loyalists), the patriotic fighters of the Meiji Restoration (1868), and attempted to carry out a violent Shōwa Restoration aimed at bringing the military to power in the 1930s. Using the slogan "imperial absolutism–people's equality" (*ikkun no zettai to kokumnin no byōdō*) and working through organizations such as Sakurakai (Cherry Blossom Society), the group fanned flames of nationalist extremism.

Members of the movement opposed Western ideas, even while using "comrade" to address each other, accepting financial contributions from capitalists, and subscribing to a quasi-national-socialist ideology. Their anti-Western tone was caused by the economic crisis after World War I (1914–18), party corruption, and their fear of the advancement of Chinese nationalism and Soviet Communism. They advocated ultranationalistic moral education (*seishin kyōiku*) and state reform (*kokka kaizō*), under the influence of the ideology of ultranationalist leaders Ōkawa Shūmei and Kita Ikki.

Prominent members or supporters included such well-known extremists as Nishida Zei, Aizawa Saburō, and Fujii Hitoshi, men with ties to most of the decade's major coup attempts. When prominent supporters in the army's Imperial Way Faction (Kōdōha) lost influence in the government in the mid-1930s, the Young Officers Movement began to decline. It fell apart after the government crackdown on extremism following the radicals' massive, unsuccessful coup attempt on February 26, 1936. The movement—particularly its role in the February 26 Incident—inspired the postwar ultranationalist writer Mishima Yukio.

Jacob Kovalio

Bibliography

Shillony, Ben-Ami. *Revolt in Japan: The Young Officers and the February 26, 1936, Incident.* Princeton, NJ: Princeton University Press, 1973.

Index

Bonin Islands, 105
Bosei Hogo Renmei (Motherhood Protection League), 81
Boshin shōsho (Imperial Rescript on Diligence and Frugality), 83
Boshin War, 21–22, 151
Boxer Rebellion, 11, 119
Brain-trusters *(Yōgaku)*, 111
Buddhism
    Nichiren, 178
    Shinto and, 234
Bund (Communist League), 249
Bunmei kaika (civilization and enlightenment), 31–32
Burakumin, 35, 133
Bureau of Rites *(Jingikan)*, 22, 156
Bureau of Thought Control, 25
Bushidō, 22–24

C

Cabinet Information Bureau *(Naikaku Jōhōkyokū)*, 25
Campaign to Clarify National Policy, 157
Capitalism, nationalism and, 41
Cardinal Principles of the National Polity *(Kokutai no Hongi)*, 25–26, 170
Censorship *(ken'etsu)*, 26–29
Central Review *(Chūō Kōron)*, 230
Centralized modern state, 3
Chang Yin-huan, 232
Charter Oath, 29, 61, 145–146
Chen Gongbo, 284
Cherry Blossom Society *(Sakurakai)*, 29–30
Chian Iji Hō (Peace Preservation Law), 67, 82, 86, 112, 139, 204, 246, 268
Chian Keisatsu Hō (Public Peace Police Law), 209
Chiang Kaishek, 12–13
Chief aide-de-camp, 89
Chifuren (National Federation of Regional Women's Organizations), 287
Chikyūsetsu (empress's birthday), 49
China, 274
    anti-Japanese boycott in, 12–13
    governments in, 283–284
Chinese characters *(kanji)*, 106
Chinese Communists, 104
Chisso (Japan Nitrogen), 57
Chokugen (Straight Talk), 35
Chonmage (topknots), 31
Chōshū, 73, 151, 224
Christ, 82
Christianity, 36, 172, 186–187, 201, 275
Chukun aikoku (loyalty to ruler and patriotism), 149
Chūō Kōron (Central Review), 230
Chūpiren (Women's Liberation League Against the Abortion Law and for the Pill), 287
Church *(kyōkai)*, 279
Church, Frank, 134
Churchill, Winston, 291
Citizens' movements *(shimin undō)*, 30

Citizenship, responsibilities of, 90
Civilization and enlightenment *(bunmei kaika)*, 31–32
Clean Government Party (Kōmeitō), 281
Clique *(batsu)*, 57
Coalition movement *(daidō danketsu undō)*, 32
Cold War in East Asia, 226–227
Colonialism, 32–34
    Western, 33
Commoner *(heimin)*, 148
Commonerism *(heiminshugi)*, 244
Commoners' Newspaper *(Heimin Shimbun)*, 35, 122
Communism, 69
Communist League (Bund), 249
Communists, 104
Compulsory education, 149
Computer technology, 92
Conciliation Movement *(Yūwa)*, 35, 133
Concordia Society *(Kyōwakai)*, 36
Conference of Three Religions *(Sankyo Kaido)*, 36
Confucian thought, 160–161
Conquer Korea Argument *(seikan ron)*, 36–37, 50
Conscription, male, universal, 149
Constitution *(Shōwa Kenpō)*, 37–38
Constitution of the Empire of Japan, *see* Meiji Constitution
Constitutional Association (Kenseikai), 4, 112
Constitutional Democratic Party *(Rikken Minseitō)*, 4, 38
Consumerism, 127
Control associations *(tōseikai)*, 54
Control Faction *(Tōseiha)*, 38–39, 165–166, 168
Cooperation and Harmony Society *(Kyōchōkai)*, 39
Cooperativism, 153
Corporatism, 127–128
Countries, interdependence among, 95–96
Crisis of 1873, 39–40
Cultural nationalism, 181
Cultural Problems Committee, 153
Culture, national, 148

D

Dai-Ajia Kyōkai (Greater East Asia Society), 71
Dai Nihon Teikoku Kempō, *see* Meiji Constitution
Dai-Tōa Kyōeiken (Greater East Asia Coprosperity Sphere), 70–71, 107
Daidō danketsu undō (coalition movement), 32
Daiichi-Kangin, 57
Daiichiji Sekai Taisen (World War I), 132, 274, 288
Daijōsai (Great New Food Festival), 70
Daijūgo Ginko (Fifteenth Bank), 101
Daimyo, 142, 230
Dainihon Aikokutō (Greater Japan Patriots Party), 7–8
Dainihon Fujinkai (Greater Japan Women's Association), 72, 85, 204
Dainihon Genron Hōkokukai (Greater Japan Patriotic Speech Association), 85
Dainihon Kokubō Fujinkai (Greater Japan National

Ishibashi Tanzan, 97
Ishihara Shintarō, 63, 97, 177, 182
Ishii Kikujirō, 132
Ishiwara Kanji, 39, 97–98, 140, 169, 267
Itagaki Seishirō, 98
Itagaki Taisuke, 99, 111, 150, 209, 243
Itai itai disease, 30
Itō Enkichi, 26
Itō Hirobumi, 63, 94, 99–100, 169, 207–208
Itō Miyoji, 100
Itō Noe, 100–101
Iwakura Mission, 61, 99, 101, 272
Iwakura Tomomi, 5, 36–37, 39–40, 101
Iwanaga Yūkichi, 43, 95, 101–102
Iwasaki Yatarō, 112, 229

J

Japan *(nippon)*, 147
    Korean minority in, 121–122
    spirit of, 247
Japan and the Japanese *(Nihon oyobi Nihonjin)*, 105
Japan As Number One: Lessons for America, 181
Japan Association of Corporate Executives (Keizai Dōyōkai), 56
Japan bashing in United States, 97
Japan Bereaved Families Association, 240
Japan Chamber of Commerce and Industry (Nisshō), 56
Japan Congress of Industrial Unions (Sanbetsu), 126
Japan Council of Private-Sector Labor Unions (Zenmin Rōkyō), 128
Japan External Trade Organization (JETRO), 157
Japan Federation of Employers' Associations (Nikkeiren), 56
Japan Federation of Labor (Sōdōmei), 129, 130
Japan National Socialist Party (Nihon Kokka Shakaitō), 7
Japan Nitrogen (Chisso), 57
Japan Socialist Party (JSP), 249
Japan Society for Expansion of the Way (Nihon Kōdōkai), 184
Japan Telegraphic News Agency *(Nippon Denpō Tsūshinsha Dentsū)*, 16, 43, 103
The Japan That Can Say No, 182, 238
Japan-U.S. Security Treaties *(Nichibei Anzen Hoshō Jōyaku)*, 9–10, 103–105, 223, 297
The Japanese (Nihonjin), 105
Japanese Communist Party (JCP) (Nihon Kyōsantō), 85–86, 222, 249, 252
Japanese Confederation of Labor (Dōmei), 127, 131
Japanese Diet, 47
Japanese-Jewish contacts, 13–14
Japanese language *(nihongo)*, 106–107
Japanese military flag, 79
Japanese military force, 15
Japanese Monroe Doctrine, 107

Japanese Romantic School *(Nihon Rōmanha)*, 107–108
Japanese Trade Union Confederation (Rengō), 128
Japanese-trained Korean troops (Kurentai), 160
Japanese uniqueness, 180
Japaneseness, 171, 177, 238
Japanism, 144
Japanists, 130
JETRO (Japan External Trade Organization), 157
Jews, 13–14
Jichi Gakkai (Self-Rule School), 68
Jietai [Self-Defense Forces (SDF)], 15, 190, 226–227
Jiji Shimpō, 65
Jimbo Kōtarō, 108
Jimmin Sensen Jiken (Popular Front Incident), 206
Jimmu (first emperor), 22, 46, 49
Jimmu Society *(Jimmukai)*, 108
Jimmukai (Jimmu Society), 108
Jingikan (Bureau of Rites), 22, 156
Jingishō (Ministry of Divinity), 156
Jisei (trend of the times), 89
Jiyū Minken Undō (Freedom and People's Rights Movement), 61–62, 150
Jiyūtō (Liberal Party), 62, 99
Jōhō sangyōron (information industry), 92
Jōhōka mirai toshi kōzō (Vision of Future Cities in the Information Age), 93
Jōhōka shakai (information society), 92–93
Joint Council of Fellow Activists on the Peace Question (Kōwa Mondai Dōshi Rengōkai), 77
Jōmon, 5
Jōyaku kaisei (treaty revision), 272–273
Jūgatsu Jiken (October Incident), 191
Jūmin undō (residents' movements), 30
Jūshin (senior statesmen), 227

K

Kagawa Toyohiko, 109
Kaientai (Naval Auxiliary Force), 163–164
Kamakura period, 19
Kamei Katsuichirō, 108
Kami (divinities), 74–75, 233
Kamikaze (Divine Wind), 109–110
Kamino Shin'ichi, 130
Kamo no Mabuchi, 173
Kanagawa Treaty, 172, 205
Kaneko Fumiko, 110, 287
Kanghwa Treaty, 241
Kanji (Chinese characters), 106
Kanno Suga, 110, 122, 286
Kanyatoi (foreigners), 60
Karafuto as Japanese colony, 32, 33
Katakana, 106
Katayama Sen, 129
Katō Hiroharu, 110–111
Katō Hiroyuki, 111–112
Katō Kanji, 134
Katō Takaaki, 112

FOR REFERENCE

Do Not Take From This Room